Martin Lut

Martin Luther designed the Luther seal in 1530 at the request of the Elector Duke John Frederick of Saxony. Luther (signed "Martinus Luther") wrote:

Since you ask whether my seal has come out correctly, I shall answer most amiably and tell you of those thoughts which now come to my mind about my seal as a symbol of my theology. There is first to be a cross, black, and placed in a heart, which should be of its natural color (red), to put me in mind that faith in Christ crucified saved us. For if one believes from the heart, he will be justified. ["For it is by believing in your heart that you are made right God, and it is by confessing with your mouth that you are saved."—Romans 10:10.] Even though it is a black cross, which mortifies and which also should hurt us, yet it leaves the heart in its natural color and does not ruin nature ... that is, the cross does not kill, but keeps man alive. For the just shall live by faith, by faith in the Savior. "This Good News tells us how God makes us right in His sight. This is accomplished from start to finish by faith. As the Scriptures say, 'It is through faith that a righteous person has life.'"—Romans 1:17.

Such a heart is to be in the midst of a white rose, to symbolize that faith gives joy, comfort, and peace. In a word, it places the believer into a white joyful rose, for this faith does not give peace and joy as the world gives. ["I am leaving you with a gift—peace of mind and heart. And the peace I give isn't like the peace the world gives. So don't be troubled or afraid."—John 14:27.] Therefore, the rose is to be white, not red, for white is the color of the spirits and of all angels. ["An angel of the Lord came down from heaven and rolled aside the stone and sat on it. His face shone like lightening, and his clothing was as white as snow."—Matthew 28:2b-3, and "She saw two white-robed angels sitting at the head and foot of the place where the body of Jesus had been lying."—John 20:12.]

This rose, moreover, is fixed in a sky-blue field, symbolizing that such joy in the Spirit and in faith is a beginning of the future heavenly joy. It is already a part of faith, and is grasped through hope, even though not yet manifest.

And around this field is a golden ring, to signify that such bliss in heaven is endless, and more precious than all joys and goods, just as gold is the most valuable and precious metal.

May Christ, our dear Lord, be with your spirit until the life to come. Amen.

Martin Luther

The Life and Lessons

LARRY D. MANSCH *and*
CURTIS H. PETERS

For the Maricelli family.
With many fond memories
of STS + Walt Disney!

Larry D. Mansch

Curtis H. Peters

McFarland & Company, Inc., Publishers

Jefferson, North Carolina

ALSO OF INTEREST

Abraham Lincoln, President-Elect: The Four Critical Months from Election to Inauguration, by Larry D. Mansch (McFarland, 2005; softcover 2008)

Rube Marquard: The Life and Times of a Baseball Hall of Famer, by Larry D. Mansch (McFarland, 1998)

All photographs by the authors unless otherwise indicated.

Frontispiece: Martin Luther designed the Luther seal in 1530 at the request of the Elector Duke John Frederick of Saxony.

LIBRARY OF CONGRESS CATALOGUING-IN-PUBLICATION DATA

Names: Mansch, Larry D., 1958– author.
Title: Martin Luther : the life and lessons / Larry D. Mansch and Curtis H. Peters.
Description: Jefferson, North Carolina : McFarland & Company, Inc., Publishers, 2016. | Includes bibliographical references and index.
Identifiers: LCCN 2016018967 | ISBN 9780786498543 (softcover : acid free paper) ∞
Subjects: LCSH: Luther, Martin, 1483–1546.
Classification: LCC BR325 .M287 2016 | DDC 284.1092 [B]—dc23
LC record available at https://lccn.loc.gov/2016018967

BRITISH LIBRARY CATALOGUING DATA ARE AVAILABLE

ISBN (print) 978-0-7864-9854-3
ISBN (ebook) 978-1-4766-2555-3

Front cover: Martin Luther, 1529, Lucas Cranach the Elder (PicturesNow); Luther Rose © 2016 iStock/tharrison

Printed in the United States of America

McFarland & Company, Inc., Publishers
Box 611, Jefferson, North Carolina 28640
www.mcfarlandpub.com

For Kim, with love.
—LDM

To my parents, my wife, Pam,
and all who have nurtured my faith.
—CHP

Acknowledgments

For all of their assistance and encouragement I gratefully acknowledge Emily Freeman, Fred Haefele, Pastor Greg Karlsgodt, Mary Jane Nealon, Linda Redfern, Pastor Molly Sasser-Goehner, Jeremy Smith, Mark Sundeen, James Swan, and Spencer Veysey.

I also wish to thank Stacey Gordon at the University of Montana School of Law. A special thanks goes to the kind-hearted congregation at Immanuel Lutheran Church in Missoula, Montana. All my love to Bethany, Lincoln, Abby, and Madison. Finally, I wish to thank Curt and Pam Peters, friends, scholars, and travel guides beyond compare.

—LDM

I wish to thank the many people who made important contributions to my work on these essays. Readers who were kind enough to read some or all of the essays and to offer helpful suggestions include John Thacker, Bruce Yungman, the Rev. John Deng Ater, Philip Eschels, Mary Eschels, Randy Fowler, the Rev. Mike Boyd, the Rev. Ron Richeson, Ben King, the Rev. David Carlson, and Dr. Stephanie Carlson. Their assistance is greatly appreciated. Very special counsel and assistance was given by Larry Mansch, the author of the biographical portion; working with him has been a great joy. Most importantly, the careful reading and the suggestions of my wife, Pam, herself a published author, have been crucial. Almost without exception, her insights are spot-on. She also provided whole-hearted support and the essential encouragement just when I needed it the most. Thank you!

—CHP

Table of Contents

Introduction

Our aim is to chronicle the life of Martin Luther in a new way—a combination of biography and commentary. The narrative of Luther's life, utilizing sources that scan hundreds of years, is told from the point of view of the historian in Part One. Luther's revolutionary thoughts on Scripture, salvation, and the proper relationship between God and man are told from the point of view of the theologian in Part Two. The chapters and essays may be read alternatively; that is, each chapter and essay will correspond one with the other of identical number. This combination of biography and analytical essays will, it is hoped, provide a valuable source of information and contemplation for laypeople, theologians, and history lovers, indeed for anyone interested in the life, times, and preaching of the man who changed the Christian world forever.

Martin Luther

That great historical period called the Renaissance—the years roughly from 1350 to 1650—saw an explosion of events and personalities that transformed Europe and lifted it out of the squalor of the Middle Ages. Columbus unwittingly discovered the New World and claimed it in the name of Spain and of God. Machiavelli's *The Prince* described how rulers might use and maintain political power effectively. Magellan circumnavigated the globe. Gutenberg's printing press allowed people to express and convey their thoughts on a wide scale. Michelangelo painted the ceiling of the Sistine Chapel. Copernicus, the father of modern astronomy, articulated that the Earth rotated on its axis and the planets revolved around the sun. Elizabeth I succeeded to the throne of England and launched her nation's Golden Age. Galileo formulated the laws of motion and changed the way people viewed the universe. The most versatile and brilliant mind of all, Leonardo da Vinci, was an artist, inventor, and scientist with no equal. But for all these historic figures and their accomplishments, the greatest event of the Renaissance was the Protestant Reformation—because it shook the foundation of the Roman Catholic Church, the most powerful institution in the world. God's holy Church, founded by Christ himself, permeated all aspects of religious, political, and social life in medieval Europe. It was unchanging; its constancy, in fact—and its ability to survive scandal and disruption—was what made it perfect. The Reformation dismantled and restructured the Catholic Church. It was nothing short of religious revolution, and it began with Martin Luther.

Germany and Lutherland (courtesy Tim Mosbacher).

Luther was born in 1483 in Saxony, Germany, the heart of the Holy Roman Empire. A brilliant young man of peasant stock who aspired to study law, Luther deeply disappointed his father by suddenly entering an Augustinian monastery. He threw himself into a life of strict discipline and structure. Dedicated and earnest, by the age of 29 Luther had received his doctor of theology degree and assumed his duties as professor of religious philosophy at the University of Wittenberg. He busied himself with lecturing, preaching, and advising, but even as his professional responsibilities increased, he found little solace in his faith. He was terrorized by demons and evil spirits and felt the presence of Satan in every waking moment. He lived in misery because he knew he could never overcome his own sinfulness and live up to God's demands. No amount of fasting, prayers, or penance could gain His favor. Called to worship and serve God, he felt only anger. Hoping that a trip to Rome would bring inspiration and enlightenment, Luther came away sickened by the rampant ungodliness of the Holy City and its inhabitants. He saw that the sacred Church did not provide the path to salvation but instead hindered it through corruption and abuse, all at the expense of its members. Called to care for the souls of his parishioners, Luther was instead terrified for his own, and lived in absolute fear of eternal damnation.

Gradually, however, Luther came to view God in a new way. Building on the works of Ambrose and Augustine and through his dissection of the New Testament, he began to believe that God's mercy would overcome man's failings. Through the defining words of St. Paul— "He who through faith is just shall live"—Luther came to realize that faith alone, receiving the gift of God's grace, justified sinners and assured their salvation. Justification came from God's righteousness, not from man's misguided efforts of goodness or the Church's rigid mandates and procedures. Paul's words were to Luther "flashes of lightening, frightening me each time I heard them." He had entered "the open doors into paradise." Justification by faith alone became, for Luther, "the summary of all Christian doctrine" and "the article by which the church stands or falls." Transformed, he began his life's work.

Emboldened by his new conviction, Luther challenged Catholicism's traditional doctrines. He began, in 1517, by proclaiming that the Church's fund-raising scheme of indulgences (whereby peasants could purchase salvation and release suffering souls from purgatory with their alms) was an abomination. He issued his challenges publicly by posting Ninety-Five Theses on the door of Castle Church in Wittenberg; what was meant as an academic exercise, however, merely a call for debate, quickly set off a firestorm in Germany. Galvanized by peasant and parishioner support, and protected by the sympathetic Elector Frederick the Wise, Luther soon took on other basic tenets of the Church. He rejected the righteous God, defined by the Church, who stood only in terrible judgment, always ready to punish the unworthy. Instead he found a loving God, a benevolent creator whose power and glory, and whose promise of salvation, were manifested by grace and mercy. He dismissed the hierarchical structure of the Church, and maintained that all believers were as priests, since all were equal in God's sight. He called for a reexamination of the liturgical Mass and the Sacraments, dismissing those parts, no matter how venerated, not sanctioned by Scripture. He taught that Christ was present in the bread and wine of the Eucharist, negating the need for priestly intervention. He criticized the Church's obsession with relics and its devotion to Mary the mother of Christ, and he scoffed at its cult of saints. He even challenged the doctrines of papal authority and infallibility. The tyrannical Church had become a den of thieves, he thundered, the Vatican a shameless brothel, its leader the Antichrist. Luther was branded a heretic by Rome, bullied, threatened, and finally excommunicated. "Here I stand," he said defiantly, and most of Germany eagerly, and adoringly, stood with him. His call for reform resulted in revolution. Luther and his legions of followers—"Protestants," "evangelicals," and then "Lutherans," they called themselves—uprooted fifteen hundred years of religious tradition in less than a decade. He watched as the whole edifice of the Catholic Church "came crashing down in the most awesome historical cataclysm."

For thirty years Luther remained the most vocal, and visible, leader of the Reformation. His energy and passion for his cause was unending. He was a prolific writer, capitalizing on Gutenberg's invention to distribute volumes of his sermons, lectures, commentaries, and letters. His works included *On the Babylonian Captivity of the Church*; *The Freedom of the Christian Man*; *The Smalcald Articles*; and *Large* and *Small Catechism*, all mainstays of Protestant theological thought today. His *Table Talk*, a series of musings and opinions on dozens of secular and non-secular topics, was a best seller. Luther translated Holy Scripture into German, and his magnificent version made the Bible truly "the people's book" for church, school, and home. Drawn by the power of music, he composed "A Mighty Fortress Is Our God" and "Lord, Keep Us Steadfast in Thy Word," among many other rousing and inspirational hymns. His colleague Philip Melanchthon wrote, with Luther's approval, the *Augsburg Confession*, the apex of the Reformation, which became (and remains) the primary confessional doctrine for Lutherans. He surprised himself by falling in love at age forty-two, and adored his wife and six children. He was an electric speaker, an opportunistic propagandist, and a charismatic leader who reveled in his role as the Great Reformer. Luther celebrated his faith and urged others to do the same: "God does not save people who are only fictitious sinners," he astonishingly said. "Be a sinner and sin boldly, but believe and rejoice in Christ even more boldly." Some thought he was Elijah reincarnate; others felt he was the greatest man since Peter and Paul. He became comfortable in his own celebrity and enjoyed it. "We have become a spectacle," he said of himself and his followers.

Luther was also famously hot-tempered, profane and unapologetic. He remained stubbornly nationalistic, saving his most colorful proclamations for the papacy ("When the Pope farts in Rome," he sneered, "we smell it in Germany"). Late in life he endured periods of bitterness, regretting that his movement had in many ways brought divisiveness rather than unity. He watched in dismay as thousands of his countrymen, mistakenly believing his doctrines called for civil revolution, died in the Peasants' War. Protestant churches divided again and again over basic theological issues he had raised. Luther railed particularly against the Jews, using language that would taint his legacy for generations. He found other reformers such as Zwingli and Calvin contemptible and proclaimed their opinions, to the degree they differed from his own, the work of the Devil. But he never wavered from his conviction that the Bible, and not ritual or doctrine or papal decree, was the sole, true means by which one could know the word of God. Humbled by his heroic reputation and proud of it as well, Luther acknowledged that he was both saint and sinner. Above all else, he hoped, he was a servant of God and His people.

Luther's movement irrevocably divided the Catholic Church, reordered and redefined it, while at the same time ending the social, economic, and political stranglehold it had exerted so long over so many. Relations between layperson and clergy, and between citizen and government, were transformed forever. The Reformation's legacy was bloody, as well. The Peasants' War, the Thirty Years' War, and the French Wars of Religion, among others, were fought between Catholics and Protestants. Europe was left permanently divided between north and south, east and west. Provincial boundaries melted, merged, and melted again. Kingdoms fell away. Through the stubborn actions of a despotic king, Great Britain established the Church of England. A Protestant strain of dissidents called Puritans took their version of the Reformation across the Atlantic Ocean and settled the New World. The seminal event of the Renaissance, Luther's Reformation lifted Christianity up from the despair of the Middle Ages and shaped the modern age. Martin Luther, the "wild boar of the Roman vineyards," as Pope Leo X called him, had inspired much more than he would ever know.

—Larry D. Mansch

The Essays

The "lessons," or "essays," that comprise Part Two present Luther's views on key topics using Luther's own words as much as possible—relying almost exclusively on writings which he published during his lifetime. Luther was never one to mince words, so this method can be trusted, I believe, to show his genuine views. On some points, of course, his positions modified over the course of his life. In the essays I have tried to present what appear to be his considered, mature judgments, but I have always indicated the dates when he expressed those positions so that the reader can also make judgments about this. The fact that I focus on a "mature" or developed position marks one difference between these essays and the descriptions of his developments in the biographical portion in Part One. Another difference is, of course, that the "life" and "lessons" parts of this work have two authors with complementary but different purposes. While we have worked in partnership and usually agree, this is not a given, and we are each answerable for our own sections.

I have thoroughly enjoyed working on this project and have learned a lot. I am impressed anew by the wealth of scholarship on Luther, but I am even more impressed by the richness and depth of Luther's own writings. As the essays will reveal, I base my presentations not on the secondary sources but rather on Luther's own words.

This raises an important point about the sources that I quote. Because the English edition, *Luther's Works, American Edition*, published by Concordia (vols. 1–30) and Fortress (vols. 31–55), is so extensive, so well-done, and so readily available, I have chosen to quote from this edition. A second reason for this choice is that this book is intended for a broad audience, and many of the readers might not find it so easy to check the sources in the Weimar edition or in another German edition.

It should also be said that these essays are intended to present an "unfiltered" version of Luther's views. While his positions are often brilliant, spectacular, and admirable, this is not always the case. He could be caustic, overly harsh, and, for lack of a better word, stubborn. Occasionally, I do express my disagreements or disappointments, but I try never to hide or soften what Luther actually wrote. That being said, my admiration for Luther is greater than ever.

The reasoning behind the order of the essays may not always be obvious. My intent has been always to choose an essay topic that relates to the material in the corresponding chapter in Part One. These essays may, to be sure, be read in any order. Below I give some additional comments relevant to the ordering.

Essay 1, "Luther on Church History." Chapter 1 in the biography offers a brief overview of the history of the Church leading up to the condition of the Church in Luther's day. The essay gives Luther's own perspective on church history with emphasis on the reliance upon Church Councils and the Church Fathers.

Essay 2, "Luther on Children's Education." Chapter 2 describes Luther's youth including his education. In the essay, Luther's progressive views on education that he developed in the 1520s are explored.

Essay 3, "Luther on Monasticism." Chapter 3 presents Luther's vow to become a monk and his life as a monk at Erfurt. In the corresponding essay Luther's position on monasticism, more complex than is usually recognized, is developed.

Essay 4, "Luther on the Central Issue: Law and Gospel." In Chapter 4 Luther's theological "awakening" during the early years in Wittenberg is described. Essay 4 deals with a crucial aspect of this awakening—the development of his views on Law and Gospel.

Essay 5, "Luther on the Divisive Issue: Indulgences and Church Finances." Chapter 5 concerns Luther's challenge to the Church in 1517. In the fifth essay the heart of the challenge, indulgences, is explored.

Essay 6, "Luther on the Authority Issue: Papacy/Scripture." Chapter 6 offers a general perspective on the papacy at the time of Luther. The sixth essay examines Luther's position on the papacy.

Essay 7, "Luther on the Theologies of Glory and the Cross." Chapter 7 describes Luther's activities in the months following the posting of the Ninety-Five Theses. In Essay 7 the provocative theses he presented at Heidelberg in early 1518 are explored.

Essay 8, "Luther Against Scholasticism: Was He a Humanist?" In Chapter 8 the Roman Church's early counterattack is presented. In the essay Luther's fundamental rejection of scholasticism, so dominant in the Roman Church's theology, is examined.

Essay 9, "Luther Debating the Key Issues: Luther vs. Eck." Chapter 9 presents Luther's ongoing battle with the Church leading up to the important Leipzig debate of 1519. The essay explores Luther's crucial and amazing power in debates.

Essay 10, "Luther on the Sacraments: The Die Is Cast." Chapter 10 describes Luther's increasingly broad and vehement attacks in the period leading to Worms. The essay focuses on a key and devastating attack—on the Roman Church's theology of the sacraments.

Essay 11, "Luther on the Oneness of the Church: The *Una Sancta*." Chapter 11 presents the circumstances surrounding Luther's historic stance at the Diet of Worms. In the essay his position on the oneness of the Church and how he viewed his impact on that oneness are explored.

Essay 12, "In Need of Comfort and Strength: Luther on the Psalms." In Chapter 12 Luther's period in hiding at the Wartburg is described. Because this was a time of special stress for Luther, the essay deals with the help he found in the Psalms at such times.

Essay 13, "Luther on Spiritual Growth in a New Church." Chapter 13 explores the active and crucial period when Luther returned to Wittenberg. Luther then realized that a new Church was necessary, so the essay examines the spiritual aids Luther developed for this new Church.

Essay 14, "Luther on Free Will: Against Erasmus—A Failed Alignment of the Stars." In Chapter 14 attention is given to the many significant writings which Luther published in the 1520s. The essay is devoted to Luther's very important *The Bondage of the Will*, 1525.

Essay 15, "Luther on Marriage, Celibacy and His Dear Kate." Chapter 15 focuses on Luther's marriage. In the essay, Luther's religious views on marriage and celibacy are explored.

Essay 16, "Luther on Church and State." Chapter 16 describes the Peasants' War of 1525 and Luther's role in it. The essay examines Luther's theology of church and state.

Essay 17, "Luther on Other Reformers." In Chapter 17 Luther's efforts to strengthen the faith in the late 1520s are presented. In the essay focus is on his views on other reformers with whom he contended during this period.

Essay 18, "Luther on the Jews." Chapter 18 presents key theological contributions made in the 1530s. The essay addresses one of the most controversial aspects of his later writings— his position on the Jews.

Essay 19, "Luther on Melanchthon." Chapter 19 describes the closing years of Luther's life, including his death. In the essay Luther's judgments on his closest colleague, a colleague who would be severely criticized by Lutherans after Luther's death, are examined.

Essay 20, "The Capstone Essay: A Contemporary Perspective." Chapter 20, "Legacy," treats the impact Luther had on developments after his death. The essay presents reflections that develop out of the essays.

For anyone who wishes to read the essays from a topical perspective, the following may be helpful:

Theological positions:
> Luther on the Central Issue: Law and Gospel (Essay 4)
> Luther on the Theologies of Glory and the Cross (Essay 7)
> Luther on the Sacraments: The Die Is Cast (Essay 10)
> Luther on the Oneness of the Church: The *Una Sancta* (Essay 11)
> Luther on Church and State (Essay 16)
> Luther on Marriage, Celibacy and His Dear Kate (Essay 15)

Critiques of the Roman Catholic Church:
> Luther on the Divisive Issue: Indulgences and Church Finances (Essay 5)
> Luther on the Authority Issue: Papacy/Scripture (Essay 6)
> Luther on Church History (Essay 1)
> Luther on Monasticism (Essay 3)

Historical topics:
> Luther Debating the Key Issues: Luther vs. Eck (Essay 9)
> Luther on Free Will: Against Erasmus—A Failed Alignment of the Stars (Essay 14)
> Luther on Other Reformers (Essay 17)
> Luther on Melanchthon (Essay 19)

Spiritual life:
> In Need of Comfort and Strength: Luther on the Psalms (Essay 12)
> Luther on Spiritual Growth in a New Church (Essay 13)

Social and cultural issues:
> Luther on Children's Education (Essay 2)
> Luther Against Scholasticism: Was He a Humanist? (Essay 8)
> Luther on the Jews (Essay 18)

Reflections:
> The Capstone Essay: A Contemporary Perspective (Essay 20)

—Curtis H. Peters

"They are trying to make me into a fixed star. I am an irregular planet."—Martin Luther

· **Chapter 1** ·

Christendom

Christendom is God's kingdom here on earth. The term comes from the Latin *Christianus*, and refers to the Christian world, the community of believers who have accepted Jesus as God's son and as the Christ, or Messiah, the Savior of mankind. Through his suffering and death Christ atoned for the sins of man; his resurrection three days later was proof of victory over Satan and death, and is thus the starting point for Christianity. While singular faith is the cornerstone of Christianity, the concept of Christendom has geopolitical connotations as well, referring to those nations and political entities that embrace Christianity even when, aside from a predominant religion, they hold little else in common. Through the ages the exact relationships between political leaders, clergy, and populace have varied widely and dramatically.

From the time of Christ until Martin Luther's appearance in the 16th century, Christendom might be roughly divided into periods of growth, expansion, and sporadic unity. The first was a heroic, if not primitive era, those years immediately after Jesus' time on earth, where a small group of believers (Jews, like Jesus himself, and then Gentiles) shared their common faith through worship and fellowship. Led by the first apostles and inspired by martyrs, the early Christians persisted in the face of brutal Roman persecution and oppression, shaking off the trappings of secrecy and evangelizing the story of their Savior, while steadily becoming more visible and vocal.

The conversion of the Roman Emperor Constantine in the early years of the 4th century ushered in the next great era of Christendom. Under his rule the Church was officially recognized by the Empire and Christians were granted full legal and citizenship rights. Constantine established the concept that a political leader was responsible to God for the spiritual wellbeing of his subjects, and was further charged with rooting out heresy or misbehavior to ensure order in society. Once persecuted by government, church leaders now allied with it and came to share in its burgeoning power and wealth. The age of church as defining institution had begun.

With legitimatization came structure. In AD 325 a council of bishops convened by Constantine in Nicaea, Bithynia produced the Nicene Creed, the Christian profession of faith which declared allegiance to "one holy catholic [universal] and apostolic Church." Over the next one hundred and fifty years basic features of Christianity emerged: the mystery of the Holy Trinity; the belief in Christ as God and man; the designation of Holy Scripture; the identification of the Sacraments, including the structure of the Mass and the manner of distribution of the Eucharist; canon law; monasticism; the liturgical calendar; missionary expansion; and division into sees, dioceses, and parishes. The status of clergy was elevated and eventually organized into a hierarchy of bishops (the Bishop of Rome said to be first among equals), priests, and deacons, some of whom could be traced back to the apostles themselves. Although the exact nature and extent papal authority was often a source of dispute, eventually the concept of papal supremacy emerged, and the pope's absolute authority came to dominate Western Europe for centuries.

Constantine's empire gave way to the rise of the Germanic Franks, and with it came the emergence of feudalism and the continued, if uneven, expansion of the faith. The Christian world underwent a dramatic transformation on Christmas Day 800, when Pope Leo III crowned Charlemagne Emperor of the Holy Roman Empire. This unexpected event represented a new and cataclysmic ideal: all of central Europe would now be united by a common faith and moral culture, a single society within a wide variety of peoples. And indeed Christendom was triumphant in the medieval age, reaching the heights of its prestige and power, corresponding with the new artistic and intellectual achievements of the emerging Renaissance. Even as the Empire itself faltered, the Catholic Church firmly established itself as the main civilizing force in Europe and its most powerful institution. Its influence manifested itself throughout the continent: Christianity took root in the British Isles, and then spread to multiple countries and populations: Franks, Lombards, and Angles converted in the sixth and seventh centuries; next came Hessian Germans and Saxons; then northern Germans and Slavs; and finally the Baltics and the Scandinavians of Denmark, Norway, and Sweden.

Owing to divergent populations, languages, and cultures, expansion necessarily brought controversy, secular and non-secular alike. Great divisions within the Church, called schisms, highlighted the theological differences between the Byzantine and Orthodox Christians of the East and the Latin and Roman Catholics of the West. In 1305 Pope Clement V moved the Holy See to Avignon in southeastern France, and there it remained until 1372 when Gregory XI returned it to Rome. After Gregory's death, however, the college became hopelessly split. The same church that had united Europe was now ruled by two Vicars of Christ in two different countries, a scandal that persisted for thirty years.

Conflict was also inevitable, evidenced most notably by the bloody Crusades of the 11th, 12th, and 13th centuries. Designed to stop invading Muslims and reclaim Christian holy places in and around Jerusalem, the Church's forces also battled to control the lucrative trade routes of the Middle East. The series of inquisitions which begin in the 12th century were designed to discover and punish heretics and to reestablish fundamental theological thought. All too often, however, the Church was guilty of authorizing and condoning theft, plunder, imprisonment, torture, and death as it carried out its missions.

Yet for all her struggles the Church remained the dominant institution in European life. The four great powers of the age, France, Germany, England, and Spain, all rivaled for military and economic power while at the same time embracing, to one degree or another, their religious roots and traditions. But it was Germany that was set apart, because of its unique political system, and it was Germany that would give rise to the Reformation.

By the High Middle Ages of the 15th century, Germany and her surrounding territories—essentially central Europe—made up the Holy Roman Empire of the German Nation. This cultural nation of twenty million people, known historically as the First Reich, consisted of some three hundred sovereign states and free cities. Unlike neighboring France, however, which benefitted from the strong centralized government of the monarchy, the authority of the German emperor was limited; real political power was held by the princes, nobles, lords, dukes, margraves, counts, and knights in the various states. In many places—perhaps about one-sixth of the empire—Catholic bishops, archbishops, or abbots, appointed by the pope in faraway Rome, held political power as well. Three of these (the archbishops of Cologne, Treves, and Mainz) joined four other non-ecclesiasticals (the King of Bohemia, the Margrave of Brandenburg, the Count Palatine, and the Elector of Saxony) to form the college of electors that chose the emperor, a fact that would play a monumental part in Luther's rise.

The vast majority of Germans were peasants who lived in small villages of fewer than one hundred people. Some worked in shops or markets but most worked to scratch out meager livings in fields and pastures. All were accountable to the Catholic Church, which permeated every aspect of peasant life. The largest building in the village was the church, and the clergyman was the village's most prominent resident. Every birth, baptism, communion, marriage, and death was marked by the Church's rules and formalities. Devout Christians were admired as upstanding members of the community, while slackers were ostracized. The week centered on Sunday Mass (conducted in Latin, which peasants could not understand), and attendance was essentially mandatory. One could achieve salvation only through adherence to the teachings of the Church, and through receipt of the Sacraments, which the Church administered. The Eucharist was offered once per year, as was repentance or confession. The Bible existed, but since only clergymen could read, its contents were more or less a mystery to the peasantry. Most remained ignorant even of the lessons of the Gospel. Yet prayer was a constant feature in every home, and the Rosary was faithfully recited. Picture books, illustrating the life of Christ and prominently featuring the Virgin Mary, were popular. The Holy Trinity, it was often suggested, had become "the Virgin, the Father, and the Son."

But the Church that dominated peasant life was unquestionably corrupt. Over the centuries the papacy had become obsessed with ceremony and form over substance. Popes lived beyond their means in divine opulence, constructed magnificent buildings, and patronized the arts. They financed wars and defended their territory, which included vast holdings of property throughout the continent. Accordingly, popes constantly needed cash, and they found a steady stream of revenue in Germany, the wealthiest country in Christendom. With no strong central government to protect them, German peasants had no alternative but to grumble and comply.

Popes collected their monies through bishops, who imposed taxes through their dioceses. Bishops established transactional taxes on contracts, mortgages, marriages, probates, and disputes in papal courts between clergy and parishioners. Rome even found a way to impose taxes on the new bishops the pope had just appointed. But these appointees who would now hold political and ecclesiastical power were seldom, if ever, Germans, a fact that did not sit well with the increasingly nationalistic populace. In fact, the new appointees often didn't even travel to Germany, but sent vicars to fulfill their duties instead. These lower clergy, as they were called, were often poorly educated in both spiritual and non-spiritual matters. Worse, they behaved not as men of God, but as men of the world.

Bribery was rampant at all levels of the Church, and avarice was commonplace. Clerical concubinage was an open secret throughout the regions, and many parish priests held common law wives and children. Monastic compliance with their vows varied from order to order. (The Benedictines and Teutonic Knights seemed to have been most worldly, while the Dominican, Franciscan, and Augustinian friars were known to more strictly cling to their vows and perform regular acts of charity and benevolence.) For generations, even popes had been less than discreet with their own dalliances, and Pope Alexander, for one, had publicly acknowledged his own child. Historians agree that the condition of the Church as a whole, from top to bottom, gave great cause for alarm.

At the height of the Church's power, and perhaps of its corruption, the Plague struck Europe in 1347. In just a dozen years nearly two hundred million people, somewhere between one-third and one-half of the population, perished. If the Black Death was not the end of the world, as many thought, then it surely was a sign of God's wrath. Catholics believed what they were taught, that their God had two sides: one loving and merciful, the other judgmental and vengeful. Perhaps, then, the Church insisted, if parishioners could please God, they might avoid the awful punishment God was now inflicting. In order to accomplish this, priests devised lists of transgressions, catalogs of sin which warranted confession. Each and every sin had to be atoned for: sins of words and thought, of action and inaction. Sin could take the form of gluttony, or lust, or sloth, or temptation. Pride, ambition, tyranny, laziness, gambling, blasphemy, seduction, profanity—all sins could be identified, categorized, and confessed. Increased emphasis was then placed on the sacrament of penance, and thus the peasant parishioner relied even more on the priest.[1]

It was a fearful time, and fear was not limited to calamitous disease or invading enemies. Christians in the Middle Ages lived in terror of Satan and his depraved powers. The devil was a real, tangible force of evil, taught the Church, ever present and pervasive. The word *Satan* itself is Hebrew, meaning "adversary" or "destructor." The Devil was said to be God's archenemy, a wickedly powerful spirit of iniquity. After a monumental battle in heaven, according to Scripture, Satan had been hurled to earth, along with his dark angels, to continue his eternal struggle with God for the souls of men. Now he perched on the shoulder of every peasant and prince, old man or young child, heinously whispering, cajoling, and tempting his prey. He lurked in every cottage and shop, in every orchard and field. Jesus had conquered death, believed the Christian, but black Lucifer still roamed, spreading his poison and disrupting God's holy reign.

Satan commanded all manner of minions who did his evil bidding. They sometimes took the form of demons, with tongues of fire and teeth of iron. They often inhabited swine, crows, and cats. They were present in strange noises. They were howling winds in the treetops and rafters. They were present in creaking floorboards and wisps of smoke, in the scurrying of rats and the bellowing of cattle. They took the form of headaches and bellyaches and all manner of unexplained circumstance. Satan was the Prince of Darkness, a lurking villainous mystery, truly the scourge of mankind.

Fear of Satan corresponded with superstition, and most people in the late Middle Ages believed firmly in witchcraft. Witches had frightening powers. They cast spells and produced illnesses of all kinds. Witches possessed elderly, defenseless people, providing a convenient explanation for odd behavior. They also lived in innocent children and manifested themselves in misbehavior or naughtiness. Witches were the cause of all kinds of mischief. They ruined orchards and vineyards. They caused pastures to wither, streams to go dry. They could sour the milk, spoil the meat, spill boiling water on the children. Witches turned butter to dung, eggs to stones. They caused fruit to fall prematurely from orchard trees, and then inhabited the bellies of horses that ate it. Witches turned conversation to argument, musings to murder. They caused distemper and perversion of thought. By their incantations witches caused men to become impotent and women to fail to conceive or worse, miscarry. Witches were sexual predators, taught Saint Augustine. Sometimes witches took the form of angels, and coupled with unsuspecting women, producing disease or a scandalous pregnancy.

While Satan was everywhere on earth, and witches and demons lurked unseen, the German peasant remained in his village. All the protection he needed, he was told, was provided by the Church, for despite its many imperfections, it remained the unchanging constant in medieval life.

Thus was Germany in the 15th century, a land far north of Rome, yet at the heart of the Holy Roman Empire. It was filled with hardworking people whose allegiance was given without question to the only Church they had ever known, a Church unsurpassed in power and influence, a Church that prescribed the way to salvation and provided the only sure refuge against evils, both real and imagined. German medieval life had stood still, it seemed, for five hundred years, but it was about to be torn apart by challenge, crisis, and tumultuous reform. In the north central part of Germany was Saxony, a region that contained flat land and mountains, rivers and black forests, cities and hamlets. In the center of Saxony was the tiny village of Eisleben. And it was here, at just a few minutes before midnight on Friday, November 10, 1483, in a modest, half-timbered two-story house on Lange Strasse, where Martin Luther was born.

• Chapter 2 •

Young Martin

Martin Luther never forgot that he was of peasant stock. His father, Hans Luder, or Ludher—Martin changed his name to Luther years later after he became famous—was from the small Saxon village of Möhra. It lay in the Werra valley, in harsh Thuringia forest country, at the base of the Harz Mountains. Möhra had no priest, just a chapel and neighborhood parish that served its hundred or so residents. Like his father and grandfather before him, Hans was a tenant farmer. Although he was the eldest son, he did not stand to inherit his father's farmhouse, cattle and horses. Due to an odd Saxon law the youngest son was heir to the family estate. When his father died in 1483, rather than stay and work the fields for his younger brother, Hans took his wife Margarethe and infant Jacob to Eisleben, where Martin, the second son, was born.

On November 11, the day after his birth, Martin was baptized at Saints Peter and Paul Church in Eisleben, just a block from the family home and across a stream called Böse Sieben. It was the feast day of Saint Martin of Tours, one of the most celebrated figures of the Church and the patron saint of soldiers. In the 4th century Saint Martin had famously cut his military cloak and shared it with a beggar. Later he organized early churches and monasteries, and worked for the poor. Young Martin was named in his honor.[1]

Six months later Hans again moved his family, this time to Mansfeld, five miles away, where he quickly found work as a quarrier, working the silver and copper mining shafts that ran below the valley. Eventually the industrious Hans earned the trust of the counts, who lived in castles above the town and owned the mining operations, and he was able to lease two smelting furnaces. While the work was never easy, Hans made steady progress toward improving his lot and his family's station. Perhaps with the assistance of Margarethe's family, Hans came to own six mine shafts in addition to his smelters. He became a respected member of the community, a *Burgher*, whose economic station lifted him a notch or two above the peasantry. Hans even served as part of the local government; in addition to the *Schultheiss*, or municipal judge, and the lords of the valley, the magistracy also included four "from the community." Hans was listed as one of these distinguished four as early as 1491. He bought a handsome home in the center of town; above the entrance gate was a sandstone arch that boasted the family coat of arms, a crossbow flanked by roses. In the coming years Margarethe delivered four more children, although at least two died of the Plague. The family worshipped at St. George's Church in Mansfeld, routinely taking part in the sacraments and other rituals, and dutifully giving thanks to St. Anne, said to be the mother of the Virgin Mary and the patron saint of miners, protector of men like Hans.

The uncertainty of mining life, with its inherent dangers and erratic economic markets, left little time for leisure. Hard work and discipline were demanded in Hans and Margarethe's household, and obedience was expected; the prevailing German attitude was that children were mere beasts who needed to be tamed. Martin's parents were as strict as they were pious, and the rod was not spared. Martin later noted that his authoritarian father "once whipped me so that I ran away and felt ugly toward him until he was at pains to win me back."[2] Margarethe matched her husband's stern and serious nature. She regularly ventured out to the forests and carried firewood home on her back. Like her husband, Margarethe suffered no misbehavior. Martin remembered that "for the sake of a nut my mother once beat me until the blood flowed."[3] Reflecting her grim outlook on life, Margarethe used to sing her children little songs:

Luther was born in this house in Eisleben on November 10, 1483.

Mir und dir is keiner hold;
das is unser beider Schuld.

For me and you, no one cares;
For that we are both guilty.

and

Wenn Volk nicht wie du und ich,
Die Schuld bei uns ist wie sein.

If folk don't like you and me,
The fault is with us as with them.[4]

Hans and Margarethe were painted by famed Renaissance artist Lucas Cranach the Elder in 1527, when Martin was at the peak of his fame. The portraits reveal two plainly dressed,

Luther was baptized at the Church of Saints Peter and Paul in Eisleben (courtesy the Church of Saints Peter and Paul).

unsmiling people, neither figure offering a clue that their son was now the most famous man in Europe. Hans is stout, scowling, one hand clutching his coat. Margarethe is lean, a white kerchief wrapped tightly across her head, her hands folded in front of her. Judging by his later writings, Martin seemed to have held a certain respect for his parents, a dutiful devotion perhaps, but nothing further. He recalled only that his parents were "well intended." When his father lay dying in 1530, Martin did not make the short trip to visit him; when he heard the news of Hans' death, he wept alone.

But whatever his parents may have lacked in affection, they were ambitious—for themselves and certainly for Martin. They noted that he was particularly bright, and seemed unusually inquisitive, from an early age. There is no indication that Hans urged his son to follow in his footsteps and work in the mines; rather, he believed that education was the key to a prosperous future. Margarethe agreed. She taught Martin to read at home and then, even though he was only four and one-half years old, fully two years younger than the norm, he was enrolled in the Latin school in Mansfeld. A family friend, Nicolas Oehmler, escorted his son Georg and Martin to school each day. Martin attended the school for the next eight years, and there the lessons he had begun to learn at home—of diligence, structure, and fundamental Christian thought—were reinforced; indeed, they became cemented in his psyche and shaped his entire life.

Each student was given a Latin primer, the language deemed essential to scholastic and religious endeavors (with minor exceptions, students were punished if they spoke in German). In addition to Latin, Martin studied basic literature, mathematics, and history. Martin was also given music lessons, for he showed aptitude on the piano and lute, and displayed a fine singing voice. He happily joined in the youth choir, which memorized and performed the *Sanctus* (Holy, holy, holy, Lord God of hosts, Heaven and Earth are full of thy glory); the *Benedictus* (Blessed be the Lord God of Israel, for he hath visited, and redeemed his people); the *Agnus Dei* (Lamb of God, you who take away the sins of the world, have mercy upon us); the *Confiteor* (I confess to almighty God, and to you my brothers and sisters, that I have greatly sinned); and the *Magnificat*, which he particularly loved (My soul doth magnify the Lord, and my spirit hath rejoiced in God my savior). The students were allowed to read only those parts of the Bible used in the Mass. They memorized the Ten Commandments, the Lord's Prayer, and the Apostles' Creed in both German and Latin. They attended daily Masses and vespers—evening prayer services—and celebrated the numerous Holy Days. Each day the students watched as the sick were brought to a nearby convent, and prayers were offered for cures, or for devils to leave the bodies they inhabited. The prevailing Church doctrine was constantly reinforced to Martin and his classmates: Jesus was the loving Savior who had been sent from God to redeem mankind. But he was also the terrible master who sat in judgment of all people, whose perfect example could never be achieved, and who instilled great fear in all who believed. Martin recalled: "From early childhood I was accustomed to turn pale and tremble whenever I heard the name of Christ mentioned, for I was taught to look upon him as a stern and wrathful judge."[5]

Reflecting the authoritarian nature of the German culture, and the strict doctrinal demands of the Church, the Latin school was not a sentimental place. Lessons were drilled into the students and those who fell behind were punished, forced to wear a dunce's cap, or *asinus* (donkey) mask. Misbehavior brought consequences, often severe ones. Students were encouraged to tattle on their classmates; one secret "wolf" student was chosen by the teacher to report any wrongdoing. The teachers marked their pupils' mistakes with slashes on a chalkboard, and at the end of each week the students received spankings for every mark accumulated. On one occasion, Martin later recalled, he was punished severely for a grammatical error: "At school I was caned in a single morning fifteen times for nothing at all. I was required to decline and conjugate and hadn't learned my lesson."[6]

In 1497, at the age of 13, Martin left Mansfeld for the river city of Magdeburg, sixty miles away, where he would spend a year at secondary school. Situated on the Elbe River, with a population of about 12,000 people, Magdeburg was one of the largest cities in Germany. It had once been the home of Otto the Great, the first emperor of the Holy Roman Empire. It contained so many churches, steeples, and spires that it was sometimes called "Little Rome." Martin attended the Cathedral School with his friend Johan Reinecke, who was to be a lifelong confidant. The school was run by the Brothers of the Common Life, sometimes called "null-brothers," a pious group of mystics who banded together in the simple life of prayer, labor, and benevolence, and who believed they could best serve mankind through instruction and pastoral care. The minimalist lifestyle of the Brothers was passed on to their students. It was customary for them to wander the streets, singing and begging for food crumbs: (*panem propter Deum*, "bread for God's sake").[7] Martin joined in this activity enthusiastically. He witnessed something that left an impression on him and must have, to some degree, influenced his future. He saw Prince William of Anhalt, who had forsaken his title and life of privilege to become a Franciscan monk, beg for food from strangers. And it was here too, at the Cathedral School, where Martin saw a Bible for the first time.

But Martin stayed in Magdeburg for just one year. He then transferred to St. George's secondary school in Eisenach, probably because his mother had relatives in the area. Eisenach was a walled city of perhaps 2,000 people in the northern foothills of the Thuringia Forest, about ninety miles from Eisleben. It was home to the Wartburg Castle, a prominent landmark which, though in disrepair, rose 1200 feet above the town and would play a huge part in Martin's later years. St. George's School, like the Cathedral School, was a college preparatory institution and devoted to the trivium of medieval liberal arts: grammar, or the mechanics of language; logic or dialectic, which was tied to thought, analysis, and philosophy; and rhetoric, the art of public speaking, instruction and persuasion. Mastery of each of these disciplines would serve Martin well in years to come.

Martin appears to have blossomed in Eisenach. He looked back fondly on his three years there. He made good friends, both in and out of school. The rector, or principal, of St. George's was John Trebonius, who showed great confidence in Martin and strongly encouraged him to continue his pursuit of academic achievement. Martin served as tutor to a grade school boy named Henry Cotta, and in exchange stayed at the Cotta family home. He grew so close to the family that he referred to Ursula as his "adopted mother." He also was befriended by the Heinrich Schalke family and sometimes took his meals with them. Both the Cottas and Schalbes would remain Martin's friends and supporters for the rest of his life.

In May 1501 Hans insisted that his son enroll at the University of Erfurt, considered to be the finest university in Germany and, as with his prior schools, close to home. Hans believed that Martin would someday become a lawyer, and could then provide a comfortable income for himself and his parents. Martin was grateful for the opportunity to continue his education and embraced his father's dream. "My dear father," he said, "'maintained me there with loyal affection, and by his labour and the sweat of his brow enabled me to go there.'"[8] Erfurt was a walled city, known for its markets and international trade. It was also a city of believers. Of its 20,000 people, about one thousand were priests, monks, and nuns, and it boasted no less than twenty-two monasteries, twenty-three churches, thirty-six chapels, and six hospitals. For Erfurt's citizens, faith was a public matter; displays of piety and expressions of Christian zeal were commonplace, and religious parades and festivals were regular events. Luther called it "a new Bethlehem."[9]

The University of Erfurt was divided into four disciplines, or faculties. Candidates for Bachelors and Masters of Arts degrees, as Martin was, were instructed by the liberal arts faculty. The three professional faculties of law, medicine, and theology were a level above; the professors of these curricula were *doctors*, or the highest order of teachers.

Conformity was the rule. The students lived in a *bursa*, a dormitory of sorts where they ate, slept and studied, all under the watchful eye of the house master. Each day began at four a.m. Students dressed alike, said common prayers, worshipped together, and studied the same core subjects. Two professors of philosophy—Bartholomaus Arnoldi von Usingen and Jodocus Trutfetter—made a particularly profound impression on Martin. They focused on Aristotle (whose views on logic and reason had been adopted by the Church, and who Martin would, in time, come to loathe), and the lesser-known philosophers William of Ockham and Gabriel Biel. Under the instruction of these men, and others, students learned the art of debate, or disputation; that is, they learned to frame the issues, define their terms, identify weaknesses, and build logical arguments. All of man's great questions gave cause for examination: What was truth if not universal? How can one find beauty? What was real or imagined?

How could right and wrong be measured? What was the purpose of existence? And most important, how might one please God? Aristotle's logic could be used to resolve any and all contradictions. In the inquiry itself, the idea was to confirm the Christian faith by showing that its doctrines fit together in a coherent whole.

In this atmosphere, and within this structure, Martin thrived. He quickly gained a reputation as a gifted and serious student. His debating prowess earned him the nickname "The Professor." While he was on friendly terms with a group of students who gave themselves over to Humanism and called themselves "the poets," he did not align himself with them, preferring to go his own way. Along with the study of philosophy he remained a devout Catholic, finding the time each day to study the Psalms until he had all 150 memorized. He graduated with a Bachelor of Arts degree in September 1502, ranking thirtieth of fifth-seven students. By 1505 he received his Master of Arts degree, ranking second of seventeen graduates. He had, at the age of twenty-two, earned the title "Master Martin," and he could now teach the trivium of the liberal arts. He was proud of his accomplishments. He later wrote: "How marvelous it was when the masters were promoted and the tapers were presented to them! I contend that there is no temporal or worldly joy to compare with it!"[10] His father was equally pleased. He presented his son with a costly graduation gift, a copy of *Corpus Juris Civilus*, the principal legal textbook of the day. Martin would immediately begin the study of law. Six months later, however, a thunderstorm, and St. Anne, intervened, setting Martin on a course that would change the world.

• Chapter 3 •

"Help me, St. Anne"

At the age of twenty-one Luther's path seemed clear. He had been the recipient of a secure, if not overly affectionate upbringing, surely better than what most peasant children received in the High Middle Ages. His parents, through their examples of hard work and dedication, had instilled in him the importance of discipline and the determination to improve one's social standing. He had always appreciated the value of education, and as he grew older he recognized his own potential, and challenged himself to excel. Success in his law studies seemed assured, and with it would come the certainty of a healthy income and the fulfillment of his father's dreams. Again following the example of his parents, Luther had always taken his faith seriously, as well. He applied the same discipline to religion as he had to his studies. He said his required prayers each morning. He regularly attended Mass, and took part in the rituals and observances as demanded. He venerated the saints and longed to view someday their holy relics that had been preserved throughout the ages. He admired the pope from afar. He did not question what he had been taught about the almighty God and his perfect holy Church.

But Luther was a sorrowful soul. He had also been taught, since his birth, to fear all that could not be understood. He was terrorized at the thought of Satan and constantly wary of his minions, the demons, spirits, and apparitions that wreaked havoc across the land and sought to poison the thoughts and deeds of humans. Luther was haunted by the fear that he was an easy prey for Satan and for all evil forces. He believed that God was locked in an endless struggle with the Devil for the souls of men. Luther saw himself as a helpless victim, a citizen of a world in which this monumental and never-ending struggle took place. While it was true that God had sent his son to save mankind, he also demanded adherence to his law. Like all Catholics—like all wretched sinners—Luther lived in fear of God's wrathful judgment. Even when immersed in his studies, this fear never left Luther's thoughts. Luther felt—he *knew*—that only through strict piety and adherence to God's commandments could he reconcile himself to the Father and escape his holy wrath. He could not possibly live up to God's expectations, he fretted, the model of which was established through the perfect life of Christ. All of the assistance the Church offered, including the intercession of Mary and the saints, observance of the sacraments, penance, and good works, could not sufficiently negate his sinful disposition. He was subject to innumerable faults, sins in thought, word, and deed, some major and some minor, but sins nonetheless. He committed so many sins that he could never atone for them all. "The more we wash our hands," he told himself, "the fouler they become."[1] If he could not gain forgiveness for his many sins, Luther feared, he could not live a godly life. And if he failed to live up to God's standards, he was surely not deserving of eternal salvation.

But it was not just damnation in hell that Luther feared; it was death itself. The wages of sin is death, St. Paul had written, and Luther interpreted this fate to mean a suffering in "everlasting nothingness." He contemplated death as a place of tormented sleep, a "grave of the soul." What would happen to him, Luther wondered, when he died? Would he have earned salvation through prayers and good works (this seemed to him unlikely), or would the Terrible Judge sentence him, an unworthy sinner, to the horrors of eternal darkness? He called the horrible fears of unworthiness before God "*Anfechtungen*," and he articulated these "assaults of terror" as though he was under attack from almighty God himself. This constant brooding over the uncertainty of the afterlife—his "melody of death," as some biographers have described it—was the stream of fears that ruled, and then transformed, Luther's life.[2]

After receiving his master's degree, Luther took a break from his studies for three months and then spent a month lecturing in the Arts faculty. On May 20, 1505, he began his law studies at Erfurt. Barely a month into his studies, however, he took a sudden leave and returned home to Mansfeld. Perhaps he was unhappy in law school and wanted to discuss his future with his parents. Perhaps he wanted to grieve the recent death of a young companion. Perhaps he merely wanted to celebrate the summer church festivals, including the Feast of St. Mary, with his family. But whatever the reason for interrupting his academic endeavors, he was on the verge of a tumultuous event. On the warm and humid afternoon of July 2 he was walking back to Erfurt. Just outside the tiny village of Stotternheim, a violent thunderstorm appeared. Terrified of the lightning's fury and fearful of death, Luther fell to the ground and cried out in desperation, "Help me, St. Anne, I will become a monk!" Many years later, recalling the awful event, he claimed that the promise was forced from him, *Terrore et agone mortis subitae circumvallatus*: "Suddenly surrounded by the terror and the agony of death," he wrote and then continued, "I felt constrained to make my vow."[3] He would enter a monastery and devote his life to God.

It was not Luther's first brush with death. Once, as a student at Erfurt, he had accidently cut himself with a knife while walking in a field. As the blood from the wound gushed, Luther called out to the Virgin Mary for help. Miraculously someone happened on the scene and managed to stop the bleeding. That night, however, the wound reopened, and once again Luther called to Mary for help, and he survived. On other occasions he had been seriously ill and bedridden for weeks. One sickness in particular necessitated that a priest be called to his bedside, and Luther later related that he got well only after he was advised, "Take courage, God will yet make you the means of comfort to many others."[4]

Whether the thunderstorm was God's will or the work of a demon, Luther could not ignore his vow. While he temporarily regretted it, he ultimately held steadfast to his promise. His many friends tried to talk him out of it to no avail. Luther was given only two weeks to prepare for his new life. Since he could enter a monastery with nothing but the clothes on his back, he gave away nearly everything he owned: most of his clothes, personal possessions and books (including the *Corpus Juris Civilus* his father had given him), and even his lute. Then, in the evening of July 15, 1505, the eve of St. Alexis Day, Luther held a farewell party at his residence hall in Erfurt. Again his friends tried to dissuade him, and again he refused. In the early morning hours they accompanied him to a group of buildings known as the Black Cloister (so named for the color of the monks' clothing), not far from the Gera River, and

Top: Site of the fateful lightning strike, just outside of Stotternheim. *Bottom:* "Help me, St. Anne, I will become a monk."

then to the thick wooden doors of the Augustinian monastery entrance. "You see me today, but never more," Luther said to them.[5] He knocked on the door and was admitted. He longed for peace, and he sought spiritual satisfaction, but felt little joy. While he believed he would never leave the monastery, he felt "quite dead to the world."[6]

He had not told his parents. Once safely ensconced behind the high monastery walls he wrote to his father and informed him of his decision and his new residence. Predictably, Hans was furious. He had sacrificed so that his son would complete his studies and become a lawyer, improving the family's social status and providing financial security. He also hoped to contract an honorable (and perhaps wealthy) marriage for Martin. All his efforts had now been wasted. He did not believe that the life of a monk would bring his son happiness. Hans' own friends tried to console him; perhaps, they reasoned, it was all for the best. If Hans wanted to please God, he should offer up his "dearest and best," his own son. But Hans believed that his son's immaturity would destroy all that he had worked for. Luther insisted that his vow, while originating in the terror of death, was no less than a promise registered in heaven. Hans reacted bitterly and wrote, "Grant that it is not an illusion and deception!" Luther later recalled that his father was "near mad about it; he would not allow it. He sent me an answer in writing, addressing me in terms that showed his displeasure, and renouncing all further affection."[7] These words of indignation, Luther wrote, "penetrated and lodged in my inmost being" and I "steeled my heart as much as I could against you and your words." Luther was "clothed in burning youth" and righteously clung to his decision, and the contempt that father and son felt for each other was a long time in healing.[8]

There were twenty-two monasteries within the city walls of Erfurt, including the Benedictines, Franciscans, and Dominicans, and Luther's choice, the Augustinians. Traditionally, monasteries (often called convents, chapters, or cloisters) were located in rural areas, the idea being that in remote places the dedicated could more effectively pray, study, work, and seek the Lord's grace. Gradually the Church hierarchy realized that, with the growth of cities and the attraction of wealth and worldly pleasure, urban areas needed sacred study places as well. Beginning in the 12th century, monasteries (and grandiose cathedrals) were built in places like Erfurt.

The founder of the order Luther chose was St. Augustine, a strong and fascinating defender of the faith who lived and wrote in the 4th century. For the rest of Luther's life Augustine would remain his theological hero. He would much admire Augustine's teachings on God's mercy and grace, and the proper relationship between God and man. "Augustine was a thinker," said Luther. "He wants to know and he doesn't want to assume, and he also teaches accordingly. He is the greatest theologian among those who wrote since the apostles."[9] There were two Augustinian orders in Erfurt: the Canons Regular, and the more moderate Order of the Hermits (reflecting the rural heritage), sometimes known as the Observants. Luther joined the latter. The orders had been incorporated by Pope Innocent IV in 1245, and now numbered over 2,000 chapters scattered across Europe. In the Saxon-Thuringia province alone some fifty Augustinian cloisters existed. All orders revered their founder, of course, and their members went about their spiritual business with an earnest combination of piety, contemplation, and discipline. Luther's order also had a reputation for scholarship and teaching, elements which certainly attracted him.

Luther joined about fifty other monks at the cloister. His initial admittance was just temporary. For the first month he was the monks' guest, and they assisted him in examining his soul: were the reasons for his application legitimate? Once this initial period of time passed, and Luther had satisfactorily displayed his sincerity, he was offered the chance to be elevated to novice status, another temporary station that would last a year. As the other monks watched, Luther presented himself to the prior, or the head of the monastery, at the cloister altar for questioning.

"What are you looking for?" asked the prior.

"God's grace and your mercy," Luther answered.

"Are you married?"

"No."

"Do you owe anyone work or money?"

"No."

"Your life here will be a hard one. Are you willing to give up wealth, marriage, and material possessions? Will you vow poverty, chastity, and obedience? Are you willing to spend long hours in prayer, in meditation, and sacrifice? Are you ready to accept the hardships of loneliness and carry on with God's wishes?"

"Yes, with God's help and insofar as human weakness allows."[10]

As the choir of monks chanted, a circle of hair on the top of Luther's head was tonsured, or shaved, and he was given a black skullcap—a mark of God surely stronger and more protective, it was said, than any helmet that could be worn in battle. He put on a white woolen shirt, then a frock and cowl made of black cloth, and finally a leather belt. A narrow strip of cloth was placed over the cowl and hung from his shoulders down to his feet; it signified the

St. Augustine Monastery, Erfurt.

words of the Savior: "My yoke is easy, and my burden is light." A prayer was then pronounced that the Lord might put off the old identity and put on the new, as God had fashioned. Luther knelt as the prior blessed him, and then lay flat on the floor, arms outstretched in the form of a cross. "Not he that has begun," said the prior, "but he that endures to the end shall be saved."[11]

Monastic life began immediately, and Luther joined other novices, brothers, monks, and priests in a numbingly monotonous routine. The Black Cloister was a collection of buildings. The church was the most imposing structure, its nave able to hold 300 worshippers and its altar set up high in the chancel, purposely unreachable to them. Just outside was the *Kreuzweg*, a small, arched courtyard that housed the order's Stations of the Cross and was designed for quiet contemplation and reflection. Next to the courtyard stood the building that housed the monks. On the first floor was the common room, where the men took their meals. On the second floor were the individual

Cathedral at St. Augustine Monastery, Erfurt.

rooms, called cells, where the monks slept. Each cell measured only three feet by seven feet, barely enough room for a tiny cot. A small window in some of the cells looked out at the *Kreuzweg* below. Each morning at two a.m. the first of the daily church bells rang, awakening the men and signaling the day's first prayer session. The men quickly dressed—they were not allowed to leave their cells unless they were dressed in their black and white garb—and made their way silently to the church. There they were sprinkled with holy water and took their places in the nave or choir loft. The choir cantor chanted the *Salve Regina*:

Save, O Queen, Thou Mother of Mercy, our life, our delight, and our hope. To Thee we exiled sons of Eve lift up our cry. To Thee we sigh as we languish in this vale of tears. Be Thou our advocate. Sweet Virgin Mary, pray for us. Thou holy Mother of God.[12]

The brethren were then required to say twenty-five *Paternosters*, or Our Fathers, and the *Ave Maria*. They filed out of the church silently, their thoughts their own. These nearly identical hours of prayer, or *horae*, were demanded seven times daily, to conform to the seven sacraments of the Church: Baptism; Eucharist; Penance; Confirmation; Marriage; Ordination;

Top: Altar at the Cathedral at St. Augustine Monastery. Here Luther took his final vows to become a monk, and here his father watched him offer his first Eucharist. *Bottom:* Monk's cell at St. Augustine Monastery, Erfurt (courtesy Erfurt Evangelical Augustinian Monastery).

and Extreme Unction, or Last Rites. Each session was somber and strictly regimented, and deviation, no matter how slight, was not allowed.

Novices were assigned two superiors who watched over them, counseled them, and introduced them to Bible studies (for nearly all of the brethren, this was the first serious look at the Scriptures they had ever had). Luther was given a Latin Bible, bound in red leather. As much as he wanted to devour its entire contents, however, he was discouraged from reading all but selected portions. One of the senior monks, a man named Usingen, told Luther that he must instead focus on the "ancient writers," for they had sufficiently "extracted the essence of truth from the Bible. The Bible is the cause of all disturbances."[13] In future years Luther would wholeheartedly reject this proposition; for now, he did as he was told.

Every hour of the day was regulated by prayer, worship, penance, study, vigils, and meals. "Not even one leaf in the garden is allowed to be plucked without permission," said Luther.[14] The monks rarely left the buildings' cluster. Work was limited

View of the meditation courtyard from the monk's cell, St. Augustine Monastery, Erfurt (courtesy Erfurt Evangelical Augustinian Monastery).

to cleaning, building repair and maintenance, and gardening. The Augustinians were a relatively wealthy order, benefitting from healthy endowments from townspeople, and while monks did not seek employment they did occasionally participate in begging on Erfurt's streets, a sign more of humility and piety than financial necessity.

For all the routine it appears that Luther enjoyed his first months at the monastery. He enthusiastically fulfilled every duty, performed every task, and met every requirement placed before him. In the overwhelming silence he found a measure of the spiritual satisfaction he was looking for. He later wrote, "I know from my own experience, and from that of many others, how mute and quiet the Devil usually is during one's first years as a priest or a monk."[15] He believed the austerity was good for him, and he liked to imagine that he was walking the same path as the famed saints of centuries past, St. George, perhaps, or Anthony, or Bernard. "I used to picture such a saint," Luther wrote, "who would live in the desert and abstain from food and drink and exist on a few vegetables and roots and cold water."[16]

He easily passed the Novitiate and took his final vows to become a monk: "I, Friar Martin Luther, make profession and promise obedience to God Almighty, and to Holy Mary, ever virgin ... to live without property, in chastity, and after the rule of Holy Father Augustine until death."[17] Again the prior blessed him and said a prayer for him:

> Lord Jesus Christ, who didst deign to clothe thyself in our mortality, we beseech thee out of thine immeasurable goodness to bless the habit which the holy fathers have chosen as a sign of innocence and renunciation. May this thy servant, Martin Luther, who takes the habit, be clothed also in thine immortality, O thou who livest and reignest with God the Father and the Holy Ghost, God from eternity to eternity. Amen.[18]

By all accounts, Luther was a dedicated and conscientious monk. Driven by his desire to please God, Luther took it upon himself to carry out his duties with unending devotion. He enthusiastically performed menial tasks, the more humble and humiliating the better—he enjoyed scrubbing and cleaning, even the cloister privy. He was on a quest for personal perfection, and there is no indication that he violated his vows of poverty, chastity, and obedience. He later said, "I was a good monk, and kept strictly to my order, so that I could say that if the monastic life could get a man to heaven, I should have entered."[19] His contemporaries concurred in that assessment. Years later one associate reflected, "Martin Luther lived a holy life among them, observed the Rule most meticulously, and studied diligently."[20] But he was far from content. His battles with God, his *Anfechtungen*, continued. Still, within short order, in April 1507, Luther was ordained a priest. He was just twenty-three years old.

Ordination was in and of itself an honor, for only the most conscientious and dedicated monks—and certainly, it was hoped, the most intellectually gifted—were selected to become priests. "I was congratulated by the prior, the convent and father confessor," wrote Luther, "so that I was now like an innocent child who had just come forth pure from baptism."[21] As mediators between God and mankind, priests were considered to be a select group of spiritual leaders. They occupied a position of superiority over the laity; in fact, only priests could administer the sacraments. Luther's first official act as a priest was to celebrate the *Missa,* or Mass, which included administration of the Eucharist.

Next to Baptism (which was the means and method by which one became a member of the Holy Church, and considered the essential doorway to spiritual life), the Eucharist was the most important of the seven Christian sacraments. From the first centuries of Christendom, the Church taught and Christians believed that in partaking of the Eucharist they were consuming the flesh and blood of Christ himself. "Take, eat, this is my body," Christ had said to his disciples at the Last Supper, and "Drink of it, all of you, for this is my blood of the covenant, which is poured out for many for the forgiveness of sins."[22] Centuries later, in the year 1215, the Fourth Lateran Council officially proclaimed what remains today an essential component of the Catholic faith: during the miracle of the Mass, ordinary bread and wine become the body and blood of the Savior through the doctrine of transubstantiation. Raising the host before the cross, the ordained priest utters the transforming words: *"Hoc est enim corpus meum"* (This is my body), and *"Hic est calix novum testamentum in sanguine meo"* (This cup is the new testament of my blood). At that moment God physically manifests himself, becoming the redeeming body and blood of Jesus Christ, actually present in the outstretched hands of the priest. In this way, prescribed by the Church and realized through the holy work of the priest, God's salvation, as offered by the sacrifice of his own son at the crucifixion, is renewed once again for ordinary people. The Mass, and particularly the Eucharist, was made effective, said the Church, *ex opere operato*, or by virtue of the work having been done. The Eucharist thus was the most basic way in which the commonplace could connect to the sacred. While Luther would, in future years, have much to say about the Church's procedures and the ways in which the Eucharist could be administered, the body and blood would always remain a central part of his faith.

Luther celebrated his first Mass on May 2, 1507. It was Cantate Sunday, the fourth Sunday after Easter. Luther prepared himself carefully by studying the eighty-nine lessons of the *Sacri canonis missae exposito*, an instructional manual written by the theologian Gabriel Biel. The work was so comprehensive, said Luther, that "when I read it, my heart bled."[23] Luther made a special confession prior to the service. Aside from the solemnity of the occasion, and the importance of his duties as first-time celebrant, he had another reason to be anxious: Hans Luther had managed to put aside, at least perfunctorily, the resentment he harbored against his son and attended the service. He arrived at the cloister leading a party of twenty family members and friends, and carried with him a gift of twenty gulden, which he dutifully presented to the prior. "You must have a very fine friend, that you visit him in such style," someone remarked.[24] Hans took his seat in the church and looked at his son for the first time in over a year. He still disapproved of the decision to enter the monastery, but he would be present for this important day.

Jerome Scultetus, the Bishop of Brandenburg, offered the ceremonial words of consecration: "*Accipe potestatem sacrifis viventis et mortuis*" (Receive the power to offer sacrifice for the living and the dead)."[25] At first Luther handled himself well. As the bells chimed and the choir chanted, "O sing unto the Lord a new song," Luther approached the altar and completed the Introductory Rites of the Greeting and the Blessing. But then he stumbled. As he began to recite, "We offer unto Thee, the living, the true, the eternal God," a desperate feeling of hopelessness and unworthiness overtook him. How dare he, a miserable sinner, approach the almighty God? What made him worthy to address the Father? He later wrote of the experience: "At these words I was utterly stupefied and terror-stricken. I thought to myself, 'With what tongue shall I address such Majesty, seeing that that all men ought to tremble in the presence of even an earthly prince? Who am I, that I should lift up my eyes or raise my hands to God? The angels surround Him. At His nod the earth trembles. And shall I, a miserable little pygmy, say, 'I want this, I ask for that?' I am dust and ashes and full of sin, and I am to speak to the living, eternal, and true God."[26]

The familiar awful feelings of panic and despair, *Anfechtungen*, nearly paralyzed him with fear. Humbled at the thought of calling upon God, terrified of the prospect of holding the Almighty in his hands, and likely humiliated at his performance in front of his father, Luther trembled, spilled a drop or two of wine and nearly dropped the bread, and then halted altogether. Shaken, he briefly considered fleeing the scene and indicated such to the prior who assisted him at the altar. But the prior would have none of that; to him, Luther's hesitation was merely stage fright. "Get on with it," he growled impatiently. "Keep going! Faster! Faster!" Somehow Luther managed to complete the Mass. He felt that the prior's words had rescued him, but "it was clear recognition to me that all was not right."[27]

Later that afternoon a banquet was held, and Luther sat down to the meal with his father. Surrounded by brethren, masters and guests, and hopeful of some kind of reconciliation, Luther quietly brought up the subject of their dispute. "Dear father," he asked, "why were you so contrary to my becoming a monk? And perhaps you are not quite satisfied even now. The life is so quiet and godly."

Hans reacted bitterly, as if the question had caused the smoldering anger inside him to boil over. "You learned scholar," he said sarcastically, "have you never read in the Bible that you should honor your father and your mother? And here you have left me and your mother to look after ourselves in our old age."

Taken aback by his father's retort, Luther fell back on his spiritual training. "But father," he said patiently, "I could do you more good by prayers than if I had stayed in the world. And don't forget that a voice from Heaven called me to this life when I was in the storm."

But Hans was ready for this explanation. "God grant it was not an apparition of the Devil," he said. For this Luther had no answer. Years later, however, he wrote to his father and explained what had gone through his mind: "But I was so secure in my own righteousness that I heard you as just a man and was boldly contemptuous."[28]

Luther retreated into the monk's world of discipline, order, and extreme self-denial. He sought to love God with all his heart and soul, and to do so he had to reject all that the world had to offer. In joining the cloister he had already rejected his family and his possessions; now he had to reject his very self. Seeking to purify both his body and his mind, and to cleanse his heart, he deemed that his daily routine of vigil, prayer, meditation and work was insufficient. He now regularly fasted, sometimes for three days at a time, and often slept on the floor, uncovered, in chilling cold. He engaged in self-flagellation, a practice not uncommon among dedicated monks and priests but, for Luther, less a test of physical endurance than a demonstration of commitment to God and request for his approval. Contact with women was, of course, extremely limited. In all his time at Erfurt Luther never heard a woman's confession. Luther later wrote that he sometimes was filled with "evil thoughts and dreams" and "evil lust," and admitted to nocturnal emissions. But his sexuality was no more of a problem than that. And Luther took the rule of St. Augustine to heart: "Tame your flesh through moderation in eating and drinking, insofar as health permits."[29] Monks were summoned to their meals twice each day, and they ate in silence. They fasted once per week; on some occasions they consumed only gingerbread, salted bread, and small amounts of beer or wine, for days at a time. Luther followed all of these rules precisely. He made a habit of invoking the names of the saints and selected twenty-one saints as his particular helpers, three for each day's morning Mass. And he became obsessed with self-examination and confession.

The confessions of sins (*Schuldbeicht*), and subsequent acts of penance, were important parts of every monk's life. Most confessed once each day, sometimes more, for if one truly aspired to be holy, sins could be purged through confession almost as fast as they were committed. For the peasantry, confession was a relatively simple matter: the sinner entered the confessional box, admitted his sins to the priest and asked forgiveness. The priest judged the seriousness of the offense and the sincerity of the sinner, and then pronounced God's forgiveness, or absolution.

For Augustinians like Luther, however, the mere acknowledgement of wrongdoing, even if sincere, was not enough. Rather, they sought to uncover motive and desire, emotion and feeling. Augustinians looked to the source of the sin in their pursuit of piety and holiness. Taking the sacrament to the extreme, Luther's confessions became marathon sessions, dragging on for hours and hours. No sin was too small, no transgression too insignificant, and no error of thought or questionable expression of emotion could be overlooked. Tardiness at choir or meals; restlessness; frivolity; breaking objects; spilling food; cursing; grumbling: all these and more were considered minor sins to be confessed and as punishment, one or more

Bust of Luther, cloister hall, St. Augustine Monastery, Erfurt (courtesy Erfurt Evangelical Augustinian Monastery).

psalms had to be prayed. More serious transgressions such as lying, cheating, stealing, gossiping, or having lustful thoughts, merited three days of fasting and recitation of psalms. Sometimes Luther would finish his confession and then think of a sin on the way back to his room, and turn around and return to confession. He might conclude a session and then feel a small sense of satisfaction that his confessions were complete; the pride that he felt, though, was a new sin that needed to be confessed. His confessors, the other priests, shook their heads with consternation at his actions. But Luther's feelings of inadequacy before God were constant, and his belief that he could never earn God's favor was unending. The very idea that God's mighty and awful wrath was at his doorstep, a mere breath away, tormented him. "When it is touched by this passing inundation of the eternal," he wrote, "the soul feels and drinks nothing but eternal punishment.... Who knows whether (good works) please God? It is God's eternity, holiness and power which thus continuously threaten man throughout the whole of his life.... God's ever-present judgment clutches man in the loneliness of his conscience, and with his every breath conveys him to the Almighty and Holy One to prosper or destroy."[30]

Luther was assigned a mentor, the vicar-general of the Augustinian Order, Johan von Staupitz. Fifty-six years old and a Doctor of Theology, Staupitz was a measured, practical man whose beliefs matched his temperament. Luther felt fortunate that a man in Staupitz's position, and of his stellar reputation, had the time and energy to counsel him. Early on, Staupitz recognized Luther's enormous intellectual potential but also saw that his constant brooding was holding him back. Staupitz attempted, regularly, to ease Luther's mind, to soothe the "temptation and trial" that Luther obsessed over. "Do you not realize that such trial is good and necessary for you?" he asked Luther. "Otherwise nothing good would come of you?"[31] Luther appreciated the message, maintaining that Staupitz was the only one who truly understood his problems—without Staupitz he would have "sunk into hell"—but he was not easily consoled. "God's word is too high," he complained, and he sank deeper into despair.[32]

Staupitz was just as patient as Luther was exasperating. He once suffered through a Luther confession that lasted six hours. He advised his charge that these drastic practices went far beyond the order's requirement, and God's. Luther later reflected, "On one occasion, my father confessor said to me when I was constantly bringing stupid sins to him: 'Look here, if you expect Christ to forgive you, come in here with something to forgive—parricide, blasphemy, adultery instead of all these peccadilloes!'" But the idea that he might neglect to confess a transgression, or minimize its importance, haunted Luther. He would not risk losing God's favor, could not bear facing God's anger. "You are a fool!" Staupitz told him. "God does not rage at you, but you rage at him; God is not angry with you, but you are angry with him! Don't you know that God commands you to hope?" Luther did believe in a loving God, a saving God, and a merciful God. But the image that dominated his thoughts, that fueled his obsessions, was of Christ the avenger, the wrathful judge. "Rest assured that God loves you," counseled Staupitz, but Luther remained fearful.[33] "The name of Christ often frightened me," he wrote. "When I looked at Him and the cross, He seemed to me like a flash of lightning. When people mentioned His name, I would rather have heard the devil mentioned. For I believed that I would have to do good works until they made Christ love and forgive me."[34]

The exhausting confessions and the painful, ultra-disciplined self-denial remained the focus of Luther's tortured existence. Despite his herculean efforts to become the perfect priest, for the most part he was miserable. The terrors of *Anfechtungen* continued to plague him. "I was myself more than once driven to the very depths of despair so that I wished I had never been created," he wrote. "Love God? I hated him!"[35] Not even solitary, contemplative prayer would always calm Luther's fears, for at times he was uncertain God was listening to him. The creeping doubt was surely the work of the Devil, who perched on Luther's shoulder and whispered in his ear, "What are you praying for? Why do you think the Lord might consider your prayers?"[36] The unanswered questions and the torment of uncertainty were almost too much to bear. "You can rely on the Means of Grace," Staupitz told him. But these words did not quiet Luther's insecurities. "At last I became like a dead body," he wrote. "I interpreted the situation according to Paul's remark: 'I was given a thorn in my flesh to keep me from being puffed up by such revelation' (2 Cor. 12:7). And so I received it as the word and voice of the Holy Spirit. I was very holy under the papacy: I was a monk! And yet I was so sad and depressed that I thought that God was not gracious to me. There I celebrated mass, and I prayed, and I had no wife—you never saw or experienced such a member of an order or monk as I was."[37]

Luther spent a few months at the new University in Wittenberg, where he acted as a substitute professor of moral philosophy. While there he also passed a series of academic requirements and was awarded successive theological degrees: *Biblicus, Formutus,* and *Sententiarius*. As he learned, he lectured, and wrote, on the teachings of Aristotle and Augustine and Peter Lombard, the Italian bishop whose *Four Books of Sentences* was the most celebrated theological textbook of the age. Then, an exciting opportunity arose: Luther was to travel to

Rome and assist in settling a controversy. A proposal had been submitted that all the Augustinian monasteries in Saxony be united and placed under Staupitz's administrative rule. The most conservative of those, including Luther's Erfurt Observants and a few others located in Nuremberg, objected—not to Staupitz, who was universally respected, but to the prospect that they become affiliated with Carthusians, Franciscans, and Dominicans, who would dilute their strict Observant traditions. While it seemed that Staupitz had already been given the authority, at least on paper, Luther and another monk were selected to travel to the papal curia and argue their case to Egidius Canisius of Viterbo, the General of the entire Augustinian order. Luther was to serve as the secondary spokesman, the *socius itinerarus*, essentially a traveling companion for his mate, whose name has been lost to history. Tradition dictated that monks not travel alone, and the pair was matched with a lay-brother who acted as escort. The trip would last about twelve weeks, and would be the first and only time in Luther's life when he would leave Germany.

The thought of visiting the holy city, the center of the Christian world, thrilled Luther. (In feeling this he was not alone; in the Middle Ages more Christians made the pilgrimage to Rome than to the Holy Land.) Not only would Luther fulfill his duties on behalf of his cloister, but he would make a full confession of all his sins and receive sufficient absolution. In this way, he hoped, he might find some measure of the spiritual relief he so desperately wanted, but which continually eluded him. Sometime in November of 1510 Luther and his companions set out on foot for Rome, 850 miles away. They walked for four weeks through the snowy mountain passes of the Alps, through Bavaria and the northern Italian cities of Milan and Florence. They enjoyed the hospitality of various monasteries along the way and were provided lodging and meals. When at last the trio viewed the city from the outlying hills, Luther fell to his knees and proclaimed, *"Salve, sancta Roma!"* (Hail to thee, Holy Rome!").[38] They hurried into the city and were received at the Augustinian monastery of Maria del Popolo.

Nearly 2,000 years old, and with a population of some 40,000, Rome had long ago lost much of its ancient splendor but was still venerated. Some called Rome the Eternal City; to others it was the capital of the world. Rome was home to the cardinals and of Pope Julius II, the so-called "warrior pope" whose active foreign affairs were nearly as ambitious as his building projects and artistic vision. Rome claimed about seventy monasteries and dozens of churches, including the "sacred seven," most notably the San Pietro in Vaticano, built on the site of the martyrdom of St. Peter, and the San Paolo fuori le Mura, built near St. Paul's tomb and the location of his shrine. (St. Peter's Basilica, designed chiefly by Michelangelo, had only been under construction since 1506, four years earlier.) The blood of martyrs flowed through Rome. Some 76,000 martyrs and forty popes were buried in the crypt of St. Callistus alone (then, as now, the largest public Christian burial ground in Rome), and the bones of many thousands more Christians were sheltered in the caves and catacombs that ran under the city's streets.

Luther spent a month in Rome, waiting for an audience with Egidius, and trying to ignore the cold, rainy weather. He had little interest in visiting any of Rome's remnants of antiquity, although he did take notice of the Pantheon; this famous pagan temple had been converted to a church, a sure sign, Luther knew, of Christ's enduring triumphal power. He would have liked to observe Michelangelo painting his masterpiece on the Sistine Chapel ceiling, or Raphael's work at the Stanza of the Vatican, but as a foreigner, merely a visiting monk, he did not merit the privilege. Instead, he busied himself by racing from church to church, holy site to holy site. Luther viewed as many relics as he could, hoping to earn indulgences for his many sins, both real and imagined, and decrease the amount of time he would have to spend in purgatory. He saw a piece of the burning bush through which God had spoken to Moses; the crucifix that had once spoken to and inspired St. Francis of Assisi; the chains that had enslaved St. Paul; a coin, one of the infamous thirty pieces of silver, paid to Judas for betraying the Lord (viewing this relic alone offered an indulgence of 1400 years). And Luther saw much more: a piece of the rope that had dragged Jesus to the cross, a thorn from his crown, the tip of the spear that had wounded him, a sample of blood from his side, a nail from the cross. He prayed over a strand of the Virgin Mary's hair, stared in awe at a stone that had rested in front of Jesus' tomb. He recited Mass at a number of churches, hoping to relieve his parents from suffering after death. So fervent was Luther's desire that he later said that he wished they were already dead, so that future sins would not be nullified by his actions. "I was a foolish pilgrim," he later wrote, "and believed all that I was told."[39]

But for all its promise, and for all his anticipation at finding redemption in Rome, Luther came away disappointed and uninspired. It is doubtful that Egidius Canisius ever granted the two visiting monks an audience; if he did, Luther never spoke of it. For all of its impressive architecture and splendor of the Renaissance he found the city chaotic, dirty and foul-smelling. He thought the Italian people rude and boorish, and resented the anti–German sentiments they expressed. He was appalled at their habit of urinating in public. Prostitution flourished and the streets were filled with beggars. Worse, the clergy seemed to flaunt their disdain for the faithful, and for their faith. Homosexuality among priests was openly practiced. Even the pope's sexuality was questioned, and it was whispered he suffered from syphilis, a disease transported from the New World. Luther gladly took his turn in performing Augustinian duties but was shocked to find that many Italian priests were skeptical about the most basic tenets of Catholic thought, many even refusing to believe in an afterlife. They were paid to perform masses and recited seven in the same amount of time it took Luther to say one. "*Passa, passa!*" they hissed at him condescendingly when he took his turn at the altar. "Get on with it!" Even the holy Eucharist was subjected to their mocking tones. "Bread thou art, and bread thou shalt remain," they sneered in Latin to unsuspecting congregations.[40] To Luther this was worse than profane; it was blasphemy.

Even the most sacred site in Rome left Luther unfulfilled. In front of the Lateran Palace stood the *Scala Sancta*, twenty-eight white marble stairs that had once stood in front of Pontius Pilate's court, and upon which Jesus had ascended on his way to trial and condemnation. Following blessed custom Luther crawled up the stairs on his hands and knees, reciting a *Paternoster* at each one, hoping that his reverence could then release the soul of his grandfather from purgatory. But at the top of the stairs Luther could only ask what was in his heart: "Who knows whether this is really true?"[41]

In late February 1511 Luther and his companions began the long trek back to Germany. He had come to Rome anxious to ease his troubled soul, to quench his thirst for spirituality and enlightenment. Instead he found filth, immorality, and irreverence. Rome was a whore, he thought. If there was a hell, she was built on it. Three decades later, when he spoke of his experiences in Rome, he realized that the negativity of the visit was a necessary precursor to his eventual disdain for papal abuses and so many of the Church's practices: "I would not take a lot of money in exchange for having been in Rome. I would not have believed it if I had not seen it myself. For the ungodliness and evil there are so huge and shameless that no one pays any regard either to God or to man, either to sin or to shame. All godly men who have been there testify to this, and so do all the ungodly who come back from Italy worse than before!"[42]

• Chapter 4 •

Wittenberg

Most of the monks at the Black Cloister in Erfurt were disappointed in Egidius's decision to merge all the monasteries in Saxony, and wanted to again appeal the issue to Rome. Luther did not join in the clamor, believing it better to put the matter to rest. His recalcitrance led his fellow monks to believe that he had abandoned them and was personally aligned with Staupitz, and Luther saw no point in arguing. Perhaps there was some truth to it. In the spring of 1512 Staupitz had Luther transferred back to the Augustinian house in Wittenberg, this time permanently.

Located in north-central Germany on the banks of the River Elbe, Wittenberg—sometimes sarcastically called the Gem of Thuringia—was a small, bland city of about 2000 people. Just nine-tenths of a mile in length, it was built on a sand dune called the White Hillock, *Witten-Berg*. City streets were narrow and unpaved, rutted and often muddy. Many peasants lived in tiny one-room houses, built with wooden sides and thatched roofs, which stood close together. Some wealthier merchants owned more elaborate homes of brick and mortar. They were most often heated by coal, which was cheaper than wood but fouled the air. Most of the daily activity centered around the market and the guild hall, from which the local government operated haphazardly. In true German tradition, Wittenberg's residents enjoyed their beer: when Luther arrived, 172 of 400 households had brewing licenses, and taverns were located on most street corners. A small shop boasted a newly-invented printing press. Game was plentiful in the nearby woods, although most peasants dared not often venture into the foreboding darkness. The region's soil was just rich enough so that farmers could produce fruit, vegetables, and grain in sufficient quantities to feed their families and, it was hoped, pay their landlords the monthly rent. In time Luther grew to love Wittenberg and even wrote a little poem, poking fun at its unremarkable trappings:

> *Ländle, ländle.*
> *Sie sind nur ein Haufen Sand.*
> *Wenn ich Sie graben, ist der Boden Licht.*
> *Wenn ich Sie ernten, ist der Ertrag gering.*
>
> *Little land, little land,*
> *You are but a heap of sand.*
> *If I dig you, the soil is light.*
> *If I reap you, the yield is slight.*[1]

The city's most prestigious resident was the Elector Frederick the Wise, who lived in a reconstructed castle, bustling with servants and decorated with fine tapestries, on the western edge of the city. Frederick's ambition was to transform Wittenberg into "the Rome of Germany." The *Schlosskirche*, or Castle Church, was Wittenberg's greatest treasure, and Frederick had stocked the church with relics that he had procured from years of barter, exchange, and negotiation with princes throughout Europe. He envisioned that visitors would flock to Wittenberg and pay for the privilege of viewing holy articles and thereby receive years off from their time in purgatory. In 1509, three years before Luther's arrival, Frederick's collection numbered an impressive 5,005 relics, including the thumb of St. Anne, hay stalks from the manger of Jesus, milk from the Virgin Mary, a tooth of St. Jerome, one piece of gold brought to Bethlehem by Wise Men, a piece of bread eaten at the Last Supper, and a stone upon which Jesus had stood before he ascended into heaven. It was calculated that if a sinner paid the required fees and viewed each and every relic on display, his purgatorial punishment would decrease by 1,443 years. Within ten years Frederick counted 19,013 relics in his collection, and the potential decrease in purgatory time totaled exactly 127,799 years and 116 days. Frederick's entire collection was put on public display each year on November first, All Saints Day.[2]

Wittenberg's second attraction—and Frederick's other treasure—was the University itself, comprised of a few small buildings in the center of town. It was founded by Imperial Charter in July 1502—Frederick's support of the institution was a challenge to his cousin Duke George's university at Leipzig—and was approved by papal decree. Frederick worked strenuously to bring the most distinguished faculty to Wittenberg and it included, at the time of Luther's arrival, the theologians Andreas Karlstadt, Nikolaus von Amsdorf, and Jodocus Trutfetter, in addition to Staupitz. Luther was particularly pleased to see Trutfetter, who had been one of Luther's instructors at Erfurt, where he also served as rector.

Luther moved into the cloister, settling in a small room above a connecting arch, at the opposite end of town from the Castle Church. In May he accompanied Staupitz to Cologne, where both men participated in an assembly of Augustinians. Upon their return, on a warm June day, Staupitz took Luther outside the monastery and the two men sat down under a pear tree. By now Staupitz had seen and heard enough of Luther to give him some career advice. Luther should study for his doctorate degree, counseled Staupitz. He should become a professor of theology there, at the University of Wittenberg, and should become the preacher at the adjoining Castle Church, as well. Predictably, Luther balked, and he stammered out a dozen reasons why he was not up to the task. He was too young, too inexperienced. He doubted that he would last three months on the job. But Staupitz persisted. He needed Luther's help, for he was falling behind in his own duties. He was constantly travelling from monastery to monastery throughout the region. He was expected to lecture on the Bible to the university's theology faculty and preach several times each week. In effect he now proposed to groom Luther to be his successor. When Luther argued that all the work might kill him, Staupitz laughed at Luther's habit of looking at things too seriously. If Luther did die, Staupitz joked, "there was plenty of work for doctors to do in heaven."[3]

Luther's deep sense of indebtedness to Staupitz, and his irrepressible belief in duty and commitment, finally led him to agree. "With a joke Staupitz refuted me," he said. "I have been called to this work, and I was compelled to become a doctor without any initiative of my own but out of pure obedience."[4] Luther worked quickly to meet his remaining academic requirements, and then had only to apply for his doctorate licensure, an expensive undertaking at the cost of fifty gulden. With some effort Staupitz persuaded Frederick the Wise that Luther

was a remarkably gifted theologian and would make an excellent addition to the faculty, and therefore deserving of financial backing. Frederick had heard Luther preach a time or two, and had been impressed with his oratorical skills. He mulled over Staupitz's request for nearly a year, and then agreed; he would pay the licensure fee on condition that Luther remain at Wittenberg for the rest of his life, where he would be responsible for "lectureship on the Bible in the theological faculty."[5]

In early October 1512 Luther travelled to Leipzig and collected the monies from Frederick's representatives. On October 18 he appeared before the Wittenberg faculty for the presentation ceremony. He promised to "teach only true doctrine" of the Catholic Church, and to report all who "promoted falsehood."[6] (Curiously, no specific oath to Rome or to the Pope was required, perhaps a foreshadowing of Germany's eventual move to religious independence.) A brown woolen doctor's cap was placed on Luther's head, and the silver doctor's ring was placed on his hand. Luther took careful note of the doctorate's insignia, which included an open and closed book. The open book was of course the Bible, and represented the ways in which God revealed himself to man. The closed book represented the secrets that God kept from man. A few days later, as the Castle Church bells chimed, Dr. Martin Luther was received by the full Senate of the theology faculty at the University of Wittenberg. He would hold this position until his death in 1546.

For the next five years of his life Luther immersed himself in the study of theology. In the Middle Ages theology was known as "the Queen of all disciplines" because its primary purpose was to support the church and its teachings. All other subjects, including philosophy, language, rhetoric, logic, and even mathematics, existed only to assist the understanding of prevailing Christian doctrine. The orthodox theologian did not rely primarily on the Bible. Rather, he utilized the medieval strategy of exegesis, relying upon biblical commentaries such as Lombard's *Sentences*, which interpreted the literal meaning of the sacred text in a sea of allegory. These commentaries were by nature burdensome, systematic, and inflexible. There was little room for original thought or debate in this framework. Intellectual or humanistic initiative, to the extent that it questioned or contradicted tradition and structure, was neither accepted nor encouraged. University courses taught in this matter were painstakingly tedious; some instructors took a year or more to cover one book of the Bible.

The rigidity of the system offered Luther the intellectual challenge he expected, but not the spiritual enlightenment he craved. Commentaries did not adequately address the great mystery, the central question that plagued and terrorized him: How could a sinful man, much less a conscientious Christian, stand before a judgmental God with any assurance of gaining eternal salvation? Luther wanted desperately to find solace in a loving, merciful God, but God's unfathomable omnipotence frightened him. "It is God's eternity," he wrote, his "holiness and power which thus continuously threaten man throughout the whole of his life…. God's ever-present judgment clutches man in the loneliness of his conscience, and with his every breath conveys him to the Almighty and Holy One to prosper or destroy."[7] Luther's turmoil began to manifest itself by taking a toll on his health. He slept poorly, often waking up in cold sweats, and suffered from headaches and constipation. The only hope for a remedy, he believed, was to work harder.

Opposite: **Elector Frederick the Wise, flanked by Luther and Melanchthon. Painting by Lucas Cranach the Elder, circa 1530 (The Granger Collection, New York).**

Not content to constrict himself to the traditional framework but still, at this early stage of his academic career, unwilling to stray too far from it, Luther looked for ways to expand. Determined to better understand the true meaning of the Bible, he came to reject the prevailing method of exegesis. Instead, he was certain that Holy Scripture, standing alone, was solely authoritative. Armed with this conviction he spent many months studying Greek and Hebrew, thus gaining a full understanding of original languages in which the Bible was written. He insisted on a literal translation of the Bible, the *sensus literalis, grammaticus, historicus,* for in this way, he reasoned, the literal, and not allegorical, truth could be gained.

He also familiarized himself with the writings of St. Augustine, whose ideas about the nature of faith, God's grace, and the sinful nature of man, among others, formed the backbone of early Christian thought. Luther felt that the teachings of Augustine, however, had diminished in importance through the centuries and been forced to give way to the theories of the philosophers Averroes, Aquinas, and Aristotle, whom he despised. He then turned to the book of Genesis, ruminating on the Almighty, the world's creator and, for Luther, the source of all his pain and pleasure he had come to know in life. In 1513 he began an analysis and then a series of lectures on the Psalms, his first detailed study of the book since he had memorized them in the early days of monastic life. He truly loved the Psalms, looking to them for inspiration and guidance. Indeed, all one needed to know about living a Christian life, Luther thought, might be found in the Psalms. "Would you see the Holy Christian Church portrayed with living color and form, fastened together in one place?" he wrote. "Take your Psalter, and you have a fine, crystal-clear mirror which will show you what Christianity is."[8] Confident in his methodology of literal interpretation of Scripture, aided by the guiding words of St. Augustine, and inspired by Genesis and the Psalms, Luther was slowly but steadily developing his own personal, spiritual inquiry: he sought "that theology which extracts the nut from the shell, the grain from the husk, the marrow from the bone."[9]

*

In the fall of 1515 Luther began a series of lectures on the *Epistles of St. Paul,* for Luther (and most Christians then and now), the greatest of all theologians and the man most responsible for delivering and explaining God's Word. In November Luther turned to St. Paul's *Epistle to the Romans,* lectures that would conclude nearly a year later in September 1516. He then analyzed *Galatians* and *Hebrews.* In his work Luther utilized a brand new edition of the New Testament, printed in Greek, which had been prepared by the Dutch theologian Desiderius Erasmus. As he read, he recorded his notes in the oversized margins of the text; many of those notes survive and provide fascinating insight into his thought process and the revolutionary doctrines that he was formulating. Steadily, he began to work through what was to be a new understanding of man's relationship with God.

Meanwhile, Luther's obligations at the University increased. He was given new responsibilities, new tasks, and new duties. When the town priest of Wittenberg became ill, Luther served as substitute preacher. This meant that on some Sundays he preached three times in one day. He was appointed the Provincial Vicar for Meissen and Thuringia. He took over administrative superintendent duties of eleven convents, which he personally visited once each year. He was also charged with the spiritual welfare of all monks and nuns in the region, correcting their missteps, comforting their malcontent, advising their temptations, and even tending to the legal affairs of the different locales. "I could use two secretaries," he wrote to a friend. "I do almost nothing during the day but write letters…. I am a preacher at the monastery, a reader at meals…, a parish preacher, director of studies, supervisor of eleven monasteries, superintendent of the fish pond at Litzkau, referee of a squabble at Torgau, lecturer on Paul, a collector of materials for a commentary on the Psalms, and then, as I said, I am overwhelmed with letters. I rarely have time for the required daily prayers and for saying Mass, not to mention my own temptations with the world, the flesh, and the devil." He could not resist poking a little fun at himself. "You see how lazy I am!" he wrote. Luther later remembered that at the end of the day that it was all he could do to fall into bed, exhausted, upon sheets that he did not have time to wash.[10]

His dynamic lectures at the University quickly became popular. Luther was regimented in his work, addressing his students at six o'clock each morning and often again in the afternoons. "I sense with certainty the weight upon my neck of this task," Luther wrote, "which for a long time, all in vain, I was reluctant to undertake and to which I agreed only when compelled to do so on orders."[11] He had a memorable presence in the classroom, towering over his students from a perch at the front of the lecture hall, bundled up in bulky layers against chilly German mornings, a wool cap on his head. His unusual appearance aside, he impressed his students with his clarity and earnestness, and he drew the constant admiration of his peers, as well. One friar from Cologne, a fellow Augustinian named Augustine Himmel, attended some of Luther's early lectures. "He was a man of middling height, with a voice both sharp and gentle," recalled Himmel. "It was soft in tone, sharp in the enunciation of syllables, words and sentences. He spoke neither too rapidly nor too slowly, but evenly and without hesitation, as well as very clearly and so logically that each part flowed naturally out of what went before. He did not get lost in a maze of language, but first expounded the individual words, then the sentences, so that one could see how the content of the exposition arose and flowed out of the text itself. For it all hung together in order, word, matter, natural and moral philosophy … there was never anything in his lectures that was not relevant and full of meaning."[12]

Luther's ideas and biblical interpretations evolved slowly during these early years of his academic career. "I did not learn my theology all at once," he recalled, "but had to search deeper for it, where my temptations took me. Keep in mind that…. I was all alone and one of those who, as St. Augustine says of himself, have become proficient by writing and teaching. I was not one of those who from nothing suddenly becomes the topmost, though they are nothing and have neither labored nor been tempted nor become experienced, but have with one look at the Scriptures exhausted their entire spirit."[13] He was feeling his way, trusting his instincts, and formulating a new, personal theology.

Luther examined the problem that had plagued him for so many years. How could man, a pathetic sinner, satisfy an angry God who demanded perfection? Luther's image of God was the image all Christians had, the image that the Church itself had for centuries perpetuated. God was a terrible, frightening, all-powerful being whose purpose, whose very existence, was to sit in terrible judgment of the world he had created. God was the Divine Majesty who expected the impossible of his children, and who then sentenced them to eternal damnation for failure to measure up to the unreachable standards he had established. Death and damnation seemed a certainty, and under this fear Luther lived his life.

Yet there was the promise of salvation. The hope for eternal life in God's heaven was the centerpiece, the distinguishing mark of Christian belief. And the key to salvation centered on the concept of justification, or God's act of declaring a sinner righteous. Gaining an understanding of the righteousness of God lay at the root of Luther's quest, his obsession, for personal holiness. It is also what tormented him. He wrote, "I hated those words, 'the righteousness of God,' which, according to the custom and the use of all teachers, I had been taught to understand in the philosophical sense with respect to the formal or active righteousness, as they called it, with which God is righteous and punishes the unrighteous sinner." The idea of a punishing God tore at Luther's soul and rendered worthless all his earthly efforts at piety and goodness. "I did not love, indeed I hated that God who punished sinners," said Luther. "Though I lived as a monk without reproach I felt, with the most disturbed conscience imaginable, that I was a sinner before God…. Secretly I was angry with God." He described his anger as "monstrous, silent, if not blasphemous" and a "murmuring" of his heart. He obsessed over the "fierce battle" that raged in "his troubled conscience." Luther fumed, "As if indeed it is not enough that miserable sinners, eternally lost through eternal sin, are crushed by every kind of calamity by the law of the Ten Commandments," now God added "pain to the gospel ... by threatening us with his righteousness and wrath!"[14] He recognized the horrible irony of his life: he hated the same God he was devoted to serving.

But then a light illuminated the darkness that enveloped him. As Luther "meditated night and day" on St. Paul's writings, he focused on Romans 1:16–17: "For I am not ashamed of the gospel: it is the power of God for salvation to every one who has faith, to the Jew first and also to the Greek. For in it the righteousness of God is revealed through faith for faith; as it is written, 'He who through faith is righteous shall live.'" The true meaning of these words struck Luther like a lightning bolt. "God had mercy on me," he later wrote. "I realized the significance of the context, namely: In it the justice of God is revealed, *as it is written, "He who through faith is righteous (just) shall live."*[15] Here, in that phrase, was the very meaning of the gospel, the explanation for Jesus' life and death and resurrection. Here the intention of the Lord was revealed. And here, for Luther, at last came relief from the torment, from his hell on earth, and from his paralyzing fear of death. Luther now understood that the justice of God meant justice through God's gift of faith. God's justice did not depend on human action. It was not the mighty and punishing justice that, the Church taught, was to be feared. Rather, God's justice is passively received. It could not be earned because it had already been given; it could not be attained because it was already present. Believers—Christians—were justified by faith alone. Their salvation, their standing before God, was in no way related to personal merit. They were received by God, justified by Christ for them. Luther now believed, absolutely, that the righteousness of God was not to be feared, but embraced. "He who through faith is just shall live."

It was for Luther a most joyous revelation. "Now I exalted in that sweetest phrase," he said, "with as much love as I had previously hated the words 'justice of God.'" Through this new interpretation of St. Paul's declaration, Luther felt that he "was altogether born again and had entered paradise itself through open gates." He excitedly examined biblical passages in light of his discovery, working day and night, verifying what he already knew. He found, in Romans, Corinthians, Philippians, and Colossians, "analogies in other terms, such as 'the work of God,' by which he works in us; 'the power of God,' by which he makes us strong; 'the wisdom of God,' by which he makes us wise; 'the strength of God,' 'the salvation of God,' 'the glory of God.'"[16]

Luther pressed on. "Afterwards I read Augustine's *On the Spirit and the Letter*, and contrary to expectation I found that he also interprets the justice of God in a similar manner: the justice in which God clothes us when he justifies us. And even though this was still expressed imperfectly, and concerning imputation Augustine did not explain everything clearly, yet it was a delight to find a justice of God by which we are justified being taught."[17] In the transforming words of St. Paul, Luther was finding answers to his spiritual cravings. From Augustine came intellectual vindication, as well.

Now Luther's real work began. Emboldened by his new interpretation of God's righteousness, he examined salvation. For this he looked to the cross. God had sent his son, the Christ, to save the very world he condemned. Thus God the Terrible was at the same time God the Merciful. Why, after all, would God desire that sinners should die? Why had he sent his son if he did not desire that sinners should live? Luther concluded that just as there must be a connection between these dual natures of God, there must be a connection between poor sinners (God's children) and Jesus the Savior (God's only begotten son). Jesus, of course, had been rejected by his Father. Alone on the cross of Calvary, suffering the agony of persecution and mercilessly tortured in front of his family and followers, Jesus believed he had been abandoned. "My God, my God, why hast thou forsaken me?" he cried out from the cross, just moments before he died and descended into hell. God's own son had felt humiliation, anger, desolation, betrayal, and rejection—and God was the source of all of it. Jesus had known, a thousand times more, infinitely more, the very pain Luther had known. Jesus Christ had his own *Anfechtungen*.

This same Christ, while the Son of Man, was also the Son of God, and therefore perfect and without sin. Thus, in his duality he was of mankind and yet the opposite of mankind. He could only have felt the incalculable weakness and desperation of the cross because he had shouldered the burden of mankind's sins as he suffered his horrible death. He had not just taken on sin, surmised Luther, he had *become* sin, the sin of all God's children. In his agony, and through it, Christ became the Redeemer. The great and mysterious God had sent his son to die, not for himself, but for mankind. There on the cross was the message. God in his weakness—manifested in the suffering and death of his son—was also God in his almighty strength, dying so that the world might live. Luther loved the concept of God's dual nature. The Savior of the world had been born, after all, in a filthy stable, attended not by royalty and magnificence but shepherds and lowly animals. He had expressed the power of God not with displays of thunder and might but messages of love and peace. The duality of God was made apparent everywhere. God's power, understood Luther, was in fact hidden in his weakness, and it went further: "God's wisdom (was hidden) in folly, his goodness in severity, his justice in sins, and his mercy in anger." Luther's ruminations would ultimately become known as his Theology of the Cross, the bedrock of his Christian belief.[18]

For Luther, God's righteousness was more than the quality and manner by which he judged mankind. God's righteousness was also something that God *gave* to believers. It was a gift, given in mercy to the undeserving. God's justice was his grace. And it made sinners acceptable in his presence. God judged, to be sure, but he did so solely for the purpose of giving sinners his justice in Christ, his son, the Savior. This was, to Luther, "passive righteousness," for to receive it a sinner only had to believe.

And if righteousness was truly a gift, it simply could not be earned. Sinners, then, need not strive to attain what was unattainable. Luther, by his own words a pious monk, knew that he had fallen woefully short in this endeavor, even after years of struggle. The Church, thought

Luther, was wrong to teach that salvation had to be earned, that it could *only* be earned. In fact it could not be earned at all, any more than it could be bought or sold. Righteousness was a gift from a merciful and loving God, not a threat from an angry and damning God. Man could not, on his own or through his own efforts, earn that which could never be earned. No matter how well- intentioned, monastic life—a life that included sacrifice, self-denial, vows of poverty and chastity, the numbing routine of prayer and service, strict adherence to Catholic doctrine, all of which Luther referred to as the attempt to become humble before God—was of no avail. And if one believed that he had achieved the impossible, that he had, on his own, reached some acceptable level of goodness and purity, he was deluding himself dangerously. For then, warned Luther, "very soon smugness takes hold of us, and as soon as this happens God's imputation of sin returns."[19]

The Church taught that there had to exist in man a spark of goodness. This tiny spark, if fanned properly (by strict obedience to the decrees and mandates of the Church), could ignite into a genuine love for God and for neighbor, and could nurture the ultimate Christian goal of salvation. By his own powers, the Church decreed, "a person can love God above all things and can perform the works of the law according to the substance of the act, but not according to the intentions of him who gave the command, because he is not in a state of grace."[20] This was, to Luther, insanity. Man had no such ability, with or without the Church's instruction or assistance. For human beings were surely, absolutely, mired in sin. They were by nature, from birth, so sunk in sin that they could not even begin to recognize their own dreary condition without God's grace. There was no room in a sinful countenance for a "spark of goodness." The idea was a fiction, a creation of the Church.

Luther portrait by Lucas Cranach the Elder, circa 1526 (Library of Congress).

For Luther, it all came back to St. Paul. The lectures on Romans focused on the will of God, and the idea that man was deceiving himself if he believed he could win God's favor, for he was but a poor sinner. "The sum and substance" of *Romans*, Luther taught, "is to disperse and eliminate all the righteousness and wisdom of the flesh and on the other hand to confirm, increase, and magnify sin and nothingness, so that finally Christ and his righteousness may enter into us in place of those things which are wiped out. For in God's presence man does not become just by doing just works, but by being just, he does just deeds."

The Church had it exactly wrong, Luther thought, when it taught that good works, in addition to faith, were required in order to achieve salvation. Rather, the very faith that brought about salvation would generate good works. "Why does man take pride in his merit and his works," wondered Luther, "which in no way please because they have merit or are good, but because they have been chosen by God from eternity that they should please Him?" The constant endeavor to live a godly life was misguided; perhaps the Church's interpretation of what constituted that life was mere folly. "Therefore we have no good works except the search for grace," wrote Luther, "because our works do not make us good, but our goodness, or rather the goodness of God, makes us and our works good." Sinful man could never earn salvation through his own behavior. He had already been given it, as a gift from a loving God. "God wills to save us," repeated Luther in a theme he returned to again and again, "not by a righteousness and wisdom from within but from without. Not that which comes and is born from ourselves. But that which comes from without into us. Not that which rises from the earth, but that which comes down from heaven." And now Luther could recognize the duality of mankind, sinful but saved, undeserving recipient but, through grace, a recipient nonetheless. "Just is a man reckoned so to be by God, but because he is reckoned to be just by God, therefore he is just," he wrote. "Always a sinner, always a penitent, always right with God. In our ignorance [man is] justified, in our knowledge unjustified; sinners in fact, but righteous in hope."

Luther never lost his belief, impressed upon his psyche since childhood, that the world was an evil place, and that Satan remained the dark, tempting force behind all earthly desires. What he began to realize, however, was that God alone provided the means to conquer evil. He now understood that his time spent as a monk, in endless hours of self-sacrifice and penance, had been all but wasted. He wrote, "It is a mistake to believe that this evil is remedied by works, since experience proves that in spite of all our good works the desire for evil persists and that no one is free from it, not even a day-old child. But God's mercy is such that, although this evil endures, it is not reckoned as sin for those who call upon Him and with signs beseech Him to deliver them…. Thus we are sinners and yet we are accounted righteous by God through faith."[21]

Luther now came to another revelation. He had always contemplated God's law and God's gospel as the same thing. He had understood that the horrors of righteousness and the elusive promise of salvation were intertwined. Now his thinking changed. He wrote, "When I discovered the proper distinction—namely, that the law is one thing and the gospel is another—I made myself free."[22] The proper use of the law—God's law—was that of a hammer or anvil. It smashed human pride, crushed human vanity, and cleared the way for God's love and mercy. God's law was also a *Spiegel*, or mirror, that revealed to humans their sin indicating their desperate need for God's loving grace. God's law was both hammer and mirror—terrible, judgmental, and harsh but also preparing one for the Gospel, which was merciful, righteous, and gracious. All man had to do was believe. All man needed was faith.

And what of faith? That too, for Luther, was a mystery that could not be credited to man. Faith was another gift from God. Faith trusted God's promise. It was, in and of itself, "knowledge of things invisible and trustworthy. It is a hidden understanding, for it is one of those things that a man cannot know by his own powers." Faith alone was Christ alone. St. Paul made this clear. Paul had scoffed at "those presumptuous persons who think they can come to God apart from Christ, as though it were sufficient for them to have believed and … then having once accepted the grace of justification, not needing him." Faith, like righteousness, came from God alone. In fact, sinners could only know of their sin through faith.

Without faith, theorized Luther, "we are not conscious of the fact. Thus we must stand under the judgment of God and believe his words with which he has declared us unjust, for he himself cannot lie."[23]

No one knew better than Luther that the gift of faith could be wasted, hopelessly lost in a sea of doubt and despair. But God's love was limitless, and never-ending. That fact, too, had been proved on the cross. Luther wrote, "The cross of Christ is distributed through the whole world; each person is always allotted his portion. Do not therefore cast it aside but rather take it up as a holy relic to be kept not in a golden or a silver case but in a golden, that is, a gentle and loving, heart." Luther offered this advice to those who despaired, who felt the same anguish he had felt for so long: "Learn Christ and him crucified; despairing of yourself, learn to pray to him, saying, you, Lord Jesus, are my righteousness, but I am your sin; you have taken on yourself what you were not and have given me what I was not. Beware of aspiring to such purity that you no longer wish to appear to yourself, or to be, a sinner."[24]

This most basic understanding of man's sin would cause him to repent of them. "For because he repents," said Luther, "he becomes just from being unjust. Therefore repentance is a medium between unrighteousness and righteousness. And thus he is in sin as a beginning point and in righteousness as an end point. If therefore we are always repenting, we are always sinners, and yet at the same time we are just and we are justified, partly sinners, partly just, that is, nothing more than penitent." For Luther, one basic truth had to be acknowledged and had to be understood: "in the Scriptures righteousness depends more on the imputation of God than on the essence of the thing itself. It is not he who possesses a certain quality who possesses righteousness; rather, this one is altogether a sinner and unrighteousness; but he has righteousness to whom God mercifully imputes it and wills to regard as righteous before him on account of his confessing his unrighteousness and his imploring God's righteousness. Thus we are all born and die in iniquity, that is, unrighteousness. We are just solely by what the merciful God imputes to us through faith in his Word."[25]

Luther's theology, still developing, still in need of much polish and definition, started with this: Man's salvation began by knowing his own sin. For the moment when man was at his most sinful, his most unworthy, his most guilty and fragile, was precisely the moment when God was his most gracious. The goodness that could then characterize the human condition did not reside in humans, but outside of them, in Christ alone, and "yet through faith also in them." Mankind was justified, sanctified, saved—and the work had already been done. It was the message of St. Paul: "He who through faith is just shall live." Luther's groundbreaking new understanding of God's righteousness, this revolutionary new way of contemplating the road to salvation, this radical interpretation and explanation for man's relationship to his Creator—all were concepts that had never before been explored. Luther's theology—now little more than intellectual exercises in personal spirituality, meant to spark a dialogue with divinity students—was bound to shake the very foundations of the dominant Christian Church that ruled all of Western Europe. It was to become, very quickly, the genesis of the Protestant Reformation. It would ignite a massive reform movement, first in Germany and then across Europe. It would consume the Church, disrupt and divide it, inflicting wounds that would never be healed.

But in 1517 Luther was still just a poor monk, a little-known professor of theology, all but unknown outside his tiny university in the outback of Saxony, a thousand miles from the power and glory of Rome. It would take more than just fresh interpretations of ancient biblical verses to bring the Holy Church to its knees. It would also take the reckless and scandalous actions of another monk, this one a cheap showman who would stumble unwittingly into Saxony and deliver a misguided message of greed and false promise to gullible believers. For without the papal-blessed actions of this charlatan there would likely have been no Reformation. He was a Dominican Friar named John Tetzel, and he would soon feel Martin Luther's wrath.

• Chapter 5 •

When the Coffer Rings

Sacraments are sacred Christian rites, defined by the Roman Catholic Church as "efficacious signs of grace, instituted by Christ and entrusted to the Church, by which divine life is dispensed to us."[1] The Church teaches that sacraments are essential to salvation. They nourish and strengthen faith, functioning to illuminate the very lives of believers. Because sacraments are so important their administration must be properly understood and monitored. The Church recognizes seven sacraments: Baptism; Confirmation; Eucharist; Anointing of the Sick; Matrimony; Holy Orders; and Penance. The last, penance, is the sacrament of spiritual healing. It is intended to aid the baptized Christian who, because of sins committed, has become distanced from God.

The Church's understanding of sin—and the manner in which sin could be absolved—had grown very complicated by the Middle Ages. Sins were evaluated by the Church in terms of their gravity: mortal sins, or those that ruptured the link between man and God's grace and thus killed the soul, were classified as more serious than venial, or lesser, sins. Every sin, however, no matter how serious or how trivial, was a turning away from God. Sin was more than just bad behavior. It was also an unhealthy attachment to any earthly thing, for it meant that the sinner's will had been influenced by something other than God. Thus, the Church taught, the soul of the sinner had to be purified, or made free to love and unite with God again. True penance meant forgiveness, a restoration of the link to God's saving grace. Penance consisted of three steps, or stages, that had to be performed by the penitent: contrition (true sorrow, or the desire to be forgiven); confession (disclosure of the sin); and satisfaction (making amends for the transgression).

Catholic doctrine held that, upon death, some souls were ready for heaven because all unhealthy attachments had been purified on earth. These believers had died in a state of grace and had become members of the communion of saints. Other souls were beyond hope and were delivered directly to hell. But some souls, while still salvageable, were not yet ready for heaven because they were not completely free from the temporal effects of sin. First, just as in any earthly civilized society, the guilty party (the sinner) had to make restitution to the injured party (God). Only then would their sins be not only forgiven, but paid for. Particularly, venial sins were to be accounted for; that is, transgressors could be purified after death and still achieve the holiness necessary to be received into the joys of heaven. Those souls were bound for a state that lay somewhere between heaven and hell, a terrible transitional condition called purgatory. The existence of purgatory was, the Church taught, identified in Scripture: Jesus had given to Peter (the first pope), and hence to papal successors, the power to lose or bind sinners. Loosing sanctified the soul, ready to enter heaven. Binding meant remitting souls to purgatory.

How long a soul had to spend in the flames of purgatory depended upon the number and the severity of the sins. Although only God knew the exact amount of days and years any individual had to serve in this transitional state, the term could be estimated by the Church. Furthermore the Church, because of its perfection and infallibility, could intervene on behalf of individual Christians and lessen purgatorial time. The Church claimed it possessed a "treasury of merit," a righteous savings account, built up over the ages from the innumerable good works of Christ and the saints, and headed by mother Mary. The validity of these merits was without question, for Christ had lived a perfect life, and the saints were known to reside in heaven. The Church, or more specifically the pope, as the Vicar of Christ, had the right—if not the solemn duty—to distribute the benefits of these merits, to work on behalf of those souls seeking heaven, in consideration for prayers, sanctity, and pious acts or actions. The granting of such a benefit—officially called an indulgence—to the faithful, would serve to shorten one's time of penance in purgatory.

Indulgences had a checkered history. Plenary indulgences were promised and distributed in the 12th century for those who volunteered for the Church's crusades. In 1300 Pope Boniface VIII instituted a "jubilee indulgence" for all who visited the tombs of the Apostles in Rome for fifteen consecutive days. Eventually financial contributions qualified for indulgence distribution. In 1476 Pope Sixtus IV first declared that souls languishing in purgatory could benefit from indulgences. And of course, many churches and church officials collected relics and then encouraged believers to view and revere them—for a price. Anxious sinners were more than happy to take advantage of the offering and lessen their purgatorial sentences. Now, in 1517, the concepts of penance, indulgences, and questionable financial dealings became intertwined, and together they played primary roles in igniting the Reformation.

Luther's town of Wittenberg lay within the jurisdiction of the Bishop of Brandenburg, whose superior was, in turn, Albrecht, the Archbishop of Magdeburg. A member of the prestigious Hohenzollern family, Albrecht was also administrator of the nearby Halberstadt diocese, which included a monastery and massive cathedral. By the tender age of twenty-four, Albrecht had already accumulated nearly 9,000 relics, which brought in a steady stream of income. Albrecht wanted to add another title to his status, and sought to purchase the Archbishopric of Mainz, an important office since it carried with it the right to vote for the election of the Holy Roman Emperor, one of only seven such electoral positions in Germany. This important see (or episcopal throne) also carried with it the Office of Imperial Chancellor and would make him the holder primate of Germany. These titles and offices were regularly put up for sale by the Catholic Church. But in this case Albrecht needed Rome to ignore its own canon law, which stipulated that an Elector had to be at least thirty years old.

The fee for all that Albrecht coveted was significant: 21,000 gulden for the office, plus another 10,000 for a special papal dispensation that allowed him to hold a plurality of offices. Albrecht was well off, but did not have that kind of cash. He approached Jakob Fugger of Augsburg, head of the largest bank in Germany, a family operation that financed the country's most powerful people. Fugger was eager to broker a deal and an ingenious method of repayment was then devised, the details of which reached all the way to Rome. Indulgences would be sold within the region (under authority of the papal bull *Sacrosanctis*, a proclamation issued by Pope Leo X in 1515), and the proceeds would be split: half would go to the Fuggers to liquidate the debt, and the other half to the Vatican. Specifically, the monies collected therein would be used to finish construction of St. Peter's Basilica, which had begun over seventy years earlier and was not close to completion. The pope's bull had made it clear that the indulgences were not to be distributed simply via payment of money, for proper absolution depended upon genuine repentance and confession of sins. But in the end, it appeared that everyone would win: sinners, or their departed relatives, would benefit from the indulgences received; St. Peter's would finally be completed, solidifying both Leo's reputation and legacy; the Fugger banking house would be repaid, with considerable interest; and Albrecht would become an Archbishop twice over, while also gaining the Elector position.

Indulgences didn't sell themselves. Albrecht needed to employ an agent, a salesman, who could preach the benefits of the indulgence. Luckily for him, the perfect candidate was available: one Johann Tetzel, a Dominican friar. Tetzel was born in Pirna, Saxony in 1465. Educated at Leipzig, Tetzel eventually rose to become prior of the Glogau monastery, and then inquisitor for Poland. By 1503, however, Tetzel had found his calling and his life's work: preaching indulgences. For the better part of the next two decades he travelled throughout Germany, from province to province, visiting Magdeburg, Bremen, Riga, Nuremburg, Würzburg, and Bamberg, among others, making money for himself and his Church. He was a skilled orator whose ability to enflame crowds of gullible listeners was exceeded only by his showmanship. Now he was hired by Albrecht to hawk indulgences in Germany.

Tetzel's formula was well-established. He began by writing letters to priests of the various parishes he planned to visit. "Tell your people," he wrote, "that for every mortal sin a man commits he must, after making a good confession, suffer seven years in purgatory, unless he has done seven years penance. Bid them think how many mortal sins a day are committed, how many each week, each month, each year. All but infinite, then, are the pains they must undergo in the flames of purgatory. This indulgence will mean for them full remission of all the punishment due to them up to the time they gain the indulgence. And for the rest of their lives, whenever they go to confession the priest will have the power to grant them a similar indulgence; and they will receive an indulgence again in the very moment when they pass from this life to the next." Although Tetzel later denied it, contemporaries reported that his claims reached absurd heights when he guaranteed that any sin, no matter how terrible—murder, rape, even a heinous violation of the Virgin Mary's purity—could be absolved through the purchase of an indulgence.

Tetzel appealed as well with financial logic. To the priests he wrote, "If you are going to Rome, or on some other dangerous journey, you would put your hundred gulden in the bank here, and when you got to Rome present your receipt and be paid the deposit. And you would gladly pay the banker five or six or ten gulden for the convenience. You would willingly give so much to make certain of your hundred gulden. And will you grudge a quarter of a gulden to bring your soul that is immortal safely to the fatherland that is paradise?"

Next Tetzel sent agents, or scouts, to visit the village or town and announce his arrival. The scout would also compile a list of the town's wealthiest citizens and make certain they knew of the visit. How much could a parishioner expect to pay for an indulgence? Albrecht dictated the amounts, and Tetzel agreed (he would receive a percentage of each indulgence sold). Kings, queens, princes, and bishops were required to pay twenty-five gulden. Abbots, counts, barons and nobles had to pay twenty gulden. Lower nobility paid six, burghers and merchants paid three, and laborers, shopkeepers and farmers would pay up to half a gulden.

Johan Tetzel and the sale of Indulgences, print circa 1870 (The Granger Collection, New York).

Those who were destitute simply had to provide proof of offerings of prayers and fasting and received their indulgence certificate, for Rome had decreed: "The kingdom of heaven ought not to be more accessible to the rich than to the poor."

Now that the stage was set, Tetzel made his triumphant entry into the village. He arrived on horseback, just behind a cross bearing the papal insignia, accompanied by a large entourage, flags waving and trumpet music splitting the air. He was usually met by local dignitaries and a large crowd, who accompanied him to the town square with great fanfare. There he gave an introductory message, reminding his listeners of the fiery terrors of purgatory that they were all but certain to face. "Have you considered that you are lashed in a furious tempest amid the temptations and dangers of the world, and that you do not know whether you can reach the haven, not of your mortal body, but of your immortal soul?" Even worse, Tetzel reminded the crowd, was the fate of their dead loved ones already suffering. "Can you not hear the voices of your dead father and mother pleading with you? 'Tiny alms and we shall be free from this torment. Pity us, pity us. We are in dire torment from which you can redeem us for a pittance.' Do you not wish to? Open your ears. Hear the father saying to the son, the mother to her daughter, 'We bore you, nourished you, brought you up, left you our fortunes, and you are so cruel and hard that now you are not willing for so little to set us free. Will you let us lie here in flames? Will you delay our promised glory?'"

Tetzel then concluded his harangue with the rehearsed lines that have reverberated through history as emblematic of his personal zeal, and of the Church's corruption:

> *Sobald das Geld in Kasten klingt*
> *Die Seele aus dem Fegefeuer springt.*
>
> *As soon as the money in the coffer rings,*
> *The soul from the purgatory's fire springs.*

Believers eagerly came forward, money in hand. Their gulden was examined and weighed (Tetzel's assistant traveled with a scale), and they received a certificate of indulgence. This paper was official assurance that the bearers no longer had to pay restitution or otherwise make satisfaction for their sins—or those of their departed relatives. Later in the day Tetzel repeated his message, this time in the form of a sermon, from the village parish, in front of another large and gratefully generous crowd. By sundown he was on his way to the next town, "his chest filled with gold, his saddlebags bursting."[2]

*

Tetzel's presence in the region was sensational news. But as lucrative as Tetzel's indulgence enterprise had become in the spring and summer of 1517, he ran into a jurisdictional problem. The secular lord of Wittenberg, the Elector Frederick the Wise, was a relentless collector of relics. He compiled the holy objects by the thousand not only to satisfy his own considerable sense of personal piety, but, more practically, because they brought in a steady stream of faithful who paid handsomely for the privilege of viewing them—and thus received forgiveness. While the *Sacrosanctis* of 1515 had suspended all other forms of indulgences, the edict proved to be nearly impossible to enforce, and Frederick displayed his relics once per year, on All Saints' Day. Frederick had no theological objection to indulgence trafficking, of course. He had once engaged Tetzel to sell them to finance the building of a bridge at Torgau. And he had raised funds through indulgence sales to assist Pope Alexander VI's planned crusade against the Turks in 1502, keeping the money when the crusade did not materialize and investing it in his university. But Frederick was concerned that increased indulgence trafficking in his district would threaten the money magnet that his relic collection had become, and he was fiercely protective of it. Also, he had no interest in seeing a Hohenzollern, a political rival, get a second Electorate. Thus he expressly forbade Tetzel, or any other indulgence peddler, to preach within his Saxon boundaries.

In October 1517 Tetzel brought his company as close to Wittenberg as he could, to the town of Jüterbok, across the Elbe River and just twenty miles to the northeast. Some members of Luther's Castle Church eagerly made the journey to Jüterbok and purchased their indulgences. Believing themselves duly sanctified, and confident that they had also improved the lot of their deceased ancestors, they returned home and asked that Luther attest to the validity of the indulgences. Some also demanded that they be given the Lord's Supper without first making a confession. Certain that his parishioners had been led astray, Luther was appalled at the requests. He felt that as the pastor of his flock he was obligated to intervene. That the source of the problem, Friar Tetzel, was a Dominican, an order generally looked down upon by Luther's Augustinians because of their preoccupation with financial matters, only added fuel to Luther's fire.

On a larger level Luther was outraged that almighty God had been turned into a common shopkeeper, that his holy redemption could be bought and sold. Everything about Tetzel's operation—the sales pitches, the passing of coins, money chests, and town square charades, all conceived and conducted in the name of Christ and thrust upon the gullible faithful— reeked of deceit and scandal. It was a cheapening of salvation, Luther fumed, a trivialization of God's grace, and encouraged a weakening of contrition. It was blasphemy, he believed, to teach that the merits of the saints were equal to Christ's merits. He rejected the idea that the saints had compiled a treasury of merit from which Rome could dip into and—for a price— apply to the sins of the faithful or the departed. Sinful humans, still living, could not earn or purchase salvation for themselves. Neither could it be purchased for souls of the dead. The ideas were contrary to Luther's emerging concept of justification by faith and his theology of the cross. The very words of St. Peter were being ignored: "Thy money perishes with thee, because thou hast thought that the gift of God may be purchased with money."[3]

Eventually Luther would come to reject the notion of purgatory itself, believing that death was final and absolute, and that those who loved and trusted God had no reason to fear it. For now, however, he focused on the scandalous idea that indulgences could lessen purgatorial time. He was convinced that Rome had no knowledge of Tetzel's corruption. Indeed, Luther did not believe that his positions necessarily contradicted the Church. He merely felt that one of its doctrines was being abused, and that that abuse needed to be brought to light. His calling as theologian and priest demanded that he speak out. When Tetzel's scandalous activity corrupted Luther's own congregation, it was time for him to act.

Luther took two steps, simultaneously. First, he wrote ninety-five theses, or statements, setting forth his positions about the indulgence scandal taking place in Germany. The statements were carefully constructed, dutifully written in Latin to appeal to the educated elite, and meant to promote academic debate. Luther's students had already heard some of these points during his lectures. Now they were presented to a wider audience. His statements were all at once provocative, bold, witty, and sarcastic. In them he managed to show his respect for the Church yet also mock those who acted recklessly on its behalf. The statements were not meant to be taken as Luther's literal positions, but were merely assertions, or propositions, meant to stir discussion; therefore he was not risking heresy (a crime then punishable by death) in presenting them. Luther was careful to strike narrowly and at the heart of the problem. His aim was to call attention to the problem of indulgence abuse, not necessarily to challenge the indulgence doctrine itself. He certainly had no idea that his writing would spark a revolt.

Castle Church, Wittenberg.

In the early afternoon of Wednesday, October 31, 1517, Luther walked to the main door of Castle Church in Wittenberg. He carried his theses, rolled up on parchment and titled *Disputatio pro clarificatione virtutis indulgentiarum* (*Disputation for Clarification of the Power of Indulgences*), and a hammer and nails in his hands. He passed through a sizeable crowd that was milling around the streets and church grounds, peasants and farmers who were celebrating the recent harvest and who were looking forward to viewing Frederick's relic collection the next day. Luther nailed his document on the door, which acted as a sort of public bulletin board for parish notices and university announcements.

The document began with a formal and respectful introduction:

> *Out of love and zeal for making the truth clear, the following theses will be debated at Wittenberg, the Reverend Father Martin Luther, Master of Arts and Sacred Theology, presiding. He begs that those who cannot be present at the oral discussion will communicate their views in writing. In the name of our Lord Jesus Christ. Amen.*

Luther's Ninety-Five Theses are inscribed on this bronze door at Castle Church, Wittenberg.

Luther's first two theses were simple in language but rich in meaning. He issued a call to action meant to rouse believers from their lethargy. Christians must follow the Lord's instructions and repent of their sins, and should spend their whole lives doing so. Repentance was a humble action, an inward acceptance of God that would produce outward action and prepare the believer to receive God's forgiveness and grace. Repentance, however, was different than the earthly doctrine of penance, which was merely administered by the Church and its officials. True forgiveness, Luther believed, could only come from God:

> *Theses 1. When our Lord and Master, Jesus Christ, says "Repent," he means that all the life of the faithful man should be in repentance.*
> *2. The Pope cannot forgive any sin; he can only make known and testify to God's forgiveness.*

Luther next turned to indulgences and the idea of purgatory. He wrote that canon, or Catholic Law, applied only to the living and not the dead. A priest had no business threatening the near-dead with the punishment and horrors of purgatory. False warnings of purgatory cultivated a crop of weeds (tares) that took away from the true message of the Gospel. Luther did not deny the power of the keys, or the pope's authority to forgive sins. But he believed that the pope had only the limited authority to absolve a confessing sinner from earthly penalties; that is, from the Church's penalties. The pope did not have the power or authority to free souls from purgatory or lessen any punishment there. His power did not and could not reach beyond the grave. When a believer dies, Luther insisted, his debts die with him, and he owes no more. It is natural for a person, when dying, to fear death, but this fear is punishment enough. Further, people are being deceived by the false promise of indulgences, which can save no man and no dead soul.

Luther wrote that the concept of indulgences was a human, not a godly one. It was nonsensical blasphemy to preach that dead souls, languishing in purgatory, can be saved by money. Money can only cause greed. Those who buy and sell indulgences, and those who believe that indulgences are genuine, will earn not salvation but damnation. Luther warned that papal promises of forgiveness, made through indulgences, were not genuine:

> 27. *They preach only human doctrines who say that as soon as the money clinks into the money chest, the soul flies out of purgatory.*
> 28. *It is certain that when money clinks in the money chest, greed and avarice can be increased; but when the church intercedes, the result is in the hands of God alone.*
> 32. *Those who believe that they can be certain of their salvation because they have indulgence letters will be eternally damned, together with their teachers.*
> 33. *Men must especially be on guard against those who say that the pope's pardons are that inestimable gift of God by which man is reconciled to him.*

Luther turned to Christ's example, and his teaching, which emphasized works of charity, kindness, and compassion. He wrote that true penitents feel sorry for their sins, and do not need to pay for them through the purchase of trivial indulgences, which are no substitute for Christ's forgiveness. It is better for a Christians to give money to the poor than to purchase indulgences. In fact, Luther argued, a person who buys an indulgence rather than helping a beggar earns God's anger, not his forgiveness. Therefore, Christians should not rely upon indulgences, for they are wasteful and not needed:

> 42. *Christians are to be taught that the Pope does not intend that the buying of indulgences should in any way be compared with works of mercy.*
> 43. *Christians are to be taught that he who gives to the poor or lends to the needy does a better deed than he who buys indulgences.*
> 45. *Christians are to be taught that he who sees a needy man and passes him by, yet gives his money for indulgences, does not buy papal indulgences but God's wrath.*
> 46. *Christians are to be taught that, unless they have more than they need, they must reserve enough for their family needs and by no means squander it on indulgences.*

Luther could not bring himself to believe that the pope knew of Tetzel's corrupt practice. And if His Holiness knew, he certainly would not tolerate it:

> 50. *Christians are to be taught that, if the Pope knew the exactions of the preachers of indulgences, he would rather have St. Peter's Church in ashes than have it built with the flesh and bones of his sheep.*

Luther believed that God's word, the holy Gospel of the Lord, was the true treasure of the Church, and it belonged to all believers. Indulgences were not treasures, and neither were they a substitute for God's boundless grace:

> 62. *The real, true treasury of the Church is the most holy Gospel of the glory and grace of God.*
> 66. *The treasures of indulgences are nets with which one now fishes for the wealth of men.*

Luther spoke to Tetzel's ridiculous claim that indulgences could absolve even a sinner who had committed an all-but unspeakable offense:

> 75. *To consider papal indulgences so great that they could absolve a man even if he had done the impossible and had violated the mother of God is madness.*

Luther could not resist the opportunity to take aim at a pope who seemed to have little interest in caring for the faithful under his charge:

> 82. *If the Pope lets the souls out of purgatory for the sake of filthy lucre, why does he not do so for the sake of holiest love and the direst need of the souls?*
> 86. *Again, "Why does not the Pope, whose wealth is today greater than the wealth of the richest Crassus, build this one basilica of St. Peter with his own money rather than with the money of poor believers?"*

Luther concluded with two statements that seemed to sum up his long years of inner torment. Perhaps every sinner, he thought, needed to experience his own personal *Anfechtungen*. And then those sinners could emerge from the darkness as he had, and realize the promise of salvation:

> 94. *Christians should be exhorted to be diligent in following Christ, their Head, through penalties, death and hell.*
> 95. *And thus be confident of entering into heaven through many tribulations rather than through the false security of peace (Acts 14:22).*

In addition to posting his theses on the Castle Church door, Luther also took a more direct second step. He sent a letter, along with copies of his theses, to Archbishop Albrecht (he also sent the documents to Bishop Schulze of Brandenburg). The letter began with a showing of Luther's humility: "Forgive me, most reverend Father in Christ, illustrious prince, that I, the off-scouring of men, have such temerity that I dare to consider sending a letter to your exalted Highness." Luther was "conscious of my own insignificance and unworthiness" and "a mere speck of dust" but the matter was urgent. Luther explained the indulgence controversy, sure that the Albrecht had no knowledge of the scandal. He asked that they now take on their duties responsibly and address the problem. (Perhaps Luther was unaware that Albrecht had hired Tetzel to preach indulgences. More likely, though, he simply pretended not to know.) In his letter Luther did not directly blame Tetzel and claimed that he had not personally heard him preach. Luther was sure that Albrecht and Schulze would agree, however, that Tetzel's practices were improper and dangerous, for indulgences detracted from the Lord's Gospel and from works of charity. Luther politely invited them to read and consider his theses. He wrote:

I am not finding fault here with the declarations (which I have not myself heard) of those who are preaching these indulgences, but I grieve at the utterly false understanding which the people are deriving from them and which they are promoting everywhere amongst the populace. Plainly if the unhappy souls believe that if they buy letters of indulgence they are sure of their salvation, and again that souls immediately fly from purgatory when they throw their contribution into the chest. Next, they believe that the grace of indulgences is so great that there is no sin so enormous that it cannot be forgiven, even if (as they say) against all possibility one were to rape the Mother of God.... O great God, souls committed to your charge, excelling Father, are thus educated for death! ... Indulgences confer absolutely nothing of value to souls for their salvation or holiness, but remove only an individual external penalty previously imposed canonically.... In short, works of piety and love are infinitely better than indulgences. And yet these are

not the things they preach with much pomp and zeal…. Christ never ordered that indulgences be
preached, but vigorously ordered that the gospel be preached…. If your fatherly Reverence please, you
could look at these disputation Theses of mine to see what a dubious thing is the view of indulgences
which they are disseminating as entirely certain.[4]

With his Ninety-Five Theses and letter to Albrecht, Luther had begun his journey down
the road that would lead to a cataclysmic break from Catholic tradition and power. In coming
months he would write a series of essays and deliver sermons in which he further articulated
his positions, and then clarify his reasoning in a small book he called *Explanation of the Ninety-
Five Theses*. He repeatedly warned against an over-reliance on indulgences. He believed that
they would cause believers to become complacent and place their trust in the indulgence system rather than in God. St. Paul had written that believers would "fear and tremble" as they
worked towards their salvation; Luther had already observed that his own parishioners did
not tremble when they returned to Wittenberg with their indulgences. Luther had no use for
the lazy Christian. "He who sincerely contributes to the building of St. Peter's for God's sake,"
he wrote, "acts much more securely and better than he who buys indulgences for it, because
there is the danger that he may make a contribution for the sake of the indulgence rather
than for the sake of God."[5]

There was, for Luther, another motivating factor. Luther did more than simply call attention to the abuses of one misguided friar; he also protested on behalf of those exploited
believers who marched unwittingly to the drumbeats of foreign religious domination. Luther
carried with him always a strong sense of *Volk*, a feeling of German cultural and ethnic unity.
His nationalistic feelings had been offended when he had first visited Rome in 1510 and was
exposed to the Italian sense of superiority. He resented the stereotypes that labeled Germans
as drunks and simpletons. Proud of his heritage, he would write and speak of *wir Deutschen*,
the German community to which he belonged, for the rest of his life. Significantly for Luther,
the dictatorial powers that ruled religious life in Germany resided outside of her borders, in
far-off Rome. Luther was not just a Catholic, but a *German* Catholic, and it was German
Catholics that he ministered to. He saw, in the construction of St. Peter's Basilica, no benefit
for Germans. "The revenues of all Christendom are being sucked into this insatiable basilica,"
he wrote. "The Germans laugh at calling this the common treasure of Christendom. Before
long all the churches, palaces, walls and bridges of Rome will be built out of our money. First
of all we should rear living temples, not local churches, and only last of all St. Peter's, which
is not necessary for us. We Germans cannot attend St. Peter's. Better that it should never be
built than that our parochial churches should be despoiled."[6]

With his writings and preaching against indulgence abuses Luther ignited much more
than a mere academic debate. To be sure, Luther's views did raise some eyebrows among his
intellectual peers. More importantly, however, within a month his theses had been translated
into German and then, thanks to the ready availability of the printing press, distributed
throughout the country. Much to Luther's amazement, his work was immediately and enthusiastically received by the peasantry, read and discussed with much excitement in cottages,
parishes, taverns, and public houses. Suddenly this obscure Saxon monk became the talk of
Germany and great champion of the people. Luther's Ninety-Five Theses were the first in a
chain of events that would shake the foundation of the Catholic Church and inspire rifts that
have remained for five hundred years (October 31, 1517, is celebrated worldwide as the birth
of the Protestant Reformation). But at the time Luther had no idea what his work would

mean or how much of a celebrity he would become. Much later in his life Luther acknowledged that he had been naïve, that "he had entered the fray against indulgences without knowing where he was going." Had he known the consequences of his actions he might not have acted at all. He had been, he believed, a tool for God's almighty purposes. His actions, so simple in origin, became monumental in effect. They were, he wrote, akin to an "assault on the heavens," and they "set the world afire."[7]

• Chapter 6 •

Popes and Heretics

St. Peter is recognized by the Roman Catholic Church as the first pope. Born Simon, or Cephas, near Lake Tiberius in Bethsaida, he was a fisherman like his father John and his brother Andrew. "I will make you a fisher of men," Jesus said to him, and Simon left his business and his home to follow his Lord. Often called the First Disciple, Simon is mentioned more than any other disciple in the New Testament. According to scripture, Simon saw Jesus walk on water, witnessed the raising from the dead of Jairus's daughter, and confessed Jesus as the Messiah. He was present at the Transfiguration, partook of the Last Supper, was present at Gethsemane, and protested his master's arrest by cutting off the ear of a Roman guard. He denied Christ three times and wept bitter tears of shame when he realized what he had done. Simon was the first disciple to whom Jesus appeared after the resurrection. He performed the first recorded miracle after the Pentecost in the name of the Lord, and spread the Good News to other Jews and then, along with St. Paul, to Gentiles. According to the account of St. Matthew, at Caesarea, Philippi Simon proclaimed Jesus as "the Christ, the Son of the living God." Jesus replied, "Thou art Peter, and on this rock I will build my church; and the gates of hell shall not prevail against it. And I will give unto thee the keys of the kingdom of heaven. Whatever you bind on earth shall be bound in heaven; and whatever you loose on earth shall be loosed in heaven."[1] These words of Jesus, now inscribed around the base of the dome of St. Peter's Basilica in Rome, promoted Peter, it is claimed, from first disciple to first pope. Thus on the shoulders of St. Peter, the simple fisherman from Galilee who became the Vicar of Christ, rests the entire structure of the Roman Catholic Church.[2]

St. Peter began a line of papal succession, an apostolic tradition that, by the time of Martin Luther's appearance 1500 years later, numbered some 212 popes. Under the leadership of these men, through the centuries the Church gained unprecedented power and accumulated staggering wealth. It managed to withstand the Great Schisms, from 1305 to 1370, when papal headquarters were located in Avignon, France, bringing about constant warfare with Italy, and from 1378 to 1415, when two, and sometimes three men simultaneously claimed title as pope. By the High Middle Ages papal jurisdiction, or *plenitude potestatis*, had expanded into the governmental, judicial, and financial realms of the various states. The Church's holdings included vast real estate properties; palaces and cathedrals filled with magnificent and priceless works of art; large standing armies and their attachments; businesses, banks and financial institutions; and massive revenues from ever-increasing rates of taxation. Exploitation of the alum deposits at Tolfa, discovered in 1461, brought unprecedented sums to the papacy. The sale of dispensations and indulgences brought vast further riches. Holy offices were routinely offered for purchase; in this practice, known as simony, an appointee paid the Roman Curia fully half of his first year's salary and one-tenth of it from then on. Upon his death, all of the office-holder's personal possessions went to Rome. By 1520, some 2000 such offices represented an invested capital of 2½ million gulden (about $500 million in today's terms), with an annual interest of about 300,000 gulden. It was estimated that in the early days of the 16th century the Catholic Church owned three-quarters of all the money in France and fifty percent of the wealth in Germany.[3]

With tremendous wealth came opportunity for abuse, beginning with the pontiff and extending down through the Curia to all levels of the ecclesiastical hierarchy. In his *A Concise History of the Catholic Church,* historian and priest Thomas Bokenkotter notes that "morally and spiritually (the High Middle Ages) was a time of terrible decline…. The papacy wallowed in corruption unparalleled since the tenth century. These men virtually bought the tiara and used it mainly for the furtherance of personal and dynastic interests—filling the College of Cardinals with relatives and unworthy candidates. They completely subordinated the religious functions of their office to unworthy temporal aims. Politically there were great successes… . But it was all achieved at a tremendous cost to the integrity of the Popes' spiritual mission. The evil fruits would be abundantly reaped."[4] While St. Peter, the first pope, had toiled in poverty, popes of the Middle Ages were the wealthiest men in the world, and they lived like emperors, in magnificent and conspicuous splendor.

Contemporary observers bemoaned the corruption that great wealth brought to the Church. Giles (Edigio) of Viterbo, who served as Prior General of the Augustinian Order in the early 1500s and was later elevated to cardinal, described the Church this way: "No law, no divinity; Gold, force and Venus rule." In 1513 Machiavelli referred to "papal decadence" when he wrote, "the nearer the people are to the Roman Church, the head of their religion, the less religious they are. And whoever examines the principles on which that religion is founded, and sees how widely different from those principles its present practice and application are, will judge that her ruin or chastisement is near at hand." Renaissance statesman and historian Guicciardini wrote succinctly about the sorry state of affairs: "Reverence for the papacy has been utterly lost in the hearts of men."[5] Pope Pius II himself recognized the widespread abuses and spoke candidly in 1465: "The priesthood is a laughing stock; the very name of cleric is an infamy. They say we live for pleasure, hoard up money, serve up ambition, sit on fat mules or pedigree horses, spread out the fringes of our cloaks and go about the city with fat cheeks under our red hats and ample hoods; that we breed dogs for hunting, spend freely upon players and parasites, but nothing in defense of the faith. Nor is it all a lie. Many of the Cardinals and other courtiers do all these things and, to speak the truth, the luxury and extravagance of our Curia is excessive."[6]

Two men, Julius II and Leo X, served as pontiffs during the years of Luther's rise from monk to professor to reformer. They followed the disastrous eleven-year term of Alexander VI (a pope unsurpassed in personal scandal, corruption, and criminal activity, father of seven children, and known for his fondness for orgies and depravities). Julius and Leo ruled over their Christian empires with different styles and temperaments, but both were filled with earthly desires, made manifest in different ways.

Julius II reigned from 1503 to 1513. He had once been an altar boy and was educated under the guidance of his uncle, Pope Sixtus IV. Through this familial influence he was quickly elevated to cardinal and then archbishop, and eventually acquired no fewer than eight bishoprics.

Upon the unexpected death of Pius III, and thanks to a comprehensive scheme where all but one cardinal was successfully bribed, Julius was elected pope in just a few hours, the shortest election in papal history. As pope he proved to be an effective tactician and built important alliances; his "Holy League" which included Kings Luis XII of France and Ferdinand II of Aragon, and Maximilian I, the Holy Roman Emperor, strengthened and secured, at least temporarily, the Holy See.

Julius also convened the Fifth Lateran Council in 1512, where one hundred of his bishops issued several important decrees which increased the Church's financial standing. The Council established the *Monti di pieta*, a system of institutional pawnbrokers that exploited needy parishioners. It decreed that local bishops had to give permission (and could charge for that permission) before books could be printed. The Council also sanctioned the levying of special taxes against the peasantry, the money then used to wage Julius's war against the Turks to reclaim the Holy Land. And it amplified the concept of the immortality of the soul and the place of purgatory (necessary for, among other things, furthering the legitimization of indulgences); those who did not accept this doctrine would be guilty of heresy and put to death.

Controversy did not worry Julius. For example, he issued a special dispensation in 1505 that allowed King Henry VIII to marry Catherine of Avignon. (Twenty years later, when Pope Clement VII refused to annul the marriage so that Henry could marry Anne Boleyn, the English Reformation began.) He also expanded the practice of indulgences, further alienating an increasingly disgruntled and wary public. Julius had his critics, but no one questioned his courage. "The Warrior Pope," as he was sometimes called, was a ferocious fighter who was determined to reunify the Papal States; his battle cry was "Drive out the barbarians." Not for 500 years had a pope led his forces into battle, but in 1511 Julius II donned full armor and marched through the snow and ice of the Italian peninsula to recapture Mirandola from the French. His ability to lead, in fact, made him the ideal model Machiavelli immortalized in *The Prince*.

Julius reigned in the years when Rome became the center of the Renaissance. Utilizing considerable revenues gained in part from the sale of indulgences, he spent huge sums on art and architecture and became the most enthusiastic patron in the history of the papacy. He began the rebuilding of the new St. Peter's Basilica, which would become the largest church in Christendom. His great passion was classical statuary, and he procured the *Apollo Belvedere* and the *Laocoön*, among other masterpieces. He ordered that the Vatican Gardens be redesigned and amassed a magnificent art collection. He hired Raphael to complete his *Stanze*, a series of magnificent frescoes designed specifically for Julius's private apartment. And most famously, he commissioned Michelangelo to paint the ceiling of the Sistine Chapel. Michelangelo had to be bullied into the project—"I'm a sculptor, not a painter," he protested—but reluctantly set to work. Michelangelo was not impressed with Julius's methods or the hypocrisy of the papacy, however, and wrote a sonnet that expressed his feelings:

> *Of chalices they make helmet and sword*
> *And sell by the bucket the blood of the Lord*
> *His cross, his thorns are blades in poison dipped*
> *And even Christ himself is of all patience stripped.*[7]

For all his military and artistic accomplishments, Julius II had many faults. He paid far more attention to his military resources and their progress on various campaigns in Perugia, Bologna, the Romagna, and other regions, than to the needs of millions of Christians in

Europe. He was more concerned with his grandiose self-image and the perceived majesty of his office than the spiritual well-being of the faithful. His vanity led him to order his image placed on coins, medals and medallions, and he established the Swiss Guard, mercenaries who provided him personal protection. He formed a "college" of 101 secretaries who had little or no responsibilities but paid him 7,400 gulden each for the positions.[8] Julius was crude and often displayed a violent temper; he was sometimes called *il terribile* and beat those who displeased him with his papal staff. He was described as "so impetuous that he would have been brought to ruin had he not been helped by the reverence felt for the church, the discord of the princes and the condition of the times."[9] His rumored sexual misbehavior while pope cannot be substantiated; it is known, however, that Julius fathered three children while a cardinal, and in 1513 died of a fever brought on by the syphilis that had plagued him for many years.

Julius's successor, Leo X, was born Giovanni de' Medici in Florence in 1475. His father was the wealthy banker Lorenzo the Magnificent who, by virtue of his power and influential abilities as a statesman, was also the *de facto* leader of the Republic of Florence. A relative of Pope Innocent VIII, Lorenzo secured for his son the position of cardinal-deacon of Santa Maria in Dominica when he was just 13 years of age. In 1492 Leo moved to Rome and was formally admitted to the Sacred College of Cardinals. Later that year, after he opposed the papal election of Cardinal Borgia (Alexander VI), he said, "Flee, we are in the clutches of the world," and returned to Florence. For the next several years Leo traveled, studied, and, at times, sought refuge when the Medici family was being persecuted for financial impropriety. By 1511 he was back in good standing with the Curia, if not Alexander, and was named diplomatic legate to Bologna. Within a year he was able to reestablish Medici control of Florence, and he remained its ruler throughout his pontificate.

The conclave that elected Leo pope on March 9, 1513, was notable for its lack of bickering, testimonies to Leo's amiable nature and the fact that the French cardinals were absent. He was ordained a priest six days later, and then consecrated as bishop, making him the last non-priest to be elected pope. Leo gave himself a celebratory procession through the streets of Rome, from the unfinished St. Peter's to the Lateran Palace, where popes had resided for twelve hundred years. Rome had rarely seen such pomp and splendor. Leo rode a brilliant white horse, followed closely by 112 equerries, personal honor attendants, and dozens of cavalry and infantry detachments. Papal chamberlains of various rank tossed gold crowns in to the crowd, less a gesture of magnanimity than of Leo's careless view of money. "God has given us the papacy," he wrote to his brother Giuliani. "Let us enjoy it."[10]

And enjoy it he did. Hardly a spiritual leader, Leo was described by British papal historian John Norwich as "less a pope than a Renaissance prince."[11] Accustomed to the trappings of luxury, his lavish spending marked his papacy, squandering the surpluses left by Julius in less than two years. Leo was grossly self-indulgent and considered himself a gourmet and connoisseur; he loved to host extravagant banquets for guests numbering in the hundreds. He spent 75,000 gulden on gold and silver tapestries imported from Brussels, and commissioned Michelangelo to construct an enormous façade honoring the Lorenzo family in Florence. He appointed nearly a hundred professors to the *Sapienza*, Rome's long-neglected university. He loved riding and hunting and would take excursions into the country with an entourage of 300. As recounted by Brian Moynahan in *The Faith: A History of Christianity*, when traveling Leo was attended "by almost 700 courtiers, an orchestra, a midget friar, a theater company, and a menagerie; his processions were graced by Persian horses, a panther, two leopards, and Hanno the white elephant, whose portrait he had painted by Raphael."[12] Leo created 141 squires and 60 chamberlains for a price of 202,000 gulden, and a record 31 new cardinals in one day alone, but these sums barely dented the enormous debts he accumulated.[13] His extravagancies left the papacy deeper and deeper indebted to the bankers of Rome and Florence, and compromised the integrity of the papal office accordingly.

Leo's rise in the Church had been the direct result of nepotism, and he was happy to continue the tradition during his time as pope. He made cardinals of two of cousins and three nephews. He summarily excommunicated Francesco della Rovere (the nephew of Julius II) so that a nephew of his own could become the coveted Duke of Urbino. The action ignited a war that lasted two years and cost hundreds of lives.

Leo's preoccupations with his own pleasures had another price. He tended to minimize or ignore arising issues in the outer reaches of the Holy Roman Empire, preferring to let his bishops and sympathetic princes handle problems. It was this tendency that caused him to underestimate the protestations of Martin Luther in far-off Saxony, which he initially viewed as a minor squabble between monks. "Luther is a drunken German," Leo reportedly said. "He will feel different when he is sober."[14]

*

Although he would gain by far the most notoriety of all reformers, Martin Luther was not the first to speak out against the authority of the papacy and the abuses of the Holy Church. In the 14th century, John Wycliffe, an Oxford scholar from Yorkshire, England, taught that Scripture, not papal ruling or Church doctrine, was the only authority Christians were obligated to follow. Anything not found in the Bible, therefore, was untrustworthy, and that included, in Wycliffe's view, the idea of pope, who he labeled a "thief, the most cursed of dippers and purse-heavers" who had "vilified, nullified, and utterly defaced" God's commandments. Wycliffe abhorred the proposition that the Church should be so incredibly wealthy. After all, Christ had demanded that his disciples forsake their earthly possessions. Any church official who accumulated wealth was living in a state of sin and not worthy of administering the sacraments. Wycliffe stressed the necessity of a personal faith in Christ, for belief was the "first virtue" and it flowed from the heart of the individual, not through the intercession of the Church. He challenged the doctrine of transubstantiation, not mentioned in the Bible but proclaimed by the Church in the Lateran Council of 1212, and he criticized the Church's practice of administering only the host, and not the wine, to the laity. Wycliffe and his followers (derogatorily called "Lollards," from the Dutch, meaning to "lolly" or mumble), were understandably shunned by Rome, and his books, particularly the groundbreaking *De Civili Dominio*, were destroyed. Wycliffe escaped direct punishment thanks to underground supporters, but forty-four years after his death in 1428 the Church exacted its revenge. It exhumed his body and burned it.[15]

In Belgium, a Prague University priest and theologian named John Huss was inspired by Wycliffe's ideas. Huss, too, was disgusted by what the office of the pope had become. He called them "heretics or otherwise evil." Huss denied that the pope was without sin (the doctrine of papal infallibility was not formally recognized and defined until 1870, but the concept went back to the early days of the Church). Huss preached that "it is our Father, the Lord God, who alone cannot sin…. Be it known to you that papal power is limited by God's law."

He scorned the ornate religious rites and ceremonies held sacred by the Church, viewing them as unnecessary obstructions to faithful living. Believing it his duty to make known the corruption and perversion he had witnessed, he wrote that "to rebel against an erring pope is to obey Christ."[16] Huss was charged with heresy and imprisoned for seven months in 1415. At his trial the General Council in Rome insisted that individuals, no matter how learned, could not interpret Scripture; that power was solely within the province of the Church and its leaders. Huss was excommunicated and burned at the stake, and he chanted hymns as the flames engulfed him, the books and writings of John Wycliffe used as kindling for the fire.

Also in the 15th century, a Dutch theologian named Wessel Gansfort (Johan Wessel) formulated ideas that in some ways served as precursor to Luther's development. In protest of the practice of simony, he once turned down the offer of Sixtus IV to become a bishop. Gansfort believed strongly that the Bible was inspired by the Holy Spirit and was the only authority for Christian life. He did not believe that the Church, or the pope, had the ability to forgive sins; in fact, he did not think it necessary to confess one's sins to a priest in order to be forgiven. In a superstitious age Gansfort opposed all belief in the unexplained, preferring to rely upon God's grace for justification. While he created only a minor stir in the Netherlands at the time, Luther later declared the he had "borrowed everything from Wessel, so great is the agreement between our spirits."[17]

Some traces of these reformers' ideas drifted into Luther's Germany. Most Germans, over the years, had been grudgingly willing to defer to Church leaders on spiritual issues, and had even tolerated clerical misbehavior and hypocrisy (including the fact that many priests had concubines or common-law wives). By 1500, however, their chief complaint was financial in nature. According to Will Durant's *The Reformation*, Germans were "drained of their money by a thousand cunning devices," and their anger was directed at Rome.[18] As much as one-third of all lands were owned by the Church, and the German Church was the richest in all of Christendom. In most towns the largest and grandest buildings, including, of course, the parishes, were owned by the Church. Roman taxation on German citizenry was oppressive, and dues, fees and tithes were demanded of the peasantry, regardless of income. Monies were to be collected "without delays," and often more sums were collected than were due. Lawsuits were referred to apostolic tribunals rather than civilian courts, and the financial judgments they imposed were sent to Rome. Cardinal Diether von Isenburg refused to pay the 20,500 gulden fee demanded before he would be confirmed as archbishop (he preceded Albrecht of Mainz) and was excommunicated. Emperor Maximilian grumbled that the pope demanded a hundred times the German revenue than could possibly be collected. He wondered if the German Church could secede from Rome, but his princes could not reach an agreement. Some remained loyal and the allegiance of others was purchased.

Germans knew they were being exploited, and they resented the fact that their money was used to construct magnificent buildings in Italy and conduct wars on foreign soil, endeavors that did not benefit them or their country. Steadily "a revolutionary spirit of hatred for the Church and the clergy" took hold of the German masses, wrote Durant. "The cry of 'Death to the priests!' which had long been whispered in secret was now the watchword of the day."[19] This was overstating the situation a bit, but certainly Luther summed up the feeling of many when he wrote, "German money, in violation of nature, flies over the Alps."[20]

By the time of Luther's appearance all of these religious, moral, and economic factors had at last come together, pushing Germany's populace to the breaking point. Meshed with a rising German nationalism and growing disdain for outside interference, the opportunity for revolt was at hand. Now, in Martin Luther, dissatisfied and angry Germans had found their voice.

• Chapter 7 •

Heidelberg

No one within the university community at Wittenberg responded to Luther's challenge to debate the merits of his Ninety-Five Theses. Indeed, most of the faculty was in general agreement with Luther's assertions. Large segments of the increasingly nationalistic German population, hungry for relief from Roman ecclesiastical rule, tired of all-too frequent displays of clerical corruption and scandal, and eager to send a message of protest, rose up in support of Luther. He became the main topic of conversation in shops, taverns, and residences. Public demonstrations and rallies took place throughout the country. Groups of peasants, holding torches and chanting Luther's name, marched down village streets and congregated in front of churches and parish houses. Medallions bearing his likeness were struck. The torrent of sentiment and feeling Luther had exposed, and the explosive nerve he had struck among so many of his fellow Germans, was quickly becoming a tide that would carry him out and away from the Catholic Church.

Luther remained loyal to the Church on the surface—his goal was always to reform Catholicism and correct its missteps, not break away from it—but his writings and sermons reflected the simmering feelings of dissatisfaction and protest that would quickly lead to rupture. At first Luther was unsettled by his sudden notoriety, but he felt a growing sense of pride in his mission. "Nobody will go to a lecture unless the lecturer is teaching my theology," Luther boasted, "which is the theology of the Bible, of St. Augustine, and of all true theologians of the church."[1] By posting his theses Luther had done the unthinkable, the impossible: he had "defied the organized Church ... broken the dam of medieval discipline ... flouted the ruler of the universe."[2]

The Elector Frederick the Wise supported Luther's actions. As president of the Council of Regency (the *Reichsregiment*), and often mentioned as a potential future candidate for Holy Roman Emperor, any unrest in Frederick's province, civil or religious, brought great risk. He was also the proud owner of an extensive relic collection and Luther had, at least by implication, argued that in terms of personal salvation relics were all but worthless. But Frederick appreciated the fact that Luther's actions had caused the national spotlight to shine on his sleepy little town. The obscure monk had garnered attention for Wittenberg and its university, and that is what Frederick valued above all else. As events unfolded in the months and years to come, Frederick's favor would prove to be one of Luther's most valuable assets.

The printing press was another. Because of the printing press Luther's ideas quickly reached all segments of European society, "far beyond my expectation," he said. His friend Friedrich Myconius, a Bavarian theologian who would later help spread the Reformation to

England, wrote that "hardly fourteen days had passed when these propositions were known throughout Germany and within four weeks almost all of Christendom was familiar with them.... It was as though the angels themselves carried the message."[3] Luther's Ninety-Five Theses and his subsequent sermons and commentaries, translated to German and then other languages, spread throughout Europe and then across the English Channel, stretching all the way to Scandinavia. Luther did not profit monetarily from his work, (his monk's vow of poverty was still in place), but its distribution had his tacit approval. Luther's popularity, as demonstrated via the medium of print, could be measured in other ways. Soon a pamphlet entitled *Karst Hans (Pitchfork John)* appeared which celebrated Luther as an emerging folk hero and champion of the masses. Within a few months a few particularly zealous German scholars published leaflets and introduced a new word into the language: they proclaimed themselves "Lutherans."

Challenges to the Church's authority had emerged previously, but without printing presses those challenges had been small in scope and scale, and had been easily squelched. Now, however, because printed versions of Luther's works so quickly appeared, a new, stronger public opinion was galvanizing. And as the production and sales of printing presses increased, ecclesiastical and civil authorities found that they could not control the proliferation of this new medieval media. Materials were not limited to Luther, of course. Fragments of the New Testament were published, an important occurrence since, for centuries, only clergy had been allowed to read Scripture. Now the people could read and hear the Lord's message for themselves, in their own language, free from (or in addition to) priestly interpretation. The peasantry learned that Christ had lived and died for them, the oppressed and the down-trodden, and not just for the privileged few that had established and maintained an earthly church. Luther was keenly aware of the power of the printing press and gladly put his literary talents to work. "I am hot-blooded by nature," he wrote, "and my pen gets irritated easily,"[4] In the first decade after his Ninety-Five Theses were posted, some six million pamphlets would be printed, fully one-quarter of them Luther's.[5]

As Luther's popularity soared, and indulgence sales flattened, John Tetzel and his fellow Dominicans were outraged. In December 1517 the University of Frankfurt hurriedly awarded Tetzel a Doctor of Theology degree, so that he might stand on equal academic footing with Luther. Assisted by colleague Conrad Wimpina, a theologian at Frankfurt, and supported by 300 other Dominicans called to a hastily-organized academic conference, Tetzel published his response to Luther in a document he called *One Hundred and Six Anti-Theses*. He made no concessions to Luther, flatly denying that any of Luther's points might be valid. Relying largely upon the work of St. Thomas Aquinas (the 13th century philosopher and scholar whose works were, and are, hugely influential within the Catholic Church), Tetzel made the power and supremacy of the pope his central argument. Taking a sarcastic swipe at the language Luther used in his Theses, Tetzel wrote, "Christians must be taught that in all that relates to faith and salvation, the judgment of the Pope is absolutely infallible."[6] Perhaps Tetzel was being prophetic; although Luther had been careful not to challenge papal supremacy in his Theses, he would argue the point much more strongly in the future.

Tetzel also attacked Luther's main contention, that any religious doctrine not founded upon the Bible was faulty. "All observances connected with matters of faith on which the Papal see has expressed itself, are equivalent to Christian truths, even if they are not to be found in scripture," he asserted. And while Tetzel never mentioned Luther by name, he made obvious reference to him: "Whoever defends heretical error must be held to be excommunicated," Tetzel warned, "and if he fails within a given time to make satisfaction, incurs by right and law the most frightful penalties." How could it be otherwise, Tetzel wondered? "If the authority of the Church and Pope should not be recognized, every man would believe only what was pleasing to himself and what he found in the Bible, and thus the souls of all Christendom would be imperiled." Protests like Luther's, Tetzel proclaimed, were attacks on the very existence and authenticity of the Holy Church itself. Luther must be silenced. Tetzel and the Dominicans demanded a result, not more theology and debate. Luther wanted to discuss God's grace; his adversaries obsessed over authority and obedience to God's Church.[7]

When Tetzel's retaliatory theses reached Wittenberg, the Dominican legate who distributed them was mobbed by students loyal to Luther, and 800 copies were publicly burned in the market square. Luther watched disapprovingly and fretted that "the song was pitched in too high a key for my voice."[8] He greatly preferred discourse to demonstration, and responded to Tetzel in a sermon he called *On Grace and Indulgence*, which became so popular it was reprinted twenty times in runs of 1000 copies each. In it Luther reiterated his disdain for indulgences; the idea that believers could purchase their salvation, he believed, made for lazy Christians and invited ecclesiastic abuse. The doctrine of indulgences was founded on the Church's need for money, not for the saving of souls. "I am called a heretic by those whose purses will suffer from my truths," he concluded. "I care not for their bawling; for only those say this whose dark understanding has never known the Bible."[9] This was to be Luther's main contention in years to come: everything he wrote, and said, and relied upon, was based upon Holy Scripture. Time and again he would challenge the authorities: "Show me where the Bible says I am wrong."

Luther's detractors dismissed his work as the ravings of a dissatisfied academic. Others saw no reason to doubt the long-established authority of the only church they had ever known. Still others remained intimidated by the pure power of the Church and did not dare express support for Luther, at least not publicly. An old friend of Luther's and now professor of theology at the University of Ingolstadt, Johan Maier von Eck, likened Luther to John Huss: in his essay *Obelisci* (Obelisk) Eck called Luther "a Bohemian heretic, an insolent rioter, and a heretic."[10] Eck would spend the rest of his life supporting papal supremacy, relentlessly attacking Luther and his doctrines. Jacob van Hoogstraaten, Dominican prior at Cologne, branded Luther a dangerous revolutionary and demanded that he be burned at the stake. (This was no false threat; just five years later Hoogstraaten, in his role as Inquisitor General, sentenced to death two Protestants, Johann Esch and Heinrich Voes, making them the first two Lutheran martyrs.) Another Dominican, Sylvester Mazoline of Prierio, who had been appointed Master of the Sacred Palace in Rome by Pope Julius II, served as papal censure of literature. He wrote that Luther's words "bite like a cur" and ridiculed Luther as a foolish German priest who had recklessly challenged papal authority. In his *Dialogue* Mazoline wrote that Luther had exaggerated, "especially stretching his theory to an unwarrantable point in dealing with indulgences."[11] Mazoline's writings sparked a back-and-forth argument with Luther that would last a decade. But this grumbling aside, for the first few months of 1518 at least, no one in the ecclesiastical community was ready to take up Luther's challenge for personal debate on spiritual or theological grounds. He referred to his critics with contempt, for he was supremely confident in his knowledge of Scripture, and they were not as learned as he was. They were "a few morons who never smelled the Bible or read a word of Christian doctrine."[12]

Pope Leo X had been advised of Luther's Ninety-Five Theses almost immediately (Archbishop Albrecht had sent a copy to him), but he underestimated the uproar they had generated in Germany and was slow to react. Advised only that there was a "rebel within the ranks" and assuming it was a squabble between monks of competing orders, Leo incorrectly calculated that the matter would be settled quickly, and within Saxony. He had other, more pressing concerns: the cardinals were feuding over numerous political issues; his princes had to be united and convinced to launch a crusade against the Turks; and he wanted to capture the wealthy city of Urbino for his nephew, Lorenzino de Medici. Eventually Leo did, however, take a few steps meant to muzzle Luther. He directed Bishop Schulze of Brandenburg to soothe, if not quiet, Luther, but left the details to Schulze's discretion. Also, one Equidius of Viterbo, who served as Augustinian General, had recently been made a cardinal, and Leo replaced him with Gabriel Venetus, who was then dispatched to Saxony with orders to "quiet that man," as Leo put it. Equidius needed time to put together his plan for dealing with Luther, and it would be several months before the plan was put into place. Leo's reluctance to immediately take more serious and direct action against Luther allowed German anti-papal sentiment to continue to grow.

Every three years the Augustinian chapters in Germany met to discuss issues and doctrine that affected the order. In April 1518, just after the Easter celebration, the meeting, called a disputation, was held in Heidelberg, a city in the Rhineland Palatinate about 250 miles from Wittenberg. Luther was to attend and give a report on his term as vicar, which was expiring. Luther's old colleague Johan von Staupitz, still head of the order, also wanted Luther to give an explanation of his Ninety-Five Theses. It would be Luther's first chance to fully explain his views to his fellow monks, and to defend them as compatible with the teachings of St. Augustine, the founder of the order. It would also mark Luther's first trip outside the safe academic haven of Wittenberg since he had posted his Theses. Luther was happy to serve as disputant and left Wittenberg on April 12, travelling on foot with two companions. There was an element of danger in Luther's trip. Dominican supporters, friends of Tetzel, had issued veiled threats against Luther. Not content merely to criticize Luther's attack on indulgences, they also claimed that Luther had called for the abolition of the Rosary and denied the divinity of Jesus' mother Mary, false rumors that were sure to rouse the passions of many peasants. But Luther held a letter of safe passage from Frederick the Wise, and stayed at inns and private homes in Coburg, Würzburg, and Erfurt, among other places. He arrived in Heidelberg on April 21, and was warmly greeted by the 24 year-old Prince Wolfgang (younger brother of Frederick), who presided over the grand castle that sat 300 feet above the city. Here Luther rested for three days, residing with his fellow monks at the *Mönchhof*, in the *Neuenheim* section of the city, enjoying the hospitality of his hosts and preparing for the disputation.

Surprisingly, Luther did not discuss his controversial views on indulgences, purgatory or papal authority at Heidelberg. Rather, he chose "sin, free will, and grace" as his topics, taking the opportunity to expand on his Scripture-based theology and his revolutionary views of justification by faith. Specifically, Luther delivered two sets of theses, twenty-eight theological and twelve philosophical, setting forth his *theoligia crucis* or "theology of the cross"— ideas he had been working on since his early days at Wittenberg—as opposed to the Church's "theology of glory." Speaking to fellow monks, church officials, and divinity students, Luther set out to answer the very question that had plagued and perplexed him for so many years:

how could man know and please God, and be assured of salvation? Luther examined the relationships between Church law (canon law), man's works, and God's grace, and in doing so brazenly upended reigning Catholic theology.

Luther posited that one could not know God—and therefore could not know salvation—except by receiving him, acknowledging him through Christ. God had, after all, revealed himself through his son, the Messiah. But he had revealed himself in the completely opposite way of what might be expected: not in power and majesty (as a theologian of glory would have it), but in the persecution he had endured. God's son had not appeared on earth in a magnificent display of might and splendor. He had not conquered Satan by the strength of his eternal weapons. Rather, he had mysteriously chosen to conceal himself in suffering, humiliation, and death. His power was hidden in the crucifixion; his strength was thus revealed by his weakest moment. The crucified Christ, to Luther, was the only pathway to God. Salvation could only occur through faith. God is particularly known through suffering—Christ's and ours. And our suffering—our *Anfechtungen*—leads us to Him and confirms us in Him. Why God acted as he did was part of the mystery, solvable only by faith. There was no other way.

Luther believed that the Church had strayed from faith-based theology, and was far the worse for it. For centuries the Church had mistakenly relied on Aristotle and his famed logic as a means to support its own authority. Christ had established his Church, to be built on the rock of St. Peter. Christ had promised to be with his Church throughout all the ages, and in fact the Church had endured, unbroken, for 1500 years. True reasoning—Aristotelian logic, or inference—could be utilized, not only to prove the existence of God, but the sole authority of his holy Church. The Church could not be wrong, and its authority could not be questioned. The Church demanded good works. Theologians of glory, in turn, believed that humans possessed the ability to do the good that could be found within them, and that this goodness, when combined with God's righteousness, meant salvation.[13]

Luther despised Aristotle's logic when used in spiritual matters and could find no use for it in his theology of the cross. Luther argued that the key to understanding God and his saving grace must come from the cross and not from human endeavors or through human reason. Works of the law, as demanded by the Church, could never improve one's standing with God, for without grace they were meaningless. Luther's theology of the cross held that humans could not earn righteousness; in fact, righteousness did not come from within, but from outside of man. It was folly to think otherwise. While human works might seem "attractive and good" they were merely mortal sins. God's grace was given to the humble, not to the arrogant who took pride in their own actions. After Adam's fall in the Garden of Eden, man's so-called free will could only choose evil, and never good. After the fall, the will was held captive and bound to sin. But all is not lost, for in man's utter despair he was left only to look to God and find his grace. Luther argued that man was *simul iustus et peccator*: simultaneously sinner (he could be nothing else), and just (through his faith). There was surely a place for good works, but they did not lead to righteousness. Rather, they came about *because* of righteousness. Luther put it this way: "Not that the righteous person does nothing, but that his works do not make him righteous, rather that his righteousness creates works. For grace and faith are infused without our works. After they have been imparted, the works follow."[14]

It was a remarkable presentation and offered a future perspective on Reformational theology (many modern scholars believe that Luther's theology of the cross, unveiled at

Heidelberg, was more significant than his Ninety-Five Theses). Luther's arguments were warmly received, particularly by the younger monks and students, the very generation that would most enthusiastically embrace the Reformation in years ahead. And at least one older theologian, Martin Bucer (who would later carry Luther's reform movement to Strasbourg), was particularly impressed. Luther's "sweetness in answering is remarkable," Bucer said, "his patience in listening is incomparable … his answers, so brief, so wise, and drawn from the Holy Scriptures, easily made all his hearers his admirers."[15] Luther's views, first roughly conceived at Wittenberg, were now evolving, sharpening, becoming more defined. He had never felt more confident. It was as if he was breathing new life into St. Paul's message: "He who through faith is just shall live."

Triumphant, Luther returned home to Wittenberg, now by wagon. He stopped for a brief visit in Erfurt, but found that his old colleagues still held a grudge over the Staupitz affair. Luther was not inclined to engage them in old debates. He only asked that they not believe "every slander heaped upon his head."[16] For the first time in many years he found he was sleeping well, eating well. He was far from content—that emotion would almost always elude him. But he felt a growing sense of satisfaction. He saw himself as a warrior for God's truth, a role he very willingly embraced. He steeled himself for the battles that he knew lie ahead. Luther had conquered Heidelberg, but he could hear the drumbeat of Rome, fast approaching.

• Chapter 8 •

"The goose that squawks among the swans"

When Luther returned to Wittenberg from Heidelberg he attempted to carry on with his duties as monk and professor. In particular, he worked to reform and retool the curriculum at the University. Many of the faculty wished to move away from scholasticism and its use of Aristotelian logic (which was the foundation for much of St. Thomas Aquinas' work and which, Luther believed, applied to worldly problems but had no place in theology), to the Renaissance-inspired study of ancient Christian and biblical texts (an aspect of the rapidly-developing doctrine of humanism). But primarily Luther's thoughts, and his heart, were with the reform movement he had sparked. He knew his bold actions had caused him to "come to the front," but he was determined to move further. Despite his popularity among the German peasantry, ominous signs were evident. He heard murmurings that John Tetzel's Dominican order was rallying against him, and that members of the theology faculty at the universities in Leipzig and Frankfurt were criticizing his work and questioning his academic credentials. Count Albrecht of Mansfeld warned Luther that papal supporters had sworn to "seize, hang or drown" him.[1] But he remained resolute: "The more they threaten, the more confident I become," he wrote. "I, who have ever loved obscurity—and would vastly prefer obscurity, and would vastly prefer being a spectator of the lively game which these worthy and learned men are carrying on at present, than being the centre of observation and ridicule…. I take the entire responsibility for all that I do. May Christ judge whether what I have said is His" Luther found some solace in the words of a man he much admired, Johan Reuchlin, a humanist and Germany's leading Greek and Hebrew scholar. "For the rest, I can only answer through with Reuchlin's words," Luther quoted. "He who is poor need fear nothing, for he has nothing to lose."[2]

In late April 1518 Luther produced a pamphlet, written in Latin, which he called *Resolutions of the Arguments Concerning the Virtues of Indulgences*, or *Resolutiones*, and which explained the meaning of his now celebrated Ninety-Five Theses. In his longest publication to date, Luther repeated his criticisms of the practice of indulgences and declared that the three centuries-old papal policy which endorsed them was null and void. He scoffed at extravagant claims of the powers of saints, and argued that a treasury of saintly merits, from which the Vatican could dip, simply did not exist. Luther could not resist taking matters a few steps further, now questioning the value of relics and pilgrimages and of special masses for the dead. Nothing in Scripture supported these, he said. And he targeted the holy city itself:

"Rome ... now laughs at good men; in what part of the Christian world do men more freely make a mock of the best bishops than in Rome, the true Babylon?"[3] He questioned whether the Roman Church was superior to all others, for that proposition, he believed, was due more to the circumstances of history than divine ordination. More specifically, Luther began to reject the notion that Christ had established the doctrine of papal authority. An examination of early Church tradition showed, he believed, that an ecumenical council of leaders held ultimate authority over churchly matters. Fully aware that his enemies were calling for his excommunication from the Church, he stated that only God could sever a spiritual communion. Further, if any Church official excommunicated a parishioner over a monetary matter, the act could be disobeyed, for no earthly institution could withhold or deny the love and mercy of God.

And in his *Resolutiones* Luther took up the issue of penance, one of the Church's most venerated sacraments, which was based on the idea that God had commanded the sinner to confess and perform a satisfaction, or penance, imposed by the priest. This Luther now rejected. In what he described as a "glowing" discovery, Luther believed that the Church had for centuries relied on a misinterpretation of Scripture. The Latin translation of Matthew 4:17, relied upon by the Church, *penitentiam agite*, meant "do penance, for the kingdom of heaven is at hand." But the Greek interpretation was "be penitent." Luther wrote that "they are wrong who make more of the act in Latin than of the change of heart in Greek."[4] Thus, priestly commands of penitence and satisfaction, required for forgiveness, were enjoined by the Church, but not by Christ. Dismissing what he called a "coercion of conscience," Luther believed that God demanded not outward deeds, but a changed heart and mind.[5]

Luther also believed that forgiveness was more simply attained. Just as salvation came through faith, he wrote, so too did forgiveness. The sinner need only turn with faith to God, to his son the Savior, and receive the Word. For through the Word, said Luther—through faith and acceptance of God's mercy—the believer was surely forgiven. He wrote: "For you will have peace only insofar as you believe the Word ... for Christ is our peace—but in faith. Anyone who does not believe this Word, even if he is absolved a million times by the pope himself and confesses to the whole world, will never find rest."[6] Luther stated that since Christ had suffered and died for all sinners and their sins, there was no need for further penance. There was, to be sure, a role for the priest, for God's offer of forgiveness could be conveyed through his priestly servant. But while a priest could declare forgiveness in Christ, he could not *absolve* sin. Luther was coming to the conclusion that forgiveness could be conveyed to a believer through *any* fellow Christian. (Indeed, in a few years Luther would proclaim that all believers were God's priests and ministers of his holy word. Further, God's Church was a community of believers, not an earthly and hierarchical institution.)

For now, in denying that a priest alone could hear confession and order the necessary penance—and in denying that penance was necessary at all—Luther was breaking the powerful bond that the authoritative Church held over its parishioners. He was challenging the very nature of Church tradition, the idea that centuries of sacred Church practices were equal to Scripture. Such groundbreaking challenges to the Church's authority would be central themes to the Reformation. In the claims of his *Resolutiones* Luther was clearly on the edge of heresy. He sent a copy to his bishop, Jerome Scultetus, who ordered Luther not to publish it. But relying again upon the protection of Frederick the Wise, Luther ignored Scultetus. Soon the treatise was widely distributed, along with a printed version of his popular sermon entitled *On Indulgences and Grace*. All across Germany the works of Martin Luther were read in astonishment, and for good reason. One of their own was taking on the all-powerful Church.

His confidence growing, Luther next took the bold step of contacting Pope Leo X directly, sending him a copy of his *Resolutiones*. Luther cleverly dated his correspondence Trinity Sunday, the first Sunday after Pentecost, solemnly celebrated by the Church since the 4th century; in doing so he was making clear his continued allegiance to the Church, despite its errors. If the Church made mistakes, Luther believed, "we should still honor her, as Christ honored Caiaphas, Annas, and Pilate."[7] His accompanying letter to Leo was curious, for while he did not hesitate to criticize the Church—in fact he felt it his duty—his words indicated that he was not yet ready to challenge the pope or question his authority. He was astounded, he wrote, to find himself being accused of heresy and apostasy, and of rebelling against the authority of the Church. He wanted to live quietly, anonymously, but events had dictated that he speak out. For it was not that long ago when preachers of indulgences, "thinking that the protection of your name made anything permissible," came to Germany and turned the Church into "a scandal and a laughing-stock." Luther reminded Leo that he was, after all, "by your own apostolic authority a Master of Theology," and had by custom the right to initiate public disputations about any issue of theology. He therefore believed he was obligated, "since he could do nothing else," to offer "a gentle resistance to them" and "question and discuss their teachings," and so had published his theses. His present desire was to explain himself and appeal to the wisdom and authority of the pope. Luther now humbly cast himself at the feet of the pope, "with all that I have and all that I am." The pope could do with Luther what he pleased, "quicken, kill, call, recall, approve, reprove, as you will." Luther would recognize the voice of Christ speaking in the pope, and if he deserved death, he would not refuse it. But although Luther was "unlearned, dull of brain, empty of scholarship in this brilliant age of ours … necessity compels me to be the goose that squawks among the swans." He would not retract one word of what he knew to be true.[8]

Luther's apparent inconsistencies here have been debated for centuries. How could he be so publically critical of long-established Church practices, taking great delight in the uproar his message was creating as it spread across Europe, while at the same time writing privately to the pope and professing allegiance, humility, and respect? Catholic apologists, then and now, argue that Luther was dishonest and deceitful, and that his actions betrayed his intentions. Some Protestants believe that Luther simply felt that any reasonable Christian, to include the pope himself, would surely see the validity of his arguments if they were laid out and presented, as Luther only desired, for scholarly debate. Others think that Luther's colleague at Wittenberg, George Spalatin, who served as personal chaplain and political advisor to Frederick the Wise, edited Luther's letter and inserted the submissive language. But while for a very brief time Luther hoped the pope might become his patron and accept his suggested reforms, such feeling did not last. For no matter how conciliatory his rhetoric might seem, in reality the clear message he sent to Leo was this: "I cannot retract." Luther's self-confidence now bordered on arrogance. "I do not care what pleases or displeases the pope," he said privately. "He is a man like other men. There have been many popes inclined to errors, vices, and even strange things." He was growing increasingly skeptical that his views would gain favor in Rome. "I am absolutely convinced," he wrote, "that it is impossible to reform the Church, unless the Canon Laws, the decretals, the scholastic theology, philosophy, logic as they now are, are taken up by the roots, and other studies put in their place."[9]

Luther preached many times in City Church, Wittenberg (courtesy Jürgen M. Pietsch, JMP-Bildagentur).

Luther was cheered, temporarily, when the University expanded its faculty in July 1518. The chair in Greek went to Philip Melanchthon, a brilliant young humanist scholar from Baden-Württemberg, Germany (his great uncle was Johannes Reuchlin), who would become Luther's greatest supporter for the next several decades, and who would author the *Augsburg Confession*, perhaps the seminal Protestant document of the age. Luther found admirers in places outside of Wittenberg, as well. Martin Bucer, who had been impressed with Luther at Heidelberg (and was one of the few Dominicans persuaded by Luther's arguments), went home to Strasbourg on the French border and, along with influential politician Jacob Sturm von Sturmeck, advocated ecclesiastical reform. Johannes Brenz, a theologian from Heidelberg, eagerly embraced Luther's concepts and worked tirelessly to promote them even in the face of harsh criticism from the Church. (Brenz would later write the first Lutheran catechism for children). Even the controversial Dutch theologian Desiderius Erasmus, who would later debate fiercely with Luther, took note of Luther's efforts in Saxony and approvingly sent a version of his Ninety-Five Theses to Thomas More, a staunch Catholic and advisor to King Henry VIII. Obviously discounting More, Erasmus wrote that Luther was "supported by all the best men without exception."[10] All of these figures would play important roles—as Luther's allies, to one degree or another—in the turbulent days ahead.

But Leo, too, had loyal supporters. Unimpressed with Luther's letter and urged on by the angry Dominicans, whose general chapter met in Rome in mid-summer, Leo finally became convinced he had to act on Luther's challenges. He again turned to Sylvester Prierias, Master of the Sacred Palace at Rome and the Bishop of Ascoli, and asked for a written report on Luther's activities, along with a summary of theological findings. In just three days, Prierias composed his *Dialogos in Presumptuosas Martini Lutheri Conclusiones de Potestate Papae* (*Dialogue against the Presumptuous Conclusions of Martin Luther on the Power of the Pope*). (While Prierias boasted that he had completed his work so quickly, some Church officials, however, quietly wondered if he had paid proper attention to detail in his work.) In his report Prierias relied upon Thomas Aquinas, a leading theologian and a champion of Aristotelian reasoning: the idea that God had given man both faith and reason, which led to truth, and which were inseparable and not subject to conflict. This school of thought, of course, relied upon by the Church for centuries, was the very same dogma that was falling out of favor at Wittenberg. Ignoring Luther's controversial positions on indulgences, which had touched off the uproar in the first place, Prierias instead emphasized the special authority and prerogatives of the pope. The Roman Church, he declared, was both in essence and practice the true and universal Church. It could be represented by the various other churches and by the cardinals, but it existed virtually in the pontiff. Further, it was impossible for the pope—and therefore the Church—to err on matters of faith, morality, and doctrine. The pontiff thus established the infallible rules of faith, sacred and authoritative as Scripture, and anyone who dared deny the truth of that fact was a heretic. Luther was merely an impudent foreign monk, wrote Prierias, a fool who had embarrassed the Church with his theses and subsequent actions. He was nothing more than "a leper with a brain of brass and a nose of iron."[11] Prierias made certain that his findings were immediately sent to Luther.

Luther was outraged by Prierias's document, which he considered to be amateurish and ill-founded. He had the *Dialogue* printed and distributed, confident that Germans and others in Europe would agree that its arguments were weak. And as if to vanquish Prierias's record, he published his own reply in two days. In it Luther rejected the earthly logic of Aristotle and

Thomas. He staked his faith on St. Paul, who taught in *Thessalonians* that Christians should "test everything, holding onto only what is good."[12] This was the position of St. Augustine, the founder of his own order, who also wrote that Holy Scripture was infallible and the only authority man was bound to respect. Luther would never agree that the actions of the Church could usurp the power of God. Prierias's grant of authority to the pope ran counter to everything Luther had come to believe about man's relationship to God and how he could be saved. "He who through faith is just shall live."

Swiss theologian (and Benedictine) Wolfgang Capito wrote to Luther and urged him to then let the matter rest. But Luther was still incensed and determined to reply to Prierias personally. When he did, scornful words flew from his pen:

> I am sorry now that I despised Tetzel. Ridiculous as he was, he was more acute than you. You cite no Scripture. You give no reasons. Like an insidious devil you pervert the Scriptures. You say that the Church consists virtually in the pope. What abominations will you not have to regard as the deeds of the church? Look at the ghastly shedding of blood by Julius II. Look at the outrageous tyranny of Boniface VIII, who as the proverb declares, 'came in as a wolf, reigned as a lion, and died as a dog.' If the Church consists representatively in the cardinals, what do you make of a general council of the whole Church? You call me a leper because I mingle truth with error. I am glad you admit there is some truth. You make the pope into an emperor in power and violence. The Emperor Maximilian and the Germans will not tolerate this.[13]

Pope Leo was losing all patience with the outspoken reformer. He quickly instituted a tribunal in Rome, the purpose of which was to identify heretics; Luther of course was the prime target. Only one theologian was to serve on the panel of judges (the rest being administrative officers), and that was none other than Sylvester Prierias. Some thought was given to putting Luther on trial *in absentia*, but the idea was abandoned; better to confront the German in person and gain an admission of his wrongdoing. On August 7, 1518, Luther was served with a summons, ordering him to appear before the Papal Court in Rome in sixty days and answer to the charge of heresy. Just two days earlier the Holy Roman Emperor, Maximilian I, had given Rome his assurances that he would support whatever disposition might be handed down. The general of the Augustinian order, however, Gabriel Venetus, decided he could not wait for Luther to appear personally, and on August 25th he directed that Luther be "seized and incarcerated, to keep him in custody with fettered hands and feet, and to send him thus to Rome."[14] Venetus had no jurisdiction over Luther and the order was ignored. But Leo, too, was anxious to resolve the matter. He sent a letter to Frederick the Wise, expressing great concern that Frederick might be providing support for Luther, who he called "a son of iniquity" and "a child of evil" who had been "hurling himself upon the Church of God." Frederick was to immediately "place Luther in the hands of the Holy See lest future generations reproach you with having fostered the rise of a most pernicious heresy against the Church."[15]

A complicated tangle of European politics saved Luther from immediate arrest and from appearing in Rome altogether. Luther believed he was not being treated fairly, and he wrote to Spalatin, begging him to advise Frederick the Wise to negotiate a different venue for the hearing. "So you see," he wrote, "just how subtly and maliciously these preachers (Dominicans) are working for my swift death!"[16] Luther offered a ruse: he would request a security escort to Rome, to assure his safety. Frederick would refuse, and Luther would then have a valid excuse for ignoring the summons to appear in Rome. Spalatin did not like the idea and refused to forward it to Frederick. He did, however, make alternative suggestions: the hearing should be conducted at any university in Germany, with the exceptions of Leipzig, Erfurt, or

Frankfurt, which were openly hostile to Luther, and that either the bishop of Würzburg or Freising should preside.

Frederick, however, had other plans. As an elector he was in a good position to bargain on behalf of his controversial professor. The Emperor, Maximillian I of the House of Habsburg, who had served since 1508, was in poor health and had just months to live. Called "the German Hercules" for his success on the battlefield as a young man, Maximillian's best days were far behind him, and he had seen his diplomatic influence dwindle and his reform efforts crumble. Now obsessed with his own demise (he travelled around his kingdom with a coffin), Maximillian desperately wanted to preserve his legacy by ensuring that his sixteen-year-old grandson Charles V, the King of Spain, succeed him. Maximillian also wanted to prevent his most prominent rival, Francis I of France, from gaining the throne. With massive financial assistance from the Fugger family (almost one million gulden), Maximillian had been systematically bribing the prince-electors for two years, but Frederick the Wise was still undecided. Would he support Charles? Francis? Was he a candidate for Emperor himself? The pope was keenly interested and monitored the situation closely. As a Medici he was not anxious to see Charles elected, but he was not willing to alienate Frederick, certainly not at the expense of a German monk, no matter how notorious and unsettling the monk had become. And he needed tax revenue from Saxony to fund future military operations against the Muslims, who were set to attack Vienna and other places in Europe.

Bribery and negotiation were called for. When Frederick insisted that, jurisdictionally, he had no interest in having one of his subjects tried in a foreign court, Leo granted two concessions. First, he announced that he would grant the Golden Rose, a special ornament solemnly blessed, to Frederick. This special award had its origins with Charlemagne in the 8th century, and was formally instituted in 1036. The Golden Rose was only rarely bestowed upon deserving royalty, military leaders, theologians, or churches. In making Frederick the 36th honoree, and just the second in his reign, Leo was publicly acknowledging Frederick, appeasing him, and showing his favor. Second, Leo agreed that Luther could remain in Germany for his hearing. He would appear at Augsburg in September at the Imperial Diet, or general assembly of territorial princes, and face the accusations against him. But there would be no German judges. A special papal legate and cardinal, Jacopo di Vio de Gaeta, more commonly known as Thomas Cajetan, would conduct the judicial examination and give Luther, the suspect, the opportunity to recant his reckless positions.

Luther had mixed feelings about the compromise. While he was relieved to learn that he would remain on German soil, he found it nearly impossible to believe that what had begun as a sincere call for academic debate had become a trial for his life. The stakes could not be higher, he believed, for the very future of Christianity was in the balance. He believed that a fair hearing would vindicate him, but who could predict what might happen? If it could be shown that he was in error, he would abandon his views, but that seemed unlikely, for he remained resolute in his positions. "I will never be a heretic," he wrote to Spalatin on August 28. He was not unmindful of the awesome power and might the Church had at her disposal. "I clearly saw my grave ready," he later wrote, "and kept saying to myself, 'What disgrace I shall be to my poor parents.'"[17] In late September he left Wittenberg on foot for Augsburg, 240 miles to the south, accompanied by Leonhard Beier, a brother in the order. Two others, Johann Rühel and Philipp von Feilitzsch, would meet him in Augsburg and assist him.

It was not an easy trip. Frederick refused to provide Luther a safe conduct assurance but did allot him twenty gulden for expenses. Luther first stopped in Weimar on September 29, where his Franciscan colleagues at the monastery warned him that his plight would be the same as Jan Hus a century ago: "They will burn you. Turn back."[18] Unmoved, he replied, "Let Christ live, let Martin die," and then delivered a guest sermon at the castle church, preaching on the fallacy of gaining righteousness through good works. At Nuremburg he met the abbey prior Wenceslaus Link, who insisted that Luther change into more acceptable attire—his monk's habit was torn and tattered—and then agreed to travel on with him and serve as counsel and advisor. Just a few miles outside of Augsburg, Luther was inflicted with severe abdominal cramps, or perhaps an intestinal infection, and luckily was able to hitch a ride in a wagon into the city. When he finally arrived at Augsburg on October 7, exactly sixty days after he had received the summons, he was welcomed at St. Anne's church within the walls of the Carmelite monastery. The prior there was Johann Frosch, who was only too happy to supply the accommodations. Frederick had promised Frosch a doctoral promotion from the University at Wittenberg for his trouble. Luther was warned to stay inside and wait to be called to the Diet. How would he answer the query that was sure to come, his friends asked him: "Are you alone wise and all the ages in error?"

In a few days he was feeling better. He was relieved to learn that Frederick, who had arrived weeks earlier, had approved a safe passage so that Luther could freely move about within the city, unmolested by Dominicans or anyone else. Several old friends and colleagues, including Augsburg cathedral canons Konrad and Bernhard Adelmann, and Veit Bild from the Benedictine order, called on him and expressed their support. Unaware of Frederick's belated safe passage guarantee, these men appealed to Cajetan, who was still finishing up other Diet business. Cajetan was not impressed with the request. "If you don't trust me," he complained, "why do you ask me? And if you do, why is a safe conduct necessary?"[19]

Luther was also the dinner guest of Konrad Peutinger, one of Augsburg's most influential citizens. Peutinger was a lawyer, publisher, curator and diplomat, and most important, a confidant of Maximillian. Though he was intrigued by Luther's celebrity and at first professed sympathy for the Protestant cause, he would ultimately remain with the Church. Now, though, he gave Luther reason to hope for a positive outcome with Cajetan. "I know now what will happen," Luther wrote that evening to Spalatin. "Friends ... are taking care of matters prudently and diligently."[20]

The next morning, October 9, Luther was surprised to receive a visit from Cajetan's emissary, Urban de Serralonga, who was ambassador of the Margrave of Montferrat and who wanted to broker a deal. All the drama could easily be avoided, Luther was told. All he needed to do was recant, and everything would be forgiven. He could then return to his work at Wittenberg as if nothing had happened. Others, in similar situations, had done as much. Luther resented the visit but kept his emotions in check. He would only recant, he said, if he could be convinced that he contradicted Scripture. He anticipated that Cajetan would rely upon St. Thomas Aquinas, but he did not consider Aquinas a legitimate biblical or doctrinal authority.

"Do you want to have a joust?" Serralonga asked him, to which Luther said nothing. Serralonga pressed Luther. Even if certain Church practices might be seen as technically incorrect, (the indulgence trade, for example), were they not permissible if they filled the Church's treasuries and therefore contributed to the Church's holy calling and mission? "Lies are good as long as they filled the box," Serralonga laughed.[21]

Luther could not agree to this. He was familiar with Rome's greed, had seen it firsthand, and could never reconcile it with the Lord God. Finally, Serralonga suggested Luther look to the practicalities of the situation. Frederick the Wise could not be counted on to protect Luther forever, he cautioned. Where would Luther be then? "Under heaven," said Luther, and bid his visitor goodbye, dismissing Serralonga as "just an Italian," which to Luther was derogatory.[22] He steeled himself for his interview with Cajetan, which would finally begin on Tuesday, October 12th. He was, he wrote, "now suspended between hope and fear."[23]

Cajetan had gained the reputation as an outstanding and dedicated Catholic scholar and advocate for Rome. He was born in Naples in 1468, making him 15 years older than Luther. He had entered the Dominican order at the age of 16 and eventually became a professor of metaphysics at the university in Padua. He was devoted to the teachings of St. Thomas of Aquinas, and when he moved to Rome to teach theology in 1501 he began his masterwork *Commentary on Saint Thomas' Summa Theologiae,* to be followed by similar treatises on Aristotle. Cajetan also was a noted papist, working to discover and discredit any opposition to papal authority and power. He successfully defended the pontiff at the schismatic Council of Pisa, and again at the fifth Council of the Lateran. For his efforts he was made a cardinal in 1517. (Much later Cajetan became known as a spokesman for papal reform, although he never joined the Protestant movement.)

Cajetan had important papal business to attend to at Augsburg, and the Luther matter was last on the schedule. He had arrived in Augsburg with great pomp and splendor, and was welcomed at a great private house owned by the Fuggers. His suite of rooms was lavishly decorated in purple, he was attended by a dozen footmen, and his food was served on silver plates. At the opening ceremonies the twenty-eight year old Albert, the Archbishop of Mainz, was made a cardinal, and Maximillian was honored as Protector of the Faith. When the pageantry was over Cajetan got down to business. War with the Turks was imminent, he told the Germans, and new taxes were necessary; the pope estimated that at least 800,000 gulden were required to fight off the threat. Cajetan told the princes that Pope Leo was also proposing that every clergyman should pay a tenth of his income, and every laity should pay a twelfth. Additionally, every fifty households should furnish one man to join the holy army.

But the German princes could not be convinced, and the tax proposal was shouted down. A document of grievances—such boldness had never before been witnessed, said observers—was presented to Cajetan:

> These sons of Nimrod grab cloisters, abbeys, prebends, canonates, and parish churches, and they leave these churches without pastors, the people without shepherds. Annates and indulgences increase. In cases before the ecclesiastical courts the Roman courts smile on both sides for a little palm grease. German money in violation of nature flies over the Alps. The pastors given to us are shepherds only in name. They care for nothing but fleece and batten on the sins of the people. Endowed masses are neglected, the pious founders cry for vengeance. Let the holy Pope Leo stop these abuses.[24]

Maximillian sent a message to Rome, noting the anti–Roman sentiment that persisted and advising caution in dealing with Luther. Then he left for a hunting trip. The Augsburg Diet was his last official duty as Emperor.

Now the matter of Luther's behavior took center stage. His hearing, which took place at the palatial new home of financier Jakob Fugger in the center of town, lasted three days. He first presented himself on Tuesday, October 12th, prostrating before Cajetan. The cardinal was surrounded by aids and adjutants from Rome. He took a fatherly tone, calling Luther "my son" and speaking with kindness and, he hoped, reason. He assured Luther that he had read all of his works and understood their serious nature, by implication distinguishing himself from the unprepared Prierias. He saw only three issues: the treasury of merits, justification through faith alone, and papal authority. Luther, advised Cajetan, was wrong on all three. He was not sent by the pope to debate the poor, confused monk. Just as he saw three issues, he had three expectations: "First, repent your errors and recant them. Second, promise not to preach them again. Third, refrain from doing anything that might disturb the peace of the Church." Cajetan was simply to secure from Luther one word—*revoco*—I recant. All would then be well, said Cajetan, and "we can sleep in peace."[25]

"I did not come to Augsburg to do what I could have done in Wittenberg," answered Luther. He was interested in scholarly debate. Which errors, specifically, was he to recant? Cajetan was intrigued, and took the bait. First, he said, Luther misunderstood the Church's treasury of merit, which was clearly set forth in the papal bull *Unigenitus* (a bull was a decree affixed with a lead seal, or *bulla*), issued in 1343. Luther quickly denied the validity of the *Unigenitus*, for in that document, he said, Scripture had been incorrectly applied. Cajetan said that the pope's bull had stated "that the merits of Christ are a treasure of indulgences." Luther stated he would recant if that is what the document said. Believing he had Luther trapped, Cajetan quickly found the language that said Christ had acquired a treasure by his sacrifice. "Oh yes," said Luther. "But you said the merits of Christ *are* a treasure. This says he *acquired* a treasure. To *be* and to *acquire* do not mean the same thing. You need not think we Germans are ignorant of grammar."

Cajetan said he had not come to Augsburg to "wrangle" with Luther, but to extract a recantation. He merely wanted "to reconcile you with the Roman Church." Luther's second error, he said, was his idea that justification came not through sacraments administered by the Church, but through faith. This was a new doctrine, not sanctioned by the Church, and was therefore false. Luther denied that his teachings were new. "I prefer the passages from Scripture, which I quote in my theses," he said. Cajetan gently explained that only the pope could interpret Scripture, and that the pope held sole authority in Christendom. But, asked Luther, was it not possible that a pope could err? Shouldn't there be oversight by the Council? Cajetan replied that Pope Nicholas V had condemned the Council of Basel nearly a century ago. The issue was far from settled, countered Luther. Surely Cajetan was aware that recently his old university in Paris had requested that a General Church Council be convened. "And the Parisians will have to answer for it," grumbled Cajetan. His fatherly patience was beginning to wear thin.

The back-and-forth continued. Setting aside his directive to avoid a debate, Cajetan was interested in testing Luther and his theory of justification. How could a communicant receiving the sacrament be certain that his faith was sufficient? How could he know he was receiving grace? This was the role of the Church. It could put the uncertain soul to rest through its objective authority, manifested through the sacrament. Certainty came from the Church, which could not err. Compare this fact to the soul of the sinner, who erred by nature. But Luther stood on faith, not reason. For he was a sinful soul, he said, and his salvation was certain. Thus, the one who comes to the sacrament must only believe: "It was not the sacrament, but faith in the sacrament that justifies." Cajetan relied upon the traditional view: contrition was necessary before one could "worthily" receive, and contrition was always uncertain. In fact, all who came to the Lord's Table were in fear of the Lord and uncertain if they might receive a state of grace. But to Luther, faith meant certainty. To receive the sacrament with doubt was to accuse Christ of lying, he told Cajetan, "and with your doubt you make Christ a liar, which is a horrible sin."

Cajetan next turned to Luther's letter to the pope, written the past summer from Wittenberg. He had given assurance that he was prepared to submit unconditionally to the pope's authority. "Do you or do you not believe?" asked Cajetan. "Recant, acknowledge your errors; this and nothing else is what the pope desires you to do." Luther replied that he believed, subject to what the Bible said, and asserted passage after passage that supported his views. Luther later recalled that every time he cited a verse from Scripture one of the Italian members of Cajetan's entourage, seated nearby, snickered. At one point Serralonga tried to intervene, although Cajetan waved him back. Cajetan was exasperated now. It was the pope who interpreted the Bible, he repeated. The argument had come full cycle, and neither man had made a concession. Luther was dismissed for the day. As he left the room and walked through the courtyard outside, Serralonga chased after him. Now it was Luther's turn to wave him away.

Luther appeared again before Cajetan the following day. This time, as if to match Cajetan's entourage, he was accompanied by Staupitz (who had just arrived), four imperial counselors, a notary, and several witnesses who would testify to his character and good intentions. Luther began by declaring that he had always been faithful to the Church, and had done his best to follow its doctrines in his teaching. Further, he intended to continue that practice in the future. He was not conscious "of teaching anything contrary to the Scriptures or the church fathers, the canon law or the correct faith." If there were any objections from Rome, or for that matter, from the universities of Basel, Freiburg, Louvain, or Paris, he would respond appropriately. Cajetan would hear none of it. He insisted that Luther bow to *Unigenitus*, and acknowledge the right of the pope to authorize indulgences, including those of John Tetzel. Now the hearing stalled. Staupitz came forward and suggested that Luther be allowed to respond in writing. Cajetan smiled at this request, and granted it, reminding Luther that his role was not to argue but to reconcile. He wanted Luther's document by the next morning.

Luther delivered his answer as promised. In the lengthy document he answered both of Cajetan's points, arguing that the *Unigenitus* was not based on Scripture. St. Peter (the first pope) was capable of mistakes, as pointed out in the book of Galatians; therefore any pope was subject to error, as well. "In the matters of faith not only is a council above a pope, but so is any one of the faithful, if armed with better authority and reason," he read, and then he went further. "His Holiness abuses Scripture. I deny that he is above Scripture." Similarly it was Scripture that set forth the doctrine of justification by faith. True faith was connected to the Word, and was in fact inseparable from the Word. Luther would obey God and not man. He would not recant.

Cajetan was contemptuous in his reply. Luther's views were inaccurate and weak, he thundered. He did not comprehend the issues that had been raised, and he continually misinterpreted Scripture. His absurd beliefs meant that "one must build a new church." Cajetan's voice rose to a shout, "*Revoco! Revoco!*" This he demanded over and over, ten times in all. Luther also lost his patience. "I refuse!" he insisted. What had begun as a gentle conversation two days earlier had fallen to a shouting match. "Go, and do not come back to me, unless you want to recant!" cried Cajetan. In the heat of the moment he forgot about having Luther arrested. "I will dispute no more with this beast," he said. "It has deep eyes and amazing speculations in its head."

That night, alone in his room, Luther wrote letters to some of his friends, including Phillip Melanchthon and Andreas Bodenstein von Karlstadt, colleagues in Wittenberg: "There is no news here, except that the town is full of talk about me..." Cajetan, he said, wanted to avoid debate and intimidate Luther "by might and power." But the cardinal, Luther wrote, was no more fit to handle the case "than an ass to play on a harp."[26]

That same night, Cajetan met with Staupitz and Link, and acting upon Serralonga's suggestion, drafted a written recantation for Luther to sign. Staupitz promised that he would discuss the matter with Luther, but prospects for success were slim. In the meantime, a rumor circulated throughout Augsburg that Cajetan was to have Luther and all of his friends arrested. John Hus had been carried to Rome and burned, and the same scenario would play out again. Staupitz quietly absolved Luther of his monk's vow of obedience, effectively relieving each from responsibility for the other. Luther, however, felt betrayed, writing later that he felt that Staupitz had "excommunicated him."[27] Then Staupitz and Link quietly left the city (Frederick had already departed), leaving Luther to an uncertain fate.

Luther agonized for several days, hearing nothing from Cajetan. Finally he wrote the cardinal a letter which served as an apology of sorts. He admitted he had shown a lack of respect and humbly begged forgiveness for any rudeness or loss of temper. He suggested a settlement: he would never again speak of indulgences or preach against them, if his opponents would do the same. His conscience, however, would let him go no further, and he would not retract anything. Luther also requested permission to appeal the matter "from a pope poorly informed to a pope to-be-better-informed." He was also planning an appeal to the General Council, although he must have known that the pope had declared this kind of appeal heretical in 1460. In one way or another, Luther reasoned, his arguments would be fully debated and rightly decided. On October 18 Luther wrote another letter, advising that he had appeared in Augsburg as required and had satisfied the papal summons. He simply asked that Cajetan recognize the obedience Luther had shown, and allow him to leave in peace.

Still, for two more days, Luther heard nothing. Believing himself out of options, Luther made arrangement with friends to help him secretly escape the city. On the night of October 20, hours after the main entrance to Augsburg had been secured, Luther was taken to a small gate on the north edge of the city. He had shed his monk's attire and was dressed in peasant clothing. Supplied with a horse by the castle canon Langenmantel, but no riding breeches, spurs, stirrups, or weapon, Luther and a companion rode throughout the night to Monheim, some forty miles away. He continued his journey for the next several nights, traveling by moonlight, staying with friends and looking over his shoulder. He finally arrived back at Wittenberg, exhausted, on October 31. The next day was All Saints Day, and Luther gratefully said Mass. It was exactly one year since he had posted his Ninety-Five Theses on the Castle Church door.

Then, finally, Cajetan acted. He wrote a lengthy and vitriolic letter to Frederick the Wise, expressing his indignation at Luther's "treachery and deception." He had given Luther a full and fair hearing, he wrote, and had treated him gently out of respect to the elector. By fleeing the city Luther had forfeited all chance of settling the dispute. Although the monk professed that he merely wanted to set forth his points for debate, he had again and again insisted that his views were "indisputable" and "irrevocable truths." So now the cardinal, as the "representative of papal authority" and the "champion of ecclesiastical orthodoxy," was left with no choice. He would denounce Luther to the pope as a traitor to Christendom and a deceiver of the Holy Church. He now demanded that Frederick immediately arrest Luther and send him to Rome for punishment, or, at the very least, banish him from Saxony. If Frederick failed to do this, he would be guilty of protecting Satan's own ally, and would "stain the ancient glory of God's house."[28] And Frederick would then himself incur the judgment of glorious and terrible Rome.

• Chapter 9 •

Sola Scriptura

Frederick the Wise faced harsh repercussions—ostracism from the Church or worse, excommunication—if he did not arrest or banish Luther per Cajetan's directive. Frederick wrestled with his options. He wanted to be a faithful servant of the Church, but he was ill-prepared to rule on matters of theology within his province. Frederick knew, of course, that Luther was a respected member of the faculty of his University and that he had the general support of his colleagues. Frederick's closest advisor, Spalatin, spoke highly of Luther, as well. Frederick did not believe that Luther was a heretic, as Cajetan claimed. That determination was, it seemed, a matter for the pope, and absent such a papal decree Frederick was unsure that he should listen to Cajetan. On the other hand, the pope had called Luther a "son of iniquity," and he had dispatched Cajetan to preside over the hearing at Augsburg. Should Frederick heed the stern warnings of Rome's emissary? What should be done with this outspoken monk?

Luther was aware of Frederick's dilemma, and in late November wrote to him:

> I am sorry that the legate blames you. He is trying to bring the whole House of Saxony into disrepute. He suggests that you send me to Rome or banish me. What am I, a poor monk, to expect if I am banished? Since I am in danger enough in your territory, what would it be outside? But lest Your Honor suffer on my account I will gladly leave your dominions.[1]

He also wrote to Spalatin:

> I beseech you, dear Spalatin, be not fearful, nor let your heart be downcast with earthly cares. You know that if Christ did not watch over me I should have perished long ago…. At all events, even should I perish, nothing would be lost to the world. For my friends at Wittenberg have now progressed so by God's grace that they do not need me at all.[2]

While he waited for Frederick to make his decision, Luther wrote an account of his trip to Augsburg, entitled *Acta Augustana*. He was grateful, he wrote, that the proceedings had taken place in Germany, but he did not believe he had been treated fairly. Cajetan was a Dominican, after all, just a Roman mouthpiece whose only agenda was to gain a revocation from Luther. Cajetan "had not produced one syllable of scripture!" Luther noted.[3] Cajetan had adamantly refused to debate the issues—which was the one thing Luther desperately wanted to do. The entire trip had been a waste of time, Luther felt, and a wasted opportunity. He wrote:

> They vexed Reuchlin a long time for some advice he gave them, now they vex me for proposing questions for debate. Who is safe from the teeth of this Behemoth? … I see that books are published and various

rumors scattered abroad about what I did at Augsburg, although truly I did nothing there but lose the time and expense of the journey.... For I was instructed there that to teach the truth is the same as to disturb the Church, but to flatter men and deny Christ is considered the same as pacifying and exalting the Church of Christ.

Increasingly, Luther was becoming certain that the pope was misguided and ill-advised (*non recte consulto*). Germans had no duty to follow his faulty pronouncements. "Before long," Luther wrote, fanning nationalistic flames, "all the churches, palaces, walls and bridges of Rome will be built out of our money. First of all we should rear living temples, next local churches, and only last of all St. Peter's. Better that it should never be built than that our parochial churches should be despoiled."[4] The only absolute authority Luther recognized was Holy Scripture, and Christians were not obligated to place their standing as believers on the directives of the pope—particularly, of course, when the pope was wrong. There could be no compromise on this issue.

> Divine truth is the lord even of the Pope. I await not the judgment of men when I have already recognized the judgment of God.... On this point depends the whole *summa* of salvation. You are not a bad Christian whether you acknowledge or ignore the Bull Unigenitus. But you are indeed a heretic if you refuse faith in the word of Christ.... The Apostolic Legate opposed me with the thunder of his majesty and told me to recant. I told him the pope abused Scripture. I will honor the sanctity of the pope, but I will adore the sanctity of Christ and the truth.... I deny that you cannot be a Christian without being subject to the decrees of the Roman pontiff.... I deny that the merits of Christ are a treasure of indulgences because his merits convey grace apart from the pope.... These adulators put the pope above Scripture and say that he cannot err. In that case Scripture perishes, and nothing is left in the Church save the word of man.[5]

Despite the quiet objections of Frederick, Luther saw to it that his *Acta Augustana* was printed and distributed in early December. He then made public his appeal of Cajetan's proclamation to a General Church Council, knowing full well that the pope had declared this mechanism heretical (*Bull Execrabilus*), for it questioned the ultimate authority of the papacy. Here Luther was looking for a venue that might validate his concerns. He did not, after all, strictly recognize a council as supremely authoritative. Rather, he would only recognize Holy Scripture in this way. But he did believe a council was superior to the pope in terms of interpretation of theological issues. It mattered little if this technical but important point was lost on the public. Luther wanted to ride the groundswell of support that he had generated, and his documents continued to be snatched up as soon as they could be printed. His appeal was so popular in Saxony that it quickly went through ten printings.[6] The distance between himself and Rome was growing greater. He began to sign all his correspondence as simply "Brother Martin Luther, Augustinian."[7]

Luther forwarded his *Acta Augustana* to his friend Wenceslaus Link, who had been with him in Augsburg. His accompanying letter was telling, for his disdain for the papacy was obvious. He wrote, "I send you my trifling work that you may see whether I am not right in supposing that, according to Paul, the real Antichrist holds sway over the Roman court. I think he is worse than any Turk."[8] Biblically, the Antichrist was the singular evil that was prophesised to struggle with Christ for the soul of mankind. Luther was not ready to publicly make known his feelings about the pope, but that day was not far in the future.

Luther also sent his *Acta* to Duke George of Dresden, who was, along with his cousin Frederick, one of the electors for the Holy Roman Emperor. Hoping that George might be sympathetic to his cause, Luther requested that "a common *reformation* should be undertaken of the spiritual and temporal estates." This is the first known usage of the word that would have such historic impact and significance.[9]

As Frederick vacillated and Luther wrote and worried, Pope Leo made a move. He issued a bull *Cum Postquam* ("when after"), which officially validated and defined the doctrine of indulgences. While the bull did not specifically attack Luther, or even mention his name, it condemned "all monks and preachers" who taught anything to the contrary. This opened the door to ecclesiastical prosecution and removed from Luther the option of further debate on the matter. The bull also reaffirmed that Christ and the saints had accumulated a treasury of merits, which the Church could apply to the penitent, and it further required all Christians to believe in the pope's power to grant indulgences. The bull was, to Luther, another reason to criticize what he believed were abuses of papal power.

In the meantime, Luther's communications with Spalatin led him to conclude that Frederick was nearing a decision, and that he would reluctantly surrender Luther to the Roman authorities as directed. By mid–December Luther told Spalatin that he was ready to leave Germany. "I am expecting the curses of Rome any day. I have everything in readiness. When they come, I am girded like Abraham to go I know not where, nay, most certainly where, because God is everywhere…. Pray for me. I am in the hands of God and my friends."[10] He wrote Staupitz that Frederick "would be happier if I were somewhere else," and his old mentor, now residing in Salzburg, Austria, advised him to leave. "The world hates the truth," wrote Staupitz gloomily. "By such hate Christ was crucified, and what there is in store for you today if not the cross I do not know…. Leave Wittenberg and come to me that we may live and die together. The prince (Frederick) is in accord. Deserted let us follow the deserted Christ."[11]

Luther believed that the situation was hopeless. On December 20, just days before Christmas, Luther delivered what was meant as a final sermon to his concerned congregation at Wittenberg Church. "As you have learned," he told them, "I am a somewhat unreliable preacher. How suddenly and without farewell I have left you in the past! If this ever happens again, I want to say good-bye in case I do not return."[12] That night he shared a supper at his home with a few close friends, and said his good-byes. He would leave at first light the next day for France, where enlightened theologians could work and freely debate the important issues.

But then, suddenly, a surprising message came from Spalatin: Frederick wanted Luther to stay. His concern for the lack of fundamental fairness in Augsburg, his desire for a final disposition from the pope and not an emissary, the well-being of his university (and, of course, the wishes of a large percentage of his subjects), were the deciding factors in his decision. He would continue to provide support and protection for his professor and monk. By letter Frederick advised Cajetan that he would ignore the directive that he arrest Luther or banish him:

> We are sure that you acted paternally toward Luther, but we understand that he was not shown sufficient cause to revoke. There are learned men in the universities who hold that his teaching has not been shown to be unjust, unchristian, or heretical. The few who think so are jealous of his attainments. If we understand his doctrine to be impious or untenable, we would not defend it. Our whole purpose is to fulfill the office of a Christian prince. Therefore we hope that Rome will pronounce on the question. As for sending him to Rome or banishing him, that we will do only after he has been convicted of heresy. His offer to debate and submit to the judgment of the universities ought to be considered. He should be shown in what respect he is a heretic and not condemned in advance. We will not lightly permit ourselves to be drawn into error or to be made disobedient to the Holy See. We wish you to know that the University of Wittenberg has recently written on his behalf. A copy is attached.[13]

Luther received the news of Frederick's decision with relief and great happiness. "I have seen the admirable words of our Most Illustrious Prince to our Lord the Legate of Rome," he wrote Spalatin. "Good God, with what joy I read and reread them." Luther believed Frederick to be a courageous and inspiring leader, as well as a pragmatic one. "He is the sort of man whose grasp extends to politics and learning at the same time."[14]

And matters of the Church never strayed far from politics. Since Pope Leo's plan to impose a new tax on the Germans had been defeated, he was left scrambling to find a way to fund his planned-crusade against the Turks. Then Maximillian I died in January 12th, 1519 and for the next five months Leo spent much of his time and energy maneuvering to ensure that Charles did not become the next Holy Roman Emperor. (In this Leo would be unsuccessful; boosted by the vote of Frederick the Wise, on June 28 Charles was elected.) Leo could not yet directly intervene in the Luther situation.

In lieu of Frederick's stubborn decision and repudiation of Cajetan, faced with a growing list of German grievances and unrest, and exacerbated by Luther's popularity among the peasantry, Leo needed to take a different strategy. He appointed a mediator of sorts. Leo directed a papal cleric named Karl von Miltitz to travel to Germany and negotiate a settlement with Luther, or, as members of the Roman *curia* now called him, "that child of Satan, son of perdition, (and) scrofulous sheep."[15]

Miltitz was himself a German. Born in Meissen in 1480, Miltitz received his theological training at Mainz, studied law at Cologne, and began his career in Rome in 1514. He had achieved mid-level clerical status in the Vatican by 1519, where he served as Gentleman-in-Waiting for the pope and as unofficial nuncio, or messenger in papal affairs. While he had not been trained as a diplomat (*nuntius et orator*), Leo felt that his Saxon roots and his connections (he had relations among the German lesser nobility), along with his familiarity with Frederick, made him a good candidate to act as a papal subordinate (*nuntius et commissarius*).

He had another reason for traveling to Wittenberg. Frederick was still anticipating receipt of the Golden Rose (a special gift by which the Church honored deserving princes), and Miltitz was authorized to deliver it. He left Rome in late December and took his time, meandering through the towns, churches, and taverns of southern Germany, speaking with locals and gathering gossip. He was surprised at the amount of support Luther held among the peasantry, estimating that three out of four people approved of the monk's activities. Miltitz was loose-lipped and did his best to gain favor with everyone he met. The pope, he said, was unhappy with the entire Dominican order. Leo placed little stock in the hurriedly-written and superficial report of Sylvester Prierias the previous summer, and believed that Cardinal Cajetan had bungled his task in Augsburg. Most of all, Miltitz said, the pope blamed the entire mess on Johan Tetzel, the *Schweinehund* (dirty dog) who had improperly distributed indulgences with his outrageous promises.

To prove his point, Miltitz stopped in Leipzig, where Tetzel now lived in retirement. He confronted Tetzel with the provincial of the Dominican Order and a representative of the Fuggers' banking house. He showed Tetzel s statement of his accounts, ledgers which proved that Tetzel had pocketed extravagant amounts of money and had lived lavishly at peasants' expense. He confronted Tetzel about his two illegitimate children. He advised the provincial to confine Tetzel to a monastery, which he soon did. Tetzel, now essentially an outcast, lived his final few months in despair (he died on July 4, 1519). His depression was not lifted even when he received a letter from Luther, who told him that he shouldn't take this treatment to heart. "Don't take it too hard," Luther wrote. "You didn't start this racket. The child had quite a different father."[16]

Miltitz brought numerous documents with him on his journey, meant to convince the Saxons that the pope was sympathetic to their station, and of course, to impress Frederick. He carried certain dispensations, annulling the stain of illegitimate births of two of Frederick's grandsons, and a sheaf of appointments, thirty in all, to papal notary positions for loyal and faithful believers. He also carried a certificate attesting to the awarding of the Golden Rose (the actual statuette was deposited with the Fuggers). This was a change from the original plan: Miltitz was to carry a papal brief which made presentation of the Rose conditional upon Luther's extradition to Rome. This idea was scrapped, however, when a cardinal at the Vatican said, "You are a pack of fools if you think you can buy the monk from a prince."[17] But in any event, Miltitz apparently had authority to offer Frederick ten thousand ducats and the position of cardinal if he cooperated. "We'll have it all fixed up in no time," he bragged.[18] "Doctor Martin is in my hands."[19]

But at their meeting on December 28, Frederick found Miltitz to be a bit of a buffoon. He did not appreciate Miltitz's casual methods and detected hints of condescension. Frederick saw through Miltitz's strategy, an odd mix of cajolery and financial persuasion, and had no interest in taking a bribe. When Miltitz advised Frederick that no case in a thousand years had plagued the Church as much as Luther's, Frederick agreed. But, Frederick wondered, did not the serious issues the monk presented call for a frank and thoughtful discussion? Annoyed that the Golden Rose was still not in his hands, Frederick quickly dismissed Miltitz. Luther, Frederick advised, was conducting university business in Altenburg, about sixty miles away. Miltitz could find him at the home of Spalatin. He wished Miltitz the best of luck in dealing with the stubborn monk.

Luther met with Miltitz on January 4, 1519, the occasion proctored by Fabian von Feilitzsch, another of Frederick's counselors. Surprisingly, the men got on reasonably well. Miltitz flattered Luther, expressing surprise that the monk was so young (Luther was then thirty-five years old). "I had thought of you, Martin, as an old, grey-haired theologian debating with himself by his own fireside," said Miltitz. "Now I see before me a man in the full vigor of his youth. I would not dare to hand you off to Rome, even with 25,000 armed men at my back."[20] Miltitz was certain that the differences between Luther and Rome could be resolved. Luther had simply misled the German people when he criticized Tetzel's indulgence practices. For while Tetzel had surely overstepped his authority and had acted primarily to satisfy Albrecht of Mainz's need of money, Rome itself had not approved. To this suggestion Luther politely disagreed. Rome, too, had acted greedily. It was the pope, after all, who needed funds and had initiated the sale of indulgences in the first place.

What would make Luther recant, asked Miltitz? To this Luther repeated his familiar line: he would gladly recant all he had said and written if he could be proven wrong by Scripture. Miltitz now turned emotional and began to weep. Could not Luther see that his words and actions were driving a wedge between the Church and the faithful? History had shown that schisms within Christendom had only resulted in misery. Surely Luther would not want something like that on his conscience. Luther replied that it was not he that had disgraced the Church in Germany; rather it was the Church's spokesmen who had made absurd declarations in the name of the pope. While it is doubtful that Luther was moved by Miltitz's mournful display—he wrote later that Miltitz cried "crocodile tears"—he did agree to a compromise. It was important to restore some measure of papal dignity. He would abide by a code of silence, and would speak no more of indulgences, as long as the Church would do the same. Further, Luther would write a letter to Pope Leo, admitting that he had been "too hot and hasty," and he would advise all who listened to him in Saxony that they should follow the Roman Church, and "obey and honor her." Finally, any remaining issues would be resolved by Mathew Lang, the Archbishop of Salzburg (and, perhaps not coincidentally, a close friend of Staupitz). This last point was the suggestion of Feilitzsch.[21]

Luther made an attempt to follow the agreement. In late February he published a pamphlet called *Doctor Martin Luther's Instruction on Several Articles which are Ascribed and Assigned to him by his Detractors*. He wrote that his previous actions should not be considered an affront to the Church. But he went much further. The saints should be venerated, he wrote, but while they could be approached for spiritual desires, the real power was with God. Luther was willing to consider the possibility that purgatory existed, but indulgences could help no soul imprisoned there. He insisted that the doctrines of the Church were subordinate to God's commandments, and that good works led to salvation but only if they flowed through God's grace and rested on faith. To be sure, Christian unity with the Church should be preserved, for it was admirable and desirable. But blind adherence to its doctrines was not a precursor for eternal life.

But almost immediately Miltitz violated the agreement, taking credit for much more than had actually been accomplished. He wrote to Leo and advised that the entire matter was resolved. Thanks to his excellent work, he wrote, Luther was now ready to recant everything. Of course the pope was pleased to hear this, and in March he had a member of his Curia, the scholar Sadoleto, prepare a letter for his signature. "My dear son Martin Luther," the missive began, "The Lord says: I take no pleasure in the death of a sinner, but that he may turn from his wickedness and live." In the pope's view Luther was a prodigal son, ready to return to his home. Leo invited Luther to travel to Rome and formally recant. He would be received, and forgiven, by His Holiness.[22]

Luther never saw the pope's letter, for it was intercepted and destroyed by Frederick the Wise. It mattered little to Luther. He could not be concerned if Miltitz had misconstrued the terms of their agreement or deliberately falsified the results of their meeting. He was prepared to place his full trust in God's word, not in the actions of a pope or a papal spokesman. He had no intention of acknowledging any authority but Holy Scripture. Luther did not remain silent for long. He had faced a series of challenges in recent months. Now he would face a far more worthy adversary, a distinguished theologian named Johann Eck who came not from Rome, but from Germany.

*

For the first few months of 1519 Rome was occupied with the election of a new Holy Roman Emperor, the position finally filled, to Pope Leo's consternation, by the nineteen year-old Charles V. Luther followed the guidelines of the ceasefire agreement he had forged with Miltitz and ceased his public criticisms of the Church. He was happy to remain out of the spotlight, at least temporarily. He delivered another series of lectures on the Psalms which were quickly printed and distributed across Europe. He also completed a second commentary on Paul's letter to the Galatians, although his understanding of Paul's meanings continued to evolve, not always easily: "It does not do enough for my stomach," he wrote.[23] Luther would produce a third commentary in 1523, and a fourth in 1535. His reputation as a scholar continued to grow; other theologians called Luther's work "learned and flawless" and "a rich treasure of the dogma of true theology."[24] Luther was awarded the black cowl, which he wore proudly as a sign of his adherence to St. Augustine's teachings, and which marked his new position of dean of the theology faculty.

Luther also took the time to focus on academic matters at the University of Wittenberg. Frederick the Wise had made curriculum reform a priority at the school and Luther enthusiastically worked to purge the institution of scholasticism, those centuries-old methods of instruction based on traditional Church doctrines. Aristotelian logic might be useful in physics or the sciences, but, Luther believed, it had no place in theology, for God's grace was far beyond the human mind's ability to comprehend. Now the humanism model of study was to take root at Wittenberg, emphasizing Greek and Latin, philosophy, history, arts, and the natural sciences. The study of all of these subjects, Luther thought, surely pleased God and would bring his blessing. It certainly pleased the students, for since Luther's arrival barely a decade ago, enrollment figures at the university had tripled. By the summer of 1519 Wittenberg students were "swarming the city like an anthill," and many who sought admission had to be turned away.[25]

While Luther continued to communicate with Frederick through his advisor Spalatin, thus securing the elector's critical support in bringing about these changes in the university's curriculum, he worked most closely with two fellow professors. The new professor of Greek, Phillip Melanchthon, came to be Luther's favorite ally. Born in Bretten, Germany, Melanchthon was fourteen years Luther's junior. Just twenty-one years old when he came to Wittenberg, Melanchthon quickly earned the titles of Master of Arts and then Doctor of Theology, and just as quickly came to revere Luther. In his inaugural address just days after joining the faculty Melanchthon referred to Luther as a proclaimer of divine truth and guardian against false doctrine.[26] The two men were remarkably consistent in their positions on ecclesiastical issues. In years to come Melanchthon would become one of the age's great religious figures and, next to Luther, its greatest Protestant theologian. His quiet and thoughtful manner, and his proclivity to negotiate and compromise, was in stark contrast to Luther's bombast and quick temper, but Melanchthon was just as committed to the cause of Church reform. Frail and unassuming, Melanchthon was extremely popular at the university and his lectures, always delivered in Latin, regularly drew hundreds of students and auditors. He was also fiercely loyal to his mentor. "I would rather die than be separated from Luther," he said. Luther was, he remarked, no less than "the champion of the Lord."[27] While Luther compared himself to the warrior King David, Melanchthon reminded him of the peaceful and wise King Solomon. Luther wrote:

> I have been born to war, and fight with factions and devils; therefore my books are stormy and warlike. I must root out the stumps and stocks, cut away the thorns and hedges, fill up the ditches, and am the rough forester to break a path and make things ready. But Master Philip walks softly and silently, tills and plants, sows and waters with pleasure, as God has gifted him richly.[28]

Luther's other ally was Andreas Bodenstein, called Karlstadt after his Bavarian hometown. Karlstadt had been a professor at Wittenberg since 1505. Once a dedicated scholastic, he had been won over by Luther's argument and now advocated curriculum reform. Karlstadt's vision of reform did not end with his students. Rather, his great ambition was to transform

Wittenberg in a wholly Christian community that others might admire and emulate. He had also boisterously supported Luther's attack on indulgence trafficking. He was "hotter in the matter than I," said Luther. (In fact, Karlstadt had written about the indulgence abuses six months before Luther, but no one had paid any attention.) It was Karlstadt who figured directly in Luther's next great confrontation with Rome and with his most formidable adversary, Dr. Johann Eck.

Ironically, Luther and Eck, a professor of theology at the University of Ingolstadt, had once been friends. But two years earlier, when Luther had posted his theses on the door of the Wittenberg church, Eck rose to defend the Church and its practices. He published his *Obelisks*, comparing Luther to Czech reformer Jan Hus, who had been burned at the stake for his views. Eck called Luther "a Bohemian heretic, an insolent rioter, and a heretic."[29] While Luther responded to the attacks with his *Asterisks*, Karlstadt could not resist and jumped into the fray. He published his own tract of 406 declarations, defending Luther and outlining his belief in the natural, sinful state of man, the indispensability of grace, and God's—not the pope's—remission of sins. Karlstadt also courageously wrote that the Bible held absolute authority over Church doctrines, decretals, and traditions. Eck responded in the summer of 1518 by proposing a public debate between himself and Karlstadt, the points of contention to be decided by the pope himself, or the faculties of the universities in Cologne, Paris, or Rome.

Negotiations over the venue of the debate, and the arbiters, dragged into the winter, and as Luther busied himself with proceedings at Heidelberg and then Augsburg, it became clear that Eck's real target was not Karlstadt, but Luther. In December Eck published twelve theses which proposed that the subject matter of the disputation be greatly expanded. He wanted to debate absolution of sins, purgatory, indulgences, the treasury of merit possessed by the Church, and above all else, the supremacy of the Roman Church—and therefore the pope—itself. The last of these topics, particularly, had been on Eck's mind since Luther had published his *Resolutions*, in which he wrote:

> That the Roman Church is superior to all others is shown by the vapid decrees the Roman popes have promulgated during four hundred years; against these are the historical evidence of fifteen hundred years, the text of the Sacred Scriptures, and the decree of the Council of Nicaea, the most sacred of all.[30]

In other words, the only voice setting forth Roman superiority was Rome itself, an assertion Luther was prepared to challenge. Luther was clear that he was not questioning the office of the pope, for since the office had been established by God, it had to be recognized. Rather, he believed the papacy possessed no sacred dignity, no supreme authority. Those were attributes of *Sola Scriptura*: Scripture alone. In anticipation of the debate, and of the critical issue that would dominate it, Luther published yet another tract: *Resolution of the Thirteenth Thesis Concerning the Power of the Pope*.

Luther viewed Eck's attacks as more than sufficient cause to end his silence and was anxious to debate. In February he wrote to Eck, his contempt unconcealed:

> I wish you salutation and that you may stop seducing Christian souls. I regret, Eck, to find so many reasons to believe that your professed friendship for me is hypocritical. You boast that you seek God's glory, the truth, the salvation of souls, the increase of the faith, and that you teach of indulgences and pardons for the same reasons. You have such a thick head and cloudy brain that, as the apostle says, you know not what to say....
>
> I wish you would fix the date for the disputation or tell me if you wish me to fix it. More then. Farewell.[31]

Luther knew he was treading on dangerous ground. No one had ever publicly challenged Roman superiority, or the pervasive power of the papacy, before. He rejected his critics: "The more they rage, the bigger my strides. I give up my first position, they yap at my heels, I move on to the next, they yap at me there."[32] Spalatin, speaking for Frederick the Wise, cautioned Luther to reconsider. But Luther wrote that he was certain the Christ was guiding him; if this were not true, he would have perished long ago. Rome had become an apocalyptic beast, a Babylon, and he could not defend the truth without insulting her. His friends, said Luther, might desert him, but then the disciples had deserted Christ in the Garden of Gethsemane. Now Luther's decisive hour was approaching, and he would not flinch or hesitate. His opponent was "a crafty, arrogant, slippery, loud-mouthed sophist whose one aim is to traduce me publicly and hand me over to the Pope devoted to all the furies." He would prepare with months of study, and the truth would emerge victorious.[33]

After many months of bickering between the parties a venue for the debate was decided: the University of Leipzig. At first the school's theology faculty, under the leadership of their chancellor, the Bishop of Merseburg, was opposed to hosting the event. They reasoned that the issue of indulgences, at least, had been resolved by the recent papal bull. Why should the matter come to the forefront again? But the Bishop's position was overruled by Duke George, the Prince of Albertine Saxony. George was, like most of the faculty, a staunch traditionalist and defender of Church (and papal) doctrine. But he was also keenly interested in a good fight, and he wasn't afraid of the implications. He chastised his faculty for their timidity: "They are evidently afraid to be disturbed in their idleness and guzzling, they think that whenever they hear a shot fired, it has hit them."[34] When his Bishop also balked, George berated him as well: "Disputations have been allowed since ancient times, even concerning the Holy Trinity. What good is a soldier if he is not allowed to fight, a sheep dog if he may not bark, and a theologian if he may not debate? Better to spend money to support old women who can knit than theologians who cannot discuss."[35] More ground rules were set. Luther insisted that the pope not serve as judge; His Holiness was, after all, the subject of the central argument. Notaries would take down every word spoken so that an accurate record could be sent to the universities in Erfurt and Paris, whose theologians and canon lawyers were finally selected as judges. Correctly perceiving that the sensational nature and subject matter of the debate would attract large crowds, George cleared the largest hall at his Castle of Pleissenburg. Two of his most trusted counselors would preside, and George himself would be present. Dozens of extra police guards were dispatched throughout the city, and would serve as protective escorts for the participants. The disputation would last several weeks, and was scheduled to begin in late June 1519.

Eck was the first of the participants to arrive in Leipzig. Accompanied only by a servant, he entered the city on June 22 and was met by cheering crowds. He participated in a Corpus Christi processional, a festive parade through the streets of the town held in honor of the Holy Eucharist, the following day. On June 24 the Wittenberg entourage arrived. First came Karlstadt, alone in his wagon and surrounded by dozens of his reference books. (Unknown to him, the rules established by Duke George would prohibit their use in the debate, a tremendous advantage for the elderly and experienced Eck.) Just inside the city gate at Grimma, near St. Paul's Church, a wheel on Karlstadt's wagon broke off, sending him flying into the dirt, bruising his arm and shoulder. The superstitious Leipzig residents who viewed the incident took it as a sign from above: surely Karlstadt was destined to lose the debate. In the second wagon came Luther and his protégé Melanchthon, along with Duke Barnum of Pomerania, the rector of the University of Wittenberg, and two other professors, Nicholas von Amsdorf and Johann Agricola. This group had been accompanied from Wittenberg by two hundred students, some armed with clubs and axes, in case of trouble. (This anticipation proved correct; several skirmishes broke out between the Wittenberg students and their Leipzig counterparts.)

Luther and his associates were met with a cool reception in Leipzig, which was primarily a Dominican city. Luther first stayed at the home of a printer named Melchior Lotter, then later with a physician named Heinrich Stromer von Auerbach, but the rest of his party had to pay for their lodging or sleep in the streets. Eck was put up free of charge by the city. Eck was provided a great stag for his dining pleasure, and a team of cooks to prepare it; Luther was given nothing. For a time Luther's safe conduct pass was withheld, and he threatened to return to Wittenberg unless it was provided. It was whispered that a ring Luther wore on his finger was a sign of his alliance with Satan. When he entered a church the resident monks left in silence. For the entire three weeks that Luther was in Leipzig he was not allowed to say the Mass.

The festivities began on Monday morning, June 27, with a six a.m. service at St. Thomas Church. The boys' choir, led by cantor Georg Rhau, sang the twelve-part Mass he had composed, entitled *De Spiritu Sanctu*. This no doubt pleased Luther, for not only was he a lover of music, but Rhau had worked as a printer and publisher in Wittenberg, and the two men were friends. (Two hundred years later the music director at St. Thomas would be Johann Sebastian Bach.) Then the parties marched to the Pleissenburg, drums beating and banners waving, as hundreds of spectators waved and cheered along the city streets.

The great hall, secured by seventy-six armed guards, was lavishly decorated for the event with tapestries and ornate candles. A crowd of several hundred squeezed inside. At the front of the hall stood two podiums, facing each other. Eck's was decorated with the insignia of St. George, while the Wittenberg lectern featured St. Martin. Supporters of both parties crowded around nearby. A Leipzig Latin scholar named Peter Mosellanus, who also served as Duke George's secretary, gave the welcoming address, reminding the participants that God demanded they treat each other with respect and dignity. "A grand address," said George, "though I marvel that theologians should need such advice." The crowd kneeled and chanted *Veni, Sanctus Spiritus* (Come, Holy Ghost) three times. Then it was time for the noonday meal of venison and wine.

At two p.m. the debate proper began. For the next several days Eck and Karlstadt debated the topic of free will and grace. Eck was confident and played to the crowd, while Karlstadt, nervous without his reference books, was hesitant. Luther bided his time and planned his strategies. He had wanted the chance to debate for years, and now was his chance. On July 2 and 3 the parties took a break for the Festival of Saints Peter and Paul, and finally Luther took center stage on July 4. Mosellanus described the combatants:

> [Luther] is of middle stature, his body thin, and so wasted by care and study, that nearly all his bones may be counted. He is in the prime of life. His voice is clear and melodious. His learning and his knowledge of Scripture are extraordinary; he has nearly everything at his fingers' ends. Greek and Hebrew he understands sufficiently well to give his judgment on the interpretation of the Scriptures. In speaking, he has a vast store of subjects and words at his command; he is moreover refined and sociable in his life and manners; he has no rough Stoicism or pride about him, and he understands how to adapt himself to

different persons and times. In society he is lively and witty. He is always fresh, cheerful, and at his ease, and has a pleasant countenance, however hard his enemies may threaten him, so that one cannot but believe that Heaven is with him in his great undertaking. Most people however reproach him with wanting moderation in polemics, and with being more cutting than befits a theologian and one who propounds something new in sacred matters.

[Eck] is a man of a tall, square figure, with a voice fit for a public crier, but more coarse than distinct, and with nothing pleasant about it; with the mouth, the eyes, and the whole appearance of a butcher or soldier, but with a most remarkable memory. In power of memory and elocution he surpassed even Luther; but in solidity and real breadth of learning, impartial men like Pistoris gave the palm to Luther.

In a debate that lasted some ten days, several crucial topics were discussed that set forth the immense differences between the established Catholic doctrines and the upstart reformation movement. The first issue was papal authority, a topic so momentous that never before in the history of the Christian church had it been so seriously challenged. Eck stated that Christ himself had established papal primacy over God's church, and both Scripture and tradition offered proof. Any hierarchy, on earth or in heaven, necessitated a top position; on earth that position was held by the pope. The world mirrored the divine, Eck argued. While God was the sovereign in heaven, the pope was the sovereign on earth. Tradition supported this position, since for over a thousand years the fathers of the church, and the faithful, had acknowledged the pope as their leader. Indeed, they looked to the pope for guidance on spiritual issues. Since Christ had authorized the papal office when he established Peter as the first pope ("Thou are Peter and on this rock I will build my church ... feed my sheep ... follow thou me ... strengthen thy brethren."), and since Christ was part of the godhead, this was all part of God's will and God's plan. The papacy was established by divine right. Was God not incapable of error? Eck also produced letters credited to a Roman bishop in the first century: "The Holy Roman and Apostolic Church obtained the primacy not from the apostles but from our Lord and Saviour himself, and it enjoys pre-eminence of power above all the churches and the whole flock of Christian people."[36] To deny any of this was heretical.

Luther was forceful in his replies. He had great respect for the papacy, he declared. But it was nothing more than an earthly institution. All earthly institutions were subject to error. Certainly the church required a leader, but that leader was Christ, not the pope. There had been no pope at the Councils of Nicaea in the fourth and fifth centuries, yet those councils had equated Jesus with God, and had firmly established the truth of the Holy Trinity. The Greek Church had endured for fourteen hundred years, all without proclaiming allegiance to a pope. Were all those Greek Christians condemned to eternal punishment? "I hold it to be certain," Luther said, "that neither the Roman pontiff nor all of his flatterers are able to cast out of heaven so great a number of saints, who have never been subject to his authority.... If they are heretics because they did not recognize the Roman pontiff, I will accuse my opponent of being a heretic, who dares to assert that so many saints held in honor throughout the universal church are damned."

As for Christ's admonition to Peter, Luther asserted that "the rock" referred not to Peter as first pontiff but to his confession of faith. Christ was the real rock, a position accepted by St. Augustine and other early Christian fathers. Further, the admonitions to "feed my sheep," "follow me," and "feed my brethren" applied to all of the disciples, not just Peter. History proved that the disciples did not consider Peter to be their leader, for they all shared in the ministry. In fact, Paul had denounced Peter, as recorded in *Galatians*.

Eck insisted that tradition proved papal supremacy. God had always been present in his church, and God's truth was revealed in it. Church leaders had looked to the pope for guidance and leadership for centuries. As for those "Christians" who did not adhere to the leadership of Rome—in fact the Greek empire had been overtaken by the Turks, which was surely proof of God's displeasure. Luther scoffed at this suggestion. It was, he believed, only Eck's arrogance that could lead to such a statement.

Eck now maneuvered Luther into a corner. The infamous John Wycliffe and Jan Hus had proclaimed that adherence to Rome was not a necessary precursor for salvation. Both had been branded as heretics by Church councils at Constance, and had paid for their evil assertions. Was not Luther guilty of the same? Luther replied that he was not defending the Hussites. He did not believe that a single assertion by these men necessarily meant that all of their positions were in error. It was clear, after all, that these "heretics" believed in one universal church, the Holy Spirit, and a communion of saints. In these beliefs they were "most Christian and evangelical."[37]

When Eck charged that Luther meant to praise the Hussites, and that he had equated the Greeks with the heretics, Luther interrupted and angrily called Eck a liar. But Eck accused Luther of denying the authority of Constance, which had condemned Wycliffe and Hus. Again Luther broke in, again calling Eck dishonest. Eck insisted on an answer: was the Council of Constance, which was acknowledged to be holy and most revered by all of Christendom, capable of error?

Indeed it was, stated Luther. "That's the plague!" said a shocked Duke George, who was sitting close by. But Luther was firm. Councils were made up of men, and were, like the pope himself, subject to error. Christians were obligated to test the words and deeds of men by Holy Scripture. Scripture alone was perfect in its authority: *Sola Scriptura*, he called it. Thus, as far as Scripture contradicted the pope or any council or any church tradition, those earthly institutions were wrong.

The debate continued for another few days, the topics including indulgences, purgatory, and the priest's power to absolve sins. Luther was surprised, but pleased, to hear that Eck's views on the indulgence scandal were similar to his. With typical bluntness, Luther stated that only "the ignorant" would trek to shrines, in Rome or elsewhere, to obtain them. Just because the Church sold them, and vouched for their effectiveness, did not make it so. As for purgatory, Luther stated that while it was not mentioned specifically in the Bible, even Augustine seemed to impliedly acknowledge its existence when he prayed for souls of the dead. Perhaps, wondered Luther, the souls of the dead slept there; the matter required further study. Luther's views on absolution were already well known: forgiveness came from God. To believe otherwise was folly. Now it was Eck's turn to scoff. "Are you the only one who knows anything?" he asked. "Except for you is all the Church in error?"[38] Luther answered, "God once spoke through the mouth of an ass." Then he concluded his argument with these words: "I am sorry that the learned doctor only dips into Scripture as deep as the water spider into the water—nay, that he seems to fly from it as the devil from the Cross. I prefer, with all deference to the Fathers, the authority of Scripture, which I herewith recommend to the arbiters of our cause."

Luther's startling declarations, that the papacy and Church Councils were less than perfect, were the watershed moments of the Leipzig Debate. He had come to believe that the pope had put himself in the place of Christ, a proposition he could never accept. Leipzig made Luther one of the most famous men in all of Europe. But he returned to Wittenberg disappointed. He complained of the special treatment Eck had received, and of the partisan crowds in Leipzig. He resorted to name-calling: Eck was, he wrote, "slippery and hypocritical," and Eck's supporters were "senseless" and "shameless."[39] Eck returned to Rome, convinced that he had triumphed. The status quo—that is, the supremacy of the Church—had weathered Luther's attacks. Although no official victor was declared (the universities of Erfurt and Paris never got around to proclaiming a winner), Eck crowed about his performance to all who would listen. He wasted no time in securing an audience with the pope. The time was now ripe, he said, for curial action against the son of iniquity, Martin Luther.

• Chapter 10 •

Exsurge Domine

In January of 1520 a spectacular meteorite shower exploded over the skies of Vienna, dazzling and horrifying peasants and nobility alike. Many viewed the event as a sign either of God's wrath or Satan's evil presence, or perhaps a foreboding signal of the end of the age. Illustrated pamphlets recording the cosmic occurrence were circulated throughout Europe. Luther pondered the news in Wittenberg. He did not believe, as astrologers did, that the stars and planets dictated events on earth, for that was God's work alone. He wondered, however, if the showers were an omen of the "tragedy" he found himself embroiled in, and which would surely continue.[1]

Indeed, Luther's rejection of the pope and the pope's church was all but complete. He now believed that Papal authority had been built, over the centuries, on nothing more than false—perhaps evil—assertions and misplaced reliance upon man-made traditions. The Church was in dire need of reform, that much was clear. But more precisely, Christians needed to see what Luther had seen. They needed to be liberated from the damning influences of the Church, and from its tyranny and corruption. Only divine Word could save them from the falsehoods of the Church; divine Word offered true salvation. Luther's opponents—papal representatives like Johann Eck, theology faculties at Cologne and Louvain, and the annoying Franciscans of Leipzig and other places—were "asses" who lacked the most basic understanding of Scripture. It was almost a waste of his time to consider their arguments any further. In a sermon Luther sneered that "We must fatten up these pigs before our Lord God comes and slaughters them. We dare not keep silent about the truth, but must risk our necks for it."[2]

Rome had heard enough. After the debate at Leipzig, Eck urged Pope Leo to take action to silence Luther once and for all. The pontiff had the general of the Augustinian order, Gabriel Venetus, write to Johann Staupitz, Luther's long-time mentor and vicar of the Saxon Augustinians: "The order, never previously suspected of heresy, is becoming odious. We beg you in the bonds of love to do your utmost to restrain Luther from writing. Let him save our order from infamy."[3]

But Staupitz had had his fill of controversy. He would deal no more with Luther's actions or misbehaviors. Instead, he resigned as vicar and moved to Salzburg, where he died four years later.

Cardinal Raeffaele Riario was next instructed to bring Luther under control. Riario was anxious to do the pope's bidding. Just three years earlier he had been implicated in a plot to assassinate Leo; he was spared from the gallows but surrendered his castle. Riario wrote to Frederick the Wise:

I am sure you are not ignorant of the rancor, contempt, and license with which Martin Luther rails against
the Roman pontiff and the whole *curia*. Wherefore I exhort you, bring this man to reject his error. You
can if you will; with just one tiny pebble the puny David killed the mighty Goliath.[4]

But Frederick was no more help than Staupitz. He responded only by stating he had
referred the matter to Richard of Gleiffenklau, another elector. The matter was out of his
hands. It appearing that all attempts at negotiation were fruitless, at the pope's direction, Eck
organized a new commission of theologians, formed with the intention of further advising
the pope. Serving with Eck were cardinals Accolti and Cajetan and a professor of theology
at the University of Rome, Johannes Hispanus. Some forty other canonists and theologians,
including representatives of the Dominican, Franciscan, and Augustinian orders, were also
summoned. After four days of discussion and debate in late May, a draft bull, or directive,
was constructed. It was then approved by the College of Cardinals. While this work was going
on, Leo was recreating at his hunting lodge in the Italian hills of Magliana; when he returned
the bull was presented to him for his consideration and approval.

The document was titled *Exsurge Domine*, the phrase being taken from the Book of
Psalms, "Arise O Lord, plead thy cause." Strangely, Luther was not named in the bull, but was
referred to as "the wild boar from the forest." His followers were the "foxes that have arisen
seeking to destroy the vineyard." Forty-one grievances against the upstart German were set
forth. They detailed the heretical nature of Luther's fundamental positions on indulgences,
repentance, purgatory, and the papacy. They noted Luther's statements regarding penance,
baptism, confession, the Eucharist, the power of the keys, and the treasury of the Church.
(Notably, some of Luther's most controversial statements and writings regarding justification
by faith were omitted, probably because the commission could not agree as to their accuracy.)
The bull then condemned all of the enumerated grievances and ordered that the faithful, as
well as churches, church officials, and ecclesiastical institutions must do the same, or risk
excommunication. It declared:

> With the advice and consent of these our venerable brothers, with mature deliberation on each and every
> one of the above theses, and by the authority of almighty God, the blessed Apostles Peter and Paul, and
> our own authority, we condemn, reprobate, and reject completely each of these theses or errors as either
> heretical, scandalous, false, offensive to pious ears or seductive of simple minds, and against Catholic
> truth. By listing them, we decree and declare that all the faithful of both sexes must regard them as con-
> demned, reprobated, and rejected.... We restrain all in the virtue of holy obedience and under the penalty
> of an automatic major excommunication.

All of Luther's writings were ordered to be burned or otherwise destroyed, and the laity
was expressly forbidden to possess or read any remaining copies. Luther was forbidden to
preach or to write anything further; in fact, none of the faithful were to listen to his sermons.
The bull noted that the papacy had the power to excommunicate Luther immediately. Instead,
although Luther had squandered prior opportunities, he would be given one final chance.
Within sixty days Luther was to provide a certified recantation of his errors, or better yet,
appear in Rome and recant personally. If he did not recant in the time allotted, he was to be
seized and transported to Rome for excommunication and, perhaps, further punishment.
The bull was dated June 15, 1520; Leo chose not to sign it but instead sealed it with a mul-
ticolored ribbon of hemp. The bull was officially proclaimed on July 24 when it was posted
at St. Peter's Basilica in Rome, and at the papal chancellery in Campo de Fiori.

Johann Eck and Vatican librarian Girolamo Aleandro were designated as official papal nuncios, and dispatched to Germany to distribute the document. Eck was to publish the bull in all of the dioceses in Saxony and southern Germany. Aleandro was to make the bull known to the emperor, assist in book burnings and treatise suppression across the region, and publish the bull in western Germany and the Netherlands. Since the pope and his commission believed that there was very little chance that Luther would recant, Aleandro was given another important task. At the expiration of the allotted sixty days, he was to convince the emperor and his princes to arrest Luther.[5]

It took four months for the bull to reach Germany and Luther. He heard rumors that it had been drafted, however. Predictably, Luther waited with scorn and contempt for those who were, as he saw it, persecuting him for merely telling the truth. In July he wrote to George Spalatin:

> I almost wish that famous bull would come from Rome to rage against my doctrine…. Even if they thrust me out of Wittenberg with their furies they will only make matters worse…. My die is cast; I despise the fury and favor of Rome; I will never be reconciled to them nor commune with them. Let them condemn and burn my books. On my side, unless all the fire goes out, I will condemn and publicly burn the whole papal law, that slough of heresies…. The more I think of Cardinal Riario's letter, the more I despise it. I see they write with cowardly fear and a bad conscience, trying to put on a ferocious mien with the last gasp. They will try to protect their folly by force, but they fear they will not succeed as happily as they have in times past. But I doubt not that the Lord will accomplish his purpose through me (although I am a foul sinner) or through another.[6]

In the meantime, Luther continued to write, the words flying from his pen. His sermons, which were transcribed and published, touched on unusual topics for a priest. He spoke out against usury and accounting houses like the Fugger's, which had bankrolled the indulgences scheme. He preached about the value of farmers, and led his congregation in prayers for rain and bountiful crops. And he dismissed the idolatry of the saints and the uselessness of making pilgrimages to sacred shrines. But most of all, Luther spent the bulk of 1520 attacking the sacred teachings of the Catholic Church.

Believing that Frederick the Wise was the only German leader who supported his actions against the Church, Luther first produced, in August, his *Address to the Christian Nobility*. Luther saw no point in continuing his arguments with Church officials, for they had turned a deaf, and ignorant, ear. In a stunning mix of doctrine and nationalism, he now called on German princes, nobles, and bishops to rally their people and express their outrage at Rome. "Here and now," Luther wrote, "the German nation, its bishops and princes, should regard themselves as Christians. They should govern and defend in their physical and spiritual goods the people who have been commended to them and they should protect them from these ravening wolves who come dressed in sheep's clothing as if they were shepherds and rulers."[7] In his *Address* Luther's rhetoric against high religious officials reached new levels of spite. Papal officers were "a crawling mass of reptiles" who proclaimed, "We are Christ's agents and the shepherds of Christ's sheep, and the senseless, drunken Germans must put up with it."[8] German Catholics were locked in "walls of straw and paper," and their leaders could bring those walls down.

The Church was not the embodiment of truth, Luther wrote. Only Holy Scripture could make that claim. The Church had become bloated, in its arrogance concerned only with feeding itself at the expense of its parishioners. He noted that Germany paid 300,000 gulden to Rome each year, money which did not address the spiritual needs of the faithful but provided a life of comfort for the Curia. Luther wrote, "If 99% of the papal court was abolished and only one percent was left, it would still be large enough to provide answers to questions of faith."[9] He minced no words as he addressed Rome's corruption:

> There is a buying and selling, a change and exchange, a crying and lying, fraud, robbery, theft, luxury, whoredom, rascality, and despite of God in every way, so that it would not be possible for Antichrist to outdo Rome in iniquity. There all things are sold and all laws can be abrogated for money. Let no one think I exaggerate; it is public; they cannot deny it.[10]

Luther dismissed as nonsense the principle that the pope, when proclaiming as the head of the Church (*ex cathedra*), was speaking as the very voice of God. "If you try to ride to Heaven on the Pope's wax and parchment," he wrote contemptuously, "your carriage will soon break down and you will fall into Hell."[11] Luther hated the fact that the pope demanded homage while he lived in splendor and luxury. On the papal brow, he noted, rested a magnificent tiara laden with jewels, signifying both spiritual and temporal power. "It is horrible and terrible that the Primate of all Christendom, who boasts he is Christ's Vicar and St. Peter's follower, should live in more worldly pomp than any king or emperor, and that he who is called 'most holy and spiritual' is really more worldly than the world itself."[12] How could this man, living in such luxury, represent the holy one, who had been born in a stable and crucified while wearing a crown of thorns? Luther wrote that "the pope should live simply," and "kissing the pope's foot and other silly signs of respect should be abolished."[13] Politically, Luther despised that the pope and his minions held authority over the Emperor. The Church's high dignitaries had their place; to be sure, they were officers, chosen to fulfill their administrative duties. But their station in secular matters did not lift them to such political heights.

Most significantly, Luther rejected the proposition that priests alone could interpret the Bible, or that they held exclusive authority over the spiritual lives of the people. "Although their whole life long they learn nothing in it, yet they presume to say that they alone understand it, and juggle with such words as that the Pope cannot err; be he bad or good, one cannot teach him a letter! It is for this reason that so many heretical and unchristian, yes, unnatural laws stand in the Canon Law."[14] He denied that priests held the means of God's grace in their hands, for God's grace was everywhere. In fact Luther had developed a new understanding of "church" (*Kirche*). In his post–Leipzig writings and lectures he dismissed the proposition that God has established his earthly kingdom through St. Peter alone, and that the Roman papacy, with all its trappings and splendor, was the logical result. Rather, Christendom was more generally a kingdom of faith, a community of believers, all of whom were saints by virtue of their faith alone.

This "communion of saints" remains the cornerstone of Protestant thought today. It does not depend, argued Luther, on an ecclesiastical hierarchy situated in Rome. Its head is not a pope, but Christ himself. In Christ all believers, peasant and prince, rich and poor, are equal, and thus all are saints. This body of believers is essential and spiritual; more important, it is Scriptural, for its holy features are the gospel, baptism, and the Eucharist. It was distinguished from external Christendom (those institutions outside of Scripture) which is marked by laws, offices, and human edicts. The power of the keys, long thought to be given to Peter as the permission to rule, had been corrupted and served only to strengthen the power and tyranny of the pope. To Luther, the power of the keys came instead through repentance and absolution of sin. They offered hope and comfort rather than fear and oppression. Steadfast faith and God's sweet grace, not the pope's self-proclaimed power and might, would overcome the gates of hell. Luther's theology, first begun years ago when he was a struggling, searching monk, had matured and taken clear shape. "He who through faith is just shall live."

Luther would never waiver or deviate from these positions. He wrote:

> Let anyone who pleases slander, curse, and judge my person and my life—it is already forgiven him. But let no one expect grace or patience from me when he wants to make liars out of the Holy Spirit and my Lord Christ, whom I preach. I am not concerned about myself, but I shall defend Christ's word with a joyful heart and renewed courage, without regard to anyone. To this end God has given me a joyful and fearless spirit, which I trust they shall not harm in all eternity.[15]

Luther criticized Catholic institutions and practices that had been mainstays of the faith for centuries. He argued that "there should be no more pilgrimages to Rome," and that "shrines should be taken down." He believed that vows of poverty were meaningless, and that "begging friars are a curse." In fact, he wrote, many monasteries should be closed, "and

Luther stands at the lectern, pointing to Romans 1:16–17: "He who through faith is just shall live" (Library of Congress).

no more founded. It would be an excellent thing if the inmates were allowed to leave when they pleased." He advised that "it be left free to every [priest or monk] to marry or not as he chooses." He believed that "vigils and private masses should be abolished or reduced in number, and that all saints days and holidays should be done away with except Sundays, for now they are only spent in drunkenness, gaming, and idleness." Even some of his friends felt that his words were too strong. But Luther told them that he "hated the [pope's] kingdom, which is nothing but sin and hypocrisy.... If I have sinned, we must remedy it by prayer."[16]

In the Introduction to his *Address to the Christian Nobility,* Luther wrote humbly: "I am well aware that people will not hold me guiltless of excessive self-esteem, in that I, a poor, despised man, dare address such great and noble persons on such important affairs, as though there were none in the world except Dr. Luther who could take on himself the care of the Christian estate."[17] But Luther wrote with the faith that his words needed to be heard; there could be no more important message for his fellow Germans and Catholics, he believed, than the arguments he posed. The public, it seemed, agreed. So great was Luther's fame, and so eagerly were his writings anticipated, that the first press run of his *Address,* an unprecedented 4000 copies, sold out in two weeks.[18]

Luther's creative and passionate literary juices now gushed, and he worked at a frenetic pace. In September he published the forty-four page *The Babylonian Captivity*, again attacking the Church's theology. While his *Address*, written in German and intended for the nobility, exposed practical abuses of the Church, *Babylonica*, as it was titled, was written in Latin and was directed at Luther's academic peers. The treatise's title was a comment on the Church's enslavement of the holy sacraments (just as the ancient Jews had been carried into captivity in Babylon, so too had the Church been enslaved by Rome). *Babylonica* was easily the most radical of his writings.

His new claims were unprecedented in scope. In this work Luther assaulted the Church's exclusive grip on the sacraments as the only means of grace available to believers. He believed there were not seven sacraments, but two, for only baptism and the Eucharist (the Lord's Supper) were authorized by Scripture. Confirmation, marriage, ordinance, penance, and extreme unction were not initiated by Christ and therefore not to be treated with the highest levels of reverence. Luther's arguments struck at the heart of the Church's power. The elimination of confirmation as a sacrament meant that the Church would lose its grip on the youth. Similarly, the loss of marriage meant that the Church need not have exclusive control over this important civil institution (Luther would have much more to say about the institution of marriage in years to come). And the loss of unction meant that the Church would lose its hold on matters of death. While the confession of sins, Luther believed, was still vitally important, the Church's role in it was overstated. God had already declared his forgiveness of sins through Christ's death and resurrection, and a priest was therefore not needed to express God's will on earth. A Christian could confess his sins without a confession box. Luther believed that the Church had become "sacramentalistic." It had become an end in itself; indeed, people went to church not to worship or pray, but because they believed that if they took part in the rituals the Church prescribed, they might be saved. They had been taught that the sacraments operated *ex opere operato*; that the power of the Lord was inherent in them, alone. Luther later expressed his views more fully in a separate tract he called *Damned Through the Church*.[19]

That left baptism and the Lord's Supper as the remaining sacraments. Baptism was a necessary rite into Christianity, biblically inspired. ("He that believeth and is baptized shall be saved," was St. Mark's admonition, "but he that believeth not shall be damned.)[20] Luther wrote, "The first thing in baptism to be considered is the divine promise, which says: 'He that believes and is baptized shall be saved.' This promise must be set far above all the glitter of works, vows, religious orders, and whatever man has added to it. For on it all our salvation epends."[21] Echoing his familiar theory of justification, Luther wrote, "Even so it is not baptism that justifies or benefits anyone, but it is faith in the word of promise, to which baptism is added. This faith justifies, and fulfills that which baptism signifies."[22] He saw baptism as a necessary starting point for justification, for "when faith then comes, baptism is complete."[23] In fact, no vow need be taken past the baptismal vow.[24] Luther's views on baptism were to be points of contention even among the Protestants who followed him.

While the Eucharist was, in Luther's view, to be retained as a sacrament, it was the most corrupted of all by the Church. The Eucharist was the key component of the Mass. This holy wonder was the very reenactment of the Incarnation and the Crucifixion. Through the doctrine of transubstantiation, decreed by the Church in the 12th century, God again becomes flesh, and Christ is again sacrificed for the sin of mankind. Only an ordained priest could preside over the transforming miracle of bread to Christ's body, wine to Christ's blood. And the Church had determined that the laity could partake only of the bread, for it was fearful that the holy wine might be spilled by clumsy parishioners.

Luther now disputed all of these Church teachings. God was everywhere, he proclaimed. He need not be transformed or made present. God was revealed not through the words and actions of a priest, but simply "where he is."[25] God was the actor in the Eucharist, not the priest. When Christ had declared, "This is my body," and "This cup is the new testament in my blood," his words were manifest in the food and drink. Transubstantiation was a dangerous fiction. Since all believers in Christ were members of the priesthood, according to Luther, all should share in both bread and wine.

Luther concluded *Babylonica* with an angry reproach. The Mass as practiced was nothing short of blasphemy, he wrote, because it stood in the place of Christ. To add human works to the equation was to deny Christ. The Church, he wrote, must abandon its view that it alone possessed the means of grace for salvation. If it persisted in its wicked folly and did not "restore proper liberty to the churches of Christ," it was responsible for the countless souls that would be lost. If left unreformed, he wrote, "the papacy is identical with the kingdom of Babylon and the Anti-Christ itself."[26]

Luther's enemies thought that his defiant words might well be used against him. They saw to it that his essay was translated into German and then disseminated. They believed that if the German populace would see how radical Luther's thinking had become, they would turn against him. The opposite held true. Luther's popularity continued to rise, and he gained heroic status among many of his fellow monks, priests, and large segments of the peasantry. His works were published to adoring crowds, eager to read what the brash monk would say next, not only in Germany, but in France, Spain, Italy, Switzerland, and the "Low Countries" of Belgium, the Netherlands, and Luxembourg. (Not everyone agreed with Luther, of course. Eventually his pamphlet was made available in England, where it was brought to the attention of King Henry VIII. After consulting with his religious adviser, Sir Thomas More, Henry pronounced the work as blasphemous and produced his own short pamphlet extolling Church practices. Luther doubted that Henry had actually written it, and said so. Henry was outraged: "Although ye fayne yourself to thynke my boke not myne owne, yet it is well knowen for mine, and I for myne avowe it."[27] Henry delivered to the pope a copy of his work, bound in gold, as "a testimony of faith and friendship to Leo X." As a reward for his support His Holiness bestowed on the King the title of *Fidei Defensor* (Defender of the Faith), which Henry would claim even after he left the Church himself a few years later and became the Supreme Head of the Church of England.)

The third of Luther's significant 1520 treatises was *Freedom of the Christian Man*, published in November. In it Luther expanded on his justification theology. "A Christian is a perfectly free lord of all, subject to none," he wrote. By this he meant that a believer was righteous before God and therefore free. He needed no further contemplation or sacrifice. Good works for his neighbor would naturally follow, by and through his faith. Luther also wrote, in seeming contradiction, "A Christian is a perfectly dutiful servant of all, subject to all." Christians, contrary to the Church's teachings, "were not free from works through faith in Christ but from false opinions concerning works, that is, from the foolish presumption that justification comes by works." A believer was, then, freed from the obligation to do good works in order to please God. Yet, he was still bound (and most happy) to do them. The Church taught that faith must be accompanied by works; only then might salvation follow. For Luther, faith always came first, and salvation was assured. Good works followed naturally. True, man could never stop sinning, and he could never atone for all he had done. But justification was always present, always available through faith. In this way the Christian lived *simul justus et peccator*, always sinning, yet always justified, at the same time.[28]

Luther's three masterworks were prepared in contemplation of his separation from the Holy Church. With his life and career in the balance, he had boldly struck at the very heart of Catholic practice and theology, attacking the very foundations of the world's most powerful institution. He had urged the leadership of Germany to follow his lead and work to reform a corrupt and evil Church. He had decried the papacy and argued that its doctrine of "sacramentalism" was not properly based on Scripture. And he had reasserted his views on justification, faith, and good works, all of which contradicted the Church's venerated positions. "I know full well that I have sung high," he wrote, "and advanced many things that will be seen as impossible and that I have attacked many things too sharply. But what should I otherwise do?!" He believed that God's spirit was the driving, invisible force that galvanized the human heart. Christ had been given to assume the sin of mankind, descending and then rising again. Christ had conquered death and had emerged victorious for all believers. His righteousness "is stronger than all sins, his life more powerful than any death, his salvation more triumphant than all the lower region."[29] This was the Christ that Luther was eager to defend. It was for the "community of saints," the hidden church that lay underneath Rome's oppressive evil, that he worked. Luther had declared war on the Holy Church, and he was ready for the fight.

• Chapter 11 •

"Here I stand"

While Luther had become the most talked-about figure in all of Europe, he was particularly celebrated in Germany. To his countrymen, he was the "Champion of Christian Liberty" or the "German Hercules." He alone had the courage to take on the Roman Catholic Church on behalf of the German people. He was the subject of countless conversations in fields, shops, and homes. Printing presses churned out nothing but Luther tracts and pamphlets, sermons and lectures. His name was cheered by the peasantry and upper classes alike, in villages, towns, and cities across the country. Luther was more than the people's champion, they said; he was a prophet, a visionary, the Lord's holy warrior sent to do battle against the Devil himself. Like Moses and the chosen people of ancient times, he had been selected to lead the German people out of the pope's bondage. For many, Luther was no less than the German savior.

But Girolamo Aleandro was eager to destroy the fearless, impudent monk. A native of Venice, Aleandro may have been born a Jew in 1480, a fact that, if true, he kept hidden. A brilliant linguist, he began his career as a member of the faculty of the arts at the Sorbonne; soon he was elected Rector. He moved to Rome and became secretary to the bishop of Liége. He did not care for Pope Julius II but became a confidant of Leo, and by 1519 he had become librarian at the Palatine Library, the first Vatican Library. He assisted in the drafting of *Exsurge Domine* and would work steadily against the Protestant movement for over twenty years, first as bishop and then cardinal (for which he was appointed *in pectore*, or secretly), until his death in 1542.

Aleandro's task as papal nuncio, or diplomat, was to work with Johann Eck and bring official notice of Luther's condemnation to the Low Country region of Europe (Belgium, Netherlands, and the Rhine delta), and to Germany. This was a challenging assignment, for Luther's support, galvanized by the popularity of his many publications, was growing stronger each day. Aleandro presented the bull to Charles V at Antwerp in late September 1520, and the young emperor gladly pledged full loyalty to the pope's Holy Church. Now armed with both ecclesiastical and imperial support, Aleandro planned to impress the public with a series of spectacular Lutheran book burnings across the region. He began at Louvain. At Aleandro's direction, papal supporters gathered hundreds of Luther's works and dumped them in the market square, where the local executioner set the massive pile ablaze with a ceremonial torch. Aleandro gave a speech denouncing the city's most famous resident, the outspoken Erasmus, who had expressed halting support for Luther's movement. ("Papal bulls are weighty," Erasmus said, "but scholars attach more weight to books with good arguments drawn from the testimony of divine Scripture, which does not coerce but instructs."[1]) Faculty members of the local university enthusiastically joined in the demonstration. Similar scenes took place at Liége and Cologne, where Luther's supporters, intimidated by these showings of the Church's authority, stayed quietly out of sight.

At Mainz, however, Aleandro ran into difficulty. A pro–Luther crowd greeted him with scorn and jeers, and, when some threw stones, he ran for cover. Then the executioner refused to strike his match, and the event had to be postponed. The following day, the city gravedigger was the only public official willing to set the fire, and he did so in front of a small crowd that consisted mainly of curious women who were bringing their geese to market. To his chagrin, Aleandro found more support for Luther the farther he traveled into the interior, where some bishops refused to allow Aleandro to post the bull at their churches, and others complied only on condition that Aleandro leave town first. He calculated that "nine-tenths of Germany was for Luther, and the other tenth cry, 'Death to the pope.'"[2] From Hesse he wrote that "All Germany is up in arms against Rome ... papal bulls of excommunication are laughed at.... Martin is pictured with a halo above his head. The people kiss these pictures. Such a quantity has been sold that I am unable to obtain one. I cannot go out in the streets but the Germans put their hands to their swords and gnash their teeth at me. I hope the Pope will give me a plenary indulgence and look after my brothers and sisters if anything happens to me."[3]

Johann Eck was also learning that the Curia had seriously underestimated Luther's popularity. He traveled throughout Germany, appearing mainly at German universities, giving pro–Roman speeches and hoping to distribute the papal bull. He found support at Brandenburg and Merseburg. But officials at Vienna and Bavaria refused to post the document, and he was shouted down at Leipzig; had he not been granted refuge in the cloister, he later wrote, he would have been killed. (This event was most astonishing to Eck; after all, just a year earlier he had, he believed, defeated Luther at the Leipzig debate.) At Torgau, Döbeln, and Erfurt, Lutheran sympathizers tore down posted copies of the bull, defaced them with urine and feces, and tossed them into the river. Eck dared not appear personally in Wittenberg, Zeitz, or Erfurt, where Luther supporters had distributed pamphlets warning him of trouble if he set foot within city limits. He made arrangements for sympathetic bishops to publish the bull in Bamberg and Augsburg. At Meissen students nearly overwhelmed him, but he somehow managed to supply a copy of the bull to a school official before he fled. He celebrated his feat by having a tablet erected at a church in Ingolstadt, which read, "John Eck, *professor ordinarius* of theology and university chancellor, papal nuncio and apostolic protonotary, having published in accord of Leo X the bull against Lutheran doctrine in Saxony and Meissen, erects this tablet in gratitude that he has returned home alive."[4]

Then a familiar figure returned to the scene. The ever-confident Karl von Miltitz, who had met with Luther previously at Altenburg in hopes of negotiating a solution, again appeared. He asked Luther to write personally to Leo and set forth his ideas for reasonable reform, assuring the pope that he had not meant to attack him personally. If Luther agreed, Miltitz promised he would try to have the papal bull rescinded. Luther had come too far, however, and would give no ground. He did write another letter to Leo (backdating it to September 6, before the bull had been published in Germany), but it hardly took on the apologetic tone Miltitz desired. Luther wrote:

> The Roman Church has become the most licentious den of thieves, the most shameless of all brothels, the kingdom of sin, death, and hell.... I have always grieved, most excellent Leo, that thou has been made pope in these times, for thou wert worthy of better days...

Do not listen, therefore, my dear Leo, to those sirens who make thee out to be no mere man but a demigod, so that thou mayest command…. In short, believe none who exalt thee, believe those who humble thee.[5]

There is no record that Leo received Luther's letter; if he did, he made no reply.

Frederick the Wise also had a suggestion. Unaware that Aleandro had already secured Charles' permission to publish *Exsurge Domine* in Germany, Frederick advised Luther to write to the new Emperor and state his case. Perhaps, Frederick thought, the Emperor could intervene and a confrontation might still be avoided. Luther wrote:

That I dare to approach your most Serene Majesty with a letter, most excellent Emperor Charles, will rightly cause wonder to all. A single flea dares to address the king of kings. But the wonder will be less if the greatness of the cause is considered … therefore I, poor and needy, the unworthy representative of a most worthy cause, prostrate myself before the feet of your Most Serene Majesty.

I have published certain books, which have kindled the hatred and indignation of great men against me, but I ought to be protected by you for two reasons: first, because I come unwillingly before the public, and only wrote when provoked by the violence and fraud of others, seeking nothing more earnestly than to hide in a corner, and secondly, because, as my conscience and the judgment of excellent men will testify, I studied only to proclaim the gospel truth against the superstitious traditions of men.

Luther's letter to Charles, like his letter to Leo, did not earn a response.

Exsurge Domine finally arrived in Wittenberg on October 10, 1520, sent from Eck via courier. The sixty-day clock was now officially ticking: if Luther did not appear in Rome and recant, he would be excommunicated as a heretic. Though Luther had long known of the bull and its contents, when he viewed the document he was at first was unsure of its legitimacy. It must be a forgery, he thought, a godless product of Eck's evil cunning. He held out hope that Leo would realize he had been duped by his advisors, who, he believed, were surely under Satan's control. As always, Luther took to his pen. He quickly produced a response entitled *Adversus Execrabile Antichristi Bullam* (Against the Execrable Bull of Antichrist). Luther wrote, "whoever wrote this bull, he is Antichrist. I protest before God, our Lord Jesus, his sacred angels and the whole world that with my whole heart I dissent from the damnation of this bull, that I curse and execrate it as sacrilege and blasphemy of Christ, God's Son and our Lord. This be my recantation."

Luther eventually acknowledged that the bull was genuine. On November 29, at the suggestion of Frederick the Wise, Luther published a second response to the bull entitled *Assertion of All the Articles Wrongly Condemned in the Roman Bull*. Again Luther's tone was defiant and sarcastic. He wrote, "I was wrong, I admit it, when I said that indulgences were 'the pious defrauding of the faithful.' I recant and say, 'Indulgences are the most pious frauds and imposters of the most rascally pontiffs, by which they deceive the souls and destroy the goods of the faithful.'" Despite his anger, Luther felt a bit of relief: "Already I am much freer," he wrote, "certain at last that the pope is the antichrist."[6] To a friend he wrote, "You would scarcely believe how pleased I am that enemies rise up against me more than ever. For I am never prouder or bolder than when I dare to displease them. Let them be doctors, princes, or bishops, what difference does it make? If the word of God were not attacked by them, it would not be God's word."[7]

On December 10, exactly sixty days after he had received *Exsurge Domine*, and when the allotted time for recantation expired, Luther decided to stage his own public demonstration. He directed his trusted ally Melanchthon to invite Wittenberg faculty, students, and parishioners to assemble, posting this notice on the church door:

Let whosoever adheres to the truth of the gospel be present at nine o'clock at the church of the Holy Cross outside the walls, where the impious books of papal decrees and scholastic theology will be burnt according to ancient and apostolic usage, inasmuch as the boldness of the enemies of the gospel has waxed so great that they daily burn the evangelic books of Luther. Come, pious and zealous youth, to the pious and religious spectacle, for perchance now is the time when the Antichrist must be revealed![8]

At the appointed hour, Luther appeared before a large crowd near the Black Cloister, just outside the walls of Elster gate, so-called because the road from Wittenberg led to that town. The Elbe River flowed quietly nearby. The students had built a huge bonfire consisting of volumes of the *Decretals*, or canon law; the papal constitution; various works of scholastic theology, including the *Summa Angelica,* the Aristotle-based Catholic manual of moral theology; and numerous writings of Johann Eck. Luther stood before the fire in his monk's robe, the damning papal bull in hand. Paraphrasing Psalm 21:9 he exclaimed, "Because thou hast brought down the truth of God, he also brings thee down into this fire today! Amen."[9] With that he threw *Exsurge Domine* into the flames. As the black smoke drifted into the bleak Saxon sky the crowd applauded and cheered, and then chanted a *Te Deum*, a hymn of joy and thanksgiving. Throughout the day Luther's students paraded through the streets of Wittenberg on foot and by wagon, mocking the pope with their display of a defaced bull attached to a pole, and an indulgence on the point of a sword. Some sang funeral songs in Hebrew. The celebration

Luther burns the papal bull of excommunication *Exsurge Domine* near the city limits of Wittenberg, December 10, 1520. His colleague Philipp Melanchthon watches from over his right shoulder. The Castle Church can be seen in the background. Lithograph by Baron von Löwenstern, 1830 (Library of Congress).

The oak tree in this small city park in Wittenberg commemorates the site where Luther burned the papal bull.

lasted throughout the night and into the next day, until city officials finally ordered the students to disperse.

Later Luther admitted that he knew his actions signified an irrevocable break with the Church. Not only had he spat upon the pope's bull, but he had demonstrably rejected the whole of canon law, the documents by which the Church manifested its authority over Christendom. Further, he had denounced the teachings of Aristotle and Aquinas and others whose philosophies had been long accepted by Rome. He was trembling and praying when he stood by the fire, he said, but when it was over he "never felt more pleased than with any other act in his life."[10] Luther was quick to justify his actions: "Since they have burned my books, I burn theirs. The canon law was included because it makes the pope a god on earth. So far I have merely fooled with this business of the pope. All my articles condemned by Antichrist are Christian. Seldom has the pope overcome anyone with Scripture and with reason."[11]

Word of Luther's actions quickly reached Rome, and the prevailing sentiment was that the threat of *Exsurge Domine* now had to be carried out. On January 3, 1521, some thirty-eight months after Luther nailed his Ninety-Five Theses to the Castle Church door at Wittenberg, Pope Leo X issued *Decet Romanum Pontificem* (It Pleases the Roman Pontiff), condemning and excommunicating Luther and his followers from the Holy Catholic Church. In part the "holy curse" read:

> He has now been declared a heretic; and so also others, whatever their authority and rank, who have ... become followers of Martin's pernicious and heretical sect, and given him openly and publicly their help,

counsel and favour, encouraging him in their midst in his disobedience and obstinacy ... such men ... are to be treated rightfully as heretics and avoided by all faithful Christians...

Our purpose is that such men should rightfully be ranked with Martin and other accursed heretics and excommunicates, and that even as they have ranged themselves with the obstinacy in sinning of the said Martin, they shall likewise share his punishments and his name, by bearing with them everywhere the title "Lutheran" and the punishments it incurs.... On all these we decree the sentences of excommunication.[12]

Luther was not surprised when the "absolute bull" reached him weeks later. He disregarded it as just another foolish action of a Church that had proved to be untrustworthy. It was no longer enough to preach that the Church needed reform, he believed. He now took a radical new position in his lectures and sermons. Those who submitted to the rule of the pope, he said, could not gain salvation. "I am persuaded of this," he taught, "that unless a man fight with all his might, and if need be unto death, against the statutes and the laws of the pope and bishops, he cannot be saved."[13] The old Church, the only Church Western Europe had ever known, was beyond cleansing. It trusted its own institutions and hierarchies more than Scripture. The Church that had guided Luther's life, that had taken him in after his frightened and desperate vow to St. Anne, and that had, through his study and devoutness of purpose, elevated him to priest and doctor and professor, was now to be forsaken. A new church, Luther hoped, forged by Protestants, sanctified by faith and united as a "communion of saints," would emerge. Luther cared little that the pope had damned him to hell. He did not fear what the Church might do to him. For now, it seemed, in the words of a later historian, "the monk had excommunicated the pope."[14]

*

Against this most serious backdrop of the excommunication of Martin Luther, on October 22, 1520 Charles V was crowned Emperor of the Holy Roman Empire in Aachen, the German city that bordered Belgium to the west. The archbishop of Cologne prayed over him in the great cathedral where Charlemagne, who had been crowned by Pope Leo III seven centuries before, and who had worked to unite the Germanic peoples into one Christian kingdom, lay buried. The archbishop administered the solemn oath: Would Charles protect the Church? Preserve eternal faith? Remain loyal to the pope? Rule justly and care for the poor, the widowed, and the orphans? "*Volo*," responded Charles in Latin, "I will."[15] Charles would reign for 34 years, until exhaustion forced him to abdicate in favor of his younger brother Ferdinand. His massive empire grew to encompass some two and one-half million square miles, and included most of Europe, parts of the Far East and of the rapidly developing Americas. His armies fought continually with France and the Ottomans. But his time on the throne would be most remembered for his (mostly unsuccessful) efforts to suppress Luther's religious protest movement.

Frederick the Wise, in his role as elector, had voted for Charles the previous spring (in fact the election had been unanimous, to the dismay of Pope Leo). But now Frederick was unable to attend the coronation, for a severe attack of gout had immobilized him some fifty miles away at Cologne, where a university professor of medicine was attending him. In the midst of his efforts to publish *Exsurge Domine*, Aleandro called on Frederick and asked that Luther be arrested. The request posed interesting issues. Rome had decided Luther's fate, but what action might the State take? And how would the new Emperor, anxious to rule over all of his subjects, act in light of Luther's popularity in Germany? It was certain, Frederick knew, that a final disposition was needed. Acting on the advice of Erasmus, Frederick declined to incarcerate Luther. He insisted that Luther be allowed a hearing on German soil, before German authorities. All parties knew that Charles was convening his first Imperial Diet, or legislative assembly (*Reichstag*), in the upcoming months at Worms (pronounced *Vormz*), in southwest Germany. Present would be an "eminent assemblage" of archbishops, bishops, princes, counts, dukes and other members of the nobility. While there were important issues to be attended to—the need for additional taxes to fund the looming wars with France, led by Francis I, and with the Turks, led by Suleiman the Magnificent, for one; a potential alliance with England (Charles' aunt, Catherine of Aragon, was Queen), for another; and the establishment of a temporary authoritative council of regency (*Reichsregiment*) to rule during Charles' absence, for yet another—the Luther affair was most pressing in the hearts and minds of the German people. Perhaps, wondered Frederick, the matter could be brought to the Diet. Perhaps Charles could determine Luther's fate.

Negotiations meant to ensure Luther's appearance at Worms were drawn-out and complicated. When Frederick's request was forwarded to Charles, a surprising answer was returned. "Beloved Uncle Frederick: We are desirous that you should bring the abovementioned Luther to the Diet to be held at Worms, that there he may be thoroughly investigated by competent persons, that no injustice be done, nor anything contrary to law." What was left unsaid in Charles' message, however, was what he meant by an "investigation." Who would preside? What standards would govern? Would Luther be able to address the charges against him? Aleandro was adamant that a secular tribunal could never have jurisdiction as to matters of faith. He wrote, "As for myself, I would gladly confront this Satan, but the authority of the Holy See should not be prejudiced by subjection to the judgment of the laity. One who has been condemned by the pope, the cardinals, and prelates should only be heard in prison .... If Luther wants to be heard, he can have a safe conduct to Rome. Or His Majesty might send him to the inquisitors in Spain. He can perfectly well recant where he is and then come to the diet and be forgiven."[16]

As Luther waited anxiously for a decision, and as final preparations for the Diet commenced (it would begin on January 28, 1521), Charles waffled. As a Bergundian he was not familiar with German customs or sentiment; he did not even speak the German language. Probably acting on the advice of Aleandro, he rescinded Luther's invitation on December 17. Perhaps he was fearful of being embarrassed; Aleandro put nothing past Luther, and a newly-crowned Emperor would look foolish, after all, if the brash German monk would refuse a royal audience. But a few weeks later Charles changed his mind and sent out feelers to Frederick. Would Luther come to the Diet if he was again asked? Luther wasted no time, for he was most anxious to have an audience with His Majesty. He wrote to Spalatin: "You ask me what I will do if called by the emperor. I will go even if I am too sick to stand on my feet. If Caesar calls me, God calls me. He lives and reigns who saved the three youths from the fiery furnace of the King of Babylon, and if He will not save me, my head is worth nothing compared with Christ. This is no time to think of safety. I must take care that the gospel is not brought into contempt by our fear to confess and seal our teaching with our blood."[17] Several of his friends advised Luther not to go, for it was obviously a trap, and his life was in danger. Safe conduct had once been promised to Hus, and he had been executed. But Luther expressed no fear. "Expect anything of me except flight or recantation," he said. "I will not flee, much less recant."[18]

But the details of Luther's appearance still had to be worked out, and negotiations continued throughout the winter, as Charles alternatively listened to Aleandro, then the German electors. In mid–February Charles finally decided that he would take personal jurisdiction and decide the matter for himself, "assisted by a commission of learned and judicious men."[19] He agreed to the German electors' demands that, at Worms, Luther could attend a hearing with respect to the doctrine of his writings, but he would not have the right to comment or argue on their contents.[20] On March 6 Charles again offered a written invitation. "Our noble, dear, and esteemed Martin Luther," the letter began. ("Zounds!" said Aleandro. "That is no way to address a heretic.") The message continued, "Both we and the diet have decided to ask you to come under safe conduct to answer with regards to your books and teachings. You shall have twenty-one days in which to arrive." Left unsaid was that there would be no debate. Luther would simply have the opportunity to answer some direct theological questions posed by Charles' experts. Charles had become convinced that if Luther was not given at least a perfunctory hearing, the already strong German public opinion (both pro–Luther and anti–Rome) would only be further inflamed. And if, as expected, the replies were less than satisfactory—that is, if Luther did not recant—the council would prepare and publish an edict of condemnation. Charles directed that Kaspar Sturm, the herald of the empire, travel to Wittenberg and personally deliver the invitation to Luther in a show of respect. Growing more restless and obstinate by the day, Luther accepted. He would travel to the Diet and state his case. But he had a message of his own for Charles. "I am heartily glad that His Majesty will take to himself this affair, which is not mine but that of all Christianity and the whole German nation."[21] But tell the Emperor, he said, "that if I am being invited simply to recant I will not come. If to recant is all that is wanted, I can do that perfectly well right here. But if he is inviting me to my death, then I will come. Antichrist reigns. The Lord's will be done."[22] To a friend he wrote: "This shall be my recantation at Worms. Previously I said that the pope is the vicar of Christ. I recant. Now I say the pope is the adversary of Christ and the apostle of the Devil."[23]

Luther left for Worms on April 2, 1521. The University provided him with 20 gulden to cover travel expenses. He took a seat in a two-wheeled cart, covered with leather shades and pulled by a pair of horses, which had been donated by the Wittenberg goldsmith Christian Döring. Phillip Melanchthon wanted to accompany Luther, but his teaching duties prevented it. He joined 39 other professors in sending Luther off. Luther would travel with a colleague Nicholas von Amsdorf, who had been with him at Leipzig, and a brother monk named Johann Petzensteiner (although Luther had been released from the Order, tradition held that monks always travel in pairs). A Saxon nobleman named Peter von Swaven, and a student named Thomas Blauer rounded out the party.[24] The herald Sturm, wearing the Imperial eagle on his cloak and holding the Imperial banner, led the wagon. The 320-mile journey would take exactly two weeks.

At every stop along the way, Luther was met by huge cheering crowds and treated like a conquering hero. "Wherever he entered a city," one observer wrote, "the people flocked to meet him outside the gates, to gaze upon the wonderful man."[25] He was feted by the city council at Leipzig and given a supply of fine wine. The burgomaster honored him at Naumburg, presenting him with a portrait of the martyred Italian reformer Savonarola, whose 15th century ideas of faith and grace cost him his life. As the crowd shouted in delight Luther kissed the portrait in gratitude.[26] He accepted money from admirers at Weimar. At Erfurt, where he began his university studies and then entered the Augustinian monastery, Luther was met by the school's rector Johannes Crotus Rubianus, an enthusiastic early supporter who was the first to call Luther and his followers "evangelicals."[27] As a procession of sixty magnificent horsemen escorted him into the city walls, hundreds of cheering citizens (many of whom had spent the day drinking in Luther's honor), called his name in praise. The demonstration was so striking that Luther later compared it to Christ's triumphal entry into Jerusalem. "I have had my Palm Sunday," he said. "I wonder whether this pomp is merely a temptation or whether it is also a sign of impending passion."[28] Luther was celebrated as "the first in so many centuries who dared to tame the Roman arrogance with the sword of the Holy Scriptures."[29]

Luther obliged his admirers in Erfurt by preaching to an overflowing crowd at the City Church on April 7. He repeated now-familiar themes of the Lutheran theology: While the Catholic Church called for good works and adherence to papal doctrines, true righteousness came only through faith in the Word. Worshipping God is made manifest through actions of charity, selflessness, and concern for fellow man. Good works follow faith, and no amount of good works can earn salvation. Finally, Luther urged his listeners to celebrate his excommunication. He no longer wished to be a member of a Church that dictated false doctrines. In the middle of his sermon an outer wall of the old building gave way, and some of the crowd scattered in fear. Luther remained in the pulpit. "Ah," said Luther, "do you not perceive the finger of the devil, who wishes to prevent you from hearing the word of God, which I announce to you? Remain, Christ is with us."[30]

Luther also delivered guest sermons in Gotha and Eisenach, where, as a teenager some twenty years earlier, he had first studied Latin and sang happily in the boys' choir. In Eisenach, however, he took ill and was bled by a physician. He felt better in a few days, and at Frankfurt he enjoyed dinner with friends, drank a stout beer, and played the lute. He learned that the Diet had, at Aleandro's urging, issued an edict for the sequestration of his books and writings. The issuance had apparently been delayed until he was well on his way to Worms; the fear was that had Luther learned of it earlier, he might not attend the Diet. Luther was disappointed to learn of the edict but did not falter. He told his friends, "Unless I am held back by force, or Caesar revokes his invitation, I will enter Worms under the banner of Christ against the gates of Hell." He wrote to Spalatin that he was determined to see the matter through, no matter the consequence. He would appear in Worms "even if as many devils are in that city as tiles on the roofs."[31] Cheered, Spalatin made lodging preparations for his Luther in Worms, where most of the accommodations were fully booked in anticipation of the confrontation between upstart monk and newly-crowned Emperor.

Worms, dubbed the city of "perpetual public peace" by Maximillian, was situated on the banks of the Rhine River, halfway between Heidelberg and Frankfurt. For more than five centuries Worms had been a *Frei und Reichsstadt*, a free and independent city of the Holy Roman Empire, not governed by a prince, bishop, or lord, subordinate only to the Emperor. There were only 50 such cities in all of Germany. Its autonomy made it the perfect place to host legislative assemblies and it had, in fact, been the site of over 100 Diets through the centuries. With much fanfare Luther and his entourage arrived at Worms at ten o'clock in the morning on Tuesday, April 16. Just inside the Mainz gate, an estimated two thousand people lined the street called *Grosse Kämmerergasse*, cheering and straining from home and shop windows and rooftops, hoping to catch a glimpse of the famous man who had dared challenge

Rome. Trumpets heralded Luther from cathedral towers. An Augustinian priest embraced Luther and ceremoniously touched his monk's cowl three times as a show of respect and admiration. There being no room at the quarters of Frederick the Wise, Luther was led to his lodgings at the Knights of St. John hostel (*Johanniterhof*), where he would share a room with Hans Schott and Bernhard von Hirschfeld, two Saxon electoral officials; also in the house were other Saxon counselors and imperial Marshall, all members of the Diet. Aleandro monitored Luther's triumphal entry into the city with disgust. He noted that it seemed "the whole world" wanted to see Luther, who scanned the crushing crowd with "demoniac eyes."[32] "I suspect it will soon be said," wrote Aleandro bitterly, "that he works miracles."[33]

Luther spent most of the next day, April 17, resting and receiving visitors, including Count Wilhelm of Henneberg and Duke Wilhelm of Brunswick. He also met with Dr. Jerome Schurf, a Wittenberg jurist who specialized in canon law, who had been appointed by Frederick the Wise to serve as Luther's counselor. "Be bold," his supporters told him, "and fear not those who can kill the body, but are powerless against the soul."[34] He heard the confession of Hans von Minkwitz, a knight who was seriously ill, and celebrated the Eucharist with him. Finally Ulrich von Pappenheim, the acting imperial marshal, served Luther with the royal summons to appear, and at four o'clock in the afternoon he was led by Pappenheim and Sturm to the bishop's court, the city's great residence hall adjoining the Worms cathedral. Luther, dressed simply in his monk's robe and cowl, was informed by Pappenheim that he was to make no speeches, and only answer questions with direct answers. Perhaps this gave Luther pause. The party walked through alleys and side streets, the indirect route being necessary to avoid heavy crowds of onlookers.

The spacious hall was lavishly decorated for the event with royal flags and buntings. Johann von der Ecken, a functionary of the archbishop of Trier who had burned Luther's books, was to serve as the inquisitor. The imperial court, all the assembled princes of the empire, sat behind Ecken, in order of rank and importance. First were the abbots, or prelates, wearing vestments of embroidered flowers. Next came rows of secular rulers accompanied by their ambassadors; they were adorned in "short, furred jackets bulging at the sleeves, silk shirts with padded shoulders, velvet doublets, brightly colored breeches, and beribboned, bejeweled *braquettes*. The rulers were surrounded by titled noblemen sporting "coronets, tiaras, and diadems."[35] Finally, towering above and presiding over all, sat His Majesty Charles V, Emperor of the Holy Roman Empire, King of Spain, Italy, and Germany, Lord of the Netherlands, heir to three dynasties, and ruler of much of the American New World. Seated upon the royal throne that had traveled with him from Spain, the royal coat of arms hanging in tapestry behind him, Charles was resplendent in his magnificent red robe and golden crown, adorned with spectacular jewels, royal scepter in his hand and saber at his side.

Every available space in the hall was taken by spectators who suddenly hushed when Luther entered the room. Luther took in the surroundings, glancing toward the galleries, and walked cautiously to the center of the hall, Schurf slightly behind, facing his inquisitor. Most of the assembly, including Charles, was seeing Luther for the first time. One witness described Luther as a man "of forty years of age, more or less, vigorous in expression and physique, eyes without distinction, mobile of countenance and frivolously changing his expression. He wore the habit of the order of St. Augustine, with leather girdle, his tonsure large and recently shaven, his hair cropped close."[36] Charles turned to an advisor and said, "That fellow will never make a heretic of me."[37]

Ecken had two questions for Luther. Gesturing toward a table stacked high with Luther's books, he inquired, first in Latin and then in German: "Martin Luther, His Imperial Majesty has summoned you here for these two reasons: first to know whether you publicly acknowledge the authorship of the books there before you bearing your name; and then, whether you stand by them or retract anything in them."[38]

Before Luther could respond, Schurf interjected. "What are the titles of the books in question?" he asked. "Let them be read!"[39] Ecken's secretary read the titles, and while the collection was by no means complete it was representative of Luther's major works. As the audience leaned forward, straining to hear, Luther now spoke, also in Latin and again in German, "with a subdued, soft voice, as if frightened and shocked, with little calm in his visage and gestures, also with little deference in his attitude and countenance." Luther said:

> Two questions have been put to me by His Imperial Majesty: First, whether I wish all the books bearing my name to be regarded as my own work; second, whether I intend to stand by them or, in fact, retract anything from those which have been published by me until now. To these two questions I shall respond briefly and to the point. First, I must indeed include the books just now named as among those written by me, and I shall never deny any of them.[40]

Many in the crowd nodded their heads in approval. Of course Luther would admit the books were his. This was a simple preliminary matter. The important issue was in the second question: would he stand by what he had written? Luther spoke again:

> As for the next question, whether I would likewise affirm everything or retract what is supposed to have been uttered beyond the testimony of Scripture: Because this is a question of faith and the salvation of souls and because it concerns the divine Word, which we are all bound to reverence, for there is nothing greater in heaven or on earth, it would be rash and at the same time dangerous for me to put forth anything without proper consideration. Since without previous deliberation I could assert less than the cause demands or more than accords with the truth, I might in either case come under Christ's judgment when he said, "Whoever denies me before men, I will also deny before my Father who is in Heaven." For this reason I beseech your Imperial Majesty for time to think, in order to satisfactorily answer the question without violence to the divine Word and danger to my own soul.[41]

This was an unexpected request, and the crowd murmured in astonishment. Ecken immediately expressed his outrage. Surely Luther did not need more time, he said. Why did he think he had been summoned here? What could there possibly be to think over? The excommunicated monk did not deserve more time; he was fortunate he was not sitting in a prison cell. But Charles overruled his inquisitor and granted Luther an extra twenty-four hours. He was ordered to appear again the following afternoon.

Was Luther's surprising request for more time preconceived? Did he simply freeze under the magnitude of the moment, as he had many years ago as a young monk saying his first mass, barely able to go on? Or was he now, under the intense pressure of facing royalty for the first time, considering recantation? Most likely Luther, under the firm instruction to give no speech or argument but simply answer the question, needed time to prepare a wise and considered response. He needed time "to frame an answer that would *also* be an argument."[42] In any event, it appears that Luther received few, if any, visitors that night. Instead he spent his time alone with his thoughts, and in prayer. He most certainly would not back down. He wrote a short letter to his friend, the Vienna humanist John Cuspianus: "From the midst of this tumult," he asserted, "truly, with Christ's aid, I shall never recant one jot."[43]

The next day Luther appeared again before the assembly. This time, however, the time was moved back to six o'clock, because the overflow crowd necessitated a change in venue to a larger public hall. Luther strode confidently to the center of the room, just steps away from Charles and the rest. Ecken advised that "although you did not deserve this respite," Luther had been given his time to deliberate. Now, Ecken demanded, "Do you wish to defend all of your books or to retract part of them?"[44]

Luther was now fully prepared to make his defining oration. He reiterated that he took full responsibility for the books that had been compiled; they were his and his alone. He explained that his works could be separated into three categories, each requiring separate consideration. The first classification of his books dealt solely with practical theological matters, seen as truthful by all, including his enemies. How could he deny accepted truth? He said:

> There are some in which I have discussed religious faith and morals simply and evangelically, so that even my enemies themselves are compelled to admit that these are useful, harmless, and clearly worth to be read by Christians.... Thus, if I should begin to disavow them, I ask you, what would I be doing? Would not I alone of all men be condemning the very truth upon which friends and enemies equally agree?[45]

Luther's second classification of writings concerned papal abuses and the tyranny of the Church. Christians, and particularly Germans, had for centuries been trapped in the falsehoods of ecclesiastical traditions. If he recanted what he had written about insufferable tyranny he would be sanctioning evil: "Another group of my books attacks the papacy and the papists as those who by their doctrines and their very wicked examples have laid waste the Christian world with evil that affects the spirit and the body."[46]

"*Immo!*" shouted Charles, his sudden outburst exploding across the hall and startling the crowd. "*Absolutely no!*"[47] But Luther went on:

> If, therefore, I had retracted these writings, I should have done nothing other than to add strength to this tyranny and I should have opened not only windows, but also doors to such great godlessness.... Good God! What a cover for wickedness and tyranny I should then have become.[48]

As Ecken fumed, Charles again interrupted Luther, directing him to move on to another subject. Luther turned now to a third classification of his books, those that attacked Rome's supporters. Perhaps he had too harshly, he said, but he was human after all, and subject to human error. He would only be corrected, he insisted, on the basis of God's Word, and then, if so convinced, he would join his enemies and throw his books into the fire:

> I have written a third sort of book against some private and (as they say) distinguished individuals, namely, those who strive to preserve the Roman tyranny and to destroy the godliness taught by me. Against these I confess I have been more violent than my religion or my profession demands. But, then, I do not set myself up as a saint; neither am I disputing about my life, but about the teaching of Christ. It is not proper for me to retract these books, because by this retraction it would again happen that tyranny and godlessness would, with my patronage, rule and rage among the people of God more violently that ever before.... Testify and point out my errors. Vanquish me with the writings of the prophets and evangelists, for if I shall be thus instructed I will be most ready to recant any error and will, indeed, be the first to hurl my little books into the flames.[49]

The great hall, packed with the crowd, was breezeless and stiflingly warm in the almost-unbearable tension. It had grown darker now as the daylight faded. Candles burned in the windows of the chamber, and long shadows fell across the floor, adding to the drama of the moment. Many knew, they expressed later, that they were witnessing a turning point in history. Luther continued:

From this I think it is sufficiently clear that I have carefully considered and weighed the discords, perils, emulation, and dissension excited by my teaching, concerning which I was gravely and urgently admonished yesterday. To me the happiest side of the whole affair is that the Word of God is made the object of emulation and dissent. For this is the course, the fate, and the result of the Word of God, as Christ says: 'I am come not to send peace but a sword, to set a man against his father and a daughter against her mother.' We must consider that our God is wonderful and terrible in his counsels. If we should begin to heal our dissensions by damning the Word of God, we should only turn loose an intolerable deluge of woes. Let us take care that the rule of this excellent youth, Prince Charles (in whom, next to God, there is much hope), does not begin inauspiciously. For I could show by many examples drawn from Scripture that when Pharaoh and the King of Babylon and the kings of Israel thought to pacify and strengthen their kingdoms by their own wisdom, they really only ruined themselves. For he taketh the wise in their own craftiness and removeth mountains and they know it not. We must fear God. I do not say this as though your lordships needed either my teaching or my admonition, but because I could not shirk the duty I owed Germany. With these words I commend myself to your Majesty and your Lordships, humble begging that you will not let my enemies make me hateful to you without cause. I have spoken.[50]

Ecken now spoke up, scolding Luther for his impertinence and arrogance. Luther's statements were nothing new. By what right did he presume to be more knowledgeable than all who had come before him? How dare he criticize and question the wisdom of the learned men, agents of God, who had expounded on these matters for centuries? Ecken chastised Luther:

Your plea to be heard from Scripture is the one always made by heretics…. How can you assume that you are the only one who understands the sense of Scripture? Would you put your judgment above that of so many famous men and claim that you know more than all of them? You have no right to call into question the most holy orthodox faith, instituted by Christ the perfect Lawgiver, proclaimed throughout the world by the Apostles, sealed by the red blood of martyrs, and defined by the Church … and which we are forbidden by the Pope and the Emperor to discuss, lest there be no end to debate.[51]

His Majesty, Ecken went on, and all those distinguished men of God here assembled, had no more patience for this impudent, heretical monk from Saxony. He was now ordered to finally, simply, and directly answer the critical question put to him. "I ask you, Martin—answer candidly and without horns [*non cortunum*, i.e., sophistic reservations]—do you or do you not repudiate your books and the errors which they contain?" Luther's reply cut through the tension in the great hall, his fateful words powerful and compelling. Speaking only in German now, Luther said:

Since, then, Your Serene Majesty and Your Lordships ask for a simple answer, I will give it in this manner without horns or teeth: Unless I am convinced by the testimony of Scripture or by clear reason (for I trust neither pope nor councils alone, since it is well known that they have often erred and contradicted themselves), I am bound by the Scriptures I have cited, for my conscience is captive to the word of God. I cannot and will not retract anything, since to act against one's conscience is neither safe nor right.[52]

Tradition holds that Luther concluded dramatically and magnificently:

> *Hier stehe ich, Ich kann nicht anders. Gott helf mir. Amen.*
> *(Here I stand, I can do no other. God help me. Amen.)*

The great hall exploded in noise and confusion. Charles rose from his seat, aghast that a mere peasant dared to rebuke an Emperor and the Church. Ecken tried to restore order. "Lay aside your conscience, Martin," he pleaded amidst the din. "You must lay it aside, because it is in error; and it will be safe and proper for you to recant. Although you say the councils have erred, you will never be able to prove it…" Luther shouted back, "I am able and willing

Here I Stand: **Ceramic mural by Maxine M. Blackmer at Immanuel Lutheran Church in Missoula, Montana.**

to do that, too!"[53] But Charles intervened. "It is enough," he ruled. "Since he has denied councils, we wish to hear no more," and then he left the chamber and the bedlam.[54] The Spaniards in the crowd hissed at Luther and shouted, "To the fire! To the fire!" Luther was escorted from the hall by his supporters. Once outside he raised both arms in triumph as if he had emerged victorious from a jousting match. "*Ich bin hindurch!*" he shouted again and again as the Germans in the streets surrounded and cheered him. "*I've come through!*"[55]

*

Luther spent the several days among friends, resting, eating, and drinking. "Had I a hundred heads," he told his friends, "they should all have been cut off before I would recant a word."[56] Meanwhile, Charles weighed his options. He could not stand by as a rogue monk made a mockery of a thousand years of Christian tradition. He had sworn an oath, after all, to uphold the sacred traditions of the Catholic Church, its "sacred ceremonies, decrees, ordinances, and holy customs for the honor of God."[57] Aleandro urged him to arrest Luther immediately and transport him to Rome. But Charles remained wary of Luther's considerable support. Already rumors were swirling that a contingent of 400 knights was ready to protect Luther by force, and that a secret peasant army of Lutherans was plotting a revolt against both the civil and religious authorities. A placard appeared on the doors and walls of the city, imprinted with the *Bundschuh*, or peasants' boot, the ominous symbol of rebellion. Then Charles received a petition from members of the Diet. They wanted to meet with Luther and perhaps work out a compromise. Had Luther not stated that he would recant if he were shown his biblical errors? Perhaps he could be persuaded that he was in the wrong. If not, while His Majesty might still allow him a safe-conduct return to Saxony, his status as a heretic would at least be confirmed.

Charles agreed to give the petitioners a chance, but negotiations with Luther proved to be useless. Representing the Diet were Duke George of Saxony, the Bishop of Brandenburg, and Hieronymus Vehus, the chancellor of the Margrave of Baden. They offered to establish a papal council in Germany to hear Luther's positions and determine what remedies, if any, for reform might be called for. Luther said that he was not defending himself—he was standing up for the word of God. "I can never make the Lord Christ other than God himself made Him," he said. Holy Scripture was free from human judgment. "I would rather lose life and head than desert so clearly the word of God."[58] He reiterated a familiar refrain: "The pope is no judge of matters pertaining to God's Word and faith," he said, "but a Christian man must examine and judge for himself."[59] Finally he grew exasperated. He simply wanted to go home. He sent a message to Charles, through Spalatin: "I beg of your Grace that you will obtain for me the gracious permission of His Imperial Majesty that I may go home again, for I have now been here for ten days and nothing yet has been effected."[60] Within hours Charles granted Luther twenty-one days to return to Wittenberg under safe-conduct. He was, however, forbidden to preach or write in the meantime.

On April 25 Luther stayed up late into the night, his last in Worms, enjoying a meal delivered by Frederick the Wise and drinking Malmsey wine with his friends. He pondered his future. Many of his supporters believed that Charles' pledge of safe-conduct was a sham. Luther would be better served, they advised, to flee to Bohemia or Denmark. But Luther insisted that he would try to make it to Wittenberg. "Most gracious Lord, I cannot yield; it must happen with me as God wills," he said.[61] Frederick gave him forty gulden for traveling expenses, and early the next morning twenty horsemen, armed with sabers, escorted him to the gates of the city.

Luther traveled by wagon with five friends: Schurf, Jonas, Swaven, the monk Petzensteiner, and Amsdorf. The company rode through Friedberg, Grünberg, and Aisfelt. At Hersfeld Luther was a guest of the monastery, and he happily delivered a sermon at the five o'clock a.m. mass, in defiance of the ban against preaching. "The word of God cannot be silenced or bound," he said.[62] The next day he preached again at Eisenach. On May 3 he visited relatives, including his grandmother and his uncle Heinz Luther, in Möhra, and then traveled on, now with only Petzensteiner and Amsdorf accompanying him. (Luther had released the others, sending them back to Worms with a note indicating they had served him well.)

Suddenly, inside a dark ravine in the Thuringian Forest near Altenstein, the small party was attacked by masked horsemen armed with crossbows. A burlap sack was thrown over Luther's head. In the confusion Petzensteiner was able to escape on foot, and Amsdorf cursed and shouted in protest. Luther, however, was mounted on a horse and spirited away into the black night.

The episode had taken only a few moments. When supporters heard that the German Hercules had been kidnapped, many assumed the worst. Albert Dürer, a Nuremberg painter and ardent supporter, heard the news on May 17. In dismay he wrote in his diary, "I know not whether he yet lives or is murdered, but in any case he has suffered for the Christian truth…. O God, if Luther is dead, who will henceforth expound to us the gospel?"[63]

• Chapter 12 •

Knight George of Wartburg Castle

While the whereabouts of Martin Luther remained a mystery to nearly everyone, Charles V informed the imperial estates in Worms that he would act conscientiously as protector of the Holy Church. He wrote:

> I am descended from a long line of Christian emperors of this noble German nation, and of the Catholic kings of Spain, the archdukes of Austria, and the dukes of Burgundy. They were all faithful to the death to the Church of Rome, and they defended the Catholic faith and the honor of God. I have resolved to follow in their steps. A single friar who goes counter to all Christianity for a thousand years must be wrong. Therefore I am resolved to stake my lands, my friends, my body, my blood, my life, and my soul. Not only I, but you of this noble German nation, would be forever disgraced if by our negligence not only heresy but the very suspicion of heresy were to survive. After having heard yesterday the obstinate defense of Luther, I regret that I have for so long delayed in proceeding against him and his false teaching. I will have no more to do with him. He may return under his safe conduct, but without preaching or making any tumult. I will proceed against him as a notorious heretic, and ask you to declare yourselves as you promised me.[1]

Charles left no doubt as to how he felt about Luther. But he asked his princes and electors for their advice to finally deal with the Luther problem. Aleandro was nominated to write a mandate (officially known as an edict) against Luther, which he was only too happy to do. But the estates could not agree on the appropriate language to be included in the edict, and the matter was delayed for a month. In the meantime the Diet voted to adjourn on May 25, and the various members, including the electors Frederick the Wise and Ludwig of the Palatinate, returned to their homes. The following day Aleandro presented his final version of the edict to the Elector Joachim of Brandenburg, who pronounced it approved without discussion or modification. The document was backdated to May 6, to give the impression that it had gained approval of the entire Diet, and presented to Charles for his signature.

The Edict of Worms, as it came to be known, marked the Holy Roman Empire's official statement on the words and actions of Martin Luther. Meant to be both a political and legal document, it summarized the various proceedings that had been conducted over the past three years, and set forth the opportunities Luther had been given to recant his scandalous positions regarding the Eucharist, confession, marriage, and the other sacraments. Luther's teaching, read the Edict, paved the way for "rebellion, division, war, murder, robbery, arson, and the collapse of Christendom." Luther had chosen to "live the life of a beast." The Edict outlined the steps that had led to *Exsurge Domine*, the bull of excommunication. Luther was guilty of "innumerable evils" that had accumulated in "one stinking pool." He was an "obstinate schismatic and manifest heretic," a rotten "limb to be cut off" from the tree of Christ.[2] The Edict stated:

For this reason we forbid anyone from this time forward to dare, either by words or by deeds, to receive, defend, sustain, or favour the said Martin Luther. On the contrary, we want him to be apprehended and punished as a notorious heretic, as he deserves, to be brought personally before us, or to be securely guarded until those who have captured him inform us, whereupon we will order the appropriate manner of proceeding against the said Luther. Those who will help in his capture will be rewarded generously for their good work.[3]

Emperor Charles V signed the Edict "with his own blessed hand" in both German and Latin, signaling a popular as well as religious audience for his new orders. Aleandro was content now, he wrote, "and even greater will be the contentment of His Holiness and of all Christendom. We praise God for giving us such a religious emperor. May God preserve him in all his holy ways."[4] Aleandro had the Edict itself translated from Latin to German and took it to the printer Hans von Erfurt in Worms, paying him ten gulden to prepare the text for publication. He also made arrangements for the Edict to be published in French, Italian, and Flemish, and joyfully took it to Rome for the pope's approval.

Meanwhile, what had happened to Luther? While the details of the plot to kidnap Luther remained a secret, Luther seemed to know that a plan was afoot to get him to safety. On April 28 he had written to a friend that he might be taken away and hidden from his enemies, although he did not know where.[5] The horsemen who had seized him, probably at the direction of Frederick the Wise, took him some ten miles back toward Eisenach and delivered him to the Wartburg Castle, a stronghold that stood on a rocky precipice about 1350 feet above the city, in the heart of the Thuringian Forest. From the German *Warte*, meaning watchtower, and *Burg*, meaning fortress, the Wartburg had served as a strategic defensive position and a

Wartburg Castle, Eisenach.

View of Thuringian Forest from Wartburg Castle.

vital prince's court since its construction in the 12th century. Frederick was lord of the castle, and the custodian Herr von Berlepsch welcomed Luther warmly. Wartburg Castle, Luther discovered, would be his home for the next ten months.

At the Wartburg, Luther was removed from Charles's political activity, and isolated from the reach of the Church. Under Berlepsch's care, he settled in to a life in seclusion. He was given a high-ceilinged room at the top of the castle, the chamber of royalty, accessible only by a narrow flight of stairs. The room had its own stove, bedstead, and table, and a leaded glass window that provided a view of the beautiful countryside to the West, the same Hörsel fields where as a boy Luther had gathered strawberries with his mother. From this new residence Luther posed as a prince. He wore courtly clothes and hung a gold chain around his neck, allowed his tonsured head to fill with hair, and grew a long beard. He even took a new name: "Junker George," signifying his status as a squire or knight. In this new persona Luther was provided all the benefits of privilege. He enjoyed the finest food and drink brought by two assigned personal servants. Accompanied by an armed guard, Luther took to riding in the countryside and was introduced to hunting. But "the bittersweet pleasure of heroes," as Luther called it, brought him little satisfaction; he did not care for the yelping hounds, sympathizing more with their prey. He noted in a letter that it grieved him to witness a hare becoming a victim to one of the dogs. Even in this instance he found a theological connection. "For what else did it signify that the devil, who pursues these innocent beasts with his snares and impious dogs of teachers, the bishops and theologians?"[6]

For all the luxuries afforded him, Luther was miserable at Wartburg. He had not asked to be hidden away and cared little for his safety. In letters to friends he referred to his

The small town of Eisenach below Wartburg Castle.

surroundings as "the wilderness," "the realm of the birds," or "the Patmos" (Patmos was the Greek island where St. John, persecuted by Rome and living in seclusion, wrote the book of Revelation). Luther was certainly bored. "Here I sit with nothing to do," he wrote to Melanchthon, "like a free man among prisoners.... I should be ardent in the spirit but I am ardent in the flesh, in lust, laziness, leisure, and sleepiness.... Already eight days have passed in which I have written nothing and neither prayed nor studied."[7] He confided to Spalatin, "Here I sit lazy and drunken the whole day."[8] Even worse, Luther fretted that he had not been forceful enough at the Diet of Worms. "They would hear other things if I were before them again," he vowed. Perhaps his supporters either thought him dead or a coward. He regretted not being back "in the fray," and wrote, "I had rather burn on live coals than rot here."[9] He longed to direct the action from his beloved Wittenberg. "I am an extraordinary captive," he brooded, "sitting here willing and unwilling at the same time. Willing, because the Lord wills thus; unwilling because I should prefer to stand publicly for the word."[10]

Although Berlepsch and his guests provided occasional entertainment, for the most part Luther was left alone with his thoughts. At night he was bothered by bats and owls, surely the messengers of Satan, he believed. Strange noises startled him; perhaps demons were tossing walnuts at the ceiling, or tumbling rocks down the stairs. One story has become legend: as he sat at his desk working, he became so upset at Satan, who, he believed, mocked him from the wall above him, that he threw an inkwell in a fit of frustration. On another occasion he imagined a small dog had climbed into his bed, and he fearfully threw it out the window. The next morning no animal could be found, and Berlepsch informed him that dogs were not kept at the castle. The whole episode, Luther thought, must have been an aspiration of the devil.[11] Paranoia fed his faith and vice-versa. "I can tell you in this idle solitude there are a thousand battles with Satan," he wrote. "It is much easier to fight against the incarnate Devil—that is, against men—than against spiritual wickedness in the heavenly places. Often I fall and am lifted up again by God's right hand."[12]

Unaccustomed to the rich food he was served, chronic constipation plagued Luther terribly. He wrote about it to Melanchthon: "The Lord has struck me in the rear end with terrible pain. My excrement is so hard that I have to strain with such force to expel it that I sweat, and the longer I wait the harder it gets. After four days I was able to go once, and then I couldn't sleep all night, and still I have no relief." In a letter to his friend Amsdorf he was even blunter: "My arse has gone bad."[13] But perhaps some good could come from his ailments. "Maybe the Lord burdens me," he wrote, "so in order to push me out of this hermitage and into the arena."[14]

Despite Luther's emotional and physical struggles, his stay at Wartburg proved to be incredibly productive. He stayed in regular contact with Melanchthon, who advised him on happenings in Germany and at Wittenberg. He learned, for example, that the reorganization of Wittenberg's curriculum was progressing and that Frederick the Wise was seeking to gain a Saxon exemption from the mandates of the Edict of Worms. Other friends and colleagues reported on the activities of Charles V, who, distracted by preparations for war in France, made no attempt to locate Luther. During his time at Wartburg Luther wrote ten books and pamphlets, and began work on two others.

Luther's new writing further challenged the Church and Christian life and practice, and it further fueled the Reformation movement. For example, in previous works Luther had discussed the sacraments, claiming that only Baptism and distribution of the Eucharist were sanctioned biblically. Now he went further. In *Concerning Confession, Whether the Pope Has the Power to Order It*, Luther wrote that all Christians had the right to confess their sins to God alone. While priestly confession and absolution were not prohibited by Scripture, neither were they mandated. Christ had given the power to forgive sins to the entire Church, not just to clergy. Any claim to the contrary was fiction.

In another treatise he called *On Monastic Vows*, Luther took on the issues of celibacy and marriage. The Church's views in these regards had become distorted, Luther wrote, continuing examples of control, rulemaking, and interference. The Bible (and in fact the early Church) had clearly sanctioned marriage by priests. Celibacy suppressed the freedom of sexual expression, one of God's greatest gifts. Vows of chastity were contrary to human reason. All such vows were enemies of faith, Luther argued, for if they were considered a good work, they were outside of true faith in Christ and therefore sinful. Of course Luther was mindful of the vows he had taken when he became a monk. But he had come to believe that monks took vows in an effort to somehow achieve a higher, more meritorious plane than other believers. This was folly, and the vows should not be binding. Saints were not made in the cloister, and they were not made because they joined the cloister. Monks, Luther believed, placed more emphasis on their status as Augustinian, Benedictine, or Franciscan, than on their status as Christians.

Similarly, Luther now scoffed at vows of poverty and obedience to particular monastic orders. Individual quests for virtue had little to do with these vows, he argued. Most monks took their vows in misguided attempts to obtain ecclesiastical security and religious comfort. The true Christian, Luther wrote, need only be obedient to God, not some man-made or

Church-sanctioned institution. He offered one disclaiming point: monks and priests, he wrote, could decide for themselves whether they wanted to revoke their vows. Their own conscience and sense of freedom would guide them, as God intended. (One of Luther's former students, a man named John Bernhardi, who now was provost of Kemsberg in the Mainz diocese, was the first monk to take Luther's advice and marry. Priests in Magdeburg and Meissen soon followed.)[15]

Luther considered *On Monastic Vows* to be among his most important theological works. But clearly the project held personal significance for him, as well. On November 21, 1521, he wrote a remarkable letter to his father Hans, still living at Mansfeld:

> This book, dear father, I wish to dedicate to you, not to make your name famous in the world, for fame puffeth up the flesh, according to the doctrine of St. Paul, but that I might have occasion in a short preface as it were between you and me to point out to the Christian reader the argument and contents of the book, together with an illustrative example...
>
> It is now sixteen years since I became a monk, having taken the vow without your knowledge and against your will. You were anxious and fearful about my weakness, because I was a young blood of twenty-two, that is, to use St. Augustine's words, it was still hot youth with me, and you had learned from numerous examples that monkery made many unblessed and so were determined to marry me honorably and tie me down. This fear, this anxiety, this non-consent of yours were for a time simply irreconcilable...
>
> And indeed, my vow was not worth a fig, since it was taken without the consent of the parents God gave me. Moreover it was a godless vow both because taken against your will and without my whole heart. In short, it was simple doctrine of men, that is of the spiritual estate of hypocrites, a doctrine not commanded by God...
>
> Dear father, will you still take me out of the cloister? If so, do not boast of it, for God has anticipated you and taken me out himself. What difference does it make whether I retain or lay aside the cowl and the tonsure? Do they make the monk? ... My conscience is free and redeemed; therefore I am still a monk but not a monk, and a new creature not of the Pope but of Christ, for the Pope also has creatures and is a creator of puppets and idols and masks and straw men, of which I was formerly one, but now have escaped by the Word...
>
> The Pope may strangle me and condemn me and bid me go to hell, but he will not be able to rouse me after death to strangle me again. To be banned and damned is according to my own heart and will. May he never absolve me more! I hope the great day is at hand when the kingdom of abomination and horror will be broken and thrust down. Would to God that I had been worthy to be burned by the Pope!
>
> The Lord bless you, dear father, with mother, your Margaret, and all our family. Farewell in the Lord Christ.[16]

Luther was aware that the most zealous of his followers were taking radical steps in carrying out his reforms. In Erfurt, for example, students and peasants demolished forty parish houses and destroyed libraries, and one person was killed in the melee. But Luther saw no need for destruction and mayhem. Reformation of the Church's practices could occur peacefully and orderly, he believed. He wrote *Faithful Exhortation to All Christians to Guard Against Revolt and Tumult* as a guide to nonviolent reform, emphasizing the importance of obeying political authorities even as religious issues were addressed. He was not particularly interested in economic or even social problems except as they were affected by adherence to Christ's teachings. He meant to reform the Church, not society's underlying civic or political structure. He wrote:

> Insurrection is unreasoning, and generally hurts the innocent more than the guilty. Hence no insurrection is ever right, no matter how good the cause in whose interest it is made. The harm resulting from it always exceeds the amount of reformation accomplished.... When Herr Omnes [Sir Mob] breaks loose he cannot tell the wicked from the godly; he strikes at random, and then horrible injustice is inevitable.[17]

Luther's room at Wartburg Castle. Above the desk is a painting of Junker George by Lucas Cranach the Elder (courtesy Wartburg-Stiftung Eisenach).

Luther spent a good deal of time at the Wartburg studying Greek and Hebrew. Not only did the mastery of these languages assist him in proper translations of sacred Scripture, but it proved invaluable as he prepared an important series of sermons, or homilies. He particularly relished this task because he understood his primary mission to be a preacher, or messenger of God's word. These sermons set forth his views in plain, simple language, and were intended for the peasantry of Germany. They were all biblically based and enthusiastically written. Luther's zeal in these particular writings has caused historians to label him as the "father of the modern evangelical sermon." Perhaps he saw himself as another St. Paul, conveying the Lord's message to eager listeners. He never lost sight of Paul's central passage that had started him on his way: "He who through faith is just shall live."

Of all the work produced by Luther at the Wartburg, the most significant was his translation of the New Testament from the Greek to High German. Incredibly, he finished this project in just three months. The first edition of Luther's translation became known as the September Testament, because it was published one year later in September 1522. The first German translation to be made available to the general population (which the Church saw as dangerous and threatening), this work sold an estimated five thousand copies in two months, and two hundred thousand in twelve years.[18] Luther had become so popular, and his written work so eagerly consumed by the German population, that since his Ninety-Five Theses appeared in 1517, some 370 editions of his writings had appeared in over 300,000 copies (all this *before* his Wartburg projects were published). The appearance of the Wartburg publications kept the printers so busy that other writers often could not get their works published.[19]

For all of Luther's inspired and laborious work, his actual whereabouts remained unknown to his enemies and supporters alike. His influence, however, seemed to be everywhere. One Albert Burer of Kemberg wrote to a friend that, wherever he traveled, he met others on the road, and the question was always the same: *"Bist du gut Marteinisch?"*[20] ("Are you with Martin?") The revolutionary movement Luther had sparked was sweeping across Northern Europe, and he did not—could not—remain in seclusion much longer. Luther eagerly made plans to return to Wittenberg.

• Chapter 13 •

The Battle for Wittenberg

It had only been four years since Luther nailed his Ninety-Five Theses to the door of the Castle Church in Wittenberg. With his challenge and subsequent actions Luther had broken away from Rome irrevocably. He had exposed corruption and deceit within the Church, labeled the Pope as the Antichrist, faced his accusers at Heidelberg, Augsburg, and Leipzig, and defied the Emperor himself at Worms. He had been branded a heretic and excommunicated, and although the Edict of Worms had been published nationwide, the Church, preoccupied with war in France, seemed to lack the will to enforce it. In addition to Luther's own revolutionary writings, which were the most popular works in Germany, a sympathetic biography entitled "The Passion of Dr. Martin Luther" became a bestseller. Protected by Frederick the Wise, for nearly a year Luther watched and waited in seclusion at the Wartburg castle, safely away from his enemies. He continued to work, however, relentlessly churning out sermons and commentaries, including a new essay on the Virgin Mary and the *Magnificat*, a series sermon guides (postils) on Sunday gospels and epistles, and an exposition of the thirty-seventh Psalm. His massive translation of the New Testament into German was ready for publication and distribution. His friends kept him apprised of the events that were changing Germany—and Europe—forever. Thousands of people were anxious to put Luther's unprecedented ideas into practice; he had "put the match to the great fire," and his followers were ready to fan the flames of revolt.[1] But strangely, in many ways, the reform movement that Luther inspired was taking place without him.

With Luther in seclusion for most of 1521, reform occurred erratically, meeting with different degrees of success from church to church, city to city, region to region. While Protestants were united against the oppression of Rome and the corruption of the Church, they did not consistently stand together in ideology or in religious practice. They had remarkably different opinions as to how Luther's messages were to be interpreted, and how reform was to be implemented. Further, while Luther had limited himself to spiritual matters, the reform movement spread to other areas; in fact, a "massive civil, social, religious, and political upheaval" was taking place across the country.[2] The results were uneven at best, and much to Luther's dismay, increasingly violent.

Galvanized by their dissatisfaction with the Church and outraged by the publication of the Edict of Worms and Luther's excommunication, common people rose up against a variety of authorities. In June, peasants in Erfurt refused to pay dues to the Church and market fees to the city. One week later a group of students took to the streets, where they were joined by hundreds of peasants, in town for the midweek markets. Both church and city officials tried to silence the marchers to no avail. The protest quickly escalated into a riot, or *"Pfaffensturm"* (parson-storm). The mob sacked over forty clerical houses, all of which belonged to the town's overlord, the non-reformist Archbishop of Mainz, and at least one man was killed.

To local government officials, the rioting in Erfurt blurred social, economic, and religious lines. Anxious to restore order and wary of the heavy-handed aid of the archbishop, they worked quickly to regain control of the municipality by negotiating a compromise. Under the "treaty of protection" that resulted, destruction of property would cease, and orthodox clergy would be protected from harm. Certain church privileges, however, including the clerical exemption from taxation, would be eliminated. The clergy paid 10,000 gulden in recognition of back taxes, and in the future would pay the same rates as everyone else. Further, four priests of known Lutheran sympathies would be allowed to preach in the city. Similar protests in Memmingen, Nuremburg, Eilenburg, and many other places across Germany, resulted in similar arrangements. The tide of reform was unstoppable.

The center of the reform movement was Luther's own Wittenberg. The city had long prided itself on its independence and creative thinking. Its university (the only such institution in Germany founded without papal charter), attracted students and faculty who were open to new ideas. In Luther's absence, Andreas Karlstadt, Luther's colleague on the theology faculty, and a young Augustinian friar named Gabriel Zwilling, took charge. Karlstadt envisioned transforming Wittenberg into a "model Christian city." Embracing Luther's view of the centrality of faith—"He who through faith is just shall live"—Karlstadt denounced the trappings and the rigidity of the Church. Karlstadt believed that the mass itself, the center of worship and devotional experience, needed to be restructured. It was never meant to be a sacrifice to God, or an offering, for God needed nothing from man. Rather, the mass was an expression of thanksgiving, a joyous celebration of God's gift, and a communion of believers, or saints. Any words in the liturgy to the contrary would be removed. Similarly, private masses—said by priests with no members of the congregation present, often presented for the benefit of the souls of the dead—came under attack by the reformers. By September Zwilling proclaimed that, unless the reforms were enacted, no masses should be celebrated at all. By the end of October Church-sanctioned masses all but disappeared. Vigils ceased, as did fasting on Mass days.

Joined by Luther's ally Philip Melanchthon, Karlstadt announced that the laity should receive both cup and bread during communion. (The common Church practice was to allow the laity to receive only the bread.) Further, the Catholic notion of transubstantiation—in which the bread and wine became body and blood through the consecrating words of the priest—was rejected, as was the necessity of the elevation of the elements; neither practice was founded on Scripture. Karlstadt next declared that it was no longer necessary to confess sins or fast before communion. (In fact, Karlstadt believed to do so was sinful. He went well beyond Luther in his views here, setting a pattern for the future.) In late September 1521, Melanchthon, joined by several of his students, took the Eucharist in this way for the first time. Shocked at this break with revered tradition, Frederick the Wise appointed an investigative commission to study the matter and report to him; the commission could reach no consensus, however, and quickly disbanded.

At Zwilling's encouragement, in the fall thirteen Augustinian friars abandoned the Wittenberg monastery, denouncing the Church as the "mother of dogma, pride, avarice, luxury, faithlessness, and hypocrisy."[3] Many followed Zwilling's advice and turned to agriculture, believing that it was nobler to earn their bread by the sweat of their brows. Some sought wives, and a few quickly married; threats of arrest were ignored. The five who remained at the monastery pondered their futures warily, for there were no indications that the old ways of life and worship would ever return. The prior, who opposed any reform, reported that he felt unsafe walking about the streets of town.[4] By early November 1521, half of the monasteries in Germany stood empty.

The Wittenberg city council also acted in the spirit of reform, passing a number of social programs designed to help the less fortunate. In November it provided for a "common purse," allaying funds to be distributed to the poor. Two months later the council expanded the program: now orphans would be cared for, students would be assisted financially, and low-interest loan programs at four percent were established. Further, houses of prostitution were closed down, and poor girls were supplied with dowries. Another measure, clearly unenforceable, bound the government to make certain that only pure gospel was preached. Word of all of these reform measures met with Luther's approval. But he wanted to see for himself what was happening. Driven in part by his curiosity, and in part by his frustration that the publication of some of his writings was inexplicably delayed, in December Luther secretly traveled to Wittenberg. Still disguised as Junker George, he stayed with Melanchthon and other friends for three days, gauging the situation. He pronounced himself pleased with the reforms he witnessed, and minimized the signs that trouble was brewing. "I was disturbed by various rumors of a certain ill-will among our people," he wrote, apparently passing if off as the mischief of over-zealous university students.[5]

Karlstadt's attacks on the mass continued. On December 3 several orthodox priests were driven from the Castle Church as they tried to celebrate Mass. When some of the worshippers knelt to pray before a statue of the Virgin Mary, they were taken out to the streets and pelted with stones. The next day an altar at the Franciscan convent was destroyed. A week later more damage was done to other buildings; when the rioters were arrested, a group of students stormed the jail, forcing their release.

On Christmas Eve hundreds of agitated Protestants, some carrying daggers beneath their cloaks, swelled the Castle Church. There was no violence, but the traditional mass was disrupted by shouting, and bits of lead and mud balls were thrown at the priests. The mob took their revelry outside to the church courtyard, where they hurled rocks at windows and statues. When the choir began to sing, the rowdies drowned it out with folk songs, including "A Maid Has Lost Her Shoe," an obvious dig at the pope. The next day Karlstadt celebrated Christmas Day mass. He wore civilian clothes instead of vestments, and omitted all references to sacrifice. And to the astonishment and delight of the two thousand people in attendance, Karlstadt spoke in German. Now, for the first time in their lives, the parishioners heard these sacred words in their native language, and thus understood them:

"*Nehmen; essen. Das ist mein Leib.*"

("Take; eat. This is my body.")

"*Trink daraus, alle von ihnen. Dieses Blut ist das Neue Testament, das für viele zur Vergebung der Sünden vergossen wird.*"

("Drink from it, all of you. This blood is the new testament, which is shed for many for the remission of sins.")

Karlstadt invited all worshippers to receive the Eucharist by eating the bread with their hands, and drinking wine from the chalice. This, too, was a new experience for the parishioners, and some were terrified that they might spill a crumb, or a drop. Karlstadt assured them that they were protected by God's grace. And the Lord's Supper was offered to anyone regardless of whether they had fasted, or confessed their sins. In fact, Karlstadt now went beyond Luther again, preaching that to the extent that confession detracted from the Eucharist, it was sinful. One did not obtain forgiveness from a verbal confession, he reasoned. He knew of no absolution of sins except through the promise of the Savior's blood; that is, the cup.[6] Whether or not you have confessed, he preached, "You should go joyfully in good confidence, hope, and faith, and receive this sacrament, for it must certainly be true that faith alone makes us holy and righteous."[7] Karlstadt's words had an unmistakable effect; confessions, noted church officials, decreased significantly in the following months.

In mid–January 1522 Karlstadt (who now insisted on being called "brother Andrew") became the first priest to marry, insisting that it was his responsibility to begin a family. "I observe that in Scripture no estate is as highly lauded as marriage," he wrote to Frederick the Wise, "and for the lack of it many poor priests have suffered sorely in the dungeons of the Devil."[8] Luther knew the bride, a fifteen-year-old girl named Anna Mochau, and approved of the match. He reacted with bemusement. "Good Heavens!" he wrote. "Will our Wittenbergers give wives to monks? They won't give one to me!"[9] He remained a single man, at least for the time being, but repeated the theme he had expressed in his *On Monastic Vows*: "Marriage is good, virginity is better, but liberty is best."[10] The vows of monks, like those of priests, he believed, were not based upon Scripture and could be disregarded.

The reformers went further. Karlstadt began to openly question the worth of child baptism. If *Sola Scriptura* was the controlling doctrine, then Holy Scripture must be taken literally. The Bible clearly stated that "whoever believes and is baptized shall be saved." Since an infant did not have the capacity to believe, Karlstadt reasoned, child baptism was all but useless. For Luther, baptism was one of only two sacraments, and changes to its institution were a most serious matter; he would have much to say about it in coming months.

Next, Karlstadt and Zwilling insisted that all religious paintings and images, statues of saints, and crucifixes, be torn down. They relied upon the book of Exodus, where God had commanded against idolatry: "Thou shalt not make unto thee any graven image, or any likeness of anything that is in heaven above, or that is in the earth beneath, or that is in the water under the earth." Music was not to be spared from this iconoclastic revolt, for it had no place in worship, in Karlstadt's opinion. "Relegate organs, trumpets, and flutes to the theater," he said, "for the lascivious notes of the organ awaken thoughts of the world." Even the most venerable of Gregorian chants worked only to "separate the spirit from God."[11] It was far better to offer one heart-felt prayer, he believed, "than a thousand cantatas of the Psalms."[12] Once again, he was not in agreement with Luther in these views, for Luther believed that the arts had a place in contemplation of the Word. "I am not of the opinion" he wrote from Wartburg, "that through the Gospel all the arts should be banished and driven away, as some zealots want to make us believe; but I wish to see them all, especially music, in the service of Him who gave and created them." But under the fiery leadership of Karlstadt, the radical "Wittenberg Movement," as it came to be known, continued to gain in momentum.

For his part, Frederick the Wise believed that the problems of reform, though rooted in spiritual affairs, could be solved only through political means. Without unanimity between the government, the established Church, and the Protestants, he reasoned, there could only be chaos, not reform. He hoped that church leaders and government officials could work out their differences through more compromise. Money was at the heart of the problem. Masses, after all, were endowed; if masses ceased, if priests and monks abandoned their vows, if communicants stopped attending services—money would no longer flow. Could this be God's will? In February Frederick wrote, "We have gone too fast. The common man has been incited to frivolity, and no one has been edified."[13] The Emperor's secretary, Valdes, wrote, "I perceived that the minds of the Germans are generally exasperated against the Roman see, and they do not seem to attach much importance to the Emperor's edicts."[14] The prior at the Augustinian monastery wrote privately, "The cloisters are in the grip of the Devil."[15] Compromise appeared impossible.

From Wartburg, Luther could no longer ignore the tumult that Germany was experiencing. He was quickly losing confidence in the leadership skills of Karlstadt and Zwilling, and he was fearful of their radical views. He was concerned that his simple message of faith alone, of which he was certain rested on firm theological ground, was being misconstrued. More precisely, he was afraid that change was taking place too quickly, and through violent means. As always, he took to his pen. He wrote a tract he called *Admonition to All True Christians to Guard Themselves against Sedition*. In this remarkable document, meant to be an open letter to all Protestants, Luther urged patience, not tumult. God was on the side of the reformers, Luther wrote, because he was on the side of "the true Christian." God's word—the spirit, the rod, and the sword of his mouth—had exposed the evils of the papacy. Luther had merely served as conduit. And God's word would ultimately triumph, but in his time and on his terms.

Urging restraint and not violence, Luther also wrote an open letter to his parishioners at Wittenberg. "You have gone about the business in a way of which I cannot approve," he wrote, "using your fists, and if this happens again I shall not take your part. You began without me, so carry it on without me. What you have done is wrong, no matter how many Karlstadts approve of it…. Believe me, I know the devil well, and he is at the root of all this and has led you to attack the sacrament, etc., so that he might injure God's Word, and meantime faith and love are forgotten."[16] Any incident of public uproar, Luther continued, was a "precise and certain sign of Satan's intervention." As always, Luther looked to Scripture. "God has forbidden insurrection," he wrote, which "almost always harms the innocent…. God has said, 'Revenge is mine; I will repay.' Insurrection is nothing else than being one's own judge and avenger, and that is something God cannot tolerate. Therefore, insurrection cannot help but make matters much worse, because it is contrary to God; God is not on the side of insurrection."[17]

Luther was particularly troubled that the rioting and violence were being carried out, at least to some degree, in his name. In stark terms he blamed himself for the upheavals. "How did it come about that I, a poor stinking bag of maggots, should come to the point that anyone could give the children of Christ my godless name?"[18]

Late in 1521 an old controversy suddenly reappeared on the scene. Archbishop Albert of Mainz, long a collector of holy relics, found himself in need of funds. Albert's collection numbered some 9,000 pieces, including what were said to be one of Isaac's limbs, bits of Moses' burning bush, jars from the wedding at Cana in which Jesus had turned water into wine, and even a thorn from the Savior's crown at Golgotha. In recent months he had added to his collection: complete bodies of various saints, mud God had used to create Adam, milk from the Virgin Mary, and the very finger that Thomas had placed in the side of the risen Christ. Now Albert offered a "surpassing indulgence," as much as nine million years of purgatorial release, to anyone who viewed the exhibit at the Collegiate Church at Halle (and, of course, paid alms for the privilege). "Do not fear Luther," said the archbishop, "for we have silenced him; go shear the flock in peace, the monk is fast in prison."[19] Incensed that these scandals had resurfaced, Luther immediately wrote a scathing tract against the "Idols of Indulgences" and supplied a copy to Frederick the Wise. But Frederick thought Luther's writing unwise; he told Luther, through Spalatin, that he would not sanction Luther's attack because it might "disturb the peace," which rested on precarious grounds already.[20] (Frederick was also feeling pressure from his cousin Duke George, the very same elector who had hosted the Leipzig Debate; George wanted to enforce the Edict of Worms and also sought legal permission to prosecute any officials who endorsed changes in the Mass.)

Luther was greatly disappointed at his prince's unexpected lack of support. He wrote to Spalatin, "I will not put up with it. I will rather lose you and the prince himself, and every living being. If I have stood up against the Pope, why should I yield to this creature?" He then wrote to Albert directly. Surely the archbishop knew that indulgences were nothing but "pure knavery," the only purpose of which was to "rob poor simple Christians both of their money and their souls." Had Albert forgotten that Luther's exposure of indulgence trafficking, which was surely Satan's work, had ignited the reform movement in the first place? Perhaps, wrote Luther, "you fancy you are safe because I am out of the way," and that the pope's edict would "extinguish the monk." But he was very much alive and "shall not hold my peace." Luther gave Albert fourteen days to respond, or Luther would publish his article and the archbishop would be "plunged into disgrace."[21] Albert capitulated. He was a miserable sinner and nothing else, he wrote, and he would withdraw the exhibit. Luther doubted Albert's sincerity but let the matter rest, and did not publish his tract.

Then more controversy came from an unexpected place. Three mysterious men arrived in Wittenberg from the small town of Zwickau, 130 miles to the south. The men were Nicholas Storch, a weaver; former Wittenberg student Markus Stübner, who boasted of his ability to read minds; and a budding theologian named Thomas Dreschel. These men, who came to be known as the "Zwickau prophets," were mystics who claimed to have received direct revelations from God. They reminded crowds that God had always spoken directly to people and offered instruction, and it was happening again, with them. Scripture could now be overlooked, the men claimed, because their conversations with the Holy Spirit had taken its place. They preached that all external pleasures of the earth could be left behind, so that the soul could become centered with the Divine. In what was to eventually become the Anabaptist doctrine, they taught that infants, incapable of true faith, need not be baptized. Further, the prophets were certain that the apocalypse was nigh. Godless men would be destroyed, they warned, and the new, true kingdom of God, to be called the "third heaven," would be established. All distinctions between Catholics and Protestants no longer mattered. In Wittenberg the prophets found a wide audience, including Karlstadt. A skeptical Melanchthon, however, wrote to Luther instead. What would the reformer advise?

Luther responded by wondering if the so-called prophets had been tested in their "encounters" with God? The Bible told of how all those who had spoken with God had been terrified, afraid, threatened by God's awesome might. What suffering, what anguish, had they experienced? Luther himself had experienced his *Anfechtungen*. Could these prophets say the same? In short order Luther would meet the mystics personally. He had heard and read enough of riots and chaos. Indulgences had resurfaced, and false prophets had appeared, confusing the faithful and leading them astray. In its disorder the young Reformation—Luther's Reformation—seemed close to ruin and he would have none of it. "They push on blindly ahead—there is no listening or reasoning," he wrote. "Well, I have seen ... such an outrageous smoke that it managed to blot out the sun, but the smoke never lasted, and the sun still shines. I shall continue to keep the truth bright and expose it."[22]

The Wittenberg parish council recognized that only Luther could bring order from the chaos. Ignoring the Edict of Worms ban, they sent a message to Luther at Wartburg: please return, as quickly as possible. Despite Frederick the Wise's protestations that the journey would be unsafe, and that the precarious non-enforcement of the Edict would be in jeopardy, on March 1, 1522, Luther left the castle and returned to Wittenberg. He no longer felt the need for the prince's protection; he was, he wrote Frederick, under "a far higher protection than the Elector's .... I say you have done too much, and you should do nothing but leave it to God."[23] Frederick asked only that Luther draft a letter advising the Diet, scheduled to convene again that spring, that Luther was returning to Wittenberg of his own free will and only to quiet the protesters, and that Frederick had nothing to do with the matter. Luther gladly did so.

At the core of Luther's return to Wittenberg were both philosophical and practical considerations that would ultimately determine the course of the German Reformation. He was genuinely concerned with the escalating chaos that had emerged in his absence. He believed now that Melanchthon was too young and inexperienced to shoulder the burden of reform by himself. (For his part, Melanchthon agreed. "The dam has broken, and I cannot stem the waters," he said.)[24] Karlstadt was proving to be too inclined to mysticism and trends of the moment. Luther was troubled by the rising voice within the reform movement itself, which he called *Schwärmer* (enthusiasts), the radical faction that, in his view, was stretching the Christian liberty he espoused to make new—and incorrect—theological law. Ultimately, he recognized that a power vacuum existed in Wittenberg, and he felt the calling to minister to his flock, in his city. The ideas of the Reformation needed practical application. Wittenberg was his home, filled with his people. The very future of Christendom, he was sure, rested in the balance. Could order come from the confusion? Would there be reform, or revolution? Would Holy Scripture be the guide, or would fanaticism rule the day? Would God's love and grace emerge triumphant, or would his faithful sink back into oppression and corruption? Would all of Luther's work be for naught? He saddled a horse and rode alone to Wittenberg.

Luther's first public appearance in Wittenberg came on March 7, 1522, *Invocavit*, the first Sunday in Lent. He ascended the familiar pulpit at Castle Church and addressed an overflow crowd of some 2,000 students, faculty, and peasants, many of whom were surprised to see that he had again tonsured his hair and was wearing monastic garb. But his appearance was designed to remind his listeners that the course of the reform he had championed would be best accomplished through patience and moderation. He delivered sermons on eight straight days, models of cool reason and understated elegance. His language was gentle, his delivery pleasant. These *Eight Sermons of Wittenberg*, as they came to be known, were examples of Martin Luther, preacher, at his very best.

He touched repeatedly on the themes of faith, love, and freedom, concepts that defined the evangelical movement as he saw it. The Gospel of the Lord, the saving grace of God himself, revolved around these basic principles; without them, there was nothing. For Luther, faith was a private matter up to each individual; it could not be hoisted upon anyone. "I will preach, speak, write, but I will force no one," he said, "for faith must be voluntary." God delivered his son for us, he explained, and our task was to believe. Faith did not come from following a specific set of rules or from meeting obligations. Rather, true faith came from the heart. Because we are mere humans, however, levels of faith varied from individual to individual. It was the duty of those with stronger faith to help those who faltered, for that was the essence of Christian love and charity. Faith without love was no faith at all. In fact, "it is a false faith, just as a face seen in a mirror is not a face but merely an image of one."[25] He urged tolerance and patience in others. Some Christians would embrace reform quickly, enthusiastically. Others would be more cautious, afraid perhaps of abandoning the old ways that had been instilled in them since birth. Luther himself had no use for so many of the customs and procedures of the past. But he respected the wishes of others who still felt affection for them. Be mindful of each other, Luther preached. All reform would come in God's own time.

Luther insisted that with faith came order. He saw no need for rioting or destruction. "Take me as an example," he said. "I stood up against the Pope, indulgences, and all papists, but yet while I was asleep or drinking Wittenberg beer with Philip Melanchthon and Amsdorf, the Word inflicted greater injury on popery than any prince or emperor ever did. I did nothing, the Word did everything." Luther would never condone civil unrest if it led to chaos. "Had I appealed to force," he said, "all Germany might have been deluged with blood; yea, I might have kindled a conflict at Worms, so that the Emperor would not have been safe. But what would have been the result? Ruin and desolation of body and soul. I therefore kept quiet, and gave the Word free course through the world."[26] Luther had unshakable confidence in the power of Scripture. He believed that it would take time, however, for people to come to understand the true message; after all, they had spent their lifetimes being told what to believe, and how. They now had the opportunity to hear the Word for the first time. Once the Gospel was understood and accepted, Luther believed, anything inconsistent with it would fall away.

Luther believed, moreover, that there was room for flexibility in reform. While it was true that the Mass, traditionally practiced as an exercise in sacrifice, was an evil that had to be eliminated, there was no need to do so by extreme measures. To great degree these matters were better left to God. Luther reminded his listeners that while God was watching his people, so too was Satan. "Do you know what the Devil thinks when he sees men use violence to propagate the gospel? He sits with folded arms behind the fire of hell, and says with malignant looks and frightful grin: 'Ah, how wise these madmen are to play my game! Let them go on; I shall reap the benefit. I delight in it.' But when he sees the Word running and contending alone on the battlefield, then he shudders and shakes for fear. The Word is almighty, and takes captive the hearts."[27]

Christians were to be forever free from the domination of Rome. That great truth had been proven over and over these past few years. No man—and no corrupt institution—had the right to tell another how to live or how to practice his faith. Luther referred to the "tyranny of popery," a meaningless set of rules and obligations that had little or nothing to do with faith, but were better left free: marriage, fasting, eating meat on Fridays, confession of sins, living in convents, and the like. God had blessed his people with the freedom to choose in these matters; that was why monks were free to break vows of chastity or poverty—or to keep them if they preferred. Christians were also free from the tyranny of radicalism, Luther said. He was not in favor of replacing one oppressive institution with another. Christians could decide for themselves whether they wanted to include images in their worship. Individual churches were free to choose their own pastors. Outward signs of faith included the sacraments of baptism and the Eucharist. The sacraments need only be accompanied by faith; all else mattered but little. God did not demand a single, binding form of practice of these tenets of faith; he only required faith.[28]

Luther's soothing sermons were welcomed by Wittenberg's city and university officials. More important, his parishioners eagerly embraced his moderate messages. "Oh what joy has Dr. Martin's return spread among us!" wrote Jerome Schurf (who had served as Luther's legal counsel at Worms), to Frederick the Wise. "His words, through divine mercy, are bringing back every day misguided people into the way of the truth. It is as clear as the sun, that the Spirit of God is in him, and that he has returned to Wittenberg by His special providence."[29] Immediately the rioting stopped, and calm was restored. Mobs of students and peasants no longer met to destroy churches or ridicule monks. One of Luther's students wrote, "Like St. Paul, Luther knows how to feed [the people] with milk until they have matured and are ready for solid food. To judge him by his face, Luther is a kind man, mild and good-natured. His voice is pleasing and impressive, and you would be amazed at his winning way of speech." Another student wrote, "All week long Luther did nothing other than to put back in place what we had knocked down, and he took us all severely to task."[30] Even the representative of the Archbishop of Mainz was impressed. Fabricius Capito was sent to Wittenberg to monitor Luther's return. Initially skeptical, he came away pleasantly surprised. "He is preaching daily and he plucks at his followers," Capito reported. "At the same time he is not forgetting to contribute what he contributed in the beginning. Already, the people are flowing together as if into a procession and then continuing on into the liberty of Christ."[31] Luther had his *Eight Sermons at Wittenberg* immediately published, and he considered it his best book to date.

Luther followed his Wittenberg sermons with addresses to adoring crowds in Erfurt, Weimar, and other towns. Just as he had in his home city, he calmly reassured his listeners that God was in control, and that there was no need for unrest or uproar. Predictably, different towns made different ecclesiastical choices. Some retained the manners of the traditional mass, while others rejected them. Some continued to adorn their churches with paintings and statues, and some did not. Music played a large part in some worship services, and was all but absent at others. Luther himself oversaw a traditional celebration of the Eucharist at one Wittenberg church; at another only bread was administered at the high alter, while both bread and wine were distributed at a side chapel. Form was not important, Luther taught. What mattered was the substance of the Lord's Supper, and the spirit in which it was taken.[32]

Luther met with the Zwickau prophets and challenged them: if they were truly conversing with God, as they claimed, would God produce a miracle? "Within seven years," the mystics answered. "My God keeps your god from doing a miracle," Luther scoffed.[33] One of the men claimed he could read Luther's mind. Secretly, he said, Luther sympathized with them and was intrigued by their claims that God was speaking to them. Luther laughed and said the only conversations they were having were with the Devil. He ordered the men out of town and they left, ridiculing Luther's obviously powerful standing in Wittenberg. He had not merely challenged the authorities, they charged. He had himself become a new king of the Protestants.

Karlstadt, the prophets' most visible follower, was also envious of Luther's prominence. His association with mysticism was one theological difference Luther could not overlook, and their friendship ended. He was removed from his position by the town council and also left Wittenberg. He renounced his academic degrees and, believing that God favored the common people, dressed in peasant clothing and took up farming. He became pastor at a small church in Orlamünde, where he called Luther "a gluttonous Ecclesiastic" and "the Wittenberg pope." Karlstadt and Luther would meet again, however, in years to come. Gabriel Zwilling, with Karlstadt the other reform leader in Luther's absence, renounced his radical ideas and became a faithful adherent to Luther's theology.

For the time being Luther was satisfied with the results of his return from exile. By his presence and calming influence he had managed to control and moderate the very forces of reform that he had set in motion. He was gratified that the unruly behavior had stopped, and he felt certain that Rome's oppressive grip on Germany, which had existed for hundreds of years, was ending. He was a hero in Wittenberg, he was home, and he doubted that he would ever leave again. "Here there is nothing but love and friendship," he wrote.[34]

Luther also was beginning to feel that God had trusted him to be the movement's leader. It was more than a blessing, and more than a calling. He was fulfilling his destiny—God's plan for him—and he believed that success in Wittenberg justified the suffering and torment he had experienced. "Follow me," Luther preached. "I was the first whom God entrusted with this matter. I was the one to whom he first revealed how his Word should be preached to you."[35] There was a hint of truth in a point made by Karlstadt and the mystics. More and more, Luther saw himself as the Lord's prophet.

• **Chapter 14** •

A Culture of Persuasion

Triumphant in his return to Wittenberg in the spring of 1522 and securely established as leader of the Reformation, Luther settled in at his old quarters on the second floor in the Black Cloister residence hall of the Augustinian Monastery. He lived with another monk and a single personal assistant, who was also one of Luther's students. He happily resumed his duties as priest at the Castle Church, and as professor of theology and biblical studies at the university. He was paid a modest annual salary of 200 gulden, and received a small honorarium for delivering additional lectures.

He continued his work with remarkable energy and devotion, preaching twice each Sunday, and twice more during the week, usually focusing on a single book of the Bible or one of the Ten Commandments. Once each week Luther spoke to a select group of friends and associates he called his "familiar colloquium." These private lectures, beginning with the Old Testament book of Deuteronomy, were later published as commentaries. Luther preached, exhorted, wrote, prayed, and counseled his parishioners, and reveled in the hard work. "My bed was not made up for a whole year," he said, "and became foul with sweat. But I worked all day, and was so tired at night that I fell into bed without knowing that anything was amiss."[1] For relaxation he found time in the evenings to play an occasional game of chess, or strum on his lute. He had a small single-lane bowling alley installed on the side of his hall. Since the fifth century, Germans had played the game as part of a religious ritual: the number of pins knocked down reduced the penance owed for sins. Now, the nine pins representing devils and demons, or papal officials—to Luther they were the same thing—and he enjoyed knocking them down with rounded rocks or balls. He loved to have company for dinner, usually university colleagues and students, with whom he could enjoy hearty foods and dark beer. "I eat like a Bohemian and drink like a German," he said, "thank God, Amen."[2]

Luther was in great demand all across Germany, and his popularity was matched only by his influence. He lived in open defiance of the Edict of Worms, for the authorities, fearful of renewed protest, did not dare arrest him. In May he went on another speaking tour, visiting Altenberg, Borna, Eilenberg, Torgau, and Zwickau. Overflow crowds, often numbering in the tens of thousands, filled churches, city halls, and town squares. Everyone, it seemed, was anxious to see and hear the man who had challenged Rome and whose messages had changed their lives. Luther was confident, he said, that his listeners knew they could not rely on good works for their salvation. But did they understand the importance of love? "Without love," he said, "faith is nothing. As St. Paul says, 'if I had the tongues of angels and could speak of the highest things on faith, and have not love, I am nothing.'" Luther also insisted upon patience in reform, for some things were moving too fast, or worse, superficially. "There are some who can run," he said, "while others must walk, and still others can hardly creep." Still he enjoyed blasting the Roman Church and ridiculing papal traditions, rules, and customs that detracted from the true essence of Christianity. "No, my dear friends," he said, "the kingdom of God does not consist in outward things, which can be touched or perceived, but in faith." And he continued to reject the idea that only a pope could tell him how to be a faithful Christian. "I refuse to go to confession simply because the Pope has commanded it and insists upon it," he said. "For I wish him to keep his hands off confession.... I will not let private confession be taken from me. But I will not have anybody forced to it."[3]

Sometimes local orthodox bishops arranged rallies and special masses to counter Luther's personal appearances in their towns, but attendance was sparse. Luther's

Martin Luther, the German Hercules (courtesy Stiftung Luthergedenkstätten in Sachsen-Anhalt).

followers came to him for more than just his views on theology, justification, and salvation. He was asked about everything: politics, government, civic affairs, taxation, interest rates, agriculture, marriage, family. A Swiss university student wrote, "As far as one can tell from his face, the man is kind, gentle and cheerful. His voice is sweet and sonorous so that I am struck by the sweet speaking of the man. Everyone, even though not Saxon, who hears him once, desires to hear him again, such tenacious hooks does he fix in the minds of his listeners."[4] Another admirer gushed, "He combines heaven and earth into one morsel when he speaks."[5] Luther was a celebrity with no equal in Germany, and in all of Europe as well.

The writing flowed. Luther was appalled at the "deplorable, wretched deprivation" of basic biblical knowledge many Saxons exhibited.[6] This was not their fault, he said however, for they had never been properly instructed. At the heart of Luther's theology was each believer's personal connection to God. Prayer was an indispensable feature of faith, and Luther meant to teach believers how to pray; so in 1522 he wrote a small tract called *A Little Prayer Book*. Luther hoped that the common man and woman would benefit from basic guidance on the utility of prayer (he continued to pray earnestly, several times each day, as he had learned in monk's training). Catholic prayer books were not uncommon in medieval days, and were in fact quite popular with the small percentage of the population that was "devout and literate." These books, the Church taught, were to be "regarded as essential for any layman who wished to save his soul, and often promised forgiveness, and indulgences from the pains of purgatory, as well as other rewards such as protection in childbirth and at the time of death for those who used them."[7] But of course Luther disapproved of such dogma. Luther's prayer book was written with the aim of reforming orthodox books on prayer. In a cover letter that accompanied the book's release, Luther wrote that Catholic prayer books "need a thorough reformation if not total extermination…. To begin with, I offer this simple Christian form of prayer and mirror for recognizing sin, based on the Lord's Prayer and the Ten Commandments."[8] *A Little Prayer Book* became one of Luther's most acclaimed and enduring works.

Luther's book was a guidebook to the essential components of the Christian faith. The book had three components. First, the Ten Commandments, God's eternal and compelling instructions that told man what he should and shouldn't do. Next, the Christian Creed, which pointed the believer to God, served as an expression of belief in the Holy Trinity, and made clear the everlasting grace and mercy given through Christ. Finally, the Lord's Prayer (the "Our Father" or *Paternoster*), which teaches that everything man could want and need would be provided by God. In these three components Luther found the summarized content of the entire Bible. (Later editions of his *Prayer Book* would include meditations on the Psalms, selected epistles, and the story of the Passion.) Luther's book was meant to memorialize and sustain faith, and his emphases are still vital for much of the Christian Church today.

For Luther everything came from faith, and faith alone (*sola fides*). Faith assured salvation. From faith came love, and love brought about good works—there was no greater commandment, Christ had said, than "Love your neighbor as yourself." In writing his prayer book, Luther noted that while the Christian could never know the doctrines well enough, prayer would provide all the assistance he might need. Later he would develop his prayer book further into a "catechism"—a book of questions and answers on the fundamentals of the faith. He wrote, "There are still many benefits and fruits to be gained, if it is daily read and practiced in thought and speech. For example, the Holy Spirit is present in such reading, repetition and mediation. He bestows ever new and more light and devoutness. In this way the catechism is daily loved and appreciated better."[9] His book differed from Catholic prayer books in one other respect: it actually omitted most prepared prayers. Luther said, "You will never pray well from a book. You may certainly read it and learn how and what you should pray for, and it may kindle the desire in you. But prayer must come freely from the heart, without any made-up or prescribed words, and it must itself form the words that are burning in the heart."[10] *A Little Prayer Book* became a milestone of evangelical piety.

Luther proudly noted that his prayer book was free from all papal influence, and not "puffed up with promises of indulgences."[11] But it did include comments which, even today, stir controversy between Protestants and Catholics. As regards the Virgin Mary, Luther wrote, "She is full of grace, proclaimed to be entirely without sin—something exceedingly great. For God's grace fills her with everything good and makes her devoid of all evil." Luther's preferred that the saying of the rosary be eliminated. He could tolerate it, however, if the Christian kept Mary's role in proper perspective. Luther explained that "what the Hail Mary says is that all glory should be given to God, using these words: 'Hail Mary, full of grace. The Lord is with thee; blessed art thou among women and blessed is the fruit of thy womb, Jesus Christ. Amen!' You see that these words are not concerned with prayer but purely with giving praise and honor. We can use the Hail Mary as a meditation in which we recite what grace God has given her. Second, we should add a wish that everyone may know and respect her…. He who has no faith is advised to refrain from saying the Hail Mary."[12] Luther's views on the Virgin Mary, deeply rooted in his Augustinian training, would continue to evolve.

Luther's *A Little Prayer Book* was immensely popular, quickly moving through nine editions in 1522 alone, fifteen more before the decade was over, and thirty-five in Luther's lifetime.[13] Prayer remained central to his theology, and he would have much more to say about it in years to come. In the book's preface he wrote that "I just don't have the time to undertake such a reformation; it is too much for me alone. So until God gives me more time and grace, I will limit myself to the exhortation in this book."[14] Luther would revisit the topic of prayer several more times in the remaining twenty-four years of his life. He would publish his *Booklet for Laity and Children* in 1525, the *Large* and *Small Catechisms* in 1529, and *A Simple Way to Pray for a Good Friend* in 1535, among others. Theological historian William R. Russell notes that Luther saw prayer and catechism as inseparable: prayer enacts doctrine, and doctrine informs prayer. The two were intertwined, meaningless one without the other, "like two chambers of a single heart working together to give life to [Luther's] understanding of evangelical theology."[15] In this sense, prayer stood at the center of Luther's Reformation.

Luther continued to attack the Catholic Church. Anxious to rid communities and churches of Roman control, he wrote that congregations had the right to appoint their own ministers.[16] Another pamphlet exposed the sexual hypocrisy of Church leaders. Bishops, Luther noted, received substantial funds because of the dalliances of priests, who paid one gulden each year per mistress they kept. These arrangements were commonplace, and Luther mocked the open secrets by quoting the "proverb" that acknowledged them: "Chaste priests are not liked by the Bishop—indeed they are his enemies."[17] This tract too was a bestseller.

When his opponents attacked him, Luther scoffed. In an essay called *A Letter of Consolation to all who Suffer Persecution* he wrote, "They threaten us with death. If they were as smart as they are stupid, they would threaten us with life."[18] When two reform Augustinians were burned at the stake in Brussels, Luther grieved for them but wished he had been in their place. "I thought I would be the first to be martyred for the sake of this holy gospel," he wrote, "but I am not worthy of it."[19] He seemed to relish the idea that more martyrs would be forthcoming and said as much in *Letter to the Christians in the Netherlands*. He was inspired by the two monks and wrote his first hymn about them.[20] His lyrics celebrated the men's death, for they had died in defense of the gospel:

> *Leave all their ashes never will,*
> *Into all lands they scatter;*
> *Stream, hole, ditch, grave—naught keeps them still*
> *With shame the foe they spatter.*[21]

The next few years saw the release of even more of Luther's works. Though still very much a single man, his writing often concerned marriage and family. He disapproved of the legal system regarding marriage that the Church had developed over the centuries. He believed that these rules of canon law—who could marry, and when, and how—were not founded on Scripture. He found such a basis in Leviticus, however, and contemplated to what extent these Old Testament laws ought to be followed. He compromised, ultimately holding that Levitical law set up *natural law* guidelines, and wrote accordingly. Natural law, Luther believed, consists of an objective and universal moral code, embedded in human nature and common to humanity. While not a sacrament, Luther wrote, he saw marriage as a great and mysterious thing, "divine in its source, but worldly in its sphere."[22] He believed that God was pleased when a man and a woman married, and he believed that it was the duty of married couples to have children and rear them properly. Luther worried that refusal to marry might lead to sexual sin or depravity. The union between man and woman was both a natural and divine right. Vows of celibacy were human inventions, and therefore non-binding—for priests, monks, nuns, and even the pope's crusaders, the celebrated Teutonic Knights.[23] He watched with some satisfaction as monks and priests broke their vows of celibacy and celebrated their freedom with public weddings. As he approved of marriage for all, Luther also seemed to approve divorce, when adultery, abandonment, or impotence were present.

Luther was willing to take on any subject in his work. He wrote of the Christian's duty to comply with government, and of the necessity for citizens to provide for the disadvantaged. He encouraged Protestant education and took on banks and lending houses. Indifferent to money and ignorant of all but basic medieval economic practices, Luther believed that greed was a sin, that avarice was the Devil's work, and that using money to make more money (*"Zinskauf"*) was evil. He saw little value in wealth and viewed the pursuit of wealth as a waste of time and talent. With this basis, of course, he disdained all of the Church's efforts in that regard.[24]

Responding to the papal accusation that he did not believe that Jesus was born to a virgin, Luther produced a tract called *That Jesus Christ was Born a Jew*. He asserted his belief—a basic tenet of Christianity—that Christ was the Messiah as foretold in the Old Testament. The topic also allowed Luther to condemn persecution of Jews in Europe (many Catholics and Protestants alike believed that Jews were unclean and in league with Satan). Luther wrote:

> If I had been a Jew and had seen such dolts and blockheads govern and teach the Christian faith, I would sooner have become a hog than a Christian. They have dealt with the Jews as if they were dogs rather than human beings; they have done little else than deride them and seize their property.... If the apostles, who also were Jews, had dealt with us Gentiles as we Gentiles deal with the Jews, there would never have been a Christian among the Gentiles.... When we are inclined to boast of our position [as Christians] we should remember that we are but Gentiles, while the Jews are of the lineage of Christ. We are aliens and in-laws; they are blood relatives, cousins, and brothers of our Lord. Therefore, if one is to boast of flesh and blood the Jews are actually nearer to Christ than we are.... If we really want to help them, we must be guided in our dealings with them not by papal law but by the law of Christian love. We must receive them cordially, and permit them to trade and work with us, that they may have occasion and opportunity to associate with us, hear our Christian teaching, and witness our Christian life. If some of them should prove stiff-necked, what of it? After all, we ourselves are not all good Christians either.[25]

Originally optimistic that Jews would convert to Christianity after the truth of his Reformation was revealed to them, Luther's attitude—and public writings—towards Jews would change dramatically in later years.

Gutenberg's printing press led to a large increase in printed literature, and over 150,000 items were printed in Germany in the 16th century. But sales of Luther's works—or works inspired by Luther—dwarfed all others. Nearly one thousand books were published in Germany in 1522; four-fifths of those were sympathetic to the Reformation. Some six thousand pamphlets—sermons, essays, and letters meant for public consumption—were printed in the first ten years of the Reformation; more than one-quarter of those were Luther's. When Church authorities and local governments advised that it was illegal to print Lutheran matters, printers complained that without Luther they would have no businesses at all. Their customers,

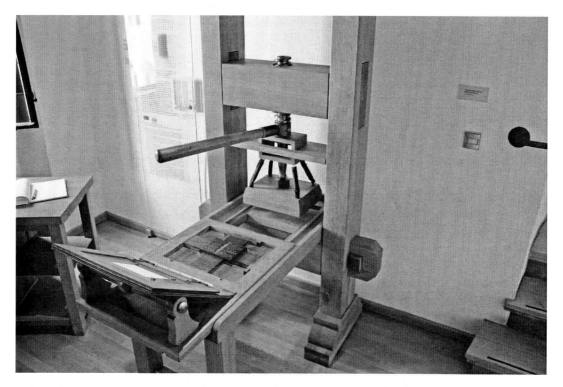

Gutenberg printing press displayed at St. Augustine Monastery, Erfurt (courtesy Erfurt Evangelical Augustinian Monastery).

they said, were not interested in Catholic publications: "what they have in over-abundance is desired by no one and cannot even be given away."[26] A book might take several weeks to produce, while a 6m × 9m pamphlet could be printed in two days. Editions were generally produced in batches of 1,000. Printers in other towns eagerly reprinted their own copies for sale. A pamphlet cost one *Pfennig* (about the same as a chicken), and was sold in large cities and small towns, at markets and fairs, by bookshop owners and traveling peddlers. Preachers gladly passed out copies, or sold them cheaply. "Luther's books were everywhere," wrote the Dutch humanist theologian Erasmus. "No one would believe how widely he has moved men."[27]

The printed word was illuminated by woodcuts or carvings. Bold graphics accompanied the text of books and pamphlets, and were sometimes printed as broadsheets. Luther was aware of the value of illustration. "Without images we can neither think nor understand anything," he said. Many woodcuts were produced by famed printmaker and portraitist Hans Holbein of Augsburg, and by Luther's close friend, the Wittenberg artist Lucas Cranach the Elder. The messages of these woodcuts were easily conveyed to the illiterate and served as visual aids for preachers. One series of images called "Passional Christi und Antichristi" ("Passion Book of Christ and Antichrist"), for example, contrasted the piety of the Lord against the decadence and corruption of the pope. Many woodcuts portrayed Luther as the German Hercules crushing his papal opponents and causing Satan to flee in shame. Others were far more crude and, at times, astonishingly graphic. "The Origin of the Monks," for example, depicted three devils excreting a pile of orthodox monks. In another, called "The Papal Belvidere (Beautiful View), or "Kissing the Pope's Feet," a group of peasants scornfully receive a papal bull with sneers and farts. The caption reads: 'The Pope speaks: Our sentences are to be feared, even if unjust.' Peasant Response: 'Be damned! Behold, o furious race, our bared buttocks. Here, Pope, is my "Belvidere."'

Luther's opponents attempted to counter his popularity with illustrations of their own. While the Church did not have, at least in Germany, an artist as renowned and beloved as Lucas Cranach the elder, several well-known illustrators, including Martin Eisengrein and Johan Jakob Rabus, carried out the propaganda work of the pope.[28] One woodcut entitled "Luther's Game of Heresy" shows him stirring a pot of stew to a boil, assisted by devils. The fumes of the stew are labeled falsehood, unbelief, pride, envy, scandal, disobedience, contempt, heresy, blasphemy, unchastity, fleshly freedom, disorder, and disloyalty.[29] The illustration purported to reestablish that the Church held supreme power, and that it was Luther, not the pope, who associated with Satan. On the whole, however, the Church's propaganda was far less effective than that of the reformers, owing both to Luther's unprecedented popularity and the widespread contempt of Rome he had inspired.

The fine arts had its role in the wave of reform media and propaganda. Hans Sachs was a shoemaker from Nuremberg who wrote more than 6,000 poems and songs, earning him the title of *Meisterlieder* (master songster). Caught up in the tide of the Reformation, in 1523 Sachs wrote a poem in honor of his hero Luther, "The Nightingale of Wittenberg, Which is Heard Everywhere," which became a national sensation. The Nuremburg council at first forbade Sachs from publishing further, but quickly realized the futility of the action and rescinded the ban.

Music was a popular method of spreading the reform message. Often, lyrics or poems were circulated from town to town via pamphlet or broadside, and were then set to the melody of traditional folk songs, a method known as *contrafacta*. One common theme centered on an idea called *verkehrte*, or, the world turned upside down: because of Luther, nothing was as it seemed, or as it used to be, and spiritual leaders had become transgressors. Another theme characterized the pope as Lucifer, or the antichrist. Using this message, Luther wrote a poem called "Nun treiben wir den Pabst hinaus" ("Now we drive out the Pope"). When set to music, his words became lyrics:

> Now we drive out the pope
> from Christ's church and God's house.
> Therein he has reigned in a deadly fashion
> and has seduced unaccountably many souls.
>
> Now move along, you damned son,
> you Whore of Babylon.
> You are the abomination and the Antichrist,
> full of lies, death and cunning.
>
> Your indulgence, bull and decree,
> now they receive their seal in the toilet.
> Thereby you stole the good from the world,
> and defiled Christ's blood as well.
>
> The Roman idol is cast out.
> We accept the true pope.
> He is God's Son, the Rock and Christ
> on whom His church is built.
>
> He is the sweet highest Priest,
> who was sacrificed on the Cross.

He shed His blood for our sins,
true indulgence flowed from his wounds.

He rules His church through his word,
God the Father Himself invests Him with power.
He is the head of Christianity,
to Him be all praise and glory for eternity.

As dear summer goes past,
grant us Christians joy and peace.
Give us a fruitful year, Lord,
and preserve us from pope and Turks.[30]

While the content of Luther's reform messages was eagerly embraced by his audiences, he ingeniously included another component of persuasion. In the prefaces to his works, he urged his readers to discuss the contents with others and read them aloud to the illiterate. In this way Luther's works were read in homes, discussed in shops, and debated in taverns. They were read in "spinning bees in Saxony and bakeries in Tyrol," church historian John A. Hartmann described. "In some cases entire guilds of weavers or leather-workers in particular towns declared themselves supporters of the Reformation, indicating that Luther's ideas were being propagated in the workplace." It was said that "better sermons could be heard in the inns of Ulm than in its churches."[31]

Before Luther's death in 1546, more than three million copies of his writings, excluding his Bible translations, were printed. Luther's popularity as a writer was even more impressive considering the fact that the Edict of Worms had banned the sale and ownership of his books.[32] The Edict had warned that the spread of Luther's message must be prevented, otherwise "the whole German nation, and later all other nations, will be infected by this same disorder." But it was too late—the infection had taken hold in Germany and beyond. Thanks in large part to the printing press, much of Germany had become Protestant; or more specifically, Lutheran. As Will Durant puts it, "Printing was the Reformation. Gutenberg made Luther possible."[33]

This massive popularity of Luther's works in the 1520s showed Rome there would be no stopping the Reformation movement in Germany. Andrew Pettegree, noted Reformation scholar at St. Andrews University, calls it the "Culture of Persuasion." He writes, "It was the superabundance, the cascade of titles that created the impression of an overwhelming tide, an unstoppable movement of opinion.... Pamphlets and their purchasers had together created the impression of irresistible force."[34]

*

For all of Luther's accomplishments, perhaps his most important contribution to the Reformation was his translation of the Bible from Greek and Hebrew to German. He had completed a first draft of the New Testament while at the Wartburg, but now, upon his return to Wittenberg, he set out to revise and polish it. Already he had acquired a complete Latin Bible from the University Library at Erfurt, and he continued to improve his understanding of the original languages of the Scriptures. His working knowledge of Greek and Hebrew was moderate at best, however, so he enlisted the assistance of his friend Melanchthon, who was an accomplished Greek scholar, and also sought the advice of Erfurt's Professor George Sturz and his old confidant Spalatin.

Translation involved new tongues as well as old, so Luther took to the streets and fields of central Saxony and studied the characteristics of the German vernacular. He intended that his New Testament be read and understood by his people, the German people, and so he "looked them on the mouth."[35] He visited with peasants in the field and mothers in their homes. He listened to tradesman and artisans in their shops, and to butchers, shoemakers, and blacksmiths. He drew on the rhythm and cadence of the people, following his own love of poetry and music. While painstakingly mindful of the original biblical text, Luther wanted his translation to acknowledge how German people spoke in their homes, their marketplaces, their streets and fields. He wanted the people to be able to relate to Holy Scripture. In a country where different German dialects were spoken in different regions—so much so that some people struggled to understand others—Luther's goal was a lofty one; he meant to equip every German-speaking Christian with the ability to hear and understand the Word of God.

Luther compared his translation work to that of teaching a bird to sing a new song. "Oh God," he said, "What great and hard toil it requires to compel the writers against their will to speak German. They do not want to give up their Hebrew ... just as though a nightingale should be compelled to imitate a cuckoo and give up her glorious melody, even though she hates a song in monotone." Luther's efforts brought a rare display of humility. "I have undertaken to translate the Bible into German," he said. "This was good for me; otherwise I might have died in the mistaken notion that I was a learned fellow."[36] Luther was meticulous in his work. While translating, he spoke his sentences out loud, so that the cadence would be satisfactory. Luther wanted his translation to "ring through all the senses into the heart" so that those hearing it might "rightly conceive of the word[s] and the feeling behind [them]."[37] He hoped that people would look to the Bible "so that we might seize and taste the clear, pure Word of God itself and hold to it, for there alone God dwells in Zion."[38] He knew that some in his audience might be skeptical. "Then they began to say: 'Yes, but how can we know what God's Word is, and what is right or wrong? We must learn this from the Pope and the councils.' Very well then, let them conclude and say what they please, yet I will reply, you cannot put your confidence in that nor thus satisfy your conscience, for you must determine this matter yourself, for your very life depends upon it. Therefore God must speak to your heart: This is God's Word; otherwise you are undecided." Luther wanted Protestants to experience what he had experienced. "The Bible is alive, it speaks to me; it has feet, it runs after me; it has hands, it lays hold of me."[39]

Luther took liberties in his work. He arranged the books in a different order than they appeared in the Vulgate Bible. He separated Hebrews, James, Jude, and Revelation from the other books. He named John as the most important of the gospels, "the one, fine, true, and chief gospel, far superior to the other three," because it contained the passage "For God so loved the world that He gave His only begotten Son that whosoever shall believe on Him should not perish but have everlasting life." (John 3:16). He listed Paul's epistles—particularly Romans—among the "truest and noblest" books. This was no surprise, for it was Paul who proclaimed the basis for Luther's entire theology: *He who through faith is just shall live.* And because the book of James seemed to "have nothing of the nature of the gospel in it," he considered it to be "an epistle of straw," and wished that it had not even been included in the Bible. Luther also criticized the mysterious book of Revelation, for it was neither gospel nor faith-based. Still, he invited others to disagree. "I leave everyone free to hold his own opinions," he wrote. "I would not have anyone bound to my opinion or judgment. I say what I feel."[40]

Luther sent the initial New Testament proofs to Spalatin, his "foretaste of our new Bible," he called it, and it met with enthusiastic approval. Luther's final version was delivered to Wittenberg printer Hans Lufft, who, anticipating high demand, employed two other local printers and generated an initial press of three thousand copies. Luther's *Das Neue Testament* was released in September 1522 to tremendous acclaim. It was "a noble monument of literature, a vast enterprise," writes theologian William R. Russell. "The poetic soul finds in this translation evidence of genius and expressions as natural, as beautiful, and melodious as in the original languages."[41] Even Johan Cochlaeus, the dean of the *Liebfrauenkirche* (Church of Our Lady) in Frankfurt and one of Luther's most outspoken critics, recognized the work's power. "Even tailors and shoemakers, yea, even women and ignorant persons who had accepted this new Lutheran gospel, and could read a little German, studied it with the greatest avidity as the fountain of all truth," he wrote. "Some committed it to memory, and carried it about in their bosom. In a few months such people deemed themselves so learned that they were not ashamed to dispute about faith and the gospel not only with Catholic laymen, but even with priests and monks and doctors of divinity."[42] This was exactly what Luther wanted; in his view all Christian men and women who had been baptized were priests, and were capable of understanding and discussing the Scriptures. Despite the relatively high cost of a gulden and a half per book, in a matter of weeks the New Testament was the most popular printed work in Germany. A second edition, which contained a few corrections and improvements, appeared in December.

Roman Catholic authorities were stunned by the success of Luther's New Testament, and immediately issued orders forbidding the book. Local orthodox representatives were authorized to confiscate it, but there were too many books in circulation, and directives to deliver up the books to Church officials, so that they could be destroyed, were ignored. The Church then sought to attack the book's errors or falsehoods, although the majority of those proved to be the result of mistranslations in established Latin versions rather than Luther's mistakes. One issue arose over Luther's translation of the beginning of the Lord's Prayer. He had substituted *"Unser Vater in dem Himmel"* for *"Unser Vater, der du bist im Himmel"* ("Our Father in Heaven," for "Our Father which art in Heaven"). But this criticism fell upon deaf ears; indeed, subsequent Catholic versions of the New Testament followed Luther's editions in this and most other respects.

Another translation was not dealt with so easily, and remains controversial to this day. Luther inserted the word *"allein"* ("alone") into the text of Romans 3:8, so that the verse now read: "Therefore we conclude that a man is justified by faith *alone* apart from the deeds of the law." This addition seemed to significantly affect the meaning of the verse, shaping it to confirm to Luther's key interpretation of the significance of good works. Here was the proof, the Romanists charged, that Luther was more interested in his own personal theology than what the Bible actually said, and what the Church taught. Luther's doctrine of faith alone—*sola fides*—was a false one.

Luther fully acknowledged that the word "alone" did not appear in the original Greek or Latin at Romans 3:28. He wrote, "I know very well that in Romans 3 the word "sola" is not in the Greek or Latin text—the papists did not have to teach me that. It is fact that the letters s-o-l-a are not there. And these blockheads stare at them like cows at a new gate, while at the same time they do not recognize that it conveys the sense of the text—if the translation is to be clear and vigorous, it belongs there. I wanted to speak German, not Latin or Greek, since it was German I had set about to speak in the translation."

What mattered for Luther was placing the words in an interpretive context. His translation was meaning-oriented; it was the meaning of the Scripture, he believed, that had to be communicated to the reader. He wrote, "The text itself, and Saint Paul's meaning, urgently require and demand it. For in that passage he is dealing with the main point of Christian doctrine, namely, that we are justified by faith in Christ without any works of the Law. Paul excludes all works so completely as to say that the works of the Law, though it is God's law and word, do not aid us in justification. ..So, when all works are so completely rejected— which must mean faith alone justifies—whoever would speak plainly and clearly about this rejection of works will have to say 'Faith alone justifies and not works.'"

Luther's intellect, and his ego, afforded him the opportunity to ridicule the skeptics who dared challenge his work. He wrote:

> If your papist wishes to make a great fuss about the word sola (alone), say this to him: "Dr. Martin Luther will have it so, and he says that a papist and a donkey are the same thing." ... For once, we also are going to be proud and brag, with these blockheads; and just as Paul brags against his mad raving saints, I will brag against these donkeys of mine! Are they doctors? So am I. Are they scholars? So am I. Are they preachers? So am I. Are they theologians? So am I. Are they debaters? So am I. Are they philosophers? So am I. Are they logicians? So am I. Do they lecture? So do I. Do they write books? So do I.
>
> I will go even further with my boasting: I can expound the psalms and the prophets, and they cannot. I can translate, and they cannot. I can read the Holy Scriptures, and they cannot. I can pray, they cannot. Coming down to their level, I can use their rhetoric and philosophy better than all of them put together. Plus I know that not one of them understands his Aristotle. If any one of them can correctly understand one preface or chapter of Aristotle, I will eat my hat! No, I am not overdoing it, for I have been schooled in and have practiced their science from my youth. I recognize how deep and broad it is. They, too, are well aware that I can do everything they can do. Yet they treat me as a stranger in their discipline, these incurable fellows, as if I had just arrived this morning and had never seen or heard what they teach and know. How they do brilliantly parade around with their science, teaching me what I outgrew twenty years ago! To all their noise and shouting I sing, with the harlot, "I have known for seven years that horseshoe nails are iron."
>
> Let this be the answer to your first question. Please do not give these donkeys any other answer to their useless braying about that word sola than simply this: "Luther will have it so, and he says that he is a doctor above all the doctors of the pope." Let it rest there. I will from now on hold them in contempt, and have already held them in contempt, as long as they are the kind of people (or rather donkeys) that they are.[43]

Even while his New Testament was still in the press, Luther began work on the Old Testament. Again he sought the assistance of colleagues. He founded a *Collegium Biblieum,* or Bible Club, to discuss matters of translation and interpretation. Each member of the group had a particular field of expertise. Luther excelled in modern German. Phillip Melanchthon was an expert on the Greek language; Justus Jonas, the scholar and lawyer who had accompanied Luther to Worms and who had guided the Wittenberg Reformation in Luther's absence, was proficient in Hebrew; Johann Bugenhagen was a master on the Vulgate Bible, the 4th century Latin Bible that the Catholic Church had adopted as its official version; Caspar Cruciger and Matthäus Aurogallus were Hebrew scholars; and Castle Church Deacon Georg Röer served as proofreader. Occasionally local Jewish rabbis, or non–German biblical scholars who were passing through Wittenberg, joined in the discussions. This group of learned men met once each week, at Luther's residence; their meetings took them past the supper hour and well into the night. Arguing, discussing, and working together, sometimes the men might spend three days to translate a single Biblical line. Sometimes they searched weeks for the correct translation of a single word. As with his New Testament, Luther endeavored to make the Old Testament reader-friendly for his countrymen and women. He hoped, he said, "to make Moses so German that no one would suspect he was a Jew."[44]

By Christmas 1523, the Pentateuch, or first five Books of the Old Testament, went to press. Next came the Psalter, or Book of Psalms (always Luther's favorite), which came out a year later. The entire Bible, containing both Testaments and lavishly illustrated with woodcuts, finally was completed a decade later, in 1534. For twenty years Luther would continually edit and modify his German Bible. Five new and original versions were released in his lifetime; Luther saw the last edition of his German Bible appear in 1545, just a year before his death.

Luther's translation won readers with *kraftvolles Deutsch,* its forceful Germanic vigor and strength. He succeeded in transforming sacred text into the language of the common people. His Bible was so popular, and was distributed so thoroughly, that it extended into the daily life and work of so many Germans. Luther even insisted that large-print Bibles be released for the benefit of those with poor eyesight. The German Bible became (and remains today), an esteemed part of the national heritage, facilitating the emergence of a standard, and modern, "High German" language. While it was officially printed in Wittenberg, countless other editions were distributed through black market presses in Strassburg, Augsburg, Nuremberg, Cologne, Lübeck, and Halberstadt, among other places. In forty years, over one hundred thousand copies of Luther's Bible were sold.

Almost immediately Luther's Bible was printed in other countries and in other languages. It served as the primary source of translations in France, Holland, Sweden, Iceland, and Denmark. It had a particular impact in England; William Tyndale, considered to be the father of the English Bible, utilized Luther's work extensively in both the King James and Revised Standard versions. For Protestants, the Bible was no longer a foreign book written only in Latin to be read and interpreted only by Catholic priests. Over the generations, many millions of Europeans read Luther's words. Luther's Reformation would no longer depend upon the words and actions of the Reformer. It was now rested on his translation of the Word of God which every person could read and consider for himself. Luther's mastery of the common vernacular perfectly complimented his steadfast enthusiasm for the gospel. He recognized his own gifts; he had, he said, "a truly devout, faithful, diligent, Christian, learned, experienced, and practiced heart." He recognized the magnitude of his achievement. "I do not wish to praise myself," he said, "but the work speaks for itself." He referred to himself as a "Doctor of the Sacred Scriptures."[45]

For Luther, however, there would be no rest. There were many challenges still before him; some would come from his enemies in Rome and others from supposed allies in Europe. In short order he would surprise all who knew him by taking a wife and starting a family. And more perilously, despite all the lessons he had taught of Christian love and political moderation, legions of Protestant faithful would ignore his pleas and go to war.

• **Chapter 15** •

"I have made the angels laugh and the devils weep"

When Martin Luther was a young boy in the late 1490s a macabre rumor circulated around Saxony. It was reported that a grotesque beast was living along the Tiber River near Rome. The monster had the head of an ass, a woman's breast and stomach, and fish scales on its legs, chest, and arms. It had one foot of a griffin and one of an ox, and instead of hands it had elephants' feet. A fierce dragon's head protruded from its back, next to the face of an ugly old man. Few doubted that stories of the mysterious creature's existence were true, but no one knew what to make of them. In June of 1522 a sickly whale stranded itself on the North Sea beach of Holland, frightening the superstitious citizenry. Six months later a deformed calf was born in Freiberg, Saxony. Alarmed by the appearance of the monsters, and concerned that the beasts might be omens of divine wrath or an imminent Judgment Day, worried Germans asked Luther to explain the events. Luther and his colleague Phillip Melanchthon quickly published a pamphlet describing the "*Horrible Figures,*" complete with woodcuts by Lucas Cranach.

Luther did not believe that the appearance of the monsters signaled the end of the world. Rather, he likened them to the evil corruptions of the Catholic Church. In his view, each part of the river creature (or "Papal Ass," as he called it), held meaning. The head was the pope himself; the female body represented the body of the papacy, or cardinals, bishops, monks, and clerics; the elephant's foot-hand signified the oppressive power of the Church; the ox foot represented the servants of the Church, or priests and orthodox theologians; the scales represented the secular rulers who defended the pope. Even the hideous backside of the monster was significant: the dragon represented papal bulls and other decrees of papal infallibility, and the old man signified the end of the papacy. In Cranach's woodcut the beast stands in front of a castle tower, the papal keys displayed on the flag.

The humanoid calf figure, Luther wrote, represented monasticism. Unsteadily standing on its hind legs, the calf signified idol worship from Old Testament days. Its coat, a hideous growth around the back of its neck, resembled a monk's cowl, and the indentation on its head replicated the monk's tonsure. The holes in the coat symbolized disunity among the various monastic orders. The monster's appearance, Luther thought, did not mean that God was angry with the world. Rather, it signified that monks and nuns should leave the shackles of monastic life, repent and become true Christians, meaning Protestants.[1]

Luther had certainly left monastic life far behind him. He no longer dressed as a monk, preferring the secular garb of breeches, banded shirts, vest, overcoat, and boots or, when preaching or lecturing, cape, vestments, and cap. He let his hair grow over the tonsure. He believed that the sheltered life of monks and nuns was often incompatible with Holy Scripture. Living a life of dedicated service did not bring one closer to salvation, for God's grace had already provided that gift to believers. The Bible gave a man or a woman everything that was needed to form a relationship with God, Luther thought, and the demanding regulations of monasticism were unnecessary. He knew that sometimes younger people were placed in monasteries or nunneries solely because their families could not provide for them. Vows extracted through fear, force, or financial necessities were not consistent with God's plan or scriptural instruction. Luther's own terrified promise to St. Anne, made long ago in the midst of a thunderstorm—"Help me St. Anne, I will become a monk"—no longer bound him, and in fact never had.

Further, Luther believed, the harsh lifestyle of the cloister might very well interfere with other, more Godly, pursuits, namely marriage and procreation. For fifteen hundred years of the Christian era, celibacy, and not matrimony, had been wrongly exalted as a higher, holier state of spirituality. Sexuality was too often condemned by association with the evils of original sin and too seldom celebrated as a blessing of family life.[2] But Luther was convinced that it was simply not natural to suppress healthy sexual desire, which was, after all, a gift from God. The Scriptures said that it was not good for man to live alone; Adam needed a helpmate, and was given Eve. "The longing of a man for a woman is God's creation," Luther said. "The act of which attracts sex to sex is a divine ordinance."[3] He had written at length on these subjects in his pamphlet *On Monastic Vows,* and his personal experience as a young man had convinced him that far too often monastic life only led to a selfish, prideful existence and a misplaced belief in good works. Inspired by Luther's "Freedom of the Christian" concepts, by the mid–1520s hundreds of monks and nuns from all across Europe had repudiated their vows and, violating canon law, left the monasteries and convents. Sometimes, monks and nuns married each other.

Luther encouraged the exodus from the cloister and tried to ease the return of former monks and nuns back into German society. He preached that wealthy parishioners should donate to special funds earmarked for assistance for those who had given up their monastic vows. He found families to host them. He encouraged merchants to give them jobs and help them learn trades. "The runaway monks and nuns steal many hours from me," he complained good-naturedly.[4] Never overly concerned with his own finances, Luther often gave financial assistance to those who left. Sometimes he gave virtually all he had, and on at least one occasion he could not pay the malt debt (no doubt a most painful sacrifice for Luther: malt was a necessary ingredient for brewing beer). Sometimes Luther's assistance paid off in unusual ways. One nun, Florentina von Oberweimar, fled her convent near Eisleben and made her way to Wittenberg. Luther encouraged her to write an account of her escape and, with his assistance, *A Story of How God Rescued an Honorable Nun* was published to minor acclaim. Another fugitive from the convent managed to escape in particularly dramatic fashion and then, improbably, became Luther's wife.

Katherine von Bora was born on January 29, 1499, in Lippendorf, Saxony, a village about twenty miles south of Leipzig. Her father was Hans, her mother Anne. They were "impoverished nobility"; that is, the family held a title and a few small parcels of land but very little else. Katherine had three brothers: Hans, Jr.; Clemens; and a third, whose name is unknown and who likely died when an infant. She also had a sister, Maria.

Anne died shortly after giving birth in 1505. Hans quickly remarried, and Katherine, just five years old, was sent to a Benedictine convent school in Brehna, about thirty-five miles to the north. Four years later she was transferred to a Cistercian cloister called *Marienthron* (Mary's Throne) at Nimbschen near Grimma, where she joined an aunt, her father's sister Magdalena von Bora. Because Katherine had no dowry, she began preparations to become a nun. She was bright, stubborn, and practical. She was devoted to learning and did well in her lessons, which included theology and literature and a bit of Latin. At the age of sixteen Katherine took her vows and became a nun, and settled into a life of devotion, charity, and prayer.

She also grew accustomed to hard work. The Cistercians were noted for their dedication to physical labor, and all nuns regularly toiled in the grain fields of the several estates the convent owned. Katherine gained a practical knowledge of the business of farming. She also helped out in the beer brewery the convent maintained, and found time to organize the nunnery's business books. Two years after she took her vows, when she was nearing the age of eighteen years, the Augustinian monk Martin Luther nailed his Ninety-Five Theses to the door of the Wittenberg Castle Church, just fifty miles away. Over the next several years some of Nimbschen's monks joined in Luther's movement, and Katherine and many of the other nuns began to embrace his doctrines of reform, as well. By 1523 Katherine was ready to leave the convent.

But the Cistercian monastery at Nimbschen fell under the jurisdiction of Duke George the Bearded, prince of Saxony, who retained his strict Catholic ideology and threatened defectors with execution. (This was no idle threat: George had a Protestant from Mittweida named Heinrich Keiner decapitated for helping a nun escape from her convent.)[5] A Protestant businessman named Leonard Coppe, of nearby Torgau, was sympathetic to the plight of the nuns, and agreed to assist twelve nuns, including Katherine, escape the cloister. On the night before Easter Sunday, April 4, 1523, three nuns were transported secretly to private homes in Saxony. The other nine, Katherine among them, were loaded into wagons that had been used to transport herring, and were taken to Wittenberg. Their arrival was big news. One university student wrote, "A wagon load of vestal virgins has just come to town, all more eager for marriage than for life. God grant them husbands lest worse befall."[6] On April 10 Luther wrote a letter to Spalatin, who was still working for Frederick the Wise:

> Grace and peace. Nine fugitive nuns, a wretched [because of what they had endured] crowd, have been brought to me by honest citizens of Torgau. I mean Leonard Coppe and his nephew Wolf Tomitzsch; there is therefore no cause for suspicion. I pity them much, but most of all the others who are dying everywhere in such numbers in their cursed and impure celibacy. This sex so very, very weak, joined by nature or rather by God to the other, perishes when cruelly separated. O tyrants! O cruel parents and kinsmen in Germany! O Pope and bishops, who can curse you enough? Who can sufficiently execrate the blind fury which has taught and enforced such things? But this is not the place to do it.
>
> You ask what I shall do with them? First I shall inform their relatives and ask them to support the girls; if they will not I shall have the girls otherwise provided for. Some of the families have already the girls otherwise provided for. Some of the families have already promised me to take them; for some I shall get husbands if I can. Their names are: Magdalene von Staupitz, Elsa von Canitz, Ave Gross, Ave von Schönfeld and her sister Margaret, Laneta von Goltz, Margaret and Catharine Zesehau and Katherine von Bora. Here are they, who serve Christ, in need of true pity. They have escaped from the cloister in miserable condition. I pray you also to do the work of charity and beg some money for me from your rich courtiers, by which I can support the girls a week or two until their kinsmen or others provide for them. For my Capernaans have no wealth but that of the Word, so that I myself could not find the loan of ten gulden for a poor citizen the other day. The poor, who would willingly give, have nothing; the rich either refuse or

give so reluctantly that they lose the credit of the gift of God and take up my time begging from them. Nothing is too much for the world and its way. Of my annual salary I have only ten or fifteen gulden left, besides which not a penny has been given me by my brothers or by the city. But I ask them for nothing, to emulate the boast of Paul, despoiling other churches to serve my Corinthians free. Farewell and pray for me. Martin Luther.[7]

Luther's efforts to assist the women were successful. Three of the nine were quickly married, and three others were returned to their families. That left three whose futures were still in doubt: the sisters Margaret and Ave von Schönfeld, and Katherine von Bora. All were either unwilling or unable to return to their families. It was rumored that Luther was romantically interested in Ave, but the feeling, if it existed, was not returned. Within a few months the sisters found mates, and that left only Katherine alone.

For about a year Katherine roomed at the home of the Reichenbach family on Bürgermeister Street, and worked as a maid. Master Reichenbach was a pharmacist, a scribe, and a jurist. Later he served as Mayor of Wittenberg. He was also friends with Lucas Cranach the Elder, and Katherine became friends with the artist's wife, Barbara, who worked with Luther to find Katherine a spouse. Katherine was courted briefly by a patrician named Jerome Baumgärtner, who was studying at the university. But when he returned to his home in Nuremberg the romance fizzled; his family objected to a possible union between their son and a runaway nun. Luther tried to salvage the match. "If you want to hold onto Kate von Bora," he wrote to Baumgärtner, "get busy before she's taken by someone else who is at hand. She has not yet conquered her love for you. I would rejoice for this marriage on both sides."[8] But Luther got no response to his plea.

Luther recommended that Katherine consider for a husband Nicholas Amsdorf, the theology professor who had supported Luther at Leipzig and Worms. She was receptive to the idea, but Amsdorf had no desire to marry, and politely declined. Next Luther suggested Dr. Kaspar Glatz, the aged rector of the university, and now Katherine objected. She then let it be known that she would consider marriage to the great reformer himself, Martin Luther.

While he was a strong proponent of marriage, Luther had never seriously considered it for himself. He thought he would remain single since, as an outlaw from the Church, his death at the hands of his enemies might come at any moment. Still, he did not deny his own sexuality and thoughts of love. "It is not that I do not feel my flesh and my sex," he wrote, "I am neither wood nor stone; but I have no thoughts of marrying, because I am preparing myself for the punishment inflicted on heretics."[9] He often made jokes about his bachelorhood. "I find so many reasons for urging others to marry," he said, "that I shall soon be brought to it myself, notwithstanding that enemies never cease to condemn the married state, and our little wiseacres ridicule it every day." The 'wiseacres' he was thinking of were professors and theologians of his circle at Wittenberg, some of whom supported the idea, and others who worried that marriage might distract him from his leadership duties of the reform movement. "Watch out that I, who have not thought of marriage at all, do not someday overtake you too-eager suitors," he told them, "just as God usually does those things which are least expected."[10]

Luther went home to Mansfeld as part of another speaking tour, and there met with his parents. His father Hans, while impressed with his son's accomplishments (unsurprisingly, both Hans and his wife Margarethe had become Protestants), still hoped that Martin would pass on the family name. He encouraged his son to marry Katherine. Luther protested mildly.

He wasn't sure that he loved her, he said. She had a very strong personality and her pride, he thought, bordered on arrogance. But he could not deny that he had affection for her. He went home to Wittenberg, but told few friends what he was thinking. 'It is not good to talk much about such matters,'" he said. "A man must ask God for counsel, and pray, and then act accordingly.'[11] But there was no denying his affection for her. By the spring of 1525 Luther was referring to Katherine as his future bride and wrote, "If I am able to spite the devil, I will marry my Kate before I die."[12]

On June 13, 1525, Luther was betrothed to "his Kate" at the Wittenberg Friary.[13] It was a Tuesday, the traditional day for ceremonies in medieval Europe. Johann Bugenhagen, pastor of St. Mary's Church and who would later introduce Protestant reforms to Denmark, presided over the ceremony. Witnesses included Lucas and Barbara Cranach, and Justus Jonas, provost of the All Saints Chapter House. Also on hand was the lawyer Johann Apel. Apel had an interesting career. He was ordained a priest in 1523 and appointed as cathedral canon at Würzburg. He then studied law and assumed both pastoral and legal duties for Conrad, Bishop of Würzburg and Duke of Francken. At least three other priests kept concubines there, but Apel secretly married a nun from the St. Marr cloister. When she became pregnant, scandal ensued, and Apel was put on trial for violating canon law. Convicted of "participating in Luther's damned teachings," Apel was defrocked and excommunicated, and briefly jailed in the city's castle tower. When Protestant civic leaders protested, Apel was released from custody and evicted from town. He was welcomed at Wittenberg and joined the law faculty, and quickly became one of Luther's closest friends.

The couple joined right hands and exchanged promises of faithfulness. Then, in full view of all the witnesses and in accordance with medieval tradition, the betrothed couple lay down on the nuptial bed, a symbolic fulfillment of consummation. They were now married in the eyes of God. Plans were then made for the actual marriage. Luther insisted it take place as quickly as possible, to minimize any dangers and to put an end to unwarranted gossip. (One rumor was that Luther had abandoned the reform movement in favor of self-indulgence. Another said that his bride was pregnant; the child, sneered Catholic apologists, would surely be the Antichrist.)

Exactly two weeks later on June 27, 1525, Luther, the forty-two year old former monk, married twenty-six year old Kate, a former nun. After a spirited procession through the streets of town, Bugenhagen solemnized the wedding, which took place at the Castle Church. The event was cause for great celebration in Wittenberg. Luther wrote the guest invitations himself, and he planned the *Festmahl,* or great feast, that followed the ceremony. He made certain that his parents attended. He wrote to Marshal Dolzig of the Saxon High Court: "It is without doubt an adventurous occasion to which I invite you as I am to become a bridegroom. How strange that idea is to me! I still can hardly believe it, but the compunction is so strong that I must believe that I am to serve and honor it."[14] The city council provided seven tankards of Franconian wine. Luther asked some of his guests to bring fresh venison for the feast, and Torgau and Einbeck beer. "If the beer is not good," he warned his friends, "you will be obligated to drain the keg yourself."[15] The invited guests included many of Luther's friends and associates who had supported him through the years: Lucas Cranach the Elder, Phillip Melanchthon, Jerome Schurf, Justus Jonas, George Spalatin, Nicholas Amsdorf, Wenzel Link, and Gabriel Zwilling. Even Andreas Karlstadt showed up, although his radical reforms and mystical leanings had estranged him from Luther.

Martin and Kate Luther, oil paintings by Lucas Cranach the Elder, 1529 (courtesy Morgan Pierpont Library, New York).

After the feast, gifts were presented. The university gave the couple a silver goblet bearing the inscription at the base: "The honorable University of the Electoral town of Wittenberg presents this wedding gift to Doctor Martin Luther and his wife Käthe von Bora." The city council gave 100 gulden. Many people donated gold coins, and someone gave Luther a medal decorated with his likeness, as though he were a king or emperor. The new Saxon elector, John the Steadfast, donated the monastery building, and the old Black Cloister, once the home of dedicated monks sworn to vows of poverty, steadfastness, and chastity, became the Luther home.

Because the wedding had been arranged so hastily, no rings were exchanged. But eventually the couple had custom rings designed by Lucas Cranach the Elder. Luther gave Kate a golden ring set with a ruby and decorated with symbols of the Christ's Passion: the crucified savior, a spear, and crown of thorns. Engraved on the inside of the ring are the names of the couple and the date of the wedding, "der 13 Juni 1525." Luther wore a unique double ring, mounted with a diamond and a ruby, and the initials of the couple (Luther's initials were followed by the letter "D," to mark his academic title). On the inside of the ring were engraved the words of St. Matthew: "What God has joined together, let no man put asunder."

And so this unlikely pair began married life. Kate immediately changed almost everything in Luther's world. He watched in amazement as Kate arose every day at four a.m. and went about her duties. She put all of her organizing skills to work, transforming the old monastery into a comfortable home, scrubbing and cleaning each room by hand, preparing the extra rooms as an inn for students and visitors. She established gardens, an orchard, and a vineyard. She had a pond built and stocked it with pike, bass, and trout. She fenced off acres for horses, pigs, chickens, and cattle, dug a well, and upgraded the brewery. She kept bees and grew flowers.

Luther wrote how wonderful it was that his once empty bed was now graced with pigtails. "My Kate is in all things so obliging and pleasing to me that I would not exchange my poverty for the riches of Croesus," said.[16] Within a few months Kate was pregnant with her first child. Shortly after the wedding Luther wrote to a friend: "Suddenly, and while I was occupied with far other thoughts, the Lord has plunged me into marriage." He found great and unexpected joy in what had happened. "With my wedding," he said, "I have made the angels laugh and the devils weep."[17]

• **Chapter 16** •

The Devil's Work

While Luther was settling into unexpected domestic bliss with his new bride, Germany was experiencing the chaos of war—not with another nation, but with itself. The Peasants' War of 1524 and 1525, a widespread revolt by commoners against the aristocracy, was the largest uprising in Europe until the French Revolution of 1789. Sparked by economic disparities among the classes, and fueled by the incendiary words and actions of the Reformation, the war cost many thousands of lives but, in the end, brought about very few substantive changes. Strangely, though, the charismatic Luther, who so many Germans looked to for leadership and inspiration, harshly turned his back on the peasants who adored him, resulting in an estrangement that never fully healed, and that tarnished his reputation for centuries to come.

For hundreds of years peasant groups across Europe had sporadically protested against the feudal system. Their complaints were many: the tyranny of the ruling classes (patricians, burghers, and plebeians all enjoyed supremacy over serfs); high taxes paid to support the government; mandatory tithes turned over to the Church; an unfair leasing system that offered no way-of-life alternative to poor, working families; inadequate hunting, fishing, and grazing rights; and the impossibility of upward mobility. Yet a lack of organization and leadership, along with insufficient military experience and basic weaponry, had doomed each and every prior uprising.

By the 1520s, Germany was beginning a slow but steady march toward industrialization. The lower classes, however, saw little improvement in their income or their way of life. More people moved from the countryside to cities and towns, looking for work in textile plants, mining and metalwork plants, and small shops and marketplaces. Commercial items of cloth, linen, and wool were manufactured for trade with other nations. Governments needed increased revenue to pay for newly-expanded trade routes along with their armies and increasing bureaucracies. The Church, historically in partnership with government, relied upon taxes to feed its construction projects and its own military machine. And, increasingly, the upper nobility was developing a taste for luxury; more cash was needed to purchase fancier clothes, sturdier and more refined household items, and objects of fine art. As a result, tax rates increased—and fell disproportionately on the lower classes: the serfs, tenants, and shopkeepers. Sometimes tax revenues were increased in creative ways. A "great tithe" was enacted for livestock sales, and a "small tithe" for fruits, grains, and vegetables. The purchase of cheese was taxed, as was wine and beer, and even acorns. Any transfer of ownership of feudal property was taxed. A death duty was installed, payable by the tenant when either landlord or tenant died. An investiture tax was enacted for every new bishop who was installed. Increasingly, hard-earned money went from the peasant and his family into the pocketbooks of the nobility. Germany was reaching new heights of economic prosperity, but only the Church, the city and regional governments, and the aristocracies were reaping the benefits.

But the peasants of 16th-century Germany were motivated by more than their stagnant social and economic stations. They were also inspired by Luther's anti-authoritarian rhetoric. Their hero, the "German Hercules," had dared to defy the Church and its fifteen hundred-year orthodoxy of domination and oppression. In exposing the hypocrisy of its leaders, he had denied the existence of a God-given right of ecclesiastical privilege and authority. He had boldly presented the argument that the Church, for its own ugly and self-sustaining purposes, had deliberately misinterpreted Christ's message and God's plan for his people. All believers were priests, Luther said. If all men were equal in God's sight, the peasantry reasoned, surely they also deserved equal treatment on the earth God had created for them. Luther's written version of the New Testament, wildly popular and available for everyone to inspect and consider for themselves, was seen as nothing less than a civil manifesto. Since the machinations of Church and state were so intertwined, it was impossible to imagine a sustaining civil authority without both institutions. Luther's chastisements against one were attacks on the other, for he targeted both prince and bishop alike. His proclamation of a brand new concept—the freedom of the Christian man—gave new hope to the commoners. Christ had, after all, sympathized with the poor and the oppressed. He had promised that they would inherit the earth. The time for fulfillment of that promise, it seemed, was now. But while Luther's words and actions inspired the common folk in the 1520s, it would be another reformer who led the peasants into battle.

Thomas Müntzer was born in Stolberg, Thuringia, in 1489. Educated at the universities of Leipzig and Frankfurt, Müntzer became a scholar of Biblical literature and, for a short time, a monastery resident at Frohse. Luther's posting of the Ninety-Five Theses in 1517, and the uproar that ensued, motivated Müntzer to vocalize his own ideas for radical, and political, reform. He was not merely interested in reforming a corrupt Church. True Protestantism, he argued, extended far beyond spiritual matters; it reached into civil affairs and politics, as well. He hoped that Luther would use his popularity and influence to carry reform from the pulpit to the streets.

Luther and Müntzer met at least once in those early Reformation days at Wittenberg, and argued over the levels and depths of reform. Luther would not extend his way to thinking to comply with Müntzer's vision of civil disobedience for he believed that there could be no Christianity without order. Acting upon Luther's advice, the ailing Frederick the Wise, ever cautious, had Müntzer removed to Zwickau. There, however, Müntzer was further influenced by the mystics and the Anabaptists. He found temporary homes in Prague, and then in Halle, where he preached at a small church, married a former nun and had two children. His ideas developed further, and his growing band of eager followers, whom he christened the "League of the Elect," pledged their allegiance to him. They migrated with him to Glaucha and Allstedt, where he became pastor at St. John's Church and produced the first liturgies in the German language, *Das Deutsche Kirchenamt* and *Deutsche Evangelische Messe*. He began to see himself as the *Nuntius Christi*, God's true prophet of the holy word. "The living God is sharpening his scythe in me," he said, "so that later I can cut down the red poppies and the blue cornflowers."[1] In the summer of 1524, Müntzer delivered a sermon in which he compared himself to Daniel of the Old Testament, who could interpret dreams and foretell the end of earthly kingdoms. He made sure that a copy was given to Duke John of Saxony, Frederick's brother, for he believed that he should replace Luther as the Duke's primary spiritual advisor. The apocalypse, Müntzer preached, was at hand.

Müntzer skillfully blended his end of times vision and radicalized Protestantism with the emerging unrest of the peasantry. Unlike Luther, he was not content to be guided by *sola scriptura,* or Scripture alone. Rather, he believed that God's word was manifested via an "inner light" that came from the Holy Spirit, and was juxtaposed with the Lutheran doctrine of justification by faith. Müntzer claimed knowledge of a new way to salvation, not through faith and grace, but through rebellion and violence. The common people, he believed, would now arise and take their rightful place as stewards, or God's elect, of the new kingdom on earth. This inevitable utopia would be free of class and nobility, for all were equal in God's sight (although a small group of chosen ones, to include Müntzer, would be authorized to lead the way). There would be no private property, no wealth—indeed, no monetary system—, and no oppressive government to trample the faithful. The wickedly anti–Christian earthly government, and its allied Catholic Church, had to be vanquished. Müntzer called on princes to assist the peasantry in destroying all remnants of Roman clergy and capitalism, and in restoring Christendom to the splendor of its founders. Nobles and priests must leave the protection of their palaces and reside as commoners. Those who still clung to the "godless orthodoxy," as he called it, would be destroyed by the sword. "The godless have no right to live," Müntzer thundered, "except insofar as they are permitted to do so by the elect." Any prince, count, or baron who, "after being reminded of this truth, and shall be unwilling to accept it, is to be beheaded or hanged."[2] From his headquarters in Allstedt he ordered his followers to destroy a statue of the Virgin in the Mellerbach Chapel of the convent of Naundorf, and instructed the townspeople to cease paying their tithes there. Luther's vision of reform suddenly seemed conservative by comparison.

Müntzer's bloody vision was too much for the authorities in Allstedt, and he was stripped of his pastorate. Forsaking his family, he gathered up his followers and drifted from town to town throughout Saxony, spewing his apocalyptic dream of the deliverance of "Israel," and foretelling of the coming of Heaven on Earth. In September 1524, in the textile town of Mühlhausen, Müntzer rallied the proletariat and took over the village council, establishing a ruling "Eternal Council of God," with himself in charge. The Council destroyed all Church property and drove out the monks, and then organized the region's peasants, farmers, and industrial workers into an army. A foundry was established in the monastery of the Barefoot Friars, and soon artillery was being cast from its works. From its tower flew the peasant banner decorated with the *Bundschuh,* or peasant boot, signifying the onward and relentless march of the common man against tyranny. Müntzer sent an open letter of invitation to the peasantry, imploring them to join his utopian society and prepare for the final battle. "Join the uprising," he wrote. "Be there only three of you, but if you put your hope in the name of God—fear not a hundred thousand …. Forward, forward, forward! It is high time …. Look not upon the sufferings of the godless! They will entreat you touchingly, begging you like children. Let not mercy seize your soul, as God commanded to Moses; He has revealed to us the same …. Forward, forward, while the iron is hot. Let your swords be ever warm with blood!"[3] He also wrote to Luther and urged him to join his movement. "When the spirit of truth is come," he wrote, "he shall guide you into all truth." Luther was astounded at Müntzer's radical interpretation of Scripture, and appalled that so many Germans were adhering to it. He wrote to his friend Spalatin that Müntzer was either "mad or drunk."[4]

Müntzer published a pamphlet he called *The Explicit Unmasking of the False Belief of the Faithless World,* which repeated many of the themes of his earlier published sermon. In the tract he called upon his followers to "drive Christ's enemies out from amongst the Elect … the sword is necessary to exterminate them … the ungodly have no right to live further than the Elect shall accord them." Under his own divinely-inspired leadership, they would "sweep Christendom clean of ungodly rulers." But now for the first time he also lashed out at Luther, whom he viewed as the "beast of the Apocalypse." By refusing to join in the struggle, Luther had proven himself to be a defender of the privileged nobility. "The wretched flatterer is silent about the origin of all theft," wrote Müntzer. "Luther says that the poor people have enough in their faith. Doesn't he see that usury and taxes impede the reception of the faith? He claims that the Word of God is sufficient. Doesn't he realize that men whose every moment is consumed in the making of a living have no time to learn to read the Word of God? The princes bleed the people with usury and count as their own the fish in the stream, the bird in the air, and the grass of the field, and Dr. Liar says, 'Amen!' What courage has he, Dr. Pussy-foot, the new pope at Wittenberg, Dr. Easychair, the basking sycophant! He says there should be no rebellion because the sword has been committed by God to the ruler, but the power of the sword belongs to the whole community. In the good old days the people stood by when judgment was rendered lest the ruler pervert justice. They shall be cast down from their seats. The fowls of the heavens are gathering to devour their carcasses."[5]

Thousands of peasants rallied around Müntzer and other leaders in the southern parts of Germany, forming an "Evangelical Brotherhood" and dedicating their lives to tearing down the feudal system. In many regions peasants refused to pay taxes and tithes, and demanded that land rental contracts be renegotiated. Surprisingly, in Werdenburg, Montfort, Lupfen, and Sulz, a handful of counts joined in the movement, protesting against the unfair treatment of their subjects. Even the bishop of Constance pledged his support. By some estimates as many as 30,000 peasants, scattered across the region and armed only with pitchforks, scythes, axes, and other crude farming tools, stood ready to fight for their cause. But first, the peasants took an unusual step. They articulated their demands in written form.

In March 1525, in the city of Memmingen, a group of delegates, guided by devotees of Swiss Protestant leader Ulrich Zwingli, drafted a set of Twelve Articles. The Articles repeated the demands that peasants had made many times over the years, but this time they took on a formal, constitutional tone. According to the Articles, each municipality must have the right to hire its own preachers, who would be paid from a general tithe; surplus funds would go to the poor, not the Church. Further, since God created man and gave him dominion over all animals, peasants must have the right to hunt and fish freely, and the forests were to revert back to localities for all to use. The rate of the feudal form of indentured servitude, called *corvees,* would not be raised, and neither would levies or lease fees be increased. Common meadows, meant for the sole use of peasants and not nobles, would be restored. Finally, death taxes would be abolished. In two months the Twelve Articles were printed over 25,000 times, and distributed throughout Germany. The document was sent to Charles V, the Holy Roman Emperor. A copy was also delivered to Luther. Meanwhile, the peasants' army continued to grow, particularly in the Black Forest region along the Rhine River, and in the low mountains of Baden-Württemberg along the Danube.

But Luther could not bring himself to support civil upheaval and quickly published a pamphlet called *Admonition to Peace*, explaining why. He certainly sympathized with the condition of the commoners, he said, and he did not hesitate to criticize the ruling classes for the long-standing and unbearable conditions. "We have no one on earth to thank for this mischievous rebellion," he wrote, "except you, princes and lords, and especially you blind bishops and priests and monks, whose hearts are hardened against the Holy Gospel, though you know that it is true and that you cannot refute it. Besides, in your temporal government, you do nothing but flay and rob your subjects, in order that you may lead a life of splendor and pride, until the poor common people can bear it no longer. Well, then, since you are the cause of this wrath of God, it will undoubtedly come upon you, if you do not mend your ways in time. The peasants are mustering, and this must result in the ruin, destruction, and desolation of Germany by cruel murder and bloodshed, unless God shall be moved by our repentance to prevent it."[6]

Nevertheless, Luther would not condone talk of rebellion or violence. He hoped living conditions for peasants might improve, he wrote, but he cautioned them not to take up arms to achieve their goals. They would surely be defeated, he warned, and would end up in a far worse state than before. When he had written of Christian freedom, he meant spiritual freedom and the liberty that salvation brought. Luther believed in order and harmony. Rebellion against order was nothing more than a strike against the roots of divinely-structured society. He suggested compromise from both sides. "Choose among the nobles certain counts and lords, and from the cities certain councilmen," he wrote, "and have these matters dealt with and settled in a friendly way."[7] In April and May 1525, Luther traveled the region surrounding Wittenberg, urging anxious listeners to keep the peace. Müntzer's path was madness, he told crowds, and would lead to chaos. "These are strange times," he said, "when a prince can win heaven with bloodshed better than other men can with prayer."[8]

But far too many commoners were committed to Müntzer's violent scheme to turn back now. If Luther would not back them in their struggle, so be it. He was no better than a traitor to them, and to their country. There would be no negotiations. Instead, the revolt intensified in dozens of locations, particularly in the southern region of the country. Municipal governments that had not taken the peasants' threats seriously were unprepared to defend themselves, and were overthrown at Heilbronn, Rothenburg, Würzburg, and Frankfurt-am-Main. Monasteries and castles were favorite targets of the peasants. Seventy monasteries were razed in Thuringia alone, and fifty more in Franconia. There was little coordination from city to city, however, and the peasant marauders showed no restraint in their actions. Church officials were beaten and left for dead. Nobles were tortured in front of their families, and many were killed. Priests were thrown into the streets. Nuns were raped. Buildings were looted, noble houses were burned, and parishes were desecrated. City and church coffers were emptied, as were clerical wine cellars, and drunken peasants ransacked churches and destroyed sacred objects. As Müntzer watched in delight, a large swath of Germany fell into the chaos that Luther had predicted.

The authorities quickly answered the call. Since the late 15th century, the *Schwäbischer Bund,* or Swabian League, had operated as a mutual defense and peacekeeping military contingent. Organized by the Imperial Estates (free cities, principalities, and prelates), and financed by the Fugger bank of Augsburg (the same financial house that had bankrolled Rome's massive building projects that led to the indulgence scandal in previous years), the

League was made up largely of mercenaries. In 1525 the Swabian League numbered some 13,000 men, of which nearly 2,000 were *Landsknechte*, or mercenaries, and, under the command of General Georg von Truchsess, they now mobilized to put down the peasants' rebellion.

The first large scale encounter between the peasants and League forces was at Leipheim, on the Danube River. On April 4, 1525, 3000 peasants led by radical priest Jakob Wehe stormed the town. The rebels pillaged the church, drank the sacramental wine, smashed the organ, and mockingly made leggings from sacred vestments. They apparently were not aware that League forces had gathered nearby. The army laid siege to the city and quickly took back control, taking about 250 peasants as prisoners. Another 400 peasants drowned as they tried to escape across the river, and mercenary forces cut down another 500 rebels. Wehe and a few other leaders were beheaded, and, while the surviving peasants were allowed to disperse, many of their cottages were burned.[9]

It would take far more than one defeat to break the peasants' spirit. April 15 was Good Friday. Peasant contingents surrounded the town of Weinsberg, where Count Ludwig von Helfenstein, was a much-despised leader known for his cruel treatment of commoners. The Count regularly threw peasants into dungeons if they neglected to bow their heads properly when he passed, for example. He once cut off the hands of a man who killed a rabbit on one of his fields, and he loved to trample the peoples' crops for sport while out on hunting expeditions. On Easter Sunday the angry peasantry, led by tenant farmer Jäcklein "Little Jack" Rohrbach, stormed the walls, killed forty guards, and then took the Count and his family as prisoners. As the rebel piper played, the mob forced the Count's wife and child to watch as they ran him down a deadly gauntlet of whips, clubs, and spears, taunting him with reminders of his own brutality as he died.

The peasants met more success in Bamberg, Zabern, Brixen, and in small pockets of Bavaria, Austria, Alsace, and the Swiss Cantons, where the Reformation had progressed in recent years. In Mainz, the Archbishop Albrecht was forced to flee in the face of a peasant assault; he was only allowed back into his see after he signed the Twelve Articles and paid a ransom of 15,000 gulden. While Luther's Wittenberg, and much of the surrounding region, was not subject to upheaval, it seemed to some, including Luther, that the peasants might prevail. He suggested the possibility that "the peasants might get the upper hand (which God forbid!); and that God perhaps willed that, in preparation for the Last Day, the devil should be allowed to destroy all order and authority, and the world turned into a howling wilderness."

With portions of his country in near shambles, and particularly horrified by news of the killing at Weinsberg, in May 1525 Luther published one of the most controversial pamphlets of his career. *Against the Robbing and Murdering Hordes of Peasants* was a shockingly harsh diatribe against the peasants that startled prince and rebel alike with its frankness. Luther noted that, in his earlier tract's call for calm and negotiation, he "did not venture to judge the peasants, since they offered to be set right and be instructed…. But before I look around they, forgetting their offer, betake themselves to violence, and rob and rage and act like mad dogs. It is the Devil's work … and in particular the work of the Devil's architect [Müntzer]."

But Luther was not content merely to lecture the rioters. It was his wish, rather, that they be put down by force. "Any man against whom sedition can be proved is outside the law of God and the Empire, so that the first who can slay him is doing right and well…. For rebellion brings with it a land full of murder and bloodshed, makes widows and orphans, and turns everything upside down." Then Luther wrote, in furious tone, the words that shocked even his most enthusiastic followers and that remain controversial among Catholics and Protestants to this day: "Therefore let everyone who can, smite, slay, and stab, secretly or openly, remembering that nothing can be more poisonous, hurtful, or devilish than a rebel. It is just when one must kill a mad dog; if you do not strike him he will strike you, and a whole land with you."[10] Luther advised the princes to "swiftly grasp the sword." A prince or a lord was "God's minister," he wrote, "and the servant of His wrath, to whom the sword is committed for use upon such fellows." The civil authorities need not worry that their violent actions would be unforgiven, he wrote, for "rebellion is intolerable."[11]

Luther went further, proclaiming that the very ideological foundation of Müntzer's vision of a classless society was faulty. His utopian idea, social redistribution of wealth for the sake of the common good, was not warranted by Scripture. "The Gospel does not make goods common," Luther wrote, and the Apostles and disciples "did not demand, as do our insane peasants in their raging, that the goods of others—of a Pilate or a Herod—should be common, but only their own goods. Our peasants, however, would have other men's goods common, and keep their own goods for themselves. Fine Christians these! I think there is not a devil left in hell; they have all gone into the peasants."[12] Luther believed that some of the rebellious peasants were mindless dupes who followed Müntzer's movement blindly. These poor souls, Luther felt, deserved some sympathy. "Dear lords," he wrote, "help them, save them, take pity upon these poor men." But those brutes who knew their actions were wrong, and who rebelled and plundered on behalf of a madman's twisted vision, deserved to die. "As to the rest," he wrote, "stab, crush, and strangle whom you can."[13]

Luther believed he was justified in his vitriolic writings, for he felt that the peasants were horribly misguided in their actions. As he had so many times in his theology, Luther turned to St. Paul. It was not the peasants' place to seek revenge, for as Paul had written, "Vengeance is mine; I will repay says the Lord." Scripture taught that rebellion against authorities was a mortal sin. The gospel was full of examples of how Christians were to behave: turn the other cheek; love thy neighbor; render unto Caesar what is Caesar's. Further, Luther reasoned, it was the plight of Christians to suffer as Jesus had suffered on the cross. Paradise would come to the faithful eventually, but there were no guarantees of earthly bliss in the here and now. "Suffering, suffering, cross, cross is the Christian law, and nothing else," was the mantra Luther lived by, and so he wrote.[14]

The worst of the peasants' rebellion, thought Luther, was that Müntzer had managed to convince thousands of peasants that upheaval was justified by the Bible, and that true Christians had the scriptural right—God's blessing, as it were—to revolt. To Luther, the very idea that individuals, no matter how downtrodden, could murder and rob and plunder *in the name of Christ* was infuriating. The rebels were turning the world, imperfect as it was, upside down in the name of the Lord.

And Luther knew well what St. Augustine had written: any government—and that included unfair and oppressive government—was preferable to no government. Without civic obedience there would be chaos and perpetual strife. God had not placed man on the earth to live in such a state. Natural law demanded some sense of structure and obedience to authority. So too did God's law. While the Church had long abandoned Augustine's great principles, Luther thought, he would turn to them. Luther had become a great champion of the people. But when the people turned to rebellion, he would have no part of it.

Just before Luther's indictment of the peasantry went to press, his protector Frederick the Wise died, on the evening of May 5, 1525. Unmarried and childless, Frederick had been ill for some time, and the upheavals in recent months had led him into a deep depression. He had written to his brother John that "if it was God's will" that the common man should rule, perhaps it was better not to resist.[15] On his deathbed he said to a servant, "Dear child, if I have ever injured you, I beg you in God's will to forgive me. We princes do to the poor people much that is not good."[16] Luther advised his assistant Spalatin to refrain from any Catholic observances at the funeral, such as singing during a vigil over the corpse as it lay in state.[17] Luther preached two sermons in honor of Frederick, one at the funeral service, and the second at the burial. The Christian community, he said, had lost "a peaceful man and ruler, a calm head." Frederick's passing was "the most grievous sorrow of all," and with Germany in peril because of the upheaval, it could not have come at a worse time. Even in this time of grief, however, Luther could not resist a warning to the peasants. Those who rebel against the authorities, he told Frederick's mourners, "shall receive to themselves damnation. This text will do more than all the guns and spears."[18]

But Luther was glad, he said, that under Frederick's term the people of Saxony had finally received the true gospel. Comforting the flock, Luther spoke of Christ's resurrection and of the faith and hope that distinguished the Christian from the heathen. As Christ conquered death, he said, so too would the believer. There is no reason to fear death, he said. He even recalled his own fears, the *Anfechtungen* that had plagued him in his youth, but which worried him no more. Faith made it all possible, he said. "He who through faith is just shall live."

As he preached, Luther could not help but recall the important role Frederick had played in his past. It was Frederick, after all, who had stood by Luther in the early days of controversy, when Luther had dared post his Ninety-Five Theses, and then had defied papal authorities at Augsburg and Leipzig and Worms. It was Frederick who had secreted Luther at the Wartburg Castle and had given him free license to preach his revolutionary theology. It was Frederick who had refused to turn him over to the Catholic authorities, while Rome fumed over the "wild boar" who had "invaded the Lord's vineyard." Without Frederick, Luther surely knew, there would have been no Reformation. Would his successor be as supportive?

As Frederick was laid to rest, his brother, Duke John, took over as Elector. To Luther's relief, the new prince would become known as Duke John the Steadfast, because he so avidly supported the Protestant cause that had developed during his brother's reign. And now John moved quickly to quell the peasants' uprising, centralizing the command of the League forces and urging swift, decisive action. Having lost the element of surprise, the peasants were out-maneuvered and unprepared to face better equipped, tightly organized and disciplined forces. By the middle of May the authorities had firmly turned the tide against the peasants. The decisive battle of the war took place on May 15 at Frankenhausen in Thuringia. Nearly 10,000 peasants, by far the largest concentration of rebel fighters of the war, gathered in the fields outside of town. Believing that this was Armageddon, and that the Lord himself would come down from the heavens and, as the prophets foretold, slay his enemies, Müntzer arrived from Mühlhausen, escorted by three hundred of his select force. From the wagon that carried him flew the rebel flag, adorned with a rainbow, symbolizing God's covenant with Noah and his people after the flood. While considerable in sheer numbers, the peasants were armed only with their farming weapons and some scant homemade artillery. Within days some 6,000 mercenaries of the Swabian League, under the command of Philipp of Hesse and assisted by

George, the new Duke of Saxony, and Duke Henry of Brunswick, surrounded them. An emissary from the League offered terms: the lives of the peasants would be spared if they surrendered Müntzer. Miraculously, a rainbow appeared in the sky, which Müntzer took as a signal from God that the peasants would be victorious. Let the soldiers advance, he told his followers. He would catch the army's cannonballs in the sleeves of his coat. He led his army in prayers and hymns as the League battalions began their assault.

The awesome power of the League's combined infantry, cavalry, and artillery turned the battle into a route. The initial cannon volley terrified the peasants, and many of them fled into the temporary safety of Frankenhausen. League forces followed, slaughtering hundreds. Three hundred peasants were taken prisoner and summarily condemned to death. When a group of wives pleaded for the lives of their husbands, Phillip granted leniency only upon condition that the women stone to death two radical priests who had encouraged the revolt. This was done immediately. In all, at least 5,000 peasants were killed that day. Several hundred citizens of Frankenhausen who had not fought, but were suspected of harboring the rebels, were spared, but only on condition that they pay 40,000 gulden.[19]

Müntzer fled Frankenhausen and hid in the woods, but was quickly captured. He was tortured until he renounced his revolutionary teachings and swore allegiance to the Pope's Church. He was then dragged, shackled, to an open field aside the princes' headquarters. There, in front of the few horrified peasants who had managed to survive the battle, he was beheaded.

More slaughters followed. Thousands of peasants were killed in engagement after engagement as the Swabian League displayed its overpowering might. Just a day after Frankenhausen, 3,000 peasants perished at Böblingen. There were more one-sided defeats at Turmberg, Königshofen, Pfeddersheim, and Freiburg. At Würzburg over 8,000 peasants died in just two hours. The skulls of scores of peasants were ripped from their lifeless bodies and piled on a high hill outside of Colmar, Alsace. Even today, the town's residents call the place *Blutberg*, the blood mountain. At Neckargartach, Jäcklein Rohrbach, who had led the peasant victory at Weinsberg, and his piper Melchior Nonnenmacher, who had gleefully played while Count Helfenstein had been forced to run the gauntlet of death, were arrested. Sentenced to death by burning, the two men were chained to a tree, wood piled around them. Noblemen gladly started the fire, which slowly roasted the rebels to death. By the end of June the war was over. In less than one year nearly 130,000 peasants had died. And embittered survivors on both sides of the conflict blamed Luther.

*

To many Roman Catholics, Luther had spurred the uprising. He was nothing but a loudmouth and a coward. He was happy to incite rebellion with his words, they said, but stood idly by as the very people he inspired marched to their deaths. A good number of Protestant evangelicals, as well, saw him as the cause of the senseless slaughter. His violent rhetoric, they felt, was inexcusable.

Luther replied to his critics in a pamphlet called *An Epistle on the Hard Little Book against the Peasants*. He did not apologize for his comments, and he did not retract them. He continued to justify the use of force, but also wrote: "I had two fears: if the peasants became lords, the devil would become abbot (father, or head of a monastery); but if these tyrannical princes became lords, the devil's mother would become abbess."[20] In other words, no good result could possibly have resulted from warfare. The princes who had slaughtered peasants even after they had surrendered were "senseless tyrants" who would one day endure their own "hellfire." Yet those peasant rebels who had justified their own bloody deeds in the name of God deserved the same fate.[21] Perhaps, Luther wrote, his critics were merely rebels themselves at heart. He believed that both sides, carried away by bloodthirstiness, had gone too far. He reminded his readers that his pleas for compromise and negotiation had been largely ignored. But there had been no bloodshed, after all, in and around Wittenberg.

Perhaps though, he continued, some good may have come from the uprising. Nobles had certainly learned that tyranny bred unrest, and with unrest came rebellion. And the peasants might now be content in peace, for they could realize more fully that it was spiritual salvation that mattered, not the contents of their pocketbooks or the bounty of their harvest. Luther continued to believe that God had assigned to all people particular stations in life. It was the duty of the Christian to accept his position willingly, for with contentment came an orderly society. There was no shame in a lowly status, no pride in a higher one. One could best serve God by going about his business with dignity and cheerfulness. Further, the consequences of social dissatisfaction would always be bloody. Luther outlined again for his readers the doctrine of two kingdoms that he had long advocated. The kingdom of the world (God's "kingdom of the left hand") depended upon law and civil order so that truly evildoers might be restrained. The spiritual kingdom (God's "kingdom of the right hand"), however, all was peace, grace, mercy, and goodness. Luther believed that one could, and should, reside in both kingdoms at the same time. But the kingdom of the right hand was far more important.

It is likely, of course, that Luther was outraged not only by upheaval but by the very threat to his Reformation that the war posed. For all his rhetoric against the "papal antichrist" and the "Devil's whores" who corrupted God's word and scandalized the German people, he did not envision, when he nailed the Ninety-Five Theses to the church door at Wittenberg, castles in flames or churches being ransacked. Only years later did Luther seem to accept some responsibility for the carnage that the war had produced. In 1532 he told a group of visitors to his house in Wittenberg, "In the rebellion, I struck all the peasants. All their blood is on my neck. But I know it from our Lord God that he commanded me to speak."[22]

In the aftermath of the Peasants' War, social classes persisted. Living conditions for peasants and serfs in Germany remained unchanged. The fight for and against the Reformation, however, intensified. The Catholic princes Duke George and Archbishop Albrecht of Mainz mounted an effort to destroy Protestantism. They were countered by Phillip of Hesse and Duke John the Steadfast, who together with other Protestant princes formed the *Torgauer Bund,* or League of Gotha, to revoke the Edict of Worms (which had become, in the wake of Luther's immense popularity, all but meaningless) and promote Protestantism. Eventually, much of Germany would officially become Protestant. But the alliances formed after the Peasants' War, and their successors, ensured that the country would know no peace for the next one hundred years or more.[23]

The Peasants' War inspired ideologues of a different sort three centuries later. Karl Marx admiringly referred to it as "the most radical act in German history," and Frederick Engels, while discounting the religious aspect of the war, nonetheless asserted that socio-economic, or class, conflict, was the real motivating force behind the struggle. The failure of the uprising underscored, for Engels, the need for a working proletariat-peasantry alliance. Münzter's utopian classless and wealth-free society, where all shared equally, is seen by some today as the forerunner of modern communism.

Without question Luther's reputation was tarnished. Historians often point out that, to some degree, the heroic status he enjoyed before the war faded, and his political and religious influence diminished. But the roots of the Reformation had been planted so deeply, and nourished so thoroughly, that the movement he fostered would continue no matter what role Luther might play in his later years. He still had the backing of a sizeable number of faithful followers and a healthy contingent of admiring princes, including the new Elector. There was still much work to do, and Luther would not rest, but his future, as always, was uncertain.

• Chapter 17 •

The Faith Alive

Although the Peasants' rebellion had been put down and the Catholic presence in Germany remained sizeable, by the late 1520s half of the country was Protestant. Support for the Reformation continued to grow, rapidly stretching across northern Europe and gaining footholds in England, Scotland, and even France. Now that the war was over, Luther returned to the questions still unanswered in the decade since he had posted his challenging Ninety-Five Theses on the door of Wittenberg's Castle Church. How would these thousands of new Protestants organize themselves? What exactly would the new church look like? Now free from the domination of Rome, how were Protestants to live and worship in light of the changes that the Reformation had brought? Luther pondered his role in the emergence of the Protestant era. How could he best use his gifts of intellect and purpose and unshakable faith? Would his thunder from the pulpit, his charisma in the classroom, and his powerful and persuasive literary voice, continue to inspire his followers? Could he withstand the criticisms that had come his way for his seeming betrayal of the peasants and their cause? In short, was he still the leader of the Reformation? Luther would spend the next five years answering these questions, as he continued on his spiritual journey and sought to mold the emerging Protestant church.

Luther realized that while there had been a Reformation, there existed no actual Reformation Church in Germany. Many thousands of Protestants throughout the country were united in their faith. They had accepted Luther's vision of a faith-based religion of truth, but there was no visible structure—no unified institution—to nurture and instruct them. "These Christians," insisted Luther, "must be gathered into a family, and built up into a kingdom—a holy and spiritual kingdom."[1] Acting upon Luther's request, Duke John ordered a "visitation" of all churches in Saxony. The Elector authorized teams of visitors, or commissioners, acting under the general supervision of Luther, Melanchthon, and Spalatin, to spread out into the various provinces and observe, inquire, and measure the spiritual health of congregations and parishioners. It would be a general survey of ecclesiastical affairs, a decade after the Reformation began and fresh from the end of the Peasants' War.

In the fall of 1528 the first results of the visitations were delivered to Luther, and they were not encouraging. Luther thought that Saxons had been inspired and reborn into lives of faith and piety. He expected that parishioners, led by dedicated pastors, would be eagerly attending church services, listening enthusiastically to the Word, and partaking of the Eucharist. Instead, he learned that "in our area visitation of the area around Wittenberg, we have discovered so far that all the pastors are living in harmony with their peasants, but the

170

"**Life of Martin Luther and the Heroes of the Reformation!**" **Breul and Brückner, lithographers, circa 1873. Luther burns the papal bull at center. Also pictured, interspersed with scenes of his life, are Hus, Wycliffe, Melanchthon and Bugenhagen, among others (Library of Congress).**

people are lazy when it comes to Word and sacrament."[2] There seemed to be little enthusiasm for social justice or outward displays of good will between neighbors. Instead he found that many Germans were living exactly as they were before the Reform movement. Too many former priests, now pastors, abused alcohol and lived in sloth and immorality. Some lived openly with their mistresses. Luther saw old familiar signs of corruption; in some cases greedy officials had seized lands in the name the church, and in others the old systems of mandatory tithing had been renewed. Abandoned monasteries belonged to noblemen. Worst of all, the common people seemed to have accepted the listless state of affairs. Doctrinal cleansing alone, Luther realized, could not erase the remnants of hundreds of years of Roman control and abuse.

Assisted by Melanchthon and with the consent of Duke John and other princes, Luther moved to address the stagnation and regain the early momentum of the Reformation. The first step was asserting local control. He repeated his insistence that community churches call their own pastors, to be chosen democratically and not appointed by Roman directive. These men who would hold power were the church's servants, not her masters. They held their positions because they had been chosen by parishioners, and they could be recalled by their parishioners; in this way corruption could be held in check. Immoral pastors must be removed. They must be encouraged to marry their mistresses and become fathers to their children. In some cases they had to give public declarations of their changed behavior. Most important, pastors needed to provide proof that they were preaching the pure Word of God, free from Roman interpretation, guided only by Scripture and the Holy Spirit.

Still, Luther was a bit uneasy with unrestrained local control, and so the provinces began to build an organization. An episcopal structural system was established, and the most talented of pastors were given supervisory duties. These supervisors, or bishops, were not provided positions of power because of special favor or ecclesiastical procession, and they were not beholden to a central power. Rather, they were individuals who could be trusted to ensure that the reforms of the movement would be carried out. They were to make sure that the Gospel was preached and that the sacraments were properly distributed. They were to live lives free from scandal and corruption. While Luther was wary of any structure that might bear similarity to Rome, he had to strike a balance between unfettered local control and an all-powerful centralized authority. He was uneasy with the prospects of locals acting as their own superintendents. "It is true that all Christians are priests," he said, "but not all are pastors."[3]

Education of the people, never a priority of Rome, became a central component of Luther's organizational reform. He looked first to his university. While Wittenberg had managed to escape the rioting and carnage that marked the Peasants' War, the city felt the destructive effects of the uprising in other ways. Some peasants, members of Luther's own Castle Church congregation, had ignored his advice and left to join Müntzer's ill-fated rebellion, never to return. While only a few university students left town to join the fight, others left school after the war was over and returned to their homes outside Wittenberg, helping get their family farms and shops back in operation. When the fighting finally stopped in the summer of 1525, only forty students were enrolled at the university, down from a high of nearly six hundred just a few years before. Alarmed at the decreased numbers, Luther wrote to Duke John, Frederick the Wise's successor. He asked for help in "putting the university in order," and noted that "it would be a shame that such a university as this, from which the gospel has gone out over the whole world, should perish." Luther urged John to carefully consider the important work that went on at the university. "We need men everywhere and must take the necessary means to train them," he wrote. "The world cannot be ruled by force alone, but there must be learned men to help with God's work and keep a hold on the people with teaching and preaching, for if there were no teachers or preachers the civil power would not long stand, not to mention the fact that the kingdom of God would entirely leave us."[4]

In response to Luther's pleas, Duke John ordered that the university be reorganized. New students were recruited, and enrollment rebounded to healthier levels. New faculty were hired, men who were, as Luther insisted, learned in the Augustinian tradition and dedicated to Reformation ideals. Most important, Duke John pledged to increase financial support for the university. Luther was given a raise to 200 gulden per year making him, along with Melanchthon, the highest paid professors at the institution.

Luther resumed his lectures on the books of the Bible, focusing on Jude, Genesis, Exodus, and Deuteronomy. He also produced a comprehensive series of commentaries on the twelve Minor Prophets. Usually his lectures coincided with his sermons at Castle Church, so that students and parishioners alike heard his messages. In 1527 he began a three-year inquiry into Ecclesiastes, which he thought to be one of the most difficult and misunderstood books of the Bible. He concluded that Solomon's masterwork condemns "man's depraved affections and desires." In essence, Luther wrote, Ecclesiastes was a book about economics and the all-important social order, for it teaches that "we may with Thanksgiving use the things that are present and the creatures of God that are generously given to us … without anxiety about the things that are still to come."[5] Solomon's message, Luther argued, was relevant for current times.

Luther diverted briefly into the New Testament with lectures on Peter, Timothy, and the first book of John. Next to St. Paul, Luther held John in the highest esteem of all biblical figures. John's writing, he wrote, was "able to raise up afflicted hearts, so fairly and sweetly does it depict Christ for us."[6] Luther then returned to the Old Testament with an exhaustive study of Isaiah. For all of his courses, lectures, and commentaries, Luther utilized his German Bible, for he thought it important that the next generation of German scholars, priests, and teachers be prepared to pass on God's words in the language of the people. Luther continued to enjoy the admiration of his students. "He always had the material for his lectures well in hand," wrote one, "so that they never contained anything that was not sharp and to the point."[7]

Luther was not content merely to improve the conditions of his university. Indeed, he campaigned to transform the entire German educational system. He believed that the principal reason for education was to produce *theodidacti,* or people taught by God. Men, women, and children, Luther thought, were to become informed of God's message of hope and salvation through Christ. Since generations of Germans had not received proper religious instruction, he wrote, "the schools are declining, the universities becoming weak, and the cloisters are ruined. Such grass dries up, and the flowers fall, as Isaiah says, when God does not move upon them by his Word."[8] Abandoned monasteries, Luther reasoned, should become Christian schools that German youth—all German youth, not just the children of wealthy merchants and aristocracy—could attend. He was a proponent of the liberal arts: languages (particularly Greek and Latin), history, mathematics, art, music theory, and select philosophy. He believed that this subject matter provided the best context for proper study of Holy Scripture. Educated believers, believed Luther, could better know God and better serve Christ in this world.

Relying on Solomon, Luther was convinced that education played another important role: it was essential for an ordered society. Luther cited the example of ancient Rome in a 1524 tract called "*To the Councilmen of all the Cities of Germany on the Erection and Maintenance of Christian Schools.*" He wrote, "The Romans brought up their children so that by the time they were fifteen, eighteen, or twenty they knew marvelously well Latin, Greek, and all the liberal arts, so that they were straightway fitted for war or government, and were brilliant, reasoning, able persons, polished in all the arts and sciences." Luther's penchant for social order—the same reasoning he used in refusing to back the peasants in their recent uprising—remained a steadfast component of his theology. "A city's best and greatest welfare, safety, and strength," he wrote, "consists rather in its having many able, learned, wise, honorable, and well-educated citizens." Justice and social order—indeed, the very preservation of civilized life—depended upon the exercise of the temporal government. And for that, the citizenry had to be properly educated. For Luther, the true function of the secular realm was to "make men out of wild beasts."[9]

Luther had practical suggestions to achieve his educated society. Luther recommended that children—both boys and girls—go to school for two hours each day; the rest of their time could be spent learning a trade as their parents saw fit. In addition to converting vacant monasteries and convents to schools, he believed that libraries should be built in every town, financed by tax revenues, and new and better books be purchased each year. Later he wrote that "We ought properly to give a hundred gulden to this cause for every gulden we would give to fight the Turk, even if he were breathing down our necks."[10] Luther also believed in a highly educated clergy, and thus young boys should be encouraged to consider pastoral vocations. God's church needed "even those of lesser ability ... for we need not only highly learned doctors and masters of Holy Scripture, but also ordinary pastors who will teach the gospel and the catechism to the young and the ignorant and who will baptize and administer the sacrament."[11]

Luther, now a family man, did not overlook parental responsibility in education. He noted Psalm 78: 5–7, where the Lord "commanded our fathers to teach to their children, that the next generation might know them ... so that they should set their hope in God and not forget the works of God." Luther exaggerated the harsh conditions of his own childhood learning. "Our schools are no more the hell and purgatory in which we were martyred by declension and conjugation, although we learned nothing of value with all our whipping, trembling, aguish, and crying. If people now take so much time teaching their children to play cards and dance, why should they not take an equal amount to teach them to read and learn other things while they are young, idle, and curious?" His own children, he added, "would have to learn not only the languages and history but also singing, music, and the whole mathematics." His support for the liberal arts was unwavering. For all of his own educational achievement, Luther felt his own learning was lacking. "It is a sorrow to me that I was not taught to read more poetry and history."[12] In a 1530 sermon called *"On Keeping Children in School"* (which was later published and distributed, as were many of his sermons and lectures), he wrote, "If I could leave the office of preacher and my other duties, or were forced to do so, there is no other office I would rather have than that of schoolmaster or teacher of boys. For I know that next to the office of preaching, this is the best, the greatest, and the most useful there is. In fact, I am not absolutely certain which of the two is better."[13]

*

For all of his interests in matters of faith and society, Luther still relished theological challenges above all. Indeed, for Luther, living his faith meant testing his own convictions and challenging the assertions of others. He was accustomed to disagreement with other religious scholars and often relished the opportunity for debate. In the later years of the 1520s, Luther faced two significant theological issues, one from within the Catholic Church and another from fellow Protestants.

Desiderius Erasmus of Rotterdam was a Catholic priest and scholar who aggressively attacked a few of Luther's positions. Brilliant and witty, Erasmus was the leading humanist of the age, acknowledged by many as the Renaissance titan of philosophy. While Erasmus was in many ways a dedicated Catholic—he accepted the authority of the pope, for example, adhered to seven and not two sacraments, and believed in the perpetual virginity of Mary— he also agreed with Luther that the Church was in need of certain reforms. It was proper, he thought, for lay believers to access the Bible. He rejected the importance of relics, pilgrimages, indulgences, vows, fasting, the invocation of the saints, and other Church-based precepts. His book *In Praise of Folly* was an attack on many of these practices, which he compared to the most frivolous superstitions of European society. His notions, charged monks who rejected the Reformation, "prepared the way and were responsible for Martin Luther. Erasmus laid the egg and Luther hatched it." (But Erasmus dismissed this claim with typical wit. "Luther," he wrote, "had hatched a different bird entirely.")[14]

Erasmus disagreed with Luther's assertion that Catholic sacred tradition was useless, and was offended by a notion that there could be, in his words, "no pure interpretation of Scripture anywhere but in Wittenberg."[15] While Luther admired Erasmus' intellectual abilities, he was angered that Erasmus would recognize many of Rome's obvious flaws but not break from the Church. In 1524 Erasmus challenged Luther directly with his *Dialogue on Free Will*, noting that in taking on the great Reformer he was like a fly landing on an elephant. His tract, however, caused a great commotion.

Like others before him, Erasmus was troubled that Luther seemed miraculously to possess the wisdom to challenge the Holy Church. What gives you this right, Erasmus asked? How is it that you alone can are wiser and more learned that all of the saints and theologians through the centuries? Was it not possible that Luther, and not the Church, was in error? Erasmus' primary contention was that mankind did indeed possess a measure of *liberum arbitrium*, or free will. Man could make choices, could choose to accept God or reject him. Did not Adam make his choice with Eve in the Garden of Eden? Erasmus argued logically that man could choose to avail himself to the instrumentalities of faith and therefore accept salvation, or reject it. The doctrines of repentance, baptism, even conversion to Christianity itself, depended upon the free will of humans. Grace assisted man and allowed him to come to the knowledge of God. Therefore, Erasmus claimed, grace and free will worked hand in hand. Further, Erasmus praised the sincerity of skeptics and doubters. He believed that the Bible was full of contradictions that puzzled the most learned of scholars, much less the common man. In the face of such doubt, he wrote, man should look to the authority of the Church and submit to it.

For nearly a year Luther seethed quietly at Erasmus. "I vehemently and from the very heart hate Erasmus," he told Kate.[16] Erasmus was a "Lucian," an "Epicurean," (both medieval terms for atheist). Then, with the Peasants' War over, the organization of the Reformation Church begun, and, not insignificantly, with his Kate's urging, Luther fought back. In late 1525 he published *The Bondage of the Will*, which he thought to be the finest work of his career, and which is considered still today as a classic doctrine of the Reformation.

Luther began modestly. He was merely "a minor academic," he wrote, "from a fairly new faculty in a small town in an obscure part of eastern Germany ... an uncultivated fellow who has always moved in uncultivated circles."[17] Luther readily acknowledged, as he always had, that he harbored the same doubts as Erasmus. What if he, and not the Church, was in error? Had he "seduced so many others ... to be damned into eternity?" He had asked himself repeatedly, "Shall you, an individual and insignificant man, dare such momentous undertakings? What if you are the sole sinner? If God permits so many great ones to err, might he not permit one individual to do so?"[18] But for all his limitations and his own self-doubt, Luther rested, as always, on faith and Scripture. After all, he wrote, "no man perceives one iota of what is in the Scriptures unless he has the Spirit of God."[19]

There was no ambiguity in the Bible, Luther wrote. Any confusion was the fault of the reader, not with the text. "Truly it is stupid and impious," he wrote, "when we know that the subject matter of Scripture has all been placed in the clearest light, to call it obscure on account of a few obscure words…. It is true that for many people much remains abstruse; but this is not due to the obscurity of Scripture, but to the blindness or indolence of those who will not take that trouble to look at the very clearest truth." If Scripture was obscure or ambiguous, Luther wondered, why had God given it to us? Attacks on the clarity of Scripture were a tired Roman ploy designed to keep submissive Christians in line. Believers did not need Rome to interpret the plain language of God, he wrote. They were themselves empowered to do that. Augustine had said much the same thing centuries ago. The assertions of Erasmus revealed him to be "vile," a "viper," a "child of Satan," and worst of all, a non–Christian.[20]

Luther returned to the heart of the matter, the very foundation upon which the Reformation rested: a rejection of all human works, and dependence on the grace of God alone for salvation. Man was, Luther insisted, absolutely helpless in his sin and sinful nature. He could do nothing to rise above his natural, squalid state. Contrary to Erasmus' assertion of the free will of human beings, Luther argued that mankind's sinful nature rendered them slaves to depravity and wickedness. Man was free to sin—only to sin—unless blessed by the miraculous intervention of God's sovereign and saving grace. Luther argued that sin incapacitates humans from achieving their own salvation, or even from working toward it. Man cannot choose between good and evil because he is overwhelmed by evil. For Luther, the central issue of Christianity was: what does God do in salvation, and what does man do? His answer was straightforward, as clear as the Scripture he loved. Since we are by nature slaves to sin and to Satan, if we are to be saved, it comes not through choice—not through an exercise of human will, as Erasmus claimed—but by faith alone. It is possible to please God, Luther wrote, "only once he has freed us."[21]

In his own life, Luther had faced the demons that tormented him in his youth—that still tormented him on occasion—but he had not done it alone. He had not met his *Anfechtungen* by himself. His uncertainty had given way to his content. "But I by the grace of God see these things clearly," he wrote, "because I see other tumults greater than these which will arise in ages to come, in comparison with which these appear but as the whispering of a breath of air, and the murmuring of a gentle brook." There was no need to question the eternal mystery of God, Luther concluded. That is the Lord's concern alone. "For as the saying truly applies," he wrote, "'things above us are no business of ours.'"[22] Luther's *Bondage of the Will* was a song of celebration, a "raucous hymn to the freedom of God."[23] Luther's rejection of Erasmus' concepts of free will, and his defense of justification by grace and faith, became known as "the Manifesto of the Reformation."[24]

Less easily dismissed was another Protestant reformer, Ulrich Zwingli of Zurich. Born just seven weeks after Luther in 1484, Zwingli led the reform movement in Switzerland. There were many similarities between the two men. They were the same age. Both were of peasant stock whose parents had achieved middle-class status: Luther's father became a successful miner, Zwingli's a prosperous farmer. Both studied at prestigious universities: Luther at Erfurt and Zwingli at Basel, Bern and Vienna. And both men were at the forefront of the break with Rome in their countries. Each rejected papal authority and Catholic tradition, and each scoffed at the worth of relics, indulgences, saintly intercession, and the veneration of the Virgin Mary. Each man stood in favor of *sola scriptura;* divine Scripture alone.

But here the similarities ended. For Luther the starting point of reform came as a result of his inner struggle as a monk, and finally his breakthrough, the realization that God's righteousness mercifully justifies sinners through faith and grace. Zwingli's fear was not personal.

Rather, he was concerned with the plight of his countrymen. While Luther was mindful of social reform, Zwingli gave it his highest priority. He saw religion as means for the ends of social justice (a trait that would be carried on by his reform successor, John Calvin). But the most serious disagreement between the two reformers was their view of Christ's presence at the Eucharist, the Lord's Supper. While the two sparred over their theological differences through their writings and preaching, it took a political crisis to bring them face to face.

In 1526 the Roman Catholic Emperor, Charles V, was at war against the French and Ottoman empires. Because he needed the support of Protestant regions and their princes, at his urging the Diet of Speyer had effectively suspended the Edict of Worms, which had outlawed Luther and his messages of reform. But when the fighting subsided, Pope Clement VII pressured the legislators at the second Diet of Speyer, held in 1529, to reinstate the Edict. Luther and his followers once again faced persecution.

This reimplementation of the Edict alarmed Protestant princes across northern Germany. Philip of Hesse, in particular, saw the dangers and feared that Catholic military forces would move against Protestants. Philip had met Luther in 1521 at the Diet of Worms, and with the encouragement of Melanchthon became a Protestant three years later. He was the very same man who had helped put down the Peasants' uprising and had defeated Thomas Müntzer at the Battle of Frankenhausen. Now Philip saw a chance to galvanize Lutheran princes from the north and east and forge a united front, a display of power that would give pause to Catholic thoughts of armed conflict. He forged an alliance of Protestant princes and powers, including representatives from Hesse, Nuremberg, Saxony, Strasburg, and Ulm.

In the first week of October 1529, Hesse invited Luther, Melanchthon, Zwingli, and sixty other Protestant leaders to his castle at Marburg, set on a high hill above the Lahn River. While Philip's primary objective was to unite the Protestant states in a political alliance, the summit held important theological implications, as well. Most particularly, Philip felt the need to reconcile the views of Luther and Zwingli, for it was essential to solidify emerging Protestant doctrines in the face of Catholic oppression.

In fact, the reformers in attendance found agreement on almost all theological issues. They were united in *sola scriptura*, justification by faith and grace, the Holy Trinity, the life, death, and resurrection of the Lord, original sin, and the number of sacraments. They opposed papal authority and the idea of papal infallibility. They rejected standard Catholic positions on Church tradition, intercession of the saints, glorification of Mary, indulgences, relics, and pilgrimages. But they found no agreement in the meaning of the Eucharist, and the debate between Luther and Zwingli was the highlight of the colloquy.

Luther had long advocated the real presence of Christ in the bread and wine. He had rejected the Catholic doctrine of transubstantiation, whereby the elements are changed into the body and blood of Christ. He believed, rather, in what came to be known as "consubstantiation"; that is, the body and blood are present "in, with and under" the bread and wine. Luther took the words of Christ at the Last Supper literally: *"Hoc est corpus meum,"* ("this is my body) and "this is my blood." To emphasize the point in front of Zwingli and the other reformers, Luther wrote the words in chalk on a table, and then covered the writing with a cloth. Repeatedly throughout the debate he lifted the cloth to show the words of Christ were still there. Luther embraced the dual nature of the elements—bread and body, wine and blood—as the perfect illustration of Christ as both human and divine. The *finite,* the bread and wine of the Lord's Supper, Luther argued, was capable of bearing the *infinite*, the resurrected body and blood of Christ.[25]

Zwingli rejected the Catholic Church's views—and Luther's. He, too, cited biblical passages for his assertion that the bread and wine merely symbolized Christ's presence at the meal. For Zwingli, the language of John 6:63 was instructive: "It is the spirit that gives life; the flesh is of no avail." Zwingli held that this language negates the necessity—even the usefulness—of Christ's physical presence at the meal. He further relied on the Christian belief in the Lord's ascension and aftermath. According to Acts 1:9, forty days after his resurrection, Christ ascended into heaven "and sits at the right hand of God." It was impossible for the humanist-leaning (with its emphasis on reason) Zwingli to believe that Christ could reside in both heaven and in the elements of the Eucharist simultaneously. The *finite* could not bear the *infinite*. The words that Luther took literally: "this is my body," were to be taken figuratively. For Zwingli, the Lord's Supper was a celebratory feast, a blessed commemoration of Christ's victory over sin and death.

At the end of the four-day summit, the various groups of Protestants had agreed on fourteen points, which were drawn up in a formal document called the Marburg Articles. They did not agree on the presence of Christ in the Eucharist. As usual, Luther took it personally when colleagues did not agree with him in theological matters. When Zwingli extended his hand at the end of the summit Luther refused to shake it. "We are not of the same spirit," he said. He predicted calamity for the humanists. "We are not of one mind," he told Zwingli's followers. "We commend you to the judgment of God."[26]

Zwingli continued with his humanist views. He came to believe that all good people, Christians and non–Christians alike, would be together in Paradise. "In short," he said, "there has not been any good man, or any holy mind, or any faithful soul, from the very beginning of the world even to its end, whom you will see there with God. What could be imagined more joyful, pleasing, and noble, than this sight?" To Luther this was proof that Zwingli was a heathen. In 1531, Zwingli was killed by Catholic forces in the War of Kappel in Switzerland, where he was serving as a military chaplain. His body was burned and tossed on a pile of dung. Luther believed that Zwingli's death was a judgment from Heaven, and called it "a victory for us.... I wish from my heart that Zwingli could be saved, but I fear for the contrary, for Christ has said that those who deny him shall be damned."[27]

Besides the Lord's Supper, the only other sacrament Protestants recognized was baptism. This, too, became a controversial subject in the late 1520s. The Anabaptist movement began in Switzerland, probably as an offshoot of Zwingli's reform preaching, although it also had roots in the earlier German mysticism activities such as with the Zwickau prophets. Anabaptism means "one who baptizes again." Anabaptists believed that infants could not form or express the acceptance of Jesus as their Savior; they simply could not yet have faith. Thus, those who had been baptized as infants needed to be baptized again.

Anabaptists were persecuted by Catholics and other Protestants, as well. By 1528 the Holy Roman Empire considered Anabaptists to be subversive, and instituted the death penalty for those involved in the rebaptism practice. At first Luther opposed the death penalty law, believing that coercion could never be forced upon matters of faith. Later, however, he modified his views; he continued to support the death penalty for the most radical Anabaptists, but preferred that they be exiled instead, so that they would not spread their radical views. (Zwingli also supported the death penalty and in fact looked on with satisfaction as some Anabaptists were drowned in Zürich in 1528.)

While Luther had long been a proponent of infant baptism, over the years he had gone through a series of changing rationales for upholding the practice. At first he likened baptism to the biblical concept of a covenant, or promise of salvation, between God and person. Later he emphasized that the parents, family, godparents, and supporting Christian community expressed their faith on behalf of the child when they presented him or her for the baptismal rite. For a short time, Luther also believed that infant baptism was proper since it had been utilized for centuries, but this argument was weak: Luther had, after all, rejected the very same rationale as regards priestly celibacy and other Church traditions. In the end Luther came to the conclusion that the vehicle of baptism was provided as yet another example of God's grace. Therefore, there was no need for the infant to bring his or her faith, for how could one be sure that the faith was strong or sincere enough? It was God's gift, and it was God who did the necessary saving work. Further, Christ's great commission to his followers was specific: "Go therefore and make disciples of all nations, baptizing them in the name of the Father and the Son and the Holy Spirit, teaching them to observe all that I commanded you."[28]

In another example of irreconcilable splits in the Protestant faith, the Anabaptists clung to their beliefs even though they were effectively shunned by most of the rest of Christendom. They were content in this separation, however, and set up communes and settlements where they could live disciplined and non-violent lives. Their practices live on today in the Mennonite, Hutterite, and Amish denominations of Europe and America. As for Philip's dream of a united Protestant front, the disagreement over the presence of Christ in the Eucharist prevented this from happening. It signaled a split in Protestant denominations which continues to modern times.

Luther never stopped writing and teaching. Appalled at the "deplorable, miserable condition which I discovered lately,"[29] (he was referring to the visitations), Luther wrote two *catechisms* or doctrinal summaries, to be used as basic instructional guides for Christians. His *Kleine Katechismus (Small Catechism)*, written for children in 1529, examines the Ten Commandments, the Apostles' Creed, the Lord's Prayer, the sacraments of Baptism and the Eucharist, and the Office of the Keys with the Confession of Sins. It was written in a clear and concise style and generally followed a question-and-answer format. Luther's explanation of the meaning of the First Commandment, for example, was presented as follows:

> The First Commandment.
> *Thou shalt have no other gods.*
> What does this mean?
> *We should fear, love, and trust in God above all things.*[30]

Similarly, Luther's *Große Katechismus (Large Catechism)* covered the same tenets of Lutheran doctrine but was intended for pastors that they might educate their congregations properly. Luther was extremely proud of his catechisms. He considered them, along with *The Bondage of the Will*, his most important and enduring works. Five hundred years later, Luther's catechisms are still in print and are used as essential guides in Lutheran instruction, for children, families, pastors, and congregations around the world.

Luther next took on a project that had been simmering in his mind for several years: utilizing his justification doctrine and the purity of the Gospel, he reworked the medieval liturgy of the Church. His groundbreaking *Deutsche Messe* (German Mass) provided a framework for a basic worship service in the language of his people. The outline of his liturgy has remained essentially unchanged for Lutherans and many other Protestants through modern times.[31]

Music played a key role in Luther's liturgy. He viewed it as an expression of faith to be used both in prayer and praise. Luther appreciated the Catholic tradition of music in worship, but he thought that Catholic music reflected the view of Church as an institution separate from and above the congregation. For Luther, music served a different purpose. While music did not promote justification—that came about only through grace and faith—it did share in the work of the Holy Spirit. By praising God in music, humans might "relish with amazement God's absolute and perfect wisdom." God was "excellently honored ... by the art of music," Luther believed. It even had supernatural qualities. Music, Luther wrote, is a great enemy of Satan, and an instrument to drive away temptations and evil thoughts." It certainly served Luther as an antidote for *Anfechtungen*.[32] Luther wrote:

> Music is a fair and lovely gift of God which has often wakened and moved me to the joy of preaching.... I have no use for cranks who despise music, because it is a gift of God. Music drives away the devil and makes people happy; they forget all wrath, unchastity, arrogance and the like.... Experience proves that next to the Word of God, only music deserves to be extolled as the mistress and governess of the feelings of the human heart.... My heart bubbles up and overflows in response to music, which has so often refreshed me and delivered me from dire plagues.[33]

Luther had loved music since his childhood days in the boys' choir in Erfurt. As an adult he became a prolific hymn writer. The first Lutheran hymnal, *Achtliederbuch*, was published in 1524, and Luther supplied four of its eight songs. He followed this effort with eighteen more in the *Erfurt Enchiridion*, and twenty-four more in *Ein Geistliches Gesang-Buchlein*, the first choral hymnal featuring settings by Johann Walter, the celebrated composer, cantor, and director of Frederick the Wise's chapel. In his lifetime Luther wrote thirty-six hymns. He usually wrote both words and lyrics; sometimes he borrowed melodies from traditional German folk songs. Luther wrote about specific themes and stories of the Bible, the Christian calendar, and the message of the Gospel. He also found inspiration in the people and events of the Reformation he had sparked.[34]

For all of his musical creativity, *Ein feste Burg ist Unser Gott* ("A Mighty Fortress Is Our God"), written around 1529, is Luther's masterpiece. It is based on the reassuring words of Psalm 46:

> God is our refuge and strength, an ever-present help in trouble.
> Therefore we will not fear, though the earth gives way and the mountains fall into the heart of the sea,
> Though its waters roar and foam and the mountains quake with their surging.
> There is a river whose streams make glad the city of God, the holy place where the Most High dwells.
> God is within her, she will not fall; God will help her at break of day.
> Nations are in uproar, kingdoms fall; he lifts his voice, the earth melts...
> The Lord Almighty is with us; the God of Jacob is our fortress.

Luther's powerful words and rousing melody makes *A Mighty Fortress* perhaps the most famous hymn in the history of Christianity. Often called the Battle Hymn of the Reformation, its themes capture the meaning of the Reformation itself: faith in a loving and powerful God, the futility of mankind's effort without God's saving grace, and the ultimate triumph over Satan. It also reflects Luther's lifelong belief that God and the Devil were locked in a fierce battle for the souls of humans and that the Lord would emerge victorious. Luther's hymn has been adopted and incorporated into works by Bach, Handel, Mendelssohn, Wagner, Debussy, and many other classical composers. Translated into eighty languages, *A Mighty Fortress* remains a staple of Protestant hymnals to this day, and can be found in some Roman Catholic hymnals, as well. A popular English translation is by Frederick Hedge:

> A mighty fortress is our God, a bulwark never failing;
> Our helper he amid the flood of mortal ills prevailing.
> For still our ancient foe doth seek to work us woe;
> His craft and power are great, and armed with cruel hate,
> On earth is not his equal.

> Did we in our own strength confide, our striving would be losing,
> Were not the right man on our side, the man of God's own choosing.
> Dost ask who that may be? Christ Jesus, it is he;
> Lord Sabaoth, his name, from age to age the same,
> And he must win the battle.

> And though this world, with devils filled, should threaten to undo us,
> We will not fear, for God hath willed his truth to triumph through us.
> The Prince of Darkness grim, we tremble not for him;
> His rage we can endure, for lo, his doom is sure;
> One little word shall fell him.

> That word above all earthly powers, no thanks to them, abideth;
> The Spirit and the gifts are ours, thru him who with us sideth.
> Let goods and kindred go, this mortal life also;
> The body they may kill; God's truth abideth still;
> His kingdom is forever.

• Chapter 18 •

A "great and constant disturbance"

In terms of religion and politics, Germany knew no rest. In 1530 yet another Diet, or legislative assembly, was called, this one at Augsburg in Bavaria. The split between Catholics and Protestants had become so pronounced that Emperor Charles V felt he had to take steps to somehow bring the reformers back in line and reunify the Holy Roman Empire under the Catholic faith. He left Spain and met with Pope Clement VII in Rome, and then came to Augsburg, marking his first appearance in Germany since the 1521 Diet at Worms. Two matters were on the agenda: the defense of Christendom against the Turks, who were now threatening to take control of Vienna, and the state of theological reform in the empire. Charles sensed that Germans were more interested in religious matters than military affairs. Surprisingly, Charles issued a conciliatory public statement that preceded his arrival in Augsburg. He would urge the legislators to "give charitable hearing to every man's opinions, thoughts, and notions, to understand them, to weigh them, to bring and reconcile men to a unity in Christian truth."[1] Although the thought of compromise angered the pope (he threatened to cancel the Diet, but finally relented), Charles asked that religious leaders from both sides join Germany's politicians and meet at Augsburg in the summer.

Luther was skeptical that any good could come from another legislative assembly, and, like the pope, he was of no mind to compromise. Still, at the bidding of the Elector Duke John, Luther made plans to travel. In his farewell sermons he told his parishioners at Castle Church that matters of great importance would be discussed at Augsburg (the "tyranny of the Turks, and the false sects of the papists") and asked for their prayers. This Diet, he cautioned, "concerns all of us."[2] Just before Easter in early April he set out on the journey with Melanchthon, Johann Bugenhagen (pastor of St. Mary's church in Wittenberg, and Luther's confessor), Justas Jonas, Spalatin, and Johann Agricola (a schoolteacher from Eisleben who had acted as recording secretary for Luther at Leipzig). Also along were Luther's nephew Cyriac Kaufman and a graduate student named Veit Dietrich, who would act as Luther's attendants.

The party traveled by wagon through the green German countryside, passing through the familiar towns of Grimma, Altenburg, Eisenburg, and Jena, all Lutheran strongholds. At Weimar, on Palm Sunday, Luther preached at the local church, as he did in successive days at Saalfeld, Gräfenthal, and Neustadt an der Heide. Duke John met the group at Torgau and initial plans and strategies for Augsburg Diet were laid out. On April 24 (Good Friday), the group reached Coburg on the Thuringian border, where they stayed for ten days. Luther preached six times in that span, but his topics did not touch on the pending political crisis;

rather, he criticized the pope and his bishops ("fanatics of self-chosen righteousness," he called them), and their denial of Christian freedom. As he so often did, he coupled his attacks on Rome with the good news of God's grace and Christ's triumph over death.

At Coburg the Wittenberg group was tasked by Duke John with drafting a formal document setting forth the Lutheran articles of faith and church order, for presentation at the Diet. Luther compiled a working list of contrasts between the "church of Christ" and the "church of the pope." Within the week the document was nearly finished, and it was agreed that Melanchthon would polish it, and deliver it, in Augsburg. Ordinarily, that job would go to Luther by virtue of his leadership position within the reform movement, but now Duke John informed Luther that the Reformer would not be attending the Diet. John had learned that the town council of Augsburg was concerned that, in view of the presence of Charles and his entourage, Luther's safety could not be guaranteed. Luther would have to remain behind in Coburg while the other theologians addressed the assembly. Messengers would keep Luther posted on the Diet's progress, and in this way he could be available for consultation. Grudgingly, Luther accepted the plan.

Along with his student and nephew, Luther was given quarters at the Coburg Castle, set high on a hill above the town. The *Festung*, or fortress, had been built in the tenth century and was one of Germany's grandest castles. Luther settled into two rooms in the *Hohe Kemenate* (high lady's bower), overlooking the Thuringia Forest. Unhappy that he was not in Augsburg, and depressed to be away from Kate for so long, Luther instructed orderlies to paint some of his favorite Psalms on the walls of his room: "I shall not die, but I shall live, and recount the deeds of the Lord," and "For the Lord knows the way of the righteous, but the way of the wicked shall perish."[3] He called his sanctuary "the realm of the birds," and wrote that "the jackdaws and crows" were holding a Diet of their own in the trees and shrubs outside his window. "They fare in and out," Luther wrote, "and keep up a racket without ceasing, as if they are drunk…. They care nothing for palaces, their hall is vaulted with the broad vault of Heaven, and its walls are as wide as the world."[4]

Here Luther lived for the next five months, a stretch that surely reminded him of his exile at the Wartburg Castle nine years before (he even grew back his beard, as he had when disguised as *Junker George*). Coburg Castle was a dark, imposing place, fortified with thirty soldiers who manned the triple walls and towers day and night. As it was not generally known that he was staying there, Luther lived quietly, relying upon Dietrich and Cyriac for company. Castle vicar Johann Grosch heard Luther's confessions and administered the Eucharist. Although he was on good terms with Paul Bader, the *Gerichtsvollzieher* (bailiff), Luther did not get along with Arnold von Falkenstein, the castle administrator, and complained about him to the Elector.

Luther was lonely and uncomfortable at the castle. He slept poorly and suffered from a steady variety of ailments. He had recurring headaches and toothaches. He complained of dizziness and ringing in his ears, and his circulation was poor. An open cut on his shin refused to heal. His limbs were so sore that he had difficulty moving about. He was constipated and required medication for release. He needed glasses but could not be fitted with a satisfactory pair. He ate and drank too much and gained weight. Luther blamed the heat and the wind— and of course, the Devil—for all of his maladies. He was frustrated and listless. "I don't want to do anything more," he wrote, "for I see well that the years are going by."[5] Eventually as the weeks and months passed, word of his whereabouts got out around Germany, and he began to receive visitors. He was happy to see old friends and colleagues but the constant entertaining exhausted him.

Then on June 5 Luther received word that his father Hans had died in Mansfeld. Luther took to his room and grieved alone for several days. He had last written to his father in February, when he had learned of Hans' illness. If the end was near, Luther wrote, "we shall shortly see each other again in the presence of Christ."[6] Now he wrote to Melanchthon in Augsburg. "Although it is a solace to me to know that he fell asleep softly, strong in the faith of Christ, nevertheless mercy and the memory of his most delightful companionship have stricken my heart so that I have ever scarcely so despised death." Remnants of *Anfechtungen*, the dreaded depression that had plagued so much of his youth, resurfaced temporarily. Luther pondered his own mortality as well as his legacy. "How often we die before we really die! I succeed now to the heritage of his name, being almost the oldest Luther of my race.... I will not write more now, for I am sad."[7] He mourned for two days, alone in his tower rooms. But within the week Luther's younger brother James visited him at the castle, and his spirits were lifted. With Dietrich acting as his secretary, he went back to work, dictating commentaries on the Psalms and various books of the New Testament.

Meanwhile the Diet at Augsburg commenced. The Protestants' document, placed in final form by Melanchthon, was called the *Augsburg Confession,* or *Augustana.* One of the most important documents of the Reformation (and still used today by Lutherans), the *Augsburg Confession* summarized the basic theology of Lutheran reform. It also set forth, in plain style, the common ground that Protestants found with Catholicism while at the same time articulating their doctrinal differences. Melanchthon presented the *Augsburg Confession* to the Diet on June 25 at the chapel of the Episcopal Palace. The main body of the *Confession* consisted of twenty-eight statements, or articles. The first twenty-one articles set forth basic doctrines of Lutheran belief and practice, including statements of faith on: "God," "Original Sin," "The Son of Man," "Justification by Faith," "Baptism," "The Lord's Supper," "Confession," "Free Will," "Good Works," "Worship of the Saints," and others. The other seven articles summarized familiar expressions of Luther's views of areas of Catholic abuses, including "Of the Marriage of Priests," "Of the Mass," Of Confession," "Of Monastic Vows," and "Of Ecclesiastical Power." The document was signed by many of Germany's most prominent reform leaders, including the Elector Duke John, Margrave George of Brandenburg-Ansbach, Duke Ernest of Lüneburg, Philip of Hesse, Duke Wolfgang of Anhalt, and representatives of several German cities. These leaders were anxious not only to publish their religious views, but also to exercise the significant political clout the movement now wielded; they referred to their jurisdictions as the Protestant Imperial States of the Realm. When Luther received his copy of the *Augsburg Confession,* he wrote Melanchthon that "it pleases me very much." He was particularly happy that it was presented "before kings" and the Emperor Charles V. He worried, however, that Melanchthon might bend to Catholic pressure and negotiate some of the document's provisions, and he wished to avoid that at all cost. In fact, he advised the contingent that if anyone felt the urge to negotiate, they should return home immediately (although no one did).

The Catholic representatives (headed by Luther's old Leipzig Debate rival Johan Eck) drafted their response to the *Augsburg Confession,* which they called the *Confutation.* While Luther waited anxiously to receive and review this document, he completed projects that he had been neglecting for some time. The first, his refutation of a long-held Catholic doctrine, was a pamphlet he called the *Disavowal of Purgatory.* This concept, Luther knew, had grown out of the practice of *Seelenmessen,* or saying masses for the languishing dead. The only apparent biblical reference for this practice came from the apocryphal book of Maccabees (the passage spoke of prayers for the dead but did not directly mention purgatory), which Luther did not consider to be binding Scripture. He believed that the souls of Christian, upon their death, did not travel to a vague, suspended state between heaven and hell but instead went to be with the Lord. Purgatory, Luther calculated, had been invented by the Catholic Church as a scheme to raise money and prey on innocent, and ignorant, faithful.

Luther's second writing project that summer was called simply *The Keys,* a treatise on the proper authority of the church. Papal authority rested on Christ's statement to Peter: "And on this rock I will build my church…. I will give you the keys of the kingdom of heaven; whatever you bind on earth will be bound in heaven, and whatever you loose on earth will be loosed in heaven."[8] Luther believed, however, that the power to loose and bind applied only to the forgiveness of sins. Further, this "power of the keys" was not an expression of papal power, and it did not endow Rome with ecclesiastic authority. Because the Lord's church was not an institution, he argued, but existed wherever a community of believers resided, the Keys were intended for the benefit and admonition of repentant sinners. The mighty empire that the Church had constructed over the centuries could not be justified or sustained upon Jesus' admonition to Peter. The Catholic corruption of Scripture was an unholy abrogation of power, for Luther the most outrageous and obvious example of Roman abuse at the expense of believers. Along with the *Disavowal of Purgatory,* Luther's *The Keys* was published to great acclaim and was disseminated widely across Germany and large parts of Europe.

Finally, after six weeks of internal debate, the Church's representatives at Augsburg issued their 280-page *Confutation.* Charles' promises of openness and tolerance, made at the start of the Diet, were ignored or forgotten. The writers refuted, point-by-point, the *Augsburg Confession's* articles of faith. They insisted that the papal Church had the absolute right and duty to deny and suppress any criticism of its divinely instituted authority. Such criticism would not be tolerated, from German Protestants or anyone else. The clear implication of the *Confutation* was that Roman military force might be necessary to put down the reformers once and for all. The Emperor Charles V wrote to Pope Clement VII: "The Protestants are more unyielding and more obstinate than ever—while the [German] Catholics are generally lukewarm and but little inclined to lend a hand in the forcible conversion of those who have fallen away." Charles called for, at the very least, a discussion in Rome to discern a plan to deal with the problem. He noted that the Germans had long advocated a "Free Council" whereby they could air their grievances and make their demands known directly to the pope. Now, wrote Charles, "The welfare of Christendom absolutely requires a Council."[9] But there would be no such meeting until the Council of Trent fifteen years later, convoked by Pope Paul III.

Two more months of debate before the Diet followed the issuance of the *Confutation.* Melanchthon tried to find common ground with the papal representatives, but all efforts failed. Luther grew extremely impatient and advised his colleagues to leave Augsburg. "Our case has been made and beyond this you will accomplish nothing better," he wrote to Melanchthon. When Luther learned that Lorenzo Campeggio, an Italian cardinal who had been appointed legate (special representative of the pope) to Augsburg, had been boasting to Melanchthon of his power of dispensation, he exploded. "I shit on the legate and his lord's dispensation," wrote a furious Luther. "Home, home!"[10]

Duke John and his party finally arrived back at Coburg on October 1 and discussed with Luther what had transpired at Augsburg. They feared that military force might be used against the German Protestants. Before he left for home, Luther wrote a pamphlet called *Warning to His Dear German People*. In it he backed down from the pacifist beliefs he had articulated during the Peasants' War, and from his complete adherence to respect for secular law. The Emperor and his supporters, wrote Luther, "cannot take it for granted that no one will attack them just because we wrote and taught so emphatically not to resort to rebellion." The Peasants' rebellion had taken place under different circumstances. "I will surely hold my pen in check and keep silent and not intervene as I did in the last uprising," he wrote. "But I will not reprove those who defend themselves.... I will accept their action and let it pass as self-defense."[11]

Luther was angered by Catholic obstinacy at Augsburg. He wrote, "They thought that when they brought the Emperor in person to Germany, all would be frightened and say, 'Gracious lords, what is your wish?' When they proved mistaken and the Elector of Saxony was the first to make his appearance, my heavens, they dirtied their breeches in their terror." Luther reminded his readers that the corruption of Rome, which he had first witnessed so many years ago on his first visit to the Vatican, still continued. The decade of Reformation had seen much progress in Germany, he went on. People now "know how to believe, to live, to pray, to suffer, and to die." If Roman soldiers forced Protestants to abandon the ways of reform, Luther continued, "you will have to help burn all the German books, New Testaments, psalters, prayer books, hymnals, and to keep everyone ignorant about the Ten Commandments, the Lord's Prayer, and the Creed ... baptism, the sacrament, faith, government, matrimony, or the Gospel. You will have to help keep everyone from knowing Christian Liberty ... from placing their trust in Christ and deriving comfort from him. For all of that was nonexistent.... I swear again that I do not wish to incite or spur anyone to war or rebellion or even self-defense, but solely to peace ... if the papists ... insist on war ... may their blood be on their heads!"[12]

Luther's words of aggression could not have been predicted, and they startled his followers. Martin Bucer, who headed the Reformation in Strasbourg, France, described Luther as a man "who often loses his way and nevertheless is insufferable about returning to it; who fears the true God and seeks to glorify him from his heart, but who only becomes more agitated when admonished. This is the way God has given him to us, and this is how we must accept him."[13]

Wary of what they believed to be imminent Catholic military action against Protestants, Philip of Hesse and Duke John of Saxony called their colleagues together at Schmalkalden, in Thuringia. There the leaders of eleven German states, including Hesse, Saxony, Anhalt, Wurttemberg, and Pomerania, and eight free imperial cities, including Augsburg, Frankfurt, and Kempten, formed the Schmalkaldic League. The entities were united in their subscription to principles set forth in the *Augsburg Confession*. The League (which eventually gained pledges of support from France, England, and Denmark), was designed as a defensive alliance; its members promised to defend each other in the event of Catholic attack. The League initially consisted of 10,000 infantry and 2,000 cavalry troops, and League leaders expected battle in the spring or summer of 1531. But just as intense preparations for war were underway, a large Ottoman army attacked Roman forces in Hungary and other places in the Eastern Europe, and Charles V was forced to divert his forces there. Charles had to cancel his planned campaign against the Protestants, and the Treaty of Nuremberg, the first in a series of truces, postponed a religious war. The treaty was a "turning point," wrote Catholic historian Philip Hughes. It marked a latent recognition that "the new thing—the Protestant state, and so Protestantism—had come to stay."[14] The treaty held as long as the League existed. For another fifteen years, then, war between Catholic and Protestant forces was averted.

*

Luther returned to his world in Wittenberg. In 1533 he turned fifty years old, an elderly man by Middle Age standards. The theologian and family man was financially secure. His salary jumped from 200 to 300 gulden per year, and he sometimes received additional payments in kind; one hundred bushels of wheat, one hundred cords of wood, and two carloads of hay were usual stipends. The Elector often sent Luther items—wine, game, fruits, and kegs of cider—that were to be used for entertaining guests. Luther also received bushels of malt for beer brewing.[15] Kate looked after the books and supplemented the family income with her gardening and cattle raising.

His marriage to Kate was a happy one, and their family steadily grew. Hans, the first of six children, was born in 1526, followed by Elizabeth in 1527, Magdalene in 1529, Martin in 1531, Paul in 1533, and Margareta in 1534. Four of the children survived into adulthood, and as if to replace them, over the years the Luther's took in four orphaned children of a friend and helped raise at least ten nieces and nephews. Luther considered childbirth a blessing from God; his children were "more precious to me than all the kingdoms of Ferdinand."[16]

Luther home, Wittenberg.

When Elizabeth died before she was a year old, Luther lamented, "Never have I thought a father's heart would be so tender for his children."[17] Magdalene died in 1542 at the age of thirteen, and Luther's faith helped him overcome the deep sorrow he felt as she lay ill. "I love her very much," he prayed, "but dear God, if it be thy will to take her, I submit to thee." Magdalene died in her father's arms, and he cried out, "*Du liebes Lenchen,* you will rise and shine like the stars and the sun. How strange it is to know that she is at peace and all is well and yet to be so sorrowful."[18] For Luther, faith and family were intertwined. But the scourge of Rome, as he considered it, was never far from his thoughts. Children were "the fruit and joy of marriage," he wrote, "of which the pope is not worthy."[19]

Luther's theology guided his family life. Just as he believed in an orderly and civilized society, he also believed in the importance of structure and obedience in the home. He regarded the Fourth Commandment—"Thou shalt honor thy father and thy mother"—as "the backbone of all civil authority and social welfare in the kingdom of men on earth."[20] He believed that he was the head of his family, but he acknowledged that Kate was in charge of daily operations. While Luther held the ultimate authority, which included discipline of his children, he knew that Kate was better suited to deal with misbehavior. "A woman handles a child much better with one finger than a man does with both fists," he said. "Therefore let everyone continue to perform the work to which God has called him and for which he was destined."[21] His wife was so busy and so full of energy, Luther teased, that he called her "Lord Kate," and he did not take her for granted. He often made a point to give thanks for such a "pious and true wife on whom the husband's heart can rely…. If I had to take care of the building, brewing, and cooking, I'd soon die."[22]

Daily life took on a relatively structured routine. Before sunrise Katherine was the first to waken—Luther called her the "morning star"—and she began preparations for breakfast. Luther

Luther home, Wittenberg.

rose at five or six and spent an hour in private prayer. When all the children awoke they were gathered for an hour in family devotions, true to Luther's belief that training and educating children was noble work, looked upon with favor by God. He used his *Small Catechism* almost exclusively for these daily lessons. "You see how rich the estate of marriage is in good works," he wrote, "for into the bosom of the family God places children who are conceived from the parents' own bodies and in need of their Christian works. For example, in making known the Gospel message to them, parents act as the children's apostles, bishops, and pastors."[23] After the morning lesson Luther spent several hours writing or lecturing, or both.

At 10:00 a.m. the family gathered again for the main meal of the day, which Kate prepared in true, stout German style: chicken, pork, or fish, potatoes, vegetables, bread, fruit, and pudding. It was not unusual for the meal to last an hour or two. Luther spent the entire afternoon in his work, reading, writing, lecturing, and preaching. Katherine went about her various duties, gardening, tending to animals, brewing beer, cleaning, washing, cooking, and looking after the children. At 5:00 p.m. the family came together again for supper. This meal was relaxed and conversational. Luther selected a daily lesson from Scripture,

Statue of Kate Luther in the courtyard outside the family home, Wittenberg.

and the topic was discussed as the food was eaten. After the meal Luther often led his family in song, playing his beloved lute as the chorales, hymns, or folk songs were sung. As daylight faded Luther spent time with his children, sometimes engaging them in biblical lessons but more often conversing, discussing school lessons, or playing games such as chess or marbles. He was gentle and kind with his children. "A father should handle his children in the manner in which we observe God handling us," he wrote. "God at times afflicts and chastises us, but He does not kill us; and in the midst of the affliction He consoles, strengthens, confirms, nourishes, and favors us."[24] Bedtime for everyone came at 9:00 p.m. Luther was relieved to lie down and not just because he was tired; he loved to offer his evening prayers. "I have to hurry all day to get time to pray," he said. "It must suffice me if I can say the Ten Commandments, the Lord's Prayer, and one or two petitions besides, thinking of which I fall asleep."[25]

More than family members filled the Luther home at the old Black Cloister. The building

Kate Luther had this door installed as a gift for her husband, Luther home, Wittenberg.

was also home to a constant stream of orphans, widows, and the destitute. Traveling pastors and visiting professors often stayed with Luther, sometimes for weeks at a time. Dozens of Luther's students also lodged there at no charge, for they typically could not afford to pay for room and board. "A miscellaneous and promiscuous crowd inhabits Dr. Luther's home," a friend wrote in 1542, "and on this account there is great and constant disturbance."[26] The Luther home was well known throughout Germany as more of an inn than a family residence, and that is how Luther and Kate preferred it.

He was seen as the moral leader of the community and was increasingly asked to settle disputes between civil litigants, bickering couples, or disagreeable neighbors. He negotiated better interest rates or extended repayment plans for people who were behind on their loans. He assisted people who could not gain clear title for their land. He appeared before magistrates and pleaded for mercy on behalf of peasants who had committed crimes. Often congregations from across Saxony asked that he approve the pastors that they called to serve, or discipline pastors who had misbehaved. Luther was often eager to defend those pastors whose reputations were sullied by gossip or spite. "It is true that perhaps we preachers are not pious," he said, "but because everyone is our enemy, Paul preaches—perhaps from experience—that one should not accept everyone's complaint against the preachers."[27] One pastor, Johan Gülden from Weida, was arrested for rape. Luther looked into the accusation, found it to be valid, and insisted that the man express his remorse and ask forgiveness; the elector was not persuaded and had the man executed. An advocate of local control, Luther was not enthusiastic about the various roles he was asked to fill. "I do not intend to be a new pope, appoint

The Luther room at the home in Wittenberg. Here the family took their meals, and here the Table Talk conversations took place (courtesy Stiftung Luthergedenkstätten in Sachsen-Anhalt).

all pastors, fill all pulpits, etc."; he said, "but I grant that I am obligated to give my counsel and help to those who need it."[28]

A good deal of what we know of Luther comes from the recorded conversations at home, particularly from around the supper table. The theologian John Mathesius was often present and recalled the spirited discussions that took place there:

> Although our doctor often took weighty and profound thoughts to table with him and sometimes maintained the silence of the monastery during the entire meal, so that not a word was spoken, yet at appropriate times he spoke in a very jovial way. We used to call his conversation the condiments of the meal because we preferred it to all spices and dainty food.
>
> When he wished to get us to talk he would throw out a question, "What's new?" The first time we let this remark pass, but if he repeated it—"You prelates, what's new in the land?"—the oldest ones at the table would start talking.
>
> If the conversation was animated, it was nevertheless conducted with decent propriety and courtesy, and others would contribute their share until the doctor started to talk. Often good questions were put to him from the Bible, and he provided expert and concise answers. When at times somebody took exception to what had been said, the doctor was able to bear this patiently and refute him with a skillful answer. Reputable persons often came to the table from the university and from foreign places, and then very nice talks and stories were heard.[29]

Some of Luther's supper guests (many of them students) took notes of the conversations. Throughout the 1530s and until his death in 1546, a treasure trove of Luther's remarks—thoughtful comments, controversial opinions, salty language and all—were thus recorded. While the notes were not in Luther's own hand, thus rendering their exact accuracy questionable,

Luther knew that his comments, which came to be called *Table Talk*, were being written down, and still he spoke freely on a wide variety of topics. Combined with the massive amount of speeches, lectures, sermons, and letters Luther left behind, *Table Talk* has afforded historians a rich and unique insight into Luther and his views on hundreds of topics, religious and secular. First published in 1566, *Table Talk*, in one version or another, has been in print ever since.[30]

Chapter 19

"Look at what he is doing now"

In the final years of his life Luther was convinced that the end of the world was at hand. This apocalyptic outlook produced a great sense of urgency and profoundly influenced his work. He grew impatient with what he saw as a lack of progress in the Reformation, and he lashed out at his enemies—real and perceived—with a vitriol that eclipsed the language of some of his earlier work. He saw no reason for moderation or compromise and he eagerly dismissed his critics as imbeciles or demons. "I was born to go to war," he said, "and give battle to sects and devils. I must root out the stumps and the bushes and hack away the thorns and the brambles. I am the great lumberjack who must clear the land and level it."[1] As Luther aged, his stubborn nature and absolute certainty in the virtue of his cause led to some of his most notable achievements. But Luther's obstinacy also gave rise to missteps that embarrassed his supporters and stained his legacy. Still, he remained unshakeable in his faith and unapologetic for his methods. He saw himself as God's avenger, and he would fight to the end. "I will do all I can with prayer," he said, "and if need be, also with my fist."[2]

For a brief time after Pope Paul III ascended to the Vatican throne in 1534, it seemed that Protestants and Catholics might finally find common ground. Born Alessandro Farnese in the papal state of Latium, Paul was a humanist and lover of the arts (he later commissioned Michelangelo to supervise the completion of St. Peter's Basilica and approved his famed "Crucifixion of St. Peter" and the "Conversion of St. Paul"). Paul fathered five children while still a cardinal. He was a charming and intelligent man, and his charisma paid great dividends; he was named Dean of the College of Cardinals in 1513 and, when Clement VII died in the fall of 1534, was easily elected pope.

Paul's predecessors had displayed little interest in reforming the Catholic Church. Leo X had downplayed Luther's movement as a "monk's quarrel" in Germany and concerned himself with military matters. Adrian VI's brief reign of less than a year afforded him little opportunity for meaningful action, and Clement VII, preoccupied with France's threat to Italy, was indifferent to religious affairs in northern Europe. But Paul III was impressed with the growing number of princes, particularly in northern Germany, who had embraced Luther's movement, and he saw a need to address the issues of reform. He issued a bull convening a general council—an assembly of ecclesiastical dignitaries, including the bishops, for the purpose of discussing policy and doctrine—in May of 1537 at Mantua, Italy. Paul III wanted Protestant representatives to appear and present their theological case; perhaps, he thought, both sides could learn to coexist together.

The papal order, however, was silent on the rules that would govern the council and how business might be transacted. Then, under pressure from his cardinals who continued to believe that the Reformation should be crushed and not tolerated, Paul III sharpened his rhetoric. The purpose of the council, he said, would be "the utter extirpation of the poisonous, pestilential Lutheran heresy."[3] Many Protestants, including the electors John Frederick and Landgrave Phillip, saw no purpose in attending the council. It would not be a free and open council, they were certain. It would not even be safe for them to appear.

Undeterred by critics and skeptics, Paul III sent *nuncios,* or ecclesiastical diplomats, to various regions across Europe to drum up support for his plan. Pietro Paolo Vergerio, who had honed his skills as a lawyer before embarking on an ecclesiastical career, and who had served with distinction as King Ferdinand's nuncio, was hand-selected to meet with Luther at Wittenberg. Vergerio was given only one directive: gain the cooperation of the Protestant leader as regards the upcoming council. If Luther promised to attend, surely other Protestants would, as well.

Vergerio arrived in Wittenberg in November 1536, where he was formally received by Hans Metzsch, the mayor, and offered lodging in the town's finest hotel. Luther treated his meeting with Vergerio as a solemn and dignified event. He put on his finest clothes, a doublet with satin sleeves and a fur-lined coat of wool, and hung a heavy gold chain and medallion around his neck. He said later that he wanted to present a youthful appearance to give the nuncio the impression that his Reformation was fresh and vigorous. To further display his virility, Luther made a point of telling Vergerio that he was happily married and had five children. He hoped, he said, that the officials in Rome did not think he was just a German drunkard.

But Vergerio was not particularly impressed with Wittenberg, or with Luther. The so-called great reformer spoke only in German, causing Vergerio to doubt that Luther had written his many Latin treatises by himself. He thought that Luther was coarse and too often used blunt language; this did not surprise Vergerio, he sniffed. He had heard that Luther was the simple "son of a Saxon coal miner and bath maid of ill repute."[4] Vergerio let it be known that he considered himself to be Luther's intellectual superior.

Vergerio advised Luther that Rome still considered him to be a confused soul who had

Luther the young theologian. Drawing by Fr. Müeller (Library of Congress).

abandoned the faith. The Church was not ready, would never be ready, to accept the theological positions of the Reformation. Luther was not intimidated. He told Vergerio that he expected nothing but condemnation of the truth from the papal hierarchy. He had "found out" the pope, he said. He knew that the pope "would see all Christendom perish and all souls damned rather than suffer either himself or his adherents to be reformed even a little, and his tyranny to be limited." The pope was evil, Luther said, and had no conscience, "but money, honors, power are everything."[5] Luther expressed his disappointment that the general council would probably not address the key issues of faith and justification. At best the bishops would discuss "useless matters," such as "laws concerning meats, the length of priest's garments, exercises of monks, etc." His evangelicals, he boasted, did not need a council; the Roman Catholics were the ones who were confused.

Vergerio then decided to challenge Luther. A general council, he said, would be convened by His Holiness the pope and therefore would hold the blessing and sanction of the Holy Spirit. Thus assembled, the council would clearly and finally point out the error of Luther's ways. The strategy worked. Luther believed that the Holy Spirit worked through *him*, not the

Reformers (foreground from left: Luther; Johann Bugenhagen; Desiderius Erasmus; Justus Jonas; Caspar Creuziger; and Philipp Melanchthon). Detail of the Reformers from the Meienberg Epitaph, Blasiikirche, Nordhausen, Germany, by Lucas Cranach the Younger (The Granger Collection, New York).

pope. Feeling provoked, Luther declared that he would attend the council "even if it were to burn him." Further, he was willing to leave German soil and risk his life for the truth. He would come, he said, "with head and neck."[6] Vergerio returned to Rome satisfied that he had successfully completed his mission.

John Frederick was not sure that Luther would be allowed to attend the council in Mantua. He would leave the final decision to Luther's colleagues. He instructed Luther to write a final and definitive theological statement, a complete and useful summary of the Lutheran position. While a group of Protestant theologians would assist, edit, and review the material, it was to be Luther's "testament of religion," or ultimate profession of faith. The document would then be presented to a group of Protestant leaders from across Germany, who would consider the work and determine whether it should be presented to a council, or whether Luther or others might even attend at all. Sensing that this work would forever define him, Luther began his writing immediately with great determination and energy. He looked upon the assignment as an opportunity to sum up his life's work.

In late December a distinguished group of Protestant theologians and long-time Luther supporters, including Melanchthon, Justus Jonas, George Spalatin, and Nicholas Amsdorf, assembled at the Black Cloister in Wittenberg. Comfortably lodged in the old monk's quarters that had been refurnished as guest rooms, and well nourished by Kate's cooking, the men reviewed and discussed Luther's work, which he called "his articles," or the "sufficient teaching for the life of the church."

The first section expressed the ancient Trinitarian doctrine of divine majesty—Father, Son, and Holy Spirit—upon which Lutherans and Catholics agreed. The second section, wrote Luther, was "about the articles that pertain to the office and work of Jesus Christ, or to our redemption." This section set forth the heart of the Reformation, the idea that had struck Luther like a thunderbolt so long ago. Jesus Christ, Luther wrote, was "handed over to death for our trespasses and was raised for our justification.... Now because this must be believed and may not be obtained or grasped otherwise with any work, law, or merit it is clear and certain that this faith alone justifies us." Here again was that "sweetest phrase," the joyous revelation that had illuminated Luther's darkness and delivered him from the terrors of *Anfechtungen*, and that had driven, inspired and sustained him for nearly thirty tumultuous years. "He who through faith is just shall live." For Luther this was the very meaning of the Gospel, the explanation for the great mystery of Christ's life, death and resurrection. Justification through faith and grace was "the sun, the day, the light of the church." From this basic precept Luther had never wavered. "On this article," he wrote, "stands all that we teach and practice against the pope, the devil, and the world. Therefore we must be quite certain and have no doubt about it. Otherwise everything is lost, and the pope and the devil and whatever opposes us will gain victory and be proved right."[7]

In the subsequent sections of his testament Luther repeated his attacks on familiar targets: the doctrines of purgatory, pilgrimages, monastic life, relics, the sacraments, and the papacy itself. His colleagues made minor suggestions, adding criticisms of the invocation of saints and clarifying language concerning the Lord's Supper. Luther was pleased when, after three days of analysis, the theologians unanimously endorsed his work. Through Spalatin, he sent the document to John Frederick, who read it, reflected on the political implications, and then read it again. He accepted Luther's writing in its entirety, and wrote Luther a personal note of thanks: "But we know, praise God, that the things which you have drawn from the Word of God and we have declared right and godly, are not human but divine things, and we want them to be confessed before the world and not denied."[8] Luther had high hopes that his articles would be endorsed by Protestants from across the country, and then presented at Mantua.

In February 1537 the leaders of the German reform movement met in Schmalkalden. It was an unprecedented gathering: thirty-eight Protestant theologians, princes, and reformers, from eighteen territories and cities, including representatives from Württemberg, Erfurt, Hamburg, Nuremberg, Magdeburg, Schwäbisch Hall, Strasbourg, and, of course, Wittenberg.[9] They met to discuss the state of the reform movement and the pope's call for a council, scheduled to convene in just three months. Luther was scheduled to present his articles, and his work would then be reviewed and considered.

But while traveling to Schmalkalden Luther became ill. Still weakened by a mild heart attack he suffered in December, on February 8 he passed a kidney stone and experienced bleeding. He arrived in Schmalkalden weakened and in extreme pain, and the personal physician of Landgrave Phillip attended to him. An enema produced repeated diarrhea but did not ease his discomfort. On February 19 he found himself unable to urinate, a condition that lasted for eight days. Dr. George Sturtz, a physician from Erfurt who Luther trusted, arrived with medications, but Luther got no relief. In agony now, Luther feared he was near death. Kate was notified; she could not travel to Schmalkalden, but sent her love and prayers and recommended that her husband be given broth made from almonds. If that didn't work, she instructed, perhaps a *Dreckapotheke*, a mixture of garlic and raw manure, would. A *Chirurg* (surgeon) was summoned from Waltershausen, who prescribed more fluids. "They gave me as much to drink as if I had been a big ox," Luther wrote to Kate.[10]

By February 25, as the theologians began their work, Luther's condition was deemed critical. He wished to die in Saxony, he said, and against the doctor's recommendation plans were made to transport him home. John Frederick came to visit and wished for God's grace and healing. But Luther had long since conquered his fear of death. Better to pray against the devil, Luther advised the Elector, for he was the real adversary. Luther thanked him for his support over the years, and requested assurances that his work would be carried on without him. Frederick was concerned, however, that should Luther die "God's precious Word" would die with him. Luther replied that there was no need to worry, for the many learned theologians who had gathered in Schmalkalden were evidence that the reform movement would remain strong. Frederick did not have the heart to tell Luther that those same theologians were bickering over trivial matters and having trouble reaching consensus. The Elector assured Luther that he would see to it that Kate and the children would be cared for. "For your wife shall be my wife," he said, "and your children shall be my children."[11]

Now the pain was so severe that Luther thought he was losing his mind. He vomited repeatedly and cried out in agony, hoping that death would come. Melanchthon came to visit, and seeing the horrible condition of his friend reduced him to tears. Luther said to him, "When I am dead and gone, remember this: if the Pope should lay aside his crown, if he should descend from the papal throne and renounce his primacy, and if should confess that he has erred and has plunged the Church into destruction, then receive him into our church; but otherwise he shall always be considered by you as the Antichrist."[12] A wagon was outfitted for Luther's trip home. He was carried outside, where a crowd of city residents had gathered to get a glimpse of him. Luther made the sign of the cross and said, "The Lord fill you with his benediction and with hatred of the pope."[13]

Five men walked beside the wagon as it started on the bumpy, tortuous trip. Every jolt from the road sent shock waves of pain through Luther's body—but probably saved his life. That first night, at an inn in Tambach (just nine miles from Schmalkalden), the urinary blockage finally opened and Luther gained relief. He immediately sent a message to Melanchthon that his "silver stream" had been restored. "Here the Lord appeared to me," he wrote on the wall of his room. His colleagues in Schmalkalden received the good news with exultation. "Luther lives!" became the celebratory cry. Luther also wrote to his Kate and described how fruitless all of the doctors and their remedies had been. The Elector had "ordered people to run, ride, fetch, and with all his might tried his best to help me. But it was not to be." Luther could not resist teasing his wife. "Your manure cure didn't help me either," he wrote. He was happy to be coming home to her.[14]

While the great majority of theologians at Schmalkalden concurred with the contents of Luther's work, which eventually came to be known as the *Smalcald Articles,* the document was not formally adopted. Luther believed that, had he presented them personally, they would have been endorsed. But there was disagreement among the delegates as to the true meaning of the Eucharist. Also, Melanchthon successfully argued any lack of unity, particularly among elements of the militaristic Schmalkaldic League, might be would be seen by the Catholics as a sign of weakness. The theologians and princes voted to take a more cautious route and re-certify Melanchthon's *Augsburg Confession,* which of course contained a good deal of similar, if not slightly dated, material. Regardless of the theological doctrine to be adopted, the delegates also decided they would not attend the pope's general council, because they did not believe their ideas could be freely presented or would be seriously considered. They could never trust a pope who insisted that a council take place in non–German lands. "We are not going to walk into the Pope's trap," they declared. With the approval of Frederick and Phillip, they instead proposed a counter-council of their own, a Protestant-led council that would include English and French representatives. For safety, an army of eighteen thousand men would be mustered. When Luther heard of this plan he thought it was madness, and an invitation to violence. By refusing to sanction his trip to Mantua, he believed, the reformers had missed a chance to convince the pope of their righteousness.

In the end, the counter-council plan did not materialize. Neither did the pope's Mantua council. The governor of the city insisted upon a papal police force for security purposes, and the council was postponed. Then Francis I of France balked at attending, believing that a council held in Italy would increase the power and influence of his rival, the Holy Roman Emperor. Military concerns over the threat of the Turks continued to preoccupy Rome. Paul III did not get his general council until 1545, at Trent. By then the opportunity for compromise and settlement, if it ever existed at all, was long gone.

*

Luther was sorely disappointed that he would not get another chance to take on his Roman Catholic rivals directly at Mantua, as he had twenty years earlier in the glorious days of his confrontations with Cajetan at Augsburg, Johann Eck at Leipzig, and Charles V at Worms. But a new series of controversies quickly arose and served to occupy his time.

Luther had known the Elector Philip of Hesse since their meeting at the Diet of Worms in 1521. After Philip's forced marriage to Christina, the daughter of Duke George of Saxony, in 1524 (a common occurrence among nobility), he began to take an active interest in the cause of the Reformation. He encouraged the spread of Luther's doctrines, and approved of Luther's controversial position during the Peasants' Rebellion. Over the subsequent years he openly and enthusiastically championed Protestant efforts in Hesse and became an outspoken critic of the papacy. Philip was the driving force behind the formation of the Schmalkaldic League, designed to protect Protestant interests from military interference from the Emperor or other Catholic forces. Luther came to rely upon him, as he did the electors Frederick and John of Saxony, as critical allies. But Philip's reckless personal life, and the ill-fated advisory role Luther would play in it, resulted in one of the more scandalous episodes of the Reformation.

Philip complained that he was not attracted to his wife from the beginning of their marriage (although she bore him ten children over the years), and often strayed from his vows. He lived, Luther noted later, "constantly in a state of adultery and fornication."[15] Knowing that divorce was not an option for royalty, Philip considered the possibility of taking a second wife. He sought advice from Luther, who initially advised that unless some extreme necessity existed—if Christina was leprous, for example, or in other ways abnormal—a bigamous marriage could never be sanctioned. Bigamy, Luther wrote confidentially, might be acceptable for "Heathens and Turks," but not for God-fearing Christians. Philip would not change his lifestyle, however. He was likely encouraged by the cavalier behavior of England's Henry VIII, who changed wives—and religions—to suit himself.[16] Although Philip suffered from syphilis, he wanted to marry the daughter of one of his sister's ladies-in-waiting, nineteen-year-old Margarethe von der Salle, and even gained Christina's permission to do so. But he would not proceed without Luther's approval.

Eventually, he got it. Philip argued that bigamy ran throughout the Old Testament and was not specifically banned by the New Testament. Philip also apparently implored that adultery was worse than bigamy and kept him from communing. Luther could not abide divorce under Philip's circumstance and reluctantly conceded that bigamy was a preferred alternative in these circumstances. He counseled Phillip to go ahead and marry Margarethe, but to keep the marriage a secret. (The marriage took place at Fulda on March 4, 1540, and was witnessed by Melanchthon; the prolific Philip sired nine more children over the years.) Word of the scandal quickly leaked, however, probably by Philip's disapproving sister. The Emperor threatened the death penalty for Philip, which was the standard punishment for bigamy. Philip avoided this fate by agreeing to suspend his religious and political activism. For his part, Luther initially denied any involvement. But the entire embarrassing episode cost Philip a number of important political and military allies and tarnished Luther's reputation. He later weakly acknowledged that Philip had confided to him within the confidence of the confessional, and in any event he had only wanted to spare Philip's first wife public shame. Eventually he admitted he had been played for a fool.[17]

The scandal over Philip's bigamy was far from Luther's only mistake in judgment. He soon found himself embroiled in another controversy that carried far more sinister connotations and continues, even today, to stain his legacy. In the mid–1540s Luther turned his caustic tongue and pen against the Jews.

Luther's first known mention of the Jewish people and their faith came early in his career, in 1514, when he was just thirty-one years old. He speculated on whether they might ever accept Christ as their Savior and thus convert to Christianity. Either way, he'd play no role himself, he thought. "Conversion of the Jews will be the work of God alone operating from within," he wrote, "and not of man working—or rather playing—from without."[18] Luther's conciliatory theological view was, in those early days, a product of the widespread and historic biases he witnessed against the Jews—an environment that surrounded him. Throughout Germany (and much of Europe), Jews were ostracized and segregated from mainstream society and limited in their abilities to travel, conduct business, and participate in civic matters. "What Jew would consent to enter our ranks," Luther wrote, "when he sees the cruelty and enmity we wreak on them—that in our behavior towards them we less resemble Christians than beasts?"[19]

In his minor work of 1523, *That Jesus Christ Was Born a Jew*, Luther again lamented the fact that anti–Semitic beliefs led to suppressive treatment and ridicule. "If I had been a Jew and had seen such dolts and blockheads govern and teach the Christian faith, I would sooner have become a hog than a Christian. They have dealt with the Jews as if they were dogs rather than human beings; they have done little else than deride them and seize their property.... When we are inclined to boast of our position [as Christians] we should remember that we are but Gentiles, while the Jews are of the lineage of Christ.... If we really want to help them, we must be guided in our dealings with them not by papal law but by the law of Christian love. We must receive them cordially, and permit them to trade and work with us, that they may have occasion and opportunity to associate with us, hear our Christian teaching, and witness our Christian life."[20]

But Luther's attitude and opinions changed over the years. While he thought that the Reformation he had sparked would usher in a new era of glory and righteousness for Roman Catholics who would no longer be deceived by papal lies, he also believed that scores of Jews would finally recognize the truth of the Christian doctrine. He fully expected that Jews would again become God's people and enter into the kingdom. But when no large-scale conversion took place, Luther joined in the chorus of hatred and scorn that had oppressed Jews for generations. Throughout the 1530s Luther campaigned against the rights of Jews, joining John Frederick's campaign that prohibited Jews from traveling through Saxony or engaging in business activities. Even when Jewish leaders personally appealed to Luther, the great reformer, to intercede on their behalf, Luther refused. He would not "contribute to your (Jewish) obstinacy by my own kind actions," he told Rabbi Josel of Rosheim. "You must find another intermediary with my good lord."[21]

Then, sometime in 1538, Luther received word from a "good friend," Count Wolfgang Schlick of Falkenau, that Jews in Bohemia and Moravia had been proselytizing Christians, advising them that the Messiah had not yet come, and encouraging them to be circumcised pursuant to Jewish law. Schlick also inferred that some Christians had been convinced to observe the Jewish Sabbath. Incensed, Luther took no steps to determine if there was any accuracy to Schlick's reports. Instead he hurriedly produced a pamphlet he called *Against the Sabbatarians.* Luther wrote that the Jews had not kept their covenant with God and had grievously sinned by rejecting the Messiah. They were living in exile, Luther wrote, outside of God's holy temple. Some Jews were reasonable, Luther noted, but in general they were "given to babbling and lying."[22]

In a pamphlet Luther read that a Jew had blasphemed the Lord and called the Virgin Mother a whore, slandering the very core of Christianity. Luther exploded in anger, his early commitment to patience and moderation now a distant memory. In 1543 he wrote *On the Jews and Their Lies,* one hundred and thirty-five pages of venom, crudeness, prejudice, and hate. This work was roughly divided into four segments. First, Luther described the "false boasts" of the Jews; that is, that they claimed to be the true children of Abraham. Next, he described relevant biblical passages relating to the promise of the Messiah. Third, Luther repeated the purported Jewish blasphemies of Jesus the Savior, and his mother, the Virgin Mary. Finally, Luther made numerous bigoted allegations and then set forth, for both religious and governmental authorities, a series of oppressive actions that should be taken against the targets of his wrath.

It is this final segment that contained Luther's most offensive rages. Jews, he wrote, were "stiff-necked, disobedient, prophet-murderers, arrogant, usurers, and filled with every vice." Repeating centuries-old stereotypes and myths, Luther accused Jews of outrageous behavior. They cursed Christians in their synagogues. They practiced witchcraft. They defamed the Virgin Mary as "a tool of the devil" and labeled Jesus a "whore's son." As punishment for these vile misbehaviors, Luther made severe recommendations. Their synagogues, schools and houses should be burned. Their prayer books should be confiscated, and rabbis must be forbidden from teaching. Jews should be forbidden to travel between German regions and forced to remain in their isolated communities. Their money should be taken from them and they should not be allowed to continue their usurious practices. Finally, those Jews who violated these conditions or caused any disturbance should be subject to harsh labor.[23]

An offensive artistic display, and the inspiration for one of Luther's anti–Semitic rants, can still be seen in Wittenberg. High on an outside wall of the City Church, where Luther had preached on many occasions, where he had been married and had his children baptized, is a *Judensau*, a shocking image of Jews in obscene contact with a large sow. The stone carving dates to 1305, some two hundred years before Luther's time. In another 1543 tract Luther described the profane image:

> Here in Wittenberg, in our parish church, there is a sow carved into the stone under which lie young pigs and Jews who are sucking; behind the sow stands a rabbi who is lifting up the right leg of the sow, raises behind the sow, bows down and looks with great effort into the Talmud under the sow, as if he wanted to read and see something most difficult and exceptional.[24]

Luther claimed to know God's will as regards the Jews. When one of his students asked him why Jews refused to convert to Christianity, Luther replied, "Because God hardened their hearts and deserted them because of their stubbornness." While Luther's hatred of Jews was based on theology and not on race, it was hatred nonetheless. Many of his colleagues were embarrassed by his cruel statements. Melanchthon, in particular, was alarmed at the venom Luther displayed. "Look at what he is doing now," he sadly told his friends.[25] He urged Luther to retract his work, to no avail. And even his beloved Kate quietly counseled her husband that his rhetoric, meant to incite persecution, went too far. Most of Luther's recommendations were ignored, but restrictions were placed on Jews' travel and ability to enter into certain business practices in some German regions. Luther's legacy was tarnished forever.

In March 1545 Luther published his last major work, a treatise called *Against the Papacy at Rome, Founded by the Devil*. As he had done for many years, in this writing Luther attacked the institution of the pope. The papacy had rejected his views, his arguments, and—to Luther—the proof of the correctness of Protestant positions. The Roman Catholic Church remained unreformed. Believing that the End Days were at hand, Luther thought it important to make a concluding statement—another final testament—setting forth what was for him the undisputed truth: the pope was the Antichrist, God's darkest enemy on earth. While the attacks on the papacy were nothing new, (it had been, after all, twenty-five years since his words and actions had led to denouncement and excommunication from the Church), now his writing took on an angrier tone, a viciousness that nearly rivaled his comments about the Jews. It was as if Luther was searching for new ways in which his words could become weapons:

> [The Pope] is the head of the accursed church of the very worst rascals on earth; vicar of the devil; an enemy of God; an opponent of Christ; and a destroyer of the church of Christ; a teacher of all lies, blasphemy, and idolatries; an arch-church-thief and church-robber of the keys and al the goods of both the church and the secular lords; a murderer of kings and inciter of all sorts of bloodshed; a brothel-keeper above all brothel-keepers and all lewdness, including that which is not to be named; an Antichrist; a man of sin and child of perdition; a true werewolf.[26]

The treatise is also remarkable for Luther's repeated scatological references. While coarse language was common in the Middle Ages (among the learned as well as the peasantry), Luther's crude descriptions of the pope, full of flatulence and feces, went well beyond spirited discourse. The "dearest little ass-pope" not only worshiped Satan, Luther wrote, but also "licked his behind." The pope farted so loudly and powerfully that "it is a wonder that it did not tear his hole and belly apart." Luther referred to the practice of selling indulgences, which had in essence started the Reformation, as "an utter shitting with which the Hellish Father fooled all the world and cheated them out of their money." It was amazing, he went on, that people (particularly secular leaders) continued to "tolerate such things from such a rotten paunch, crude ass-pope in Rome."[27] And for special emphasis, Luther commissioned his artist-friend, Lucas Cranach the Elder, to produce a series of woodcuts, equally crude, that accompanied the text.

Luther was not just angry with popes and Jews. He was increasingly angry, as well, with his own people of Wittenberg. He believed that decades of persistent preaching and evangelizing had borne little spiritual fruit among his parishioners and neighbors. He was dismayed at their laziness and indifference. He saw signs of moral corruption, pettiness, jealousy, and greed. Drunkenness was rampant. Luther was shocked at women who dressed immodestly and at men who shamelessly flaunted their lust and desires outside of marriage. He regularly chastised his Sunday congregations for their shortcomings. He had had enough of Wittenberg. In July 1545 Luther left on a short trip to Leipzig and Zeitz, where he had been called to settle disputes between feuding clergymen of the Naumburg diocese. From an inn he wrote a sorrowful letter to Kate:

> I should like to arrange not to have to go back to Wittenberg. My heart has grown cold so that I do not care to live there, but wish you would sell garden and the farm, house and buildings, except the big house, which I should like to give back to my gracious lord.... It looks as if Wittenberg and her government would catch, not St. Vitus' dance or St. John's dance, but the beggar's dance and Beelzebub's dance; the women and girls have begun to go bare before and behind and there is no one to punish or correct them and God's word is mocked. Away with this Sodom.... I will wander around here and eat the bread of charity before I will martyr and soil my poor old last days with the disordered life of Wittenberg, where I lose all my bitter, costly work.[28]

Kate was alarmed enough to notify Melanchthon and other town and university officials. A contingent immediately traveled to Zeitz to convince him to reconsider. The Elector John Frederick was also advised and, sensing that physical infirmities had brought on Luther's angst, dispatched his personal physician to examine him. Luther was cheered by these displays of affection and returned home. He carried on with his normal duties but at a slower pace. He confided to friends that the end was near.

It is likely that Luther's ever-increasing ill health contributed to the anger and discontent of his last years. In 1545 he was sixty-two years of age, a very old man for the era. He was sick and uncomfortable almost all of the time. He suffered from vertigo, phlebitis, headaches, viruses, fevers, cramps, arthritis, hemorrhoids, constipation, infections, poor circulation, limited eyesight, and a weakened heart. He escaped his bouts of depression and melancholia, and the *Anfechtungen* that still flared occasionally, with prayer and Bible study. (Sometimes, he said, he would ruminate for hours at a time on the phrase, "I am baptized," and would then find solace.) But the age's common remedies for his variety of physical ailments were far less reliable. "I am sluggish, tired, and cold," he wrote to a friend, "that is, I am an old and useless man. I have finished my race. It remains only that the Lord calls me to my fathers, and that my body be handed over to decomposition and the worms. I have lived enough, if one may call it living. Please pray for me that the hour of my passing will be pleasing to God and a blessing for me." He repeated his apocalyptic vision. "It looks," he wrote, "as if the whole world, too, has come to its passing."[29]

Still he worked. In the final year of his life Luther published eleven pamphlets and several collections of lectures and sermons. At least seventy of his letters still exist; doubtless he wrote countless more. His followers could not get enough. In response to one request he wrote:

> You often urge me to write a book on Christian discipline, but you do not say where I, a weary, worn old man, can get the leisure and health to do it. I am pressed by writing letters without end; I have promised our young princes a sermon on drunkenness; I have promised certain other persons and myself a book on secret engagements; to others one against the sacramentarians; still others beg that I shall omit all to write a comprehensive and final commentary on the whole Bible. One thing hinders another so that I am able to accomplish nothing. Yet I believe that I ought to have rest, as an emeritus, to live and die in peace and quietness, but I am forced to live in restless action. I shall do what I can and leave undone what I cannot do.[30]

On November 10 Luther celebrated his last birthday. The next day he concluded what was to be his final lecture, on the book of Genesis, at the university. His parting words to his students were, "This is dear Genesis; God grant that others do better with it after me; I can do no more, I am weak. Pray God to grant me a good, blessed hour."[31]

A testamentary dispute arose between two brothers, Albert and Gebhard, both counts in Mansfeld. Luther's father had been a miner there, and Luther had attended the town's Latin School as a boy. Thus he felt a certain sentimentality about the place, and although he was tired and in ill health he agreed to serve as mediator. Along with Melanchthon he traveled to Mansfeld and began his work. Progress was made, and he celebrated Christmas there with old friends and relatives. But Melanchthon took ill, and the men returned to Wittenberg in early January.

A few weeks later Luther again left for Mansfeld, this time accompanied by his sons and John Aurifaber, an assistant. Bad weather forced the party to take lodging at Eisleben, the town of Luther's birth. The counts and their attorneys also came to Eisleben, and negotiations continued for the next several weeks. Over that time Luther wrote a series of letters to Kate. His spirits improved, and his writing took on a playful and pleasant tone. He called her his "housewife of the heart," "Mrs. Brewmaster," and "Madame Doctor," and signed his letters "your old lover," and "your holiness's obedient servant." He joked about the weather, complained about the lawyers, and teased her about how he spent his time. He was drinking plenty of good beer, he wrote, and "I am so well that I am sore tempted by fair women and care not how gallant I am." He urged her not to worry about him or his health, for he was in God's hands. "Pray for us and be good," he told her. "God bless you."[32]

On February 16 the disputing parties reached an agreement and signed a treaty of good intentions. In celebration Luther preached a sermon at St. Andrew's church, taking his text from Matthew. God's word confounded mankind's understanding, he told his listeners. Turn away from the wisdom of the world and turn to Christ. He chastised his oldest enemy, the pope:

House where Luther died, February 18, 1546, Eisleben.

> So the pope, too, wants to be a very wise man, indeed, the wisest of the wise, simply because he has a high position and claims to be the head of the church; whereupon the devil so puffs him up that he imagines that whatever he says and does is pure divine wisdom and everybody must accept and obey it, and nobody should ask whether it is God's Word or not. In his big fool's book, he presumes quite shamelessly to say that it is not likely that such an eminence, meaning himself, could err. So, too, the emperor, kings, and cardinals; because they sit in such high places, they too think they cannot err or be wrong.[33]

But suddenly he felt ill, and was taken to his room, where he tried to rest. On the night of February 18 he complained of dizziness and pain in his chest. He took some sips of brandy, and warm towels were laid upon him, and his breathing became slight. Sometime around two o'clock in the morning, his sons Martin and Paul were summoned, joining Aurifaber, a Mansfeld clergyman named Cölius, and his longtime colleague Justas Jonas. Jonas later reported that Luther briefly rallied and made final declarations. "O my heavenly Father," he said, "one God and Father of our Lord Jesus Christ, though God of all comfort, I thank thee that thou hast given me thy dear son Jesus Christ, in whom I believe, whom I have preached

Luther died in this room (courtesy Stiftung Luthergedenkstätten in Sachsen-Anhalt).

and confessed, loved and praised, whom the wicked Pope and all the godless shame, persecute, and blaspheme. I pray thee, dear Lord Jesus Christ, let me commend my soul to thee. O heavenly Father, if I leave this body and depart, I am certain that I will be with thee and can never, never tear myself out of thy hands."

Luther then repeated the soothing words of John 3:16 three times:

"God so loved the world that he gave his only begotten son, that whosoever believeth in him should not perish but have everlasting life."

"Father," Luther said, "into thy hands I commend my spirit. Thou hast redeemed me, thou true God."

Jonas and Cölius leaned closer to the dying man and asked him, "Reverend father, will you stand steadfast by Christ and the doctrine you have preached?"

"*Ja*," said Luther. "*Yes*." Then he whispered, "Who hath my word shall never see death," and with that he died.[34]

Portrait of Luther in the house where he died (courtesy Stiftung Luthergedenkstätten in Sachsen-Anhalt).

Chapter 20

Legacy

On the morning after his death, the body of Martin Luther was taken back to St. Andrew's church in Eisleben, where Justus Jonas preached a sermon and a small crowd stood vigil. The next day, February 20, Luther's body was wrapped in white linen and placed in a hearse. Fifty horsemen escorted the corpse back to Wittenberg. On February 22 Johan Bugenhagen presided over the funeral service at Castle Church before a crowd of several thousand people that included, of course, Kate and the children Hans, Paul, Martin, and Margareta. Philip Melanchthon gave the eulogy. Luther was a noble figure, he said, the modern equivalent of the Old Testament prophets and Peter and Paul, the founders of the early Christian church. "It was clear," Melanchthon said, "that the light of the Gospel was recognized with greater splendor when Luther spoke." Melanchthon repeated the apocalyptic theme that had dominated Luther's last days. "Dead is the horseman and chariot of Israel," he said, "who ruled the Church in this last age of the world!"[1] Luther's casket was buried at the front of the church, below the raised pulpit from which he so often preached, where it remains to this day.

In July 1546, just five months after Luther's death, war broke out between the Schmalkaldic League, led by Philip of Hesse, and the Holy Roman Empire. The fighting lasted less than one year, and the 52,000-strong Catholic Army emerged victorious. At the decisive Battle of Mühlberg the Elector Duke John Frederick, who had been, along with his predecessor Frederick the Wise, Luther's great protector, was captured, court-martialed, and sentenced to death. In exchange for life imprisonment he relinquished his electoral status to his cousin Maurice, and signed the Capitulation of Wittenberg in May 1547. Luther's home city, where he had posted the Ninety-Five Theses that began the Protestant Reformation exactly thirty years earlier, fell back under Catholic control. Standing at his tomb, Emperor Charles V considered disinterring Luther's remains and dishonoring them; he decided against it, saying, "I war not with the dead, but with the living."[2] He then ordered that Lutherans be reintegrated back into the Catholic Church.

But the roots of Protestantism were too deeply established in the hearts and minds of many Germans. Pastors, in particular, refused to go along with the new order. A few were banished, some were executed, and many others—perhaps as many as four hundred—were imprisoned. Some fled to England, where they were influential in the English Reformation, some strains of which the Puritans carried across the Atlantic Ocean to America. After more fighting, finally the Treaty of Augsburg was signed in 1555. This agreement officially ended religious struggles in Germany and established the concept of *cuius regio, eius religio* (who rules, his religion). Princes of the Holy Roman Empire could now select Lutheranism or

Catholicism within their domains, and subjects would be allowed to travel to any region they preferred.

Kate Luther had a difficult time after her husband died. Who would not mourn, she asked her sister, "for so noble a man as was my dear lord, who much served not only one city or a single land but the whole world?"[3] Luther left Kate some nine thousand gulden in real estate and another thousand in personal property, but the farm and outbuildings were destroyed in the war, the animals were confiscated, and, save for occasional boarders, she had no regular income. For a time she received a small pension from Frederick. Kate shuttled between Wittenberg, Braunschweig, and Torgau, and then back to Wittenberg. Then the Plague resurfaced, and in the autumn of 1552, all but destitute and surrounded by sickness, she was forced to leave Wittenberg for good. Her horse shied on the road near a shallow ditch, and Kate either jumped or fell out of the little wagon that carried her. She never recovered from the internal injuries she suffered and died on December 20 at the age of fifty-three. She was laid to rest at St. Mary's Church in Torgau, some thirty miles from her husband.

Philip Melanchthon continued to work tirelessly for the Protestant cause. He died in 1560 and is buried near Luther in the Castle Church. Melanchthon was a "divine instrument," Luther had said, and had worked "to the great rage of the devil and his scabby tribe." Luther had called himself the "rough pioneer who must break the road," but the intellectual Melanchthon "comes along softly and gently, sows and waters heartily, since God has richly endowed him with gifts."[4]

The wooden door of the Castle Church, upon which Luther had nailed his Ninety-Five Theses in 1517, burned in 1760, a casualty of the Seven Years' War. It was replaced by a 2,200 pound bronze door, the Ninety-Five Theses inscribed in Latin thereon. Luther and Melanchthon's portraits are portrayed above the door, flanking the figure of Christ on the cross; Luther holds a German Bible, and Melanchthon holds his *Augsburg Confession*. The door remains, for tourists, theologians, and historians, the most popular stop on Germany's "Luther Trail." Wittenberg city officials proclaim it to be the "most photographed door" in all of Europe. Although the Emperor's Palace at Worms, where Luther defied the Roman Catholic Church in 1521, no longer stands, other historic sites from Luther's time—including the houses where he was born and died in Eisleben, the Augustinian monastery in Erfurt, the Wartburg Castle, and the Black Cloister (now *Lutherhaus*) in Wittenberg, among many others—can still be visited.

In 1580, some thirty-five years after Luther's death, a group of Lutheran scholars and theologians published the *Book of Concord*, a compilation of doctrinal standards of the Lutheran Church. First published on the fiftieth anniversary of the presentation of the *Augsburg Confession* to Charles V, the *Book of Concord* contains the *Apostles' Creed*, the *Augsburg Confession*, and Melanchthon's *Treatise on the Power and Primacy of the Pope*, among other documents. Luther is represented by his *Small and Large Catechisms*, and the *Smalcald Articles*, the "quintessence of his faith and his doctrine, the fruit of twenty years of theological struggle and maturing."[5] The *Book of Concord* forever memorializes Luther's criticisms of the Roman Catholic Church, and his calls for reform. It remains "the basic definition of what it means to be a Lutheran."[6]

In the 1500 years of its existence, the Church had faced many crises: persecution by the Roman Empire; barbarian invasions; and the Great Schism, for example. But Luther's Reformation was different. This movement resulted in mass defections from the parishes, abandonment of dozens of cloisters by priests and nuns, and the loss of half of Europe's allegiance to Rome. The Church had no choice but to examine itself.[7]

But Catholic leaders were slow to address topics of reform. The papacy feared losing its power, and the Curia stubbornly resisted any mention of change. Further, the political threats from Spain and France, and the military threat of the Turks, preoccupied Rome. In 1536 Pope Paul III, Clements's successor, took the first necessary steps and established a commission on papal reform. The following year a scathing report was delivered. The commission found that widespread abuse and corruption had spawned the Reformation. The papal hierarchy lacked spirituality, the report said. Its officers were open to bribery and cronyism. Canon law was avoided when convenient. Rome itself hosted the same immoral and iniquitous activities that Luther had seen firsthand back on his visit to the city in 1510. The Curia attempted to suppress the report, but it leaked out, to the delight of Protestants. The Swiss reformer John Calvin stated that mere "traces" of Christianity were all that existed in the Roman Catholic Church.[8]

The Church reacted defensively. In 1542 Paul III established the Supreme Sacred Congregation of the Roman and Universal Inquisition, meant to defend and promulgate Catholic Doctrine and defend the Church from heresy or "unacceptable and false doctrines." The office still exists, headquartered in Rome.

Finally in 1545, just a year before Luther's death, Paul III convened the general council at Trent, which met sporadically for the next eighteen years. But there would be no concessions to or compromise with the reformers. Acting in the light of three decades of Protestant criticism, the council drew a line of demarcation between Catholic and Protestant teaching, and it reaffirmed all the traditional doctrines that Luther had challenged. The Church retained its authority as the sole interpreter of Scripture, and its hierarchical nature remained in place. The Bible and Church tradition were equally authoritative. The number of divinely-inspired sacraments remained at seven, and transubstantiation of the Eucharist was reaffirmed. Purgatory existed, indulgences were legal (although "all evil gains for the obtaining of them" were to be abolished), and the clergy would remain celibate. The divine institution of the priesthood was reaffirmed, as was the sacrificial character of the Mass. There would be no "priesthood of believers" as Luther had taught; rather, the bishop would keep absolute control over his diocese, and the laity would continue to have little or no participation in the business of the faith. The pope's power was not only reaffirmed but enhanced. He was now given authority to enforce conciliar decrees, and clergy were forced to take oaths of loyalty to him. Luther's most important doctrinal claim, that justification occurred by faith alone through the grace of God, was rejected. Justification, decreed the council, was actualized by faith *and* good works, the cooperation of human will and God's grace. In short, the Council of Trent decreed that Luther and his Protestants were wrong on every count.

But if the council rejected any doctrinal reform, it did, in its "Counter-Reformation," install new and strict measures of internal discipline. It formed seminaries to educate the clergy. It unified its liturgy by standardizing the Tridentine Mass, which remained in effect for four centuries.[9] The Church became more spiritual, perhaps, and certainly more intellectual. This mixture gave rise to the influential Jesuits of Ignatius Loyola, a former soldier, and Francis Xavier, who traveled across the globe, "wherever there is hope of giving greater service to God," and established schools, orphanages, and colleges with military precision and order. "I have never left the army," Ignatius said. "I have only been seconded for the service of God."

The Jesuits pursued evangelism, apostolic ministry, and service; obedience to the pope was also required. The Jesuits became the largest male religious order in the world, carrying on their work in over one hundred countries. For all of its worldwide success, however, the Jesuits' attempts to take back Germany for Catholicism failed. In most regions of Luther's country the pope's "black horsemen," as Jesuits were called, were not welcome.

While Luther's movement continued to spread after his death, his vision of unity would never be realized. The Scandinavian kingdoms of Denmark, Norway, and Sweden embraced Lutheranism (eventually naming it as the official state religion). In Switzerland John Calvin and his followers adopted many of Luther's ideas, but insisted that God "predetermined" who would and would not be saved. Many Protestants in the Netherlands, France (Huguenots), and Scotland (Presbyterians) followed similar doctrines. During the reign of King Henry VIII, the Anglican Church of England (the mother church for America's Episcopalians), was established.

Christendom—to believers, God's spiritual kingdom here on earth—is now well into its third millennium. Over two billion people, or nearly one-third of the earth's population, are Christians, making Christianity the largest religion in the world. The Roman Catholic Church claims about 1.1 billion members worldwide.[10] The theological differences among Christians have not lessened since the Reformation.

There are over 800 million Protestants in the world, including Baptists, Presbyterians, Methodists, Pentecostals, and Evangelicals, among many others. The Lutheran Church, divided itself into many different denominations, numbers some seventy-two million members.[11] While these denominations all have their differences in structure, points of emphasis, and social and doctrinal interpretation, they hold important positions in common. All Protestants reject the authority of the papacy and the trappings of the Catholic Church. Protestants are united in theological conviction by the "Solas" first identified by Luther and the other medieval reformers: *Sola Scriptura* ("Scripture alone"), *Sola Fides* ("faith alone"), and *Sola Gratia* ("grace alone"). Some now add *Solus Christus* ("Christ alone") and *Soli Deo Gloria* ('to God alone be glory").[12] And all Protestants acknowledge the founder of the movement that resisted and then broke with Rome: Martin Luther, the Father of the Reformation.

Luther was as amazed as anyone when his academic challenge to debate the Church's corrupt practices ignited the most momentous events in the history of Christendom. His bold accusations, and his unwillingness to back down from them even in the face of the Church's mighty power, was far more than astonishing—it was unprecedented. It was, after all, *his* Church, his way of life, his own path to salvation that he questioned. Luther had no desire to destroy the institution that had been his very reason for living. But he also sought relief from his personal hell, the *Anfechtungen* that had so tormented and terrorized him. How could one love an avenging God who punished the very sinners he had so imperfectly created? He found his relief in the comforting message of St. Paul: "He who through faith is just shall live." We are not saved through the merits of our works, Luther believed, but through the grace and mercy of a loving God. Christians need not look to, or rely upon, the Church for salvation. For the faithful, it was already there.

In Paul's message Luther also found the strength to carry out his mission of challenge and reform. He was mistaken in his belief that the Church would listen, or could be healed. Luther could not have predicted the tumult that his arguments would bring. Nor could he have imagined that the most powerful institution in the world would be crippled, hopelessly

Statue of Luther, Wittenberg.

and irrevocably split—in "the most awesome historical cataclysm"—all over the new theology he pronounced.[13] The very foundations of public and private behavior would be transformed. Luther's Reformation shook the pillars of Christendom. The world would never again be the same.

Luther was fully aware of his fame. He enjoyed his status as founder and primary spokesman for the Reformation. He took pride in his work, and he took on every challenge with vigor and unwavering courage. So sure was he of his convictions that he did not hesitate to arrogantly chastise those who dared criticize him or take issue with his message. Luther spoke freely, rashly, often graphically, and sometimes to the detriment of his cause and his legacy. (It might have been better, wrote Luther biographer Roland Bainton, if Luther had died before he slandered the Jews.) But for all his faults, Luther remained humble before God. His legacy was not his primary concern. "I ask that my name not be spoken," he said, "and that you do not call yourselves Lutherans, but Christians. What is Luther? The teaching is not mine. And I was not crucified for anybody. Paul refused to let Christians name themselves Pauline or Petrine, but simply Christians. How can I, a stinking bag of maggots, have come to this, that the children of Christ should name themselves with my imperfect name? But if it is your opinion the Luther's teaching is that of the Gospel, then you should not merely throw Luther away. If you do so, then you will be throwing away his teaching as well, which you recognize as the teaching of Christ."[14]

Martin Luther's teachings have not, of course, been thrown away. Rather, his doctrine—Christ's doctrine, he would say—has persevered through the centuries. Conscious or not of Luther's personal imperfections, millions of people revere him and hold fast his message of hope and faith, calling his theology their own. "Here I stand," Luther supposedly said at the Imperial Diet of Worms, boldly defying the Holy Roman Emperor and Roman Catholic Church. "I can do no other." Spoken or not, the sentiments of courage and pure conviction were unmistakably present. Five hundred years later Protestants around the world, Lutherans and otherwise, say: we remember you, Luther, and we stand with you.

• Essay 1 •

Luther on Church History

Because Chapter 1 of Part One addresses the historical background for the Reformation and the ecclesiastical context in which Luther lived, it is instructive to examine how Luther himself viewed this background and context. By 1517 he knew that crucial changes needed to be made in the Church if she were to be faithful to Scripture and to its Gospel as he had come to understand and embrace that message. But what about the Church's first fifteen centuries? How much of it was misguided? Did it need to be respected as God-directed and God-blessed? If not, how could that be justified?

In the early years of the Reformation, Luther did not address these and related issues in a major writing, but he did work out his responses through the next several years, and in 1539 he published his most considered judgments on church history. This work, *On the Councils and the Church,*[1] addressed the role that the Councils have played and should play in the Church, but it did much more than that. It offered answers to such key questions as:

- Does the Early Church serve as the guide to how the Church should be?
- Can we look to the Church Fathers for definite truth and wisdom?
- Is there a God-given structure for the Church?
- Can the papacy serve God's purposes for the Church?

And, of extreme importance for understanding Luther's break with the Roman Church:

- Do Church Councils show the work of the Holy Spirit in properly guiding the Church?

For several years after 1517, Luther and the other leaders in the Reformation believed that a Church Council properly called and run would make the necessary modifications in the Church so that she would be more faithful to her God-given purpose. This was his position, for example, in his 1520 open letter, *To the Christian Nobility of the German Nation*; in this work he laid out a number of particulars that a Council could and should address.[2] The *Augsburg Confession* of 1530 offered a willingness to participate in a broad church council: "we obediently offer, in addition to what we have already done, to appear and defend our cause in such a general, free Christian Council."[3] Even Luther's *Smalcald Articles* of 1536 listed items for a general council on which discussion "with learned and reasonable people" might be possible[4]—though by that time Luther had, no doubt, lost hope for a constructive ecumenical council.

On the Councils and the Church, written three years after *The Smalcald Articles*, begins on the point of that lost hope. Luther wrote of a trick that people played on a dog. The trickster would hold out a piece of bread on the tip of a knife and then as the dog bit for it would pull it back and spin the knife rapping the dog on its beak with the knife handle. This trick, he claimed, is exactly what the church leaders had done repeatedly in teasing the reformers and the political leaders with an offer to call a church council and then rescinding the call. This had happened frequently in the 1530s. Luther's *Smalcald Articles* was written for The Council of Mantua, but that council never took place. When the Council of Trent was finally called and began to meet in 1545, one year before Luther's death, it was soon obvious to him that there would be no reform or renewal based on Scripture and the Gospel. The council met periodically until 1563 (1545–49, 1551–52, and 1562–63), and Luther's negative expectations were not wrong. In the end, the decrees of the council present virtually the complete antithesis to Luther's positions on key Reformation issues.

Luther's Analysis

On the Councils and the Church contains three major sections in addition to the introduction described above. In Part I Luther discussed the limited value of councils and the church fathers for reforming the church. Part II offered an examination of the Jerusalem Council recorded in Acts as well as of the major councils of early church history: Nicaea (325), Constantinople (381), Ephesus (431), and Chalcedon (451). In Part III Luther presented his views on the nature and marks of the church.

Luther cited several cases of the church fathers and the councils disagreeing with one another as well as of their many statements and ideas that had been totally disregarded. He could not see any of them, church fathers or councils, as a definitive voice of God guiding the Church in doctrine or practice. That voice, he argued vehemently, is to be found only in Scripture. "If it had not been for Holy Scripture, the church, had it depended on the councils and fathers, would not have lasted long."[5]

But can church councils serve a useful function? Yes, they can, Luther judged, and he offered extensive analyses of the four major councils mentioned above to demonstrate this. They did not offer new articles of faith but reaffirmed established biblical teachings: "I think that my conscience is clear when I say that no council … is authorized to initiate new articles of faith, because the four principal councils did not do that."[6] Then he offered ten principles for a proper church council, beginning with a repetition of the above point:

1. "A council has no power to establish new articles of faith, even though the Holy Spirit is present."[7]
2. "A council has the power—and is also duty-bound to exercise it—to suppress and condemn new articles of faith, in accordance with Scripture and the ancient faith."[8]
3. "A council has no power to command new good works; it cannot do so, for Holy Scripture has already abundantly commanded all good works."[9]
4. "A council has the power—and is also duty-bound to exercise it—to condemn all good works that oppose love, according to all of Scripture and the ancient practice of the church, and to punish persons guilty of such works."[10]
5. "A council has no power to impose new ceremonies on Christians, to be observed on pain of mortal sin or at the peril of conscience—such as fast days, feast days, food, drink, garb."[11]

6. "A council has the power and is bound to condemn such ceremonies in accordance with Scripture; for they are un–Christian and constitute a new idolatry or worship, which is not commanded by God, but forbidden."[12]

7. "A council has no power to interfere in worldly law and government."[13]

8. "A council has the power and is bound to condemn such arbitrary ways or new laws, in accordance with Holy Scripture, that is, to throw the pope's decretals into the fire."[14]

9. "A council has no power to create statutes or decretals that seek nothing but tyranny, that is, statutes on how the bishops should have the power and authority to command what they will and everybody should tremble and obey."[15]

10. "A council has the power to institute some ceremonies, provided, first, that they do not strengthen the bishops' tyranny; second, that they are useful and profitable to the people and show fine, orderly discipline and conduct."[16]

As a capstone comment, Luther wrote, "Finally, a council should occupy itself only with matters of faith, and then only when faith is in jeopardy."[17]

And what of the "Church" itself? How did Luther describe this sacred body? Surprisingly, Luther disdained the word "church" ("ecclesia") because it suggested an institution rather than people.[18] The Church is nothing other than people, he insisted. It is the *people* of God. Luther believed that a lot of trouble could have been avoided if the Creed had simply said, "I believe that there is a holy Christian people." The Church is fundamentally not an institution with a structure, a head (other than Christ), a hierarchy, and the like. It is merely God's people.

This holy, Christian people can be recognized by seven visible marks: first, by their possession of the holy word of God; second, by the holy sacrament of baptism; third, by the holy sacrament of the altar (holy communion); fourth, by the office of the keys exercised publicly (confession and absolution); fifth, by the fact that it consecrates or calls ministers; sixth, by prayer, public praise, and thanksgiving to God; and seventh, by the holy possession of the sacred cross (bearing suffering patiently). Luther called these the "seven principal parts of Christian sanctification or the seven holy possessions of the church."[19]

In summary, *the church is the people of God sanctified by the Holy Spirit and grounded in Sacred Scripture; the church displays the seven holy marks.*

Answers to the Five Key Questions

Luther answered all of the questions posed above.

1. *Does the Early Church serve as the guide to how the Church should be today?*

The Early Church also experienced disagreement and conflict. It only functioned as God's people when it relied fully on Scripture to define doctrine and practice. It is a guide for us to the extent, but only to the extent, that it is based on a total reliance on Scripture.

2. *Can we look to the Church Fathers for truth and wisdom?*

The Church Fathers often disagreed with each other. There is much to admire in them when their views are based on Scripture but much also to reject when they are not. No less a figure than Augustine, Luther claimed, held this view—even about himself as a prominent theologian.[20]

3. *Is there a God-given structure for the Church?*

This question is answered by the fact that the church is people—not an institution. It has been given the seven visible possessions and is empowered by the Holy Spirit. So long as the people of God display these possessions and rely solely on God's Word, there are no further structural requirements. There is no God-given structure.

4. *Can the papacy serve God's purposes for the Church?*

No. The church functioned beautifully for centuries without any bishop having primary authority over all others. The papacy is a human invention that stands in the way of a primary reliance on God's Word.

5. *Do church councils show the work of the Holy Spirit in properly guiding the Church?*

The councils show the work of the Holy Spirit if and only if they rely fully on Holy Scripture for guidance and limit themselves by the ten principles cited earlier. When they go beyond this, they are merely human assemblies with no special authority.

The Council of Trent

The canons and decrees of the Council of Trent present a strong contrast, even an antithesis, to Luther's positions. Already in the first of the three Council of Trent periods, decisions were made on Scripture, original sin, justification, the sacraments in general, baptism and confirmation that defied the Reformers in the strongest terms.

- On the Church and Scripture: The Church is the official interpreter of Scripture. The Bible and official church tradition are equally authoritative. The deuterocanonical (apocryphal) books were officially included in Scripture. Thus, Scripture does not stand above the Church; rather, the Church, in its official decrees from the pope and from Councils, stands above Scripture.
- On Justification: Human cooperation with divine grace was affirmed. Salvation by grace alone and through faith alone were rejected.
- On the Sacraments: Seven sacraments were reaffirmed in contrast to the Lutheran position which emphasized baptism and holy communion as the visible means through which the Holy Spirit works.[21]
- On a few other disputed points (made in the third period): The doctrines of purgatory, invocation of saints, veneration of relics, and use of indulgences (with modifications) were all reaffirmed.[22] This was the final "slap in the face" of Luther and his coworkers.

It is probably not an exaggeration to say that Luther's worst fears about the harmful use of a church council were realized.

In conclusion, church history, according to Luther, shows the hand of God leading His people through the work of the Holy Spirit when those people rely on Scripture, make full use of the Sacraments, and display the other visible marks. But church history shows opposition to God when anything is substituted for Scripture and when the proper use of the Sacraments is lacking and the other marks are not displayed.

We may safely assert that Luther's understanding of church history emboldened him to stand against the basic trends of the previous few centuries. His defiant reliance on Scripture gave him the confidence to stand up to the hierarchy of the Roman Church and to denounce it as in opposition to God's Word. His conviction in *Sola Scriptura* made it possible for Luther to see himself as "on the right side of history."

- **Essay 2** -

Luther on Children's Education

Chapter 2 of Part One deals with Martin's youth, so in this second essay we will examine his progressive views on children and their education, which are remarkable. Luther brought his wisdom and insights not only to topics that were theological or church-related but also to many social topics. His views on such topics played a crucial role in bringing society as a whole out of a medieval framework into a modern era. Societies today still struggle with issues of child abuse and inadequate opportunities for many children. Moreover, Luther's ideas on education are relevant to contemporary issues regarding public vs. private schooling and the role, if any, that religious teachings should have on what is taught in public schools.

Children: Precious to God

One of my favorite passages from Luther's *Small Catechism,* indeed from all of his writings, is from his introduction to the Lord's Prayer: "Our Father who art in heaven. What does this mean? By these words God would tenderly encourage us to believe that He is our true Father and that we are His true children, so that we may ask Him confidently with all assurance, as dear children (*liebe Kinder*) ask their dear father."[1]

Luther viewed children *spiritually* and saw them as precious in God's eyes. In his treatise, *The Estate of Marriage* of 1522, written when Luther was 38—three years before his marriage, he wrote,

> But the greatest good in married life, that which makes all suffering and labor worthwhile, is that God grants offspring and commands that they be brought up to worship and serve him. In all the world, this is the noblest and most precious work, because to God there can be nothing dearer than the salvation of souls. Now since we are all duty bound to suffer death, if need be, that we might bring a single soul to God, you can see how rich the estate of marriage is in good works…. Most certainly father and mother are apostles, bishops, and priests to their children, for it is they who make them acquainted with the gospel. In short, there is no greater or nobler authority on earth than that of parents over their children, for this authority is both spiritual and temporal.[2]

Parents are authority figures, but they are to use their authority for the well-being and salvation of the precious children God has entrusted to them.

Luther married in June of 1525, and he and Kate had six children born between 1526 and 1534. With respect to his own children, Luther knew both joy and heartache. The second child, Elizabeth, died during her first year, and another daughter, Magdalena, died in Luther's arms when she was only thirteen. Luther's love for Magdalena is beautifully shown in passages in his *Table Talks*. About Luther, it was written, "When his daughter was in the agony of death, he fell on his knees before the bed and, weeping bitterly, prayed that God might will to save her. Thus she gave up the ghost in the arms of her father."[3] And this is a quote from Luther: "Dear daughter, you have another Father in heaven. You are going to him."[4] Luther was a strict father with high expectations of his children, but he exhibited great love and care for them.

Luther's high regard for children was perhaps best shown by two works in which he emphasized their education. In 1524 Luther wrote a famous letter *To the Councilmen of All Cities in Germany That They Establish and Maintain Christian Schools*,[5] and in 1530 he penned *A Sermon on Keeping Children in School*.[6]

Political Leaders: Establish More Schools

In 1524 Luther looked on the situation of elementary education in Germany as deplorable. The schools that did exist were primarily for the children of the middle and upper classes; most children received little or no schooling. The schools were controlled by the Catholic Church and stressed learning Latin. With the focus of the elementary schools on the medieval curriculum of grammar, logic, and rhetoric, and with their strict discipline, they did not provide a valuable education, spiritual or otherwise, according to Luther, and he saw that more parents were deciding not to send their children to school. Luther decried the monastery and cathedral schools as "devil's training centers" and as offering "asses' dung."[7] In his own view, if they were the only choice, "I could wish that no boy would ever study at all, but just remain dumb."[8] But he stressed that they cannot be the only choice.

Luther felt no remorse that the monastery and cathedral schools were disappearing, but he argued that the worst possible reaction to this was leaving the education gap unfilled. Satan would love an uneducated people who would not be able to study Scripture, discern false teachings, or provide a qualified clergy.[9] In addition, a society will always need strong, educated leaders in the secular realm.[10] Furthermore, it is a great mistreatment of children not to offer them the gift of a quality education.[11]

To remedy this situation, Luther offered the following among the points included in the 1524 document:

1.   The responsibility to provide good educational institutions now falls upon the secular leaders. The Catholic Church has failed and parents are not providing the education; the nobility and council members must step to the fore.[12]

> It therefore behooves the council and the authorities to devote the greatest care and attention to the young. Since the property, honor, and life of the whole city have been committed to their faithful keeping, they would be remiss in their duty before God and man if they did not seek its welfare and improvement day and night with all the means at their command.[13]

2.   Education is not only important for those going into the learned professions of law, ministry, and medicine. All children including those who will become workers should receive basic schooling.

> This one consideration alone would be sufficient to justify the establishment everywhere of the very best schools for both boys and girls, namely, that in order to maintain its temporal estate outwardly the world must have good and capable men and women, men able to rule over land and people, women able to manage the household and train children and servants aright.[14]

3. Girls as well as boys should receive education.

Now such men must come from our boys, and such women from our girls. Therefore, it is a matter of properly educating and training our boys and girls to that end.[15]

4. Basic to good education is a strong grounding in the languages including Greek, Latin, and Hebrew.

Languages and the arts, which can do us no harm, but are actually a greater ornament, profit, glory and benefit, both for the understanding of Holy Scripture and the conduct of temporal government—these we despise. But foreign wares, which are neither necessary nor useful, and in addition strip us down to a mere skeleton—these we cannot do without. Are not we Germans justly dubbed fools and beasts?[16]

5. Education will take place better without the harsh discipline that has been so common.

By the grace of God it is now possible for children to study with pleasure and in play languages, or other arts, or history. Today, schools are not what they once were, a hell and purgatory in which we were tormented with *causalibus* and *temporalibus,* and yet learned less than nothing despite all the flogging, trembling, anguish, and misery.[17]

6. The political leaders need also to establish libraries containing collections of high quality works.

Finally, one thing more merits serious consideration by all those who earnestly desire to have such schools and languages established and maintained in Germany. It is this: no effort or expense should be spared to provide good libraries or book repositories, especially in the larger cities which can well afford it. For if the gospel and all the arts are to be preserved, they must be set down and held fast in books and writings.[18]

Luther was not about to give in to the anti-intellectual and anti-education voices that were being heard. Instead, he offered a progressive antidote to the situation. And we know that leaders in such communities as Magdeburg, Gotha, Eisleben, and Nürnberg responded positively to his suggestions.

Parents: Send Children to School

Luther's other key writing on education was his 1530 *Sermon on Keeping Children in School.* It was written from the Coburg Castle, where he remained because he was under the ban, while Melanchthon and others were defending Lutheranism before the Diet of Augsburg. Coburg was as close as he could get to Augsburg while still under the protection of John the Steadfast, Elector of Saxony (the brother and successor of Frederick the Wise).

He wrote this as a sermon that Lutheran pastors could preach. It was written in July and was published in August. I doubt, though, that Luther expected the sermon to be preached verbatim, for I calculate that it would have lasted ninety minutes.

While the earlier writing called for the establishment of new schools and is addressed to political leaders, this one focused on parents and the duty they have to send their children to school. Luther was harshly critical of parents too little concerned about the wellbeing of their children, of the church, and of society to provide for the education of their sons and daughters. He chastised them for their focus on making money and for accepting the common anti-intellectual adage, "Die Gelehrten, die Verkehrten" ("The learned, the crazy").[19] How will the Gospel and the Church survive in Germany, he believed, if none are educated to become pastors and schoolteachers? How will there be a strong society if none are educated to know, develop, and enforce civil law? How will young people realize their full ability if they are not taught?

In his argument, Luther added an important and innovative twist. He was not satisfied if only the sons of the privileged study. His focus was on the "common people" far more than it had been in the 1524 *"To the Councilmen"* cited above.

> Therefore go ahead and have your son study. And even if he has to beg bread for a time, you are nonetheless giving to our Lord God a fine bit of wood out of which he can carve you a lord. That is the way it will always be: your son and my son, that is, the children of the common people, will necessarily rule the world, both in the spiritual and the worldly estates, as this psalm [113] testifies. For the rich misers cannot and will not do it; they are the Carthusians [known for their austerity] and monks of Mammon, whom they must serve day and night. The born princes and lords cannot do it alone; they are particularly unable to understand anything at all about the spiritual office. Thus both kinds of government on earth must remain with the middle class of common people, and with their children.[20]

It is a message to the lower class. Here is your chance, through education, to lift yourselves up and to take control of things for the betterment of society.

Luther was not only a spiritual leader. He was remarkably progressive, even revolutionary, on other topics important for society. One such topic was the education of children. He supported state-established schools, general education for all classes, education of both boys and girls, and the reduction of harsh discipline. Beyond this, he even looked to the lower and middle classes to provide leadership in both the spiritual and the secular fields thus mirroring his own development.

His views on education, though, were never far from his spiritual focus. Indeed, one can argue that it was his understanding of the Gospel with its liberating power that opened the door to his remarkable insights on education.

*

The full list of Luther's children is: Hans (b. June 7, 1526, d. 1575), Elizabeth (b. Dec. 10, 1527, d. August 1528), Magdalena (b. May 5, 1529, d. Sept. 20, 1542) Martin (b. Nov. 9, 1531, d. 1565), Paul (b. Jan. 28, 1533, d. Mar. 8, 1593), and Margarethe (b. December 17, 1534, d. 1570). Hans became a lawyer, Martin studied theology, and Paul became a physician and a professor at Jena.[21]

Luther on Monasticism

When Luther developed a critique on an issue, he not only had done careful research on the biblical basis for his views; he generally also had extensive first-hand experience on which he drew. Nothing illustrates this better than Luther's eventual attack on monasticism.

There is no doubt that as a young man Luther dedicated himself wholeheartedly to the monastic life—and was even fanatical about it. The worship services several times each day, the intense prayer life, the devotion to his work responsibilities, and the obligatory control of his thoughts and actions were his ritual. He was a "monk's monk," so to speak. As such a monk, Luther was a supremely devout Catholic committed to the teachings and practices of 16th-century Roman Catholicism. In this essay we will explore how and why that changed so completely—and even violently.

Luther: A Monk's Monk

In 1533, long after he had left the monastery and had also been excommunicated, Luther, as part of his defense against the charges of Duke George of Saxony, said the following about his earlier life as a monk:

> It is true, I was a pious monk, and so strictly did I observe the rules of my order that I may say: If ever a monk got to heaven through monasticism I, too, would have got there. To this all my associates in the cloister, who knew me, will bear witness. If this life had lasted longer, I would have martyred myself to death with the vigils, praying, reading, and other labor.[1]

It is reported that John Nathin, Luther's monastic instructor, would point to Luther as a model monk and another St. Paul.[2]

Luther was twenty-one and had begun graduate studies in law and philosophy when in 1505 he entered a monastery of the Augustinian Order. After his transfer from Erfurt to Wittenberg, he maintained his close contact with the Erfurt monks as is shown by his 1512 invitation to them to come to his graduation as Doctor of Theology. For a time he also served as a vicar, inspecting the spiritual and financial conditions at various Augustinian monasteries and reporting his findings back to Erfurt. His life as a monk could become quite hectic as the following excerpt from a letter to John Lang, the prior at Erfurt, shows:

> I am a preacher at the monastery, I am a reader during mealtimes, I am asked daily to preach in the city church, I have to supervise the study [of students], I am a vicar (and that means eleven times prior), I am

caretaker of the fish [pond] at Leitzkau, I represent the people of Herzberg at the court in Torgau, I lecture on Paul, and I am assembling a commentary on the Psalms.[3]

Even after the posting of the Ninety-Five Theses in 1517 and the vehement rebuff Luther received from the Church, he continued to live as a monk in the Augustinian Monastery at Wittenberg. He became upset that so many monks around the country, acting, no doubt, on things Luther had written, were fleeing the monasteries in a sudden and disorderly way. In a letter written from the Wartburg in December of 1521 to John Lang at Erfurt, Luther wrote, "the monks could have parted from each other in a more peaceful and friendly way."[4] Luther himself wore the cowl and habit as a monk until October of 1524—a full seven years after posting the Ninety-Five Theses!

Luther's Attack on Monasticism

Later, however, guided by the Gospel of grace and faith proclaimed in Scripture, Luther denounced monasticism in the strongest terms, and he analyzed its flaws in detail. In his *Smalcald Articles* of 1537, a document in which the later Luther summarized his mature positions on the key theological issues, he gave his basic objection succinctly in Article XIV:

> Since monastic vows directly conflict with the first chief article [of the *Smalcald* Articles, a clear statement of salvation only through Christ's redemption], they must be absolutely abolished. It is about them that Christ says, "Many will come in my name, saying, 'I am the Christ,' and they will lead many astray" (Matthew 24:5, 23–24). He who makes a vow to live as a monk believes that he will enter upon a way of life holier than ordinary Christians lead. He wants to earn heaven by his own works, not only for himself, but also for others. This is to deny Christ. They also boast from their St. Thomas Aquinas that a monastic vow is equal to Baptism. This is blasphemy.[5]

Luther's primary criticism of monasticism was that it promoted, whether explicitly or implicitly, work righteousness and thus stood in direct opposition to a doctrine of salvation made possible solely through God's grace. Luther saw it as a flagrant attack on the Gospel. And, of course, the criticism applied not only to the monastic life but also to all of the work-righteous deeds that were promoted by the Church at that time and were a part of monastic life. This included devotional use of relics, going on pilgrimages, buying indulgences, purchasing masses, saying a large number of prayers, doing penance by self-flagellation, and others.

Luther also offered many other criticisms of monasticism:

1. The monastic life offers no inner peace, for monks are never certain that they are doing enough to merit God's favor. In his 1535 *Lectures on Galatians*, Luther wrote:

> I saw many who tried with great effort and the best of intentions to do everything possible to appease their conscience. They wore hair shirts; they fasted; they prayed; they tormented and wore out their bodies with various exercises so severely that if they had been made of iron, they would have been crushed. And yet the more they labored, the greater their terrors became. Especially when the hour of death was imminent, they became so fearful that I have seen many murderers facing execution die more confidently than these men who had lived such saintly lives.[6]

2. People often enter the monastic life for all of the wrong reasons including doubts about themselves. In 1532, Luther wrote in his exposition of Matthew 5:6 ("Blessed are those who hunger and thirst for righteousness, for they will be filled."):

"Despair makes a monk" is a saying that has always been true. It means that a man either has no confidence in his ability to make a living and runs into a monastery for the sake of his stomach, as most monks have done, or that he despairs of the world and is not sure of himself that he will remain pious or help other people become better.[7]

3. A Christian's calling is not to run from society and other people but to serve God where they are. In a 1533 sermon on Luke 2:15–20 (the shepherds at Bethlehem at the time of Jesus' birth), Luther wrote:

These shepherds do not run away into the desert, they do not don monk's garb, they do not shave their heads, neither do they change their clothing, schedule, food, drink, nor any external work. They return to their place in the fields to serve God there![8]

4. Living a chaste life within marriage is far better in God's eyes than the false "chastity" of forced celibacy. In 1532, Luther wrote:

What have I promised with my chastity? I have renounced marriage; for the unchasteness outside marriage—such as adultery, fornication, impurity, etc.—I need not renounce in a cloister; God has already forbidden these things to the layman as well as to monks. Nay, precisely with this promise I have *renounced* chastity; for God Himself calls the estate of matrimony chastity, holiness, and pureness (I Thess. 4:3)…. The monk, therefore, who can renounce no more in his vow of chastity than marriage must of necessity renounce marriage as unchasteness.[9]

5. The vow of chastity and the other aspects of the monastic vow do not change our human nature. The following comment was attributed to Luther:

Aristotle uses fire, which burns whether it be in Ethiopia or in Germany, as an illustration of something. It signifies that nature is not changed by circumstances of place or time. So a monk, if his nature is evil, is the same inside or outside a monastery.[10]

6. A normal, domestic life can be far more godly.

Let the monks and nuns glory in their works. For a husband, let it be enough if he rules his house properly; for a wife let it be enough if she takes care of the children by feeding them, washing them, and putting them to sleep, if she is obedient to her husband and diligently takes care of the household affairs. These works far surpass those of all nuns. Nevertheless, nuns are exceedingly proud of what they do.[11]

7. Monastic vows are human ordinances and go beyond anything God commands. In his 1521 attack on monastic vows, Luther wrote:

We need only abide within the limits of the humbler chastity of marriage and not walk according to the flesh. After all, it was not God who commanded chastity, nor did he counsel or recommend it. It was introduced by human temerity and ignorance.[12]

Several of these points, especially the "primary criticism" and #7 above are addressed extensively in the *Augsburg Confession*, Article XXVII, and in the parallel Article of the Apology of the *Augsburg Confession*. Although these sources were written by Melanchthon, they certainly had Luther's approval. One additional point is emphasized in them—the improper nature of the monastic vow itself—that it is made, for example, by people far too young for such a vow.

A Slight Qualification

In the last twenty years of his life, Luther's attacks on monasticism seem relentless. But that is not entirely the case. In the very *Smalcald Articles* of 1537 cited above he also stated the following:

Monastic colleges and communities were formerly founded with the good intention of educating learned men and virtuous women. They should be used for that again. They could produce pastors, preachers, and other ministers for the churches. They could also produce essential personnel for the secular government in cities and countries, as well as well-educated young women for mothers, housekeepers, and such.[13]

These passages can be reconciled only if Luther judged that the monastic life was not inherently contrary to the Gospel and to a proper Christian life. In other words, a proper reform (consistent with Luther's intent on "reform"—not "revolution") would make it clear that the life in a monastery or nunnery is not based on work-righteousness, that it is not superior to any other Christian calling, that the focus should not be on rituals, penance, poverty, celibacy, vows, and the like, but rather on Christian service beneficial to society. Without such change, the doors of monastic institutions should be closed without hesitation.

It is worth noting in conclusion, that there are a handful of Lutheran monasteries in the world today—in Sweden, Germany, and Finland, and there is also one in Oxford, Michigan. Visiting the Lutheran St. Augustine's House in Oxford, Michigan, and the Roman Catholic Cistercian Abbey of Our Lady of Gethsemani near Bardstown, Kentucky, made somewhat famous as the monastic home of Thomas Merton, revealed that in a monastery there can be an emphasis on outward Christian service and the gospel can be proclaimed. Nevertheless, the dangers to which Luther pointed, were real and his demands for reform were necessary.

- **Essay 4** •

Luther on the Central Issue: Law and Gospel

Both before and after the posting of the Ninety-Five Theses in 1517, the crucial issue for Luther was always how, if at all, can we be right with God. How can we be saved from eternal damnation? How can we be legitimately relieved from the terrible burden of sin, from our fear of a righteous God, and from our cases of spiritual turmoil—our *Anfechtungen*? How can we live with genuine confidence and hope?

In the wording of these questions, key words are "legitimately" and "genuine." Luther could not be satisfied with such easy answers as "Just do your best; God doesn't expect any more than that" or "You do your part and God will do his" or "Trust in the goodness of a caring God" or "The Church's answers have always been good enough for everyone else."

Fortunately, Luther was not satisfied with easy answers. If he had been, he never would have dug so deeply into Scripture.

It was fortunate, too, that he was urged by his mentor, Johann von Staupitz, to earn a doctorate in theology and to teach biblical studies at the university level. This gave him the perfect opportunity to dig deeply.

And it was *extremely* fortunate that near the very beginning of his academic career, he focused on the Pauline letters to the Romans and Galatians.

The insights that Luther gained from his careful study of these writings were the crucial points that shaped Luther's entire theology and his entire life. Those insights also freed him from his inner own *"Anfechtungen,"* and gave him the courage to speak out with amazing strength and directness. All of this was made possible by his pre–1517 work as a young theology professor at the University of Wittenberg.

Luther's earliest lectures in 1513–14 were on the Psalms, and these were followed by lectures on Romans in 1515 and on Galatians in 1516 and early 1517. Preparation for the lectures forced him to explore and meditate on such passages as "The righteous will live by faith" (Romans 1:17 & Galatians 3:11), "We maintain that a man is justified by faith apart from observing the law" (Romans 3:28), and "All who rely on observing the law are under a curse" (Galatians 3:10). In the process, Luther became a vigilant opponent of any form of Pelagianism, the heresy condemned by the Church in the fifth century according to which a person still has a free will uncorrupted by the fall and can earn righteousness,[1] or of Semi-pelagianism, the heresy that free will is only partially impaired and a person must do his part which is then supplemented by God's grace.

225

The *Lectures on Galatians* was prepared by Luther for publication in 1519. He lectured on the epistle again in 1531 with publication in 1535. The *Lectures on Romans* was not published during Luther's lifetime but the manuscript survived and was published in its fullness in the 20th century. In 1522 Luther did, however, write for publication the important "Preface to the Epistle of St. Paul to the Romans," in which he clearly laid out his understanding of Law and Gospel.

These lectures and writings provide a perfect introduction to both the early and mature views on his most central theological position. It is also worth noting that Luther's exegetical studies, in distinction from his polemical writings, can provide a helpful introduction to his theological views because the latter are often addressed to specific situations and are colored by personalities, context, and emotion.

In his early lectures on Galatians and Romans, Luther was critical of many practices of the Church as man-made and inconsistent with Scripture, but his language shows that he presented these criticisms as those of a loyal son seeking to promote renewal and reform from within. In his interpretations of specific verses, he made frequent positive use of Jerome, Augustine, and other Church Fathers respected and used in the Roman Church—and even of the contemporary Humanist, Erasmus. Later, however, he was critical of his early commentaries for being too soft in its criticisms of church practices and doctrines and for accepting too much of Jerome and Erasmus.

We will highlight Luther on Law and Gospel by looking at his early lectures on Romans, his early lectures on Galatians, the "Preface" to Romans, and finally to his later lectures on Galatians.

The Early Lectures on Romans

In his 1513–14 lectures on the Psalms, Luther had given special attention to the Penitential Psalms and to the picture of an obedient and suffering Christ that he saw in them. Then when he turned to Romans in 1515, he was struck by the significance of that picture of Christ for our own spiritual lives. It becomes, he realized, the basis for our own righteousness. Jesus was obedient and suffered *for us that we might be made righteous in God's eyes*. A believer is still a sinner, but through faith is forgiven, is made righteous. A believer is humbled before God. This humiliation does not make people more distant from God but actually brings them closer to him "for in humility they will seek Christ and confess that they are sinners and thus receive grace and be saved."[2]

When Luther compared the practices of the Church, including monasticism, with all of this, he was dismayed.[3] There is no humility before God. There is no recognition that acts prescribed by the Church's leaders are themselves sinful and do not result in the faith Paul described. There is no proper recognition of the Law. There is no proper respect for the Gospel.

The Early Lectures on the Epistle to the Galatians

Luther likewise loved Paul's letter to the churches of Galatia. He once said, "The Epistle to the Galatians is my epistle, to which I have wedded myself. It is my Catherine von Bora"[4]— a reference to his beloved wife.

Luther caught Paul's emphasis on grace and the Gospel in this letter and gave it a poignant application:

> Certainly today, too, the Gospel has been perverted in a great part of the church, since they are teaching people nothing but the decrees of the popes and the traditions of men who turn their backs on the truth; or the Gospel is treated in such a way that it does not differ at all from laws and moral precepts. The knowledge of faith and of grace is despised even by the theologians themselves.[5]

Significantly, Luther was not merely claiming that the contrast is between the commands and traditions of *men* on the one hand and *Scripture's* teaching of faith and grace on the other; it is also between *God's* commandments and that teaching of faith and grace. He was dealing with the fundamental distinction between Law and Gospel. He wrote:

> The Gospel and the Law, taken in their proper sense, differ in this way: The Law proclaims what must be done and left undone; or better, it proclaims what deeds have already been committed and omitted, and also that possible things are done and left undone (hence the only thing it provides is the knowledge of sin); the Gospel, however, proclaims that sins have been remitted and that all things have been fulfilled and done.[6]

Luther included under the Law the entire law of the *Old Testament*—not merely the regulations and rules developed by the Pharisees and other Jewish religious leaders. The Law reveals our human inadequacies, our sin, and can never be a source of comfort. The Gospel, by contrast, tells us that through faith in Christ we are forgiven and freed.

> But when the heart has thus been justified through the faith that is in His name, God gives them [those who trust in the Lord] the power to become children of God (John 1:12) by immediately pouring into their hearts His Holy Spirit (Romans 5:5), who fills them with His love and makes them peaceful, glad, active in all good works, victorious over all evils, contemptuous even of death and hell. Here all laws and all works of laws soon cease; all things are now free and permissible, and the Law is fulfilled through faith and love.[7]

Works of the Law may be done and may be well and good, but one can never be justified by them. They *follow* righteousness, rather than leading to it. "Christian righteousness and human righteousness are not only altogether different but are even opposed to each other, because the latter comes from works, while works come from the former."[8]

What, then, is the purpose of the Commandments? They are necessary for sinners to reveal their sin, and they show sinners, made righteous by faith, how they should live.[9] The Law has *prepared* us for Christ and for faith; it is not our companion or custodian *with* Christ.[10]

Luther ended his commentary with a powerful statement that those who find his claim odious in any way should first set his name aside and only look at Paul and the clarity of his writing on Law and Gospel, and then compare it with "the appearance presented by the church, which today is most wretched."[11]

The thrust of these powerful lectures is that the Law, God-given or man-made (even by the Church), can never make us right with God. That can only come through the Gospel according to which God forgives us because of Christ. The Law can lead us to Christ but it can never bond us with him.

The Preface to the Epistle to the Romans

In the "Preface," Luther showed exceptionally high regard for Romans:

This epistle is really the chief part of the New Testament and is truly the purest gospel. It is worthy not only that every Christian should know it word for word, by heart, but also that he should occupy himself with it every day, as the daily bread of the soul. We can never read it or ponder over it too much; for the more we deal with it, the more precious it becomes and the better it tastes.[12]

By 1522, the date of the writing of this "Preface" (revised in 1546), Luther had developed a clearer understanding of Law and Gospel as the center of the Christian message. In this work there are no attacks or extraneous comments. There are only a concise explanation of key theological terms (law, sin, grace, faith righteousness, flesh, and spirit) and a brief chapter-by-chapter summary of the epistle.

The term that Luther explains first and most fully is "law." In this he makes the following points:

- Paul does not mean a teaching about deeds that are to be done or not done; he means having a love for the law in the depth of one's heart.[13]
- No one can love the law that God lays down even if one is determined to keep it; thus, no one can really keep the law.[14]
- Thus, all are sinners no matter what their outward deeds may be.[15]
- To fulfill the law, one must do its works with pleasure and love.[16]
- Christ has fulfilled the law for us.[17]
- Only with faith in Christ can one have this love for the law and what it requires.[18]
- Thus, only faith in Christ can fulfill the law.[19]
- This faith is given by God's Holy Spirit and is not our own product.[20]

Luther then went on to explain the other key terms. "Gospel" is not among them but is mentioned in the last paragraph as having been clarified by him. Indirectly, this is the case, for he did explicitly explain grace, faith and righteousness.

"Grace" is "God's favor or the good will which in himself he bears toward us, by which he is disposed to give us Christ and to pour into us the Holy Spirit with his gifts."[21]

"Faith" is "a divine work in us which changes us and makes us to be born anew of God .... It kills the old Adam and makes us altogether different men, in heart and spirit and mind and powers; and it brings with it the Holy Spirit. O [sic] it is a living, busy, active, mighty thing, this faith. It is impossible for it not to be doing good works incessantly."[22] "Faith is a living, daring confidence in God's grace, so sure and certain that the believer would stake his life on it a thousand times."[23]

On "righteousness," he wrote:

Righteousness ... is called 'the righteousness of God' because God gives it, and counts it as righteousness for the sake of Christ our Mediator, and makes a man to fulfill his obligation to everybody. For through faith a man becomes free from sin and comes to take pleasure in God's commandments.... [H]e serves his fellow-men willingly, by whatever means he can, and thus pays his debt to everyone. Nature, free will, and our own powers cannot bring this righteousness into being.[24]

Out of this we may define "Gospel" in the following way: "Gospel" is the good news that God in his grace gives us faith to trust in the righteousness that Christ has won for us. Through this faith we are able to live a new life of good works totally impossible without God's grace and the Holy Spirit working in us.

The Later Lectures on the Epistle to the Galatians

In his later and more developed commentary on Galatians, he showed beautifully his understanding of Law and Gospel.

He began with comments on the general argument of the epistle. "Christian righteousness," he claimed is passive and thus unlike any other kind of righteousness of which we might speak, e.g., political righteousness, ceremonial righteousness, or even righteousness of the Law, for only Christian righteousness is absolutely none of our doing and is the result purely of God's grace. Moreover, it is the only remedy that an afflicted conscience has against despair and eternal death. God, because of Christ, gives us faith and thus makes us righteous.[25]

But before this faith can have any effect, there must be awareness of the Law and of the God-given demands that we cannot fulfill. It is totally impossible for any human to achieve a righteousness by the Law. The Law can only lead to an afflicted conscience; that is, however, a good thing, for it makes us ready for the divine gift of faith and the total righteousness that is bequeathed on us because of Christ.

The comfort that the Christian finds in the Gospel is stated elegantly by Luther near the end of the opening section on the epistle's argument:

> I am baptized; and through the Gospel I have been called to a fellowship of righteousness and eternal life, to the kingdom of Christ, in which my conscience is at peace, where there is no Law but only the forgiveness of sins, peace, quiet, happiness, salvation, and eternal life. Do not disturb me in these matters. In my conscience not the Law will reign, that hard tyrant and cruel disciplinarian, but Christ, the Son of God, the King of peace and righteousness, the sweet Savior and Mediator. He will preserve my conscience happy and peaceful in the sound and pure doctrine of the Gospel and in the knowledge of this passive righteousness.[26]

Summary

What, then, in the end is Luther's understanding of Law and Gospel—what he understood to be the central pillar of Christian faith?

Law is the entire body of God's commands given to guide into holy living and righteousness but demanding at all times pure devotion and love. It is totally beyond our reach and properly condemns us daily. But it serves the wonderful purpose of making us desperate and preparing us for the passive reception of the Gospel.

The Gospel is God's gift to us whereby he gives us faith and makes us righteous through the pure righteousness won for us by Christ. It remakes us and leads us gladly to do God's will and the good works which God demands. While the Law condemns us every day, the Gospel assures us that we are forgiven and made righteous. The Gospel holds out for us the promise of new life now and in eternity.

It is not too much to say that Luther sought to bring all of his other positions under this central doctrine. All other teachings were to be consistent with and flow from the basics of Law and Gospel, sin and grace.

Rejection by the Roman Church

It is little wonder that the Roman Catholic Church of Luther's day could not accept this. The problem wasn't only that Luther objected to indulgences, corruption, wickedness in the priesthood, and the like. He was objecting to any theology that made room for humans to please God, even in the smallest way, through their own initiative. His vigilance opposed *any* form of Pelagianism—*any* effort to show that a human can cooperate and do some things that lead God to declare that person righteous.

Thus, all of canon law would crumble. The structure of ecclesiastical authority with its dependence upon human directives and punishments would collapse. And any effort to motivate people to act in certain ways in order to placate or to please God would be doomed.

Luther's understanding of Law and Gospel is of great relevance today, for it is a constant temptation in various church bodies to promote a form of Christian moralism and legalism. The Gospel is wonderfully liberating, but for people who seek to control or manipulate others or for people who think that it goes against human reason, it is still an obstacle.

• Essay 5 •

Luther on the Divisive Issue:
Indulgences and Church Finances

Luther, we can be sure, had no idea that his posting of the theses and his challenge for a debate would cause such a major upheaval. But we know why it did. It was about *the money*. The money led both to *the ecclesiastical* and to *the political hierarchy*. The hierarchy led to *the pope*. Perhaps unwittingly, Luther had placed his challenge where it hurt the most. If "Law and Gospel" was the "central issue," "Church finances" was the "divisive issue."

Luther's Insistence on Arguments from Scripture

A little over two years after the Ninety-Five Theses had been posted, in January of 1519, when Karl von Miltitz traveled from Rome to Germany to put pressure on Frederick the Wise to force Luther to back down, Luther sent a letter to Frederick. He wished to assure everyone, he wrote, that he was not attacking the Church but only wished to point out the theological wrongs of indulgences as practiced. His letter included the following as one of the offers he was willing to make to Miltitz:

> I was willing to issue [a little book] to admonish everyone to follow the Roman church, to be obedient and respect it, and to understand my writings as having been intended to bring not dishonor but honor to the holy Roman church. [In this little book] I also wanted to confess that I had pointed out the truth too heatedly and brought it to the attention of the public at what was perhaps the wrong time. [I wanted to demonstrate] that while the issue is quite important, I had done enough, and that in this matter it is sufficient for everyone to know the proper difference between indulgences and good works.[1]

In the letter, he also made it clear that he was unwilling to recant without Scriptural evidence that he was wrong, but he denied that he was attacking the Roman Church or the Papacy per se. We can see, however, that *money* did tie indulgences to the Church, Luther's assurances notwithstanding.

Indulgences, Repentance and Forgiveness

The Roman Church had, it must be noted, issued indulgences for centuries. Indulgences were intended to be assurances to the penitent that they had indeed demonstrated the

231

requisite sorrow for their sins. As such, they were linked to the Roman Church's practice of penance—of repentance (and, perhaps, deeds which would show genuine sorrow, sacrifice, and devotion) that would prepare the way for forgiveness.

Repentance and forgiveness are, of course, tied tightly together in Scripture. John the Baptist preached "a baptism of repentance for the forgiveness of sins."[2] In his Pentecost message, Peter proclaimed, "Repent, and be baptized, every one of you, in the name of Jesus Christ for the forgiveness of your sins."[3] In the Old Testament, Nathan confronted David with his adultery and murder: "Then David said to Nathan, 'I have sinned against the Lord.' Nathan replied, 'The Lord has taken away your sin.'"[4]

"Repentance," "*metanoia*" in Greek, means literally, to turn around, to change direction 180 degrees. It involves a complete reorientation of one's life. It is linked also to faith in God's goodness and forgiveness. Genuine repentance includes contrition—a sorrow in one's heart,[5] faith, trust in His forgiveness, and change in one's life.

Scripture indicates that there should be signs of genuine repentance in a person's life. John the Baptist is quoted as saying, "Produce fruit in keeping with repentance."[6] Here is where indulgences entered the picture. They were intended originally to certify that a person had shown a genuine repentance in the heart thereby opening one to God's forgiveness.

Nevertheless, it all became a slippery slope. Already at the time of the First Crusade, indulgences were given by the Roman Church to warriors who had shown great courage and success in defending Western Christianity. Later they were extended to those who paid for others to fight. Subsequently, they were made available to people who went on pilgrimages, offered special prayers, gave alms, or performed similar acts of piety.

In the theology of indulgences developed by the scholastic theologian Thomas Aquinas, a distinction was made between temporal and eternal punishment for sin. In the account of David and Nathan, Nathan said, "The Lord has taken away your sin. You are not going to die. But because by doing this, you have made the enemies of the Lord show utter contempt, the son born to you will die."[7] In Thomistic theology, indulgences were not intended to guarantee anything involving eternal punishment (in hell) but rather were confined to the relief of temporal punishment in this world—*or in purgatory*. Purgatory was seen as an extension of the temporal punishments that had to be satisfied before one could enter heaven. If a person were genuinely penitent and did what was necessary to receive an indulgence, then the treasury of surplus merit accumulated by Christ and the great saints could be applied as compensation and relieve the penitent person of some or all temporal punishment in this life and in purgatory. Eventually, it came to be claimed that one could buy an indulgence for someone already in purgatory on the assumption that the person was genuinely penitent.

The Need for Money

It is also very significant that the Roman Church found indulgences to be a great moneymaking device. Indulgences could be sold to genuinely penitent people, it was claimed, and the payment of the money would be the "fruit in keeping with repentance." Thus was opened the door for tremendous graft and corruption.

Pope Leo X needed money and lots of it for his lavish lifestyle and for continuing the work on the elaborate St. Peter's Cathedral, begun by his equally extravagant predecessor,

Julius II. In addition, Albert of Brandenburg of the house of Hohenzollern needed money to pay back the Fuggers for a loan he had made to pay the fee for becoming the Archbishop of Mainz.

The solution, as described in Chapter 5, was a special plenary indulgence with the money to be split between the pope and Albert. The indulgence would be advertised as benefitting the construction of St. Peter's in Rome. The person responsible for selling the indulgences was a Dominican, John Tetzel. Until Luther entered the fray, the enterprise was very successful.

Luther's Attack

It should be noted that Luther did not attack this special indulgence on the basis of the financial issues; in fact, he claimed in a work written in 1541 that he "did not know at that time who would get the money."[8] Indeed, on the financial issue, Luther would also have tangled with his own Prince Frederick, who was the recipient of money for his kingdom and the university through a special Wittenberg indulgence. Frederick had accumulated a huge number of relics in Wittenberg, and people who made a pilgrimage there and venerated the relics could buy an indulgence; the highlighted day for this was All Saints' Day, November 1. Thus, it is not by chance that Luther posted the Ninety-Five Theses on October 31. Although the sermon is lost, Luther had apparently preached against the fallacies of these indulgences on All Saints' Day in 1516—a year before his posting of the Ninety-Five Theses.[9]

Luther may not have known in 1517 about the financial arrangements surrounding the indulgences, but he had heard about several outrageous things that Tetzel reportedly was saying. He wrote about some of them in the same 1541 writing mentioned above:

> I heard what dreadful and abominable articles Tetzel was preaching, and some of them I shall mention now, namely:
>
> That he had such grace and power from the pope that even if someone seduced the holy Virgin Mary, and made her conceive, he [Tetzel] could forgive him, provided he placed the necessary sum in the box.
>
> Again, that the red indulgence-cross, bearing the papal arms, was, when erected in church, as powerful as the cross of Christ.
>
> Again, that if St. Peter were here now, he would not have greater grace or power than he [Tetzel] had.
>
> Again, that he would not change places with St. Peter in heaven, for he had rescued more souls with indulgences than St. Peter had with his preaching.
>
> Again, that if anyone put money in the box for a soul in purgatory, the soul would fly to heaven as soon as the coin clinked on the bottom.
>
> Again, that the grace from indulgences was the same grace as that by which a man is reconciled to God.
>
> Again, that it was not necessary to have remorse, sorrow, or repentance for sin, if one bought (I ought to say, acquired) an indulgence or a dispensation; indeed, he sold also for future sin.[10]

Despite the scandalous nature of these claims, Luther focused on more theological issues in his various polemics against the Roman Church's practice of indulgences.

1. First and foremost, he sought to present his case solely on the basis of clear *Scriptural* passages. Biblical citations are not mentioned in the Ninety-Five Theses themselves, but the *Explanations of the Ninety-Five Theses,* published in 1518, is replete with Scriptural quotations and references.

2. Repentance must be a *sincere inner repentance*. It is not enough to go through a ritual or to pay an amount of money. Repentance is to be a matter of the heart.[11]

3. It is wrong to think that the pope has power over sin and the punishment of sin. Only *Christ* himself has this power.[12]

4. It is only through *faith* that the forgiveness of sins, the removal of guilt, and the satisfaction for punishment are received.[13]

5. Penance and the remission of sin can only apply to *the living* and only to *the one repenting in faith*.[14]

6. No human, including the pope, can impose penalties after death in purgatory, and so no human including the pope can remove them, either.[15]

7. Indulgences endanger souls by leading people to think that they are certain of salvation without any need for genuine repentance or faith.[16]

8. Indulgences are never preferable to Christian acts of love.[17]

9. Purgatory is a non-biblical fabrication developed as a moneymaking ploy.[18]

Luther's Position on Confession and Absolution

One might ask, what is the role of the pastor and the church in absolution—the pronouncement of the forgiveness of sins? Luther was well aware of Matthew 16:19, "I will give you the keys of the kingdom of heaven; whatever you bind on earth will be bound in heaven, and whatever you loose on earth will be loosed in heaven" and of John 20:21ff., "Again Jesus said, 'Peace be with you! As the Father has sent me, I am sending you.' And with that he breathed on them and said, 'Receive the Holy Spirit. If you forgive anyone his sins, they are forgiven; if you do not forgive them, they are not forgiven.'"

Indeed, one of the "six chief parts of Christian doctrine" in Luther's *Small Catechism* of 1529 is The Office of the Keys—Confession and Absolution. Luther described genuine confession of a person of faith and gave a brief form of confession at the end of which the confessor (the one hearing the confession) says, "Do you believe that my forgiveness is God's forgiveness? ... As you believe, so let it be done for you. And by the command of our Lord Jesus Christ I forgive you your sins, in the name of the Father and of the Son and of the Holy Spirit. Amen. Depart in Peace."[19]

In his *Large Catechism*, also dated 1529, Luther wrote the following:

> So notice then, that Confession, as I have often said, consists of two parts. The first is my own work and action, when I lament my sins and desire comfort and refreshment for my soul. The other part is a work that God does when He declares me free of my sin through His Word placed in the mouth of a man. It is this splendid, noble, thing that makes Confession so lovely, so comforting.[20]

In the end, Luther held that the absolution or forgiveness that comes to the repentant person of faith is *from God*. The person pronouncing the forgiveness is only the spokesperson for God. And what about the hypocritical person who has no faith or who only feigns repentance? The words spoken by the confessor cover that, too: "As you believe, so let it be done for you" or, as it is sometimes put, "Be it unto you according to your faith."

Luther on the Authority Issue: Papacy/Scripture

Luther did not shy away from difficult issues; neither did he show hesitation to expressing his judgments in very strong ways—that were almost certain to raise the hackles of Church officials. A vital issue was, of course, *who* has the authority. Who ultimately decides how the Church should function? Who has the authority to declare some views or practices wrong? Who settles doctrinal disputes? Who has the authority to make the biggest fiscal decisions? Who is the head of the Church?

If not the pope, then who? Or should the goal be to reform the papacy so that Scripture can be followed and God's will be done?[1]

A Change in Luther's Views on the Papacy

In 1545, near the end of his life, Luther wrote that as a monk he had been a "rabid papist."[2] He compared himself to Paul before his conversion:

So intoxicated, nay, so immersed in the doctrines of the pope was I, that I would have been quite ready to kill all, if possible, or to help those and to hold with those who killed the people who with a single syllable refused to render obedience to the pope.[3]

He went on to indicate how very much he regretted his earlier "concessions" to the pope after the Reformation began:

In these writings of mine you will, therefore, find how many great concessions at first I made to the pope in all humility—concessions which in later times and in these days I regard and execrate as supreme blasphemy and abomination.[4]

Luther did, of course, become extremely vehement and even coarse in his attacks on the pope and the papacy. But one thing is quite striking. Many others including Wycliffe and Hus had railed against the corruption, sinfulness, and outrageous wealth of the popes, but these were *not* the emphasis that Luther gave. Whether one looks at relatively early attacks on the papal office or at his later writings, Luther focused on how the papacy stood in the way of the *Gospel and the authority of Scripture.*

There is reason to believe that in 1517 Luther thought he was doing Rome a service by pointing out the sensationalistic practices of Tetzel. This point shouldn't be pushed too far,

though, for some of the theses themselves emphasized the limits of the pope's power in for-
giving sins. Nevertheless, Luther's harshest attacks would only come a little later, prompted
as they were by Rome's quick condemnations. Those counterattacks were fostered, no doubt,
by the immediate hostilities against Luther by Archbishop Albert of Mainz, who was receiving
money from the indulgences, and by Tetzel's fellow Dominicans. Luther was dismayed and
outraged by the Church's response.

The Theological Attack on the Papacy, 1520

By the time of the Leipzig Debate against Eck in 1519, the handwriting was on the wall.
Luther knew that the problem was not in the particular individual who happened to be the
pope at any given time, but was rather in the office itself as it had evolved in negative ways
over several centuries. In 1520 he used the occasion of a somewhat inept document written
by a Franciscan monk in Leipzig, Augustine Alveld to write a rebuttal tract entitled, *On the
Papacy in Rome Against the Most Celebrated Romanist in Leipzig*. In this tract he began to for-
mulate a fuller position on the Papacy. Also in 1520 he gave his more expanded judgments
on papal reform in *To the Christian Nobility of the German Nation Concerning the Reform of
the Christian Estate*.

The earlier piece, *On the Papacy in Rome…*, shows how highly he regarded Christ and
Scripture relative to the pope.

> First, I will not tolerate it that men establish new articles of faith and scold, slander, and judge as heretics,
> schismatics, and unbelievers all other Christians in the whole world only because they are not under the
> pope…. Second, I shall accept whatever the pope establishes and does, on condition that I judge it first
> on the basis of Holy Scripture. For my part he must remain under Christ and let himself be judged by
> Holy Scripture. But the Roman knaves come along and put him above Christ, make him a judge over
> Scripture, and say that he cannot err.[5]

*To the Christian Nobility of the German Nation Concerning the Reform of the Christian
Estate* went further. It reveals that Luther had lost all confidence that the Church could be
reformed from within. He now placed his hope in the new young Holy Roman Emperor,
Charles V, and on the nobility. They were the only opportunity for again placing Christ and
Scripture above any ecclesiastical office.

Some in the German nobility were delighted to see Luther take up the papacy issue
because of the so-called *Gravamina*—grievances over Rome's fleecing of the German areas.
These were the injustices they believed they had to endure in the huge amounts of money
that they were required to send to Rome for the building of elegant Italian churches and for
the exorbitant lifestyles of the pope and Curia. People such as Knight Ulrich von Hutten
loved Luther's attacks, but they didn't understand that Luther had spiritual concerns rather
than financial issues at heart.

To Luther the need for major reform seemed obvious on *theological* grounds. In *To the
Christian Nobility of the German Nation*, Luther expressed his dismay that a "wall" had been
built around the pope and that he was above the governments and other authorities, above
Scripture, and above the councils. This meant that there was no obvious way to reign in the
pope. The most serious issue was that he was held to be above Scripture and could interpret
or ignore passages according to his liking; he could also add doctrines and necessary practices

that were not even hinted at in Scripture. The terrible upshot of this was that *the Gospel of forgiveness through God's grace because of Jesus Christ was being destroyed.* In Luther's words, the problem was stated as follows:

> The Romanists have very cleverly built three walls around themselves. Hitherto they have protected themselves by these walls in such a way that no one has been able to reform them. As a result, the whole of Christendom has fallen abominably.
>
> In the first place, when pressed by the temporal power they have made decrees and declared that the temporal power had no jurisdiction over them, but that, on the contrary, the spiritual power is above the temporal. In the second place, when the attempt is made to reprove them with the Scriptures, they raise the objection that only the pope may interpret the Scriptures. In the third place, if threatened with a council, their story is that no one may summon a council but the pope.[6]

The theological basis that Luther used for pulling down the Papacy was the doctrine of the "priesthood of all believers." God's Church, he held, is not a hierarchy but rather a body in which all Christians have direct access to God including their Lord and Savior Jesus Christ.[7] This means that *all* Christians *including the pope* are, in the political realm as distinct from the Church, under the political leaders, who have been designated by God for that role. The pope is not above the political leaders, so the latter can initiate reforms consistent with Scripture and with sound political practice.[8] The pope can, for example, be punished by the political authorities as much as anyone else for illegal, corrupt practices.

Second, the "priesthood of all believers" means that God the Holy Spirit is available to all Christians and opens up Scripture to them.[9] The pope stands *under* Scripture as does every Christian and must be enlightened by the Holy Spirit the same as all other Christians. Moreover, the distinction between clergy and laity means that the power to forgive and retain sins has been given to the Church and can be administered by all pastors and not just the pope.

Third, the "priesthood of all believers" means that any God-fearing Christian can properly reprimand any other for conduct and teachings contrary to Scripture. This certainly means that an assembly of Christians, a church council, may do so and is not under the control of a pope or anyone else.[10]

Luther concluded the treatise with a call for twenty-six (twenty-seven in the second edition) reforms that the Emperor and the Nobility should make.[11] Several had to do with limiting the pope's and the church's authority in the secular and political realm. But he also called for drastic reforms of such things as pilgrimages, masses for the dead, saints' days, indulgences, monasteries, and even universities. Luther expected the Christian *political* authorities to initiate (or at least to demand) these changes, for he didn't see any alternative; for him it was the only viable, God-given means to bring reform to the church.

The Established Position, 1537

Melanchthon, not Luther, wrote the *Treatise on the Power and Primacy of the Pope*, 1537. It was formally adopted by the Smalcaldic League that year. Although thirty-two people signed it, Luther was not one of them—probably only because he was too ill at the time to take part in the meetings or to sign the document.

But Luther did write the *Smalcald Articles,* which were considered at the same assembly—

and signed by forty-three though not formally adopted—, and he did give his considered judgments on the papacy in a section of that document. We turn to it as a reflection of Luther's later views on the subject.

The *Smalcald Articles* were written by Luther as his "last will and testament" since he was so ill at the time that he expected to die any moment. He did live several more years, but the articles have retained their place as a clear, forthright, and "final" statement of Luther's positions on a broad range of issues.

Luther titled one of the articles, "The Papacy." Its place in the document shows the great importance he placed on the topic, for it is one of only four articles in "The Second Part." Part One was on the Trinity and was brief, for in this, he held, there was no dispute with Catholicism. Part Two was on "The Office and Work of Jesus Christ; That Is, Our Redemption." It was dedicated to the Gospel—the saving work of our Lord Jesus Christ, and on this there were huge points of disagreement. The four articles in Part Two were "The Chief Article" (justification by faith through Christ's redemptive sacrifice), "The Mass," "Chapters and Cloisters," and "The Papacy." Part Three included fifteen articles covering a whole range of doctrines including the law, baptism, holy communion, confession, and much more.

There are at least three major reasons given why the Papacy, in Luther's judgment, undercut the gospel of salvation through Christ. The first is that the pope was treated as the head of the church and thus stood in opposition to Christ. The second is that the pope makes salvation depend upon obedience to his commands and decrees rather than to faith alone in Christ. The third is that the pope attacks and kills those who commit themselves to a pure gospel rather than to the Pope's authority and system. We note again that Luther grounded his entire attack on the Gospel and commitment to Christ; the conduct of the popes, their lifestyle, their wealth, their sins, and their corruption were *not* the focus of his criticism. He was willing to call the pope the Antichrist because the office of the papacy stood in place of Christ.

Luther began the article with his fundamental point:

> The pope is not, according to divine law of God's Word, the head of all Christendom. This name belongs to One only, whose name is Jesus Christ (Colossians 1:18). The pope is only the bishop and pastor of the Church at Rome and of those who have attached themselves to him voluntarily or through a human agency (such as a political ruler). Christians are not under him as a lord. They are with him as brethren, colleagues, and companions, as the ancient councils and the age of St. Cyprian show.
>
> Today, though, none of the bishops dare to address the pope as "brother" as was done in the time of Cyprian.[12]

Luther believed he had both Scripture and history on his side:

> It is clear that the holy Church has been without the pope for over five hundred years at least.[13] To this day, the churches of the Greeks and of many other languages neither have been nor are presently under the pope. Besides, as is often remarked, the papacy is a human invention that is not commanded and is not necessary but useless. The holy Christian Church can exist very well without such a head.[14]

Even if it would be agreed that the papacy is a human institution solely to serve good order, it could not be accepted, for the only head of the church is Christ. We should live as a brotherhood.

> The Church can never be better governed and preserved than if we all live under one head, Christ. All the bishops should be equal in office (although they may be unequal in gifts). They should be diligently joined in unity of doctrine, faith, sacraments, prayer, works of love, and such. According to St. Jerome,

this is how the priests of Alexandria governed the churches, together and in common. So did the apostles and, afterward, all bishops throughout all Christendom, until the pope raised his head above all.[15]

Luther followed this with some of his most scathing comments:

This teaching shows forcefully that the pope is the true Endchrist or Antichrist (I John 2:18). He has exalted himself above and opposed himself against Christ. For he will not permit Christians to be saved without his power, which, nevertheless, is nothing, and is neither ordained nor commanded by God.... The pope ... bans [genuinely Christian] faith. He says that to be saved a person must obey him.... When we distinguish the pope's teaching from, or compare it to, Holy Scripture, it is clear that the pope's teaching at its best has been taken from the imperial and heathen law. It deals with political matters and decisions or rights, as the decretals show. His law also teaches ceremonies about churches, garments, food, persons, and childish, theatrical, and comical things without measure. But on all of this, nothing is taught about Christ, faith, and God's commandments. Finally, the papacy is nothing else than the devil himself, because above and against God the pope pushes his falsehoods about Masses, purgatory, the monastic life, one's own works, and false worship.[16]

Luther continued with a brief statement of the third major reason mentioned above, about attacking and damning those with genuine Christian faith:

He also condemns, murders, and tortures all Christians who do not exalt and honor his abominations above all things. Therefore, just as we cannot worship the devil himself as Lord and God, so we cannot endure his apostle—the pope or Antichrist—in his rule as head or lord. For what his papal government really consists of (as I have very clearly shown in many books) is to lie and kill and destroy body and soul eternally.[17]

Luther was very forceful in his attack, but he thought that he should be—even *had to be* because the very Gospel was at stake. *There could only be one head of the church—Jesus Christ—, and no one may undo the Gospel of grace by adding rules and regulations required for spiritual wellbeing.*

It is often asked whether Luther's arguments and attack apply only to the papacy of his day or to the papacy in general. Some have assumed, or at least wanted it to be true, that with the appropriate reforms, the papal office could indeed be an appropriate "earthly" head of the Church and perhaps a focal point for the unity of all Christians.

But it must be recognized that Luther's attack was against the very office and that he did not suggest reforms that would again make it consistent with the Gospel, with the Lordship of Christ, and with the priesthood of all believers. Luther's understanding of Christianity was so egalitarian in nature by virtue of a common baptism, creed, faith, Lord, and Holy Spirit that even an "earthly" head was unacceptable. While there may be different functions and different forms of service, ultimately the only "head" can be Jesus.

Finally, it must be said that Luther was concerned not at all about the "practicality" of his position. He was concerned, rather, about faithfulness to the Gospel, to Scripture, and to the Lordship of Christ.[18]

Luther on the Theologies
of Glory and the Cross

By early 1518, Luther had moved beyond a critique of particular Church practices or even of the authority structure of the Church. He now began his criticism of the Church's theological foundation and of the theologians. In a later essay, we will examine Luther's still developing attack on Scholasticism, the dominant intellectual methodology and structure in the universities at the time, but his fascinating assertions in the Heidelberg Disputation of April 1518 show a deep new theological foundation—in the distinction between a "theology of glory" and a "theology of the cross."

Luther's underlying concern behind this distinction was that theologians were allowing an abstract, "philosophical" understanding of God's essential nature to shape their theology and to open the door to a "works righteousness" perspective; he labeled this a "theology of glory." For Luther it was no genuine Christian theology at all and its adherents were not real "theologians."

The contrast is to see God's essential nature in concrete, biblical details—particularly about Jesus—, and to let this lead naturally to a "faith righteousness." He labeled this a "theology of the cross." The distinction was made explicit in the Heidelberg Disputation.

The Heidelberg Disputation

Staupitz, as head of the German congregation of the Augustinian Order, used the occasion of the triennial conclave of the congregation to have Luther present several debate theses on some of his theological points in the Ninety-Five Theses. He likely wanted the other monks to be aware of what Luther was teaching, undistorted by his opponents, and he no doubt wanted them to make a fair appraisal of the strengths and weaknesses of his claims. But he didn't think Luther should be the defender of the theses; Luther was already branded as a heretic in too many circles. Brother Leonhard Beier, a fellow member of the Augustinian Order, was selected as the person to defend them.

Luther presented forty theses—the first twenty-eight were labeled "theological theses" and the other twelve "philosophical theses." The theological theses focused on the ineffectual nature of all human works and the absolute importance of God's grace. Not only do our human works not lead to righteousness (thesis #2); they are "likely to be mortal sins" even if they "seem attractive and good" (thesis #3).[1] This is especially true when human works are done with a sense of "self-security" (thesis #8) and "arrogance" (thesis #11). Being aware of this is helpful, for it arouses "the desire to humble oneself and seek the grace of Christ" (thesis #17). Thesis #18: "It is certain that man must utterly despair of his own ability before he is prepared to receive the grace of Christ."[2] The next theses (especially #19–24) are on the theology of glory and the theology of the cross.

The philosophical theses (#29–40) focus on the serious mistake that theologians made by relying on the philosophical structure of Aristotle. Thesis #29 states: "He who wishes to philosophize by using Aristotle without danger to his soul must first become thoroughly foolish in Christ."[3] For Luther, there was no placing of Aristotle alongside Christ (as Aquinas did), or placing of any other philosopher with Christ; Christ was always superior. The foolishness of the Gospel was always superior to the wisdom of any human.

In six of the theses, Luther dealt with the theology of glory and the theology of the cross. In thesis #19, Luther wrote: "That person does not deserve to be called a theologian who looks upon the invisible things of God as though they were clearly perceptible in those things which have actually happened."[4] In his *Proofs of the Thesis Debated in the Chapter at Heidelberg*, May 1518, it is clear that these "invisible things of God" are abstract, philosophical concepts such as "virtue, godliness, wisdom, justice, goodness."[5] Perhaps such notions as omnipotence, omniscience, and omnipresence would have served his purposes even better. The point is that "theologians" try to know God in terms of such abstract notions instead of the concrete ways in which God reveals himself.

Thesis #20 gives the contrast: "He deserves to be called a theologian, however, who comprehends the visible and manifest things of God seen through suffering and the cross."[6] If we want to know the true nature of God, we need to look where we might least expect to find it, but where Scripture and Jesus lead us: to his suffering and death on the cross. The love of God is made manifest in the sacrifice that Jesus made on the cross. Quoting again from the *Proofs...*, "Now it is not sufficient for anyone, and it does him no good to recognize God in his glory and majesty, unless he recognizes him in the humility and shame of the cross.... True theology and recognition of God are in the crucified Christ, as it is also stated in John 10 [John 14:6]: 'No one comes to the Father, but by me.'"[7]

Thesis #21: "A theology of glory calls evil good and good evil. A theology of the cross calls the thing what it actually is."[8] Anyone who sees "good" and something God-pleasing in the deeds that people produce is calling the "evil good." Likewise, to think that Jesus' suffering and his death on the cross were bad is calling the "good evil," for they show the God of love in his full beauty and perfection. A theology of the cross, however, sees our human actions and God's gracious redemption for what they really are.

The following, also from the *Proofs...*, amplifies his points:

> This is clear: He who does not know Christ does not know God hidden in suffering. Therefore he prefers works to suffering, glory to the cross, strength to weakness, wisdom to folly, and, in general, good to evil. These are the people whom the apostle calls "enemies of the cross of Christ" [Philippians 3:18], for they hate the cross and suffering and love works and the glory of works. Thus they call the good of the cross evil and the evil of a deed good. God can be found only in suffering and the cross, as has already been said. Therefore the friends of the cross say that the cross is good and works are evil, for through the cross works are dethroned and the old Adam, who is especially edified by works, is crucified. It is impossible for a person not to be puffed up by his good works unless he has first been deflated and destroyed by suffering and evil until he knows that he is worthless and that his works are not his but God's.[9]

In Thesis #22, Luther brought out the theology of glory's folly in likening human actions to the true nature of God: "That wisdom which sees the invisible things of God in works as perceived by man is completely puffed up, blinded, and hardened."[10] If we seek to know God in the abstract concepts and to imitate him in our own actions, we are doomed to failure—both because the true nature of God can best be seen in the concrete suffering of Jesus and because our actions are always touched with sin.

Thesis #23—The futility of seeking to lift ourselves up to God through our deeds is brought out by the law. "The law brings the wrath of God, kills, reviles, accuses, judges, and condemns everything that is not in Christ."[11]

In Thesis #24, Luther again referred to the theology of the cross: "Yet that wisdom is not of itself evil, nor is the law to be evaded; but without the theology of the cross man misuses the best in the worst manner.[12] The theology of the cross allows the law to do its work and the gospel likewise to become clear and full of grace.

In Thesis #25–28, Luther went on to argue that God works in us to make that which is righteous. God's grace is seen in the cross, and our response is actually a product of God in us. Thesis #28 includes the statement, "The love of God does not find, but creates, that which is pleasing to it."[13]

Explanations of the Ninety-Five Theses, 1518

Only a month after the Heidelberg Disputation, Luther published his *Explanations of the Ninety-Five Theses,* and he made reference to the theology of the cross. He wrote:

> A theologian of the cross (that is, one who speaks of the crucified and hidden God), teaches that punishments, crosses and death are the most precious treasury of all and the most sacred relics which the Lord of this theology himself has consecrated and blessed, not alone by the touch of his most holy flesh but also by the embrace of his exceedingly holy and divine will, and he has left these relics here to be kissed, sought after, and embraced.[14]

Luther thereby tied his provocative distinction between the two theologies to his earlier famous attack on indulgences and related practices. It is far better to embrace the redemptive suffering of Christ than to puff ourselves up through our own pious deeds.

The Sermon "Two Kinds of Righteousness"

There is at least one other reference that should be mentioned. In a sermon entitled "Two Kinds of Righteousness," preached in 1518 or 1519, Luther brought out the importance of servitude rather than glory in our own lives. The text for the sermon was Philippians 2:5–6, "Your attitude should be the same as that of Christ Jesus: Who, being in very nature God, did not consider equality with God something to be grasped."

The righteousness that justifies a person comes as a gracious gift from God made possible by Christ's suffering and death on the cross. This righteousness, for which we can take no credit, changes us and makes it possible for us to live in humility and produce our "proper righteousness," which consists in (a) slaying the flesh and crucifying one's desires, (b) loving the neighbor, and (c) living in meekness and fear toward God.[15] It is the life of service consistent with the theology of the cross—*not* the theology of glory.

Luther illustrated his point using the account about Simon, a Pharisee, in Luke 7:36–50. Simon was described by Luther as "pretending to be in the form of God and perching on his own righteousness." He thought that his own deeds were so wonderful that he was in "the glory of the form of God." In his "glory" he "was arrogantly judging and despising Mary Magdalene, seeing in her the form of a servant."[16] Simon, trusting in his own works, was living a life of dominance and pride consistent with the theology of glory.

Luther's own words make his points clearly:

> Christ ignores the form of God in which Simon was superciliously pleasing himself; he does not recount that he was invited, dined, and honored by him. Simon … is now nothing but a sinner. He who seemed to himself so righteous sits divested of the glory of the form of God, humiliated in the form of a servant, willy-nilly. On the other hand, Christ honors Mary with the form of God and elevates her above Simon, saying: "She has anointed my feet and kissed them. She has wet my feet with her tears and wiped them with her hair." How great were the merits which neither she nor Simon saw. Her faults are remembered no more. Christ ignored the form of servitude in her whom he has exalted with the form of sovereignty. Mary is nothing but righteous, elevated into the glory of the form of God, etc.[17]

Indeed, one could say that "true glory" comes only through humility, service, and suffering—not through lifting ourselves up through our own piety.

Conclusion

It is easy to think of God as high and mighty—far removed from all of us and from the pain in this world and to think that we must lift ourselves up to God through deeds patterned after his invisible, abstract nature. But a deeper theology sees God in the truest form precisely in "suffering and the cross." Luther used this understanding on how we find and know God to undercut a theology based on good works, including such things as buying indulgences, using relics, and going on pilgrimages. Reliance on *our* good works amounts to a failure to see, and an implied rejection of, God's righteousness that is won for us in God's own suffering in Christ. If, however, we see God's love in the suffering and death of Jesus, there is no need to trust in our own good works. Moreover, we can be open to our own suffering and service, knowing that God works through suffering and creates love. The person "who has emptied himself through suffering no longer does works but knows that God works and does all things in him."[18]

If we ask the question, "Where do we find God?" The answer is "In the cross." The theology of the cross understands Jesus' suffering and death as our window to seeing God most clearly. Through Jesus' obedient passion, God bestows on us His righteousness. God also changes us and remakes us so that we can follow with lives of service and humility.

By contrast, the "theology of glory" holds that *our* good works of righteousness, *our* piety, enable us to enjoy divine blessings now and through eternity. The key is our sufficient righteous works—including such "spiritual" activities as buying indulgences, reverencing relics, going on pilgrimages, and the like. In this theology, the crosses and sufferings in life are not blessings; they are best avoided or conquered.

Luther's development of these two "theologies" is grounded, of course, in the New

Testament including many recorded sayings of Jesus. It was not "new"; but his articulation was profound.

Luther continued to stress the ideas generated in the *Heidelberg Disputation* even though he did not invoke the terminology. Throughout his writings he emphasized the crucified Christ as the heart and center of our Christian faith. He continued to write of humble service. Luther also never strayed from his denunciation of indulgences, the use of relics, and trust in any good works no matter how much we admire or desire them.

The theology of the cross and the theology of glory as a fundamental theological structure influenced Luther's positions on a broad range of topics. A special example is in the beautiful explanations of the second and third articles in his *Small Catechism*:

Second Article

I believe that Jesus Christ, true God, begotten of the Father from eternity, and also true man, born of the Virgin Mary, is my Lord. He has redeemed me, a lost and condemned creature, purchased and won me from all sins, from death, and from the power of the devil. He did this not with gold or silver, but **with His holy, precious blood and with His innocent suffering and death** [emphasis added], so that I may be His own, live under Him in His kingdom, and serve Him in everlasting righteousness, innocence, and blessedness, just as He is risen from the dead, lives and reigns to all eternity. This is most certainly true.[19]

Third Article

I believe that I cannot by my own reason or strength believe in Jesus Christ, my Lord, or come to Him. But **the Holy Spirit has called me by the Gospel, enlightened me with His gifts, sanctified and kept me in the true faith. In the same way He calls, gathers, enlightens, and sanctifies the whole Christian Church on earth** [emphasis added] and keeps it with Jesus Christ in the one true faith. In this Christian Church He daily and richly forgives all my sins and the sins of all believers. On the Last Day He will raise up me and all the dead and will give eternal life to me and to all believers in Christ. This is most certainly true.[20]

• Essay 8 •

Luther Against Scholasticism: Was He a Humanist?

It may seem odd to call Luther a "humanist." "Biblical scholar," "professor," "pastor," "theologian," "reformer," and "critic" may all seem easier titles to justify, but a basis for calling him a "humanist" is less obvious.

The term is used, of course, in many different senses. It can refer to one who specializes in the humanities (literature, the arts, philosophy, history), but that is *not* the sense in which it is used here. Here it means one who helped open Western thought to new possibilities after the more structured, authoritarian, and limiting approaches of the medieval period. With this greater openness, there was a celebration of what "humanity" and individual humans could accomplish. Also central to it was a new love for and appreciation of the classical worlds of the Greeks and Romans.

Clearly, Luther lived in an age of this new "humanism." His contemporary, Erasmus, was called a humanist—as was Luther's close colleague, Melanchthon. They were Greek scholars, and they helped bring to light the works of the great Greek playwrights, poets, and philosophers *in the original language.* (Luther made use of their linguistic developments in his study of the New Testament.)

This new humanism meant far more, however, than the reintroduction of the Greek and Roman classics. It also included an attack upon the thought structure and presuppositions that dominated academia at the time. The term that is most often associated with that thought structure is "scholasticism." Literally, the term only means the approach to knowledge and learning used at that time in the "schools," *i.e.,* the universities, but it signifies a particular approach to knowledge in general.

There were, to be sure, a variety of intellectual influences and paradigms in those schools—Aquinas was very different from Scotus, and both were very different from Ockham, for example. But there were some general features:

1. Philosophy and theology were considered to be complementary or even to be wedded together.

2. It was deemed quite appropriate to bring references to God into non-theological areas of thought.

3. The universities had very strong ties to the Church, and the Church guarded against teachings that seemed to go against Church doctrine—*in any field of study.*

245

4. The primary method for establishing and maintaining truth was through *authority* with a significant emphasis on *deductive logic*.

Theology and Philosophy

Luther's attack on the use of philosophy in theology was central to the reclamation of the Gospel. In his judgment, tying Christianity and Christian theology to any particular philosophical system would only compromise biblical teachings. He affirmed, using Paul's claims in I Corinthians 1, that the cross of Christ is "foolishness" to the Greeks and to the wise of this world. For Luther there was no tie between philosophy and theology, and he judged the use Aquinas made of Aristotle in realms touching on theology to be little short of scandalous.

Through Aquinas (1225–1274), Aristotle had become extremely important in scholastic thought. Indeed, he used Aristotle as the ultimate authority in the natural realm (God being the authority in the supernatural realm); he even referred to Aristotle as "the Philosopher." But in 1517, a couple of months before the posting of the Ninety-Five Theses, Luther lashed out against Aristotle in the strongest of terms.

The document was his *Disputation Against Scholastic Theology*, a set of ninety-seven theses. Here are a few of the theses in which he attacked Aristotle—and thus Thomas Aquinas and scholasticism, in general—head-on:

41. Virtually the entire *Ethics* of Aristotle is the worst enemy of grace.
43. It is an error to say that no man can become a theologian without Aristotle.
44. Indeed, no one can become a theologian unless he becomes one without Aristotle.
45. To state that a theologian who is not a logician is a monstrous heretic—this is a monstrous and heretical statement.
47. No syllogistic form is valid when applied to divine terms.
50. Briefly, the whole Aristotle is to theology as darkness is to light.[1]

In these theses, Luther also specifically attacked John Duns Scotus, William of Ockham, and the lesser-known Gabriel Biel—a scholastic professor of theology at Tübingen in the late 15th century.

The attack on the uncritical use of philosophy by Christians continued in the *Heidelberg Disputation* of 1518. There he emphasized that the ways of God, the theology of the cross, appears foolish to humans. "No person philosophizes well unless he is a fool, that is, a Christian," he claimed in Thesis 30.[2] Thesis 29: "He who wishes to philosophize by using Aristotle without danger to his soul must first become thoroughly foolish in Christ."[3]

In his exposition of Romans and in other writings in those early years, Luther used Augustine rather than such scholastic theological/philosophical scholars as Scotus, Aquinas, and Biel. He saw Augustine not as a theologian making use of a philosophical system but as a theologian adhering to the Gospel and the teachings of Scripture. His use of Augustine was based on a theology of sin and grace. Agreeing with Augustine, Luther claimed that we have no natural ability to avoid sin, do the right, and win God's favor. Every effort to claim that man has a natural ability to do God's will and to cooperate with God in becoming worthy of God's blessing is a form of Pelagianism and is heretical.

Theology and Other Disciplines

In scholasticism, theology was often considered to be the "Queen of the Sciences." That meant that theology was at the apex of the structure of the various disciplines at the time and that the others were "logically dependent" upon her. Thus, the other disciplines were to conform to her highest principles regarding the place of God and God's creative work on all aspects of the natural order. University structure in and after the High Middle Ages reflected this. "Theology ruled."

Luther never followed in this vein. For him the issue of the place of theology vis-a-vis other disciplines was of no importance. Rather, the issue was the place of sin and grace in a person's life. Thus, Luther's *Disputation Against Scholastic Theology* begins with a defense of Augustine's position on free will—that "man, being a bad tree, can only will and do evil"[4] and that he is entirely dependent upon God's grace.

Luther, to be sure, was willing to speak out on a variety of issues outside theology. Examples include political authority, social structure, and economics, but he did so by way of drawing out the implications of the Gospel, *i.e.,* how society would either enable or hinder a person to live out life as a Christian.

Of importance here is Luther's position on "vocation." Every person has a divine calling to serve God and other people in love and in Christian humility. The homemaker or the farmer or the blacksmith has a God-given vocation just as does the pastor or any other worker in the Church.

While Luther was ready to speak out on social and other issues from a theological perspective, it was not from a position of the superiority of theology as the "queen of the sciences." He did not continue that scholastic emphasis.

The Universities and the Church

Luther was important for freeing the university at Wittenberg (and through this, other universities) from the clutches of the Church. Wittenberg was a new university established by Frederick the Wise in 1502,[5] and it very early became widely known through the work of Luther and Melanchthon. While Frederick wished to be a faithful servant of the Church, he denied the Roman Church's efforts to control his faculty, thereby initiating a degree of independence that would eventually be adopted by many universities throughout northern Europe. This independence at Wittenberg and elsewhere was greatly enhanced, of course, by the success of the Reformation and the formation of church bodies completely separate from the Roman Church.

While Luther (and Melanchthon) certainly played important roles in the separation of the university from the Church's control, an even greater part was played by Frederick the Wise and his brother and successor, John the Steadfast, both of whom defied the Roman Church and refused to allow it to control their young and important university.

The Use of Authority

Luther was committed, it is true, to the use of authority in theology, *but it was the authority of Scripture—not of the Church.*

In 1877, the American philosopher, Charles Sanders Peirce, wrote an essay entitled *The Fixation of Belief* in which he described four ways of establishing and maintaining a claim. The four are tenacity, authority, a priori, and scientific. "Tenacity" is maintaining a position without reasons or evidence; "authority" cites a figure or source as a basis for knowledge; "a priori" uses rational insight and deduction to establish a system of knowledge; and "scientific" uses empirical evidence and experiments.

Scholasticism was firmly grounded in the way of authority. The a priori way would be developed extensively later by Descartes and others; the scientific way was just beginning in the sixteenth century and would grow through the efforts of Galileo, Francis Bacon, and many others. But for scholasticism a heavy emphasis was placed on authority. The scholastics were expert logicians, to be sure, and they dealt carefully with physical evidence, but authority played a major role.

Scholastic thinkers relied heavily on accepted philosophers, especially Aristotle, and they quoted "Church Fathers" and prominent theologians as well as Scripture. Over all hovered the voice of the Church—particularly in the papacy and the decrees of the Church Councils. The Church was the final interpreter of Scripture and the Church was the final arbiter of disputes—especially, but not exclusively, in the domain of theology.

Luther, as we have seen, had no place for the quotation of philosophers in the area of faith and theology. He was willing to question the views of Church Fathers, and he disputed the final authority of the Roman Church—particularly in the papacy. But he still relied on authority. The absolute authority for Luther was Scripture, and he would quote Church Fathers (particularly Augustine) if they based their views on Scripture.[6]

Luther's disagreement with scholasticism on this point was not so much on the use of authority but rather on which authority/authorities one should use. For Luther, as stated above, the authority was *Scripture,* and it was the *only* authority. *"Sola Scriptura"* was, to be sure, a primary emphasis of the Lutheran Reformation.

Conclusion

Luther never modified his severe criticism of scholasticism and the universities of his day; if anything, his views were only solidified. The following quotation from a sermon postil (postils offered for preachers suggestions and guides on particular texts), written in 1521/1522 while Luther was at the Wartburg, is revealing:

> There is no need of Christ and of Scripture if the teachings of the pope and the universities are valid. For this reason I have said that the pope, the bishops, and the institutions of higher learning are not good enough to be heretical. No, they surpass all heretics and they are the bilge-water pool of all heresies, errors, and idolatries which have existed from the beginning of the world. With them they push Christ and the word of God completely to the side, and they only keep their names as a cover-up…. If it is true that before the birth of Christ the pagans were without Christ and Scripture, nevertheless, they did not act against Scripture and Christ as do these. For this reason the pagans assuredly are better than the papists.[7]

Luther maintained that his critique of scholasticism and of the universities was done for the sake of Scripture's teachings about Christ and the Gospel. He held further that the uncritical use of Aristotle and other philosophers has run counter to the "foolishness" of

God. The authority of the Church, he also argued, has harmed the universities and stands in the way of the true authority of Scripture. *Sola Scriptura* trumped all other avenues to truth on any issue related to man's salvation.

Was Luther a "humanist"? His reliance on authority for truth, his emphasis on Scripture as the only ultimate authority, and his emphasis on matters of faith and religion separated him from many other humanists of that period such as Pico or Erasmus. Luther knew some of the Greek classics, but he didn't value them as highly (though he relied on the Greek for his New Testament translation). And Luther placed no great emphasis on *human* accomplishments.

Nevertheless, he helped open the door to the freshness of the new humanism and the Renaissance by standing up to the authority of the Church and defending the rights of the *individual* to know and proclaim the truth. Luther was only one of many (Reuchlin, Erasmus, Montaigne, Pascal, Francis Bacon, Descartes, *et al.*) who put to an end the dominance of scholasticism—especially in Northern Europe—but he does need to be included in that list.

• Essay 9 •

Luther Debating the Key Issues:
Luther vs. Eck

It is interesting to note how important the debate format was for Luther and the reform movement. To be sure, Luther presented many ideas both in treatises and sermons, and he was called upon to defend his views in conferences, ecclesiastical hearings, and official government assemblies (diets), but his preparation for and participation in debates were central to his reform efforts and success.

The Ninety-Five Theses were, of course, assertions which Luther proposed for debate. In addition, we have seen already the debate theses in the *Disputation Against Scholastic Theology,* as well as those used in the *Heidelberg Disputation.* In this essay we will also look at the most crucial debate of all—the Leipzig debate of 1519 against Dr. Johann Eck.

As we have seen, Luther was a superb biblical scholar and a profound theologian. But if he were only a scholar and theologian, no matter how brilliant, it is likely that his commentaries and other writings would have caused little more than a ripple and that his discoveries would have languished in monastery and university libraries—even with the benefit of the printing press. Luther, however, also had another set of skills and a temperament that made for the development of concise and provocative debate theses and allowed him to be an aggressive, skilled debater. This set of skills and temperament helped propel him very quickly to the center of the European stage.

On Debate

Debate is a long-established method both for discovering the truth and for showing a position to be true or preferable. In medieval universities, debate topics would often be addressed by (1) stating a question or problem, (2) offering supportive reasons for an affirmative answer, (3) offering supporting reasons for a negative answer, (4) defending or explaining the better answer, and (5) revealing the weaknesses of the poorer answer. A professor might lead the class through the entire process. It was also possible for the students to learn the process of clear thinking and problem-solving by arguing for the alternative positions themselves.

Thomas Aquinas was a master at using debate within his own writings. In his *Summa Contra Gentiles,* he would pose a question, state both the position which he opposed and the

250

preferable position, give arguments for both positions, and present the reasons why the preferable position is superior—responding also point-for-point to the objections which the inferior position offered. In this process, careful deduction was employed and terms were precisely defined. In addition, important authorities were often cited as crucial support for the preferable position.

The skilled debater must have an exhaustive knowledge of the subject, be able to employ solid deduction, be able to present arguments cogently and articulately, and, if the debate is to be more than a game, be convinced of the superiority of his or her position. Luther possessed all of these features—the last of which being a particular strength.

The Ninety-Five Theses as a Basis for Debate

On October 31, 1517, Luther presented his challenge for a debate in the Ninety-Five Theses (points to be debated).[1] On that date Luther sent important letters to Bishop Schulze of Brandenburg and to Archbishop Albrecht of Mainz; we know that the theses were included in the letter to Albrecht, who sent them on to Pope Leo with the demand that Luther be silenced. Within a few days the theses, originally printed in Latin, the academic and ecclesiastical language at that time, were taken, translated into German, printed, and widely disseminated.

No academic or church official came forward for a disputation on the theses, but they soon became a sensation and thus the basis of a vigorous and widespread informal "debate."

Luther followed up on the theses a few months later by writing and publishing his *Explanations of the Ninety-Five Theses*. In this lengthy document, he presented his arguments for each thesis one-by-one. He employed deduction, definition of terms, and citation of authorities. He did not follow the full format of Aquinas, for he only presented one side of the case; he left it to his opponent to present the other side.

When Luther wrote the *Explanations*, there was no opponent standing across the room, but he was debating, nonetheless.

Luther's debate style can be illustrated by the presentation and defense of the first thesis: "When our Lord and Master Jesus Christ said, 'Repent,' he willed the entire life of believers to be one of repentance."[2] This, of course, was central to the indulgences issue; forgiveness, Luther claimed, requires repentance and not merely the purchase of a certificate. In the *Explanations*, he gave several arguments for the thesis. He argued from Scripture, from "reason" offering the rational understanding of forgiveness and repentance, and from a petition in the Lord's Prayer, which Christians have used for fifteen centuries and which we pray throughout our lives.

The first argument offered an analysis of the Greek word for "repent," μετανοεω, and its use in Scripture. He pointed out that the word means "assume another mind and feeling, recover one's senses, make a transition from one state of mind to another, have a change of spirit."[3] "By this recovery of one's senses it happens that the sinner has a change of heart and hates his sin,"[4] he added. Luther then quoted six passages from the New Testament (Matthew 10:34, 35, & 38; Matthew 5:4; Galatians 5:24; and II Corinthians 6:4–5) in support of the view that repentance is a basic inner transition.

The second argument was "according to reason." "Since Christ is the master of the spirit not of the letter, and since his words are life and spirit, he must teach the kind of repentance that is done in spirit and in truth."[5] This spiritual repentance cannot be just an outward show or act (Matthew 6:16), but must be an inner change performable by the mighty and the lowly, the ecclesiastics as well as the laity. "For the teaching of Christ must apply to all men, that is, to men in every walk of life,"[6] he wrote.

Luther added a third argument: We pray the Lord's Prayer petition, "forgive us our debts" throughout our lives, so there must be debts and forgiveness our entire lives and therefore we must repent throughout our lives.

Thus, Luther held, repentance does not involve buying anything or performing any act but rather it requires a change of mind and heart that is repeatable throughout one's life. Buying indulgences has nothing to do with repentance or forgiveness—nor does praying before relics or being in a religious vocation.

Although the proposed disputation on the Ninety-Five Theses never occurred, Luther's presentation and arguments began to win significant support. After some initial doubts, Karlstadt became convinced on the indulgences topic. At the disputation in Heidelberg in April and May of 1518, Luther impressed several young Augustinian monks like Bucer and Brenz, who would also become leaders in the Reformation—this despite the fact that Pope Leo had wanted the Augustinian Order to silence Luther at the Heidelberg gathering.

Luther vs. Eck at Leipzig

But the big debate or disputation did finally occur in June and July of 1519. It took place in Leipzig. It might have been an opportunity to use the debate format to allow the strongest position with the best supporting arguments to emerge and to guide the Church through this challenge, but it turned out to be more of just an acrimonious verbal fight.

The opponent in the situation was Dr. Johann Eck, a professor at Ingolstadt. He had been on friendly terms with Luther until he attacked the Ninety-Five Theses viciously in 1518. Luther responded in kind, but then things quieted down again. Karlstadt, however, picked up the battle and wrote 370 theses in defense of the Wittenberg position. Eck challenged Karlstadt to a public disputation, and the stage was set. Leipzig was selected as the site for the debate, and on December 29, 1518, Eck publicized the event along with 12 theses he wished to be debated. It was readily apparent from his theses that Eck was attacking Luther, not just Karlstadt, so Luther himself responded with thirteen theses of his own for the debate. The battle lines were drawn.

Luther's thirteen theses, some given in summary form below, included:

1. "Every man sins daily, but he also repents daily according to Christ's teaching."[7]
2. Sin remains in a person throughout life.
3. To hold that one no longer sins while doing good is Pelagian.
7. One babbles who holds that free will is the master of good or evil deeds.
10. The merits of Christ are not the "treasure of indulgences."
11. Indulgences are a hindrance to a good work.
13. "The very feeble decrees of the Roman pontiffs which have appeared in the last four hundred years [try to] prove that the Roman church is superior to all others. Against

them stand the history of eleven hundred years, the text of divine Scripture, and the decree of the Council of Nicaea, the most sacred of all councils."[8]

The long-awaited debate began with Eck and Karlstadt (defending Luther's positions) as the antagonists, but Eck's easy successes led to Luther standing in to defend his own positions. The two superb debaters went at it pointedly and ruthlessly—Eck arguing from the positions of scholastic theologians and philosophers; Luther from Scripture.

Luther's comments on the debate and its aftermath reveal no disappointment in his argumentation, but they do reveal his dismay at what a biased spectacle the disputation had become. This author would say that the *public* disputation had apparently become a kind of circus or "boxing match" with fans cheering for one side or the other. In Luther's words,

> The citizens of Leipzig neither greeted nor called on us but treated us as though we were their bitterest enemies. Eck, however, they followed around town, clung to, banqueted, entertained, and finally presented with a robe and added a chamois-hair gown. They also rode horseback with him. In short, they did whatever they could to insult us.[9]

After more than a week of formal debate between Eck and Luther, the debate was closed and the transcripts were submitted to the theological faculties of Erfurt and Paris for a decision on the winner. Erfurt refused to give a judgment, and Paris delayed for two years before giving any decision, and even then they did not declare a clear winner/loser.

The debate, perhaps surprisingly, was beneficial for Luther. It gave him new insights about the complete authority of Scripture and on the limitations of the papacy. It strengthened his convictions so that his theses were no longer points for academic discussion or debate but were now firm articles of personal faith on which he would fight to the end. It also helped him to realize that the gap between him and the official Roman church was likely unbridgeable. It did what a debate was supposed to do: it clarified.

• Essay 10 •

Luther on the Sacraments:
The Die Is Cast

In 1520 Luther "took off his gloves" and attacked the Roman Catholic Church with full force. No longer was he merely pointing out some church practices that were inconsistent with biblical theology. No longer was he seeking to persuade his opponents with straightforward theses and arguments. Now he was *on the attack*, for he was sure he had both the Bible (and thus, God) and his Saxon ruler on his side. He wrote now as a person with no fear. And if he were to die, he would have said his piece.

Luther's Attack: Introduction

The epitome of his attack was *A Prelude on the Babylonian Captivity of the Church* or, as it is often called, *The Babylonian Captivity of the Church*. It was a "prelude" apparently in the sense that it was an initial attack on the Church's sacramental theology with more expected to follow on this crucial battle. It was, to be sure, a well-reasoned piece written in formal, academic Latin. But the writing can leave no doubt: Luther was aggressive and he was attacking Roman Catholic theology at its heart. Erasmus said of this writing that it "made the breach irreparable."[1]

Luther had already sought to expose the hypocrisy of the Church in its use of indulgences and relics. He had decried the Church's disdain for the biblical doctrine of salvation by grace through faith. He had argued that the true authority for Christianity is Scripture—not the papacy or any other aspect of ecclesiastical authority.

But what he now attacked was how the Church related to its people throughout their entire lives. This is why his attack on the Church's theology and use of the sacraments had such broad implications. It wasn't merely an issue of the number of sacraments or of the definition of the term. It wasn't just an issue of transubstantiation vs. consubstantiation or of communion in one or two kinds. It was a matter of *the Church itself being captured* in a legalized system that hid the Gospel; the Church was experiencing a "Babylonian Captivity" at the hands of the prelates.

But even that isn't all. Behind the words we can see that it was also a matter of the Church's most fundamental treatment of its laity; *the Roman Church was imposing a "Babylonian Captivity" upon the people*. Thirdly, Luther made it clear the Church and *the clergy* had also been "Babylon" against the genuine sacraments and *had taken the sacraments into a "Babylonian Captivity."*

It is important to have a perspective on the Roman Catholic position that Luther was attacking. Viewed in a positive light, *the sacraments allowed the Church to be the caretaker of people from the cradle to the grave.* Beginning with infant baptism, it continued through the high points of confirmation and marriage to the last rites (extreme unction) performed on a person's deathbed. Along the way, a person was cared for on a regular basis through the Mass and through confession and absolution (penance). All of this was handled through the actions of a priest, given that power through the sacrament of ordination. Through these seven rites and practices, the Church could care for people throughout their lives assuring them of God's (and the Church's) benevolence and urging them to faithful, obedient service.

Luther saw this system, however, as something that went far beyond Scripture. To Luther, this set of seven rites and rituals was developed by the clergy as a way through which the clergy could capture the Church itself, for only the clergy was authorized to administer and dispense the Church's blessings. The Church was no longer *the people of God gathered around Word and Sacrament.* Instead, the Church was *the ecclesiastical hierarchy dispensing benefits through a man-made system.*

In addition, Luther viewed the process not as "caretaking" but rather as *captivity.* For Luther, the agent for the care of people is not properly "the Church" but rather *God himself.* While thinking that it was extending care for people, the Church was really standing in the way of God's grace and was controlling people. It was imposing a *"Babylonian captivity"* on God's people and thus was denying both God's grace and human freedom.

The original "Babylonian captivity" took place in the sixth century BC when Babylon under Nebuchadnezzar II destroyed Jerusalem (587 BC) and deported Jews to Babylon in 597, c. 587, and c. 582 BC. Exiles began to return in 539 BC after the fall of Babylon to the Persian Cyrus the Great.

The exile was traumatic for the Jews and may be compared to their slavery in Egypt as a period of great suffering. The temple had been destroyed, the independence of Judah was lost, and the people were exposed to horrible demands to reject their faith and to adopt the paganism of the Babylonians. Considerable detail on the horrendous nature of the experience can be found in the books of Ezekiel and Daniel.

In the book of Revelation, "Babylon" is the symbolic term used for the great enemy of God, the "mother of all harlots." She is the epitome of evil and is "drunk with the blood of saints and martyrs."[2]

To link the Roman Catholic Church with Babylon and to think of her as in a Babylonian captivity and of her actions as the imposition of a captivity akin to the tragedy of the sixth century BC was an exceedingly vitriolic attack.

There is one more feature to consider before looking at the details of Luther's argument. The term "sacrament" is not generally recognized as a biblical term but was developed and used by the Church to designate a "sacred act."[3] If we understand this to be an act in which *God's* blessings are bestowed, then, Luther thought, there must be a directive *given by God in Scripture* to the effect that a particular type of act gives this blessing; a sacrament must be instituted by God. More explicitly, in the New Testament Church established on Pentecost, those acts must be instituted by Christ and empowered by the Holy Spirit. Furthermore, for Luther the heart and center of all divine blessings given by Christ is found in the Gospel including the forgiveness of sins. Thus in Luther's view, a sacrament is a sacred act instituted by Christ and empowered by the Holy Spirit through which the forgiveness of sins and the blessings of the Gospel are bestowed on a believer. In Lutheran theology it would also include possession of a "sign," i.e., a tangible or visible element.

Rites Rejected as Sacraments

We begin with four rites that Luther dismissed out of hand as sacraments—confirmation, marriage, extreme unction, and ordination.

Confirmation. Confirmation is a rite in which a person makes a public confession of his or her faith as a Christian. Luther's rejection is brief and blunt: there is no biblical basis for calling confirmation a sacrament.

> We seek sacraments that have been divinely instituted, and among these we see no reason for numbering confirmation. For to constitute a sacrament there must be above all things else a word of divine promise, by which faith may be exercised. But we read nowhere that Christ ever gave a promise concerning confirmation, although he laid hands on many....
>
> For this reason it is sufficient to regard confirmation as a certain churchly rite or sacramental ceremony, similar to other ceremonies such as the blessing of water and the like.... Still, these things cannot be called sacraments of faith, because they have no divine promise connected with them, neither do they save, but the [true] sacraments do save those who believe the divine promise.[4]

Marriage. Luther offered a number of objections to calling marriage a sacrament: Nowhere in Scripture is there any indication that divine grace is given in marriage; marriage also took place long before the New Testament Church was established; and marriage still takes place outside the Church and Christianity among the general population.

Of special interest, however, is Luther's critique of the translation from the Greek in the Latin Vulgate, the official Bible accepted in the Roman Catholic Church. The Vulgate does indeed use the word *sacramentum* on occasion, and in Ephesians 5:31–32, it uses the term in connection with marriage. The English translation of this Vulgate passage is: "The two shall become one. This is a great sacrament [*sacramentum*]." Luther explains the mistranslation as follows:

> For where we have [in the Vulgate] the word *sacramentum* the Greek original has *mysterion*, which the translator sometimes translates and sometimes retains in its Greek form. Thus our verse in the Greek reads: "The two shall become one. This is a great mystery." This explains how they came to understand a sacrament of the New Law here, a thing they would never have done if they had read *mysterium*, as it is in the Greek [*mysterium* is the Latin transliteration of the Greek *mysterion*].[5]

Luther went on to point out that in I Timothy 3:16, Christ himself is called a sacrament in the Vulgate whereas the text clearly means that Christ is a great mystery "manifested in the flesh, vindicated in the Spirit, seen by angels, preached among the nations, believed on in the world, taken up in glory." Translating *mysterion* as *sacramentum* in the sense that we mean "sacrament" is a great mistake.

In short, there is no biblical basis for considering marriage to be a sacrament, the use of *sacramentum* in the Vulgate notwithstanding.

Extreme Unction. Luther's rejection of extreme unction or last rites as a sacrament is based upon his exegesis of James 5:14–15 which reads, "Is any one of you sick? He should call the elders of the church to pray over him and anoint him with oil in the name of the Lord. And the prayer offered in faith will make the sick person well; the Lord will raise him up. If he has sinned, he will be forgiven."

Luther acknowledged that this seems to give the promise of forgiveness and has a sign (the oil). But he made several objections:

- Luther questioned whether it was written by the "apostle James" and should even be in the canon.[6]
- No person has the authority to institute a sacrament; a sacrament must be instituted by Christ.[7]
- The passage makes no connection with a person's deathbed; moreover, it would seem to be capable of repetition whenever one would be ill.[8]
- The prayers, the passage says, will lead to recovery; they are not a preparation for death.[9]
- When extreme unction is administered, people **very** seldom recover, but a sacramental promise never fails.[10]
- Elders—not priests—are referred to in the passage as anointing with oil and praying.[11]
- Tying it with other passages in Scripture, it is not the anointing but the prayer that is effective—with the faith of the healed.[12]

Thus, in Luther's judgment, extreme unction cannot be a sacrament.

Ordination. There is nothing in Scripture, Luther emphasized, that even hints that ordination, the rite of being declared a priest, is a sacrament; that claim is entirely an invention of the Church. And it does not suffice to say that the Church is guided by God in its decisions: "It is the promises of God that make the church and not the church that makes the promises of God. For the Word of God is incomparably superior to the church, and in this Word the church, being a creature, has nothing to decree, ordain, or make, but only to be decreed, ordained, and made."[13]

Luther offered other arguments, too:

- The true church is not necessarily to be found in a particular body but rather in the universal Church.[14]
- True, Dionysius, a church father, did mention six sacraments including ordination, but his writings are filled with strange, mystical, and allegorical claims that are found in none of the other church fathers. It is better to focus on Paul, for example.[15]
- The exaltation of ordination has led to a disastrous chasm between clergy and laity with the result that "shepherds have been turned into wolves, servants into tyrants, churchmen into worse than worldlings."[16]

Thus, Luther's criticism of ordination as a sacrament suggested his developed position on the "priesthood of all believers," *i.e.,* that every Christian is a "priest" with direct access to God without any necessity for making this access through the clergy or through the church hierarchy.

Penance—A Special Case

In the section on penance, which involves performing tasks to demonstrate repentance, it becomes clear that the Church is not only "captured" into a Babylonian captivity but that the Church is also Babylon itself placing people into captivity. Luther calls the Catholic Church, which has placed the clergy into an exalted and tyrannical position, "*this Babylon of ours* [which] *has so completely extinguished faith.*"[17]

Luther's argument on penance is a bit subtler than those given above, for he held that forgiveness of sins does genuinely come from God through repentance and absolution. Indeed, his ambivalence on whether penance properly used is a sacrament is shown by the fact that in this very writing, Luther called penance a sacrament in the introductory section[18] but left it off the list of sacraments in the concluding section.[19]

Nevertheless, he found the Church's practice to be totally abhorrent. As the Church used penance, it was definitely *not* a sacrament, he believed.

The basic problem, Luther held, is that the Church has placed the emphasis on the *power and authority* of the priest to forgive sin rather than on the *faith* of the person receiving God's wonderful blessing of forgiveness. Luther believed that the clergy had confiscated the practice in order to have a tyrannical grip on the lives of people. His words are strong:

> For they have adapted to their own tyranny the word of promise which Christ speaks in Matt. 16 and 18: "Whatever you bind, etc.," and in the last chapter of John: "If you forgive the sins of any, they are forgiven, etc." By these words the faith of penitents is aroused for obtaining the forgiveness of sins. But in all their writing, teaching, and preaching, their sole concern has been, not to teach what is promised to Christians in these words, or what they ought to believe, and what great consolation they might find in them, but *only through force and violence to extend their own tyranny far, wide, and deep* [emphasis added].[20]

According to Luther, in talking of "contrition," a key part of penance, the Church emphasized only personal sorrow and not the faith which leads to genuine contrition. In talking of "confession," it falsely claimed that only when made to a priest can forgiveness come whereas Scripture speaks of confession before the "brother," *i.e.*, any Christian, leading to God's forgiveness. And in talking of "satisfaction," the Church stressed paying penalties for sin rather than emphasizing the assurance of forgiveness and faith in God's promises.

If, then, penance were practiced in a biblical way emphasizing the penitent's faith and God's forgiveness, it would be akin to a sacrament. On the one hand, it certainly brings forgiveness and the blessings of the Gospel. On the other, it was promoted but not instituted by Christ, and there is no (visible) sign.

Nevertheless, in what Luther called their "greed" and in their lust for power, priests transformed a wonderful blessing into a weapon of tyrannical control.

There were, however, two rites which Luther maintained were genuine sacraments in every sense: they were clearly instituted by Christ; they work faith, bring God's forgiveness and offer the full blessings of the Gospel; and they have visible signs.

Holy Communion—A Genuine Sacrament

Luther began his discussion by arguing that the Church's practice of offering to the laity the bread but not the wine is completely indefensible. The Church has no right to determine on its own that a divine blessing may be withheld from the laity. Moreover, all of the passages about holy communion speak with one accord of both the bread and the wine being offered to the recipients.[21]

In continuing on this point, Luther used the terminology that the Church had "captured" the sacrament. "*The first captivity of this sacrament,* therefore, concerns its substance or completeness, which the tyranny of Rome has wrested from us…. They are the sinners, who forbid the giving of both kinds to those who wish to exercise this choice."[22]

"*The second captivity of this sacrament*" is the *requirement* that the Thomistic view on substance and accident with respect to the communion elements be confirmed and that any contrary view is heresy. The Thomistic view, based upon Aristotle's metaphysical view on substance and accident, is that the substance or inherent nature of the bread and wine is Jesus' body and blood and that the form or accidents, *i.e.,* the sensible features, are those of bread and wine. Luther thought it unnecessary and even foolish to analyze the elements in this way (he also thought it wasn't even faithful to Aristotle) but even worse to condemn all differing views. For his part, Luther held that we could understand the elements to be both bread/wine and also body/blood, pure and simple.

"*The third captivity of this sacrament*" is that "it has been converted by the teaching of godless men into a good work."[23] Luther held that the words of Christ connected with the Last Supper are a "testament" or last wish that must be respected. Those words offered a promise that must be received in faith. Thus, the central part of the sacrament is Christ's *promise* of grace and blessing to be received in *faith*—the very opposite of a good work. He continued,

> They proceed to the very height of madness, and after inventing the lie that the mass is effective simply by virtue of the act having been performed, they add another one to the effect that the mass is none the less profitable to others even if it is harmful to some wicked priest who may be celebrating it. On such a foundation of sand they base their applications, participations, brotherhoods, anniversaries, and numberless other lucrative and profitable schemes of that kind.[24]

The Church's practice had turned the sacrament into a good work rather than an act of God's grace and has allowed priests, through their schemes and devices, even to use saying mass for the purpose of making money!

For Luther it was imperative that holy communion be offered in both kinds as an act of grace received in faith and as a free gift from God.

Baptism—A Genuine Sacrament

The tone which Luther adopted in the section on baptism is different from the rest of the work because it is so positive and downplays any criticism of the Roman Church's practice. To be sure, there are attacks on the Roman Catholic Church's theology of baptism as found in Peter Lombard's *Sentences,* on the Church's stances which undercut the lifelong saving nature of baptism, and on the Church's denial of Christian freedom through its legalistic administration of vows. Nevertheless, the central theme in this section is positive—emphasizing the grace imparted by God in baptism to the believing Christian.

Luther again brought out the important theme of promise and faith. The genuine sacraments properly understood are built on this duality. The promise is from God and cannot be abrogated by any human administering the sacrament. It is God's offer of grace and forgiveness to His people. Faith is the necessary receptor of this wonderful promise. It is not a human work but is a gift of the Holy Spirit which will affirm and trust the promises of God.

In an interesting section, Luther denied that "washing" was the best image for baptism.

Rather, he claimed, it is "dying and resurrection." In baptism, a person "dies" to the old self dominated by sin and life without God and "is raised" to a new life in forgiveness, grace, and doing good works as a *result* of faith—not as a way to win God's favor.

The fact that the Church has not completely crippled baptism, according to Luther, is only because of the baptism of infants. The Church has not been able to turn infant baptism into a gross moneymaking scheme or into a legalism because of the innocence of these small children. The deceit and schemes would come with older people who can be controlled and duped, and the Church would try to make adults doubt the lifelong efficacy of baptism and instead think they needed penance as a later, secure lifeline to God.

How do infants have the faith to receive the promises of baptism? For Luther, it is the faith of the people who surround the child that makes the reception of the promises possible in the infant:

> Infants are aided by the faith of others, namely, those who bring them for baptism. For the Word of God is powerful enough, when uttered, to change even a godless heart, which is no less unresponsive and helpless than any infant. So through the prayer of the believing church which present it, a prayer to which all things are possible (Mark 9:23), the infant is changed, cleansed, and renewed by the inpoured faith.[25]

A Theology of Sacraments

Luther's attack on the Catholic Church's sacramental theology was harsh, but the writing did contain a positive theology of the sacraments. Among its chief points would be the following:

- A sacrament brings the gracious promises of God to people.
- These promises are received by faith in the recipient; God's promises and faith are necessary corollaries.
- It is God who gives the blessings in a sacrament—not the person performing the rite.
- A person of faith will indeed receive the blessings of a sacrament no matter the spiritual nature of the person performing the rite.
- The sensible aspects of the sacraments (signs) bring blessing to a person because of the Word that is with those signs.
- A sacrament must be instituted by Christ; no human may institute a sacrament.
- The blessings of sacraments may be undercut by a church that in its teachings makes a sacrament a good work or a human endeavor.
- The gracious blessings of a sacrament are life-long and powerful.

Luther had clearly developed his own theology of the sacraments in strong distinction from that theology in the Church.

There are a couple of final comments to be made. It might be argued that Luther's theology of the sacraments actually enhanced the importance of baptism and holy communion in general by emphasizing their central role in *God's* providing grace, forgiveness, faith, and all of the other blessings of the Holy Spirit. It might further be put forward that this theology specifically increases the importance of baptism vis-a-vis the Anabaptists and holy communion vis-a-vis the Reformed.[26]

• **Essay 11** •

Luther on the Oneness of the Church: The Una Sancta

One of the thorniest issues that Luther had to face was what his protests were doing to church unity. Was he responsible for division in the church? Was he going against the "High Priestly Prayer" of Jesus in John 17? In that chapter, Jesus is quoted as praying, "Holy Father, protect them by the power of your name—the name you gave me—so that they may be one as we are one."[1] And again, "May they be brought to complete unity to let the world know that you sent me and have loved them even as you have loved me."[2]

Luther returned to this issue again and again—always maintaining that the institutional unity of the Roman Church had never been universal. He was able to indicate, of course, that the Eastern Orthodox Church with its huge number of congregations and worshipers, was not to be ignored, and that it had been effectively separated from the Roman Church since the Great Schism of 1054, though tensions had existed for several centuries before that. The issue was made all the clearer by the fact that the official name of the Eastern Church is "Orthodox Catholic Church" and that of the Roman Church is "Roman Catholic Church"; "catholic" means "universal."[3]

Faith and the Church's Oneness

But this was not Luther's main point. His central claim was, rather, that the unity of the Church was not *institutional* but instead a unity of *faith*.

In Luther's *Smalcald Articles* of 1537, often considered to be the culmination and authoritative statement of his doctrinal positions, the section entitled "The Church" is amazingly brief. Here it is in its entirety:

> We do not agree with them that they are the Church. They are not the Church. Nor will we listen to those things that, under the name of Church, they command or forbid. Thank God, today a seven-year-old child knows what the Church is, namely, the holy believers and lambs who hear the voice of their Shepherd (John 10:11–16). For the children pray, "I believe in one holy Christian Church." This holiness does not come from albs, tonsures, long gowns, and other ceremonies they made up without Holy Scripture, but from God's Word and true faith.[4]

This brief article reveals Luther's thesis: True Church unity requires a oneness of faith that is based solely on Scripture.

261

A beautiful and comprehensive description of Luther's position on the Church is best found in an unlikely source, *On the Papacy in Rome Against the Most Celebrated Romanist in Leipzig,* 1520.

This was not a writing that Luther had planned—or even anticipated in any way. After Luther had debated Eck in Leipzig in the summer of 1519, an overzealous Franciscan monk in that city, Augustine Alveld, wrote a short work which he thought would crush Luther's position on the papacy as Luther had developed it in that debate. Alveld believed he could demonstrate from Scripture that "the apostolic see was 'a divine institution'" in a way that "all scholars would have to acknowledge."[5] Luther thought that Alveld's sophomoric work was not worthy of his spending time to reply but instead gave the task to one of his students, John Lonicer, who ended his work by calling Alveld an "ass." A friend and follower of Luther, John Bernhardi, also responded to Alveld with an essay entitled, *Confutation of the Inept and Impious Booklet of Friar Augustine Alveld.* But Alveld didn't give up. In May of 1520 he wrote a treatise with the grandiose and lengthy title, *A Very Fruitful and Useful Booklet About the Papal See and About St. Peter; Also About those who Are the True Sheep of Christ whom Christ our Lord has Commanded to Be Under Peter's Protection and Rule.*

This was too much for Luther. In less than two weeks, he wrote his reply, *On the Papacy in Rome, Against the Most Celebrated Romanist in Leipzig.* In so doing, he made a new and powerful statement on the nature of the Church.

Luther bristled at Alveld's charge that he was a heretic on the grounds that he did not acknowledge the supremacy of the Roman papacy and hierarchy. Heresy, Luther argued should be associated with matters of faith—not with allegiance. Moreover, he claimed, the issue of allegiance was, for the Roman Church, really an issue about money. He believed that the Roman Church was so upset with him because it wanted to continue to fleece the Germans. The Germans need to stand up to this effrontery, Luther challenged.

Luther was determined to set the record straight on what Christendom, i.e., the Church, really is. It is for Luther a spiritual body of believers under the headship of Christ—the only way the Church is understood in the New Testament. It is *not* an organization constructed according to a human plan. Nor is it a building, a sanctuary. It is a community of faith.

Luther acknowledged that the term Christendom, *i.e.,* the Church, is used by people in various ways. But Scripture knows only one meaning, *viz.,* the people of God joined in unity by their common biblical *faith.* Here is a key passage in Luther's reply to Alveld:

> Scripture speaks about Christendom very simply and in only one way; they have brought two more ways [a man-made assembly identified by external forms such as vestments and rites, and houses of worship] into general usage.
>
> *The first* [and only genuine] *way,* according to Scripture, is that Christendom means an assembly of all the people on earth who believe in Christ, as we pray in the Creed, "I believe in the Holy Spirit, [...] the communion of saints."[6] This community or assembly means all those who live in true faith, hope, and love. Thus the essence, life, and nature of Christendom is not a physical assembly, but an assembly of hearts in one faith, as St. Paul says in Ephesians 4, "One baptism, one faith, one Lord." Accordingly, regardless of whether a thousand miles separates them physically, they are still called one assembly in spirit, as long as each one preaches, believes, hopes, loves, and lives like the other. So we sing about the Holy Spirit, "You have brought many tongues together into the unity of faith." This is what spiritual unity really means, on the basis of which men are called a "communion of saints." This unity alone is sufficient to create Christendom, and without it, no unity—be it that of city, time, persons, work, or whatever else it may be—can create Christendom.[7]

Luther based his view of the spiritual oneness of the church on Ephesians 4:3–5: "Make every effort to keep the unity of the Spirit through the bond of peace. There is one body and one Spirit—just as you were called to one hope when you were called—one Lord, one faith, one baptism; one God and Father of all, who is over all and through all and in all." The key point for Luther was that the oneness of the Church, the *Una Sancta*, is not based on the nature of an organization, its human leadership, its rituals or trappings, or its dictates. It is based on the God who loves them and on the fact that the people in the Church share a faith, a baptism, and a Savior.

For Luther, if two people have been baptized in the name of the Trinity, if they confess Jesus as their Lord, if they believe in the God of the Christian creeds, and if they confess their sinfulness and their trust in God's forgiveness, then they are both in the *Una Sancta*—the one holy Christian and apostolic Church.

Luther contrasted this "spiritual" nature of the Church with any "physical" representation. In the 1520 writing quoted above, he emphasized that the Church is not "physical" in any sense. The Church is *not* an organization with a human structure no matter what that structure is. The Church is *not* a building or a site or a set of buildings.

Implications and Ramifications of a Faith-Based Oneness

The position that the Church's oneness is not institutional but is entirely a unity based upon the oneness of biblical faith provided a foundation for Luther's many attacks on the structure, doctrines, and practices of the Roman Church including:

- The Church cannot have a human head or a group of leaders which can dictate any teaching or practice that is not a matter of Christianity's biblical faith, and because of this,
- The teachings and practices on indulgences are null and void.
- The decrees on pilgrimages need not be followed.
- The emphasis on relics is a sham.
- The papacy is not an aspect of the Christian Church.
- Monastic regulations and vows are of no import.

Luther was concerned to show that neither he nor anyone else could be branded a heretic simply because he did not acknowledge the supremacy of the papacy and curia. Heresy, he held, is a matter of faith—not of allegiance to an organization or to an individual.

Although faith might seem to be a set of doctrines or teachings such as we find in a creed or a Christian kerygma (a summary of the Christian message), that is not quite the point that Luther is making. Rather, he was emphasizing the faith, the bond with God, through which one receives the forgiveness of sins and all of the spiritual blessings that God brings to us, his people. When Jesus healed and forgave, he brought his miraculous gifts to people through their God-given faith worked in them by the Holy Spirit. This living faith unites a person with every other person of faith no matter the distance or time frame that separates them, the organizational structure in which they find themselves, or any other earthly feature.

There are important ramifications of this position. For one, Luther's position was more revolutionary than might first appear, and it had immense consequences. Many had held, and it is commonly held yet today, that the Church is both an organization and a common faith (perhaps within that organization). Thus, many church bodies would each claim today, as the Roman Church did with Luther, that it is the Church and that the people who are genuine (not hypocritical) members of the body hold to a single faith—usually understood as a set of specific beliefs. This was not Luther's position. For him it would be wrong to identify *any* organization as *the* Church—as *the Una Sancta.*

Another ramification has to do with the fact that Luther's position has often been described as presenting the Church as "invisible"—because faith and the bond that ties Christians together in the church is invisible to all but Christ, the Church's head. This misses the point, however. Christians in this world are clearly visible; the only thing that is not visible or knowable from a human perspective is the presence of faith—though there are signs of genuine faith. A better term, and more faithful to Luther's meaning, would be that the Church is "non-institutional." There is no "physical" entity that corresponds to the Church.

As he wrote in the *Large Catechism,* 1529,

> I believe that there is upon earth a little holy group and congregation of pure saints, under one Head, even Christ. This group is called together by the Holy Spirit in one faith, one mind, and understanding, with many gifts, yet agreeing in love, without sects and schisms. I am also a part and member of this same group, a sharer and joint owner of all the goods it possesses. I am brought to it and incorporated into it by the Holy Spirit through having heard and continuing to hear God's Word, which is the beginning of entering it.[8]

Conclusion

Are the church bodies, the congregations, the assemblies of Christians, the worship services, etc., then of little importance? They are of great importance! It is in those assemblies and services that the Word of God is taught and that the sacraments of baptism and holy communion are celebrated. Such assemblies and services are precious gifts of God for the establishment and growth of faith. Apart from the Word of God and the sacraments, faith is not to be found.

If one is looking, then, for a "physical" church body in which the "spiritual" holy Christian Church is prominent, one needs to examine whether the teachings are faithful to God's Word and whether the sacraments are administered in accordance with that Word. The Church stands under the Word—not *vice versa.*[9]

But even such a church body is not *The Church.* At best, such a body is parallel to what Luther says of the Christian individual of faith—that person is still *simul justus et peccator,* at the same time both saint and sinner. This church body is both a place where people of faith can be found (and identified, within limits) and a human institution not identical with the one, true Christian Church.

In Need of Comfort and Strength: Luther on the Psalms

The Great Challenges in Luther's Life

Luther frequently went through periods of inner turmoil. He was criticized on many fronts, and even some of his closest supporters questioned his actions. His life, especially after 1520, was in danger. Everything took a toll on him physically as he suffered from serious constipation, insomnia, and even bouts of depression. Luther's health would worsen considerably in succeeding years, and he often experienced intense pain. He suffered at various times in the last years of his life from heart and circulation problems, kidney stones, gout, dysentery, headaches, dizziness, and serious fatigue.

The situation was very bad during his time at the Wartburg (May of 1521 through February of 1522), due also to his isolation and loneliness. His only contact with his close friends at Wittenberg and elsewhere was through correspondence. Whereas he had been in the middle of the fray for over three years, now he was isolated—with almost no news of what was happening outside his bleak walls. His restricted diet was awful, and he had little opportunity for exercise. He had been brought by others with no say in the matter (and probably against his will) to the Wartburg for his safekeeping, but to him it was like being in jail. His letters referred to his being "in the wilderness" and on "the Isle of Patmos."

On top of everything else, there are indications in his writings that he was seething over his treatment by the officials at Worms.

He combatted the situation with intensive work. He wrote nearly a dozen significant works in less than ten months of seclusion. Even more amazing, in a period of only eleven weeks, he completed the first draft of his translation of the New Testament into German— an accomplishment that was not only of great significance for the Church but played a major positive role in the development of the German language.

Luther's Source of Comfort

Of course, all of this hard work was not just "any work," but rather it immersed Luther in his true source for guidance—Holy Scripture. Within Scripture, there was for Luther a special source for comfort and strength. If his inspiration for the clarity and beauty of the

265

Gospel was in the letters of Paul, particularly Romans and Galatians, the place where he turned to be close to God was in the Psalms. In Scripture we find not only "Leseworte" (words to read and study), but more importantly, "Lebeworte"—words to *live by*; for Luther this was particularly true of the Psalms. In his "Preface to the Psalter" (1524) as part of his *Prefaces to the Old Testament*, he wrote,

> In a word, if you would see the holy Christian Church painted in living color and shape, comprehended in one little picture, then take up the Psalter. There you have a fine, bright, pure mirror that will show you what Christendom is. Indeed you will find in it also yourself and the true *gnothi seauton* ["know thyself"—words on a temple in Ancient Delphi, Greece and important words for Socrates], as well as God himself and all creatures.[1]

The Psalms were the heart and soul of Luther's personal spiritual life.

As a monk praying the offices, Luther had, of course, prayed the Psalms countless times. He began his teaching career by lecturing on them from 1513 to 1515. His first publication was a work on the seven penitential Psalms. Psalm 46 was the basis for the great Reformation hymn, "A Mighty Fortress," composed between 1526 and 1529. Indeed, several of Luther's great hymns were based on particular Psalms: "If God Had Not Been on Our Side," Psalm 124; "From Depths of Woe I Cry to Thee," Psalm 130; and "O Lord, Look Down from Heaven, Behold," Psalm 12.

Psalm 68—A Psalm for Courage and Strength

At the very beginning of his Wartburg year, he wrote extensive pieces on Psalms 68 and 37.[2] He desperately needed strength and guidance, and he found both in the Psalms. His comments on those Psalms still ring with personal conviction and personal faith—not with the commentary of a scholar.

Psalm 68 is a liturgy celebrating the glorious and triumphant rule of God. It includes many clear references to the march from Mount Sinai (v. 8) at the time of the Exodus to Mount Zion (e.g., v. 26) at the time of David. But for Luther the historical references of the Psalm were even broader. For him the vivid historical references were also to the time of Jesus. In fact, Luther titled this writing "Psalm 68 About Easter, Ascension, and Pentecost"[3] and no doubt chose this Psalm because he came to the Wartburg in that part of the church year. He also saw in this and other Psalms vivid references to his own time.

On verse one, for example, "May God arise, may his enemies be scattered, may his foes flee before him," Luther wrote:

> When Christ died, ... the ranks of the Jews divided; some believed and obtained favor, while others incurred the disfavor of God and were dispersed by the Romans. The prophet viewed this judgment ... and he cried: "Let the rejoicing of God's enemies come to an end! Let God arise and effect a change! Let Him raise Christ from the dead!"[4]

Luther saw in the term "arise" an indication of the Resurrection of Christ. He saw in the term "fire" and in an allusion to wind in verse two ("As smoke is driven away by the wind, so drive them away; as wax melts before fire, let the wicked perish before God") reference to the Holy Spirit and to Pentecost. This Christocentric interpretation of the Psalm continued throughout with emphasis upon God's victory and His greatness.

But this wasn't all. The strength and comfort of the Psalm came also from his seeing that God was active and victorious in Luther's own time. God would arise also in that period and be with the people of faith and strike down His enemies. The Gospel and God's truth would prevail, Luther was sure.

It must be emphasized that for Luther the Bible not only addressed the issues of the periods when it was written; its truths also applied fully to every age. Thus, the proclamation of God's protection and ultimate victory over evil and unfaith gives assurances at any time and in any situation.

- Did Luther see God's enemies in power in the Roman Church?—They would be dealt with and would fail.
- Did Luther see threats to his own life?—God would protect him spiritually (from Satan's wiles), which is all that really counted.
- Was the Church in turmoil?—God would see the true Church through unharmed.
- Was Luther suffering?—God would uphold His servant through everything.
- Was Germany in chaos?—God would punish the evildoers and be with His true followers.

The key to all of this certainty and comfort is found in God's victory in the Resurrection, Ascension, and Pentecost. "To God be praise and glory!" he could say.

Some key passages bring out the essence of his understanding and the basis for his comfort and strength. They show both his devotion to Christ and his hatred over what had become of the Roman Church.

On verse three, "But may the righteous be glad and rejoice before God; may they be happy and joyful,"

> Though the dear disciples and all lovers of the truth have been mourning while the enemies gained the upper hand and triumphed, now they find their great delight in Christ's resurrection and in the victory of the truth. Their joy is pure and God-pleasing; for they exult before God over the truth and over spiritual matters, while the enemies rejoice over their own wickedness.[5]

On verse six, "God sets the lonely in families, he leads forth the prisoners with singing; but the rebellious live in a sun-scorched land,"

> Apart from faith, all doctrine and life separate and disunite mankind. The formation of sects is the inevitable result.... You will find one abounding in this prayer, one in that. One is a Carthusian monk, one a barefoot friar. One goes on pilgrimages, one endows institutions, one fasts. If hearts cling to any of these, discord, hatred, pride, and all sorts of misery will follow. Therefore there is no god, no doctrine, no life, no means that produces unanimity other than this God with His agency of faith.[6]

On verse ten, "Your people settled in it [the promised land], and from your bounty, O God, you provided for the poor,"

> Since the members of Christ's flock are subjected to much suffering for their faith's sake and are humbled and oppressed and despised by all, God manifests His loving-kindness toward them so that after much humiliation they taste and experience ever more how good, loving, and kind God is. Thus the many abasements and sufferings teach the simple believers to become ever better acquainted with God, to trust him and believe in Him and thereby grow strong and rich and established in their confidence in God's kindness.[7]

On verse twenty-three, "That you may plunge your feet in the blood of your foes, while the tongues of your dogs have their share,"

St. Paul enjoins in Romans 14:1 that the weak in the faith should be received and not rejected…. At present the bishops are biting, slashing, and devouring the weak friends, while they are licking and healing the wound of the strong enemies. Those are the devil's dogs.[8]

On verse twenty-six, "Praise God in the great congregation; praise the Lord in the assembly of Israel,"

All the Masses stacked together are worthless without the Word of God. However, today this order has been reversed miserably.[9]

On verse twenty-seven, "There is the little tribe of Benjamin, leading them, there the great throng of Judah's princes, and there the princes of Zebulun and Naphtali," Luther applied references on the tribes to the Apostles, and because Naphtali is listed and Peter was from that area, he wrote,

It may be surprising to see the Apostle Peter relegated to the end. Perhaps this was done to take the wind out of the sails of the future papists. Unfortunately it went for naught.[10]

On verse thirty, "Rebuke the beast among the reeds, the herd of bulls among the calves of the nations. Humbled, may it bring bars of silver. Scatter the nations who delight in war,"

The psalmist asks God to rebuke and punish the avaricious and the ambitious, who seize and appropriate these gifts and who are motivated in their desire for advancement by nothing but greed and ambition. In that regard, the pope, cardinals, bishops, priests, monks, and their kind have now become almost feverish. Let us hear how he portrays them. First he calls them "beasts that dwell among the reeds."[11]

Also on this verse:

If the psalmist had chosen plain German, he would have said, "O God, punish all those who push and press their way into the office of pope, bishops, cardinals, priests, monks, clerics, and do not await an urgent call to the office. For they assuredly seek only honor and wealth, gluttony, high living, and good days, and become bulls and tyrants of the people. They fabricate human ordinances to suppress Thy Gospel. They are actuated by the prospect of riches in the church, donated by kings for the sustenance of the poor. O punish, punish, resist, resist them, dear Lord, lest Christendom perish! They are evil reed finches." Behold, now you see what the prophet thinks of the papacy and papists.[12]

On verse thirty-three, "To him who rides the ancient skies above, who thunders with mighty voice,"

The greedy and ambitious … bind the worship of God to all sorts of externals, such as chapels, cloisters, churches, altars, bells, garments, vessels, tablets, tonsures, food, drink, sleeping. That is characteristic of the beast in the reeds, the papist sect, today.[13]

Luther's language became quite vehement and indicates his total disdain of the Roman Church after his treatment by Church officials and the Holy Roman Emperor at Worms. It is also worth noting that this writing, as seen in one of the quotes above, also contained strong language about the rejection of the Gospel by Jews, but that will be treated in another essay.

As stated earlier, Luther also wrote on Psalm 36 during this period. For Luther, Psalm 36 was a special Psalm of comfort, and he addressed this writing "to the poor little flock of Christ at Wittenberg."

Psalm 118—A Source of Great Comfort

Before leaving the topic of Luther's devotion to and use of the Psalms, mention should be made of Luther's writing on his very favorite Psalm—Psalm 118. In the summer of 1530

Luther would again be isolated and cut off from the action. This time he was housed in the castle at Coburg while the Diet of Augsburg was taking place and the *Augsburg Confession* was being presented and deliberated. He felt himself again "in the wilderness."

In addition, Luther learned on June 5 that his father had died. Not surprisingly, he turned to the Psalms for prayer and comfort.

He wrote in his preface to his writing on Psalm 118, which he called, "*The Beautiful Confitemini*" from its opening word in the Vulgate, "O give thanks,"

> This is my own beloved psalm. Although the entire Psalter and all of Holy Scripture are dear to me as my only comfort and source of life, I fell in love with this psalm especially. Therefore I call it my own. When emperors and kings, the wise and the learned, and even saints could not aid me, this psalm proved a friend and helped me out of many great troubles. As a result, it is dearer to me than all the wealth, honor, and power of the pope, the Turk, and the emperor. I would be most unwilling to trade this psalm for all of it.[14]

Verse one of the Psalm is, "Give thanks to the Lord, for he is good, and his love endures forever." Luther's comments offer high praise to God for His goodness. "God is good, but not as a human being is good; from the very bottom of His heart He is inclined to help and do good continually."[15] In words that remind us of his beautiful explanation of the first article of the Apostle's Creed, he continued, still on verse one:

> He unceasingly showers the best upon us. He is the Creator of our bodies and souls, our Protector by day and by night, and the Preserver of our lives. He causes the sun and the moon to shine on us, fire, air, water, and the heavens to serve us. He causes the earth to give food, fodder, wine, grain, clothes, wood, and all necessities. He provides us with gold and silver, house and home, wife and child, cattle, birds, and fish. In short, who can count it all? And all this is bountifully showered upon us every year, every day, every hour, and every minute....
>
> This verse also serves to comfort us in all our misfortunes. We are such softies, such sapless sufferers. A pain in the leg or the stirring of a little leaf can cause us to fill heaven and earth with our howls and wails, our grumbling and cursing....
>
> The good God permits such small evils to befall us merely in order to arouse us snorers from our deep sleep and to make us recognize, on the other hand, the incomparable and innumerable benefits we still have. He wants us to consider what would happen if He were to withdraw His goodness from us completely.[16]

Luther's exposition continued in lavish praise of God for His protection and goodness at all times. Along the way, he treated what some regard as his favorite Bible verse, "I will not die, but live, and proclaim what the Lord has done"—verse seventeen:

> This verse ... emphasizes the two points...: comfort and help, with which God blesses the pious and the righteous. Here you see how the right hand of God mightily lifts the heart and comforts it in the midst of death, so that it can say: "Though I die, I die not. Though I suffer, I suffer not. Though I fall, I am not down. Though I am disgraced, I am not dishonored." This is the consolation. Furthermore, the psalmist says of the help: "I shall live." Isn't this an amazing help? The dying live; the suffering rejoice; the fallen rise; the disgraced are honored. It is as Christ says: "He who believes in Me, though he die, yet shall he live" (John 11:25). Paul speaks in a similar manner: "We are afflicted in every way, but not crushed; perplexed, but not driven to despair" (2 Cor. 4:8). These are all words that no human heart can comprehend.[17]

In the closing paragraph on the Psalm, he wrote the following:

> [God] does not stop doing good because of the wickedness of men. Thus He proves that He is good by nature, and that His goodness does not stand or fall by the vice or virtue of another, as human goodness

may stand on the virtue of one and fall by the vice of another and even become worse than he is.... May Christ, our Lord, make us human beings true, perfect Christians. To Him be praise and thanks forever! Amen.[18]

Closing

Luther never tired of praying, meditating on, and writing about the Psalms. They were for him the source of strength that he so desperately needed as he faced obstacles that threatened to overwhelm his life.

• **Essay 13** •

Luther on Spiritual Growth
in a New Church

By the time of his return from the Wartburg in 1522, Luther realized that an entirely new spirituality was needed in the Reformation Churches. He knew that the old piety was almost totally foreign to Scripture and to genuine Christianity.

His protests had begun over the sale of indulgences. He was outraged by the view that if a person would spend money for a certificate of indulgence, that would bring favor from God and reduction of punishment in purgatory—even for people other than the one paying. Though the Church said that this purchase presupposed genuine repentance and faith, Luther knew that the indulgence practice sent all the wrong messages. Genuine repentance and faith were enough by themselves—no indulgences were needed; the entire doctrine of purgatory was misguided; and how could one by paying money benefit someone else who had already died?

But after Worms and his time of reflection at the Wartburg, Luther could see that virtually everything about Roman piety was wrong-headed and that a new church required an entirely new basis for spiritual growth.

The list of required or recommended practices for spiritual growth in the Roman Catholic Church included, besides purchasing indulgences: pilgrimages and veneration of relics (with payment), praying the rosary, praying to the saints, fasting and abstinence (including not eating meat of warm-blooded animals on Fridays), purchasing special masses, showing obeisance to the pope, performing various forms of penance including practices mentioned in this list, attending prescribed worship services, and the like. *It was all worthless—or even harmful.*

Roman piety urged a higher tier of spirituality which included both vows of celibacy, poverty, and obedience, and also living apart from the world in a monastery or nunnery.

Luther saw that all of this was misguided, for it was not based upon the use of Scripture and the sacraments (baptism and holy communion), and because it paid no heed to the spiritual ethics in the 10 commandments, in Jesus' moral teachings, in the Old Testament prophets or the New Testament epistles.

For genuine growth in spirituality, Luther saw that new helps were needed. The aids which Luther developed for this purpose were revolutionary: the Bible in the language of the people, hymns for worship, prayers for daily life, and a catechism of basic Christian teachings. Moreover, these aids were for everyone; no longer was there a lower class of Christians (the laity) and a higher class (the clergy, monks, and nuns), but *all* people could use these same aids to grow in faith and love.

The Bible in the Language of the People

What a spectacular gift to the Church this was! Now a person without a university education could hear a lesson read *and understand it*! Now a person who could read German could look at biblical verses directly *and understand them*!

To make this possible, Luther not only used the Latin of the Vulgate (the official Bible of the Roman Church) but he also studied Greek and made use of the scholarship of his colleague Melanchthon to translate New Testament passages from the original Greek. This he did with unswerving dedication during his Wartburg confinement. Later he did the same with the Old Testament studying Hebrew so that he could render the Old Testament passages faithfully. He continued to make translation improvements in both Testaments throughout the rest of his life. As one holds Luther's translation, *Die Bibel,* in his hand, it seems like a task for more than a single person's lifetime—yet Luther accomplished it while performing countless other tasks and did his initial New Testament translation in less than three months! He continued to work intensely on the Old Testament and had done all but the prophets by 1524, but he was not able to complete the entire Bible including several books of the Apocrypha until 1534. No doubt the task itself inspired and nourished him, for it brought him into a special closeness with God.

Luther's was not the first translation into German, but it was by far the best, and it changed the course of Christianity forever—not just in Germany but throughout the world by showing that a careful translation into the language of the people was both possible and a great blessing. No longer was God's Word hidden from the believer. No longer was it deemed too transcendent for the layperson to understand. It did as much as anything to crumble the authority of the Church hierarchy, for now a person could study for himself and wasn't at the mercy of the clergy for understanding what God said.

Luther's German translation was beautiful. "Ich bin das Brot des Lebens," Luther in his simple, straightforward German quoted Jesus as saying,[1] and this kind of everyday but almost melodic language brought Jesus and all of Scripture to life for the people. It was, many believe, his greatest contribution to the Church.

If a person were depressed, worried, angry, confused, tempted, guilty, or struggling, the individual needed only to turn directly to the Bible and read key sections by himself and for himself. God's Word was now truly an "open book."

With his translation, Luther provided prefaces to help the reader find the key points. The prefaces highlighted his theological insights. In his preface to the New Testament, for example, he wrote:

> The gospel, then, is nothing but the preaching about Christ, Son of God and of David, true God and man, who by his death and resurrection has overcome for us the sin, death, and hell of all men who believe in him....
> See to it, therefore, that you do not make a Moses out of Christ, or a book of laws and doctrines out of the gospel, as has been done heretofore and as certain prefaces put it, even those of St. Jerome [c. 340–420, Church Father, translator of Vulgate]. For the gospel does not expressly demand works of our own

by which we become righteous and are saved; indeed it condemns such works. Rather the gospel demands faith in Christ: that he has overcome for us sin, death, and hell, and thus gives us righteousness, life, and salvation not through our works, but through his own works, death, and suffering, in order that we may avail ourselves of his death and victory as though we had done it ourselves.[2]

Luther was also quite willing in his prefaces to give a ranking to the various books in the Bible. In a famous passage, he wrote:

In a word St John's Gospel and his first epistle, St. Paul's epistles, especially Romans, Galatians, and Ephesians, and St. Peter's first epistle are the books that show you Christ and teach you all that is necessary and salvatory for you to know, even if you were never to see or hear any other book or doctrine. Therefore St. James' epistle is really an epistle of straw, compared to these others, for it has nothing of the nature of the gospel about it.[3]

Hymns

Luther loved music, and he knew what it could do for one's spiritual life. He played the lute, he sang, and he composed. In so doing he was lifting up his soul and the souls of others.

Music had been a part of worship for centuries, of course, but it was the formal chanting or the choir motets—always in Latin (or sometimes in Greek). It was beautiful, but it was not music of the people, for they did little or no singing in the worship services themselves.

At a time when he was busy with the translations, 1522–24, he was also composing spiritual songs one after another—at least two dozen. A few were Latin hymns or chants that he translated into German. A couple used melodies from John Hus and the Bohemian Brethren. But most were new lyrics put to existing or new "folk song" melodies that could be sung by the people in worship, in the home, while walking or when working. Luther made use of the *Minnesänger* tradition and wrote carol-like songs that told stories or taught spiritual truths. Some of the songs were also translations of psalms.

The hymns fit particular parts of the worship service (e.g., the introit, creed, or communion), various special services (evening, wedding, funeral), seasons of the Church year (Christmas, Lent, Easter, etc.), parts of the catechism (Ten Commandments, Lord's Prayer, baptism, etc.), or the central Gospel message.

They do not fit the models of the hymns of Romanticism or contemporary praise songs, but they were extremely popular from the outset, and people loved to sing them and to memorize them.

One of the first, *"Nun freut euch liebe Christen"* ("Dear Christians, One and All, Rejoice"), has ten verses set to a cheery tune that you could dance to. In the translation of Richard Massie, the first verse is:

> Dear Christians, one and all, rejoice,
>   With exultation springing,
> And with united heard and voice
>   And holy rapture singing,
> Proclaim the wonders God has done,
> How His right arm the vict'ry won.
> What price our ransom cost Him![4]

The subsequent verses speak of the hold Satan had on us, of the futility of our good works, and of God's wonderful rescue. Verse five has God the Father sending His Son on the Messianic mission of salvation, verse six describes the Son's completing this mission to save us, and the last four verses present the Son giving comfort and instruction to us, His children. This is the closing verse:

> "What I on earth have done and taught
> Guide all your life and teaching;
> So shall the kingdom's work be wrought
>   And honored in your preaching.
> But watch lest foes with base alloy
> The heav'nly treasure should destoy;
>   This final word I leave you."

The song turns out to be almost a joyful sermon.

While this hymn is cheerful, Luther's most famous hymn, *"Ein feste Burg"* ("A Mighty Fortress"), likely written in 1527 or 1528, exudes confidence and courage with its strong beat and cadence. Out of thanks to God and respect for Luther, Lutherans stand when this hymn is sung, but the strength and drum-beat of the piece in its original format almost require one to stand, in any case.

The words, based on Psalm 46, fit the strength of the tune perfectly. Verse one is:

> A mighty Fortress is our God, a trusty shield and weapon;
> He helps us free from ev'ry need that has us now o'ertaken.
> The old evil Foe now means deadly woe;
> Deep guile and great might are his dread arms in fight;
> On earth is not his equal.

The last part of the first verse may make it sound like the devil is invincible, but then look what happens in the subsequent three verses:

> With might of ours can naught be done, soon were our loss effected;
> But for us fights the Valiant One, whom God Himself elected.
> Ask ye, Who is this? Jesus Christ it is,
> Of Sabaoth Lord, and there's none other God;
> He holds the field forever.
>
> Tho' devils all the world should fill, all eager to devour us,
> We tremble not, we fear no ill, they shall not overpow'r us.
> This world's prince may still scowl fierce as he will,
> He can harm us none, he's judged; the deed is done;
> One little word can fell him.
>
> The Word they still shall let remain nor any thanks have for it;
> He's by our side upon the plain with His good gifts and Spirit,
> And take they our life, goods, fame, child, and wife,
> Let these all be gone, they yet have nothing won;
> The Kingdom ours remaineth.[5]

Prayers

Personal prayer books had long been popular in the Roman Catholic Church, but they often included unbiblical elements that supported work-righteousness and misguided acts of piety. Because these little books were so important to so many people, Luther soon realized that a Gospel-centered and biblical prayer book was needed for the laity. The result was his *Personal Prayer Book*, first published in 1522 and continuing for several years in numerous printings and new editions. His section on sin and confession focused on the Ten Commandments. His thoughts on prayer were based on The Lord's Prayer. His summary of the Christian Gospel used as its basis The Apostles' Creed. (Much of the material in these three sections would later be used in his Catechisms.) The *Personal Prayer Book* of 1522 included eight psalms (12, 67, 51, 103, 20, 79, 25, and 10) and Paul's epistle to Titus. It also included forty-nine woodcuts of biblical scenes with the scriptural references.

The earlier prayer books had included sections on the "Hail Mary." It may seem somewhat surprising that Luther's book also included this, but he gave it a completely different emphasis and interpretation saying that in it we are praising and honoring God. It is not a petition to Mary, he claimed, but rather a glorification of God. The following gives Luther's own words:

> Take note of this: no one should put his trust in the Mother of God or in her merits, for such a trust is worthy of God alone and is the lofty service due only to him. Rather, praise and thank God through Mary and the grace given her. Laud and love her simply as the one who, without merit, obtained such blessings from God, sheerly out of his mercy, as she herself testifies in the Magnificat…. Let not our hearts cleave to her, but through her penetrate to Christ and to God himself…. You see that these words are not concerned with prayer but purely with giving praise and honor…. There are two things we can do. First, we can use the Hail Mary as a meditation in which we recite what grace God has given her. Second, we should add a wish that everyone may know and respect her.[6]

This was the wording of the "Hail Mary" in Luther's *Prayer Book:* "Hail, Mary, full of grace. The Lord is with thee; blessed art thou among women and blessed is the fruit of thy womb, Jesus Christ. Amen." And this was also the wording of the "Hail Mary" in the Catholic Church at the time. But, of course, it is not the "Hail Mary" that is recited by Roman Catholics today. That wording is: "Hail Mary, full of grace, the Lord is with thee; blessed art thou amongst women, and blessed is the fruit of thy womb, Jesus. Holy Mary, Mother of God, pray for us sinners, now and at the hour of death. Amen."

A Jesuit, Canisuis, added "Hail Mary, Mother of God, pray for us sinners" in his 1555 *Catechism,* and this was approved by the Council of Trent several years after Luther's death. The *Catechism of the Council of Trent,* 1566, included the following:

> The Church of God has wisely added prayers and an invocation addressed to the most holy Mother of God, by which we piously and humbly fly to her patronage, in order that, by her intercession, she may reconcile God to us sinners and may obtain for us those blessings which we stand in need of in this life and in the life to come. We, therefore, exiled children of Eve, who dwell in this vale of tears, should constantly beseech the Mother of mercy, the advocate of the faithful, to pray for us sinners. In this prayer we should earnestly implore her help and assistance; for that she possesses exalted merits with God, and that she is most desirous to assist us by her prayers, no one can doubt without impiety and wickedness.[7]

The "Hail Mary" still in use today in the Roman Catholic Church directly contradicts Luther's points.

Catechisms

Of his many writings, the one which Lutherans know the best (and in many cases have memorized), is *Luther's Small Catechism.* It is one of the confessions in the *Book of Concord,* and it continues to be used in Lutheran churches as an introduction to Christian faith. Its primary purpose was not to distinguish Lutherans from other Christians but rather to present the essential teachings of Christianity. Of course, some took exception to the teaching of infant baptism or of the real presence of Jesus' body and blood in Holy Communion, but Luther taught and Lutherans teach that these are basic *Christian* teachings.

Catechisms were a traditional means for education at the time. Pupils would memorize set answers to specific questions; in drills the instructor would ask the questions and the learners were to recite the answers from memory. In Luther's catechism, the typical question is "What does this mean?" The answers give brief, meaningful theological answers. A typical example is in the sixth petition of the Lord's Prayer:

> And lead us not into temptation.
> *What does this mean?*
> Answer: God indeed tempts no one. But we pray in this petition that God would guard and keep us, so that the devil, the world, and our flesh may not deceive us nor seduce us into false belief, despair, and other great shame and vice. Though we are attacked by these things, we pray that still we may finally overcome them and gain the victory.[8]

In 1520 Luther had written an abbreviated help for Christians entitled, *A Short Form of the Ten Commandments, the Creed, and the Lord's Prayer*. But an organized series of visitations made to the Reformation congregations in the latter half of the 1520s convinced him of the need for a new educational tool. He wrote in his preface to the *Small Catechism*:

> The deplorable, miserable condition which I discovered recently when I, too, was a visitor, has forced and urged me to prepare this catechism.... The common person, especially in the villages, has no knowledge whatever of Christian doctrine. And unfortunately, many pastors are completely unable and unqualified to teach.[9]

The result was the *Small Catechism*, first published in 1529. The accompanying *Large Catechism*, written both to guide the pastors and teachers and to provide deeper understandings for the people who had completed the *Small Catechism*, was published in the same year.

The *Small Catechism* was divided into three sections (a fourth, a set of questions and answers for a person preparing for Holy Communion, was added a few years after Luther's death). The first dealt with primary Christian teachings and has six parts: The Ten Commandments, The [Apostles'] Creed, The Lord's Prayer, The Sacrament of Holy Baptism, Confession and Absolution (also called The Office of the Keys) including an order for confession, and The Sacrament of the Altar (Holy Communion). Section two, "Daily Prayers," offered prayers to be taught and used in the home. Section three, "Table of Duties," presented a series of biblical passages which give responsibilities that Christians in various stations have. The thirteen categories given include bishops, pastors, and preachers; citizens; husbands; wives; children; employers; workers; widows; and several more.

The *Large Catechism* covered in detail five of the six parts in section one above. It did not include "The Office of the Keys" but it did give an order for confession.

These catechisms continue to be a great blessing. Their concise presentation of Christian teachings remain a source of insight and comfort for people throughout their lives. The table of duties shows that all people in all walks of life have special Christian callings or "vocations." And the prayers section promotes daily, rich conversation with God. The "morning and evening prayers" are still used every day by an untold number of Lutherans. These prayers are as follows:

Morning

In the name of God the Father, Son, and Holy Spirit. Amen.

I thank You, my Heavenly Father, through Jesus Christ, Your dear Son, that you have kept me this night from all harm and danger. And I pray that you would keep me this day also from sin and all evil, so that all my doings and life may please You. For into Your hands I commend myself, my body and soul, and all things. Let Your holy angel be with me so that the wicked foe may have no power over me. Amen. (Then go to your work with joy, singing a hymn, like one on the Ten Commandments, or what your devotion may suggest.)

Evening

In the name of God the Father, Son, and Holy Spirit. Amen.

I thank You, my Heavenly Father, through Jesus Christ, Your dear Son, that You have graciously kept me this day. And I pray, forgive me all my sins, where I have done wrong, and graciously keep me this night. For into Your hands I commend myself, my body and soul, and all things. Let Your holy angel be with me, so that the wicked foe may have no power over me. Amen. (Then go to sleep immediately and cheerfully.)[10]

Luther on Free Will: Against Erasmus— A Failed Alignment of the Stars

By the early 1520s Erasmus and Luther were celebrities—the two most widely known figures in all of Europe. They had some initial fairly cordial correspondence and they possessed several similarities; for example,

- Their writings were widely known and very popular.
- Both were superb, engaging writers.
- Both were highly critical of the church hierarchy and of many church practices.
- Both had been monks and priests in the Roman Church; they knew first-hand the things they criticized.
- Both opposed scholasticism as misguided and pointless.
- Both had grave misgivings about reason—especially as used in theology and philosophy.
- Both had a large following of enthusiastic adherents as well as many powerful detractors.
- Neither had any wealth or helpful family connections.

It was reasonably expected by many that they would become a team, but that was not to be.

Erasmus of Rotterdam

Erasmus was likely born in 1469, so he was approximately fourteen years older than Luther. Though he became a monk and priest, his real love was literature; he devoured the ancient classics, teaching himself Greek in the process and aligning himself with the developing humanism of key Renaissance figures. He wrote and taught in Cambridge, Paris, Basel, Louvain, Brussels, and other cities dazzling people everywhere with his brilliance, wit, and beautiful Latin.

Along the way, he became famous as a satirist, and much of his satire was directed against the clergy and the Roman Church's hierarchy. *Praise of Folly,* 1511, became a huge bestseller, and his anonymous skit about Peter's denial of Pope Julius II's entrance into heaven was both devastating and hilarious.

Erasmus also had a serious side to his scholarship. He wrote and published a critical version of the Greek New Testament with notes in which he, among other things, pointed out weaknesses in the Latin Vulgate, the official Bible of the Roman Catholic Church. Luther greatly admired it and used it for his New Testament translation from Greek into German, but traditionalists in the Roman Church accused Erasmus of heresy.

Nevertheless, Erasmus never really turned against the Roman Church. He was against indulgences, relics, a profligate papacy and clergy, and much more, to be sure, but he always hoped that humanistic learning would make its way into the Church enough that the Church would become more like the early church and Jesus himself—simpler, compassionate, and peace-loving.

Luther and Erasmus—Early Tensions

The very earliest correspondence between Luther and Erasmus showed their mutual respect but also how different their temperaments were. In March of 1519, Luther wrote a friendly and admiring letter to Erasmus in which he also appealed for the latter's friendship.[1] In May, Erasmus responded expressing his admiration and his agreement with much that Luther was doing. He mentioned, though, that some of Luther's foes had accused Erasmus of being an aid to Luther in his writings and of being a "standard-bearer" for Luther; he didn't like the accusation. He wrote, "I have testified to them that you are entirely unknown to me, that I have not read your books, and neither approve nor disapprove of your writings."[2]

Erasmus' temperament is then shown even more fully in the advice he offered to Luther much as a mentor would offer to a younger colleague:

It might be wiser of you to denounce those who misuse the Pope's authority than to censure the Pope himself. So also with kings and princes. Old institutions cannot be rooted up in an instant. Quiet argument may do more than wholesale condemnation. Avoid all appearance of sedition. Keep cool. Do not get angry. Do not hate anybody. Do not be excited over the noise you have made.[3]

The contrasts between the two became ever clearer. Erasmus used bitter satire and coupled his attacks with humor; Luther presented his attacks in straightforward, tough language. Erasmus wrote in a sophisticated, beautiful language for intellectuals in all countries; Luther used a clear German and Latin to make his points crystal-clear for all people and especially for the Germans. Erasmus was willing to hold back for the sake of peace; Luther would sacrifice peace for the sake of God's truth.

Moreover, Erasmus was a man of letters; Luther was a pastor and a theologian—even a prophet in the sense of one who boldly proclaims God's Word no matter what. It is no doubt significant, too, for understanding their differences that Erasmus was beholden to Charles V for a stipend and to the humanists in the Roman Church hierarchy for their protection and support; Luther had no such financial dependency.

Erasmus' concern for truth and his respect for Luther is shown in the fact that he had encouraged Frederick of Saxony (Frederick the Wise) to help and to protect Luther. But, as indicated above, he never became one of Luther's followers as such, despite accusations to that effect, and he felt himself trapped in the middle between Luther's adherents and ecclesiastical officials. He was criticized both by those who believed he was disingenuous for not siding with Luther (they thought he had started what Luther was continuing), and also by those in the Roman Church who thought he did side with Luther. He replied to both that he only wanted peace and healthy reform in the Church and that he was not a party in the dispute.[4] Not surprisingly, his response satisfied neither group of critics.

Luther, for his side, probably never trusted Erasmus to have the courage to stand by his convictions in the face of criticism. He saw Erasmus as a member of an elite intellectual society—far from the deeply committed person that he was.

The Battle Over Free Will

Before we turn to an examination of the key documents in the free will debate between Luther and Erasmus, it is important to realize that neither was interested in the broad philosophical issue of determinism vs. indeterminism. The *determinist* says that every event that occurs, including all human thoughts and actions, is determined by antecedent conditions, and the *indeterminist* claims that at least some events are not determined in this way but are the result either of choice or chance. This issue was *not* the issue for either Luther or Erasmus.

Erasmus' concern was with morality, for he saw morality as the essence of Christianity. As Christians we are called upon to live lives in keeping with the 10 Commandments and the injunctions of the New Testament, he believed. For him, we *ought* to live according to high Christian standards, and God would never demand this if it were not possible. "Ought implies can" is the way philosophers today would describe his point. Erasmus held, too, that God comes to our aid with his mercy and takes care of our failings. For him we could say that "ought implies can with the aid of God's mercy." He was concerned that some of Luther's earlier "assertions" undercut Christian morality by asserting that humans "cannot no matter what."

Luther, on the other hand, was not primarily concerned about morality *per se*; he did not see morality as the essence of Christianity. For Luther Christianity is about the grace of God offering salvation through Christ. He did not see how any Christian could define Christianity in terms that did not include "Christ" and "salvation" and "grace," so he disagreed completely with Erasmus' understanding. Moreover, Luther thought that by implication Erasmus was saying that a person could help win God's favor (and salvation) by the right moral effort, and this Luther denied with total conviction; it was a major part of his attack on the Roman Church.

Thus, the debate was really about whether a person could help win God's favor by moral choice and striving. For Luther this is impossible because until a person receives God's grace and forgiveness, that person is under the control of Satan and of sin. Man has no free will to begin to move close to God and to do God's will. For Erasmus man must have the free will to begin to please God for morality and for Christianity to have any meaning.

Luther's *The Bondage of the Will*, 1525, was written as an answer to Erasmus' *On the Freedom of the Will*, also called the *Diatribe*, 1524.[5] Erasmus had had serious reservations about Luther for several years, and he finally published a document that took exception to a basic element in Luther's theology and not just to his style. Erasmus did not consider himself to be a theologian, but he believed he could point out a fundamental flaw in Luther. He had indeed put his finger on a genuine cornerstone of Luther's theology, and he opened the opportunity for Luther to write what many consider to be his finest theological writing of all. Luther appreciated Erasmus' focusing on this most vital issue.

In *On the Freedom of the Will*, it is clear that Erasmus despised theological assertions and controversy. As indicated above, he believed that Christianity is fundamentally a faith of simple moral commitment based on a loving God and a life-style of love and peace. But morality requires free will. If a person is urged by a loving and gracious God to do what is morally right, that person must have a free will to be able to choose to do what is right. And God would not urge a person to do something if that person had no choice and only acted out of necessity. This is true even if we give God all praise for His grace and forgiveness. In his book, Erasmus supported his claims by offering interpretations of several key biblical passages.

Luther regarded Erasmus' position as a system of "work righteousness" and semi-Pelagian heresy according to which a person can cooperate with God to gain salvation. *The Bondage of the Will* opens with a brief greeting in which Luther acknowledged Erasmus' superior talent but expressed his disappointment and low opinion of the scholar's book, whereupon he then immediately argued that Erasmus' disdain of assertions and his preference for skeptical withholding of judgment is totally unsuited for a Christian. Christianity, Luther argued, citing many biblical passages, is grounded in assertions—God's assertions found in Scripture and confessed boldly by the believer.

Luther objected strongly to Erasmus' contention that some things in Scripture are clear but that some are obscure and unknowable. Perhaps there are flaws in our knowledge of terms and phrases, Luther claimed, but Scripture is clear in its claims. For Luther, the Bible speaks with absolute clarity about Christ and the salvation God has won for us.

At this point, the issue of free will was taken up. This is what Erasmus had written in *On the Freedom of the Will*:

> So in my opinion, as far as free choice is concerned, what we have learnt from Holy Writ is this: if we are in the way of true religion we should eagerly press on to better things, forgetting the things that are behind; if we are entangled in sins, we should strive with all our might, have recourse to the remedy of penitence and entreat by all means the mercy of the Lord, without which no human will or endeavor is effective; and whatever is evil in us, let us impute to ourselves, whatever is good let us ascribe wholly to the divine benevolence, to which we owe our very being; then for the rest, let us believe that whatever befalls us in this life, whether joyful or sad, it has been sent by God for our salvation, and that no wrong can be done to anyone by him, who by nature is just, even if some things happen that we feel we have not deserved, nor should anyone despair of forgiveness from a God who is by nature most merciful. To hold fast to these things, I say, is in my judgment sufficient for Christian godliness, and we have no call to force our way with irreverent inquisitiveness into those concealed, not to say superfluous, things, such as: whether God foreknows anything contingently; whether our will accomplishes anything in things pertaining to eternal salvation; whether it simply suffers the action of grace; whether what we do, be it of good or ill, we do by necessity or rather suffer to be done to us.[6]

In his response, Luther first summarized Erasmus' point as follows: "that we should strive with all our might, have recourse to the remedy of penitence, and entreat by all means the mercy of the Lord, without which no human will or endeavor is effective; also, that no one should despair of the pardon of God who is by nature most merciful."[7]

Luther went on to write, "These words of yours devoid of Christ, devoid of the Spirit, are colder than ice itself, so that they even tarnish the beauty of your eloquence. Perhaps they were dragged out of you, poor fellow, by fear of the pontiffs and tyrants."[8] Luther found Erasmus' position to be indecisive and confusing. How much does man contribute by his striving?

How much does God contribute by his mercy? And why shouldn't it be important to investigate this issue to reach a definitive conclusion/assertion?

Luther made his point strongly:

> When ... you order [Christians] not to be inquisitive about what they can and cannot do in the matter of obtaining eternal salvation, this is beyond question the unforgiveable sin. For as long as they are ignorant of what and how much they can do, they will not know what they should do; and being ignorant of what they should do, they cannot repent if they do wrong; and impenitence is the unforgivable sin.

Thus Luther has refocused the issue. For him the real issue is obtaining salvation.

At this point Luther was willing to take a definitive step. He was willing to accept the full consequences, as far as salvation is concerned, of God's omniscience. God knows all—without regard to time or place. He knows the future as fully as the past. And God has full free will to determine what will happen; man does not.

Scholastics had explored the logic of God's omniscience to an amazing degree. For them the issue encompasses even personal trivial choices. But this matter of logic was of no interest to Luther. His interest was in whether a person has any freedom to do God's will and thus to contribute to winning His favor and salvation. On this Luther claimed a decisive "No." Until God takes hold of a person and through Christ and the Holy Spirit brings that person to faith and salvation and the subsequent good works, a person is under the control of Satan and sin. On this there is absolutely no free will. Until God frees us because of Christ, we are under the control of Satan.

In response to Erasmus' claim that his position was in accordance with many Church Fathers and with general Church history, Luther replied that the Church has often made mistakes and that the only reliable truth is in Scripture.

After arguing against the interpretations Erasmus gave of several biblical passages, Luther offered additional passages to support his own position. He then presented his conclusions in which he reiterated five central points.

First, God's omniscience rules out any free choice in any other creature:

> I will here bring this little book to an end, though I am prepared if need be to carry the debate farther. However, I think quite enough has been done here to satisfy the godly and anyone who is willing to admit the truth without being obstinate. For if we believe it to be true that God foreknows and predestines all things, that he can neither be mistaken in his foreknowledge nor hindered in his predestination, and that nothing takes place but as he wills it (as reason itself is forced to admit), then on the testimony of reason itself there cannot be any free choice in man or angel or any creature.[9]

Second, Satan's control over us until God rescues us likewise leaves no room for free will:

> Similarly, if we believe that Satan is the ruler of this world, who is forever plotting and fighting against the Kingdom of Christ with all his powers, and that he will not let men go who are his captives unless he is forced to do so by the divine power of the Spirit, then again it is evident that there can be no such thing as free choice.[10]

Third, until God rescues us, all of our actions are necessarily directed toward evil:

> Similarly, if we believe that original sin has so ruined us that even in those who are led by the Spirit it causes a great deal of trouble by struggling against the good, it is clear that in a man devoid of the Spirit there is nothing left that can turn toward the good, but only toward evil.[11]

Fourth, the history of both Jews and Gentiles shows that without God's grace a human can only will the evil.

Again, if the Jews, who pursued righteousness to the utmost of their powers, rather ran headlong into unrighteousness, while Gentiles, who pursued ungodliness, attained righteousness freely and unexpectedly, then it is also manifest from this very fact and experience that man without grace can will nothing but evil.[12]

Finally, as Christians we must confess that Christ's redemption requires us to believe that we were necessarily lost without Him:

To sum up: If we believe that Christ has redeemed men by his blood, we are bound to confess that the whole man was lost; otherwise, we should make Christ either superfluous or the redeemer of only the lowest part of man, which would be blasphemy and sacrilege.[13]

In a parting shot, Luther wrote in all capitals: "I for my part in this book HAVE NOT DISCOURSED, BUT HAVE ASSERTED AND DO ASSERT."[14]

Luther believed that he had won the debate hands down. He considered this writing to be his greatest polemical work. The book was widely acclaimed (also denounced by many) immediately after its publication, and many theologians and others have praised it since then.

The book shows huge strengths including:

- Luther demonstrated the importance of assertions for a Christian.
- He had the courage and conviction to disagree with a popular, recognized authority.
- He was willing to accept that esteemed Church Fathers and later theologians made significant errors and sometimes strayed from Scripture.
- He saw vividly the Pelagian heresy that lies behind a moralistic version of Christianity.
- He understood the Gospel entirely in Christological terms.
- He recognized the full power of Satan's control of the unregenerated person.
- He understood the total import of *sola gratia*—that we are saved by God's grace alone.
- He showed with great skill the errors in some of Erasmus' interpretations of Scripture and offered insightful interpretations of his own.
- He demonstrated that we are totally dependent upon God's grace and that even faith is a gift of grace.
- He accepted his conclusions about our lack of free will with complete conviction even if some saw them as irrational or counterproductive.

Nevertheless, on the philosophical level, Luther did not argue how the role of Satan can be reconciled with God, who is omnipotent. Likewise, he did not propose that an omnipotent being might be able to create creatures with at least limited free choice, a more Augustinian position. In addition, Luther was willing in talking of free will to deal with a logical issue that was more akin to the approach of Scholasticism—despite the fact that both he and Erasmus viewed such thinking negatively.

Theologically, he might have acceded to Erasmus' point that there are some passages that are difficult for us to understand without implying that the doctrines central to Christianity and to salvation are unclear.

Luther was right to point out the flaws of the Pelagian, moralistic, and cautious proposals that Erasmus had made. Of course, his language could have been gentler though likely there was no way to bring Erasmus to change his views. It should be noted, too, that Erasmus' satire could be terribly disrespectful, and that Luther's aggressive approach may have been necessary to keep his points from being lost or compromised in endless back-and-forth.[15]

A word needs to be said about the doctrine of predestination. The Calvinist position of double predestination is that God's determination of events extends to his controlling who will be saved and who will not be saved. This goes further than Luther was willing to go. Luther's emphasis was that God can and does overcome Satan's total control over our will and that he graciously brings us to salvation. He protects and "predestines" his people through the work of the Holy Spirit. Luther did not purse the "logic" of the issue further.

In the end, *The Bondage of the Will* must be celebrated as a great work of Christian theology. It shows beautifully that a Christian *must* make bold assertions. It argues forcefully for the basic doctrine that we are entirely dependent upon God's unfathomable grace for every single aspect of our salvation and for all of the spiritual blessings that He showers upon us through the Holy Spirit. In a very literal sense, Luther wished to give God all glory.

• Essay 15 •

Luther on Marriage, Celibacy and His Dear Kate

One of the things that endeared Luther to a broad mix of people was that he brought Christianity to bear on the everyday aspects of life. Several times he wrote on the family and the education of children. His teachings on vocation, a Christian's calling, tied faith to virtually all walks of life; a person didn't need to become a priest or monk or nun to serve God beautifully and fully—indeed, a lay person might serve far better than someone in the clergy. And he wrote often on the subject of marriage, realizing how central this is in a Christian's life.

A few years ago this writer was surprised to learn that the anniversary of Luther's and Kate's wedding in June is the occasion for perhaps the largest annual celebration in Wittenberg and that the wedding is featured in gift shop items. Many still find his marriage, the marriage of a former monk/priest to a former nun, to be a revolutionary and wonderful event.

On Marriage

Already in early 1519, long before he married, Luther preached a sermon on marriage. The Gospel lesson for the second Sunday in Epiphany, January 16 that year, was John 2:1–11 on the wedding at Cana. An "unauthorized" version of that sermon based on a hearer's notes was published, and Luther found it necessary to publish the sermon in a corrected form.

In that corrected sermon, Luther made several important points:

- As was the case with Adam and Eve, a person should marry the person that *God* has chosen to be the spouse.[1]
- The love of marriage is a love that is superior to "false love" (love for worldly things or for a woman outside marriage) and "natural love" (love between a parent and child or between other relatives), for it seeks the other person wholly. "All other kinds of love seek something other than the loved one; this kind wants only to have the beloved's own self completely."[2]
- Mankind has been corrupted by the fall so that people now lust for someone other than their spouse.[3]
- The Church protects people from lust by making marriage a sacrament, by emphasizing fidelity in marriage, and by encouraging the production of offspring.[4]

285

- The highest purpose of marriage is the bearing and rearing of children to be Christians.[5]

On one of the above points, as we have seen in an earlier essay,[6] Luther's view was soon to change. That issue was marriage as a sacrament. In *Babylonian Captivity of the Church*, 1520, Luther upbraids the Roman Church for its shallowness of biblical study on the topic of marriage and for its financially motivated manipulations.

A "sacrament," as indicated in the earlier essay, is a means by which God gives His grace to people, but Scripture, Luther emphasized, never asserts nor even implies that this happens through marriage. Ephesians 5:31–31 is about marriage and uses the word *"sacramentum"* in the Latin translation, but the original Greek word is *"mysterion,"* which means "mystery." Properly translated into English, the Pauline passage is, "'For this reason, a man will leave his father and mother and be united to his wife, and the two will become one flesh.' This a profound mystery—but I am talking about Christ and the church."[7]

Moreover, Luther pointed out, marriage is practiced among non–Christians as well as Christians. Is God also extending grace as forgiveness of sins and the blessing of faith (the essence of a sacrament) to non–Christians when they marry? Of course not, Luther claimed, though they are practicing a special relationship instituted by God. Even if we say that God "wills" or "blesses" a marriage, that does not make it a sacrament, a sacred act in which the Holy Spirit brings the grace of God to His people.

In the powerful *Babylonian Captivity of the Church*,[8] Luther went on to attack and ridicule the Roman Church for its convoluted laws that both force and annul marriages as a scheme for filling its coffers. Luther used strong language to make his point:

> But what shall we say *concerning the wicked laws of men by which this divinely ordained way of life has been ensnared* and tossed to and fro? Good God! It is dreadful to contemplate the audacity of the Roman despots, who both dissolve and compel marriages as they please. I ask you, has mankind been handed over to the caprice of these men for them to mock them and in every way abuse them and make of them whatever they please, for the sake of filthy lucre?[9]

After 1520, Luther never strayed from the view that marriage is *not* a sacrament, but he did often emphasize how marriage is a great blessing given by God. One of his most extensive and beautiful works on marriage was *The Estate of Marriage,* published in 1522.

Parts One and Two deal with which persons may marry each other (listing, for example, the blood relationships that rule out marriage) and with the legitimate reasons for divorce.

Of special importance is Part Three, in which Luther extolled marriage as a blessing from God. He began by describing the many popular writings and sayings about married life that made it out to be burdensome and depressing. "The world says of marriage, 'Brief is the joy, lasting the bitterness.'"[10] This perspective, Luther held, must be combatted. He offered the following positive view:

> Now the ones who recognize the estate of marriage are those who firmly believe that God himself instituted it, brought husband and wife together, and ordained that they should beget children and care for them. For this they have God's word, Genesis 1, and they can be certain that he does not lie. They can therefore also be certain that the estate of marriage and everything that goes with it in the way of conduct, works, and suffering is pleasing to God. Now tell me, how can the heart have greater good, joy, and delight than in God, when one is certain that his estate, conduct, and work is pleasing to God?[11]

Doing something that is designed and ordained by God even if, or perhaps because, it includes "insignificant, distasteful, and despised duties," such as are included in marriage and in raising a family, bring joy to the one who does it in service to God. "Nothing is so bad, not even death itself, but what it becomes sweet and tolerable if only I know and am certain that it is pleasing to God."[12] In a humorous and facetious way, Luther described the menial tasks and then offered a gibe about the celibacy of priests and nuns:

> Alas, must I rock the baby, wash its diapers, make its bed, smell its stench, stay up nights with it, take care of it when it cries, heal its rashes and sores, and on top of that care for my wife, provide for her, labor at my trade, take care of this and take care of that, do this and do that, endure this and endure that, and whatever else of bitterness and drudgery married life involves? What, should I make such a prisoner of myself? O you poor, wretched fellow, have you taken a wife? Fie, fie upon such wretchedness and bitterness! It is better to remain free and lead a peaceful, carefree life; I will become a priest or a nun and compel my children to do likewise.[13]

He followed this with an appropriate Christian perspective:

> What then does Christian faith say to this? It opens its eyes, looks upon all these insignificant, distasteful, and despised duties in the Spirit, and is aware that they are all adorned with divine approval as with the costliest gold and jewels. It says, "O God, because I am certain that thou has created me as a man and hast from my body begotten this child, I also know for a certainty that it meets with thy perfect pleasure. I confess to thee that I am not worthy to rock the little babe or wash its diapers, or to be entrusted with the care of the child and its mother. How is it that I, without any merit, have come to this distinction of being certain that I am serving thy creature and thy most precious will? O how gladly will I do so, though the duties should be even more insignificant and despised. Neither frost nor heat, neither drudgery nor labor, will distress or dissuade me, for I am certain that it is thus pleasing in thy sight."[14]

Luther also offered parallel comments for the wife and mother including childbirth as one of her "truly golden and noble works."[15]

This, then, is a key point for Luther: The Christian husband and wife can in faith have a perspective on marriage and parenthood that gives joy and strength knowing that what they are doing is "pleasing to God."

An additional emphasis of Luther was that marriage is a God-given protection against the temptation of extramarital sex—and against syphilis, which was rampant at the time. In Luther's words, "It is no slight boon that in wedlock fornication and unchastity are checked and eliminated. This in itself is so great a good that it alone should be enough to induce men to marry forthwith, and for many reasons."[16]

Luther closed *The Estate of Marriage* first with the encouragement that a couple should marry without great worry about being able to afford married life, for we can trust God to provide, and then with a comment about sex that shows he had not quite freed himself from some traditional views: "Intercourse is never without sin; but God excuses it by his grace because the estate of marriage is his work, and he preserves in and through the sin all that good which he has implanted and blessed in marriage."[17]

Celibacy

This writing also reveals Luther's growing disdain for the vow of celibacy which was required of monks, priests, and nuns. At the time, Luther was bound by his own vow of celibacy, but he had come to see it as a very harmful *human* requirement—and certainly as a rule unsupported by anything in Scripture. He argued that celibates often flee from the responsibilities of marriage and family life, that marriage is not seen as the God-pleasing institution that it is, that the protection marriage offers against fornication is not used, and that celibates often engage in fornication and unchastity—thinking that their vow is more important and excuses them from those sins. On this last point and regarding the Roman Church's hypocrisy, Luther wrote in 1539,

> If someone had ravished a hundred virgins, violated a hundred honorable widows, and lain with a hundred whores before that, he may become not only pastor or preacher but also bishop or pope. And even if he were to continue this kind of life, he would nonetheless be tolerated in those offices. But if he marries a bride who is a virgin, or a make-believe virgin, he cannot be a servant of God. It makes no difference that he is a true Christian, learned, pious, competent. He is a bigamist.[18]

Luther's most important work on vows including the vow of celibacy, *The Judgment of Luther on Monastic Vows,* was written in 1921 while he was at the Wartburg. Controversy had arisen in Wittenberg over whether it was legitimate for a priest, monk, or nun to break the three vows of poverty, obedience, and celibacy. Karlstadt and Melanchthon had written on the topic defending and, in Karlstadt's case "encouraging" the breaking of these vows. Luther was not satisfied with their argumentation, so he wrote a work tying the issue to justification by faith and arguing that any vow which goes against justification by faith cannot be binding. The sections of the work argue for the following theses regarding the vows required of the religious:

- Vows Are Against Faith.[19]
- Vows Are Against Evangelical Freedom.[20]
- Vows Are Contrary to the Commandments of God.[21]
- Vows Are Against Love.[22]
- Monasticism Is Contrary to Common Sense and Reason.[23]

Luther's central claim was that the vows substitute our actions and the keeping of man-made vows for faith as the basis of our relationship with God. Luther made the point with regard to each of the three vows. With regard to celibacy or chastity, he wrote:

> In all truth chastity has a godlessness of its own, just like the other parts of the vows. Its godlessness exists in that it boasts of a faith over and above the common general faith. And this is a direct disservice to Christ.... It is not the virgin or the chaste who will be saved, but the Christian.... And where the Spirit is not present, chastity can be neither vowed nor kept in any but a godless fashion, for he who takes this vow believes that he is pleasing God by this work of chastity.... It follows then that he who takes the vow of chastity in this frame of mind is actually vowing nothing at all and is free not to fulfill the vow.[24]

Luther's Marriage

All but one of the writings cited above were written while Luther was still a monk and long before he married. After posting the Ninety-Five Theses and even after he wrote those works on marriage and vows, Luther had no intent to marry. He did not immediately renounce his vows, for he thought that this should be done only when guided by faith and when it is not harmful to others. Moreover, finding a spouse should be done deliberately and carefully—relying on God's guidance, and Luther did not think that God had led him in this direction. It must be added that Luther expected to be slain relatively soon, thus making it impossible to be a good husband and father.

That changed in 1525. In 1523 Katharina Von Bora was the leader in a group of twelve nuns who escaped from the Marienthron Convent at Nimbschen, Germany, and arrived in Wittenberg on Easter Monday of that year. Two years later she was the last of those still needing to find a spouse, and she chose Luther. He acceded to her wish, thinking that it was God's guidance, and soon found their marriage to be rich and full of love.

Kate was a wonderful helper and a very talented person. She took care of their busy household, bore him six children, and carried him through many health issues and periods of overwhelming stress. Kate cleaned and improved the former monastery which was now their home, and she was a gardener, fisher, brewer, vintner, livestock tender and breeder, cook, bee-keeper, and nurse. She was a marvelous hostess, provided housing for students, and kept the family finances in order.

Through their twenty-one years of marriage, Luther travelled a great deal, and we have many of his letters to her. The various salutations that he used show both his tender love and also his charming sense of humor, something that is too little appreciated. Here are some of those salutations:

- "To my dearly beloved Lady of the House, Katharina Luther at Wittenberg. Dear Kate" (June 1530)
- "My dear Kate" (August 1530)
- "To my dear lord, Mrs. Katharina Luther at Wittenberg. Dear Kate" (August 1530)
- "To my most beloved Lady of the House, Katharina Luther. My sweetheart Kate" (February 1532)
- "To my friendly dear lord, Mrs. Catherin von Bora, D. Lutherin at Wittenberg. Dear Lord Kate" (July 1534)
- "To my dearly beloved Kate, Doctora Lutherin, and Lady of the New Pig Market. Dear Damsel Kate, gracious Lady of Zülsdorf (and by what other names Your Grace is called)" (July 1540)
- "To my gracious damsel, Katharina Luther von Bora and Zülsdorf to Wittenberg. My true love" (July 1540)
- "To the rich lady at Zülsdorf, Mrs. Doctor Katharina Luther, dwelling physically at Wittenberg and residing in spirit in Zülsdorf. To my sweetheart" (July 1540)
- "To my friendly and dear Lady of the House, Katharina von Bora Luther, a preacher, beer brewer, gardener, and whatever other talents she may have. Dear Kate" (July 1545)
- "To my friendly, dear Kate Luther, a beer brewer and judge at the Pig Market in Wittenberg. Dear Kate" (January 1546)
- "To my dearly beloved Lady of the House, Katharina Luther, Mrs. Doctor, lady of Zülsdorf, of the Pig Market, and whatever else she might be. Dear Kate" (February 1546)
- "To my highly learned wife, Katharina Luther, my gracious Lady of the House at Wittenberg. Dear Kate" (February 1546)
- "To my dear Lady of the House, Katharina Luther, doctor, lady of the Pig Market at Wittenberg. Dear Kate" (February 1546)
- "To the holy, worrying Lady Katharina Luther, doctor, Lady of Zülsdorf at Wittenberg, my gracious, beloved Lady of the House. Most holy Ms. Doctor" (February 1546)[25]

The salutations and the letters themselves are quite charming and reveal a tender, caring marriage. They show Luther's appreciation for his wife's remarkable and varied talents. They also show his dependence on her—including her care for him through all of his serious ailments.

These letters and the information we have about Luther's marriage from the "Table Talks" and other sources also show that Luther "practiced what he preached." He clearly was intent on bringing into his marriage and home the elements of faith and a godly life about which he had written in his works on marriage.

• Essay 16 •

Luther on Church and State

In his *The Rise and Fall of the Third Reich,* William Shirer attacked Luther on two major points. One is that he called Luther a "vicious anti–Semite" and a precursor to Hitler himself. This topic is considered in a later essay in this collection.

The second point of attack is the claim that Luther held that the Christian should be passively obedient to all political rulers, for they are placed in their position of authority by God. Shirer wrote,

> Luther's siding with the princes in the peasant risings, which he had largely inspired, and his passion for political autocracy insured a mindless and provincial political absolutism which reduced the vast majority of the German people to poverty, to a horrible torpor and to a demeaning subservience.[1]

Later in the book, Shirer wrote: "The great founder of Protestantism was ... a ferocious believer in absolute Obedience to political authority."[2] He amplified his point as follows:

> In what was perhaps the only popular revolt in German history, the peasant uprising of 1525, Luther advised the princes to adopt the most ruthless measures against the "mad dogs," as he called the desperate, downtrodden peasants…. Luther employed a coarseness and brutality of language unequaled in German history until the Nazi time. The influence of this towering figure extended down the generations in Germany, especially among the Protestants.[3]

His point that Luther commanded total obedience to rulers did not originate with Shirer. It can also be found in the writings of theologian Ernst Troeltsch and writer Thomas Mann, for example.[4] The charge has been advanced by several others including William Inge, Peter Wiener, Frederick Bonkovski and Alan Davies.

The Two Kingdoms

Few elements of Luther's thought have been more misunderstood than his teaching on the Two Kingdoms. Essentially, Luther held that a Christian lives in two different kingdoms. The first is the kingdom of Christ, which is the Church of all true believers; the second is the kingdom of the world, in which the government is central and necessary. *God rules over both and neither is inherently bad.* This is *not* a distinction between a kingdom of God and a kingdom of Satan, *nor* is it the same as the separation of the religious from the secular—or the American perspective on Church and State.[5] Likewise, it is not the same as Augustine's famous distinction between the City of God and the City of Man, for in that metaphor a person is a member

291

of only one of those cities depending on whether one's primary love is directed upward toward God or downward toward self or things in this world.

Luther's Doctrine of the Two Kingdoms evolved, but it always emphasized that there are in this world a spiritual kingdom and a temporal kingdom. The spiritual kingdom, the "Kingdom of the Right" as it is sometimes called, is the true Church of all genuine believers. Christ is the Lord of this kingdom and it uses the Word of God and the sacraments to bring God's grace and forgiveness to people. The Holy Spirit builds believers up in faith, hope, and love. God uses people as shepherds and spiritual leaders to spread the Gospel and dispense the means of grace—the Word and sacraments.

The temporal kingdom or the "Kingdom of the Left" is made up of all people. God rules this kingdom, too, to promote order, justice, and peace. Because all people are sinners, various instruments are needed to maintain this order. God has established positions of authority in the state and in other institutions such as the family to secure the order, justice, and peace that are needed for all people to live alongside one another productively and in harmony. The people in authority are to govern according to the will of God as found, for example, in the moral law in Scripture.

Luther's Early Position

Luther's first major writing on Church and State, *To the Christian Nobility of the German Nation Concerning the Reform of the Christian Estate,* appeared in 1520 and was designed to encourage the Christian rulers to curb the excesses and unchristian activities of the Roman Church. Luther had completed the Leipzig debate with Eck and was confronted with the condemnations of Louvain and Cologne as well as the defense of the papacy and attacks on his position by Alfeld and Prierias. If the ecclesiastical travesty was to be halted, Luther came to believe, it would have to come from Christian rulers, and this lengthy letter/treatise offered biblical justification for the action.

The Church, Luther argued, had no authority in political matters. Its responsibility, a more important one at that, was in the spiritual realm. But the Church had attempted to become a worldly power with control over princes and rulers, and this, he believed, had to end. Luther argued that the priesthood of all believers allowed the Holy Roman Emperor and the German Christian nobility to call for a reforming church council and even to make specific reforms directly. Thus, Luther in the document sought to limit the Church's authority in the worldly sphere while at the same time exalting the state's authority—even over some ecclesiastical matters![6]

By the time he returned from the Wartburg in 1522, however, Luther's disappointment with the rulers was clear. In a strongly worded writing, *Temporal Authority: To What Extent It Should be Obeyed,* he claimed that the rulers had misused their power and had not acted as Christians:

> I fear … that they will continue to be princes and will never become Christians. For God the Almighty has made our rulers mad; they actually think they can do—and order their subjects to do—whatever they please. And the subjects make the mistake of thinking that they, in turn, are bound to obey their rulers in everything. It has gone so far that the rulers have begun ordering the people to get rid of certain books, and to believe and conform to what the rulers prescribe. They are thereby presumptuously setting

themselves in God's place, lording it over men's consciences and faith, and schooling the Holy Spirit according to their own crackbrained ideas. Nevertheless, they let it be known that they are not to be contradicted, and are to be called gracious lords all the same.[7]

Luther used this treatise to establish both the basis for civil government and its limitations. The basis is the Word of God in which God ordains a government that is under His authority. This government is to maintain law and order, justice and peace *according to God's will*. It is necessary because of the sinful nature of all people—and especially of those who are not genuine Christians guided by the Holy Spirit. Rulers are also to maintain a social condition in which it is possible for a person to become and remain a true Christian, but they are not to force this on anyone.

This last point brings up a key limitation. *Rulers are not to interfere in any way with the faith of individuals—either by command or by prohibition*. This is the interference that led Luther to write this treatise to begin with, for the rulers had, among other things, ordered certain books destroyed.

Is a Christian to obey the civil authorities? Yes—but not without restriction. A person is not to allow a ruler to exercise control over things spiritual. But, more importantly, and in direct contradiction to Shirer and others, a person is not to obey when the government is commanding or acting in an immoral way, i.e., against God's law. The following passage is crucial: "What if a prince is in the wrong? Are his people bound to follow him then too? Answer: No, for it is no one's duty to do wrong; we must obey God (who desires the right} rather than men [Acts 5:29]."[8]

Luther also had this admonition for the rulers: "A prince must act in a Christian way toward his God also; that is, he must subject himself to him in entire confidence and pray for wisdom to rule well as Solomon did [I Kings 3:9]."[9]

The Peasant Revolt

But what of the things that Luther is said to have written at the time of the Peasant Revolt of 1525? This was central to Shirer's attack and to the claim of others that Luther supported obedience to the rulers no matter what.

The condition of the peasants in Germany was extremely difficult. Under feudalism, the peasants were "tied to the land"; they were farmers who did not own the land but had the right and obligation to farm a portion of a holding for a lord, a bishop, or a monastery, for example, in exchange for rental payments or other services. Their obligations were heavy, and they had basically no mobility and little freedom.

Heartened by Luther's courageous attack on the Roman Church, they believed that they could oppose the landowning institutions of the church and still be faithful Christians. There had been uprisings by peasants in various periods—especially in the 14th and 15th centuries, but the revolt in 1525 was especially strong and violent. It also had a new "Protestant" aspect. Indeed, some more radical pastors like Thomas Müntzer actively led the rebellion.

In the early part of 1525, the peasants of Memmingen, Germany (60 miles southwest of Augsburg), adopted 12 articles in which they expressed their grievances. They ranged from the right to call their own pastors to rights for hunting, cutting wood, receiving fair rental fees, being relieved from unjust laws, and the like. The document, called simply *Twelve Articles,* made the concerns seem reasonable and justified.

Luther wrote a response, but things had turned very violent before it became available. In the document, he blamed the landowners for having caused difficulties, but he strongly urged the peasants not to resort to violence. On the first point he wrote,

> We have no one on earth to thank for this disastrous rebellion except you princes and lords, and especially you blind bishops and mad priests and monks, whose hearts are hardened, even to the present day.... Well, then, since you are the cause of this wrath of God, it will undoubtedly come upon you, unless you mend your ways in time.[10]

The violence grew, however, and Luther was appalled. The result was his short, terse writing titled, "Against the Robbing and Murdering Hordes of Peasants."[11]

The essay accuses the peasants of three terrible wrongs:

> In the first place, they have sworn [in the *Twelve* Articles] to be true and faithful, submissive and obedient, to their rulers. [Here Luther quoted Luke 20:25 and Romans 13:1] ... Since they are now deliberately and violently breaking this oath of obedience and setting themselves in opposition to their masters, they have forfeited body and soul, as faithless, perjured, lying, disobedient rascals and scoundrels usually do.[12]
>
> In the second place, they are starting a rebellion, and are violently robbing and plundering monasteries and castles which are not theirs; by this they have doubly deserved death in body and soul as highwaymen and murderers.... For rebellion is not just simple murder; it is like a great fire, which attacks and devastates a whole land. Thus rebellion brings with it a land filled with murder and bloodshed; it makes widows and orphans, and turns everything upside down, like the worst disaster. Therefore let everyone who can, smite, slay, and stab, secretly or openly, remembering that nothing can be more poisonous, hurtful, or devilish than a rebel. It is just as when one must kill a mad dog; if you do not strike him, he will strike you, and a whole land with you.[13]

(Shirer was wrong when he wrote that Luther called the peasants "mad dogs." Rather, Luther compared the situation with the peasants to one in which a "mad dog" will attack or kill you if you do not kill it first. It is an illustration, perhaps unfortunate—but not a name-calling.)

> In the third place, they cloak this terrible and horrible sin with the gospel, call themselves "Christian brethren," take oaths and submit to them, and compel people to go along with them in these abominations. Thus they become the worst blasphemers of God and slanderers of his holy name. Under the outward appearance of the gospel, they honor and serve the devil, thus deserving death in body and soul ten times over. I have never heard of a more hideous sin.[14]

Luther then went on to urge the princes to carry out their God-given responsibility and to crush the rebellion.

> The rulers, then, should press on and take action in this matter with a good conscience as long as their hearts still beat. It is to the rulers' advantage that the peasants have a bad conscience and an unjust cause, and that any peasant who is killed is lost in body and soul and is eternally the devil's. But the rulers have a good conscience and a just cause; they can, therefore, say to God with all confidence of heart, "Behold, my God, you have appointed me prince or lord, of this I can have no doubt; and you have given me the sword to use against evildoers (Romans 13)."[15]

There are several things to note about this outburst:

Luther found the chaos of the rebellion to be intolerable. Protest was one thing; violent rebellion and chaos were quite another.

Moreover, Luther was particularly outraged by the deceit and arrogance of the rebels that they disregarded their commitments of their oaths and of the "Twelve Articles" and even dared to label their rebellion as a proper, *Christian* response to their situation.

In addition, intemperate though this document is, Luther was addressing a particular situation and was not developing a position on protest in general. Indeed, there is nothing in the writing which goes against the restrictions on political power found in the 1522 document. The wrong is not in the protest. The wrong is in the violence, the destruction, and the killing. *There is no appeal here to "absolute obedience" under all circumstances.*

It must also be said that Luther's position becomes more objectionable because of the *carte blanche* that he gave to the authorities to put down the rebellion by any means necessary. This opened the door to further violence, destruction, and killing that he in all likelihood did not foresee.

Finally, as in the case of Luther's 1543 writing on the Jews (cf. the essay in this collection on that topic), we see in this document a negative character trait. When Luther committed himself to a peaceful approach to assist a suffering group of people and then thought that he had been ruthlessly betrayed (and misused) by those people, he reacted in fierce and unconstrained anger. This is shown in his vocabulary as well as in his assertions. This is a trait that must be acknowledged so that one does not take his words at such moments as his considered general judgments.

The response of the princes was swift and brutal. Estimates are that some 100,000 peasants and family members were killed. Luther was blamed by both friend and foe alike for the slaughter, though his harsh writing was probably more an excuse for the revengers than an incentive. He was also accused of contradicting his earlier *Admonition to Peace* and of betraying the peasants. After a short time, Luther wrote a response to the criticism entitled, *An Open Letter on the Harsh Book*. The response is really not a retraction of anything that he had written in *Against the Robbing and Murdering Hordes of Peasants*; indeed, he reiterated and defended many of the points. He also asserted that if his earlier advice had been heeded, there would not have been such bloodshed. *But he did render harsh judgment upon unchristian rulers for their extravagant and unnecessary brutality.* He wrote,

> But those furious, raving, senseless tyrants, who even after the battle cannot get their fill of blood, and in all their lives ask scarcely a question about Christ—these I did not undertake to instruct. It makes no difference to these bloody dogs whether they slay the guilty or the innocent, whether they please God or the devil. They have the sword, but they use it to vent their lust and self-will.[16]

In the end, Luther still felt comfortable with the theological doctrine of the two kingdoms and its faithfulness to Scripture. This must be the reason that Luther did not retract or modify his basic doctrine after the tragedy of the Peasants' War. In his judgment, it would seem, the doctrine had passed its most serious test.

Conclusion

In summary, the key points of the doctrine of the two kingdoms are as follows:

- The two kingdoms are the spiritual Kingdom of Christ and the temporal Kingdom of the World. They may also be called the "Kingdom of the Right Hand" and the "Kingdom of the Left Hand."

- God is the ruler of both kingdoms.
- The Kingdom of Christ, the true Church, is made up of all true believers in Jesus Christ as Lord and Savior.
- The Kingdom of the World is made up of all people as sinners; its primary concern is the maintenance of order, justice, and peace.
- The Kingdom of Christ is ruled directly by a compassionate Christ; the caring pastors and leaders of the church serve under him.
- The Kingdom of the World is ruled directly by a just God and indirectly by the rulers he has placed in this world.
- A Christian is a member of both kingdoms.
- The Kingdom of Christ is the kingdom of the Gospel. It is grounded in the grace and forgiveness of God. Its primary values are faith, hope, and love.
- The Kingdom of the World is the kingdom of the Law. It is grounded in the commandments of our Lord. Its primary values are justice and obedience.
- The Kingdom of Christ fills the world with compassion and grace.
- The Kingdom of the World seeks to control the sinfulness and violence in the world.
- All Christians are to live in the Kingdom of Christ with love and forgiveness.
- All people, Christians included, are to live in the Kingdom of the World with obedience and are to promote justice.
- All Christians are to honor others in the Kingdom of Christ as brothers and sisters in Christ.
- All people, Christians included, are to live in the Kingdom of the World respecting each other as people created by God.
- The Kingdom of Christ is not to exercise worldly control; its function is to nourish through Word and Sacraments.
- The Kingdom of the World is not to interfere with people's spiritual life—either through restrictions or demands.
- The Kingdom of Christ is not to punish but is to lift up and uphold, but it may withhold grace from unbelievers.
- The Kingdom of the World must punish wrongdoing. It is to maintain law and order.
- In the Kingdom of the World, rulers may not arise above God's law. People may disobey when the rulers go against the law of God.

In closing, it is worth asking what Luther's doctrine might give as a Christian's response to Hitler and Nazism—especially for a Christian living in Germany at that time.

On the one hand, the doctrine promotes obedience to a ruling authority building on Paul's words in Romans 13:

> Everyone must submit himself to the governing authorities, for there is no authority except that which God has established. The authorities that exist have been established by God. Consequently, he who rebels against the authority is rebelling against what God has instituted, and those who do so will bring judgment on themselves.

HOWEVER, the doctrine of the two kingdoms makes additional points that give a different perspective. (1) A government is to curb lawlessness and to promote peace and order. The Nazi government did not respond to disorder but fostered it and engaged in it. Peace and order were harmed—not promoted by the government. (2) A government is to rule in accord with God's law. The Nazi regime, however, engaged in murder, slander, and sin of the most egregious types. It ruled *against* God's law rather than in accord with it. (3) A government is not to interfere with the spiritual life of the Church. The Nazi government attempted to seize control of the Church and to use it for propaganda purposes. Nazi flags were to adorn the churches, pastors were considered government employees, sermons were subject to censorship, and certain worship services were outlawed.

In consideration of these points, the Nazi regime was more an anti-government in the Kingdom of the World than a government. There is little doubt that Luther would have condemned it and would have condoned the strong resistance of such pastors and believers as Dietrich Bonhoeffer.

• Essay 17 •

Luther on Other Reformers

Luther is generally recognized as the Father of the Reformation, but there were certainly others including contemporaries of Luther who were Reformers in their own right. Luther had contacts with them, face-to-face or in writing, and in this essay we will examine his judgments on some of them with whom he disagreed. In a sermon of September 21, 1544, on Galatians 5:25–6:10, he spoke of pride as a great danger for successful preachers. He indicated that this had been harmful for the Reformation and named key examples: "Zwingli, Carlstadt, and Müntzer have done much harm."[1] These are the figures we will consider as we look at Luther's views on other reformers.

Karlstadt (Carlstadt)

Andreas Bodenstein, known by his hometown of Karlstadt (Carlstadt), was a colleague of Luther's at Wittenberg and one of his earliest and most ardent supporters. He, in fact, authored a set of theses, 152 of them, against the sale of indulgences six months prior to Luther's posting of the Ninety-Five Theses. In the Leipzig debate against Eck, Dr. Karlstadt was the one who first defended Luther's position against Eck, and Luther, a superior debater, took over only after Karlstadt fared poorly against Eck.

But their relationship took a dramatic turn during Luther's time at the Wartburg. Karlstadt, also a priest, tried to take the Reformation to the next stage or beyond by both insisting on and practicing mass in the vernacular, getting rid of clergy vestments, removing all images from churches in a mob action, downplaying confession as a necessary preparation for communion, and urging the marriage of priests (at age 40 he married a girl of 15). After Luther denounced his radical actions and he was dismissed, Karlstadt advocated polygamy, helped lead the Peasant Revolt, and called Luther "the Wittenberg Pope." He railed against both the Roman Church and Luther's movement, denounced higher learning and schools of all types, and claimed that peasants understood God far better than priests or Luther did. But after the defeat of the peasants, he sought and received refuge in Luther's own home. He lived out his last years in Basel.

In Luther's view, Karlstadt betrayed the Reformation movement and sought to usurp it while Luther was secluded in the Wartburg. At first Karlstadt may have believed that he was merely taking up Luther's banner and continuing Luther's work, but Luther would have none of that justification.

After Karlstadt was expelled from Saxony by the political authorities in late summer of 1524, he went to Strassburg (Strasbourg) and continued to teach and preach. In that same year people there wrote to Luther to seek his judgment about Karlstadt, and he replied with the *Letter to the People of Strassburg in Opposition to the Fanatic Spirit.* In 1525 Luther wrote *Against the Heavenly Prophets in the Matter of Images and Sacraments,* a more extensive two-part work on Karlstadt's teachings and on critiques of Luther found in eight of Karlstadt's more recent books. Luther's counterattack was strong and included the following key points:

- Karlstadt had departed from the central doctrines of law and gospel in Scripture and had developed a new legalism thus exiting from genuine Christianity.
- Karlstadt relied on his own inspiration and mystical experience rather than on God's Word. "He would be considered the greatest spirit of all, he who has devoured the Holy Spirit feathers and all,"[2] Luther wrote of him.
- Karlstadt had deserted his position in Wittenberg and on his own went to various places to preach without a legitimate call.
- Karlstadt had been expelled from Saxony by the legitimate authorities—not by Luther.
- Karlstadt's role in the destruction of images in the churches was violent and incited mob action. (The true meaning of biblical statements about images, Luther held, is that they are not to be worshipped.)
- Karlstadt claimed that Lutheran Holy Communion wrongly retains a sacrifice of Christ on the altar only because Lutherans use the term "mass" and because they raise the host. (In the same writing, Luther also offered a careful study of the term "mass" in various languages.[3])
- Karlstadt's exegesis on why Jesus' words "Take eat, this is my body" doesn't refer to the bread but rather to his physical body is counter to all intelligent understanding of language. (Luther's treatment of the grammar was extensive and detailed.[4])
- Karlstadt denied the real presence because he relied on his own understanding "attending only to what is common to the crowd."[5]
- On his teaching about the sacrament, "Dr. Karlstadt robs God of his honor, contradicts the truth, destroys the teaching of St. Paul, and makes the passion of Christ unnecessary, since he denies, in the face of clear and strong texts, that the body and blood of Christ are in the sacrament."[6]

In the end, Luther's judgment on Karlstadt was not that he was a traitor or a usurper. *It was that he was a heretic.*

Müntzer

Unlike the relationship with Karlstadt, Luther had never been close to Thomas Müntzer, a pastor in Zwickau (south of Leipzig, 125 miles south of Wittenberg) before he was removed and wound up first in Allstedt (southwest of Eisleben, 100 miles southwest of Wittenberg) and then in Mühlhausen in Thuringia (north of Eisenach, 160 miles southwest of Wittenberg). Müntzer was an idealist who sought to establish a perfect Christian society in this world. While still at Zwickau, he and the other "Zwickau Prophets," including Nicholas Storch (a weaver), Marcus Stübner (a Wittenberg student), and Martin Cellarius (a theologian) claimed that the Holy Spirit spoke to them directly and that these "revelations" were more important than Scripture. They opposed infant baptism and believed that a divine intervention was about to take place that would establish a Christian community in which all things would be held in common. The uneducated were superior Christians to the priests and the leaders of society, they held. Müntzer believed that those who were not Christian did not deserve to continue to live and was in favor of violence against them. He urged the peasants in Thuringia to take up arms and to fight against church officials, landowners, capitalists, and rulers. In the end, the peasants were crushed and Müntzer was beheaded.

In the summer of 1524, only a few months before he wrote to the people of Strassburg about Karlstadt, Luther was so fearful of the violence that Müntzer was arousing that he wrote to the Princes of Saxony to take action against Müntzer. The document is titled *Letter to the Princes of Saxony Concerning the Rebellious Spirit.* Luther was very upset about the false teachings stemming from Müntzer, and he was careful to distance himself and his followers from Müntzer's ideas and practices. But his primary concern was different. He was willing to let the "battle of spirits" and the war between religious interpretations take place under God. God will see to it that right will win out. In a remarkable passage, he wrote,

> As far as doctrine is concerned, time will tell. For the present, your Graces [the princes] ought not to stand in the way of the ministry of the Word. Let them preach as confidently and boldly as they are able and against whomever they wish. For, as I have said, there must be sects, and the Word of God must be under arms and fight. Therefore the followers of the Word are called an "army" (Ps. 68) and Christ is designated as a "commander" in the Prophets. If their spirit is genuine, he will not be afraid of us and will stand his ground. If our spirit is genuine, he, again, will not fear either it or anyone else. Let the spirits collide and fight it out. If meanwhile some are led astray, all right, such is war. Where there is battle and bloodshed, some must fall and some are wounded. Whoever fights honorably will be crowned.[7]

Luther wrote not to attack their theology or to defend his own; some of that would take place in *Against the Heavenly Prophets,* already cited. Rather, he wrote to encourage the princes to squelch Müntzer and his gang, for they were bent on winning through violence and civil unrest:

> But when they want to do more than fight with the Word, and begin to destroy and use force, then your Graces must intervene, whether it be ourselves or they who are guilty, and banish them from the country…. For we who are engaged in the ministry of the Word are not allowed to use force. Ours is a spiritual conflict in which we wrest hearts and souls from the devil.[8]

Luther also stressed how effective the peaceful proclamation of the Word is in bringing about great change and cited his words to monks and nuns as an example.

In the case of Müntzer, Luther cited both his heresy and his use of violence to gain the upper hand.

In the end, the princes were brutal against Müntzer and the peasants who followed him. The Battle of Frankenhausen (southwest of Eisleben, 115 miles southwest of Wittenberg) on May 15, 1525, concluded the Peasants' War. Müntzer was captured, tortured, and then on May 27 beheaded at Mühlhausen.

Zwingli

With respect to Zwingli, Luther's disagreement with him on the nature of Christ's presence in the sacrament is widely known, but Luther's concerns were broader.

Ulrich (Huldrych) Zwingli became a pastor in Switzerland after receiving a strong education in Renaissance humanism; he was particularly devoted to the writings of Erasmus. In 1519 he was installed as the pastor of the cathedral in Zurich. Inspired, no doubt, by the news out of Wittenberg, he began to push strongly for reforms in the church; he attacked corruption in the hierarchy, the sale of indulgences, forced fasting, and clergy celibacy. He quickly became the acknowledged leader of the Reformation in Switzerland and formed a political (and military) league with like-minded Swiss cantons so that they might defend themselves against attack from the Roman Church. He was also very concerned about a growing Anabaptist ("Brethren") movement in his region, a movement that urged return to a simple first-century Christianity with no clergy, strict compliance with the Sermon on the Mount, and adult "believer" baptism. Zwingli promoted a violent reaction to these people that resulted in their severe persecution.

Philip of Hesse, a political leader on the side of the Lutherans, believed that the lasting success of the reform movement required an alliance of the key reformers—particularly of Luther and Zwingli, so in 1529 he arranged for a colloquy in which the spiritual leaders would meet, discuss their theological agreements and differences, and form a partnership. Many followers of both leaders believed that their differences could be overcome, and they encouraged a rapprochement between them. What a strong alliance this could make against Rome, they believed. Zwingli and his associates such as Oecolampadius of Basel and Bucer of Strassburg said yes to the colloquy, and Luther reluctantly agreed to participate, as well.

The most obvious difference between the theological views of Zwingli and Luther was on the topic of Christ's presence in the Lord's Supper. Because of the physical nature of body and blood, Zwingli held that the bread could not be Jesus' body in any literal sense but must be seen more symbolically—as, he thought, Jesus no doubt intended. Likewise, the wine should not be taken as Jesus' blood in any literal sense. For Luther, the recipient of the bread and wine did eat and drink the true body and blood of Christ—in the most literal of senses.

Luther had already written in opposition to Zwingli's position on this topic. He knew that Zwingli held, as he did, that Scripture was the only source and norm for our faith, but he also knew that the Swiss Reformer approached Scripture from a more rationalistic and humanistic perspective. Zwingli emphasized that we must use reason to understand and to interpret the Bible and that the Bible's teachings and doctrines are in accord with reason. Luther disagreed and held that we must have a faith in line with the clear teachings of Scripture whether those teachings accord with our reason or not.

In 1527, Luther wrote *That These Words of Christ, "This Is My Body," etc., Still Stand Firm Against the Fanatics* and in 1528, *Confession Concerning Christ's Supper*. These works are extensive expositions of Luther's views and show his strong disagreement with the Reformed opposition. It is little wonder that Luther believed there was little or nothing to gain by further discussion.

In the earlier work, Luther argued that it is not enough for people to agree that Scripture is the only source and norm for our faith. Satan still finds ways to tear holes in this Word and to get people to disagree and to reject things in the Bible. He went on to point out how marked and crucial the different interpretations on Christ's presence in the Sacrament are:

> It is perfectly clear, of course, that we are at odds concerning the words of Christ in the Supper. And it is well known on both sides that these are Christ's or God's words. That is one thing. So we say, on our part, that according to the words Christ's true body and blood are present when he says, "Take, eat; this is

my body." If our belief and teaching go wrong here, tell us, what are we doing? We are lying to God, and proclaiming that he did not say this but said the opposite. Then we are assuredly blasphemers and liars against the Holy Spirit, betrayers of Christ, and murderers and seducers of the world.

Our adversary says that mere bread and wine are present, not the body and blood of the Lord. If they believe and teach wrongly here, then they blaspheme God and are giving the lie to the Holy Spirit, betray Christ, and seduce the world. One side must be of the devil, and God's enemy. There is no middle ground.[9]

For Luther, the issue was clear. Do we accept the normal and clear meaning of the words of Scripture or do we not?

For Luther it was decisive that the Greek New Testament says literally, "Take, eat; this is my body," but Zwingli and others argued that "is" in this context can and must mean "signifies" or "represents" and that "body" means "sign of the body." Likewise, they held that Jesus could not be at the right hand of the Father and also be bodily present at the communion table. On this last point, Luther wrote, "The right hand of God is not a specific place in which a body must or may be, such as on a golden throne, but is the almighty power of God, which at one and the same time can be nowhere and yet must be everywhere."[10] And "is" means "is"—pure and simple. We may not understand it all with our human reason, but in faith we are to believe what God's Word says and to accept the blessings that it offers.

The 1528 work was a response to writings on the Lord's Supper that Zwingli and Oecolampadius had also published in 1527. It is Luther's most careful and profound writing on the Sacrament. It includes a response to the specific arguments made in his opponents' works, a thorough analysis of the relevant biblical passages, and a summary of articles of faith to which he was fully and finally committed. Those articles are, indeed, a beautiful confession of his personal faith patterned on the Apostles' Creed and extended over some thirty-five paragraphs or topics. In this confession, he wrote with regard to the Supper:

> I also say and confess that in the sacrament of the altar the true body and blood of Christ are orally eaten and drunk in the bread and wine, even if the priests who distribute them or those who receive them do not believe or otherwise misuse the sacrament. It does not rest on man's belief or unbelief but on the Word and ordinance of God—unless they first change God's Word and ordinance and misinterpret them, as the enemies of the sacrament do at the present time. They, indeed, have only bread and wine, for they do not also have the words and instituted ordinance of God but have perverted and changed it according to their own imagination.[11]

This paragraph is considered so beautiful and complete that it is quoted in the *Formula of Concord,* Solid Declaration, VII.[12]

The meeting of the reformers arranged by Philip of Hesse took place at Philip's elegant Marburg castle October 2–4, 1529. It was actually cut short by a day or two by the community's outbreak of a disease, the "English Sweat."

Luther did not write anything for the colloquy, and the reports on what transpired there were written by various observers. According to those reports, the discussions were reasonably cordial, at least in comparison with the documents the participants had written in the previous couple of years. The first day, Friday, Oct. 2, featured simultaneous discussions, one-on-one, between Zwingli and Melanchthon and between Luther and Oecolampadius. These were to lay the groundwork for the general discussion on the next day. Saturday featured the beginning of the official colloquy. On Sunday the discussion was brought to an end and a set of fifteen articles were considered for mutual adoption.

Among the central points on the Lord's Supper made by Zwingli and his colleagues were:

- The physical body of Christ cannot be in more than one place. It is at the right hand of God.
- John 6:63 informs us about holy communion and indicates that "the Spirit gives life; the flesh counts for nothing." The believer receives a spiritual blessing in faith. The blessing given is spiritual—not physical.
- The faith of the believer lifts one spiritually up to Jesus rather than Jesus coming down physically to us.
- "Is" in "this is my body" means "represents" or "signifies." "Body" doesn't mean "physical body."

Luther's steadfast response is seen in one of his actions. Before he spoke on Saturday, he wrote on the table with chalk, *"Hoc est corpus meum"* ("this is my body") and covered it with a cloth.[13] Late in the afternoon, Luther reinforced his response to Zwingli's logic by removing the cloth and asserting, "Here is our Scripture passage. You have not yet wrested it away from us, as you volunteered to do; we have no need of another passage."[14] "My dearest sirs, since the text of my Lord Jesus Christ reads, *Hoc est corpus meum,* I cannot pass over it, but must confess and believe that the body of Christ is there."[15]

For all practical purposes, the discussion was over. On Sunday afternoon they considered the fifteen "Marburg Articles." All signed off on the first fourteen, but they did not agree on one key aspect of the fifteenth—the one on Holy Communion. They did not agree on the real presence of our Lord's body and blood.

I doubt that Luther made the trip to Marburg with much hope that a breakthrough with Zwingli and the others was possible unless one or both parties would be willing to compromise on a central religious conviction. That, obviously, did not happen.

It might seem that the disagreement between Luther and Zwingli was only minor and about the meanings of words. Both, after all, were deeply committed Christians, concerned to reform the church according to Scripture alone. But the difference between them was far more significant.

First, there was a difference on the degree to which one should submit to Scripture. Is reason a judge over what Scripture can mean, or is it not? For Luther, the answer was a resounding, "NO!"

Second, both believed that the significance of the Sacrament lay in the *spiritual* nature of faith. We are called to a faith that is *spiritual* in nature but not worldly in any sense. But for Zwingli the "spiritual" meant the opposite of "material." The "body" as material and physical could not be any basis for growth in faith. For Luther, however, the "spiritual" meant the opposite of "wicked" or "tied to Satan." The "body," as a material and physical product of God's creation, could certainly be used by Him for the growth of faith. If God said that the (physical) body of Christ was in the Sacrament and that it could bring spiritual strength and healing, then so be it; there is nothing to gainsay that. Zwingli's view was thus more Platonic (true reality is in the Ideas; the physical world is only an imitation). Luther was far more inclined to view the physical in positive terms.

Third, very little was said in Marburg about Zwingli's combination of church and state and about his willingness to use force to promote the purity of the church. Luther held firmly to the doctrine of the two kingdoms; he allowed for the state to use force to promote peace and justice, but the church had no business in that area.

Although they had been forceful in their attacks on each other, at Marburg Luther and Zwingli also expressed respect and even admiration for each other. Certainly, Luther did not have the same hostility toward Zwingli that he had for Karlstadt and Müntzer. Nevertheless, Luther believed that Zwingli wanted him to compromise his beliefs, and he would not even consider that. In the end, Luther held Zwingli to be a misguided heretic and one who harmed the reformation of the church by his failure to accept the clear meaning Scripture, by his trust in reason, and by his "spiritualizing" of the Sacrament.

Finally, Marburg marked an end during Luther's lifetime to the efforts to combine the movements of the Swiss Reformed and the Lutherans.

• **Essay 18** •

Luther on the Jews

During the last several decades dating back to the Nazi period, Luther's hateful comments about the Jews have become increasingly widely known—and condemned. Some Nazi leaders reveled in citing Luther as a promoter of the anti–Semitism that led Nazism to the Holocaust and the death camps.[1] Since the Second World War various authors have developed the claim further that Luther is indeed the father (or *a* father) of Nazi/German anti–Semitism. Notable is, of course, William Shirer, who in his monumental *The Rise and Fall of the Third Reich,* 1960, called Luther "this towering but erratic genius, this savage anti–Semite and hater of Rome, who combined in his tempestuous character so many of the best and the worst qualities of the German—the coarseness, the boisterousness, the fanaticism, the intolerance, the violence, but also the honesty, the simplicity, the self-scrutiny, [etc.]"[2]

As we shall see, Luther, late in his life, did say some extremely harsh things about the Jews. They didn't receive much attention until the Nazi period, but then some propagandists made extensive use of them.

Luther's Statements

In 1523 Luther wrote *That Jesus Christ Was Born a Jew.* In it he encouraged Christians everywhere to show a more gracious attitude toward Jews than was being shown at the time because this would make their conversion to Christianity much more likely. Luther emphasized the special place that Jews held in God's eternal plan and that the Messiah himself was Jewish. (The writing was also devoted to Luther defending himself against a rumor which claimed he taught that Joseph was Jesus' biological father—a false rumor that was one of many wild attempts to discredit Luther.) Near the outset, Luther made his point clearly:

I will cite from Scripture the reasons that move me to believe that Christ was a Jew born of a virgin, that I might perhaps also win some Jews to the Christian faith. Our fools, the popes, bishops, sophists, and monks—the crude asses' heads—have hitherto so treated the Jews that anyone who wished to be a good Christian would almost have had to become a Jew [meaning, no doubt, that a good Christian would become so revolted by the Christian leaders that he would become entirely sympathetic with the Jew]. If I had been a Jew and had seen such dolts and blockheads govern and teach the Christian faith, I would sooner have become a hog than a Christian.

They have dealt with the Jews as if they were dogs rather than human beings; they have done little else than deride them and seize their property....

I hope that if one deals in a kindly way with the Jews and instructs them carefully from Holy Scripture, many of them will become genuine Christians and turn again to the faith of their fathers, the prophets and patriarchs. They will only be frightened further away from it if their Judaism is so utterly rejected that nothing is allowed to remain, and they are treated only with arrogance and scorn. If the apostles, who also were Jews, had dealt with us Gentiles as we Gentiles deal with the Jews, there would never have been a Christian among the Gentiles. Since they dealt with us Gentiles in such brotherly fashion, we in our turn ought to treat the Jews in a brotherly manner in order that we might convert some of them.[3]

It should be pointed out, however, that Luther did not complete the writing without also pointing out several errors of interpretation that Jewish scholars had made when dealing with such passages as Genesis 49:10–12 (viz., it is wrong to still be waiting for the coming of the Messiah), and Daniel 9:24–27.

In several of Luther's commentaries and particularly in his writings on Genesis, Luther spoke about the Jews. Because his interpretation of Old Testament passages was thoroughly Christocentric, he emphasized how privileged the Jews were to be the ones to whom God gave the promise of Christ, the Messiah. But he also stressed that they were without excuse for not turning to and following Jesus, this Messiah, when he was born. That incomprehensible turning away from Jesus is what has made the Jews such a huge tragedy according to Luther. After Jesus came, the "Chosen people" are certainly anything but "Chosen," he believed.

But in his later years, Luther wrote very hostile pieces against the Jews. It is helpful to look in particular at *Against the Sabbatarians*, 1538, and *On the Jews and Their Lies*, 1543.

The occasion for the former may have been a follow-up to a request that the Jewish scholar, Josel of Rosheim, had made of Luther in 1537 for help with receiving a safe travel permit. The following is part of the letter Luther wrote him:

> My dear Josel:
>
> I would have gladly interceded for you, both orally and in writing, before my gracious lord (the elector), just as my writings have greatly served the whole of Jewry. But because your people so shamefully misuse this service of mine and undertake things that we Christians simply shall not bear from you, they themselves have robbed me of all the influence I might otherwise have been able to exercise before princes and lords on your behalf.
>
> For my opinion was, and still is, that one should treat the Jews in a kindly manner, that God may perhaps look graciously upon them and bring them to their Messiah—but not so that through my good will and influence they might be strengthened in their error and become still more bothersome.
>
> I propose to write a pamphlet about this if God gives me space and time, to see if I cannot win some from your venerable tribe of the patriarchs and prophets and bring them to your promised Messiah.[4]

If *Against the Sabbatarians* was the "pamphlet" mentioned, Luther's focus had changed by the time he wrote it. In it he seemed bent on dealing with false, legalistic teachings that Jews were foisting on Christians. In this case the teaching he considered was that the day of worship must be Saturday. Luther's concern was probably due to a report he had received of Judaizing tendencies among Christians in Moravia.

Luther presented counter-arguments against those who were pushing Judaizing tendencies and gave points that Christians could make to Jews to convert them. Luther cited Jewish mistakes regarding several commandments and offered Jeremiah 31 and Isaiah 9 as passages to use with Jews. He emphasized that Jews should be able to look around and see that they have been experiencing a 1500-year exile, far longer than in Egypt, the wilderness, or Babylon, since the coming of Christ. This should forcefully tell them that they have missed the Messiah and are being judged for it and not for any possible "unknown" sin(s). Luther wrote with a sense of urgency and conviction but the tone is not harsh or bombastic.

Such is not the case with *On the Jews and Their Lies*. Bainton even wrote that "One could wish that Luther had died before ever this tract was written."[5]

The occasion for this offensive work seems to have been Luther's receiving an anti–Christian treatise written from a Jewish perspective. At the outset of this work, Luther made reference to it. He wrote,

> Grace and peace in the Lord. Dear sir and good friend [Count Wolfgang Schlick zu Falkenau, a friend who had reported the Judaizing efforts in Moravia to Luther], I have received a treatise in which a Jew engages in dialog with a Christian. He dares to pervert the scriptural passages which we cite in testimony to our faith, concerning our Lord Christ and Mary his mother, and to interpret them quite differently. With this argument he thinks he can destroy the basis of our faith.
>
> This is my reply to you and to him.[6]

This Jewish treatise has not been identified,[7] but we are able to discern some of its apparent arguments from Luther's responses. It is safe to say that these arguments led Luther to "blow his stack" and to release all of his anger and frustration.

First, it seems that the treatise boasted about the superiority of Jews over Gentiles on four major grounds: their lineage,[8] circumcision,[9] possession of the law,[10] and possession of Canaan, Jerusalem, and the temple.[11] This arrogance, even bragging before God, upset Luther terribly.

Second, it appears that the treatise addressed confidently the future coming of the Messiah. In his response, Luther went through a number of Old Testament passages giving his Christological interpretation. His impatience was building because he had done this in detail before and because he thought the passages to be so clear in and of themselves. In apparent frustration, he was now offering his comments not to evangelize the Jews but to protect the believers; he had given up on any significant conversion of the Jews. He couldn't believe that anyone would fail to see God's truth which he found to be so absolutely obvious. His dismay is shown in the following passage:

> If I had not had the experience with my papists, it would have seemed incredible to me that the earth should harbor such base people who knowingly fly in the face of open and manifest truth, that is, of God himself. For I never expected to encounter such hardened minds in any human breast, but only in that of the devil. However, I am no longer amazed by either the Turks' or the Jews' blindness, obduracy and malice, since I have to witness the same thing in the most holy fathers of the church, in pope, cardinals, and bishops.[12]

Among the passages he addressed were Genesis 49, II Sam. 23, Haggai 2, and Daniel 9.

Third, and most importantly, the treatise seems to have made claims about Jesus and about Mary that to Luther were utterly scandalous. "They call Jesus a whore's son, saying that his mother Mary was a whore, who conceived him in adultery with a blacksmith."[13]

> They further lie and slander him and his mother by saying that she conceived him at an unnatural time [during the menstrual period].... [Using a misinterpretation of Leviticus 20:18, they say that] whatever is conceived at such a time results in imperfect and infirm fruit, that is, in insane children, mental deficients, demon's offspring, changelings, and the like—people who have unbalanced minds all their lives. In this way the Jews would defame us Christians, by saying that we honor as the Messiah a person who was mentally deficient from birth, or some sort of demon.[14]

Luther was outraged. He began to attack Jews in general for malicious, secret misuse of Jesus' name and of secretive blasphemous greetings when meeting a Christian Gentile. He was open now to attacking Jews in all of the old wicked caricatures (anti–German conspiracy, usury, and the like).

Luther had built himself up to quite a harangue. But one is still hardly prepared for what follows. Luther's "sincere advice"[15] is as follows:

First, to set fire to their synagogues or schools and to bury and cover with dirt whatever will not burn, so that no man will ever again see a stone or a cinder of them....

Second, I advise that their houses also be razed and destroyed....

Third, I advise that all their prayer books and Talmudic writings, in which such idolatry, lies, cursing, and blasphemy are taught, be taken from them

Fourth, I advise that their rabbis be forbidden to teach henceforth on pain of loss of life and limb....

Fifth, I advise that safe-conduct on the highways be abolished completely for the Jews....

Sixth, I advise that usury be prohibited to them, and that all cash and treasure of silver and gold be taken from them and put aside for safekeeping....

Seventh, I recommend putting a flail, an ax, a hoe, a spade, a distaff, or a spindle into the hands of young, strong Jews and Jewesses and letting them earn their bread in the sweat of their brow....[16]

Later in the essay Luther added a few more vicious "recommendations":

That they be forbidden on pain of death to praise God, to give thanks, to pray, and to teach publicly among us and in our country....

That they be forbidden to utter the name of God within our hearing.[17]

Luther also admonished pastors to protect the parishioners from all contact with Jews, who will certainly try to deceive and destroy them.

Surprisingly, Luther ended the writing in this way: "May Christ, our dear Lord, convert them mercifully and preserve us steadfastly and immovably in the knowledge of him, which is eternal life. Amen."[18]

Is an Explanation Possible?

Luther cannot be exonerated for his hateful document. But what accounts for it? Is he the anti–Semite that Shirer claimed?

Some have sought to downplay Luther's vitriol against the Jews in one or more of the following ways:

- By asserting that these comments are an aberration and that his true, more positive views on the Jews are found in other writings (Siemon-Netto);
- By suggesting that in a time of weakness Luther turned against his own theology and "acted against his better judgment" (Gritsch);
- By claiming that Luther's crass vocabulary makes these comments sound worse than they really were;
- By emphasizing that Luther wished only for the conversion of the Jews and that his anger stemmed from their failure to convert (Bainton);
- By appealing to the view that Luther's horrible physical ailments and his age affected him mentally and drove him to uncharacteristic outbursts (Metaxas);
- By suggesting that the broad array of those who disagreed with Luther (papists, Anabaptists, certain humanists, other Reformers, etc.) so dismayed him that he lashed out against all whom he considered to be heretics (Eckhardt);
- By arguing that Luther was merely a child of his times and that his comments were no better and no worse than what many others were writing and saying;

- By claiming that in these comments Luther was acting not as a theologian or reformer but as a "politician" defending the faith and the society (Beinert) or as a "prophet" of the end times (Oberman); and
- By making a distinction between (1) Luther's hostility that was strictly religious in nature and (2) genuine anti–Semitism that is grounded in racism (Gutteridge).

Some (e.g., Bainton) have even tried to make aspects of Luther's diatribe look, at least in part, reasonable and charitable.

Of the explanations that have been offered, the most substantive may be Luther's dismay at how few Jews had converted (the fourth mentioned above) and Luther's terrible ailments (the fifth mentioned). Nevertheless, his outburst is still puzzling and dismaying in view of his earlier writings on the Jews and, even more, on his general views on God's grace and forgiveness and how this undergirds our Christian ethic.

There is a clue, however, in Luther's writing that is not used in the explanations offered above. It is that Luther found the anti–Christian tract to be so reprehensible and offensive that he lost his temper and lashed out in kind. Unfortunately, we do not have the treatise to which Luther was responding, but we can reconstruct it somewhat using Luther's comments that Jesus was slandered as a bastard and deranged and Mary as a whore. Nevertheless, this in no way excuses Luther for lashing out at Jews *in general* and for descending into the most hate-filled gutter language.

There is also another point to be made. Luther believed that the Jews were being stiff-necked and obstinate in rejecting truths that were gracious and obvious. Indeed, God, he believed, had been especially concerned to bring these truths to them. To use a contemporary example, it would be as though a person were faced with people who resolutely affirmed that the world is flat in the face of overwhelming evidence to the contrary. To use a more contemporary illustration, it would be as though a scientist committed to studying global climate change had to confront people who scornfully dismissed the scientific evidence that he considered to be important. Or, perhaps better, it would be as though a therapist committed to helping people with drug addictions was ridiculed by addicts for thinking that drug addiction is harmful. We can see in many situations that Luther's strong faith and commitment led him to be short and uncomprehending of those who did not share the religious convictions that he considered to be so wonderful and so obvious.

To be sure, understanding what may have been Luther's situation does not lead to excusing him. His pompous and hateful appeal to stereotypes and his vengeful attacks must be condemned. Even if the treatise to which he was responding had made offensive and outrageous claims (and had made the Christian in the dialogue appear to be a dunce), this was no longer a response to that treatise. It was allowing the treatise to release a fury of anti–Jewish superstition, anger, and hate.

Yet one would hope that Luther's egregious wrongs in this writing would not lead people to discount the other great contributions which he made for Christianity and for humanity.

• Essay 19 •

Luther on Melanchthon

Luther's closest colleague and Reformation collaborator was Philip Melanchthon—a truly remarkable person in his own right. Melanchthon was a dear friend, a brilliant scholar, a classical linguist and humanist, a theologian, the writer of several Lutheran confessions, a stand-in for Luther at critical junctures, and much more. But in many circles Melanchthon now has a tainted reputation as weak, as too willing to compromise, and as the person who "betrayed" the Lutheran movement after Luther died in 1546.

In this essay we will examine what Luther himself thought of Melanchthon. Why did he trust him so fully? Did his judgment of Melanchthon change over the years? Did Luther see any signs of weakness and betrayal? For our purposes, we will use primarily Luther's letters to Melanchthon himself. Luther was never one to avoid direct, straightforward comments to anyone, and he reveals his thoughts quite forcefully in those letters.

Background

Philip Melanchthon, over thirteen years younger than Luther, was a prodigy who studied the classics and other liberal arts at Heidelberg and Tübingen, receiving the Master of Arts in 1514. Under the influence of his great-uncle Thomas Reuchlin and Erasmus, he developed as a humanist and adopted the name "Melanchthon" as the Greek form of his family name, Schwartzerdt. In the summer of 1518, nearly a year after Luther's posting of the Ninety-Five Theses, he was called to Wittenberg as professor of Greek. Luther praised his inaugural address: "Four days after he had arrived, he delivered an extremely learned and absolutely faultless address."[1] A few days later Luther wrote of his new young colleague: "He is an excellent Greek teacher and a most learned and kind man. His classroom is jammed with students."[2] His commitment to the reform movement was soon clear. Only six weeks after Melanchthon arrived, Luther wrote on how the young man could be expected to surpass him as a reformer, "If it please Christ, Melanchthon will make many Martins and a most powerful enemy of scholastic theology; for he knows their folly and the Rock of Christ as well. As a man of might, he will prove his ability. Amen."[3]

Luther considered Melanchthon to be the best academic at Wittenberg, and they very quickly became the best of friends. Moreover, Melanchthon almost immediately became the ablest theological supporter of Luther and his reformation positions. In 1521 he published the first systematic exposition of Luther's theology, the *Loci Communes*.

Wartburg

Melanchthon had been with Luther at Leipzig and at other events, but his special place alongside Luther appears clearly during the time when Luther was hidden away at the Wartburg, 1521–22.

Melanchthon's special blessing had already become apparent through his work with Luther on Greek. While at the Wartburg, Luther completed the draft of the translation of the New Testament into German, and Melanchthon continued to assist him by offering insightful translation suggestions. Melanchthon's expertise in Greek was a necessity for Luther's translation work.

But more than that, Melanchthon was Luther's stand-in in Wittenberg at this time. Karlstadt had begun to move in different directions, and the "Zwickau Prophets," led by Müntzer, had started to divert Luther's reforms into the position of Anabaptism (against infant baptism) and direct revelation from God to these prophets.

Luther, in danger of being arrested and executed, was hidden away at the Wartburg Castle, and Melanchthon, along with Spalatin, was his eyes, ears, and mouthpiece. During the 15 months of that period, Luther's supreme trust in Melanchthon is shown. Thinking of his own danger, his letter to Melanchthon on May 12, 1521, contains the following remarkable passage:

> You, therefore, as minister of the Word, be steadfast in the meantime and fortify the walls and towers of Jerusalem until [the enemy] also attack you. You know your call and your gifts. I pray for you as for no one else, if my prayer can accomplish something—which I do not doubt. Return, therefore, this service so that we carry this burden together. So far I stand alone in the battle; after me they will seek you.[4]

It would not be the last time Luther would urge his friend to be steadfast.

By May 26, Luther was aware that trouble was brewing in Wittenberg. In a letter of that date to Melanchthon, he wrote:

> I cannot believe what you write, that you [the leaders at Wittenberg] are going astray without a shepherd. This would be the saddest and bitterest of news. As long as you, Amsdorf, and the others are there, you are not without a shepherd. Don't talk that way, lest God be angered, and we be found guilty of ingratitude. Would that all the churches, at least the collegiate churches [churches with more than one clergyman], had one-fourth of your share of the Word and its ministers! Thank the Lord who has enlightened you.[5]

On July 13, he sought to stiffen Melanchthon's backbone as he criticized him for his last letter [not extant]:

> Your letter displeased me for two reasons: First, I realize that you carry the cross too impatiently; you give in too much to your emotions and as is your way you are just too gentle. Second, you extol me so much. You err tremendously in ascribing such great importance to me, as if I were so much concerned for God's case. Your high opinion of me shames and tortures me….
>
> Since things are going so well at Wittenberg [? !], you certainly don't need me. I am unhappy with you personally, however, because you burden yourself with so much work and do not listen and spare yourself. Here you are being led by your own stubbornness. I shout this at you so often, but each time it is as if I were telling a story to someone who is deaf.[6]

In future years, Luther would often comment on Melanchthon being too gentle and considerate. He often used the saying, "A badly knotted log calls for a blunt wedge," referring to himself as a "blunt wedge" and to Melanchthon as not being "blunt" enough.[7]

By early August, Luther was quite aware of Karlstadt's new theses against celibacy, monasticism, private masses, and reception of communion only in one kind, but he did not foresee the turmoil to come. He did criticize to Melanchthon some of Karlstadt's exegesis.[8]

In his letter to Melanchthon of January 13, 1522, Luther revealed that he was aware of the direct revelation claims and the Anabaptist tendencies of the Zwickau prophets, and he gave his colleague suggestions that he could use against them. His main comment regarding Melanchthon, though is in a single sentence within the long letter: "I do not approve of your timidity, since you are stronger in spirit and learning than I."[9]

These letters reveal that Melanchthon was not only Luther's tutor in Greek. He was also Luther's second-in-command on all matters pastoral and theological. Moreover, they reveal that, although Luther praised Melanchthon's intellectual gifts and his spiritual advancement, he was very worried about the latter's caution and gentleness.

Augsburg

For the next several years, Melanchthon continued to be Luther's trusted colleague and confidante. They did not always agree. Melanchthon thought Luther was far too antagonistic in his attacks upon Erasmus, Melanchthon's fellow humanist, and he disagreed with Luther's decision to marry. Nevertheless, he was always at Luther's side supporting him with arguments and his exceptional erudition.

The crucial point came in 1530, when it was unsafe for Luther to attend the imperial diet at Augsburg, and Melanchthon led the Lutheran contingent. Luther had to remain in safety at the Coburg—over 150 miles away. Luther had prepared statements that could be used against the Catholic hierarchy and the Emperor, but Melanchthon led the writing of a new document to be read before the diet.

This document, the *Augsburg Confession*, has become a (many would say, "the") primary confessional document for Lutherans ever since. But at the time Luther had his doubts that Melanchthon was forceful enough. It is probably fair to say that Luther's strategy was to make a confession of faith that was totally faithful to Scripture and that would show in no uncertain terms how wrong the Roman Church was on several key points. Melanchthon's strategy, by contrast, seems to have been faithfully to present the Lutheran position as consistent with Scripture and with the best of Church history; the Roman Church and the Emperor should, he thought, accept it as biblical and sound. From this vantage point, the Lutherans could point out errors in the Roman Catholic practices that should be corrected. The Lutherans thus were shown to be "orthodox" and "catholic" in the original meanings of those terms.

The two strategies may seem consistent, but they were not. Luther's was to stand up boldly and separate; Melanchthon's was to stand up faithfully and to find a commonality wherever possible. In the end, the harsh response of the Roman Church made Melanchthon's faithfulness and Luther's boldness seem one and the same.

Some of the articles in the *Augsburg Confession* emphasized that the Lutherans were not "radical" reformers and that they were soundly in the best Christian traditions (e.g., the articles on God [I], The Son of God [III], and Baptism [IX]). Other articles showed the solid biblical foundations of teachings from which the Roman Church had departed but that the Lutherans were emphasizing (e.g., on Original Sin [II], Justification [IV], and The Church [VII]). A third category seems to be those which describe a harmful, unbiblical practice in the Church at that time (e.g., Both Kinds in the Sacrament [XXII], The Marriage of Priests [XXIII], and The Distinction of Meats [XXVI]).

Melanchthon's efforts to reach a commonality may best be seen in the "Summary of the Conflict" and "Review of the Abuses That Have Been Corrected" following article XXI. The "Summary" begins as follows:

> This then is nearly a complete summary of our teaching. As can be seen, there is nothing that varies from the Scriptures, or from the Church universal, or from the Church of Rome, as known from its writings. Since this is the case, those who insist that our teachers are to be regarded as heretics are judging harshly. There is, however, disagreement on certain abuses that have crept into the Church without rightful authority.[10]

The opening of the "Review" is as follows:

> Our churches do not dissent from any article of the faith held by the Church catholic. They only omit some of the newer abuses. They have been erroneously accepted through the corruption of the times, contrary to the intent of canon law.[11]

Luther's concerns about Melanchthon being too "soft" at Augsburg can also be seen in his letters. This was a difficult time for Luther. He was upset that he could not be at Augsburg, he had just learned that his father had died, he was very piqued over not receiving more updates from Melanchthon and the others at the diet,[12] he was worried about the Turkish invasion, and he continued to be tormented by painful constipation and his other ailments. His nerves were definitely on edge.

On June 29, he wrote,

> I have received your *Apologia*, and I wonder what it is you want when you ask what and how much is to be conceded to the papists.... For me personally more than enough has been conceded in this *Apologia*. If the papists reject it, then I see nothing that I could still concede, unless I saw their reasoning, or clearer Scripture passages than I have seen till now.... I shall not permit anything further to be taken away from me, come what may.[13]

Although Luther expressed his general appreciation for the *Augsburg Confession*,[14] he did continue to state some disagreements with Melanchthon—on the interpretation of some passages and on other matters. His impatience showed in a letter on July 31: "I wish you would be of a little more peaceful mind. Also, you are wearing me out with your vain worries, so that I am almost tired of writing to you, since I see that I accomplish nothing with my words."[15]

Wittenberg Controversies

In the 1530s there were occasional differences that emerged among the theologians at Wittenberg. One concerned the issue of whether repentance as a human act is a necessary aspect of justification. Conrad Cordatus, a pastor in a neighboring town, attacked the Wittenberg lecturer Caspar Cruciger (and, by implication, Melanchthon) who claimed that it was a part of justification, basing his lecture on notes from Melanchthon. The question was whether this view was akin to the Erasmus position that justification required a human contribution (repentance). Luther insisted, of course, that justification had to be entirely God's doing; to require a human contribution was a semi-Pelagian heresy. A disputation was held and Luther's views carried the day, but some suspected that Luther and Melanchthon were never quite in harmony on the point.

More dramatic was a controversy with John Agricola, a teacher and preacher from Eisleben, who held that for a redeemed Christian the law was of no significance. Indeed, Agricola thought that the gospel by itself could bring people to repentance and to faith and that the law was unnecessary as preparation for the gospel and for faith. On this issue, Melanchthon and Luther were clearly on the same side—insisting that the law is a necessary precondition for the gospel and for faith. Again there were disputations (there were three but twice Agricola failed to appear), and the position of the two most prominent Lutheran theologians was affirmed.

Luther's Last Days

Luther worked closely and respectfully with Melanchthon through the remainder of his life. But perhaps nothing shows Luther's love for Melanchthon as a dear friend better than the fact that in the final days before his death on February 22, 1546, he wrote several cordial letters to his esteemed colleague. He thanked Melanchthon for his prayers, requested that the prayers continue, and expressed the wish that Melanchthon could be with him. Moreover, in his last letters to Kate, Luther also requested that his greetings be passed on to Melanchthon. This is from his letter to Melanchthon on February 1:

> To the man of outstanding learning, Mr. Philip Melanchthon, Master [of Arts], theologian and servant of God, my dearest brother in the Lord,
> Grace and peace in the Lord! I do thank you, my Philip, for your prayers for me, and I ask you to continue to pray.... I certainly wish you were here, were it not that consideration for your health forces me instead to think it is good that we left you at home.[16]

The Aftermath

Melanchthon's fate after Luther's death was not a happy one. Only four months after Luther's death, Emperor Charles V, after making a secret pact with the pope, began attacking the Lutheran princes in the "Smalcald League" crushing them at the battle of Mühlberg on April 24, 1547. Saxon Elector John Frederick and Philip of Hesse were among those taken captive. An "Augsburg Interim" was imposed, which stripped the Lutherans of most of their reforms while granting a very few concessions such as marriage of clergy. Faithful Lutherans who refused to proclaim allegiance to the Roman Catholic Church were exiled, imprisoned, or executed.

No doubt Luther would have stood up against this, and probably would have been killed or captured because of it (Wittenberg was taken by the Emperor, who actually entered the Castle Church and stood over Luther's grave), but the intellectual, peace-loving, kind-hearted Melanchthon could not be defiant. He now called many of the Roman practices "adiaphora" meaning neither required nor prohibited in Scripture. He made concessions including alterations in the *Augsburg Confession* (many Lutheran bodies require subscription to the "unaltered *Augsburg Confession*) and was thought to be a cowardly traitor by the "Genuine Lutherans"— the "Gnesio-Lutherans." He worked on a "Leipzig Interim" document that retained some Lutheran articles and gave up others. Melanchthon died in 1560 having maintained his grace and poise but was despised by those who thought he had been a weakling and a traitor. Those who believed they had been faithful to Luther and betrayed by Melanchthon produced the *Formula of Concord* in 1580, also known as a basic Lutheran Confession.

We have no idea what Luther would have thought of all of this. No doubt he would have been disappointed with the gentle, peace-loving Melanchthon as he often was, but I think he would have continued to admire the intellectually gifted Reformer whose gentleness and peace-loving nature were too great for the situation in which he was placed.

• **Essay 20** •

The Capstone Essay:
A Contemporary Perspective

Luther's thoughts and his actions continue to attract widespread attention some five centuries after they profoundly changed Western history. But the interest is not only because of his role in history; it is also because his ideas continue to be provocative and relevant as people wrestle with questions related to being a Christian today, being the Church, and even being a citizen of the world.

A fresh study of Luther's writings has led me to develop and emphasize the following theses as a "capstone" or culmination.

1. Luther's writings are a strong witness to his amazing character.

Great courage is an obvious feature of his character. On the basis of his convictions, Luther was able to stand up against the most powerful institution of his day. He did not back down in the face of almost certain capture, imprisonment, and execution. Perhaps even more remarkable, he did not yield to attacks from respected churchmen, scholars, and friends that he was a heretic, that he was destroying the church, and that he was an enemy of God. He was criticized as an egoist, a criminal, and a corruptor of society. Yet he did not back down— before clerics, papal emissaries, intellectuals, dukes, and even the Holy Roman Emperor.

Likewise remarkable is his deep spiritual faith and trust. This is not to say that his spiritual journey was easy. He struggled early, he struggled in the middle of his life, and he struggled near the end. But he had a strategy for handling his struggles—he read and meditated on Scripture. Paul's epistles were so important to him that he no doubt read and studied Romans and Galatians hundreds of times. He turned to the Psalms to find there parallels to his every mood, his every challenge, his every heartbreak as well as the comfort, the strength, and the love that he so desperately wanted and needed. His faith and his trust remained solid through all of his personal earthquakes.

His character also displayed a very strong will. This is closely tied to his courage. He simply would not give up. The threats only made his determination stronger. So also did criticism, rejection, vicious attacks, and anything else that might come up against him. Even his extreme physical ailments and his psychological traumata did not lead him to modify or compromise. He believed that God was with him and that the "gates of hell could not prevail" against him. Some might call it stubbornness, but it should be noted that he did not hold firm simply because it was *his* view or *his* position. He held firm because it was the view or position he found in Scripture. A perfect example is his dispute with Zwingli at Marburg.[1]

316

2. Luther developed great insights that are still meaningful.

Luther is often praised for his contribution to the German language by helping to give it a consistent grammar, word choice, and spelling through his translation of Scripture. Likewise, his exceptional skills as a biblical scholar, a debater, and a persuasive writer are among his additional amazing talents.

No less remarkable are both the insights of his religious (and non-religious) views and the contributions he made for people's spiritual lives.

Theologians today are still mining his distinction between a theology of glory and a theology of the cross and are finding in Luther's position a distinction which divides Christianity (and even religion in general) along the very helpful lines of turning one's back on suffering on the one hand and of embracing suffering for the blessings and salvation it brings, on the other.

Luther's position on the Kingdom of the Right Hand and the Kingdom of the Left Hand avoids the simplistic distinction of seeing everything spiritual as good and everything worldly as evil but instead sees the spiritual and the earthly as two distinct realms that are both under God. This enables the Christian to be both a believer and a citizen who serves people in a broad variety of Christian vocations.

His understanding of the Church rejects authoritarianism, a rigid clergy/laity division, and the exaltation of an earthly institution. Instead, he focused on the faith of people that ties them together in a spiritual oneness distinct from any man-made organization—thus giving the Church a faith-based unity.

A brilliant thinker can often ground complexities of a theory in a simple way that is straightforward and easy to describe. Luther excelled in this. An example would be the three solas—that we are saved by grace alone through faith alone based upon Scripture alone. Immediately, any form of human cooperation with God, any type of justifying human activity, and any spiritual authority other than Scripture are all eliminated. On this compact basis Luther was able to attack indulgences, monastic vows and the Roman papacy among other things. Luther also built simply and effectively on the Pauline distinction between Law and Gospel: that the Law shows us our sin and helplessness and that the Gospel gives undeserved and unexpected forgiveness.

Luther's brilliance is shown, too, by offering the tools for a full spiritual life. They include (1) Scripture in the language of the people, (2) hymns that are melodic to sing, easy to memorize, and rich in teaching content, and (3) concise summaries of Christianity in catechisms.

3. Luther's writings are ecumenical in nature.

If "ecumenical" is taken to mean promoting oneness in the Church, this claim may seem to be contradictory with the divisiveness of the Reformation. But it is not. Luther intended that the Scriptural truths that he had uncovered would be for *all Christians*—even as a Christian witness for *all people*. His writings were offered to provide insights for all. This included helping those who were involved in such religious practices as buying indulgences, going on pilgrimages, reverencing relics, purchasing masses, and praying to saints so that they could reexamine those practices in the light of Scripture. Whether urging new beliefs or new actions, his writings were intended for everyone—not just his followers. His writings can be seen as an effort to unite all Christians.

Luther's writings did not merely "define Lutherans" as distinct from others. They could guide all Christians to a new oneness. The events and emphases of the 500th anniversary of the Reformation may help bring this out.

4. As with any great figure in history, one must look for both strengths and weaknesses.

In a sense, this was part of Luther's emphasis that every person is *simul justus et peccator*—at the same time saint and sinner.

One cannot expect that his writings and actions were all perfect. He could, for example, be unnecessarily harsh and ruthless. There are many examples of this including comments about Erasmus, political rulers, and church leaders.

His guidance to Philip of Hesse in which he allowed bigamy so long as it was kept secret was clearly a mistake that he came to recognize and regret. His permission to the princes to use strong violence against the peasants went beyond what he knew would restore peace and order. His diatribe against the Jews late in life was hateful and wrong.

In some respects, Luther was like Job—suffering physical ailments and both psychological and spiritual distresses that were almost unimaginable. These do not provide an excuse for any of his statements or actions, but they are important to be aware of, nonetheless.

As suggested above, the 500th anniversary of Luther's posting of the Ninety-Five Theses is a special opportunity to reexamine and reassess Luther's contributions and his place in history. It has been the impetus for this work and for many others that will enrich our understanding of this gigantic figure.

Chapter Notes

Abbreviations: The following abbreviations for sources have been used: *CTLC—Concordia: The Lutheran Confessions* (St. Louis: Concordia, 2005). *LW—Luther's Works* (St. Louis: Concordia, and Philadelphia: Fortress, 1959ff.). *WLS—What Luther Says,* Ewald M. Plass, editor (St. Louis: Concordia, 1959). Unless otherwise noted, scriptural passages are taken from the *Holy Bible, New International Version,* copyright 1973, 1978, 1984, International Bible Society, Zondervan Bible Publishers.

Chapter 1

1. Much of the information in this chapter is gleaned from the many excellent summaries of the state of the Roman Catholic Church in the Middle Ages, including: Thomas Bokenkotter, *A Concise History of the Catholic Church* (New York: Doubleday, 2004); Will Durant, *The Reformation: A History of European Civilization from Wycliffe to Calvin, 1300–1654* (New York: Simon & Schuster, 1957); Diarmaid MacCulloch, *The Reformation: A History* (New York: Penguin, 2003); William Manchester, *A World Lit Only by Fire: The Medieval Mind and the Renaissance, Portrait of an Age* (New York: Little, Brown, 1992); and Brian Moynihan, *The Faith: A History of Christianity* (New York: Doubleday, 2002).

Chapter 2

1. Preserved Smith, *The Life and Letters of Martin Luther* (Boston: Houghton Mifflin, 1911), pp. 1–2.
2. Roland H. Bainton, *Here I Stand: A Life of Martin Luther* (New York: Mentor, 1950), p. 17.
3. *Ibid.*
4. Bainton, *Here I Stand,* p. 18, and Richard Marius, *Martin Luther: The Christian Between God and Death* (Cambridge: The Belknap Press of Harvard University Press, 1999), p. 22.
5. John Louis Nuelsen, *Luther the Leader* (Cincinnati: Jennings and Graham, 1906), p. 14.
6. Bainton, *Here I Stand,* p. 17.
7. Gerhard Brendler, *Martin Luther* (New York: Oxford University Press, 1991), p. 27.
8. Martin Brecht, *Martin Luther: His Road to Reformation, 1483–1521,* trans. James L. Schaff, 3 vols. (Philadelphia: Westminster, 1895), I: 5.
9. Bainton, *Here I Stand,* p. 9.
10. James M. Kittelson, *Luther The Reformer: The Story of the Man and His Career* (Minneapolis: Fortress, 2003), p. 49.

Chapter 3

1. Julius Kostlin, *Life of Luther* (New York: Charles Scribner's Sons, 1911), p. 37.
2. Richard Marius, *Martin Luther: The Christian Between God and Death* (Cambridge: The Belknap Press of Harvard University Press), 1999, pp. 59–67.
3. Martin Brecht, *Martin Luther: His Road to Reformation, 1483–1521* (Minneapolis: Fortress, 1985), p. 48; and Marius, *Martin Luther,* p. 48.
4. George Cubitt, *The Life of Martin Luther* (New York: Carlton and Phillips, 1853), p. 43.
5. Martin Marty, *Martin Luther: A Life* (New York: Penguin, 2004), pp. 6–7.
6. *Ibid.,* p. 44.
7. Brecht, *Martin Luther,* p. 58; and Kostlin, *Life of Luther,* p. 21.
8. Martin Luther, *The Letters of Martin Luther* (New York: Macmillan, 1908), 1520–1521; V.H.H. Green, *Luther and The Reformation* (New York: Capricorn, 1964), p. 35; and Ian D. Kingston Siggins, *Luther* (New York: Barnes and Nobles, 1972), p. 38.
9. Lothar Schmelz, *Evangelical Church and Monastery of St. Augustine in Erfurt* (Erfurt: Evangelisches Augustinerkloster zu Erfurt, 2003), p. 10.
10. Frederick Nohl, *Luther: Biography of a Reformer* (St. Louis: Concordia, 2003), p. 29.
11. Roland H. Bainton, *Here I Stand: A Life of Martin Luther* (New York: Mentor, 1950), pp. 26–27; and Nohl, *Luther,* pp. 29–30. When he took his vows Luther lay on the tomb of Johannes Zachariae, who worked to condemn the reformer Jan Hus in the early fifteenth century. Hus was burned at the stake. As he died, he said, "You roast a lean goose today, but from my ashes a swan will ascend in a hundred years that you cannot roast." Ninety-one years later, Protestants like to believe, Luther fulfilled the prophecy. Schmelz, *Evangelical Church and Monastery of St. Augustine in Erfurt,* pp. 28–29.
12. Bainton, *Here I Stand,* p. 28.
13. Moritz Meurer, *The Life of Martin Luther, Related from Original Authorities* (Anon, N.Y.: H. Ludwig and Company, 1848), pp. 21–22.
14. Schmelz, *Evangelical Church and Monastery of St. Augustine in Erfurt,* p. 10.
15. Green, *Luther,* p. 36.
16. *Ibid.,* p. 37.
17. William Dallmann, *Luther: His Life and His Labor for the Plain People* (St. Louis: Concordia, 1917), p. 17.

18. Bainton, *Here I Stand*, p. 28.
19. Green, *Luther*, p. 37; and Bainton, *Here I Stand*, p. 34.
20. Green, *Luther*, p. 37.
21. *Ibid.*, p. 37.
22. *Holy Bible*, Matthew 26: 26, 27 (English Standard Version).
23. Brecht, *Martin Luther*, p. 71.
24. Siggins, *Luther*, p. 37.
25. Meurer, *The Life of Martin Luther*, p. 22.
26. Bainton, *Here I Stand*, p. 30.
27. Siggins, *Luther*, p. 37; and Marius, *Martin Luther*, p. 52.
28. Bainton, *Here I Stand*, pp. 31–32.
29. Brecht, *Martin Luther*, p. 66.
30. James M. Kittelson, *Luther The Reformer: The Story of the Man and His Career* (Minneapolis: Augsburg, 1986), p. 56; Green, *Luther*, p. 44; and Brecht, *Martin Luther*, p. 66.
31. Marius, *Martin Luther*, pp. 75, 76.
32. Bainton, *Here I Stand*, p. 34.
33. Bainton, *Here I Stand*, p. 41; and Marius, *Martin Luther*, p. 76.
34. A. Skevington Wood, *Captive to the Word* (Milton Keynes, UK: Paternoster, 1969), pp. 29–30; and Dallmann, *Luther*, p. 21.
35. Bainton, *Here I Stand*, p. 44.
36. *Ibid.*, p. 43.
37. Siggins, *Luther*, p. 43.
38. Richard Friedenthal, *Luther: His Life and Times* (New York: Harcourt Brace Jovanovich, 1967), p. 79.
39. Preserved Smith, *The Life and Letters of Martin Luther* (Boston: Houghton Mifflin, 1911), p. 18.
40. Marius, *Martin Luther*, p. 82.
41. Bainton, *Here I Stand*, p. 38; and Marius, *Martin Luther*, p. 83.
42. Siggins, *Luther*, p. 42.

Chapter 4

1. Bainton, *Here I Stand* (New York: Mentor, 1950), p. 39.
2. Carter Lindberg, *The European Reformations* (New York: John Wiley & Sons, 2011), and Brecht, *Martin Luther: His Road to Reformation 1483–1521* (Minneapolis: Fortress, 1985), p. 185.
3. Bainton, *Here I Stand*, p. 45.
4. Marius, *Martin Luther: The Christian Between God and Death* (Cambridge: The Belknap Press of Harvard University Press, 1999), pp. 84–85; and *Martin Luther Works* V 5371.
5. Brecht, *Martin Luther*, p. 126.
6. James M. Kittelson, *Luther the Reformer: The Story of the Man and His Career* (Minneapolis: Fortress, 2003), p. 85.
7. Bainton, *Here I Stand*, p. 44.
8. Martin Luther, *Preface to the Psalter*, p. 255.
9. V.H.H. Green, *Luther and the Reformation* (New York: Capricorn, 1964), p. 43; and Ian D. Kingston Siggins, editor, *Luther* (New York: Harper and Row, 1972), p. 40.
10. Siggins, *Luther*, p. 40.
11. Kittelson, *Luther the Reformer*, p. 88.
12. Klees, Emerson, *The Will to Stay with It* (New York: Friends of Finger Lake, 2002), p. 112.
13. Martin Brecht, *Martin Luther: His Road to Reformation, 1483–1521* (Minneapolis: Fortress, 1985), p. 85; and Kittelson, *Luther the Reformer*, p. 134.
14. Kittelson, *Luther the Reformer*, pp. 87–88.
15. *Ibid.*, pp. 134–135.
16. Kittelson, *Luther the Reformer*, p. 134; and Diarmaid MacCulloch, *The Reformation* (New York: Penguin, 2003), p. 119.

17. John M. Todd, *Luther: A Life* (New York: Crossroad, 1982), p. 78.
18. See Regin Prenter, *Luther's Theology of the Cross* (Philadelphia: Fortress, 1971), p. 17; Gerhard Forde, *On Being a Theologian of the Cross: Reflections on Luther's Heidelberg Disputation, 1518* (Grand Rapids, MI: Eerdmans, 1997); and Walther von Loewenich; *Luther's Theology of the Cross* (Minneapolis: Augsburg Fortress, 1976).
19. Kittelson, *Luther the Reformer*, p. 98.
20. Kittelson, *Luther the Reformer*, p. 91.
21. Martin Luther, *Lectures on Romans* (Philadelphia: Westminster John Knox, 1961).
22. Gerhard Brendler, *Martin Luther: Theology and Revolution* (New York: Oxford University Press, 1991), p. 65.
23. Kittelson, *Luther the Reformer*, p. 95.
24. *Ibid.*, p. 96.
25. *Ibid.*

Chapter 5

1. The Catholic Catechism, http://www.vatican.va/archive/ccc_css/archive/catechism/p2s1c1a2.htm, 1131.
2. Tetzel's methodology for the sale of indulgences can be seen in his own writing. The best example can be found in James Harvey Robinson, editor, *Translations and Reprints from the Original Sources of European History* (Philadelphia: University of Pennsylvania, 1902), p. 4. Here is reproduced "An Extract from Sermon Given by Tetzel to Parochial Clergy as Pattern for Indulgence Preaching. (From the Latin. Gieseler: Ecclesiastical History, Vol. V., pp. 225–26." This work notes that Tetzel sent an "Instruction summario" to the priests, directing them to "go to work in behalf of the indulgence." In this chapter, then, I have utilized Tetzel's own words and meaning.
3. Holy Bible, Acts of the Apostles, 8:20.
4. Preserved Smith, *The Life and Letters of Martin Luther* (Boston and New York: Houghton Mifflin, 1911), pp. 42–43.
5. Donald K. McKim, editor, *The Cambridge Companion to Martin Luther* (Cambridge University Press, 2003), p. 266.
6. Roland H. Bainton, *Here I Stand: A Life of Martin Luther* (Nashville: Abington, 1950), pp. 62–63.
7. Martin Luther, *Life of Luther, Written by Himself* (London: Bell & Daldy, 1872).

Chapter 6

1. Holy Bible, Mathew 16:18.
2. John Julius Norwich, *Absolute Monarchs: A History of the Papacy* (New York: Random House, 2011), p. 4.
3. William Manchester, *A World Lit Only by Fire* (New York: Little, Brown, 1992), p. 132; and V.H.H. Green, *Luther and the Reformation* (New York: Mentor, 1974), p. 24.
4. Thomas Bokenkotter, *A Concise History of the Catholic Church* (New York: Image, 2005), p. 202.
5. Manchester, *A World Lit Only by Fire*, p. 131.
6. Green, *Luther and the Reformation*, p. 24.
7. Brian Moynihan, *The Faith: A History of Christianity* (New York: Doubleday, 2002), p. 343.
8. Manchester, *A World Lit Only by Fire*, p. 133.
9. John Julius Norwich, *Absolute Monarchs*, p. 283.
10. Manchester, *A World Lit Only by Fire*, p. 38.
11. *Ibid.*, p. 289.
12. Moynihan, *The Faith*, p. 343.
13. *Ibid.*, p. 133.
14. Roland H. Bainton, *Here I Stand: A Life of Martin Luther* (Nashville: Abington, 1950), p. 72.

15. Moynihan, *The Faith*, pp. 300–304.
16. Will Durant, *The Reformation: A History of European Civilization from Wycliffe to Calvin, 1300–1564* (New York: Simon & Schuster, 1957), p. 165.
17. *Ibid.,* p. 328.
18. *Ibid.,* p. 264.
19. *Ibid.*
20. Bainton, *Here I Stand*, p. 80.

Chapter 7

1. Brian Moynihan, *The Faith: A History of Christianity* (New York: Doubleday, 2002), p. 350.
2. William Manchester, *A World Lit Only By Fire: The Medieval Mind and the Renaissance* (New York: Little, Brown, 1992) p. 143.
3. "How Luther Went Viral," *The Economist*, December 17, 2011; and Robert Kolb, *Martin Luther as Prophet, Teacher, and Hero* (Grand Rapids, MI: Baker, 1999), p. 22.
4. Moynihan, *The Faith*, p. 350.
5. "How Luther Went Viral," *The Economist*, December 17, 2011.
6. Julius Kostlin, *Life of Luther* (New York: Charles Scribner's Sons, 1883), p. 97.
7. Diarmaid MacCulloch, *The Reformation: A History* (New York: Penguin, 2003), pp. 125–126.
8. Moynihan, *The Faith*, p. 350.
9. Will Durant, *The Reformation: A History of European Civilization from Wycliffe to Calvin, 1300–1564* (New York: Simon & Schuster, 1957), p. 346.
10. William Dallman, *Martin Luther: His Life and Labor for the Plain People* (St. Louis: Concordia, 1917), p. 82.
11. Durant, *The Reformation*, p. 346.
12. V.H.H. Green, *Luther and the Reformation* (New York: Mentor, 1974), p. 60.
13. Richard Marius, *Martin Luther, The Christian Between God and Death* (Cambridge: Tthe Belknap Press of Harvard University Press, 1999), pp. 152–155.
14. David M. Whitford, *T&T Companion to Reformation Theology* (New York: Bloomsbury, 2014), p. 60.
15. Marius, *Martin Luther*, p. 154.
16. *Ibid.,* p. 155.

Chapter 8

1. James M. Kittleson, *Luther and the Reformation* (Minneapolis: Fortress, 2003), p. 116; and Preserved Smith.
2. *The Letters of Martin Luther* (Boston: Houghton Mifflin, 1911), p. 28.
3. Will Durant, *The Reformation: European Civilization from Wycliffe to Calvin, 1300–1564* (New York: Simon & Schuster, 1957), p. 346.
4. Roland H. Bainton, *Here I Stand: A Life of Martin Luther* (Nashville: Abington, 1950), p. 67.
5. Kittleson, *Luther the Reformer*, p. 113.
6. Ian D. Kingston Siggins, *Luther* (New York: Barnes & Noble, 1972), p. 84.
7. Bainton, *Here I Stand*, p. 68.
8. Project Wittenberg, Concordia Theological Seminary: *"Prostratum me pedibus tuia, beatissime pater, offero, cum omnibus quae sum et habeo. Vivifica, occide, voce, revoke, approba, reproba, ut placuerit; bocem tuam vocem Christi, in te praesidentis et loquentis, agnoscam."*
9. H.V.V. Green, *Luther and the Reformation* (New York: Mentor, 1974), p. 61.
10. Richard Marius, *Martin Luther: The Christian Between God and Death* (Cambridge: The Belknap Press of Harvard University Press, 1999), p. 158.

11. Bainton, *Here I Stand*, p. 68.
12. Holy Bible. I Thessalonians 5:21.
13. Bainton, *Here I Stand*, p. 77.
14. Dickenson's Theological Quarterly, vol. 5, 1879, p. 729.
15. Bainton, *Here I Stand*, p. 81.
16. Kittleson, *Luther the Reformer*, p. 116.
17. Green, *Luther and the Reformation*, p. 64.
18. Richard Friedenthal, *Luther: His Life and Times* (New York: Harcourt, Brace, Jovanovich, 1970), p. 176.
19. Brecht, *Luther: Luther: The Road to Reformation*, p. 251, and Bainton, *Here I Stand*, p. 70.
20. Kittleson, *Luther the Reformer*, p. 121.
21. Marius, *Martin Luther*, p. 161.
22. Kittleson, *Luther the* Reformer, p. 122; and Marius, *Martin Luther*, p. 160.
23. Friedenthal, *Luther*, p. 178.
24. Bainton, *Here I Stand*, p. 80.
25. Kittleson, *Luther the Reformer*, pp. 122–123, and Brecht, *Luther: Luther: The Road to Reformation*, p. 253.
26. Bainton, *Here I Stand*, pp. 72–73.
27. Bainton, *Here I Stand*, p. 74; and Estelle Ross, *Martin Luther* (New York: Frederick A. Stokes, 1927), p. 53.
28. J.A. Wylie, *The History of Protestantism*, vol. 1 (Harrington: DE: Delmarva, 2015), p. 285.

Chapter 9

1. Roland H. Bainton, *Here I Stand: A Life of Martin Luther* (Nashville: Abington, 1950), p. 76.
2. Estelle Ross, *Martin Luther* (New York: Frederick A. Stokes, 1927), p. 66.
3. Richard Marius, *Martin Luther: The Christian Between God and Death* (Cambridge: The Belknap Press of Harvard University Press, 1999), p. 164.
4. Martin Marty, *Martin Luther* (New York: Penguin, 2004), p. 44.
5. Bainton, *Here I Stand*, p. 75.
6. Martin Brecht, *Martin Luther: His Road to the Reformation* (Minneapolis: Fortress, 1990), p. 264.
7. Richard Friedenthal, *Luther: His Life and Times* (New York: Harcourt, Brace, Jovanovich, 1970), p. 187.
8. Will Durant, *The Reformation: A History of European Civilization from Wycliffe to Calvin, 1300–1564* (New York: Simon & Schuster, 1957), p. 348.
9. *Ibid.*
10. Kittleson, *Luther the Reformer* (Minneapolis: Fortress, 2003), p. 129.
11. *Ibid.,* p. 127.
12. *Ibid.,* p. 130.
13. Bainton, *Here I Stand*, pp. 77, 78.
14. Kittelson, *Luther the Reformer*, p. 130.
15. Bainton, *Here I Stand*, p. 80.
16. Friedenthal, *Luther: His Life and Times*, p. 191; and Bainton, *Here I Stand*, p. 81.
17. Bainton, *Here I Stand*, p. 80.
18. *Ibid.,* p. 80.
19. Mackinnon, *Luther and the Reformation* (New York: Russell & Russell, 1962), p. 184.
20. Friedenthal, *Luther: His Life and Times*, p. 191.
21. Preserved Smith, *The Life and Letters of Martin Luther* (Boston: Houghton Mifflin, 1911), p. 55.
22. Friedenthal, *Luther: His Life and Times*, p. 192.
23. Brecht, *Martin Luther*, p. 289.
24. *Ibid.*
25. *Ibid.,* p. 281.
26. *Ibid.,* p. 279.
27. *Ibid.,* p. 281.
28. Durant, *The Reformation*, p. 349.

29. William Dallman, *Martin Luther: His Life and Labor for the Plain People* (St. Louis: Concordia, 1917), p. 82.

30. Smith, *The Life and Letters of Martin Luther*, p. 59.

31. *Ibid.*, pp. 59–60.

32. Friedenthal, *Luther: His Life and Times*, p. 200.

33. Smith, *The Life and Letters of Martin Luther*, p. 61.

34. Julius Kostlin, *Life of Luther* (New York: Charles Scribner's Sons, 1883), p. 57.

35. Bainton, *Here I Stand*, p. 83.

36. *Ibid.*, p. 88.

37. Marius, *Martin Luther*, pp. 176–177.

38. Bainton, *Here I Stand*, p. 91.

39. Kittleson, *Luther the* Reformer, p. 142.

Chapter 10

1. Richard Marius, *Martin Luther: The Christian Between God and Death* (Cambridge: The Belknap Press of the Harvard University Press, 1999), p. 219.

2. *Ibid.*, and Martin Brecht, *Martin Luther: His Road to Reformation, 1483–1521* (Minneapolis: Fortress, 1985), pp. 343, 344.

3. Roland Bainton, *Here I Stand: A Life of Martin Luther* (Nashville: Abington, 1950), p. 111.

4. *Ibid.*

5. Brecht, *Martin Luther*, pp. 394, 395.

6. Preserved Smith, *The Life and Letters of Martin Luther* (Boston: Houghton Mifflin, 1911), pp. 74–75.

7. James M. Kittleson, *Luther the Reformer: The Story of the Man and his Career* (Minneapolis: Fortress, 1986), p. 151.

8. *Ibid.*, p. 152.

9. *Ibid.*

10. Smith, *The Life and Letters of Martin Luther*, p. 82.

11. Estelle Ross, *Martin Luther* (New York: Frederick A. Stokes, 1927), p. 79.

12. Smith, *The Life and Letters of Martin Luther*, pp. 81–82.

13. *Ibid.*, p. 81.

14. *Ibid.*

15. Brecht, *Martin Luther*, pp. 345, 346.

16. Preserved Smith, *The Life and Letters of Martin Luther*, p. 86.

17. *Ibid.*, pp. 79–80.

18. Kittleson, *Luther the Reformer*, p. 151.

19. Martin Luther, *Damned Through the Church*, p. 55.

20. Holy Bible, Mark 16:6.

21. Martin Luther, *The Babylonian Captivity*.

22. *Ibid.*

23. Paul Althaus, *The Theology of Martin Luther* (Minneapolis: Fortress, 1966), p. 369.

24. Bainton, *Here I* Stand, p. 107.

25. *Ibid.*, p. 108.

26. Kittleson, *Luther the Reformer*, p. 152.

27. Estelle Ross, *Martin Luther* (New York: Frederick A. Stokes, 1927), p. 81.

28. *Martin Luther*, p. 253.

29. *Ibid.*, p. 271.

Chapter 11

1. Roland H. Bainton, *Here I Stand: A Life of Martin Luther* (Nashville: Abington, 1950), pp. 122–123.

2. *Ibid.*, p. 130.

3. William Manchester, *A World Lit Only by Fire: The Medieval Mind and the Renaissance* (New York: Little, Brown, 1992), pp. 163–164.

4. Bainton, *Here I Stand*, p. 122.

5. Will Durant, *The Reformation: A History of European Civilization from Wycliffe to Calvin, 1300–1564* (New York: Simon & Schuster, 1957), pp. 355–356.

6. Martin Brecht, *Martin Luther: Shaping and Defining the Reformation 1521–1546* (Minneapolis: Fortress, 1990), p. 404.

7. Arthur Cushman McGiffert, *Martin Luther: The Man and His Work* (New York: Century, 1917), p. 187.

8. Preserved Smith, *The Life and Letters of Martin Luther* (Boston: Houghton Mifflin, 1911), p. 100.

9. *Ibid.*

10. McGiffert, *Luther: The Man and His Work*, p. 189.

11. Bainton, *Here I Stand*, p. 128.

12. Papal Encyclicals Online. "The Bull *'Decet Romanum Pontificem'*—Leo X Excommunicates Martin Luther—Rome, 1521 January 3rd."

13. McGiffert, *Luther: The Man and His Work*, pp. 129–130.

14. Durant, *The Reformation*, p. 357.

15. Richard Marius, *Martin Luther; The Christian Between God and Death* (Cambridge: The Belknap Press of Harvard University Press, 1999), p. 276.

16. Bainton, *Here I Stand*, p. 134.

17. *Ibid.*, p. 169.

18. *Ibid.*, p. 195.

19. McGiffert, *Luther*, p. 194.

20. Harold J. Grimm, *The Reformation Era 1500–1650*, 2d ed. (New York: Macmillan, 1973), p. 112.

21. Bainton, *Here I Stand*, p. 136.

22. V.H.H. Green, *Luther and the Reformation* (New York: Mentor, 1974), p. 94.

23. Bainton, *Here I Stand*, p. 139.

24. Brecht, *Martin Luther*, p. 448.

25. Estelle Ross, *Martin Luther* (New York: Frederick J. Stokes, 1927), p. 89.

26. Jean Marie Vincent Audin, *History of the Life, Writings & Doctrines of Luther* (London: C. Dolman, 1854), p. 304.

27. Marius, *Martin Luther*, p. 288.

28. Bainton, *Here I Stand*, p. 139.

29. Brecht, *Martin Luther*, p. 449.

30. Audin, *A History of the Life, Writing & Doctrines of Luther*, p. 303.

31. Brecht, *Martin Luther*, p. 450.

32. Marius, *Martin Luther*, p. 289.

33. McGiffert, *Luther*, p. 198.

34. Martin Luther, *The Life of Luther, Written by Himself* (London: Bell & Daldy, 1872), p. 86.

35. Manchester, *A World Lit Only by Fire*, p. 172.

36. Green, *Luther and the Reformation*, pp. 95–96.

37. Bainton, *Here I Stand*, p. 141.

38. De LaMar Jensen, *Confrontation at Worms: Martin Luther and the Diet of Worms* (Provo: Brigham Young University Press, 1973), p. 46.

39. Marius, *Martin Luther*, p. 290.

40. Jensen, *Confrontation at Worms*, p. 47.

41. *Ibid.*, p. 50.

42. Marius, *Martin Luther*, p. 290.

43. Smith, *The Life and Letters of Martin Luther*, p. 37; and Marius, *Martin Luther*, p. 290.

44. Smith, *The Life and Letters of Martin Luther*, p. 115.

45. Jensen, *Confrontation at Worms*, p. 50.

46. *Ibid.*

47. Manchester, *A World Lit Only by Fire*, p. 172.

48. Jensen, *Confrontation at Worms*, pp. 50–51.

49. Jensen, *Confrontation at Worms*, pp. 51–52; and Green, *Martin Luther*, pp. 97–98.

50. Smith, *The Life and Letters of Martin Luther*, p. 117.

51. Durant, *The Reformation*, p. 361; and Bainton, *Here I Stand*, pp. 143–144.

52. *Ibid.* Note that Luther's phrase "without horns" meant without any sophistic reservation.

53. Jensen, *Confrontation at Worms,* p. 56.

54. Durant, *The Reformation,* p. 361.

55. Green, *Luther and the Reformation,* p. 99.

56. Ross, *Martin Luther,* p. 94.

57. Marius, *Martin Luther,* p. 294.

58. Green, *Luther and the Reformation,* p. 101.

59. Bainton, *Here I Stand,* p. 147.

60. Julius Kostlin, *Life of Luther* (New York: Charles Scribner's Sons, 1883), p. 97.

61. *Ibid.*

62. Brecht, *Martin Luther,* p. 472.

63. Smith, *The Life and Letters of Martin Luther,* p. 120.

Chapter 12

1. Roland H. Bainton, *Here I Stand: A Life of Martin Luther* (Nashville: Abington, 1950), p. 145.

2. Martin Brecht, *Martin Luther: His Road to Reformation 1483–1521* (Minneapolis: Fortress, 1990), pp. 473–474, and Bainton, *Here I Stand,* p. 147.

3. De Lamar Jensen, *Confrontation at Worms* (Provo: Brigham Young University Press, 1973), p. 103.

4. Bainton, *Here I Stand,* p. 147.

5. Preserved Smith, *The Life and Letters of Martin Luther* (Boston: Houghton Mifflin, 1911), p. 119.

6. Estelle Ross, *Martin Luther* (New York: Frederick A. Stokes, 1927), p. 96; and Arthur Cushman McGiffert, *Martin Luther: The Man and His Work* (New York: Century, 1917), p. 217.

7. McGiffert, *Martin Luther,* p. 218.

8. Smith, *The Life and Letters of Martin Luther,* p. 122.

9. Bainton, *Here I Stand,* p. 151.

10. McGiffert, *Martin Luther,* p. 214.

11. Richard Marius, *Martin Luther: The Christian Between God and Death* (Cambridge: The Belknap Press of Harvard University Press), p. 299.

12. Bainton, *Here I Stand,* p. 151.

13. Marius, *Martin Luther,* p. 297.

14. James M. Kittleson, *Luther the Reformer* (Minneapolis: Fortress, 2003), p. 165.

15. H.V.V. Green, *Luther and the Reformation* (New York: Mentor, 1974), p. 110.

16. Smith, *The Life and Letters of Martin Luther,* p. 132.

17. Will Durant, *The Reformation: A History of European Civilization from Wycliffe to Calvin, 1300–1564* (New York: Simon & Schuster, 1957), p. 365.

18. Harold J. Grimm, *Reformation Era, 1500–1650* (New York: Macmillan, 1974), p. 121.

19. Green, *Luther and the Reformation,* p. 104.

20. Smith, *the Life and Letters of Martin Luther,* p. 120.

Chapter 13

1. Julius Kostlin, *Life of Luther* (New York: Charles Scribner's Sons, 1883), p. 100.

2. Geoffrey Rudolph Elton. *The New Cambridge Modern History: Volume 2, The Reformation, 1520–1559* (Cambridge: Cambridge University Press, 1990), 69.

3. Will Durant. *The Reformation: A History of European Civilization from Wycliffe to Calvin, 1300–1564* (New York: Simon & Schuster, 1957), p. 364.

4. Mark U. Edwards. *Luther and the False Brethren* (Palo Alto: Stanford University Press, 1975), p. 8.

5. James M. Kittleson. *Luther the Reformer* (Minneapolis: Augsburg, 1986), p. 173.

6. Ronald J. Sider. *Andreas Bodenstein Von Karlstadt:*

The Development of His Thought, 1517–1525 (Leiden: E.J. Brill, 1974), p. 160.

7. *Ibid.*

8. Bainton, *Here I Stand,* p. 155.

9. Durant, *The Reformation,* p. 364; and Bainton, *Here I Stand,* p. 155.

10. Bainton, *Here I Stand,* p. 156.

11. Richard Marius, *Martin Luther: The Christian Between God and Death* (Cambridge: The Belknap Press of Harvard University Press, 1999), p. 319.

12. Bainton, *Her I Stand,* pp. 160–161.

13. *Ibid.,* p. 162.

14. V.H.H. Green. *Luther and the Reformation* (New York: Capricorn, 1964), p. 104.

15. Bainton, *Here I Stand,* p. 155.

16. Henry Eyster Jacobs, *Works of Luther* (Philadelphia: A.J. Holman, 1915), p. 92.

17. Martin Luther, *A Sincere Admonition to All Christians to Guard Against Insurrection and Rebellion,* pp. 62–63.

18. M. Michelet, *Martin Luther Gathered from His Own Writings* (New York: A.A. Kelley, 1859), p. 262.

19. R. Weiser. *Luther By A Lutheran* (Baltimore: T. Newton Kurtz, 1830), cclix.

20. Julius Kostlin, *Life of Luther,* p. 105; and Marius, *Martin Luther,* p. 320.

21. Preserved Smith, *The Life and Letters of Martin Luther* (Boston: Houghton Mifflin, 1911), pp. 92–93.

22. Kostlin, *Life of Luther,* pp. 99–100.

23. Helmut T. Lehmann, editor, *Luther's Work* (Philadelphia: Fortress, 1955), vol. 48, p. 391.

24. Bainton, *Here I Stand,* p. 163.

25. Kittleson, *Luther the Reformer,* p. 182.

26. Philip Schaff, *History of the Christian Church, Volume VII, Modern Christianity: The German Reformation* (New York: Charles Scribner's Sons, 1901), p. 889.

27. *Ibid.*

28. Geoffrey Rudolph Elton, *The New Cambridge Modern History: Volume 2, The Reformation, 1520–1559* (Cambridge: Cambridge University Press, 1990), p. 69.

29. Schaff, *History of the Christian Church,* p. 889.

30. Kittleson, *Luther the Reformer,* p. 183.

31. *Ibid.,* p. 184.

32. Durant, *The Reformation,* p. 367.

33. Marius, *Martin Luther,* p. 335.

34. Arthur Cushman McGiffert, *Martin Luther: The Man and His Work* (New York: Century, 1917), p. 244.

35. *Ibid.*

Chapter 14

1. Will Durant, *The Reformation: A History of European Civilization from Wycliffe, to Calvin, 1300–1564* (New York: Simon & Schuster, 1957), p. 368.

2. *Ibid.*

3. John Murray Todd, *Luther: A Life* (New York: Crossroads, 1982), pp. 237–240.

4. *Ibid.,* 240–241.

5. Harry Gerald Haile, *Luther: An Experiment in Biography* (Princeton: Princeton University Press, 1980), p. 331.

6. Luther wrote these words as part of the Preface to his *Small Catechism,* published in 1529. The situation was surely far worse in 1522.

7. Charles Arand, *That I May Be His Own* (St. Louis: Concordia, 2000), p. 68.

8. LW 43:12; WA 10/2:339–406. And see William R. Russell, "Luther, Prayer, and the Reformation" *Word & World,* vol. 22, no. 1 (Winter 2002), pp 49–54.

9. Martin Luther, preface to his *Large Catechism,* 9.

10. Martin Brecht, *Martin Luther: His Road to Reformation 1483–1521* (Minneapolis: Fortress, 1990), p. 121.

11. Todd, *Luther: A Life*, p. 243.

12. Luther, *A Little Prayer Book* (1522).

13. William R. Russell, editor, *Martin Luther, Theologian of the Church: Collected Essays of George W. Forell; Words and Worlds* (St. Paul: Luther Seminary, 1994), p. 52; and Martin Brecht, *Martin Luther: Shaping and Defining the Reformation 1521–1532* (Minneapolis: Fortress, 1990), 120.

14. Martin Luther, *A Little Prayer Book,* preface.

15. *Ibid.*, 50.

16. Martin Luther, *That a Christian Assembly or Congregation Has the Right and Power to Judge All Teaching and to Call, Appoint, and Dismiss Teachers, Established and Proven by Scripture* (1523).

17. Martin Luther, *Against the Spiritual Estate of the Pope and the Bishops Falsely So-Called* (1524); and Todd, *Luther: A Life*, p. 240.

18. Martin Luther, *Letter of Consolation to All Who Suffer Persecution* (1524).

19. Brecht, *Martin Luther*, p. 103.

20. Martin Luther, "A Lovely Hymn About the Two Martyrs of Christ Who Were Burned in Brussels by the Sophists of Louvain" (1524).

21. Brecht, *Martin Luther*, p. 103.

22. Frater Alban Baker, DRNJ, "An Exposition of Luther's Views on Marriage, in Light of Both Their Adherence to and Deviation from the Catholic Faith, p. 4.

23. Martin Luther, *An Exhortation to the Knights of the Teutonic Order* (1525).

24. Martin Luther, *Temporal Authority: To What Extent It Should Be Obeyed; Ordinance of a Common Chest; To the Councilors of All Cities in Germany That They Establish and Maintain Christian Schools* (1525).

25. Martin Luther, "That Jesus Christ Was Born a Jew," translated by Walter I. Brandt, in *Luther's Works* (Philadelphia: Fortress, 1962), pp. 200–201, 229.

26. Russell, *Words and Worlds*, p. 64.

27. Durant, *the Reformation*, p. 368.

28. John A. Hartmann, Yale Divinity School, unpublished paper, "The Use of Propaganda in the Reformation and Counter-Reformation," http://www.people.vcu.edu/~jahartmann/images/Propaganda_in_the_Reformation.pdf; and see R.W. Scribner, "For the Sake of Simple Folk: Popular Propaganda for the German Reformation" (New York, Cambridge University Press), 1981.

29. "How Luther Went Viral: Five Centuries before Facebook and the Arab Spring, Social Media Helped Bring About the Reformation," *The Economist*, Dec. 17, 2011.

30. Hartmann, "The Use of Propaganda in the "Reformation and Counter-Reformation," Appendix.

31. *Ibid.*

32. See Durant, *The Reformation*, p. 368, and History of Information.com, http://www.historyofinformation.com/narrative/how-printing-changed-books.php.

33. Durant, *The Reformation,* 368.

34. *Ibid.*

35. Philip Schaff, *History of the Christian Church* (New York: Charles Scribner's Sons, 1910), vol. VII, ch. 4, sec. 62.

36. James M. Kittelson, *Luther the Reformer: The Story of the Man and His Career* (Minneapolis: Fortress, 2003), p. 175.

37. *Ibid.*

38. Martin Brecht, *Shaping and Transforming the Reformation 1521–1532* (Minneapolis. Fortress, 1990), p. 46.

39. Schaff, *History of the Christian Church*, p. 64.

40. Martin Luther, *Luther's Works, vol. 35: Word and Sacrament I* (Philadelphia: Fortress, 1994).

41. Ewald M. Plass, *This Is Luther: A Character Study* (St. Louis: Concordia, 1948).

42. Russell, *Worlds and Worlds*, p. 66.

43. Martin Luther, *An Open Letter on Translating* (1530).

44. Bainton, *Here I Stand*, p. 255.

45. Smith, *The Life and Letters of Martin Luther*, p. 264.

Chapter 15

1. Martin Brecht, *Martin Luther: Shaping and Defining the Reformation, 1521–1532* (Minneapolis: Fortress, 1990), p. 98.

2. Trevor O'Reggio, "Martin Luther on Marriage and Family" *History Research* 2.3 (2012): 195–218., pp. 1–2.

3. Martin Luther, *Table Talk*, 1659 and 4153.

4. Brecht, *Martin Luther*, p. 99.

5. Gerhard Brendler, *Martin Luther, Theology and Revolution* (New York: Oxford University Press, 1991), p. 302.

6. Bainton, *Here I Stand: A Life of Martin Luther* (Nashville: Abington, 1950), p. 223.

7. Preserved Smith, *The Life and Letters of Martin Luther* (Boston: Houghton Mifflin, 1911), p. 170.

8. Richard Marius, *Martin Luther: The Christian Between God and Death* (Cambridge: The Belknap Press of the Harvard University Press), p. 437.

9. John Parker Lawson, Translator, *The Autobiography of Martin Luther* (Edinburgh: Edinburgh Printing and Publishing, 1836), p. 259.

10. Marius, *Martin Luther*, p. 437.

11. Julius Kostlin, *The Life of Martin Luther* (Philadelphia: Lutheran Publication Society, 1883), p. 132.

12. Brendler, *Martin Luther, Theology and Revolution*, p. 304.

13. Luther always spoke affectionately of Katherine as "Kate" or "Kathe." The "e" is not silent in German, but is unaccented and has the sound of the "e" in the word "the." Many translate this as "Katy," but we have chosen "Kate" as just as accurate and more endearing, to reflect Luther's feelings toward his wife.

14. Brendler, *Martin Luther, Theology and Revolution*, p. 305.

15. *Ibid.*

16. O'Reggio, "Martin Luther on Marriage and Family," p. 198.

17. *Ibid.*

Chapter 16

1. V.H.H. Green, *Luther and the Reformation* (New York: Mentor), p. 13.

2. Will Durant, *The Reformation: A History of European Civilization from Wycliffe to Calvin, 1300–1564* (New York: Simon & Schuster, 1957), pp. 383–384.

3. Durant, *The Reformation*, p. 384; and see Igor Shafarevich, *The Socialist Phenomenon* (New York: Harper & Row, 1980), p. 57.

4. Green, *Luther and the Reformation*, p. 32.

5. *Ibid.*, pp. 136–137.

6. Durant, *The Reformation*, p. 386.

7. *Ibid.*, p. 387.

8. Jams M. Kittelson, *Luther The Reformer: The Story of the Man and His Career* (Minneapolis: Fortress, 2003), p. 191.

9. Durant, *The Reformation*, p. 388; and see generally Douglas Miller, *Armies of the German Peasants' War, 1524–26* (Oxford: Osprey, 2003).

10. Durant, *The Reformation*, p. 390.

11. *Ibid.*

12. *Ibid.*

13. Julius Kostlin, *The Life of Martin Luther* (Philadelphia: Lutheran Publication Society, 1883), p. 132.

14. Richard Marius, *Martin Luther: The Christian Between God and Death* (Cambridge: The Belknap Press of the Harvard University Press, 1999), p. 42.

15. Preserved Smith, *The Life and Letters of Martin Luther* (Boston: Houghton Mifflin), p. 160.

16. Richard Marius, *Martin Luther*, p. 428.

17. *Ibid.*

18. Kostlin, *The Life of Martin Luther*, p. 128.

19. Durant, *The Reformation*, p. 391.

20. W.V.H. Green, *Luther and the Reformation*, p. 139.

21. Kittelson, *Luther the Reformer*, p. 192.

22. Marius, *Martin Luther*, p. 433.

23. *Ibid.*

Chapter 17

1. James Aitken Wylie, *The History of Protestantism* (London: Cassell, Petter & Galpin, 1980), book 1, p. 533; and see J.A. Wylie, "Martin Luther and Church Organization," *LandMarks Magazine*, October 1995.

2. Kittelson, *Luther the Reformer: The Story of the Man and His Career* (Minneapolis: Fortress, 2003), p. 216.

3. Martin Marty, *Martin Luther* (New York: Penguin, 2004), p. 117.

4. Preserved Smith, *The Life and Letters of Martin Luther* (Boston: Houghton Mifflin), p. 184.

5. See Jaroslav Pelikan, editor, *Luther's Works, vol. 15: Ecclesiastes, Song of Solomon, and the Last Word* (St. Louis: Concordia), 1972.

6. Smith, *The Life and Letters of Martin Luther*, p. 185.

7. Kittelson, *Luther the Redeemer*, p. 248.

8. Smith, *The Life and Letters of Martin Luther*, p. 186.

9. William Henry Lazareth, *Luther, the Bible, and Social Ethics* (Minneapolis: Augsburg Fortress, 2001), p. 171.

10. Kittelson, *Luther the Reformer*, p. 243.

11. *Ibid.*, pp. 243–244.

12. Smith, *The Life and Letters of Martin Luther*, p. 187.

13. Kittelson, *Luther the Reformer*, pp. 248–249.

14. Terrence M. Reynolds, "Was Erasmus Responsible for Luther? A Study of the Relationship of the Two Reformers and Their Clash over the Question of the Will," *Concordia Theological Journal* (1977), p. 2; Reynolds references Arthur Robert Pennington, "The Life of Character of Erasmus," 1875, p. 219.

15. *Ibid.*

16. Richard Marius, *Martin Luther: The Christian Between God and Death* (Cambridge: The Belknap Press of the Harvard University Press, 1999), p. 442.

17. Lee Gatiss, "The Manifesto of the Reformation—Luther vs. Erasmus on Free Will," *Churchman* 123:3 (2009), pp. 203–225.

18. Marty, *Martin Luther*, p. 128.

19. Martin Luther, *The Bondage of the Will*, p. 112.

20. *Ibid.*

21. Gatiss, "The Manifesto of the Reformation," p. 216; and T. George, *The Theology of the Reformers* (Leicester: Apollos, 1988), p. 77.

22. Marty, *Martin Luther*, p. 130.

23. *Ibid.*, p. 133.

24. Gatiss, "The Manifesto of the Reformation," p. 203; and B.B. Warfield, "The Theology of the Reformation" in *Studies in Theology: The Works of Benjamin B. Warfield*, vol. 9 (Grand Rapids, MI: Baker, 2003 [1932]), p. 471.

25. Marty, *Martin Luther*, p. 141.

26. *Ibid.*, p. 142.

27. *Ibid.*

28. Holy Bible, Matthew 28: 19.

29. Friedrich Bente, *Historical Introductions to the Lutheran Confessions: As Contained in the Book of Concord of 1580* (St. Louis: Concordia, 2005), p. 156.

30. For example, in his *Small Catechism*, Luther's explanation of the Apostles' Creed, since the fourth century the basic statement of Christian belief in the Holy Trinity, begins this way:

The First Article (of Creation).
I believe in God the Father Almighty, Maker of heaven and earth.
What does this mean?
I believe that God has made me and all creatures; that He has given me my body and soul, eyes, ears, and all my limbs, my reason, and all my senses, and still preserves them; in addition thereto, clothing and shoes, meat and drink, house and homestead, wife and children, fields, cattle, and all my goods; that He provides me richly and daily with all that I need to support this body and life, protects me from all danger, and guards me and preserves me from all evil; and all this out of pure, fatherly, divine goodness and mercy, without any merit or worthiness in me; for all which I owe it to Him to thank, praise, serve, and obey Him. This is most certainly true.

31. Luther's outline of service:
Spiritual Song or Psalm.
Kyrie Eleison ("Lord, have mercy." From I Chronicles 16:34: "Give thanks to the LORD; for he is good; for his mercy endures forever.").
Prayer (collect).
Epistle (a reading of a portion of one of the letters of the Apostles).
Choir hymn.
Gospel (a reading from one of the Gospel accounts of the life and times of Christ).
Nicene Creed (the profession of faith in the Holy Trinity, the basis for Christianity).
Sermon (corresponding with the Gospel).
Lord's Prayer.
Exhortation to communicants.
Words of institution.
Distribution of bread (body) and wine (blood).
Thanksgiving collect.
Salutation ("The Lord be with you") and Benediction ("Go in peace)."

32. William Johnston, "Music History: Martin Luther, the German Reformation, and Their Impact on Sacred Music," https://www.manystrands.com, December 13, 2009.

33. Bainton, *Here I Stand*, pp. 266–267.

34. For example, Luther's first hymn, "Flung to the Heedless Winds," was written as a commemoration of the martyrdom of two young Lutheran monks who were burned at the stake in a Brussels marketplace. Catholics spread the false story that the two men had recanted their Protestant views before they died, and Luther wanted to tell the truth in his hymn. This work was written in folk song style, and minstrels regularly performed it as they traveled around Germany in the first years of the Reformation. One of Luther's three Christmas hymns, "All Praise to Thee, Eternal God," was written and published in 1523. It was used by Johan Sebastian Bach in his Christmas Day *Choralkantate* (Bach utilized Luther's work on several occasions). "We All Believe in One True God" expresses Luther's firm conviction in the family, or community, of Christians. Based on the words of the Nicene Creed, this Trinitarian hymn sets forth the meaning of each part of Luther's catechisms. Luther meant for families to sing together as they studied the Bible and catechism in their homes, and it became a popular church song, as well. "That Man a Godly Life Might

Live" was a tribute to the Ten Commandments, while "May God Bestow on Us His Grace" was the first missionary hymn of the Reformation. "Christ, Our Lord, Came to the Jordan" was written to commemorate the feast day of John the Baptist. One of Luther's finest works, "Our Father, Thou in Heaven Above," reinforces the simple majesty of the Lord's Prayer.

Chapter 18

1. John Murray Todd, *Luther: A Life* (New York: Crossroad, 1982), p. 300.

2. Martin Brecht, *Martin Luther: Shaping and Defining the Reformation 1521–1532* (Minneapolis: Fortress, 1990), p. 371.

3. *Ibid.,* p. 372.

4. Estelle Ross, *Martin Luther* (New York: Frederick A. Stokes, 1927), pp. 152–153.

5. Brecht, *Martin Luther,* pp. 374–375.

6. *Ibid.,* p. 378.

7. Arthur Cushman McGiffert, *Martin Luther: The Man and his Work* (New York: Century, 1917), p. 340.

8. Holy Bible, Matthew 16: 18, 19.

9. Todd, *Luther,* p. 314.

10. *Ibid.,* p. 315.

11. *Ibid.,* p. 318.

12. *Ibid.,* pp. 320–321.

13. Brecht, *Martin Luther,* p. 410.

14. Philip Hughes, *A Popular History of the Reformation* (Garden City, NY: Image, 1957), p. 132.

15. Martin Brecht, *Martin Luther: The Preservation of the Church 1532–1546* (Minneapolis: Fortress, 1993), pp. 17–18.

16. Roland H. Bainton, *Women of the Reformation, in Germany and Italy* (Minneapolis: Augsburg, 1971), p. 36.

17. Henry Jacobs Eyster, *Martin Luther* (New York: Columbia University Press, 1957), p. 276.

18. Roland H. Bainton, *Here I Stand: A Life of Martin Luther* (Nashville: Abington, 1950), p. 237.

19. Bainton, *Women of the Reformation,* p. 34.

20. William Henry Lazareth, *Luther on the Christian Home: An Application of the Social Ethics of the Reformation* (Philadelphia: Muhlenberg, 1960), p. 138.

21. Ewald M. Plass, *This Is Luther: A Character Study* (St. Louis: Concordia, 1948), p. 258.

22. Schwiebert, E.G., *Luther and His Times* (St. Louis: Concordia, 1950), p. 593.

23. Lazareth, p. 220.

24. Plass, *This Is Luther,* p. 421.

25. Preserved Smith, *The Life and Letters of Martin Luther* (Boston: Houghton Mifflin, 1911), p. 317.

26. Letter of George Held to Count George of Anhalt, February 23, 1562, in Theodor Kolde, *Analecta Lutherana* (Gotha: F.A. Perthes, 1883), p. 378; and quoted in Helmut T. Lehmann and Theodore C. Tappert, general editors, *Luther's Works, Volume 54, Table Talk* (Philadelphia: Fortress, 1967).

27. Brecht, *Martin Luther,* p. 8.

28. *Ibid.,* p. 7.

29. Lehmann and Tappert, general editors, *Luther's Works, Volume 54, Table Talk.*

30. Some excerpts from *Table Talk:*

Biblical scholarship: "I did not learn my divinity at one only time, but I was constrained to search deeper and deeper, to which my temptations brought me; for no man, without trials and temptations, can attain to the true understanding of the Holy Scriptures. St. Paul had a devil that beat him with fists, and with temptations drove him dili-

gently to study the Holy Scripture. I, said Luther, had cleaving and hanging on my neck the Pope, the Universities, all the deep-learned, and with them the devil himself; these hunted me into the Bible, where I diligently read, and thereby, God be praised, at length I attained to the true understanding of the same."

The Trinity: "And truly we find and see printed the Holy Trinity in all good arts and creatures, as the almighty power of God the Father, the wisdom of God the Son, and the goodness of God the Holy Ghost. Neither can we conceive or know how the apple of the eye doth see, or how understanding words are spoken distinctly and plainly when only the tongue is moved and stirred in the mouth, all which are natural things, as we daily see and act. How then should we be able to comprehend or understand the secret counsel of God's Majesty, or search it out with our sense, wit, reason, or understanding?"

God's power and creation: "God's power is great, who holdeth and nourisheth the whole world, and maintaineth it; and it is a hard article where we say and acknowledge, 'I believe in God the Father.' He hath created all things sufficiently for us. All the seas are our cellars, all woods are our huntings; the earth is full of silver and gold, and of innumerable fruits, which are created all for our sakes, and the earth is a corn-house and a larder for us, etc…. Thus goeth it always with God's power in our weakness; for when he is weakest in us, then is he strongest."

Faith and action: "Believest thou? Then thou wilt speak boldly. Speakest thou boldly? Then thou must suffer. Sufferest thou? Then thou shalt be comforted. For, said Luther, faith, the confession thereof, and the cross do follow one after another."

Satan's works: "The greatest punishment God can afflict on the wicked, is when the church, to chastise them, delivers them over to Satan, who, with God's permission, kills them, or makes them undergo great calamities. Many devils are in woods, in waters, in wildernesses, and in dark pooly places, ready to hurt and prejudice people; some are also in the thick black clouds, which cause hail, lightnings, and thunderings, and poison the air, the pastures and grounds. When these things happen, then the philosophers and physicians say, it is natural, ascribing it to the planets, and showing I know not what reasons for such misfortunes and plagues as ensue."

The antichrist: "Antichrist is the pope and the Turk together; a beast full of life must have a body and soul; the spirit or soul of antichrist is the pope, his flesh or body the Turk. The latter wastes and assails and persecutes God's church corporally; the former spiritually and corporally too, with hanging, burning, murdering, etc. But, as in the apostle's time, the church had the victory over the Jews and Romans, so now will she keep the field firm and solid against the hypocrisy and idolatry of the pope, and the tyranny and devastations of the Turk and her other enemies."

The Pope: "Kings and princes coin money only out of metals, but the pope coins money out of everything—indulgences, ceremonies, dispensations, pardons; 'tis all fish comes to his net. 'Tis only baptism escapes him, for children came into the world without clothes to be stolen, or teeth to be drawn… The chief cause that I fell out with the pope was this: the pope boasted that he was the head of the church, and condemned all that would not be under his power and authority; for he said, although Christ be the Head of the church, yet, notwithstanding, there must be a corporal head of the church upon earth. With this I could have been content, had he but taught the Gospel pure and clear, and not introduced human inventions and lies in its stead. Further, he took upon him power, rule, and authority over the Christian church, and over the Holy Scriptures, the Word of God; no man must presume to expound the Scriptures, but only he, and according to his ridiculous conceits; so that he made himself lord over the church, proclaiming her at the same time a powerful mother, and empress over the Scriptures, to which we must yield and be obedient; this was not to be endured. They who, against God's Word, boast of the church's authority, are mere idiots. The pope attributes more power to the church, which is begotten and born, than to the Word, which has begotten, conceived, and borne the church."

Christian living: "A householder instructs his servants and family in this manner: Deal uprightly and honestly, be diligent in that which I command you, and ye may then eat, drink, and clothe yourselves as ye please. Even so, our Lord God regards not what we eat, drink, or how we clothe ourselves; all such matters, being ceremonies or middle things, he leaves freely to us, on the understanding, however, that we ground nothing thereon as being necessary to salvation."

Government: "Germany is like a brave and gallant horse, highly fed, but without a good rider; as the horse runs here and there, astray, unless he have a rider to rule him, so Germany is also a powerful, rich, and brave country, but needs a good head and governor… God placeth his highest office very wonderfully; he commits it to preachers that are poor sinners and beggars, who do utter and teach it, and very weakly do thereafter, or live according to the same."

Music: "I always loved music; whoso has skill in this art, is of a good temperament, fitted for all things. We must teach music in schools; a schoolmaster ought to have skill in music, or I would not regard him; neither should we ordain young men as preachers, unless they have been well exercised in music."

Rest: "Sleep is a most useful and most salutary operation of nature. Scarcely any minor annoyance angers me more than the being suddenly awakened out of a pleasant slumber. I understand that in Italy they torture poor people by depriving them of sleep. 'Tis a torture that cannot long be endured."

Man and God: "There are three sorts of people: the first, the common sort, who live secure without remorse of conscience, acknowledging not their corrupt manners and natures, insensible of God's wrath, against their sins, and careless thereof. The second, those who through the law are scared, feel God's anger, and strive and wrestle with despair. The third, those that acknowledge their sins and God's merited wrath, feel themselves conceived and born in sin, and therefore deserving of perdition, but, notwithstanding, attentively hearken to the gospel, and believe that God, out of grace, for the sake of Jesus Christ, forgives sins, and so are justified before God, and afterwards show the fruits of their faith by all manner of good works."

Chapter 19

1. James M. Kittelson, *Luther the Reformer: The Story of the Man and His Career* (Minneapolis: Fortress, 2003), p. 270.

2. Martin Brecht, *Martin Luther: The Preservation of the Church 1532–1536* (Minneapolis: Fortress, 1993), p. 180.

3. Friedrich Bente, *Historical Introductions to the Symbolical Books of the Evangelical Lutheran Church* (N.p.: Quality Classics, 2010), p. 61.

4. Brecht, *Martin Luther,* p. 175.

5. Julius Kostlin, *The Life of Martin Luther* (Philadelphia: Lutheran Publication Society, 1883), pp. 455, 477.

6. Brecht, *Martin Luther,* p. 176.

7. Martin Marty, *Martin Luther* (New York: Penguin, 1994), Preface.

8. Brecht, *Martin Luther,* p. 182.

9. *Ibid.,* p. 183.

10. *Ibid.,* p. 185.

11. Wilhelm Rein, *The Life of Martin Luther* (New York: Funk & Wagnall's, 1883), p. 184.

12. *Ibid.*

13. Brecht, *Martin Luther,* p. 186.

14. *Ibid.,* pp. 186, 187.

15. Martin Luther, *The Life of Luther, Written by Himself* (London: Bell & Daldy, 1872), p. 382.

16. Luther reluctantly approved King Henry's plan to take two wives because, he reasoned, it was important that a male heir carry on the tradition of the Kingdom. He was also concerned that Hesse be able to commune. See John Alfred Faulkner, "Luther and the Bigamous Marriage of Philip of Hesse," *American Journal of Theology,* vol. 17, no. 2 (April 1913), p. 210.

17. Kittelson, *Luther the Reformer,* p. 288.

18. Henry Preserved Smith, *Luther's Correspondence and Other Contemporaneous Letters* (Philadelphia: Lutheran Publication Society, 1913), 1:29.

19. Elliot Rosenberg, *But Were They Good for the Jews?* (New York: Birch Lane, 1997), p. 65.

20. Martin Luther, "That Jesus Christ Was Born a Jew," translated by Walter I. Brandt, in *Luther's Works* (Philadelphia: Fortress, 1962), pp. 200–201, 229. The term "anti-Semitic" was first used in the nineteenth century. A more accurate term for Luther's time might be "anti–Judaic."

21. Heiko Oberman, *Luther: Man Between God and the Devil* (New York: Image, 1918), p. 293.

22. Martin Luther, "Against the Sabbatarians," *Luther Works,* 47:133.

23. See Martin Luther, *On the Jews and Their Lies* (New York: Liberty Bell, 2004).

24. The tract is called *Vom Schem Hamphoras und vom Geschlecht Christi (Of the Unknowable Name and the Generations of Christ).* Many *Judensaus* were scattered across Germany and the rest of Europe in the Middle Ages, and many have been removed or destroyed. It is uncertain why the Wittenberg *Judensau* remains. Beneath the offensive image, however, is a memorial to the victims of the Holocaust wrought by the Nazis in the 1930s and 1940s.

25. Brendler, *Martin Luther,* p. 368.

26. See Martin Luther, *Against the Papacy at Rome, Founded by the Devil.*

27. *Ibid.* Luther, *Against the Papacy in Rome, Founded by the Devil.* For an excellent summary of this aspect of Luther's writings see Danielle Mead Skjelver, "German Hercules: The Impact of Scatology on the Definition of Martin Luther as a Man 1483–1546," University of Maryland, University College, http://www.academia.edu/1016951/German_Hercules_The_Impact_of_Scatology_on_the_Image_of_Martin_Luther_as_a_Man_1483–1546.

28. Smith, *The Life and Letters of Martin Luther,* p. 416.

29. John M. Todd, *Luther: A Life* (New York: Crossroad), p. 349.

30. Smith, *The Life and Letters of Martin Luther,* p. 415.

31. *Ibid.,* p. 417.

32. *Ibid.*

33. Tappert, *Luther's Works, Vol. 51: Sermons I* (Philadelphia: Fortress, 1967).

34. Smith, *The Life and Letters of Martin Luther,* pp. 415–423.

Chapter 20

1. James M. Kittelson, *Luther the Reformer: The Story of the Man and His Career* (Minneapolis: Fortress, 2003), p. 299.

2. Henry Eyster Jacobs, *Martin Luther: The Hero of the Reformation, 1483–1546* (New York: Putnam, 1898), p. 409.

3. Preserved Smith, *The Life and Letters of Martin Luther* (Boston: Houghton Mifflin, 1911), p. 424.

4. Edward Vainio, *Reflections of Pastoral Significance* (New York: Lulu, 2010), p. 58.

5. Carleton A. Toppe, "Luther's Deathbed Confession—the Smalcald Articles," *Wisconsin Lutheran Quarterly*, Winter 1983.

6. Robert Kolb and Charles P. Arand, *The Genius of Luther's Theology: A Wittenberg Way of Thinking for the Contemporary Church* (Grand Rapids, MI: Baker Academic, 2008), p. 16.

7. Thomas Bokenkotter, *A Concise History of the Catholic Church* (New York: Image, 1977), p. 241.

8. Brian Moynihan, *The Faith: A History of Christianity* (New York: Doubleday, 2002), p. 423.

9. "Tridentine" is derived from the Latin *Tridentinus*, "related to the city of Tridentum" (modern-day Trent, Italy. The Tridentine Mass was replaced by the Mass of Paul VI in 1969.

10. There are also an estimated 225 million to 300 million members of the Eastern Orthodox Catholic Church.

11. The largest denomination is the Evangelical Lutheran Church in American, with nearly four million baptized members. The next two largest Lutheran denominations are the Lutheran Church-Missouri Synod and the Wisconsin Evangelical Lutheran Synod. All statistics in this section are from Pew Research Center: Religion & Public Life, www.pesforum.org.

12. Lutherans do not deny the accuracy or truth of the five *Solas*, but emphasize only the first three. Indeed, for many Protestants, the original three *Solas* were increased to five in the twentieth century.

13. Bokenkotter, *A Concise History of the Catholic Church*, p. 208.

14. Heinz Stade and "Thomas A. Seidel, *In the Footsteps of Martin Luther* (Eisenach: Wartburg, 2007), p. 238.

Part Two: Essay 1

1. The German title is *Von den Consiliis und Kirchen*, literally translated, *On the Councils and the Churches*, but *On the Councils and the Church* presents a more accurate reflection of the work's content. This is also the title used in *LW*.

2. Luther, *To the Christian Nobility of the German Nation*, *LW*, 44:156ff.

3. *The Augsburg Confession, CTLC*, p. 54, sentence #21.

4. *Ibid.*, p. 296. This, "The Third Part" of the *Smalcald Articles*, comprises fifteen articles: Sin, The Law, Repentance, The Gospel, Baptism, The Sacrament of the Altar, The Keys, Confession, Excommunication, Ordination and the Call, The Marriage of Priests, The Church, How One Is Justified before God and Does Good Works, Monastic Vows, and Human Traditions.

5. Luther, *On the Councils and the Church, LW*, 41:52.

6. *Ibid.*, p. 123.

7. *Ibid.*

8. *Ibid.*

9. *Ibid.*

10. *Ibid.*, p. 130.

11. *Ibid.*

12. *Ibid.*

13. *Ibid.*

14. *Ibid.*, pp. 130f.

15. *Ibid.*, p. 131.

16. *Ibid.*

17. *Ibid.*, p. 136.

18. *Ibid.*, p. 145.

19. *Ibid.*, p. 166.

20. *Ibid.*, p. 27.

21. On these points, cf. Harold J. Grimm, *The Reforma-tion Era, 1500–1650* (New York: Macmillan, 1954), pp. 396ff.

22. Cf. Will Durant, *The Reformation* (New York: Simon & Schuster, 1957), pp. 931–933. For fuller information on the Council of Trent vis-a-vis Luther's theology, cf. Martin Chemnitz, *The Examination of the Council of Trent*, vols. 1–4 of *Chemnitz's Works* (St. Louis: Concordia, 2007). The published decisions of the Council are in *The Canons and Decrees of the Council of Trent* (Rockford, IL: Tan, 1978).

Essay 2

1. *The Small Catechism, CTLC*, p. 357.

2. Luther, *The Estate of Marriage, LW*, 45:46.

3. Luther, *Table Talk, LW*, 54:431, #5496.

4. *Ibid.*, p. 432, #5497.

5. Luther, *To the Councilmen of All Cities in Germany That They Establish and Maintain Christian Schools, LW*, 45:347–378.

6. Luther, *A Sermon on Keeping Children in School, LW*, 46:207–258.

7. *To the Councilmen*, op. cit., p. 374.

8. *Ibid.*, p. 352.

9. *Ibid.*, pp. 349f.

10. *Ibid.*, p. 357.

11. *Ibid.*, pp. 351f.

12. *Ibid.*, p. 355.

13. *Ibid.*

14. *Ibid.*, p. 368.

15. *Ibid.*

16. *Ibid.*, p. 358. Luther's praise for the study of foreign languages continues for several pages.

17. *Ibid.*, p. 369.

18. *Ibid.*, p. 373.

19. *A Sermon on Keeping*, op. cit., p. 232.

20. *Ibid.*, p. 251.

21. Cf. Edward M. Plass, *This Is Luther* (St. Louis: Concordia, 1948), p. 259 and Rudolf Markwald and Marilynn Markwald, *Katharina Von Bora* (St. Louis: Concordia, 2002), p. 194.

Essay 3

1. *WLS*, p. 964, entry #3034, translated from Weimar edition, 38:143.

2. John Nathin, *Luther* (Berlin:1903), I: 55 as referenced in *WLS*, 964n.

3. Luther, Letter to John Lang, October 26, 1516, *LW*, 48:27f.

4. Luther, Letter to Cardinal Albrech, December 1, 1521, *LW*, 48:346.

5. *The Smalcald Articles, CTLC*, pp. 309f.

6. Luther, *Lectures on Galatians* (1535), *LW*, 27:13; cf. also Luther, *Sermons on the Gospel of St. John, LW*, 22:360.

7. Exposition of Matthew 5:6 (1532), *WLS*, #3038.

8. Luther, *Sermons*, The Gospel for the Early Christmas Service, Luke 2, *LW*, 52:37.

9. *WLS*, #3052.

10. *WLS*, #3041—Table Talks, #578.

11. Luther, *Lectures on Genesis, LW*, 3:204.

12. Luther, *The Judgment of Martin Luther on Monastic Vows, LW*, 44:376. Cf. also the section on celibacy in the essay "Luther on Marriage, Celibacy and His Dear Kate" in this volume.

13. *The Smalcald Articles, CTLC*, p. 293; Part II, Article III.

Essay 4

1. The heresy is named after Pelagius, a British or Irish monk who lived c. AD 354—c. 420. He was expelled c. 418.

2. Luther, *Lectures on Romans, LW,* 25:192.
3. *Ibid.,* pp. 171ff., 469ff.
4. *WLS,* #3131.
5. Luther, *Lectures on Galatians* (1519), *LW,* 27:176f.
6. *Ibid.,* pp. 183f.
7. *Ibid.,* p. 221.
8. *Ibid.,* p. 225.
9. *Ibid.,* p. 232.
10. *Ibid.,* pp. 278f.
11. *Ibid.,* p. 408.
12. Luther, *Prefaces to the New Testament, LW,* 35:365.
13. *Ibid.,* p. 366.
14. *Ibid.*
15. *Ibid.,* pp. 366f.
16. *Ibid.,* p. 367.
17. *Ibid.,* p. 368.
18. *Ibid.*
19. *Ibid.*
20. *Ibid.,* pp. 368f.
21. *Ibid.,* p. 369.
22. *Ibid.,* p. 370.
23. *Ibid.*
24. *Ibid.,* p. 371.
25. Luther, *Lectures on Galatians* (1935), *LW,* 26:4f.
26. *Ibid.,* p. 11.

Essay 5

1. Luther, Letter to Elector Frederick, January 5 or 6, 1519, *LW,* 48:98. The "little book" referred to is a pamphlet which Luther later published in February of 1519. It was titled, "Doctor Martin Luther's Instruction on Several Articles which are Ascribed and Assigned to Him by His Detractors."
2. Mark 1:4 (NIV).
3. Acts 2:38 (NIV).
4. 2 Samuel 12:13 (NIV).
5. cf. Joel 2:13, Mark 7:6, Luke 18:9–14.
6. Matthew 3:8, Luke 3:8 (NIV).
7. 2 Samuel 12:13–14 (NIV).
8. Luther, *Against Hanswurst, LW,* 41:232.
9. Martin Brecht, *Martin Luther: His Road to Reformation, 1483–1521,* translated by James L. Schaff (Minneapolis: Fortress, 1985), 186.
10. *Against Hanswurst,* op. cit., p. 232.
11. Luther, *Explanations of the Ninety-Five Theses, LW,* 31:84f.
12. *Ibid.,* pp. 97f.
13. *Ibid.,* pp. 100ff.
14. *Ibid.,* pp. 107ff.
15. *Ibid.,* pp. 119ff.
16. *Ibid.,* pp. 179ff.
17. *Ibid.,* pp. 199ff.
18. Luther, *Lectures on Genesis, LW,* 8:316. In 1517 and for several years thereafter, Luther accepted the existence of purgatory, but his view gradually changed. In 1545 in the reference cited, he called it a "lie of the devil, in order that the papists may have some market days and snares for catching money."
19. Luther, *The Small Catechism, CTLC,* p. 368.
20. Luther, *The Large Catechism, CTLC,* p. 468.

Essay 6

1. We have seen from the previous essays that Luther was gifted as a biblical scholar and as a theologian. We have also seen that he was extremely courageous. But it took more than this for him to become a renowned Reformer and noted celebrity within three years of the posting of the

Ninety-Five Theses and well before he was forty. One of those features, which we will witness over and again in these essays, is his extraordinary skill as a polemical writer. He could make his arguments clearly, forcefully, and in a way that forced reaction—either agreement or disagreement. In this essay we can see that skill in his critique of the papacy. Cf. the last note of this essay for further treatment of this topic.
2. *WLS,* p. 1006 (#3190).
3. *Ibid.*
4. *Ibid.*
5. Luther, *On the Papacy in Rome, Against the Most Celebrated Romanist in Leipzig, LW,* 39:101.
6. Luther, *To the Christian Nobility of the German Nation, LW,* 44:126.
7. *Ibid.,* pp. 127f. and 135f.
8. *Ibid.,* pp. 131ff.
9. *Ibid.,* pp. 133–136.
10. *Ibid.,* pp. 136ff.
11. *Ibid.,* pp. 156ff.
12. *The Smalcald Articles, CTLC,* p. 294.
13. Luther probably meant the first five or more centuries of the Church's existence.
14. *Ibid.*
15. *Ibid.,* p. 295.
16. *Ibid.,* pp. 295f.
17. *Ibid.,* p. 296.
18. It was mentioned at the outset of this essay that Luther was a powerful polemical writer. His success as one who wrote public documents attacking his opponents and arguing for his positions was vital for the rapid, effective development of the Reformation. It is, perhaps, not too much to say that his polemics outflanked and defeated those of his opponents virtually every step of the way.
In his polemics, Luther demonstrated the following:
• He made his points on the basis of Scriptural support and the implications of the Gospel itself.
• This foundation gave him the confidence to make them with uncommon force.
• He had nothing to hide; there was no fear in him that he had to keep his weak points or failings hidden.
• He had great confidence in the common man to understand his points and to see the truth.
• He could make his arguments either in the language of academia or in the language of the people, both in terms of German and of "salty" wording, and he *did* make his points both in academic format and in the "people's language."
• He was able to catch the support and enthusiasm of the huge numbers of people who felt oppressed and put upon by the Church.
• He was brilliant in exposing the flaws and weaknesses of the opposition.
• He was familiar with a broad range of topics and could make use of this extensive knowledge in his writings.
• He was able to arouse his followers and wear down the opposition with strong language, repetition, and lengthy presentations..
Luther was a master at winning "the public" through his powerful polemics.

Essay 7

1. Luther, *Heidelberg Disputation, LW* 31:39.
2. *Ibid.,* p. 40.
3. *Ibid.,* p. 41. Luther went on in subsequent theses to claim superiority of several Greek philosophers over Aristotle. He mentions Plato, Pythagoras, Parmenides, and Anaxagoras.
4. *Ibid.*

5. *Ibid.*, p. 52.
6. *Ibid.*, p. 40.
7. *Ibid.*, pp. 52f.
8. *Ibid.*, p. 40.
9. *Ibid.*, p. 53.
10. *Ibid.*, pp. 40f.
11. *Ibid.*, p. 41.
12. *Ibid.*
13. *Ibid.*
14. Luther, *Explanations of the Ninety-Five Theses, LW,* 31:225.
15. Luther, *Two Kinds of Righteousness, LW,* 31:299.
16. *Ibid.*, p. 303. Luther assumed that the woman in the account was Mary Magdalene, but that is not in the text.
17. *Ibid.* In this quotation, Luther called Simon "the leper" thinking that he was the same Simon as in Mark 14 and Matthew 26.
18. *Heidelberg*, op.cit. p. 55.
19. Luther, *The Small Catechism, CTLC,* p. 355.
20. *Ibid.*, p. 356.

Essay 8

1. Luther, *Disputation Against Scholastic Theology, LW,* 31:12. Luther was becoming a controversial figure even before October 31, 1517.
2. Luther, *Heidelberg Disputation, LW,* 31:41.
3. *Ibid.*
4. *Ibid.*, p. 9.
5. The University existed as an independent institution until 1817, when it was combined with the University of Halle. The main campus of what is now called the Martin Luther University of Halle-Wittenberg is in Halle, but it maintains a conference center in Wittenberg.
6. It should be added that Luther trusted reasonable argumentation to make his points, as did the scholastics, but he sought never to allow human reason to undercut anything taught in Scripture. Reason was a gift of God that should be used, but it should be used *in service of* the teachings of Scripture.
7. Luther, *Sermons, "The Gospel for the Main Christmas Service, John 2," LW,* 52:82.

Essay 9

1. The claim that Luther posted the Ninety-Five Theses on the Castle Church door on October 31, 1517, has been called into question and may not be accurate. We do know that he wrote the two letters to Bishop Schulze of Brandenburg and to Archbishop Albrecht of Mainz *on that date* and that the theses were included with the letter to Albrecht. In any case, the Ninety-Five would be widely publicized within the next days and weeks.
2. Luther, *Explanations of the Ninety-Five Theses, LW,* 31:25.
3. *Ibid.*, 31:84.
4. *Ibid.*
5. *Ibid.*
6. *Ibid.*
7. Luther, *The Leipzig Debate, LW,* 31:317.
8. Luther, Letter to Spalatin Concerning the Leipzig Debate, July 20, 1519, *LW,* 31:319.
9. *Ibid.*, p. 323.

Essay 10

1. Luther, *The Babylonian Captivity of the Church, LW,* 36:9.
2. Revelation 17:5–6.
3. *Cf.* the discussion in the section on marriage below.

4. *The Babylonian*, op. cit., p. 92.
5. *Ibid.*, p. 93.
6. *Ibid.*, p. 118. The letter's authenticity had been questioned by Eusebius, Jerome, Erasmus, and Cajetan. *Cf.* LW, 36:118 footnote 213, and 35:395 footnote 55. Today the letter is most often attributed to the James who was the leader of the Church in Jerusalem in the book of Acts and the brother of Jesus.
7. *Ibid.*
8. *Ibid.*, p. 119.
9. *Ibid.*
10. *Ibid.*, p. 120.
11. *Ibid.*
12. *Ibid.*, p. 121.
13. *Ibid.*, p. 107.
14. *Ibid.*, p. 108.
15. *Ibid.*, p. 109.
16. *Ibid.*, p. 112.
17. *Ibid.*, p. 83.
18. *Ibid.*, p. 18.
19. *Ibid.*, p. 124.
20. *Ibid.*, p. 82.
21. Luther denied that John 6 is about the sacrament.
22. *The Babylonian*, op. cit., p. 27.
23. *Ibid.*, p. 47.
24. *Ibid.*
25. *Ibid.*, p. 73.
26. *Cf.* Essay 17 in this book, "Luther on Other Reformers."

Essay 11

1. John 17:11.
2. John 17:23.
3. Even before the Reformation, there were several additional church bodies. Already in the earliest centuries AD there were such separate bodies as the Assyrian church and the Armenian church. Later but still before Luther there were in central and western Europe the Waldensians (followers of Waldo) and the Moravians (followers of Huss). An example of Luther's emphasis that there was no oneness in the Church is in Luther, *On the Papacy in Rome, Against the Most Celebrated Romanist in Leipzig, LW* 39:58.
4. *The Smalcald Articles, CTLC,* p. 309.
5. Augustin Alveld, *Concerning the Apostolic See,* quoted in the editor's introduction to Luther, *On the Papacy,* op. cit., p. 51.
6. For Luther, the "communion of saints," the *communio sanctorum,* means the same as "the holy Christian (or "catholic") Church, the *una sancta.*
7. *On the Papacy,* op. cit., p. 65.
8. Luther, *The Large Catechism, CTLC,* pp. 404f.
9. In his provocative "Theses against the Whole School of Satan and All the Gates of Hell," 1530, Luther wrote:

> 1. The church of God has no power to establish any article of faith; nor has it ever established any; nor will it ever establish any.…
>
> 5. The church of God has no power to confirm articles or precepts or the Holy Writings as by a higher sanction or judicial authority; nor has it ever done this; nor will it ever do it.
>
> 6. Rather the church of God is approved and confirmed by the Holy Writings as by a higher and judicial authority.

Quoted in *WLS*, pp. 267f.

Essay 12

1. Luther, *Prefaces to the Old Testament, LW* 35:256f.
2. *Cf.* note 3 below.
3. Luther, in following the numbering of the Psalms in

the Septuagint and the Vulgate, actually numbered this Psalm as 67. In our Bibles it is Psalm 68 following the numbering in the Hebrew Old Testament. The discrepancy of one is from Psalm 9 to Psalm 147. Our Psalms 9 and 10 are combined in the Septuagint and Vulgate; our Psalm 147 is divided into two Psalms in the Septuagint and Vulgate.

4. Luther, *Psalm 68, LW* 13:3.
5. *Ibid.*, p. 4.
6. *Ibid.*, p. 7.
7. *Ibid.*, p. 11.
8. *Ibid.*, p. 25.
9. *Ibid.*, p. 27.
10. *Ibid.*, p. 28.
11. *Ibid.*, pp. 30f.
12. *Ibid.*, p. 32.
13. *Ibid.*, p. 35.
14. Luther, *Psalm 118, LW*, 14:45. Luther numbered this Psalm as 117.
15. *Ibid.*, p. 47.
16. *Ibid.*, pp. 47–50.
17. *Ibid.*, p. 86.
18. *Ibid.*, p. 106.

Essay 13

1. John 6:48, "I am the bread of life."
2. Luther, *Prefaces to the New Testament, LW*, 35:360.
3. *Ibid.*, p. 362.
4. *Lutheran Service Book* (Saint Louis: Concordia, 2006), #556.
5. *The Lutheran Hymnal* (Saint Louis: Concordia, 1941), #262.
6. Luther, *Personal Prayer Book, LW*, 43:39f. Earlier in his life, Luther had indeed prayed to Mary, but this quote shows how his position on Mary had changed to one of respecting and honoring her while giving all praise (and prayers) to God.
7. *The Catechism of the Council of Trent,* John A. McHugh, O.P., and Charles J. Callan, O.P., translators, 1923, www.saintsbooks.net/books/, p. 293.
8. Luther, *The Small Catechism, CTLC*, p. 363.
9. *Ibid.*, p. 339.
10. *Ibid.*, p. 370.

Essay 14

1. Luther, Letter to Erasmus of Rotterdam, March 28, 1519 (*LW*, 48:117–119).
2. Durant, Will. *The Reformation,* vol. VI of *The Story of Civilization* (New York: Simon & Schuster), 1957, p. 430.
3. *Ibid.*
4. *Ibid.*, p. 433. Durant quotes a letter Erasmus sent to the pope in February, 1523.
5. The Latin title of Erasmus' work is *De Libero Arbitrio Diatribe sive Collatio.* "Diatribe" means what we would call a "presentation" or "essay" and "Collatio" means a discussion. Philip S. Watson claims that Erasmus used these terms in deliberate distinction from "assertion." Translator's "Introduction" to Luther, *The Bondage of the Will* (*LW*, 33:8).
6. Erasmus, *Diatribe,* in *Erasmus von Rotteram. Ausgewählte Schriften,* quoted in *LW*, 33:30f., footnote #27.
7. Luther, *The Bondage of the Will* (*LW*, 33:31).
8. *Ibid.* These two sentences absolutely outraged Erasmus and were ridiculed in his long response to Luther titled *Hyperaspistes* (which means "protector," but "*aspis*" also means "viper"). Cf. *LW*, 33:31f., footnote. Erasmus' outrage is probably best shown in this sentence: "So in the future you can leave out those smooth appellations: 'my dear Eras-

mus, my dear Erasmus' and keep that sort of pat on the head for your sworn supporters."

9. Luther, *The Bondage of the Will, op cit.* (*LW*, 33:293).
10. *Ibid.*
11. *Ibid.*
12. *Ibid.*
13. *Ibid.*
14. *Ibid.*, p. 295.
15. Cf. among other sources, Roland Bainton, *Erasmus of Christendom* (New York: Charles Scribner's Sons), 1969, pp. 279–283.

Essay 15

1. Luther, *A Sermon on the Estate of Marriage, LW*, 44:8.
2. *Ibid.*, p. 9.
3. *Ibid.*
4. *Ibid.*, pp. 10–12.
5. *Ibid.*, pp. 12f.
6. Cf. "Luther on the Sacraments: The Die Is Cast" in this collection.
7. Ephesians 5:31–32 (NIV). The first sentence is a quote of Genesis 2:24. Cf. Luther, *The Babylonian Captivity of the Church, LW*, 36:93–95.
8. Cf. "Luther on the Sacraments."
9. Luther, *The Babylonian Captivity of the Church, LW*, 36:96.
10. Luther, *The Estate of Marriage, LW*, 45:38.
11. *Ibid.*
12. *Ibid.*, p. 39.
13. *Ibid.*
14. *Ibid.*, pp. 39f.
15. *Ibid.*, p. 40.
16. *Ibid.*, p. 43.
17. *Ibid.*, p. 49.
18. Luther, *On the Councils and the Church, LW*, 41:157.
19. Luther, *The Judgment of Martin Luther on Monastic Vows, LW*, 44:273ff.
20. *Ibid.*, pp. 295ff.
21. *Ibid.*, pp. 317ff.
22. *Ibid.*, pp. 326ff.
23. *Ibid.*, pp. 336ff.
24. *Ibid.*, p. 373.
25. Markwald, Rudolf and Marilynn. *Katharina Von Bora: A Reformation* Life (St. Louis: Concordia), 2002, pp. 102ff. Zülsdorf was an estate Kate had inherited. The last salutation in the list was written just eight days before Luther's death.

Essay 16

1. William Shirer, *The Rise and Fall of the Third Reich* (New York: Simon & Schuster), 1960, p. 91.
2. *Ibid.*, p. 236.
3. *Ibid.*
4. Cf. Uwe Siemon-Neto, *The Fabricated Luther* (St. Louis: Concordia), 1993.
5. There are important similarities, to be sure, between Luther's doctrine and the American principle of the separation of church and state. But one essential difference is that in Luther's doctrine the kingdom of the world with its leaders is ruled by God. Another is that in it God's law supersedes the state's and is to guide the latter. A third is that a Christian has a special God-given responsibility over against the state. A fourth, and very important one, is that Luther's kingdom of Christ does not apply to all religious organizations. Nevertheless, a Christian can very well live by Luther's doctrine in our society.

6. Luther, *To the Christian Nobility of the German Nation, LW*, 44:123–217.

7. Luther, *Temporal Authority: To What Extent It Should Be Obeyed, LW*, 45:83f. This writing was based on a series of sermons Luther preached upon his return from the Wartburg.

8. *Ibid.*, p. 125.

9. *Ibid.*, p. 126.

10. Luther, *Admonition to Peace, A Reply to the Twelve Articles of the Peasants in Swabia, LW*, 46:19. The *Twelve Articles* are in *LW*, 46:8–15.

11. Luther, *Against the Robbing and Murdering Hordes of Peasants. LW*, 46:49–55. The German title is *Wider der räuberischen und mörderischen Rotten der Bauern.* "Rotten" could also be translated as "Gangs."

12. *Ibid.*, pp. 49f.

13. *Ibid.*, p. 50.

14. *Ibid.*, pp. 50f.

15. *Ibid.*, p. 53.

16. Luther, *An Open Letter on the Harsh Book Against the Peasants, LW*, 46:84. Note that in this passage, Luther does actually name-call using the phrase "bloody dogs," but it is applied to some of the political authorities—not the peasants.

Essay 17

1. Luther, *Sermon on Galatians 5:25–6:10*, September 21, 1544, *WLS*, p. 635, #1950.

2. Luther, *Against the Heavenly Prophets in the Matter of Images and Sacraments, LW*, 40:83.

3. *Ibid.*, pp. 118ff.

4. *Ibid.*, pp. 154ff.

5. *Ibid.*, p. 153.

6. *Ibid.*, p. 201.

7. Luther, *Letter to the Princes of Saxony Concerning the Rebellious Spirit, LW*, 40:57.

8. *Ibid.*

9. Luther, *That These Words of Christ, "This Is My Body," etc., Still Stand Firm Against the Fanatics, LW*, 37:25f.

10. *Ibid.*, p. 57.

11. Luther, *Confession Concerning Christ's Supper, LW*, 37:367.

12. *CTLC*, p. 598. Cf. also *The Augsburg Confession*, Articles X, *CTLC*, p. 61.

13. *The Marburg Colloquy* and *The Marburg Articles, LW*, 38:64. This point is taken from the report of Osiander.

14. *Ibid.*, p. 67. This is also from Osiander's report.

15. *Ibid.*, p. 48. This is from an anonymous report.

Essay 18

1. Julius Streicher and others publicized the largely unknown bombastic comments of Luther against the Jews.

2. William Shirer, *The Rise and Fall of the Third Reich* (New York: Simon & Schuster), 1960, p. 91. In a later passage (p. 236), Shirer wrote.

This great founder of Protestantism was both a passionate anti-Semite and a ferocious believer in absolute obedience to political authority. He wanted Germany rid of the Jews and when they were sent away he advised that they be deprived of "all their cash and jewels and silver and gold" and, furthermore, "that their synagogues or schools be set on fire, that their houses be broken up and destroyed ... and they be put under a roof or stable, like the gypsies ... in misery and captivity as they incessantly lament and complain to God about us"—advice that was literally followed four centuries later by Hitler, Göring and Himmler.

The breaks in the above quotation are in the Shirer text. Interestingly, his footnote for the quotations is to a 1942 book by Franz L. Neumann titled *Behemoth*—not to the Luther writing.

3. Luther, *That Christ Was Born a Jew, LW*, 45:200 f.

4. Quoted in Luther, *Against the Sabbatarians: Letter to a Good Friend, LW*, 47:62.

5. Roland Bainton, *Here I Stand* (Nashville: Abingdon), 1950, p. 297.

6. Luther, *On the Jews and Their Lies, LW*, 47:137.

7. *Ibid.*, footnote 4.

8. *Ibid.*, pp. 140 ff.

9. *Ibid.*, pp. 149 ff.

10. *Ibid.*, pp. 164 ff.

11. *Ibid.*, pp. 172 ff.

12. *Ibid.*, p. 177.

13. *Ibid.*, p. 257.

14. *Ibid.*, p. 260.

15. *Ibid.*, p. 268.

16. *Ibid.*, pp. 268–272.

17. *Ibid.*, p. 286.

18. *Ibid.*, p. 306.

Essay 19

1. Luther, *Letter to George Spalatin*, August 31, 1518, *LW*, 48:78.

2. Luther, *Letter to George Spalatin*, September 2, 1518, *LW*, 48:83.

3. Luther, *Letter to Staupitz*, October 3, 1518, *WLS*, p. 919, #2877.

4. Luther, *Letter to Melanchthon*, May 12, 1521, *LW*, 48:216.

5. Luther, *Letter to Melanchthon*, May 26, 1521, *LW*, 48:234.

6. Luther, *Letter to Melanchthon*, July 13, 1521, *LW*, 48:257f.

7. Cf. *WLS*, pp. 920f., #2881 and #2885.

8. Luther, *Letters to Melanchthon*, August 1 and 3, 1521, *LW*, 48:277–289.

9. Luther, *Letter to Melanchthon*, January 13, 1522, *LW*, 365f.

10. *The Augsburg Confession, CTLC*, p. 70.

11. *Ibid.* p. 71.

12. Luther's brief letter to Melanchthon on June 7, 1530, begins as follows: "I see that you all have decided to torment us with silence. Consequently, so that we don't pine away unavenged, we announce to you by means of this letter that from now on we shall compete with you in the matter of silence. Should you perhaps despise this, I praise the Wittenbergers who, although they are extremely busy, write three times before you idle people write once." *LW*, 49:320.

13. Luther, *Letter to Melanchthon*, June 29, 1530, *LW*, 49:328. *"Apologia"* means "defense." Later another confession would be called *The Apology to the Augsburg Confession*, but here Luther meant the *Augsburg Confession* itself.

14. Cf. Luther, *Letter to Melanchthon*, July 3, 1530, *LW*, 49:343.

15. Luther, *Letter to Melanchthon*, July 31, 1530, *LW*, 49:390.

16. Luther, *Letter to Melanchthon*, February 1, 1546, *LW*, 50:293.

Essay 20

1. Cf. Essay 17 in this book, "Luther on Other Reformers."

Bibliography

Part One

Arand, Charles. *That I May Be His Own*. St. Louis: Concordia, 2000.

Audin, Jean Marie Vincent. *History of the Life, Writings and Doctrines of Luther*. London: C. Dolman, 1854.

Bainton, Roland H. *Here I Stand: A Life of Martin Luther*. Nashville: Abington, 1950.

Bainton, Roland H. *Women of the Reformation, in Germany and Italy*. Minneapolis: Augsburg, 1971.

Beck, Victor Emanuel. *Why I Am a Lutheran*. New York: Thomas Nelson & Sons, 1956.

Bente, Friedrich. *Historical Introductions to the Lutheran Confessions: As Contained in the Book of Concord of 1580*. St. Louis: Concordia, 2005.

Bente, Friedrich. *Historical Introductions to the Symbolical Books of the Evangelical Lutheran Church*. N.p.: Quality Classics, 2010.

Bokenkotter, Thomas. *A Concise History of the Catholic Church*. New York: Image, 2005.

Brecht, Martin. *Martin Luther: His Road to Reformation, 1483–1521*. Minneapolis: Fortress, 1985.

Brecht, Martin. *Martin Luther: Shaping and Defining the Reformation, 1521–1532*. Minneapolis: Fortress, 1990.

Brecht, Martin. *Martin Luther: The Preservation of the Church, 1532–1546*. Minneapolis: Fortress, 1993.

Brendler, Gerhard. *Martin Luther, Theology and Revolution*. New York: Oxford University Press, 1991.

Cubitt, George. *The Life of Martin Luther*. New York: Carlton and Phillips, 1853.

Dallman, William. *Martin Luther: His Life and Labor for the Plain People*. St. Louis: Concordia, 1917.

Durant, Will. *The Reformation: A History of European Civilization from Wycliffe to Calvin, 1300–1564*. New York: Simon & Schuster, 1957.

Eyster, Henry Jacobs. *Martin Luther*. New York: Columbia University Press, 1957.

Eyster, Henry Jacobs. *Works of Luther*. Philadelphia: A.J. Holman, 1915.

Forde, Gerhard. *On Being a Theologian of the Cross: Reflections on Luther's Heidelberg Disputation, 1518*. Grand Rapids, MI: Eerdmans, 1997.

Green, V.H.H. *Luther and the Reformation*. New York: Mentor, 1974.

Grimm, Harold J. *Reformation Era, 1500–1650*. New York: Macmillan, 1974.

Haile, H.G. *Luther: An Experiment in Biography*. Garden City, NY: Doubleday, 1980.

Hart, David Bentley. *The Story of Christianity: An Illustrated History of 2000 Years of the Christian Faith*. New York: Metro, 2013.

Hughes, Phillip. *A Popular History of the Reformation*. Garden City, NY: Image, 1957.

Kittleson, James M. *Luther the Reformer: The Story of the Man and His Career*. Minneapolis: Fortress, 2003.

Klees, Emerson. *The Will to Stay with It*. New York: Friends of Finger Lake, 2002.

Kolb, Robert. *Martin Luther as Prophet, Teacher, and Hero: Images of the Reformer, 1520–1620*. Grand Rapids, MI: Baker, 1999.

Kolb, Robert, and Charles P. Arand. *The Genius of Luther's Theology: A Wittenberg Way of Thinking for the Contemporary Church*. Grand Rapids, MI: Baker Academic, 2008.

Kostlin, Julius. *The Life of Martin Luther*. Philadelphia: Lutheran Publication Society, 1883.

Lawson, John Parker, trans. *The Autobiography of Martin Luther*. Edinburgh: Edinburgh Printing and Publishing, 1836.

Lazareth, William Henry. *Luther on the Christian Home: An Application of the Social Ethics of the Reformation*. Philadelphia: Muhlenberg, 1960.

Lazareth, William Henry. *Luther, the Bible, and Social Ethics*. Minneapolis: Augsburg Fortress, 2001.

Lehmann, Helmut T., and Theodore C. Tappert, gen. eds. *Luther's Works, volume 54: Table Talk*. Philadelphia: Fortress, 1967.

Lindberg, Carter. *The European Reformations*. New York: John Wiley & Sons, 2011.

Loewenich, Walther von. *Luther's Theology of the Cross*. Minneapolis: Augsburg, 1976.

Lull, Timothy F., ed. *Martin Luther's Basic Theological Writings*. Minneapolis: Fortress, 1989.

Luther, Martin. *The Life of Luther, Written by Himself*. London: Bell & Daldy, 1872.

MacCulloch, Diarmaid. *The Reformation: A History*. New York: Penguin, 2003.

MacKinnon, James. *Luther and the Reformation*, four volumes. New York: Russell & Russell, 1962.

Manchester, William. *A World Lit Only by Fire: The Medieval Mind and the Renaissance*. New York: Little, Brown, 1992.

Marius, Richard. *Martin Luther: The Christian between God and Death.* Cambridge, MA: The Belknap Press of Harvard University Press, 1999.

Marty, Martin. *Martin Luther.* New York: Penguin, 2004.

McGiffert, Arthur Cushman. *Martin Luther: The Man and His Work.* New York: Century, 1917.

Meurer, Moritz. *The Life of Martin Luther, Related from Original Authorities.* Anon, NY: H. Ludwig and Company, 1848.

Michelet, M. *Martin Luther Gathered from His Own Writings.* New York: A.A. Kelley, 1859.

Miller, Douglas. *Armies of the German Peasants' War, 1524–26.* Oxford: Osprey, 2003.

Moynihan, Brian. *The Faith: A History of Christianity.* New York: Doubleday, 2002.

Nohl, Frederick. *Luther: Biography of a Reformer.* Saint Louis: Concordia, 2003.

Norwich, John Julius. *Absolute Monarchs: A History of the Papacy.* New York: Random House, 2011.

Nuelsen, John Louis. *Luther the Leader.* Cincinnati: Jennings and Graham, 1906.

Oberman, Heiko A. *Luther: Man Between God and the Devil.* New Haven: Yale University Press, 1989.

Pauck, Wilhelm. *The Heritage of the Reformation.* Glencoe, IL: Free Press, 1961.

Plass, Ewald M. *This is Luther: A Character Study.* St. Louis: Concordia, 1948.

Prenter, Regin. *Luther's Theology of the Cross.* Philadelphia: Fortress, 1971.

Rein, Wilhelm. *The Life of Martin Luther.* New York: Funk & Wagnall's, 1883.

Robinson, James Harvey, ed. *Translations and Reprints from the Original Sources of European History.* Philadelphia: University of Pennsylvania, 1902.

Ross, Estelle. *Martin Luther.* New York: Frederick A. Stokes, 1927.

Schmelz, Lothar. *Evangelical Church and Monastery of St. Augustine in Erfurt.* Erfurt: Evangelisches Augustinerkloster zu Erfurt, 2003.

Schwiebert, E.G. *Luther and His Times.* St. Louis: Concordia, 1950.

Shafarevich, Igor. *The Socialist Phenomenon.* New York: Harper & Row, 1980.

Siggins, Ian D. Kingston, ed. *Luther.* New York: Barnes & Noble, 1972.

Smith, Henry Preserved. *Luther's Correspondence and Other Contemporaneous Letters.* Philadelphia: Lutheran Publication Society, 1913.

Smith, Preserved. *The Life and Letters of Martin Luther.* Boston: Houghton Mifflin, 1911.

Stade, Heinz, and Thomas L. Seidel. *In the Footsteps of Martin Luther.* Eisenach: Wartburg, 2007.

Todd, John M. *Luther: A Life.* New York: Crossroad, 1982.

Vainio, Edward. *Reflections of Pastoral Significance.* New York: Lulu, 2010.

Weiser, R. *Luther by a Lutheran: A Full Length Portrait of Doctor Martin Luther.* Baltimore: The Publication Rooms, 1848.

Whitford, David M. *T&T Companion to Reformation Theology.* New York: Bloomsbury, 2014.

Wood, A. Skevington. *Captive to the Word.* Milton Keynes, U.K.: Paternoster, 1969.

Wylie, James Aitken. *The History of Protestantism.* London: Cassell, Petter & Galpin, 1980.

Part Two

Althaus, Paul. *The Theology of Martin Luther.* Translated by Robert C. Schultz. Philadelphia: Fortress, 1966.

Bainton, Roland. *Erasmus of Christendom.* New York: Charles Scribner's Sons, 1969.

Bainton, Roland. *Here I Stand: A Life of Martin Luther.* Nashville: Abingdon, 1978.

Bainton, Roland H. *The Age of the Reformation.* Princeton: D. Van Nostrand, 1956.

Die Bekenntnisschriften der Evangelisch-Lutherischen Kirche, 5th ed. Göttingen: Vandenhoeck & Ruprecht, 1964.

Die Bibel nach der deutschen Übersetzung D. Martin Luthers. St. Louis: Concordia, n.d.

Boehmer, Heinrich. *Martin Luther: Road to Reformation.* Translated by John W. Doberstein and Theodore G. Tappert. New York: Meridian, 1957.

Brecht, Martin. *Martin Luther: His Road to Reformation, 1483–1521.* Translated by James L. Shaaf. Minneapolis: Fortress, 1985.

Brecht, Martin. *Martin Luther: Shaping and Defining the Reformation, 1521–1532.* Translated by James L. Shaaf. Minneapolis: Fortress, 1990.

Brecht, Martin. *Martin Luther: The Preservation of the Church, 1532–1546.* Translated by James L. Shaaf. Minneapolis: Fortress, 1993.

Carlson, David M. "Martin Luther's Influence in Nazi Germany." Unpublished manuscript, 1997.

Concordia: The Lutheran Confessions, rev. ed. St. Louis: Concordia, 2005.

Dawidowicz, Lucy S. *The War Against the Jews, 1933–1945.* New York: Holt, Rinehart and Winston, 1975.

Durant, Will. *The Reformation: A History of European Civilization from Wyclif to Calvin, 1300–1564.* New York: Simon & Schuster, 1957.

Erasmus, Desiderius. *Christian Humanism and the Reformation.* Edited by John C. Olin. New York: Harper, 1965.

Erasmus, Desiderius, and Martin Luther. *The Battle over Free Will.* Edited by Clarence H. Miller. Indianapolis: Hackett, 2012.

Erasmus, Desiderius, and Martin Luther. *Discourse on Free Will.* Translated and edited by Ernst F. Winter. London: Bloomsbury, 1989.

Gilmore, Myron P. *The World of Humanism, 1453–1517.* New York: Harper, 1962.

Grimm, Harold J. *The Reformation Era, 1500–1650.* New York: Macmillan, 1954.

Gritsch, Eric W. *Martin Luther's Anti-Semitism: Against His Better Judgment.* Grand Rapids, MI: William B. Eerdmans, 2012

Harran, Marilyn J. *Martin Luther: Learning for Life.* St. Louis: Concordia, 1997.

Kelley, Donald R. *Renaissance Humanism.* Boston: Twayne, 1991.

Kittelson, James M. *Luther the Reformer: The Story of the Man and His Career.* Minneapolis: Augsburg, 1986

Klug, Eugene F. A. *Lift High This Cross: The Theology of Martin Luther.* St. Louis: Concordia, 2003.

Lilje, Hanns. *Martin Luther in Selbstzeugnissen und Bilddokumenten.* Hamburg: Rowohlt, 1965.

Luther, Martin. *Die Hauptschriften,* 3d ed. Berlin: Christlicher Zeitschriftenverlag, n.d.

Luther, Martin. *Luthers Werke, Kritische Gesamtausgabe. Schriften.* 68 vols. Weimar: Hermann Böhlaus Nachfolger, 1883–1999.

Luther, Martin. *Luther's Works.* American Edition. General editors Jaroslav Pelikan and Helmut T. Lehmann. 56 vols. St. Louis: Concordia, and Philadelphia: Muhlenberg and Fortress, 1955–86.

Luther, Martin. *Martin Luther's Basic Theological Writings,* 2d ed. Edited by Timothy F. Lull. Minneapolis: Fortress, 2005.

Mall, E. Jane. *Kitty, My Rib.* St. Louis: Concordia, 1959.

Markwald, Rudolf K., and Marilynn Morris Markwald. *Katharina von Bora: A Reformation Life.* St. Louis: Concordia, 2002.

Martin, Bernard. *Europe and the New World,* volume two of *A History of Judaism.* New York: Basic, 1974.

Nohl, Frederick. *Luther: Biography of a Reformer.* St. Louis: Concordia, 2003.

Plass, Ewald M. *This Is Luther: A Character Study.* St. Louis: Concordia, 1948.

Pollack, W. G. *The Story of Luther.* St. Louis: Concordia, 1944.

Schwiebert, E. G. *Luther and His Times: The Reformation from a New Perspective.* St. Louis: Concordia, 1950.

Shirer, William L. *The Rise and Fall of the Third Reich: A History of Nazi Germany.* New York: Simon & Schuster, 1960.

Siemon-Netto, Uwe. *The Fabricated Luther: The Rise and Fall of the Shirer Myth.* St. Louis: Concordia, 1995.

Spitz, Lewis W. *The Renaissance and Reformation Movements.* Two vols., rev. ed. St. Louis: Concordia, 1987.

Todd, John M. *Martin Luther: A Biographical Study.* Westminster, MD: Newman, 1965.

What Luther Says: A Practical In-Home Anthology for the Active Christian. Edited by Ewald M. Plass. St. Louis: Concordia, 1959.

Index

Page numbers in **bold italics** indicate pages with illustrations.